SEVEN-FIFTY INTERCEPTOR

ALL MODELS 1962-1970
WORKSHOP MANUALS & ILLUSTRATED PARTS MANUALS

SECTION 1 - CONTENTS

MK1 or Series I WORKSHOP MANUAL
MK2 or Series II WORKSHOP MANUAL

SECTION 2 - CONTENTS

MK1 or Series I ILLUSTRATED PARTS MANUAL
MK1A or Series IA ILLUSTRATED PARTS MANUAL
MK2 or Series II ILLUSTRATED PARTS MANUAL
1970 MK2 or Series II PARTS SUPPLEMENT

A FLOYD CLYMER PUBLICATION PUBLISHED IN 2022 BY VELOCEPRESS

All rights reserved. This work may not be reproduced or transmitted in any form without the express written consent of the publisher

www.VelocePress.com

IMPORTANT

Each of the 5 individual manuals included in this publication have their own specific index and corresponding page numbers.

The numbers to the bottom center of the page is the page number within each 'Section' as referenced in the 'Section' index below.

SECTION 1 - WORKSHOP MANUALS – INDEX

MK1/Series I - Workshop Manual	Pages 1-60
MK2/Series II - Workshop Manual	Pages 61-119
Section 2 Index	Page 120

SECTION 2 - ILLUSTRATED PARTS MANUALS – INDEX

MK1/Series I - Parts Manual	Pages 1-56
MK1A/Series IA - Parts Manual	Pages 57-112
MK2/Series II - Parts Manual	Pages 113-166
1970 MK2/Series II - Supplement	Pages 167-173

WORKSHOP MAINTENANCE MANUAL

FOR THE

Royal Enfield
'Made like a Gun'

736 c.c.

"INTERCEPTOR"

MOTOR CYCLE

Published by
FLOYD CLYMER PUBLICATIONS
World's Largest Publisher of Books Relating to Automobiles, Motorcycles, Motor Racing, and Americana
222 NO VIRGIL AVENUE, LOS ANGELES, CALIFORNIA 90004

Announcement

This is a reproduction of the official and authentic factory workshop manual as originally printed in England. It covers completely the necessary procedures of servicing and overhauling the "Interceptor" models. It also covers the servicing of the latest model Indian Chiefs which were built by Enfield before being discontinued by the old Indian Company.

Royal-Enfields have been sold in the United States for many years and thousands of these quality cycles are in daily use in this country.

We suggest that the R-E owner contact his nearest authorized dealer when in need of service, as the dealer has genuine parts and factory trained mechanics.

Names and addresses of R-E dealers can be secured from Cooper Motors, 2815 West Olive Ave., Burbank, Calif. 91505, who are the U. S. importers; or from Shillingford & Sons, 1635 W. Hunting Park, Philadelphia, Pa., Eastern distributors.

Floyd Clymer
FLOYD CLYMER
Publisher

T.T. "INTERCEPTOR" U.S.A. MODEL

Royal Enfield "Interceptor" Workshop Manual

LIST OF CONTENTS

	Page
TECHNICAL DATA	5
ENGINE SPECIFICATION	6–10
1. Engine	6
2. Cylinder Heads	6
3. Cylinders	6
4. Pistons	6
5. Connecting Rods	6
6. Crankcase	6
7. Crankshaft and Flywheel	6
8. Main Bearings	6
9. Camshafts	6
10. Valves	7
11. Valve Gear	7
12. Timing Drive	7
13. Ignition and Lighting System	7
14. Carburetters	8
15. Air Filter	8
16. Lubrication System	8
17. Breather	8
18. Gearbox	8
Oil Pump Diagrams	9
19. Clutch	10
SERVICE OPERATIONS WITH ENGINE IN FRAME	10–19
20. Removal of the Timing Cover	10
21. Valve Timing	10
22. Tappet Adjustment	10
23. Removal of the Camshafts	11
24. Ignition Timing	11
25. Primary Chain Adjustment	12
26. Timing Chain Adjustment	12
27. Magneto Chain Adjustment	12
28. Removal of the Dual Seat and Rear Mudguard	12
29. Removal of the Petrol Tank	12
30. Removal and Refitting of the Cylinder Head	13
31. Removal of the Valves	13
32. Removal of the Rockers	14
33. Removal of the Valve Guides	14
34. Removal of Sparking Plugs	14
35. Removal of the Cylinders	14
36. Removal of Pistons	14
37. Decarbonising	14
38. Grinding-in Valves	15
39. Reassembly after Decarbonising	15
40. Cleaning the Oil Filters	16
41. Overhaul of Oil Pumps	16
42. Removal of the Timing Chains	17
43. Removal of Pump Worm and Timing Sprocket	17
44. Removal of Camshaft Sprockets	17
45. Removal of the Magneto	17
46. Removal of the Engine and Clutch Sprockets	17
47. Removal of Tappets and Guides	17
48. Dismantling the Breathers	17
49. Removal of the Clutch	17
50. Removal of Final Drive Sprocket	18
51. Oil Seal Behind Engine Sprocket	18
52. Oil Pipe Unions	18
53. Rocker Oil Feed Relief Valve	18
54. Fitting the Alternator	18
SERVICE OPERATIONS WITH ENGINE REMOVED	19–21
55. Removal of the Engine Gearbox Unit from the Frame	19
56. Removal of the Gearbox	19
57. Dismantling the Crankcase	19

	Page
58. Main Bearings	20
59. Fitting the Connecting Rods	20
60. Reassembly of Crankcase	20
61. Crankshaft Plugs	21
62. Pump Worm Threads	21
GEARBOX AND CLUTCH	21–26
63. Description of the Clutch	21
64. Description of the Gearbox	22
65. Removal of the Gearbox	22
66. To Dismantle the Gearbox	22
67. Removal of the Ball Races	22
Operation of Gears	23
68. Change-Gear Mechanism	24
69. Reassembling the Gearbox	24
70. Dismantling and Reassembling the Clutch	24
71. Adjustment of Clutch Control	24
Exploded view of Gearbox	25
72. Adjustment of Neutral Finder	26
73. Gearbox Oil Level	26
AMAL MONOBLOC CARBURETTER	27–31
74. General Description	27
75. Tuning the Carburetter(s)	28
Exploded View of Monobloc Carburetter	29
76. Tuning Sequence with Two Carburetters	30
77. Dismantling Carburetter	30
78. Causes of High Petrol Consumption	31
LUCAS TWIN-CYLINDER MAGNETO	31–33
79. General	31
80. Lubrication	31
81. Adjustments	32
82. Cleaning	32
83. High Tension Cables	32
84. Renewing Timing Control Cable (Manual Control)	32
85. Contact Breaker Springs	32
86. Servicing. Testing Magneto in Position on Engine	33
87. Automatic Advance Mechanism	33
GENERATOR/RECTIFIER CHARGING SET	34–36
88. General (6-volt Sets)	34
89. Maintenance	36
BATTERY	37
90. General	37
91. Technical Data	37
92. Filling and Soaking Batteries	37
HEAD AND TAIL LAMPS	38–39
93. Headlamp	38
94. Lucas Light Unit	38
95. Replacing Light Unit and Bulb	38
96. Parking Lights (Early Models with Casquettes)	39
97. Tail Light	39
FRAME	40–42
98. Description of Frame	40
99. Steering Head Races	41
100. Removal of Rear Suspension Unit	41
101. Servicing Rear Suspension Units	41
102. Removal of Swinging Arm Chain Stays	42

	Page
103. Centre Stand	42
104. Wheel Alignment	42
105. Lubrication	42
FRONT FORK	43–46
106. Description	43
107. Operation of the Fork	44
108. Dismantling the Fork to Replace Spring, Oil Seal or Bearing Bushes	44
109. Springs	45
110. Reassembly of Parts	45
111. Steering Head Races	45
112. Removal of Complete Fork	46
113. Lubrication	46
FRONT WHEEL	47–50
114. Removal from Fork	47
115. Removal of Brake Cover Plate Assembly	47
116. Replacing Brake Linings	47
117. Removal of Brake Operating Cam(s)	47
118. Removal of Hub Spindle and Bearings	47
119. Hub Bearings	48
120. Fitting Limits for Bearings	48
121. Refitting Ball Bearings	48
122. Reassembly of Brake Shoes and Operating Cam into Cover Plate	49
123. Final Assembly of Hub before Replacing Wheel	49
124. Wheel Rim	49
125. Spokes	49
126. Wheel Building and Truing	49
127. Tyre	49
128. Tyre Pressure	50
129. Lubrication	50
REAR WHEEL	50–55
130. Description	50
131. Removal and Replacement of Main Portion of Wheel for Tyre Repairs, etc.	50
132. Removal and Replacement of Complete Wheel for access to Brake	50
133. Removal of Brake Shoes for Replacement, etc.	51
134. Removal of Brake Operating Cam	52
135. Cush Drive	52
136. Removal of Ball Bearings	53
137. Hub Bearings	53
138. Fitting Limits for Bearings	53
139. Removal of Hub Driving Pins	54
140. Refitting Ball Bearings	54
141. Reassembly of Brake Shoes and Operating Cam into Cover Plate	54
142. Centring Cam Housing	54
143. Final Reassembly of Hub before Replacing Wheel	54
144. Wheel Rims	54
145. Spokes	54
146. Wheel Building and Truing	55
147. Tyre	55
148. Tyre Pressures	55
149. Lubrication	55
SPECIAL TOOLS	56–60

3

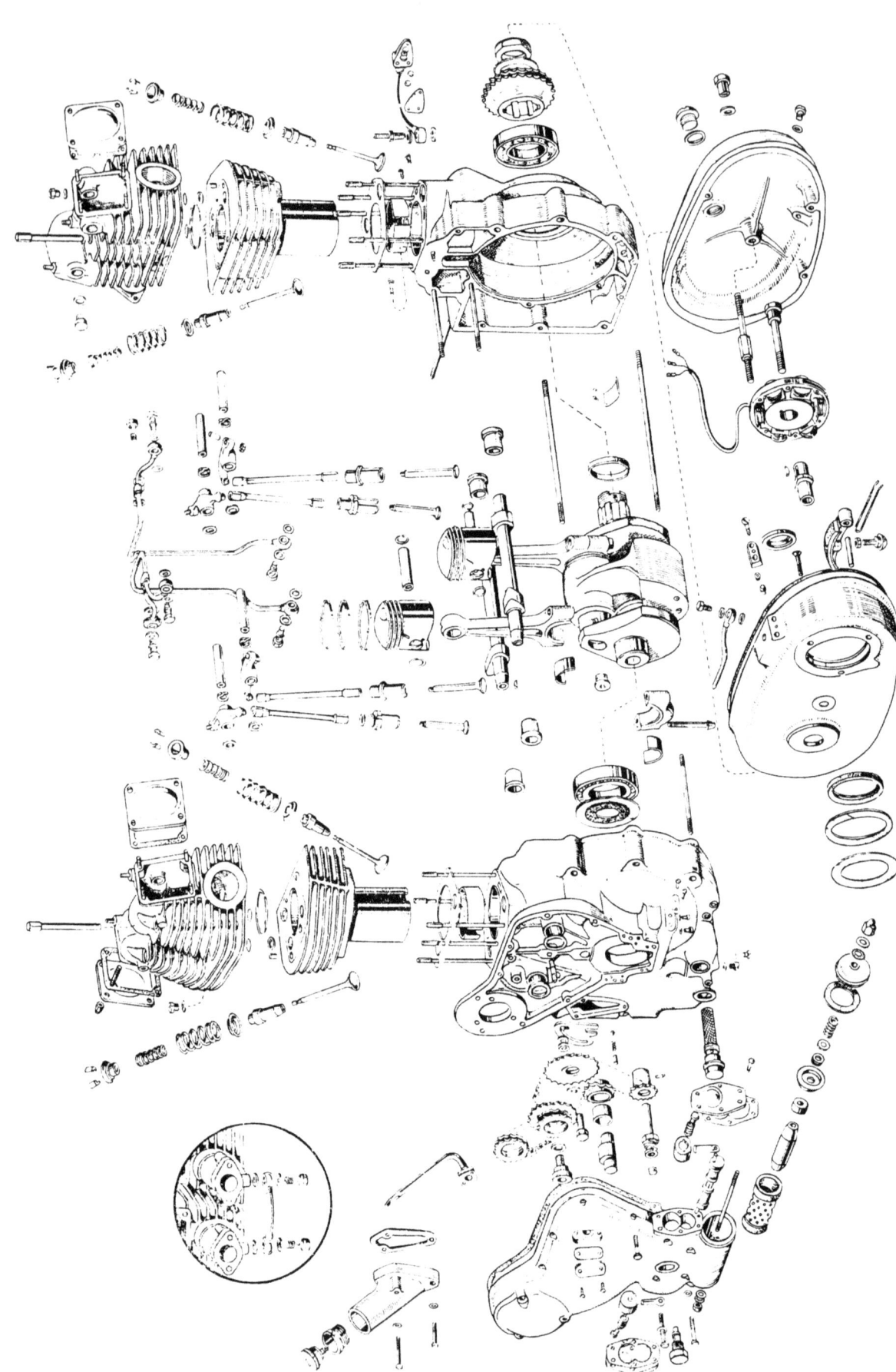

EXPLODED VIEW OF "INTERCEPTOR" ENGINE 1965-6

Fig. 1

Royal Enfield "Interceptor" Workshop Manual

Technical Data

"Interceptor" Engine

Cubic Capacity	736 c.c.
Stroke ... Nominal	93 mm.
Bore ... Nominal	71 mm.
Actual	70·92 mm./2·792 in.
Rebore to ·020 in. oversize when wear exceeds ·0065 in.	
Compression Ratio	8 to 1 or 7¼ to 1
Piston Diameter—	
Bottom of Skirt—	
Fore and Aft	2·788 in.
Top Lands	2·7635 in.
Skirt is tapered and oval turned.	
Piston Rings—	
Width—Plain Rings	·0625/·0635 in.
Single Scraper Ring	·1550/·1560 in.
Double Scraper Rings	·0781/·0776 in.
Radial Thickness	2·883/3·085 mm.
Gap when in unworn Cylinder	·015/·020 in.
Clearance in grooves	·001/·003 in.
Renew Piston Rings when gap exceeds 1/16 in.	
Oversize Pistons and Rings available	+·020 in.
Piston Boss Internal Diameter	·7498/·7500 in.
Gudgeon Pin Diameter	·7498/·7500 in.
Con. Rod Small End Internal Diameter	·7507/·7505 in.
Big End Internal Diameter Con. Rod	2·0190/2·0185 in.
Big End Internal Dia. Bearing Shells	1·8750/1·8755 in.*
Crank Pin Diameter, Timing Side	1·8744/1·8740 in.
Crank Pin Diameter, Driving Side	1·8741/1·8737 in.
Driving Side Main Ball Bearing—	
Type	Hoffman 145 or R and M—LJ45
Outside Diameter	85 mm.
Inside Diameter	45 mm.
Width	19 mm.
Timing Side Main Roller Bearing—	
Type	Hoffman R145 or R and M—LR45
Outside Diameter	85 mm.
Inside Diameter	45 mm.
Width	19 mm.
Rocker Inside Diameter	·5627/·5622 in.
Rocker Bearing Inside Diameter	·5622/·5617 in.
Rocker Spindle Diameter	·5617/·5615 in.
Inlet Valve Stem Diameter	·3430/·3425 in.
Exhaust Valve Stem Diameter	·3410/·3405 in.
Valve Guide Internal Diameter	·3437/·3447 in.
Valve Guide External Diameter	·6275/·6270 in.
Valve Guide Hole in Cylinder Head Dia.	·625/·626 in.
Tappet Stem Diameter	·3743/·3740 in.
Tappet Guide Internal Diameter	·3755/·3745 in.
Tappet Guide External Diameter	1·0125/1·0130 in.
Tappet Guide Hole in Crankcase Dia.	1·011/1·010 in.
Tappet Clearance with cold engine—	
Inlet	Nil ⎫ Normal
Exhaust	Nil ⎬ running
Inlet	Nil ⎫ Continuous
Exhaust	·005″ ⎬ high-speed running

*Assumes ·0005 in. "stretch" of eye of rod and cap due to interference fit of bearing shells.

Valve Spring Free Length—	
Inner	1½ in.
Outer	1 11/16 in.
(Renew when reduced by 1/16 in.)	
Valve Timing with ·012 in. clearance. See Page 11	
Camshaft Bearing External Diameter	·9095/·9085 in.
Camshaft Bearing Internal Diameter	·7505/·7495 in.
(Bored in position in crankcase.)	
Cam Lift—	
Exhaust	Sports—·328 in. Std.—·3125 in.
Inlet	Sports—·344 in. Std.—·3125 in.
Valve Lift (approx.)—	
Exhaust	Sports—·328 in. Std.—·3125 in.
Inlet	Sports—·344 in. Std.—·3125 in.
Timing Sprocket	12 Teeth
Camshaft Sprockets	24 Teeth
Magneto Sprocket	19 Teeth
Timing Chain—Type	Single No. 110038 endless
Length	66 Pitches
Width	·225 in.
Pitch	·375 in.
Roller	·250 in.
Magneto Chain—Type	Duplex No. 114500 endless
Length	44 Pitches
Width	8·64 mm.
Pitch	8 mm.
Roller	5 mm.
Magneto Speed	Half Engine Speed
Points	·015 in.
Timing—Advanced	11/32 in. before T.D.C. (32°)
Engine Sprocket	29 Teeth
Clutch Sprocket	56 Teeth
Final Drive Sprocket	21 or 20 Teeth
Primary Chain—Type	Duplex No. 114038 endless
Length	92 Pitches
Width	·628 in.
Pitch	·375 in.
Roller	·250 in.
Feed Oil Pump—Speed	1/6 Engine Speed
Piston Diameter	·24975/·24950 in.
Stroke length	·5 in.
Return Oil Pump—Speed	1/6 Engine Speed
Piston Diameter	·375/·3755 in.
Stroke length	·5 in.
Sparking Plug—Lodge 2HLN. Champion N5 or NA8, or KLG FE.75, Autolite AE2. For high speed running over long distances, use Lodge 3HLN, Champion N3 or NA10, or KLG FE.100, Autolite AE 901.	
Diameter	14 mm.
Reach	⅜ in.
Gap	·018/·022 in.

Engine Specification

1. Engine

The engine is an even-firing vertical twin-cylinder, having separate cylinders and heads and fully enclosed pressure-lubricated overhead valve gear. It has a dry sump lubrication with the oil tank integral with the crankcase and a massive one-piece high-strength spheroidal graphite cast iron crankshaft.

2. Cylinder Heads

The cylinder heads are die-cast from light aluminium alloy with ample finning to ensure adequate cooling. The exhaust pipe inserts are cast-in and the valve inserts are of austenitic iron and are shrunk in so that they are replaceable. The large capacity induction ports are streamlined and blended to the valve seatings.

3. Cylinders

The separate cast-iron cylinders have a nominal bore of 71 mm, the stroke being 93 mm. The cubic capacity of the engine is 736 c.c. The cylinder heads are located on the cylinders by hollow dowels and the joint between head and barrel is made by a split, triangular section steel ring which seats on a chamfer at the top end of the cylinder barrel and stands about ·005 in. proud of the joint face. The push rod tunnels are sealed by washers of special heat and oil resistant rubber bonded to metal and fitting in recesses in the cylinder head.

4. Pistons

The pistons are made of low expansion aluminium alloy, heat treated and form ground taper and oval. Standard and low compression pistons are available, the former having approximately $\frac{1}{4}$ in. dome and the latter about $\frac{3}{16}$ in. Each piston carries two compression rings, of which the top one is chrome plated. Standard compression pistons are fitted with a special dual oil control ring. Low compression pistons use a single slotted type ring.

Compression ratios are as follows:—

Standard Pistons, No compression plate—$8\frac{1}{2}$ to 1.
Standard Pistons, 1 compression plate—8 to 1.
Standard Pistons, 2 compression plates—$7\frac{1}{2}$ to 1.
Low Compression Pistons, no plate—$7\frac{1}{4}$ to 1.
Low Compression Pistons, 1 plate—6·9 to 1.
Low Compression Pistons, 2 plates—6·6 to 1.

5. Connecting Rods

The connecting rods are produced from stampings of Hiduminium RR56 light alloy. The little end bearings are of alloy direct on to the gudgeon pin. In case of wear after long service the little end can be bored out and fitted with a bush, but this is rarely necessary.

The big end bearings consist of white-metalled steel liners which are renewable. The detachable bearing caps are bolted to the connecting rods by means of high tensile socket screws, the heads of which are drilled for wiring.

6. Crankcase

The combined crankcase and oil tank is die-cast from light alloy in two halves, being split vertically.

7. Crankshaft and Flywheel

The crankshaft is cast in one piece, integral with the massive central flywheel, from high quality spheroidal graphitic cast iron. The total weight is approximately 24 lbs., and all crankshafts are dynamically balanced.

The main journals are ground, and the big end journals are ground and hand lapped. The main journal on the drive side is drilled through its centre for the crankcase breather.

8. Main Bearings

Heavy duty bearings are provided for the crankshaft, the driving side being ball and the timing side roller.

9. Camshafts

The camshafts are machined from drop forged steel stampings with the cams and bearings hardened and ground. The cam profiles are produced to give racing performance and, in order to obtain the maximum efficiency, the usual silencing ramps are omitted. Alternative camshafts with quietening ramps are available for riders who are prepared to sacrifice a little performance in the interests of mechanical silence. These were fitted to the earlier engines.

The camshafts are located in the crankcase and

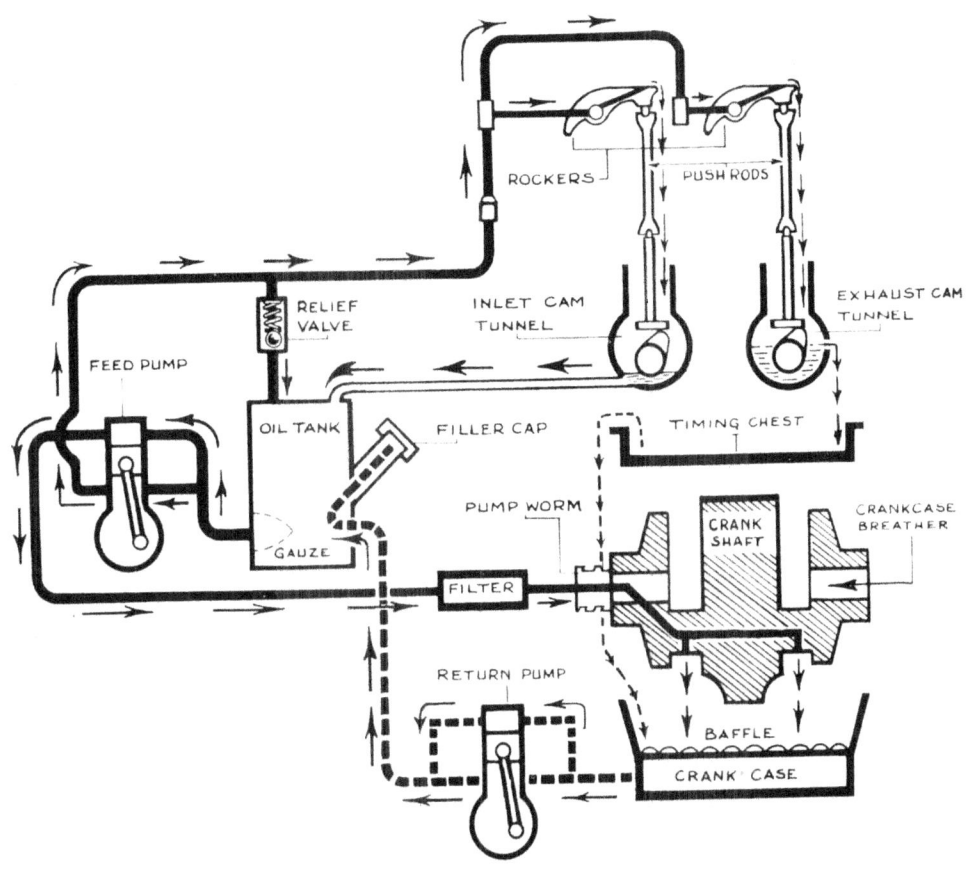

LUBRICATION SYSTEM. Diagrammatic Arrangement
Fig. 2

run in bronze bushes. The bushes on the nearside are pressed into detachable housings which are bolted to the driving side crankcase. This enables the camshafts to be changed, if so desired for tuning purposes, without the necessity of dismantling the crankcase.

10. Valves

The inlet valves are machined from stampings of special Silicon-Chrome Valve Steel and the exhaust valves are of High-Nickel-Chromium-Tungsten Valve Steel with the stems Stellite-tipped.

11. Valve Gear

The valves are operated from the camshaft by means of large, flat-based, guided tappets, tubular alloy push rods with induction hardened steel ends and overhead rockers. Two compression springs are fitted to each valve secured by Bullock Type split collets locking in high strength aluminium collars. The springs are specially designed to give a variable rate on compression.

12. Timing Drive

The camshafts are located in the crankcase, running in bronze bushes. They are driven by an endless chain from the timing sprocket on the crankshaft and the tightness of the chain can be adjusted by means of the chain tensioner in the timing chest.

The magneto is driven by a separate endless chain from the rear camshaft sprocket in the timing chest. The tension of this chain is adjusted by moving the magneto fixing bolts in their slotted holes.

A special slotted bolt securing the front camshaft sprocket provides a drive to a tachometer if this is required. This drive can be fixed to an aperture provided in the timing cover, which is otherwise covered by a small plate.

13. Ignition and Lighting System

The ignition is supplied from a Lucas K2F magneto and the lighting and other electrical circuits from a 6- or 12-volt battery which is charged through a rectifier from a Lucas alternator.

The alternator is housed in the primary chaincase, the permanent magnet rotor being mounted on the end of the crankshaft and the six coil stator fixed to the back of the chaincase. When a 12-volt battery is used the "Zener Diode" regulation system is employed. This ensures maximum charge rate when the battery voltage is low, cutting down to a trickle charge as the voltage rises.

The magneto is chain-driven from the inlet camshaft at half engine speed and the timing is hand controlled from a lever on the handlebar on the earlier models, while later models have an automatic centrifugal control incorporated in the magneto sprocket.

14. Carburetters

Twin Amal Monobloc carburetters with a bore of $1\frac{3}{16}$ in. are fitted as standard. On the earlier models only the left-hand carburetter contained a float chamber, the right-hand instrument being fed by a short flexible connecting tube joining the two jet holders. Later, carburetters with right-hand float chambers became available and were used on the right-hand side of the machine with the standard left-hand float chamber on the left.

15. Air Filter

Provision is made for housing twin 5 in. diameter Vokes Micro-Vee felt and gauze dry filters in a compartment of the toolbox, but the use of these may reduce the maximum speed slightly.

16. Lubrication System

Lubrication is by the Royal Enfield Dry Sump system which is entirely automatic and positive in action. The oil tank is integral with the crankcase, ensuring the full rate of circulation immediately the engine is started and rapid heating of the oil in cold weather.

There are two positively driven piston type oil pumps running at $\frac{1}{6}$ engine speed, one at the rear of the timing cover for pumping oil to the bearings under pressure and the other at the front for returning the oil from the crankcase to the tank. The return pump has a capacity approximately double that of the feed pump which ensures that oil does not accumulate in the crankcase.

The oil from the big ends drains into the bottom of the crankcase and is prevented by a baffle from being drawn up by the flywheel.

The oil from the rocker bearings is squirted through a small hole in each rocker on to the top ends of the push rods. It then flows down the push rod tunnels into the cam tunnels, where it lubricates the cams and tappets. Oil from the rear (inlet) cam tunnel is then returned direct to the oil tank through a drilled passage. Oil from the front (exhaust) cam tunnel overflows into the timing chest, where it lubricates the timing chains and then drains to the sump beneath the baffle plate at the bottom of the crankcase.

Both pumps are double acting, the primary side of the feed pump supplying the big ends and the secondary side the rockers and valve gear. Both sides of the return pump combine to pump oil back to the tank from the sumps at the bottom of the crankcase.

A spring loaded relief valve controls the pressure of the oil to the valve rocker gear which is through external pipes.

A gauze strainer is provided for the feed oil leaving the tank and there is a large capacity felt filter in the feed to the big ends. An aluminium cylinder is fitted over the fixing stud inside the filter element to reduce the volume of oil required to fill the filter after it has been dismantled for cleaning and to ensure the rapid flow of oil to the big ends.

A small circular magnet is also fitted over the fixing stud inside the oil filter for the purpose of collecting any ferrous particles which may be suspended in the oil.

17. Breather

Two separate breathers are fitted to ventilate the crankcase. The driving end of the crankshaft is drilled through, allowing the engine to breath into the primary chain case which is itself vented by means of a banjo union and a copper pipe running along the top. The second breather consists of drilled passages in the wall of the driving side of the crankcase. These communicate with the breather body situated on the crankcase wall just below the L.H. cylinder base. From here the gases are taken by a copper pipe to a union on top of the oil tank and thence by another pipe to the rear chain. The purpose of the connection to the oil tank is twofold. First it allows any surplus oil carried over to drain back into the tank. Secondly, it provides a vent to permit the escape of pressure which would otherwise build up in the tank due to the difference in the capacities of the feed and return pumps. Both the drilled main shaft and the side breather body contain non-return disc valves which prevent air being drawn into the crankcase on the up-stroke of the pistons and thus tend to produce a partial vacuum in the case. Excessive pressure in the case, as shown by oil leaks, may be the result of one of these discs becoming stuck.

18. Gearbox

The gearbox is bolted on to the back of the crankcase and has four speeds, which are foot controlled, and a patented neutral finder. All gears are in constant mesh, changes being effected by robust dog clutches. (See Subsection 64).

OIL PUMP DIAGRAMS

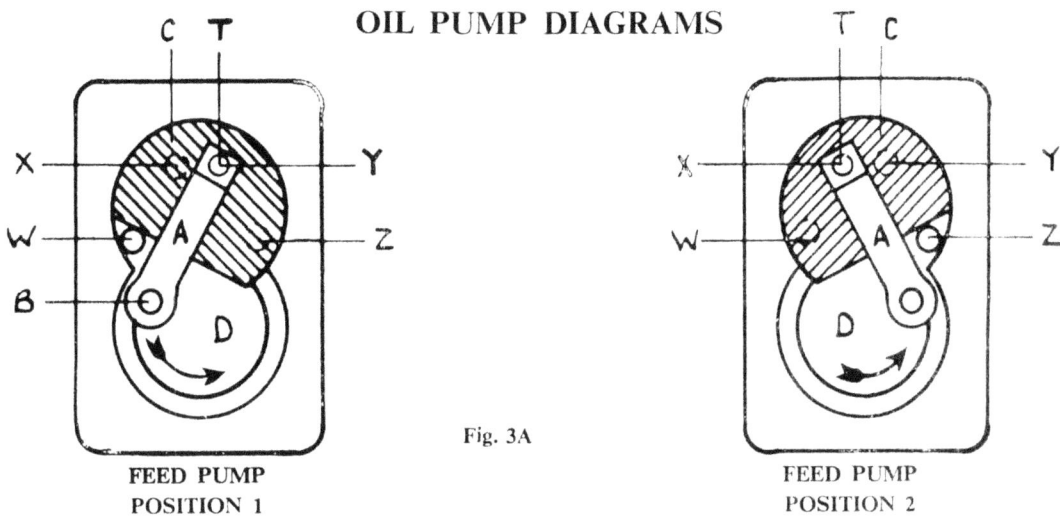

Fig. 3A

FEED PUMP POSITION 1   **FEED PUMP POSITION 2**

The ports in the housing are connected as follows:—

- W — delivery to rocker gear.
- X — delivery to big ends.
- Y — suction from oil tank.
- Z — suction from oil tank.

Position 1. The plunger A is being drawn out of the cylinder hole in the disc C by the action of the peg B on the shaft D. The port T in the disc C registers with the suction port Y in the housing, so that oil is drawn into the cylinder from the oil tank. At the same time the delivery port W in the housing is uncovered and oil below the disc in the housing is forced through W to the rocker Gear.

Position 2. The plunger A is being pushed into the cylinder hole in the disc C. The port T in the disc now registers with the delivery port X in the housing, so that oil is forced out of the cylinder to the big ends. At the same time the suction port Z in the housing is uncovered and oil is drawn into the housing below the disc from the oil tank.

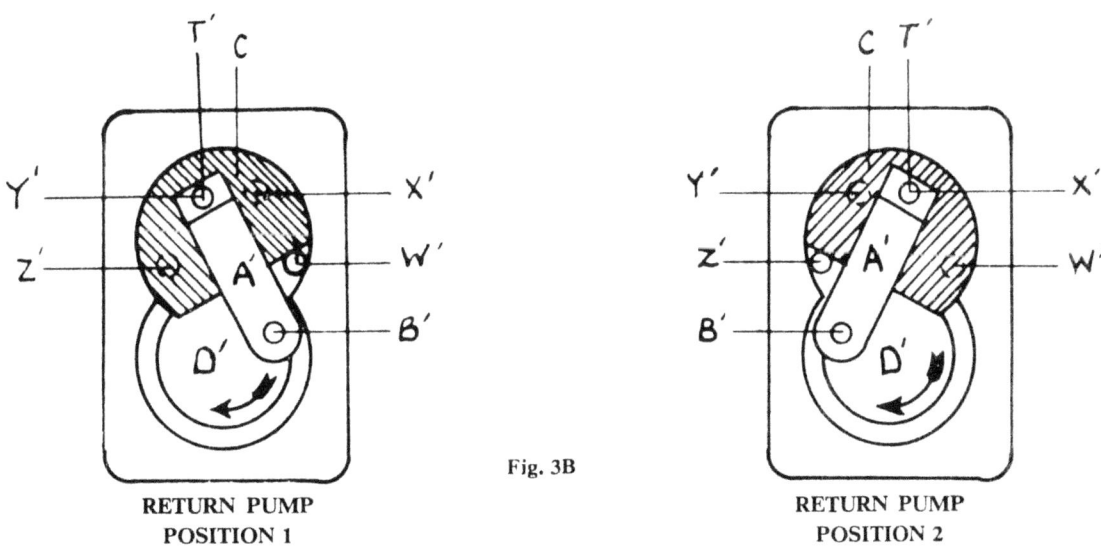

Fig. 3B

RETURN PUMP POSITION 1   **RETURN PUMP POSITION 2**

The ports in the housing are connected as follows:—

- W' — delivery to oil tank.
- X' — delivery to oil tank.
- Y' — suction from crankcase.
- Z' — suction from crankcase.

Position 1. The plunger A' is being drawn out of the cylinder hole in the disc C' by the action of the peg B' on the shaft D'. The port T' in the disc C' registers with the suction port Y' in the housing, so that oil is drawn into the cylinder from the crankcase sump. At the same time the delivery port W' in the housing is uncovered and oil below the disc in the housing is forced through W' back to the oil tank.

Position 2. The plunger A' is being pushed into the cylinder hole in the disc C'. The port T' in the disc now registers with the delivery port X' in the housing, so that oil is forced out of the cylinder back to the oil tank. At the same time the suction port Z' in the housing is uncovered and oil is drawn into the housing below the disc from the crankcase sump.

The standard gear ratios with 20T and 21T sprockets are as follows:—

	20T	21T
Bottom Gear	12·32	11·75
Second Gear	8·16	7·8
Third Gear	6·51	5·72
Top Gear	4·44	4·22

19. Clutch

The clutch has six pressure plates and five friction plates, including the sprocket which is lined on both sides with friction material. On earlier models this was a moulded material riveted on but later models employ a bonded cork based material. The four loose friction plates on the later clutches use the same cork based material bonded on. In earlier clutches the two inside plates had inserts of moulded material which, though it would stand more heat was more liable to slip if an excess of oil reached the friction surfaces.

A description of the operating mechanism is given in Subsection 63.

Service Operations with Engine in Frame

20. Removal of the Timing Cover

First place a tray under the engine to catch the oil which will escape when the cover is removed. Remove the timing side exhaust pipe. Remove the oil filler neck by taking out the three screws fixing it to the crankcase. Remove the timing cover fixing screws. Draw off the timing cover, tapping it lightly if necessary.

In refitting the cover, insert the two long screws through the cover to locate the gasket. See that the thrust washer is on the chain tensioner sprocket spindle and that the neoprene seal is in position on the oil feed plug. If the seal or plug is damaged a new one of either should be fitted. The seal is Part No. 42114 and the plug is Part No. 42113.

The refitting of the cover will be facilitated if the engine is turned gently forwards while the cover is being put into place. This will help the engagement of the pump worm with the pump spindle and prevent damage to the gears.

Always fill the filter with clean oil before refitting the timing cover and always take great care not to damage the gasket where the section is narrow.

To verify that the oil pumps are working after replacing the timing cover, start the engine and slacken the feed plug between the oil pumps. The return oil pump can be checked by removing the oil filler cap so that the oil return pipe can be seen. It may take several minutes for all the oil passages to fill and the oil to commence circulating. The feed to the rockers can be observed by removing the rocker-box covers, when oil will be seen flowing down the surface of the push rods.

21. Valve Timing

The camshaft sprockets are keyed to the camshafts so that the valve timing can only be incorrect if the timing chain is incorrectly fitted.

The correct setting is obtained with the marks stamped on the camshaft sprockets facing each other inwards on the centre line and the mark on the crankshaft sprocket pointing vertically downwards. (See Fig. 4.) If it is necessary to remove the sprockets see Subsections 43 and 44.

Remember that all three timing sprocket fixing bolts have **Left-Hand Threads.** While tightening the camshaft bolts the sprockets should be held.

The table on page 11 shows the characteristics of three alternative camshaft and sprocket arrangements which are available. The choice between these depends on whether the owner wants (1) good torque and speed with good mechanical silence or (2) maximum torque up to 80 m.p.h. or (3) maximum flat-out speed. When checking opening and closing points do not expect precise agreement with the figures quoted. The figures obtained when checking will depend largely on the method used to decide when the valve opens or closes also, if using a dial gauge, whether this is reading the movement of the tappet or spring collar. It must be remembered, too, that the precise timing of each valve depends on the accurate position of *four* keyways and on whether the timing chain is new or worn. The figures in the table are intended as a guide to which cams are fitted and enable a check to be made that the timing marks are correctly lined up. If opening and closing points on the same shaft are early or late by about 30° the sprocket is fitted one tooth wrong

22. Tappet Adjustment

The tappet clearance is adjusted by means of a screw in the outer end of the rocker. Access to the adjusting screws is obtained by removing the covers of the rocker boxes.

The inlet should be set so that the rocker is just binding, the exhaust so that it is just free. For

Ref.	Camshaft	Inlet Sprocket	APPROXIMATE TIMING AT ·012 in. CLEARANCE				Remarks
			EX. opens B.B.D.C.	EX. closes A.T.D.C.	IN. opens B.T.D.C.	IN. closes A.B.D.C.	
1	EX. 32705 IN. 32705 (Standard)	36140	82°	35°	35°	82°	Cams have quietening ramps. Least mechanical noise. Good torque and speed.
2	EX. 35345 IN. 35344 (Sports)	36140	77°	35°	37°	60°	Better torque than (1). Same maximum speed. Noisier.
3	EX. 35345 IN. 35344 (Sports)	45207 (Marked "A")	77°	35°	22°	75°	Torque as (1) up to 80 m.p.h. Better than (1) or (2) above 90 m.p.h. Noisier than (1)

continuous high speed work, however, give the exhaust ·005 in. clearance. These figures are for a COLD engine.

To adjust the clearance, loosen the locknut beneath the rocker arm, turn the screw and retighten the locknut.

The adjustment of each valve should be made with the corresponding valve in the other cylinder fully open. This ensures that the tappet is on the neutral portion of the cam.

If the heads of the adjusting screws are worn they should be replaced.

23. Removal of the Camshafts

Remove the timing cover (Subsection 20).
Remove the camshaft sprockets (Subsection 44).
Remove the three screws holding each of the camshaft bearing housings.*

Compress the valve springs and withdraw the camshafts. It is necessary to rotate the camshafts slightly while withdrawing them in order that the cams will pass through the shaped hole in the crankcase.

When replacing the camshafts compress the valve springs and hold the tappets clear of the cams. If the rocker adjusting screws are screwed right back, it is not necessary to compress the valve springs.

24. Ignition Timing

To set the ignition timing, first remove the timing cover (Subsection 20) and then remove the magneto sprocket nut and withdraw the sprocket, using Special Tool No. 14835 in the case of the earlier engines fitted with manual ignition control.

*From engine No. YB16573 onwards the fitting of detachable crankshaft bearing housings was discontinued. To remove the camshafts from these engines it is necessary to separate the two halves of the crankcase. See Subsections 55, 56 and 57.

When automatic control is fitted no special extractor is required. Merely unscrew the centre sleeve nut which secures the auto. advance coupling to the magneto and keep on unscrewing, when the coupling will be drawn off its shaft.

Set the contact points to ·012/·015 in. when fully opened. If they are worn or pitted a new set should be fitted. (See Fig. 20, Subsection 80, for illustration of contact breaker.)

Remove both sparking plugs and set the pistons $\frac{7}{16}$ in.—$\frac{11}{32}$ in. (31° to 32°) before top dead centre. Note which piston is on the compression stroke (both valves closed) and which is on the exhaust stroke (exhaust valve open).

Fit the magneto chain and sprocket, or auto. advance coupling, and tighten the nut finger tight. Set the ignition control in the fully advanced position (manual control) or, in the case of engines fitted with automatic advance, rotate the two halves of the coupling relatively to each other against the springs and hold them in this position with a piece of wire. Now rotate the magneto armature forwards (anti-clockwise looking at the contact breaker) until the points just commence to open as indicated by the fact that it is *just* possible to withdraw a piece of *thin* tissue paper from them. Tap the magneto sprocket or auto. advance coupling on to the tapered end of the magneto shaft and tighten the centre sleeve nut.

Now rotate the engine through one revolution and check the timing on the other contact breaker cam. The H.T. pick-up nearest to the contact points when they are in the open position is the "live" one and the H.T. lead from this must be connected to the sparking plug in the cylinder which is on the compression stroke. Do not forget to remove the wire holding the auto. advance coupling.

Note.—To check the timing (as opposed to resetting it) set the pistons $\frac{11}{32}$ in. before t.d.c.

with the ignition retarded. Now advance the timing either by the manual control (when fitted) or by rotating the contact breaker arm anti-clockwise (auto. advance). The points should just open in the full advance position.

25. Primary Chain Adjustment

The tension of the primary chain can be checked through the inspection cover in the primary chain case and, should it require adjustment, access to the adjuster is gained by removing the chain case cover, which is held in position by a single nut. Before removing the nut, place a tray under the engine to catch the oil from the chaincase.

Beneath the bottom run of the chain is a curved slipper on which the chain rests and which may be raised or lowered by turning the adjusting screw after having first slackened the locknut.

A rubber button is fitted to the end of the adjusting screw to prevent the transmission of chain noise to the chaincase and this is held against the chaincase by a hairpin spring, which prevents it from bouncing.

Do not adjust the chain to be dead tight but rotate the engine slowly and, while doing so, test the tension of the top run of the chain by pressing it up and down with the fingers. Adjust the tension so that there is $\frac{1}{4}$ in. up and down movement at the tightest spot.

Re-tighten the locknut on the adjusting screw, replace the chain cover and replenish with oil to the height of the level plug.

26. Timing Chain Adjustment

Before adjusting the tension of the timing chain, turn the engine until the chain is in its tightest position, checking the chain between all sprockets.

Adjust the tension so that there is $\frac{1}{4}$ in. movement of the chain.

The tension of the timing chain is altered by moving the quadrant after slackening the nut A which secures it (see Fig. 4). This rotates the eccentric spindle on which the chain tensioner jockey sprocket is mounted. Tightening of the chain is effected by moving the quadrant to the left.

It is imperative that the quadrant is fitted the right way round and that the eccentric spindle is fitted correctly in the quadrant fork. If the chain tightens when the quadrant is moved to the right, the tensioner has been wrongly assembled and may cause damage to the quadrant (see Fig. 5).

In making the adjustment, care must be taken to see that any backlash in the quadrant is taken up in the "tightening" direction, i.e. do not make the chain too tight and then move the quadrant back slightly, but tighten the chain progressively until the correct tension is obtained and then lock the quadrant. If the chain becomes too tight during adjustment, slacken it right back and make the adjustment again.

If the chain is too slack it may give rise to a loud noise which can be mistaken for a faulty bearing. If it is too tight the result will be a high pitched howl. If such noises are heard, therefore, first check the adjustment of the timing chain.

27. Magneto Chain Adjustment

To adjust the magneto chain tension, remove the timing cover (see Subsection 20), slacken the three magneto fixing nuts, slide the magneto back until the chain has about $\frac{3}{16}$ in. up and down movement, then tighten the fixing nuts.

28. Removal of the Dual Seat and Rear Mudguard

Disconnect the leads to the rear lamp by pulling out the plugs in the connectors near the tool box.

Loosen the two nuts on either side of the seat attaching the mudguard carrier to the frame and lift the seat, mudguard and carrier off together.

29. Removal of the Petrol Tank

The petrol tank is rubber mounted front and rear. The front attachment is by means of a horizontal stud passing through a rubber sleeve

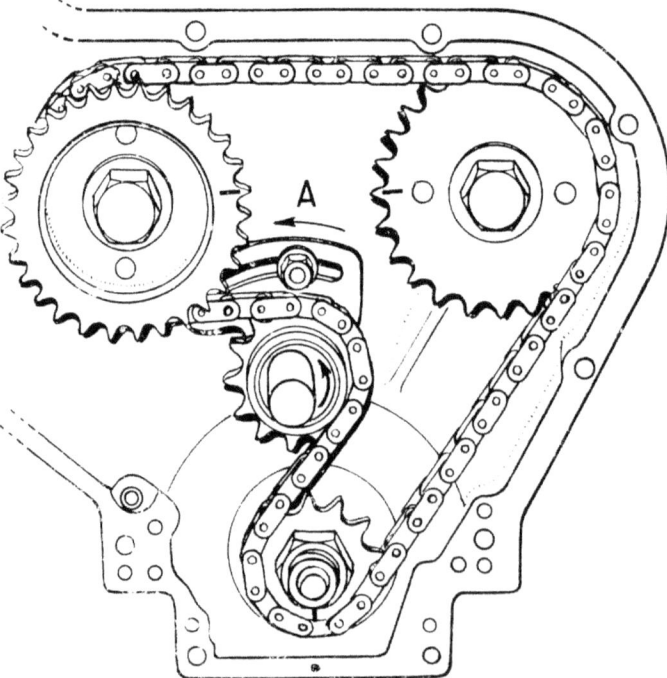

TIMING CHAIN ADJUSTMENT SHOWING TIMING MARKS
Fig. 4

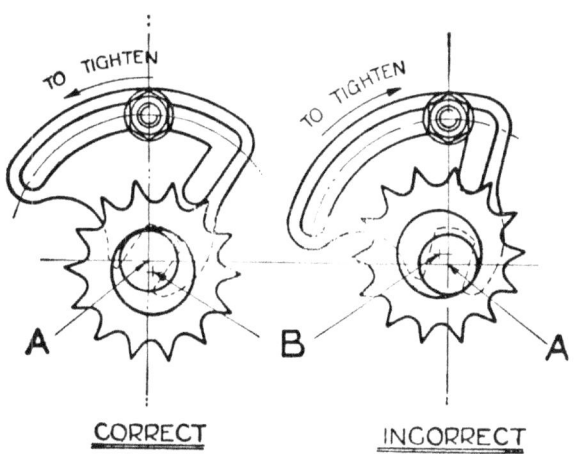

TIMING CHAIN ADJUSTMENT

Fig. 5

housed in a lug across the frame immediately behind the steering head. The rear fixing on the 4¼ gallon tank is by means of a transverse clamp and two bolts which pull the tank down on to rubber blocks above and beneath the top tube. On the smaller capacity tanks used in the U.S.A. a rubber lined metal clip is used secured by two ¼ in. diameter bolts and nuts.

To remove the tank, first disconnect the petrol pipes, then remove the nut from one end of the front attachment stud and knock out the stud. Then unscrew the nuts or bolts securing the rear end of the tank and lift it away, taking care not to damage the paintwork on top at the front end where it may come into contact with the handlebar clamp. It is preferable to remove the dual seat and rear mudguard before attempting to lift the tank.

30. Removal and Refitting of the Cylinder Head

First remove the petrol tank and petrol pipe. (Subsection 29.)

The dual seat may also be removed if desired. (Subsection 28.)

Remove head steady brackets.

Disconnect the oil pipes and plug leads.

Remove the exhaust pipes and carburetter(s). also the induction manifold on single carburetter models.

Remove the rocker box covers.

Turn the engine until both valves in one head are closed.

Remove the five cylinder head nuts from the head, hit it smartly with a hide mallet beneath the exhaust and inlet ports (not the fins) and lift it off.

Turn the engine through one revolution and repeat with the other head.

When replacing the heads, see that the dowels are in position in the cylinder barrels and that the push rods are the right way up (shallow cups upwards).

See that the taper section "Cross" sealing ring and its seatings are perfectly clean and that the rubber seals for the push rod tunnels are in good condition and correctly fitted. With the head upside down on the bench drop the packing shim into the recess first, then the seal with the metal side downwards. A little jointing compound should be applied to both sides of the "Cross" sealing ring and the rubber push rod tunnel seals.

Lower the cylinder heads over the push rods making sure that the rockers locate in the cups.

Fit the head nuts *and washers* and tighten down lightly. At this stage fit the induction pipe on single carburetter models. Do not overtighten the nuts—20 lbs. ft. is the recommended figure. Tighten each nut a little at a time in turn. Begin with the two inside nuts and the one by the spark plug, leaving the final tightening of the corners to the last.

31. Removal of the Valves

Having removed the cylinder head, remove the rocker-box covers, each held by four nuts, and swing the rocker clear of the valve. Using a suitable valve spring compressing tool, compress the valve springs and remove the split collets from the end of the valve stem. Slacken back the compressing tool and release the springs. Withdraw the valve and place its springs, top spring collar (and bottom collar if it is loose) and split collets together in order that they may be reassembled with the valve from which they were removed.

Deal similarly with the other valves in the heads.

If the valve will not slide easily through the valve guide, remove any slight burrs on the end of the valve stem with a carborundum stone. If the burrs are not removed and the valve is forced out, the guide may be damaged.

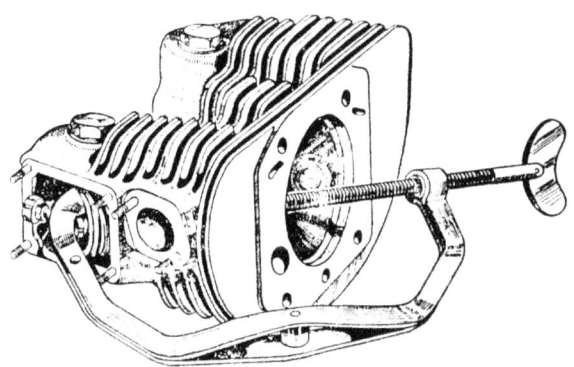

REMOVAL OF VALVES

Fig. 6

32. Removal of the Rockers

To remove the rocker, first take off the cylinder head. Remove the hexagon plug on the inner side and the rocker spindle may be drawn out by means of a bolt screwed into the rocker spindle, which is tapped $\frac{5}{16}''$ B.S.F.

On reassembling make sure that the spring washers are fitted on the sides of the rockers nearest the centre of the engine and the plain thrust washers on the outer sides.

33. Removal of the Valve Guides

To remove the valve guides from the heads two special tools are required which can easily be made.

The first is a piece of tube with an internal bore of not less than $\frac{7}{8}$ in.

The second is a mandrel about 4 in. long made from $\frac{9}{16}$ in. diameter bar with the end turned down to about $\frac{5}{16}$ in. diameter for $\frac{1}{2}$ in.

Support the cylinder head on the tube which fits over the collar of the valve guide. Using the mandrel force the guide out of the head with a hand press or by using a hammer.

To fit a new guide, support the head at the correct angle and use a hand press and the same mandrel. If a hand press is not available and the guide is replaced by a hammer, use a piece of tube of $\frac{9}{16}$ in. internal diameter to prevent damage to the bore of the guide. If a valve guide is removed for any reason, an oversize one should be fitted in order to maintain the interference. It is necessary to re-cut the valve seat and grind in the valve after a guide has been replaced. (See Subsection 38.)

A worn exhaust valve guide may give rise to slight smoking from the exhaust pipe due to oil passing down the valve stem on to the hot valve head. This may also be caused or increased by faulty operation of the breather.

34. Removal of the Sparking Plugs

Care must be taken when removing and replacing the sparking plugs not to damage the threads in the cylinder heads.

If the threads do become damaged, they can be tapped out to a larger size and steel wire inserts fitted.

Special tools are available for tapping and inserting the steel wire inserts. The latter tool consists of a piece of $\frac{7}{16}$ in. diameter tube or rod with a slot cut in the end.

The insert is placed over the tool with the tag engaging in the slot and it is screwed into the plug hole in the cylinder head from the outside until the last coil is 1 to $1\frac{1}{2}$ threads below the top face. A reverse twist of the tool will then break off the tag.

If the cylinder head has been removed, the fitting of the insert will be facilitated if the tool is put through the hole from the inside and the insert screwed back from the outside.

If the cylinder head has not been removed, care must be taken not to drop the end of the tag into the cylinder and in such a case it is better to break off the tag with a pair of long-nosed pliers.

35. Removal of the Cylinders

When the cylinder heads have been removed the cylinders can be lifted clear of the studs. This should be done with the pistons at top dead centre.

It is advisable to put a clean cloth over the mouth of the crankcase to prevent anything, such as a piece of broken piston ring, from falling in.

When replacing the cylinders, clean off the joint faces and fit new paper joints, two to each cylinder.

36. Removal of Pistons

Remove the cylinder heads and cylinders.

With a tang of a file remove the two outer circlips retaining the gudgeon pins. Remove the long central cylinder studs which come opposite the gudgeon pins.

Use Special Tool No. E 5477/T to extract the gudgeon pin or using a rod about $\frac{1}{4}$ in. in diameter insert this right through one gudgeon pin and drive the other pin out of its piston, supporting the connecting rod substantially meanwhile to prevent distortion.

Having lifted the first piston away, the other one may be readily removed in the same manner. Mark the pistons and gudgeon pins so that they go back into the same pistons the same way round and so that the pistons go back into the same barrels the same way round.

Take care not to drop the gudgeon pin circlip into the crankcase. A clean cloth should be put over the mouths of the crankcase to prevent this.

37. Decarbonising

Having removed the cylinder heads as described in Subsection 30, scrape away all carbon, bearing in mind that you are dealing with aluminium which is easily damaged. Scrape gently and avoid scoring the combustion chamber or the valve seats which are of austenitic iron shrunk into the head. Be careful while performing this work not to injure the joint faces which bed down on to the head gaskets.

Do not, in any circumstances, use caustic soda or potash for the removal of carbon from aluminium alloy.

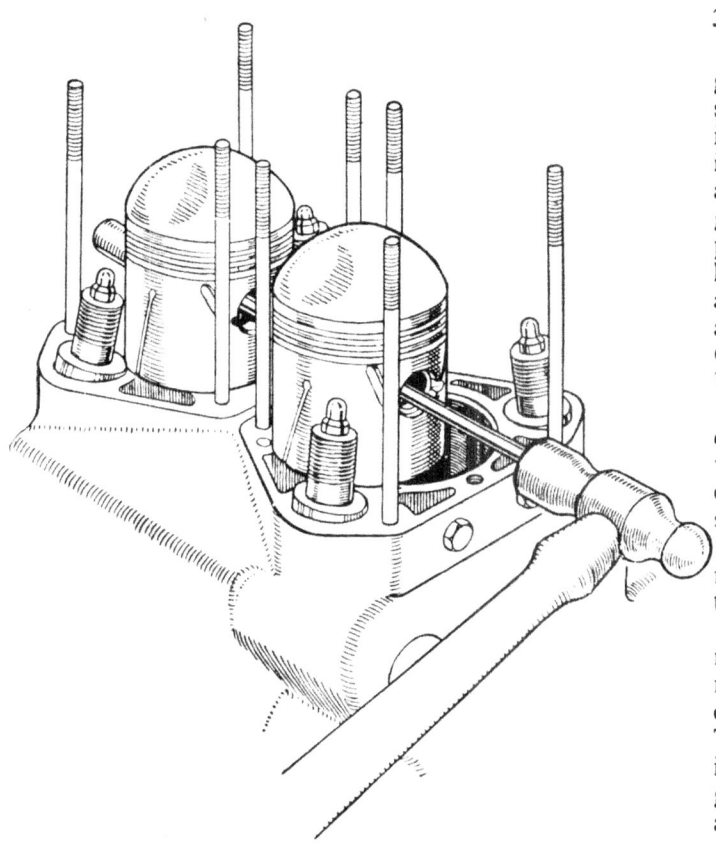

REMOVAL OF PISTONS

Fig. 7

Scrape away all carbon from the valve heads and beneath the heads, being very careful not to cause any damage to the valve faces.

If the piston rings are removed the grooves should be cleaned out and new rings fitted. For cleaning the grooves, a piece of discarded ring thrust into a wooden handle and filed to a chisel point is a useful tool.

If the piston ring gaps exceed $\frac{1}{16}$ in. when the rings are in position in the barrel, new rings should be fitted. The correct gap for new rings is ·015—·020 in. The gap should be measured in the least worn part of the cylinder, which will be found to be the extreme top or bottom of the bore.

While the cylinders and pistons are not in position on the engine, cover the crankcase with a clean cloth to prevent the ingress of dust and dirt of all kinds. Do not, of course, attempt to scrape the carbon from the pistons when the mouths of the crankcase are open.

38. Grinding-in Valves

To grind a valve, smear the seating with a little grinding-in compound, place a light, short coil spring over the valve stem and beneath the head, insert the valve into its appropriate guide, press it on to the seat using a tool with a suction cup and with a backwards and forwards rotary motion, grind it on to its seat. Alternatively, a tool which pulls on the valve stem can be used. Frequently lift the valve and move it round so that an even and true seating is obtained. If no light spring is available, the lifting will have to be done by hand. Continue grinding until a bright ring is visible on both valve and seating.

The faces and seats of the exhaust valves are cut at 45 degrees but the profiles of the inlet valves are of a special streamlined design which eliminates pockets and sharp edges and allows a smooth flow of gas without eddies.

If the inlet valves or their seats are pitted and require re-cutting, care must be taken to reproduce the correct profile as shown in Fig. 8.

The cylinder heads should preferably be returned to the Works for the inlet valve seats to be re-cut but, if this is not possible, a special tool consisting of an arbor No. T.2053 and cutter No. T.2054 is available. Great care must be exercised in using this tool as it is located off the valve guides and these may be damaged if suitable apparatus is not employed.

The inlet valve faces and seats can be cut at 45 degrees in cases of emergency but this may have a deleterious effect on the performance of the engine.

39. Reassembly after Decarbonising

Before building up the engine, see that all parts are scrupulously clean and place them conveniently to hand on a clean sheet of brown paper.

Check the piston ring gaps to find out whether excessive wear has taken place (see Subsection 37).

It is advisable to fit new gaskets to the cylinder base and cylinder head. Two paper gaskets are fitted to the base of each cylinder.

Smear clean oil over the pistons, having replaced the rings if these have been removed, lower the piston over the connecting rod and insert the gudgeon pin from the outer side. Fit the circlip and then fit the second piston in a similar manner.

Oil the cylinder bores and lower the barrels over the pistons and seat them gently on their gaskets.

Drop the push rods down their tunnels on to the tappet heads, shallow cups upwards.

Replace the cylinder heads as described in Subsection 30.

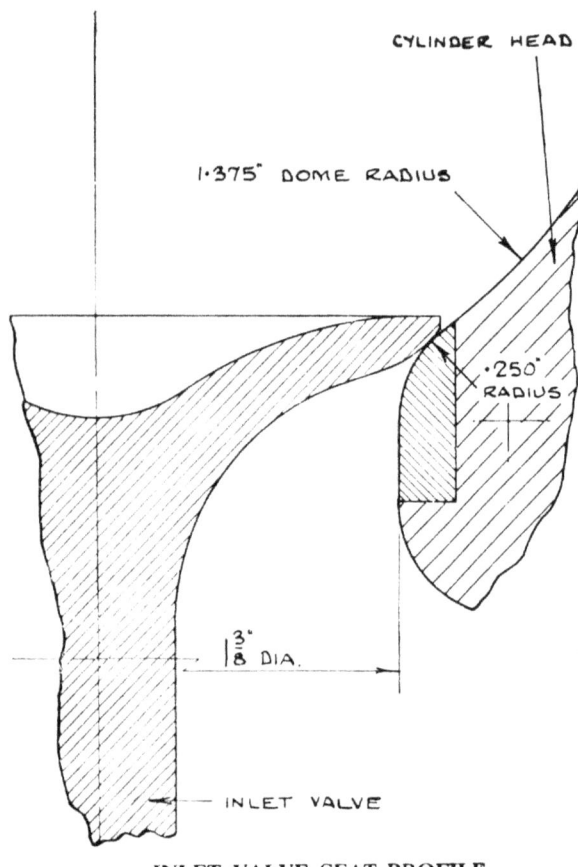

INLET VALVE SEAT PROFILE

Fig. 8

After the engine has been assembled, run it for a brief period at a speed which will ensure that the ignition has been advanced by the automatic advance device. If it is run too slowly "blueing" of the exhaust pipes may take place.

After the engine has been run for some time and has become thoroughly hot, go over **all** the cylinder head and other nuts to ensure that they are tight.

40. Cleaning the Oil Filters

The oil filter is located in the timing cover immediately below the oil pumps and is in the feed circuit to the big ends.

The filter element is removed by unscrewing the nut holding the end cap in position. When reassembling the filter after cleaning, take care that no grit or other foreign matter is sticking to it. The aluminium cylinder fitted over the rod inside the filter element is to reduce the free space which has to be filled after cleaning before oil reaches the big ends. After emptying the filter chamber it is essential to run the engine slowly for about five minutes to ensure that oil is reaching the big ends.

The felt element should be taken out and washed in petrol after the first 500 miles and after every subsequent 2,000 miles. Fit a new element every 5,000 miles.

41. Overhaul of Oil Pumps

Remove the timing cover as described in Subsection 20

Remove the end plates from both pumps.

Remove the pump discs and plungers.

Remove the pump spindle which can be pulled out from the front or return pump end after removal of the locating screw.

Check the fit of the plungers in the pump discs which should have a minimum of clearance but should be able to be moved in and out by hand.

If, when fitting a new disc or plunger, the plunger is found to be too tight a fit, carefully lap with metal polish until it is just free. If the pump disc is not seating properly or if a new pump disc is being fitted, it should be lapped to the seating with Special Tool No. E.5425, using Carborundum 360 Fine Paste or liquid metal polish until an even grey surface is obtained.

Wash all passages, etc., thoroughly with petrol after lapping to remove all traces of grinding paste.

Check the pump disc springs for fatigue by assembling in the timing cover and placing the pump covers in position. If the springs are correct, the pump cover should be held ¼ in. off the timing cover by the pump spring.

The pump spindle should be renewed if excessive wear has taken place on the teeth.

Reassemble the oil pumps, replacing the paper cover gaskets if necessary. Before fitting each cover fill the pump chamber with clean oil.

Having assembled the pumps, lay the timing cover flat and fill the oil ports by means of an oilcan. Turn the pump spindle with a screw driver in a clockwise direction looking on the front and it can then be seen whether the pumps are operating correctly.

CORRECT RELATIVE POSITIONS OF DUAL SCRAPER RINGS

Fig. 9

Fill the filter chamber with clean oil and replace the timing cover, taking great care not to damage the gasket where the section is narrow. (See Subsection 20.)

When the timing cover has been refitted on the engine, the oil feed to the big ends can be checked by partially unscrewing the feed plug in the timing cover between the oil pumps. The oil return to the tank can be checked by removing the oil filler cap. The feed to the rockers can be observed by removing the rocker-box covers, when oil will be seen flowing down the surface of the push rods.

42. Removal of the Timing Chains

Remove the magneto and chain (Subsection 45).

Loosen the chain tensioner locknut and stud.

Lift the adjusting plate clear of the chain tensioner spindle.

Remove the chain tensioner spindle and sprocket.

Lift the chain off the sprockets.

43. Removal of Pump Worm and Timing Sprocket

Remove the timing chains (Subsection 42).

Unscrew the oil pump worm by means of the hexagon head behind it. This is a **Left-Hand Thread.**

Withdraw the timing sprocket using Special Tool No. E.4869.

44. Removal of the Camshaft Sprockets

Remove the timing chains (Subsection 42).

Unscrew the camshaft sprocket fixing bolt, **which has a Left-Hand Thread,** at the same time holding the sprocket.

Withdraw the sprocket by means of a suitable extractor.

45. Removal of the Magneto

Remove the timing cover (Subsection 20).

Remove the magneto sprocket or auto-advance coupling (Subsection 24).

Remove three fixing nuts and withdraw the magneto.

46. Removal of the Engine and Clutch Sprockets

The primary chain is endless so that it is necessary to remove both the engine and clutch sprockets simultaneously.

The alternator stator is removed by undoing the three fixing nuts, after which the stator can be pulled off the three studs on which it is located.

Remove the central hexagon bolt securing the alternator rotor, which can then be drawn off, taking care not to lose the key.

Unscrew the engine sprocket nut, using Special Tool No. E.4877. The engine sprocket is mounted on splines and can then be removed with the clutch sprocket.

To remove the clutch sprocket, unscrew the three pressure plate pins and remove the pressure plate assembly, the centre retaining plate and the assembly of driving and driven clutch plates. The clutch sprocket can then be withdrawn from the centre after the removal of the large circlip which secures it.

47. Removal of the Tappets and Guides

It is only necessary to remove the tappets and guides if they have become worn.

Remove the cylinder heads and barrels. (Subsections 30 and 35.)

Extract the tappet guides, using Special Tool No. E.5790, having heated the case first.

The guides are made from Nickel Chrome Alloy Iron and if a guide should break while removing it, it can be withdrawn with a pair of pliers if the crankcase is heated locally with a blowlamp. Otherwise it is necessary to dismantle the crankcase and drive the tappet and guide out from underneath using a heavy bar in the cam tunnel.

The guide should have an interference of ·0015 to ·0025 in. in the crankcase and can be driven in with a bronze drift, care being taken when the guide is nearly home to avoid breaking the collar.

If a tappet guide is taken out it should be replaced by an oversize one.

48. Dismantling the Breathers

If the breathers are not operating efficiently, they may cause pressure in the crankcase, instead of a partial vacuum, giving rise to smoking or over-oiling.

See that the discs and backplate of the breather on the crankcase immediately below the left-hand cylinder are clean and undamaged, and that the discs are seating properly.

When reassembling the breather, apply jointing compound sparingly to the back of the steel plate, taking great care to keep the compound away from the discs and seatings.

The breather which operates through the crankshaft, may be inspected by removing the slotted plug from the head of the rotor retaining bolt. (See Fig. 10.)

49. Removal of the Clutch

Remove the engine sprocket and clutch sprocket together as described in Subsection 46.

To remove the clutch hub, hold the clutch with

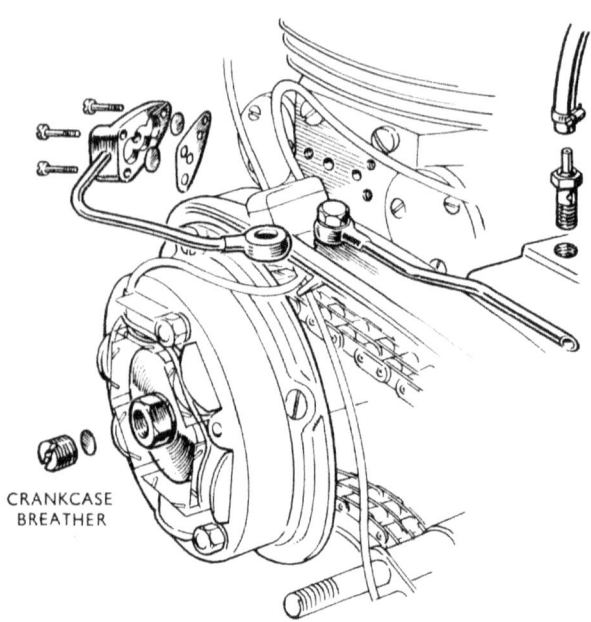

CRANKCASE BREATHERS
Fig. 10

Special Tool No. E.4871 and remove the centre retaining nut and washer with a box spanner.

The hub can then be withdrawn from the shaft with Special Tool No. E.5414.

50. Removal of the Final Drive Sprocket

Remove the clutch as described in Subsection 49.

Remove the primary chain tensioner.

Remove the rear half of the primary chain case by taking out three socket screws and the centre stud.

Remove the grub screw locking the final drive sprocket nut.

Hold the sprocket and remove the nut (**Right-Hand Thread**). The sprocket can then be withdrawn.

51. Oil Seal Behind Engine Sprocket

This consists of a neoprene oil seal, with a garter spring, backed up by either one or two steel washers. The correct order of assembly is as follows:—

(1) Press the oil seal W43382 into the chain case from the front with the garter spring facing the inside of the case. The seal should be pressed in till its outer face is flush with the inner surface of its housing in the back half of the chain case.

(2) Into the recess thus formed at the back of the chaincase fit the thicker washer W34069.

(3) If provided, fit the thinner washer W34068 so that it lies between W34069 and the edge of the outer race of the driving side main ball bearing.

(4) Fit the back half of the chain case to the engine and tighten the three socket screws W38027. This should result in the oil seal being pushed in to the chain case so that its face stands slightly proud of the inner surface of its housing.

(5) Fit the engine sprocket, taking great care not to damage the lip of the seal when pushing the sprocket through it.

52. Oil Pipe Unions

The oil feed to the rocker gear is through pipes from unions at the back of the crankcase below the cylinder base to unions on the cylinder heads.

The tapped holes into which the unions screw into the aluminium are fitted with steel wire inserts to prevent the threads in the aluminium from stripping.

The method of fitting the thread inserts is the same as that used for the sparking plug inserts described in Subsection 34.

53. Rocker Oil Feed Relief Valve

There is a pressure relief valve in the oil supply to the rocker gear, whose function is to prevent excessive pressure and whose setting is not critical.

The valve is located in the crankcase face behind the timing cover and consists of a $\frac{3}{16}$ in. diameter steel ball held in position by a spring and a brass plug.

The valve is set before leaving the Works and should not normally require to be disturbed but, if it is found necessary to dismantle it, it can be reset by screwing the plug in until it is flush with the face of the crankcase, which will cause the pressure to be relieved at approximately 10 lbs. per square inch. The plug is prevented from moving by peening over the aluminium **into** the screwdriver slot with a small centre punch.

54. Fitting the Alternator

The alternator consists of two parts, the stator and the rotor.

The stator is mounted on to the primary chaincase with three studs and distance pieces.

The rotor, which contains the permanent magnets, is mounted on the end of the crankshaft and is located by a key and secured by a special bolt and washer.

The radial air gap between the rotor and the poles of the stator should be ·020 in. in all positions and care must be taken when refitting to see that it is not less than ·010 in. at any point.

Fit the rotor first, making sure that it is located concentrically on the end of the crankshaft. Attention must be given to the seating of the key because a badly-fitting key may cause the rotor to run unevenly. Finally secure the rotor with the appropriate bolt and washer.

Place the three distance pieces over the three chaincase studs. The stator can then be fitted, with the coil connections facing outwards.

Replace the nuts and shakeproof washers only finger-tight, and insert six strips (preferably of non-magnetic material) ·015 in. thick and about ⅛ in. wide between the rotor and each pole piece.

Tighten the stator nuts and withdraw the strips.

Check the air gap with narrow feelers and, if less than ·010 in. at any point, remove the stator and set the three studs carefully until the correct gap is obtained.

An alternative, and more satisfactory, method of assembling the alternator requires the use of Special Tool No. T2055/19.

This is a gauge ·015 in. greater in radius than the rotor and fits over the adaptor on the end of the crankshaft in the rotor's place.

The stator is then put in position on the studs in the chaincase and the nuts tightened up.

Remove the gauge and fit the rotor, then check the air gap.

Service Operations with Engine Removed

55. Removal of the Engine Gearbox Unit from the Frame

Disconnect the battery leads.
Remove the dual seat and petrol tank.
Remove the engine steady.
Remove the tool box cover and slide the flexible connection to the air cleaner off the induction pipe (where fitted).
Remove the exhaust pipes.
Disconnect the electric horn leads.
Loosen the rectifier bracket and swing the rectifier clear.
Remove contact breaker cover.
Remove carburetter fixing pins.
Remove the rear chain.
Disconnect the clutch cable.
Remove the footrest bar.
Remove the bottom rear engine bolt and the bolt securing the gearbox bracket to the frame. Loosen the nuts on the chainstay pivot bolt.
Support the engine on a suitable box or wood block.
Raise the centre stand and remove the spring.
Loosen the bottom gearbox nuts and swing the lower engine plates down.
Remove the front engine plates, horn and stand.
Lift the engine out of the frame.

56. Removal of the Gearbox

Remove the engine sprocket and clutch (Subsections 46 and 49).
Remove the rear half of the primary chaincase by removing three socket screws and the centre stud.
The gearbox and gearbox bracket can now be withdrawn from the back of the crankcase after unscrewing the four nuts which secure them.

57. Dismantling the Crankcase

Drain the oil tank by removing the drain plug.

Having removed the engine from the frame as described in Subsection 55, dismantle the heads, barrels, pistons, timing gear and magneto, as described in Subsections 20, 30, 35, 36, 42, 43, 44 and 45.

Remove the gearbox as described in Subsection 56.

Remove the two hexagon-headed plugs on the driving side of the crankcase just below the cylinder base.

Access can now be obtained through the plug holes to two screws holding the two halves of the crankcase together which must be removed. (See Fig. 11.)

Remove three nuts in the timing chest, two nuts on the driving side crankcase, two loose studs through the bottom of the crankcase and two loose studs through the back of the oil tank. (The other studs have already been removed to take the engine out of the frame.)

Turn the crankshaft until the connecting rods are at bottom dead centre and the two halves of the crankcase can then be separated, tapping the crankcase with a soft mallet.

The inner race of the roller bearings on the timing side will remain on the crankshaft bringing with it the cage and rollers and leaving the outer race fixed to the crankcase.

The inner race of the ball bearing on the driving side is a tight fit on the shaft and can be removed with Special Tool No. E.5121. If this is not available, the shaft can be driven out with a hide mallet or a soft metal drift.

To avoid damage to the ball bearing the case should be heated to about 100°C. before doing this.

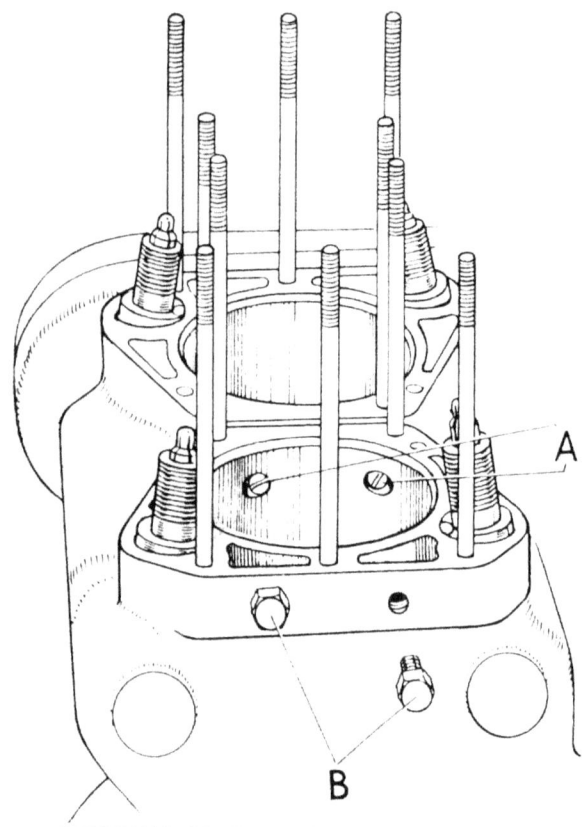

REMOVAL OF SCREWS IN CRANKCASE
Fig. 11

58. Main Bearings

To remove the ball bearing from the driving side crankcase, heat the crankcase to about 100 degrees C. by immersion in hot water or in an oven after which the bearing can be driven out using a drift **which applies pressure to the outside race only.**

When refitting a new ball bearing, heat the crankcase in the same way and use the same drift taking great care to keep the bearing square with the bore.

To remove the outer roller race from the timing side crankcase, first heat the crankcase then drive the race out using a small punch through the three holes provided.

The inner race and rollers can be withdrawn from the crankshaft using a claw type extractor.

When refitting the inner race drive it on to the shaft until just flush with the end and no further.

59. Fitting the Connecting Rods

To remove the connecting rods from the crankshaft, unscrew the socket screws in the connecting rods, having first removed the security wires through the heads (if fitted).

If the big end bearings caps are removed to examine the condition of the bearings, *make sure that the caps are refitted the same way round on the same rods and that the rods themselves are refitted the same way round on the same crank pins.*

In refitting the connecting rods, the socket screws should be tightened with a torque wrench set at 250 in. lb. (21 ft. lb.).

No cotter pins or other locking devices are fitted. If the socket screws are correctly tightened they will never come loose. If they are *not* adequately tightened they are liable to fatigue failures. Use only genuine big end screws, Part No. 47876 These have a very high fatigue strength due to the use of a special steel and the fact that the threads are rolled *after* heat treatment. Wiring the heads is not recommended.

If it is necessary to replace the big ends, a service crankshaft can be supplied with connecting rods fitted.

60. Reassembly of Crankcase

If the main bearings have been removed fit the replacement ball bearing in the driving side crankcase and the outer roller race in the timing side as described in Subsection 58. The outer race should be pressed home until it nips the steel and rubber oil seal W46200 (steel washer W36275/A on early engines) and should then be secured by making four equally spaced centre punch marks in the case so as to spread the aluminium over the radiused edge of the race.

Assembly of the two halves of the crankcase on to the crankshaft is easier if the crankcase is warmed while the crankshaft is cold. If the driving side is fitted first take particular care not to knock a roller out of the timing side main bearing when fitting the timing side case—this could cause serious damage to the engine. Risk of this is obviated by fitting the timing side of the case first but, if this is done, care must be taken not to rotate the crankshaft until it has been located endways by fitting the engine sprocket and tightening the nut right home. Rotation of the shaft before it is positioned correctly could score the inside of the timing side of the case.

It is possible to assemble the crankcase cold but the bearing clearances will then be reduced. This may necessitate wrapping a piece of thin string round the rollers of the timing side bearing to ensure their easy entry into the outer race. When cold it will be necessary to draw the driving end of the crankshaft through the ball bearing by means of the sprocket nut and a temporary distance piece used in place of the sprocket and somewhat shorter than it. The nut and distance piece must then be removed and the shaft locked into place by tightening the nut after fitting the sprocket.

Whichever method of assembly is used make sure that all parts are scrupulously clean, put clean oil on bearings, remove all traces of old jointing compound and any protruding pieces of metal from the joint face by means of a scraper and put fresh jointing compound on the face between the two halves of the crankcase. Do not forget the distance piece W34062 between the driving side ball bearing and the crank web and make sure that the camshafts are correctly fitted, exhaust at the front, inlet at the rear. Lift the tappets to clear the cams.

Bolt the two halves of the crankcase together before the jointing compound has set. Do not forget the two screws between the cylinder barrels (see Fig. 11).

61. Crankshaft Plugs

The oil passage through the big ends is sealed by two screwed aluminium plugs locked by a centre punch.

If the crankcase is taken out of the engine for any reason, the plugs should be removed and the oil passage cleared of sludge.

62. Pump Worm Threads

If the threads in the crankshaft, into which the pump worm screws, become damaged, a steel wire insert can be fitted. The crankshaft should preferably be returned to the Works for this to be done or, alternatively, the hole can be drilled out $\frac{7}{16}$ in. in diameter, using the timing sprocket as a drill bush and new threads tapped with a special tool. **Note that the thread is left-hand.**

The method of fitting the wire insert is the same as described in Subsection 34, for the sparking plugs.

Gearbox and Clutch

63. Description of the Clutch

The clutch is built into the clutch sprocket and is mounted on the gearbox mainshaft which projects through into the primary chaincase.

There are six driven plates which are plain and five driving plates, giving ten friction surfaces.

The driven plates comprise the clutch centre back plate, two dished and two flat steel plates on splines on the clutch centre drum, and the clutch front plate. (See Fig. 13.)

The driving plates include the clutch sprocket itself, which has a ring of friction material bonded to it (riveted on early models) and is located on the clutch centre drum by an anti-friction bearing consisting of 54 balls, $\frac{3}{16}$ in. diameter (in early models) or a ring of low friction material (in later ones). There are four loose friction plates splined to the clutch outer drum, which is riveted to the clutch sprocket. On early models the two plates nearest to the sprocket have keystone-shaped inserts of friction material and the two outer plates have bonded-on segments of "J.17" (a synthetic cork-based material which gives particularly good grip under oily conditions). On later models all the driving plates have bonded-on facings of J.17 material.

Pressure is applied to the clutch plates by six springs fitted between the outside of the clutch

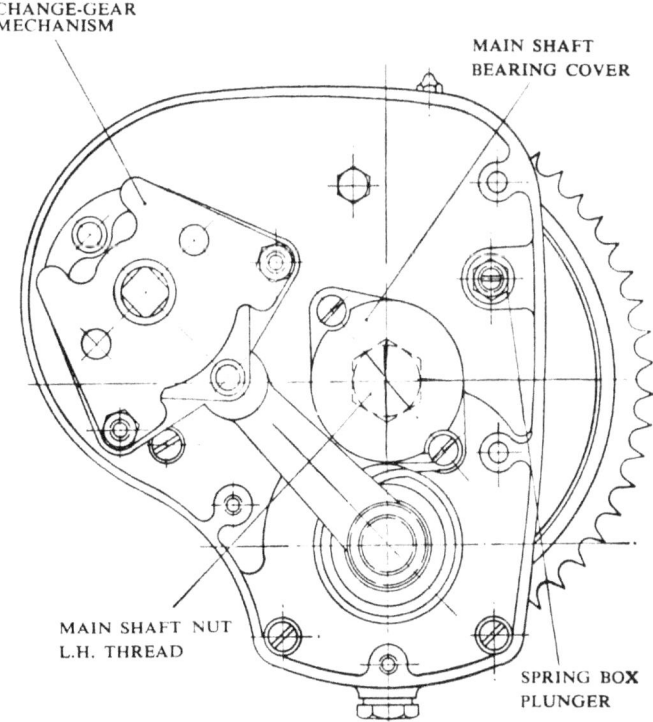

GEARBOX WITH OUTER COVER REMOVED
Fig. 12

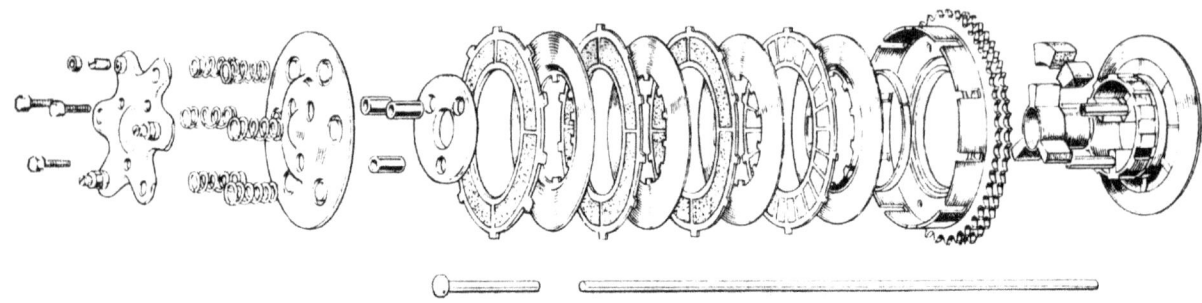

EXPLODED VIEW OF CLUTCH
Fig. 13

front plate and the inside of a star-shaped pressure plate.

The clutch operating mechanism consists of a lever mounted on the inside of the outer cover of the gearbox and operated by the control cable and handlebar lever. When the control is operated the clutch front plate is caused to move to the left, against the pressure of the springs, by means of a pad pushed by a rod passing through the gearbox mainshaft and operated by the lever in the outer cover through an adjusting screw and ball.

The clutch centre drum drives the mainshaft through a cush drive with six rubber blocks.

64. Description of the Gearbox

The operation of the gearbox is shown diagrammatically in Fig. 14.

The clutch sprocket A is mounted on the end of the mainshaft B which passes through the mainshaft sleeve C on the end of which is the final drive sprocket D.

At the other end of the mainshaft B is a pinion E which engages with a pinion F on the layshaft G. At the other end of the layshaft G is a pinion H engaging with a pinion J which runs free on the mainshaft sleeve C.

The mainshaft sleeve C has splines on which slides a double pinion KL. This double pinion KL engages with two pinions M and N which are free to rotate or slide on the layshaft G.

The double pinion KL has dogs at each end which can engage with dogs on the pinion E or on the pinion J.

The pinions M and N have internal dogs which can engage or slide over projecting dogs P and Q on the layshaft G.

The double pinion KL and the pinions M and N all slide together and are moved by the operator fork R and are located by a spring plunger S which engages with a notched plate which is part of the operator arm R.

The kickstart lever is connected to the pinion F on the layshaft by a ratchet mechanism which automatically disengages when the lever is released.

65. Removal of the Gearbox

This is described in Subsection 56.

The gearbox can, however, be completely dismantled with the engine in the frame except for the removal of the inside operator and the bearings in the gearbox shell.

66. To Dismantle the Gearbox

First remove the kickstart crank, the change-gear lever and the neutral finder and pointer.

Remove four screws and the gearbox outer cover can then be detached.

Remove the change-gear mechanism, by taking off the two nuts securing it.

Remove the mainshaft bearing cover which is attached by two screws.

Remove four cheese-headed screws and one hexagon bolt.

Remove the spring box locating plunger nut and washer.

Remove the mainshaft nut **(left-hand thread)**.

The gearbox inner cover can then be removed.

The mainshaft can be drawn straight out if the clutch has been removed, which, however, should be done before taking off the gearbox inner cover. (See Subsection 49.) The top gear pinion and dog will come away with the mainshaft.

The layshaft can then be removed and the 2nd and 3rd gears drawn off the final drive sleeve together with the operator fork.

To take out the final drive sleeve, the final drive sprocket must be removed and this is preferably done before removing the inner cover. (See Subsection 50).

67. Removal of the Ball Races

The mainshaft ball bearings can be removed by using a stepped drift $1\frac{7}{16}-1\frac{11}{64}$ in. diameter for

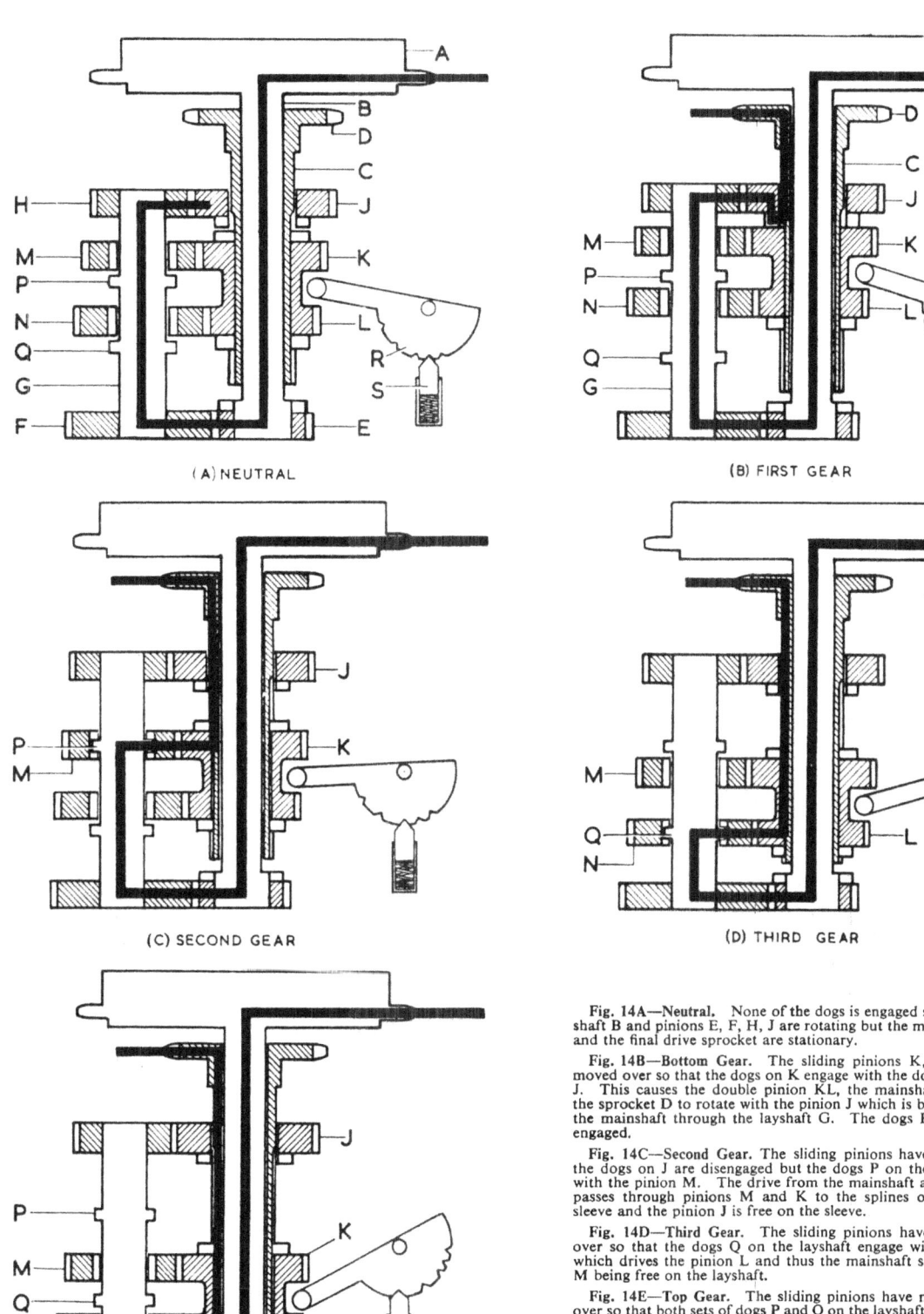

OPERATION OF GEARS
Fig. 14

Fig. 14A—Neutral. None of the dogs is engaged so that the mainshaft B and pinions E, F, H, J are rotating but the mainshaft sleeve C and the final drive sprocket are stationary.

Fig. 14B—Bottom Gear. The sliding pinions K, L, M, N have moved over so that the dogs on K engage with the dogs on the pinion J. This causes the double pinion KL, the mainshaft sleeve C and the sprocket D to rotate with the pinion J which is being driven from the mainshaft through the layshaft G. The dogs P and Q are not engaged.

Fig. 14C—Second Gear. The sliding pinions have moved so that the dogs on J are disengaged but the dogs P on the layshaft engage with the pinion M. The drive from the mainshaft and layshaft then passes through pinions M and K to the splines on the mainshaft sleeve and the pinion J is free on the sleeve.

Fig. 14D—Third Gear. The sliding pinions have moved further over so that the dogs Q on the layshaft engage with the pinion N which drives the pinion L and thus the mainshaft sleeve, the pinion M being free on the layshaft.

Fig. 14E—Top Gear. The sliding pinions have now moved right over so that both sets of dogs P and Q on the layshaft have disengaged but the dogs on the double pinion KL have engaged with those on the pinion E and the mainshaft and sleeve rotate together giving a one to one drive through the gearbox from the clutch sprocket to the output sprocket the pinions M, N, J being free to rotate.

the bearing in the box and $\frac{13}{16}-\frac{39}{64}$ in. diameter for the bearing in the cover.

When refitting the bearings stepped drifts of $2\frac{5}{16}-1\frac{11}{64}$ in. diameter and $1\frac{11}{16}-\frac{39}{64}$ in. diameter must be used for the bearings in the box and cover respectively.

Note the oil seal in the recess behind the larger mainshaft bearing.

68. Change-Gear Mechanism

If the two nuts securing the change-gear ratchet mechanism are slackened the adjuster plate can be set in the correct position. In this position the movement of the gear lever necessary to engage the ratchet teeth will be approximately the same in each direction.

If the plate is incorrectly adjusted, it may be found that, after moving from top to third or from bottom to second gear, the outer ratchets do not engage the teeth on the inner ratchets correctly.

If, when fitting new parts, it is found that the gears do not engage properly, ascertain whether a little more movement is required or whether there is too much movement so that the gear slips right through second or third gear into neutral. If more movement is required, this can be obtained by filing the adjuster plate very slightly at the points of contact with the pegs on the ratchet ring.

If too much movement is already present, a new adjuster plate giving less movement must be fitted.

69. Reassembling the Gearbox

The procedure is the reverse of that given in Subsection 66, but the following points should be noted:—

If the mainshaft top gear pinion and dog have been removed, make sure that the dog is replaced the right way round or third and top gears can be engaged simultaneously.

Make sure that the trunnions on the operator fork engage with the slots in the inside operator.

See that the mainshaft is pushed right home. It may tighten in the felt washer inside the final drive shaft nut.

The layshaft top gear and kickstarter pinion should be assembled on the layshaft and the kickstarter shaft and ratchet assembled on to it before fitting the end cover. Do not forget the washer on the layshaft between the kickstarter pinion and the kickstarter shaft.

The joint between the gearbox and the inner cover should be made with gold size, shellac or a similar jointing compound.

Make sure that all parts are clean before commencing assembly. In normal climates the recesses in the gearbox should be packed with soft grease and the box should be filled up to the correct level with engine oil. (See Subsection 73.) **On no account must heavy yellow grease be used.**

70. Dismantling and Reassembling the Clutch

The method of removing the clutch is described in Subsection 46.

When reassembling the clutch, the following sequence must be adhered to, after first securing the clutch sprocket with the large circlip.

Fit the cush rubbers, retaining plate and three distance tubes, and follow with the pressure plate assembly as follows:—

Plain dished plate (dish projecting outwards.)
Friction plate (with inserts on early models).
Plain flat plate.
Friction plate (with inserts on early models).
Plain flat plate.
Friction plate (with bonded facings).
Plain dished plate (dish projecting inwards).
Friction plate (with bonded facings).
Front plate.
Pressure plate and springs.

When reassembling the pressure and front plates, see that the three distance pieces are fitted over the pins securing the pressure plate to the clutch centre drum. These must pass through the holes in the front plate into the three recesses in the clutch centre retaining plate. Note that three strong (13g) and three weak (14g) springs are used. These *must* be fitted alternately and, in the case of later models with adjusting screws on three arms of the pressure plate, the 14g springs *must* be fitted behind the adjusting screws. The three pressure plate pins must be locked up tight.

If the clutch lifts unevenly adjust one or, if necessary, two of the adjusting screws in the pressure plate (later models). These screws can also be used to increase the spring pressure when wear has taken place on the friction surfaces but care must be taken not to screw them in too far. This could reduce the lift of the clutch by causing some of the springs to become coil bound, thus causing clutch drag.

71. Adjustment of Clutch Control

It is essential that there is about $\frac{1}{32}$ in. free movement in the clutch cable, to ensure that all the spring pressure is exerted on the plates.

There are three points of adjustment for the clutch control. The first is in the clutch operating lever in the gearbox and is accessible after removing the lower inspection cover in the front cover of the gearbox (see Fig. 16). The clutch cable should be slacked right off or, preferably, disconnected when making this adjustment. Slacken the locknut and adjust the centre screw in or out

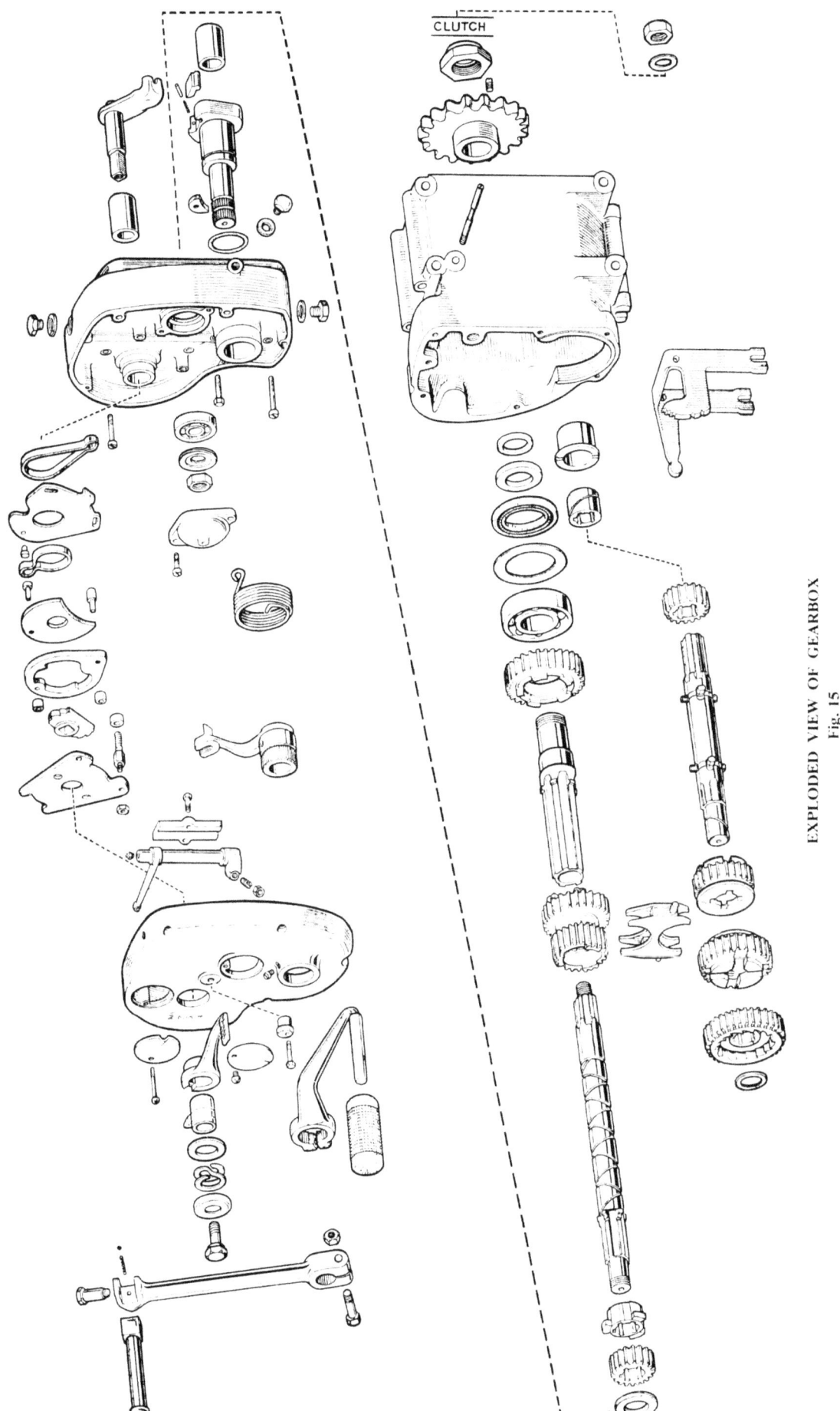

EXPLODED VIEW OF GEARBOX
Fig. 15

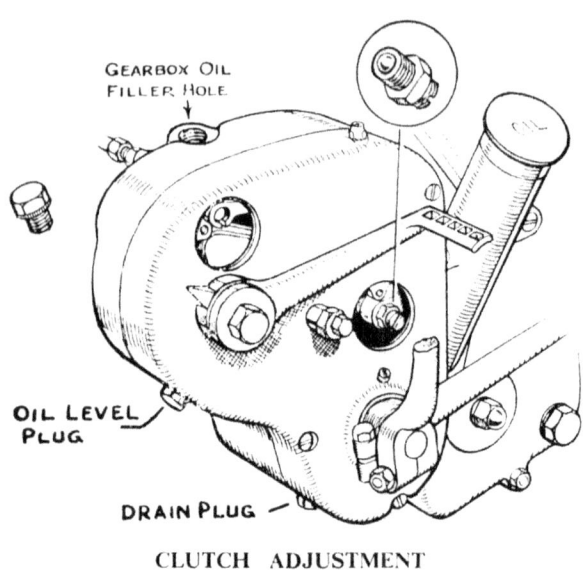

CLUTCH ADJUSTMENT
Fig. 16

until it is as nearly as possible in line with the clutch push rod. Tighten the locknut and check that no part of the lever is hard against the inside of the gear box front cover or either of the inspection covers.

The second and third adjustments are in the outer casing of the clutch control cable. There is an adjustable sleeve with a locknut forming the abutment for the outer casing at the gearbox end (in some machines this may be replaced by a mid-cable adjuster about 12 in. from the handlebar lever) and also a finger-operated sleeve and locknut at the handlebar end.

To adjust the control cable, having first set the adjuster in the gearbox clutch operating lever correctly, couple up the control cable, screw the adjusting sleeve at the handlebar end of the casing in as far as possible then unscrew it two turns. Now adjust the sleeve at the gearbox end of the casing until there is $\frac{1}{32}$ in. to $\frac{1}{16}$ in. slack in the control. If the control is adjusted in this manner the finger adjustment at the handlebar end can be used to take up any slack which may appear temporarily as the result of the friction material swelling due to heat if the clutch has to be slipped a great deal in traffic. This adjustment can also be used to give more clearance temporarily if this is necessary as a result of wear of the friction linings. This, however, should be corrected finally by adjusting the centre screw in the gearbox clutch operating lever.

72. Adjustment of the Neutral Finder

The neutral finder is adjusted by means of an eccentric stop secured to the front of the gearbox cover by a bolt which limits the travel of the operating pedal. Slacken the bolt and turn the eccentric until the correct movement of the pedal is obtained.

73. Gearbox Oil Level

The gearbox is filled with oil by removing a plug in the top and the correct level can be checked by removing a second plug lower down on the left-hand side looking at the cover. (See Fig. 16.)

Amal Monobloc Carburetter

74. General Description

Two of the well-known AMAL Monobloc carburetters are fitted direct on to the inlet ports as standard though for special purposes a model is available with a single carburetter supplying both cylinders through a branched induction manifold. A sectioned view of the carburetter is shown in Fig. 17 and an "exploded" view in Fig. 19 which actually illustrates the left-hand carburetter of a pair, or the type used when only one carburetter is fitted. On early models the right-hand carburetter had no float or float chamber but was fed with petrol from the float chamber on the left-hand carburetter through a connecting tube joining the two main jet holders. On recent machines the right carburetter has its own float chamber which is on the right-hand side of the mixing chamber, the carburetter being a mirror image of that illustrated. Each float chamber contains a metal or plastic barrel-shaped float operating on a nylon fuel needle with a powerful lever action which ensures a positive cut-off unless there is dirt on the seating.

The supply of air to the engine is controlled by a throttle slide which carries a taper needle operating in the needle jet. The needle is secured to the throttle slide by a spring clip fitting in one of five grooves and the mixture strength throughout a large proportion of the throttle range is controlled by the position of this needle in the slide and by the size of the jet in which it works. There is, however, a restricting or main jet at the bottom of the needle jet and the size of this controls the mixture strength at the largest throttle openings. At very small throttle openings petrol and air are fed to the engine through a separate pilot system, which has an outlet at the engine side of the throttle. The air supply to this pilot system is controlled by the pilot air screw and the slow running of the engine can be adjusted by means of this screw and a stop which holds the throttle open a very small amount. The throttle slide is cut away at the back and the shape of this cut-away controls the mixture at throttle openings slightly wider than that required for slow running. There is a compensating system to prevent undue enriching of the mixture with increasing engine speed, this system consisting of a primary choke surrounding the upper end of the needle jet through which air is drawn in increasing quantities as the depression in the main choke increases. This air supply and the supply to the pilot system are taken from two separate ducts in the main air intake to the carburetter so that all the air passing to the engine can be filtered by fitting an air cleaner to the main carburetter air intake.

Two small cross holes in the needle jet, at a level just below the static level in the float chamber, permit petrol to flow into the primary choke when the engine is not running or when it is running at very low speeds, thus forming a well of petrol which will be drawn into the engine on starting or accelerating from low speeds. At moderately high engine speeds the level of petrol in the float chamber falls slightly and in consequence no more fuel flows

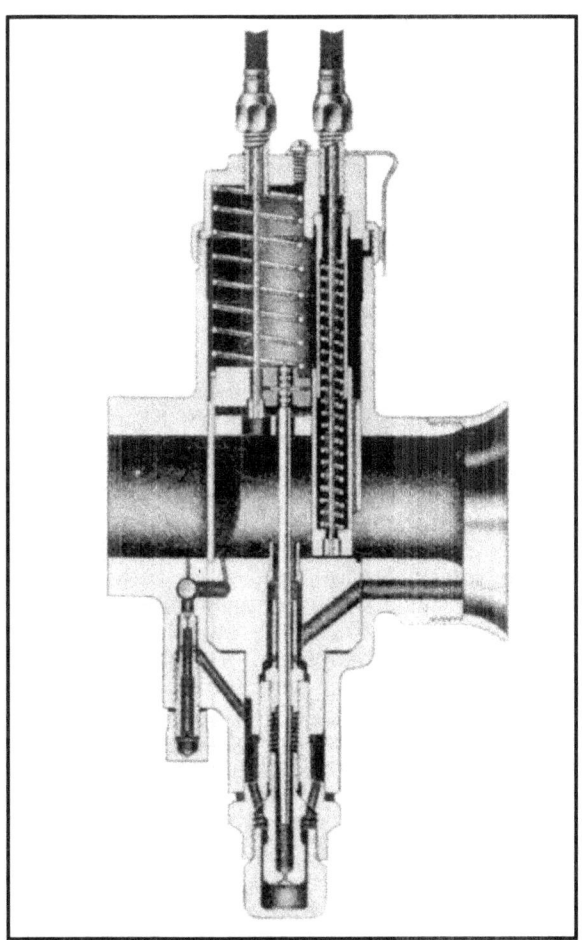

SECTION THROUGH MIXING CHAMBER, SHOWING AIR VALVE AND THROTTLE CLOSED

Fig. 17

through the cross holes in the needle jet so that the petrol well remains empty until the engine slows down or stops.

A handlebar controlled air slide is provided to enrich the mixture temporarily when required.

75. Tuning the Carburetter(s)

The throttle opening at which each tuning point is most effective is shown in Fig. 18. It should be remembered, however, that a change of setting at any point will have some effect on the setting required at other points; for instance, a change of main jet will have some effect on the mixture strength at half throttle which, however, is mainly controlled by the needle position. Similarly an alteration to the throttle cut-away may affect both the needle position required and the adjustment of the pilot air screw. For this reason it is necessary to tune the carburetter in a definite sequence, which is as follows:

First—Main Jet. The size should be chosen which gives maximum speed at full throttle with the air control wide open. If two different sizes of jet give the same speed the larger should be chosen for safety as it is dangerous to run with too weak a mixture at full throttle.

Second—The pilot air screw should be set to give good idling. Note that the pilot jet is detachable and two sizes are available, 25 c.c. and 30 c.c. If the pilot air adjusting screw requires to be screwed out less than half a turn the larger size pilot jet should be used; if the air screw requires to be screwed out more than 2-3 turns fit the smaller size of pilot jet.

Third—The throttle valve should be selected with the largest amount of cut-away which will prevent spitting or misfiring when opening the throttle slowly from the idling position.

Fourth—The lowest position of the taper needle should be found consistent with good acceleration with the air slide wide open.

Fifth—The pilot air screw should be checked to improve the idling if possible. When setting the adjustment of the pilot air screw this should be done in conjunction with the throttle stop. Note that the correct setting of the air screw is the one which gives the fastest idling speed for a given position of the throttle stop. If the idling speed is then undesirably fast it can be slowed down by unscrewing the throttle stop a fraction of a turn.

It will be noted that of the four points at which adjustments are normally made, i.e., pilot air screw, throttle cut-away, needle position and main jet size, the first and third do not require changing of any parts of the carburetter. Assuming that the carburetter has the standard setting to suit the particular type of engine any small adjustments occasioned by atmospheric conditions, changes

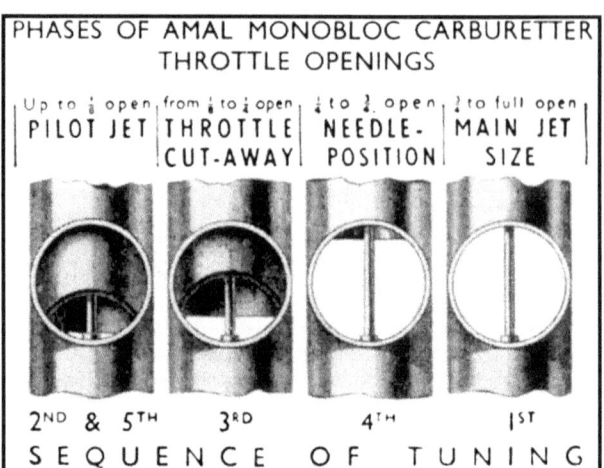

Fig. 18

in quality of fuel, etc., can usually be covered by adjustment of the pilot air screw and raising or lowering the taper needle one notch. If, however, the machine is used at very high altitudes or with a very restricted air cleaner a smaller main jet will be necessary. The following table gives the reduction in main jet size required at different altitudes:

Altitude, ft.	Reduction, %
3,000	5
6,000	9
9,000	13
12,000	17

In the case of carburetters for engines running on alcohol fuel considerably larger jets are needed. In most cases a No. 113 needle jet will be required and the main jet size will require to be increased by an amount varying from 50% to 150% according to the grade of fuel used.

If the engine is run on fuel containing a small proportion of alcohol added to the petrol, a rough and ready guide is that the main jet should be increased by 1% for every 1% of alcohol in the fuel. In most cases alcohol blends available from petrol pumps do not contain sufficient alcohol to require any alteration to the carburetter setting.

The range of adjustment of the taper needle and the pilot air screw are determined by the size of the needle jet and of the pilot outlet respectively. Standard needle jets have a bore at the smallest point of ·1065 in. and are marked 106. Alternative needle jets ·1055 in., ·1075 in., ·109 in. and ·113 in. bore are available and are marked 105, 107, 109 and 113 respectively.

The standard pilot outlet bore is ·025 in. but in some cases larger size pilot outlets are used. Since the pilot outlet is actually drilled in the body of the carburetter it is necessary to have a carburetter with

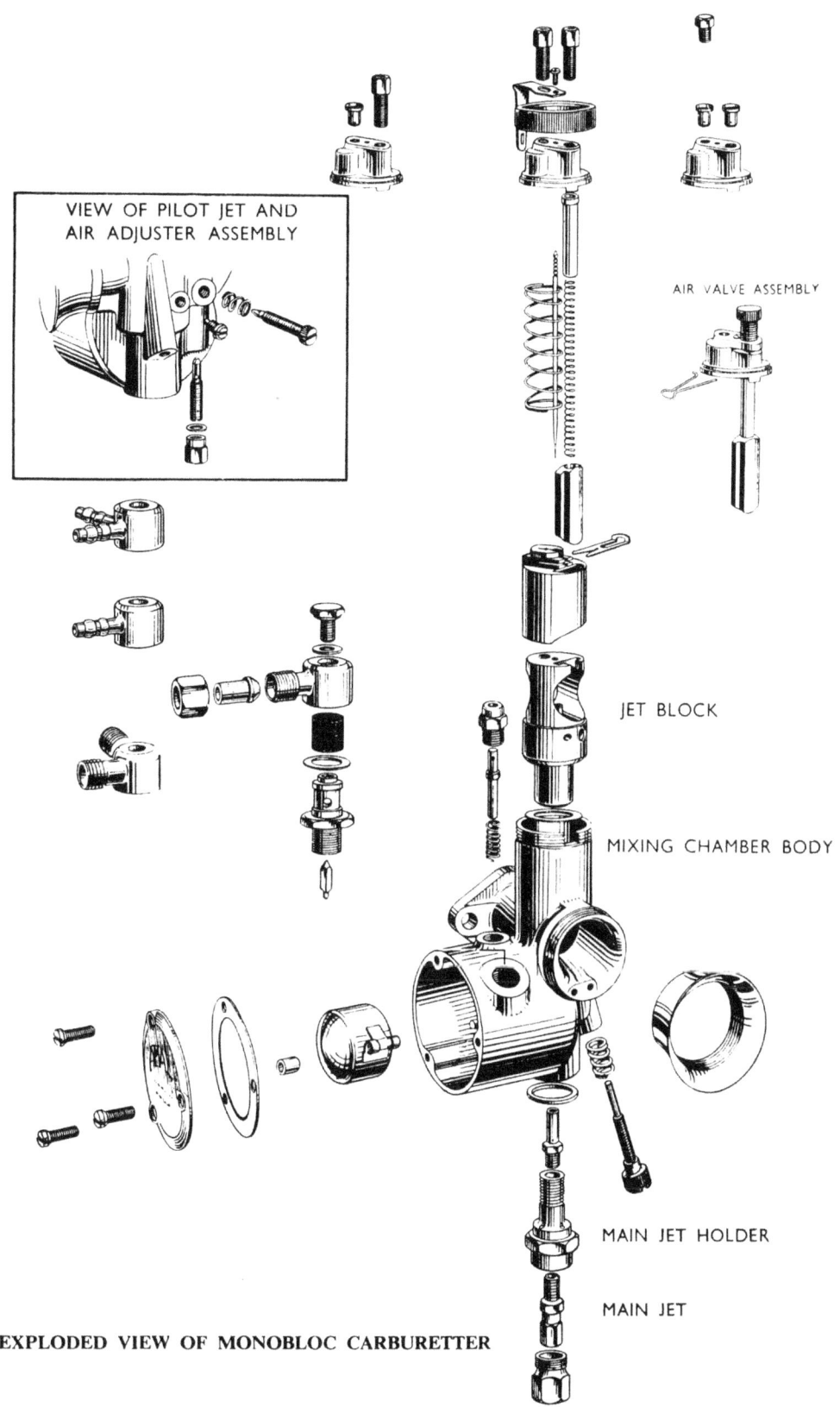

EXPLODED VIEW OF MONOBLOC CARBURETTER

Fig. 19

the correct size pilot outlet if the best results are to be obtained.

The accompanying table shows the standard settings for Amal Monobloc Carburetters used on Royal Enfield "Interceptor" motor cycles.

These may be taken as correct for all normal conditions and for practical purposes carburetter tuning consists only of setting the pilot air screw and throttle stop.

76. Tuning Sequence with Two Carburetters

When setting the slow running on machines fitted with two carburetters the following procedure is recommended —

(1) See that both throttle slides are open the same amount for any given position of the twist grip. This is most easily checked by looking into the air intakes while slowly opening and closing the throttles with the air slides wide open. Make sure that the highest point of the cut-away on the throttle valve reaches the top of the bore simultaneously in both carburetters. If necessary adjust one or both mid-cable adjusters in the throttle cables.

(2) Repeat this procedure for the air slides.

(3) Start the engine and let it run at a fast idle till thoroughly warm. Open the air slides fully and remove the H.T. lead and waterproof plug cap from the right-hand sparking plug, opening the throttle if necessary to keep the engine running on one cylinder.

(4) Adjust the throttle stop on the left-hand carburetter to hold the throttle just wide enough open to keep the engine running with the twist grip shut.

(5) Adjust the pilot air screw on the left-hand carburetter to give the maximum speed for this throttle position.

(6) Slow down the engine as far as possible by adjusting the throttle stop and reset the pilot air screw if necessary to give the maximum speed for the new throttle position. Repeat till the engine is running as fast as possible on the smallest possible throttle opening.

(7) Replace the right-hand plug cap and lead and remove the left-hand ones.

(8) Repeat (4), (5) and (6) on the right-hand carburetter.

(9) Replace the left-hand plug cap and lead. The engine should now be running steadily at a fast idle.

(10) Slow the engine down by unscrewing each throttle stop equally. If running becomes lumpy adjust each pilot air screw an equal amount. If necessary, slow engine down further by unscrewing each throttle stop equally but do not try to get *too* slow an idle with a hot engine otherwise it will be liable to stop when only partly warmed up.

77. Dismantling Carburetter

The construction of the carburetter is clearly shown in Fig. 19.

If the float chamber floods, first make sure that there is no dirt on the fuel needle seating. Owing to the use of a nylon needle and the leverage ratio between float and needle, flooding is very unlikely with this type of carburetter unless dirt is present or, of course, the float is punctured.

If it is necessary to remove the jet block note that this is withdrawn from the upper end of the

Settings for AMAL Monobloc Carburetters on Royal Enfield 736 c.c. "Interceptor" Motor Cycles

Carburetter Type No.	Choke Bore in.	Main Jet c.c.	Needle Jet in.	Needle Position	Throttle Valve	Pilot Jet c.c.	Remarks
L/H 389/85 R/H 389/86	$1\frac{3}{16}$	380	·1065	3	$389/3\frac{1}{2}$	25	Float on L/H Carburetter only. Tube connecting Jet Holders.
L/H 389/205 R/H 689/205	$1\frac{3}{16}$	380	·1065	4	$389/3\frac{1}{2}$	25	L/H Float on L/H Carburetter. R/H Float on R/H Carburetter. No connecting tube.
L/H 389/225 R/H 689/225	$1\frac{3}{16}$	400	·109	3	389/3	30	As 389/205 and 689/205 but special rich setting for Californian market.
389/226	$1\frac{3}{16}$	360	·1065	3	$389/3\frac{1}{2}$	25	For single Carburetter Model.

Notes: Some 389/205 and 689/205 were sent out with No. 3 needle position.

Some 389/205 and 689/205 were converted to 389/225 and 689/225 without renumbering.

Needle positions:—No. 1 = clip in top groove. No. 5 = clip in bottom groove.

mixing chamber after unscrewing the jet holder. Be careful not to damage the jet block when removing or refitting it. Note that the large diameter of the jet block pulls down on to a thin washer.

A single strand of an inner control cable is useful for clearing the small passages in the jet block and care must be taken not to enlarge these by forcing the wire through them. Compressed air from a pipe line or a tyre pump is preferable. A choked main jet should be cleared only by blowing through it.

78. Causes of High Petrol Consumption

If the petrol consumption is excessive first look for leaks either from the carburetter, petrol pipes, petrol taps or tank. If coloured petrol is in use this will readily indicate the presence of any small leaks which otherwise might pass unnoticed. If the petrol system is free from leaks, carefully set the pilot adjusting screw as described in Subsections 75 and 76 to give the correct mixture when idling. Running with the pilot adjusting screw too far in is a common cause of excessive petrol consumption. If the consumption is still heavy try the effect of lowering the taper needle in the throttle slide by one notch. Do not fit a smaller main jet as this will not affect consumption except when driving on nearly full throttle and may make the mixture too weak at large throttle openings, thus causing overheating. Remember that faults in other parts of the machine can have a marked effect on petrol consumption. Examples of this are binding brakes, chains too tight or out of line and, in particular, under-inflated tyres.

Lucas Twin-Cylinder Magneto

Models K2F 42369B and L.U. 54044111 (Automatic Advance)

79. General

This magneto incorporates a wound rotating armature and a high-energy permanent magnet field system, this latter being cast integral with the body. The unit is designed for 3-point flange fixing.

Small breathing holes are provided in the body of the magneto. These holes should not be allowed to become blocked.

On earlier models provision is made for altering the ignition timing by the manual control method, in which the cam ring is moved relatively to the armature. The lever controlling this movement is mounted conveniently on the handlebars and is connected by Bowden cable to the magneto. On later models an automatic advance and retard mechanism is fitted to the magneto driving sprocket.

80. Lubrication

To be carried out every 3,000 miles.

(i) Wipe the outside of the magneto to remove dirt or grease, and then take off the contact breaker cover. Unscrew the hexagon-headed screw in the centre of the contact breaker and withdraw the contact breaker from its housing. Prise off the special locking plate from the contact breaker arm pivot pin, taking care not to lose the insulating washer beneath it.

Slacken the screw which retains the contact breaker arm spring. The contact breaker arm may then be lifted from its pivot.

Wipe away any dirt or grease from the contacts with a petrol-moistened cloth. If necessary, use a very fine carborundum stone to polish the contacts, recleaning afterwards with a petrol-moistened cloth. Smear the pivot pin with a little Mobilgrease No. 2 before refitting the contact breaker arm.

In the case of magnetos with manual control remove the cam ring, which is a sliding fit in its housing, and lightly smear inside and outside surfaces with Mobilgrease No. 2. Both removal and refitting of the cam can be made easier if the handlebar control lever is half retarded, thus taking the cam away from its stop pin. Apply one or two drops of thin machine oil to the felt cam lubricator in the housing. Refit the cam, taking care that the stop peg in the housing and the plunger of the manual timing control engage with their respective slots. There is no need to disturb the cam ring when automatic advance mechanism is fitted.

Refit the contact breaker. This can be made easier if the contact breaker heel is away from the

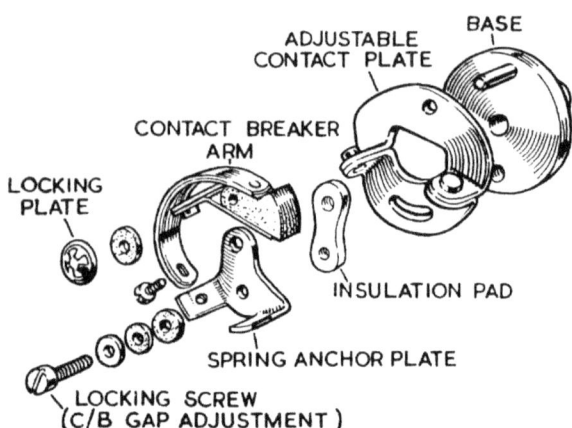

K2F (42369B) MAGNETO CONTACT BREAKER
Fig. 20

cam lobe; turn the engine until this is so. The key on the projecting part of the contact breaker base must engage with the keyway in the armature shaft. Refit the hexagon-headed screw and tighten with care. It must not be slack, nor must undue force be used.

(ii) *Bearings.* The main bearings of the magneto are packed with grease during manufacture and need no attention until a general overhaul is undertaken.

81. Adjustments

Check every 3,000 miles.

(i) *Setting contact breaker gap.* The contact breaker gap must be set to 0·012–0·015 in. when the contacts are fully separated.

To adjust the gap, turn the engine until the contacts are fully opened. Slacken the cheese-headed screw which locates the spring anchor plate; the plate on which the contact is mounted may then be moved away from or towards the contact breaker arm, to give the required clearance.

(ii) *Adjusting the Timing Control Cable.* Slackness in the manual control timing can be taken up by sliding the waterproofing rubber shroud up the cable and turning the hexagon-headed cable adjuster. After adjusting, return the rubber shroud to its original position over the adjuster and control barrel.

82. Cleaning

To be carried out every 6,000 miles.

Check the contact breaker contacts and, if necessary, clean them as described in Subsection 80. Wipe the outside of the magneto to remove dirt or grease. Check the cable adjuster and control barrel for signs of water ingress.

Remove the high tension pick-ups and polish with a soft dry cloth. Each carbon brush must move freely in its holder and, if necessary, clean it with a petrol-moistened cloth. Should a brush be worn to within ⅛ in. of the shoulder it must be renewed.

Whilst the pick-up moulding is removed, clean the slip ring track and flanges by holding a soft dry cloth against them with a suitably shaped piece of wood while the engine is slowly turned.

The high tension cables must be kept clean and dry.

83. High Tension Cables

If, on inspection, the high tension cable shows signs of deterioration, it must be replaced, using 7 mm. rubber, P.V.C. or neoprene covered ignition cable. To fit a new high tension cable, bare the end for about ⅜ in., thread the knurled moulded nut over the cable, and thread the bared cable through the washer removed from the old cable.

Bend back the strands radially, and screw the nut into the pick-up moulding.

The latest engines are fitted with special high resistance H.T. cables (green) which prevent interference with radio or television without the need for a separate mid-cable or plug cap suppressor. These cables have a non-metallic thread carrying the H.T. current and are supplied complete with metal ferrules at each end. They must not be cut or shortened and, if replaced by standard type cables, a suppressor of about 5,000 ohms resistance must be fitted as close as possible to the sparking plug in order to comply with the law in the U.K. and many overseas countries.

84. Renewing Timing Control Cable (Manual Control)

The Bowden timing control cable should be renewed if it becomes frayed, otherwise moisture may enter the contact breaker housing.

To do this, slip back the rubber shroud and, by means of the hexagon at the base, unscrew the control barrel. If the cable and plunger to which it is attached are now pulled upwards, the cable nipple can be disengaged from the plunger slot.

Soften the solder and remove the nipple.

Thread the new length of cable through the rubber shroud, cable adjuster, control barrel, sealing washer and restoring spring. Solder the nipple to the end of the cable. Engage the nipple with the slot in the plunger and screw the control barrel into the body, ensuring that the sealing washer is correctly fitted between the barrel and the body. Take up any slackness in the cable by means of the adjuster before refitting the rubber shroud in position.

85. Contact Breaker Springs

Correct contact breaker spring pressure, measured at the contacts, is 18—24 oz.

86. Servicing. Testing Magneto in Position on Engine

To locate cause of misfiring or failure of ignition, check as follows :—

(i) Remove the sparking plugs from the engine. Hold the end of the H.T. cable about ⅛ in. from the cylinder block and crank the engine. If strong and regular sparking is produced the fault lies with the sparking plug or plugs which must be cleaned and adjusted or renewed.

(ii) If no sparking is produced, examine the H.T. cable and, if necessary, renew it as described in Subsection 83.

(iii) Very occasionally, the fault may be due to a cracked or punctured pick-up moulding. This type of fault is not easily detected by inspection, and a check should therefore be made by substitution.

(iv) If the ignition cut-out switch is suspected, disconnect the cable at the magneto and retest. If the magneto now functions normally, the fault is in either the cable or the cut-out switch. Correct by replacement.

(v) If the magneto has recently been replaced or removed, it may be incorrectly timed. See Subsection 24.

(vi) Check the contact breaker for cleanliness and correct contact setting as described under Maintenance.

If the cause of faulty operation cannot be traced from the foregoing checks, the cause may be an internal defect in the magneto. The magneto should therefore be removed from the engine for dismantling.

Further ignition particulars are given in a booklet issued by the makers, a copy of which we shall be pleased to forward upon request.

87. Automatic Advance Mechanism

This forms the coupling between the magneto driving sprocket and the magneto spindle. It consists of two weights which are pivotally mounted and fly outwards due to centrifugal force when the engine speed increases, thus advancing the angular position of the spindle in relation to the sprocket. The movement is restrained by two small tension springs and is limited in both directions by positive metal stops. The rate of advance is controlled by the strength of the springs and, in order to obtain sufficient advance to suit moderate speed part throttle conditions, fairly weak springs are fitted. In consequence it may sometimes be found that the engine has stopped with the coupling in the fully advanced position. This is due to the engine having bounced back off compression when it stopped and to the springs being unable to overcome the frictional drag of the contact breaker fibre heel on the cam either when the engine was turning backwards or when it is stationary. As soon as the engine is rotated slowly forwards by the kick starter, however, the magneto should return to the fully retarded position as the frictional drag will then assist the springs instead of opposing them.

The mechanism is automatically lubricated and requires no attention beyond making sure that the springs are securely fastened and that it operates freely. If it does not, the probable reason is that the chain is too tight (see Subsection 27). For timing instruction with the automatic advance coupling see Subsection 24.

Generator/Rectifier Charging Set

88. General (6-volt Sets)

(a) Constructional Notes

The alternator consists of a spigot mounted 6-coil laminated iron stator with a rotor carried on and driven by an extension of the crankshaft. The rotor has an hexagonal steel core, each face of which carries a high energy permanent magnet keyed to a laminated pole tip. The pole tips are riveted circumferentially to brass side plates, the assembly being cast in aluminium and machined to give a smooth external finish.

As shown in Figure 21, there are no rotating windings, commutator, brushgear, bearings or oil seals and consequently the alternator requires no maintenance apart from an occasional check of the three-way connector in the three output cables to see that this is clean and tight.

If removal of the rotor becomes necessary for any purpose, there will be no necessity to fit keepers to the rotor poles. When the rotor is removed, wipe off any metal swarf that may have been attracted to the pole tips and put the rotor in a clean place.

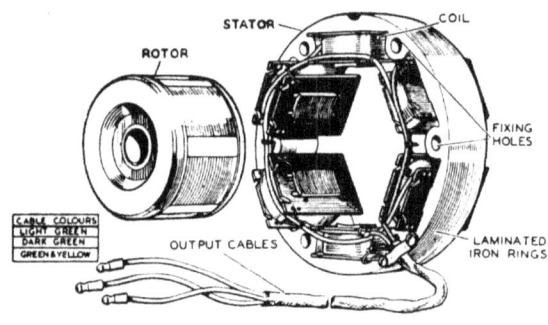

STATOR AND ROTOR OF ALTERNATOR RM19

Fig. 21

(b) Rectifier

A bridge-connected rectifier is fitted to convert the alternator output to a uni-directional battery charging current. The rectifier requires no maintenance apart from an occasional check to see that the connections are clean and tight. The nuts that clamp the rectifier plates together must never under any circumstances be slackened, as the clamping pressure has been carefully adjusted during manufacture to obtain the correct performance characteristics. A separate nut is used for securing the unit to the machine and this nut should be checked occasionally to see that it is tight.

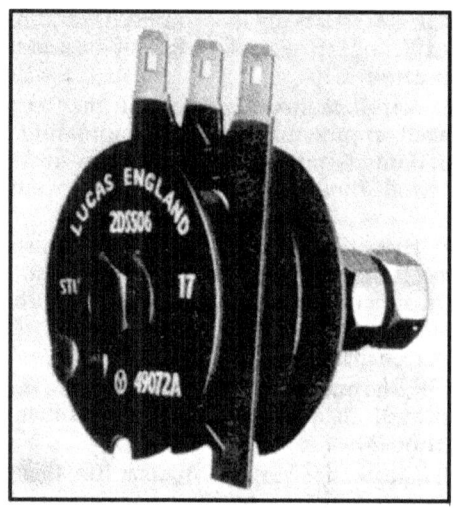

RECTIFIER

Fig. 22

(c) Operation (6-volt Sets)

The alternator stator is wound with three pairs of series-connected coils, one pair being permanently connected across the rectifier. The purpose of this latter pair is to provide a small trickle charging current for the battery whenever the engine is running.

Connections to the remaining coils vary according to the demand on the battery and, as shown schematically in Figure 23, depend on the positions of the lighting switch. When no lights are in use, the coils are short-circuited and the alternator output is regulated to its minimum value by interaction of the rotor flux with the flux set up by the current flowing in the shorted coils. In the "Pilot" or parking lights position, the shorting link is disconnected and, the regulating fluxes being consequently reduced, the alternator output increases and compensates for the parking lights load. In the "Head" position of the lighting switch, the output is further increased by all three pairs of coils being connected in parallel.

In the case of a machine frequently left standing with the lights "on" and which does only a small amount of daylight running it may be found that a higher charge rate for daylight running is desirable.

This can be achieved by disconnecting and taping up one end of the green/white lead (light green on some early models) which runs from No. 7 terminal on the earlier switch LU31491A (LU31784A/D if Airflow fairing is fitted) or No. 4 terminal on the later plug and socket switch LU34289A, to one of the outside terminals of the rectifier. This open circuits the four coils which are normally short circuited and so increases the output from the other two. If a still higher rate of daylight charge is required (as, for example, on a machine equipped with a radio transmitter) this can be obtained by cross connecting the green/white and green/black (light green and dark green on some early models) leads at the snap connectors in the leads from the alternator. This brings four instead of two coils into action both for daylight running and when running on the pilot lights, the remaining two coils being short circuited or open circuited according to whether the short circuiting lead from switch to rectifier is connected or not. The following are the approximate maximum charge rates from an R.M.19 alternator into a 6-volt battery with the various connections described above —

2 coils charging, 4 short circuited—3 amps.
2 coils charging, 4 open circuited—$4\frac{3}{4}$ amps.
4 coils charging, 2 short circuited—$6\frac{1}{4}$ amps.
4 coils charging, 2 open circuited—$7\frac{3}{4}$ amps.
6 coils charging —10 amps.

The higher charge rates should only be used in exceptional circumstances as running for long periods at these rates will overcharge the battery causing excessive gassing and loss of acid.

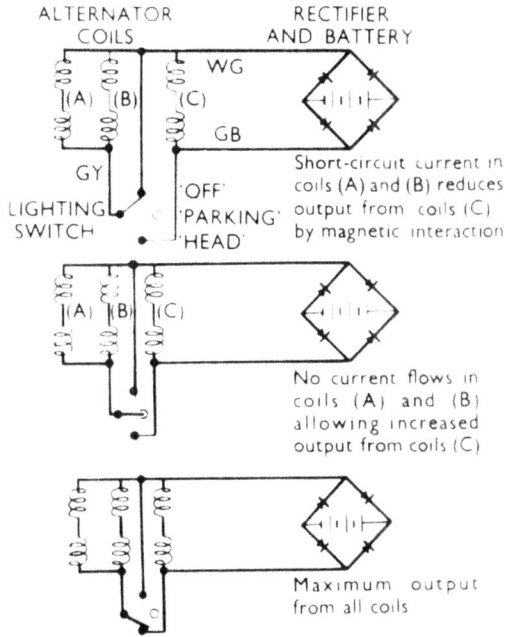

CIRCUIT DIAGRAMS FOR POSITIONS OF LIGHTING SWITCH (6-volt Sets)

Fig. 23a

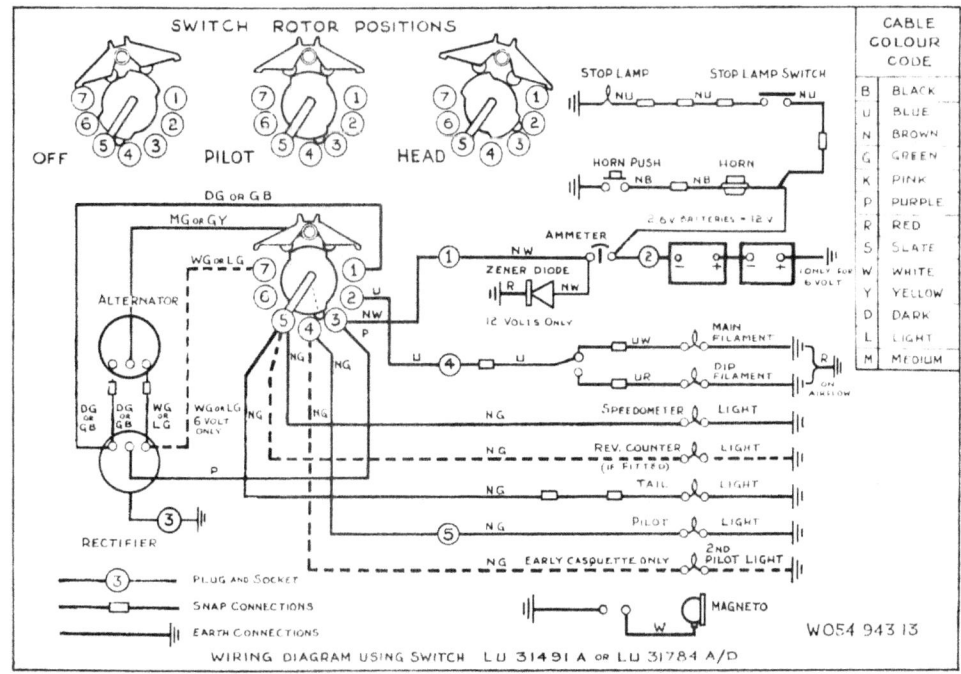

Fig. 24a

(d) Operation (12-volt Sets)

The voltage generated by a permanent magnet A.C. generator of the type fitted to the Royal Enfield "Interceptor" model is entirely dependent on the voltage of the battery to which it is connected. The same generator can, therefore, be used to charge either a 6-volt or a 12-volt battery. The current delivered against 12 volts is naturally less than it is against 6 volts but at any speed above 1,000 r.p.m. (18 m.p.h. in top) more than half the 6-volt current is delivered at 12 volts and at maximum speed the proportion is over 80%. The electrical output measured in watts is, therefore, greater at 12 volts than at 6 volts at any normal speed and is nearly twice as much at high speeds. Advantage can be taken of this to use higher wattage bulbs which consume less current, so that the voltage drop in the cable harness is less and the increase in useful light is greater than would be expected from the increased wattage of the bulbs.

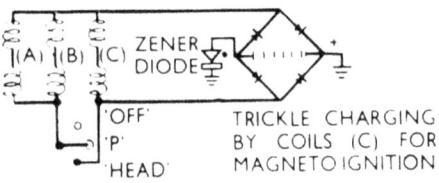

CIRCUIT DIAGRAM (12-volt Sets)
Fig. 23b

Another advantage of the 12-volt system is that it enables the Zener diode system of regulation to be used. The Zener diode has the remarkable property of changing from a non-conductor to a conductor at a critical voltage which can be arranged to be 14 volts, i.e., when the 12-volt battery is discharged, the Zener diode, which is in a circuit in parallel with the battery, does not take current, but as the battery voltage rises the diode begins to pass current so that less goes into the battery. This gives much better regulation than can be achieved by the arbitrary switching in and out of coils.

89. Maintenance

(a) Check wiring occasionally to see that all connections are clean and tight.

(b) Check tightness of rectifier securing nut.

(c) On 12-volt sets check that Zener diode is tightened securely on to a clean flat surface. When functioning, the diode acts as an earth connection for quite large currents and will overheat if not in good contact with a fair mass of metal, preferably aluminium. On the other hand, do not over-tighten as the securing bolt is $\frac{1}{4}$ in. diameter U.N.F. thread and is made of copper for maximum thermal conductivity. It can easily be stripped or broken.

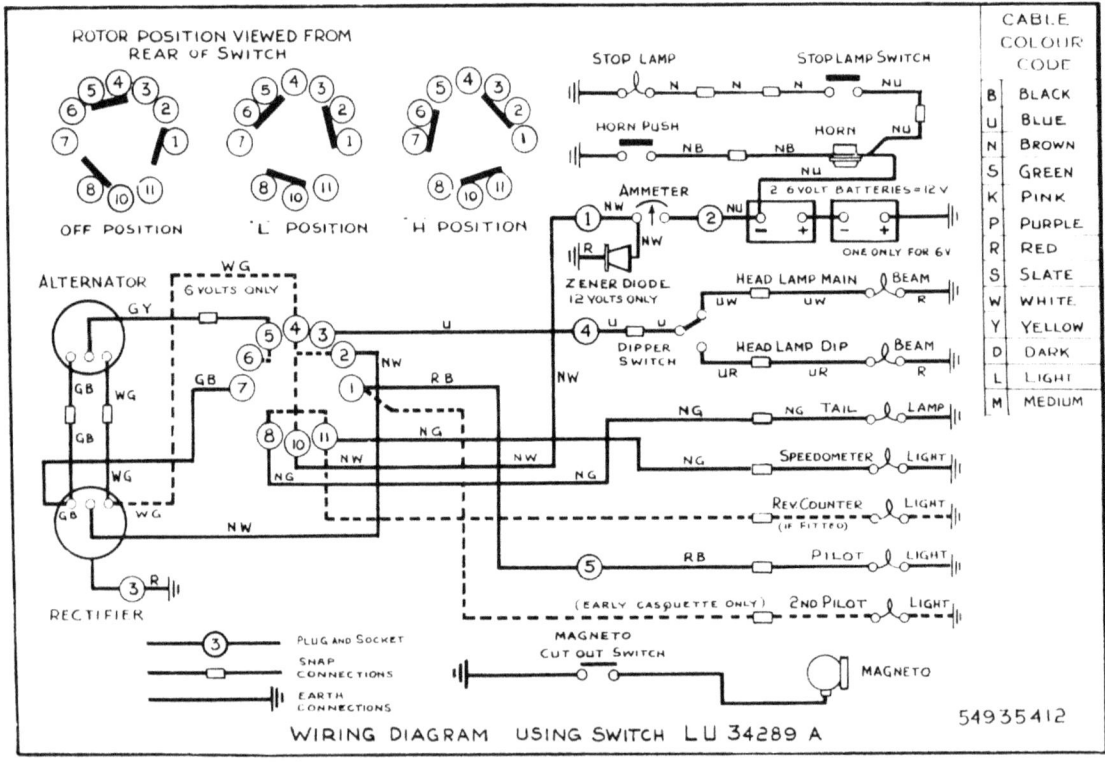

Fig. 24b

Battery—Models MLZ9E & MKZ9E-2

90. General

Both types of battery are of modern construction with translucent polystyrene cases through which the acid level can be seen. Each cell contains nine plates with separators formed from a dry inert micro-porous material which does not dilute the acid as did the wet wood separators formerly used. Special anti-spill filler plugs are fitted venting into a common chamber.

The larger MLZE battery is used with 6-volt sets. Two of the smaller MKZE—2 batteries connected in series are used with 12-volt sets.

These batteries must not be filled beyond the filling line indicated on the side of the case. This is below the tops of the plates and separators.

The acid level will rise slightly while the battery is on charge but will fall again during off charge periods when the upper ends of the plates will be kept wet by capillary attraction.

These batteries are supplied in the "dry charged" condition and must be filled in accordance with instructions in Sub-sections 91 and 92.

91. Technical Data

	MLZ9E	MKZ9E-2
Nominal Voltage	6	6
No. of Plates per Cell	9	9
Volume of Acid per Cell	90 c.c.	80 c.c.
Amp. Hr. Capacity:		
10 hr. rate	12	7
20 hr. rate	13	8
Recharge Current	1·2 amps.	0·7 amps.
S.G. of acid for filling dry charged battery:		
(a) Climates normally below 80°F. (26·6°C.)	1·260	1·260
(b) Climates normally above 80°F. (26·6°C.)	1·210	1·210

Note.—The above acid densities are corrected to 60°F. (15·5°C.).

To prepare 1·260 s.g. electrolyte slowly pour one part by volume of 1·835 s.g. acid into three parts of distilled water.

To prepare 1·210 s.g. electrolyte use four parts of water.

Always add acid to water, never vice versa, or dangerous spurting may result.

92. Filling and Soaking the Batteries

Discard the vent hole sealing tapes.

Pour into each cell in one operation pure dilute sulphuric acid of appropriate specific gravity to the coloured line denoting the maximum filling level and allow the battery to stand for one hour. Check the level and syphon off surplus acid from any cell where it has risen higher than the acid level line. Thereafter keep the acid just level with the coloured line by topping up with distilled water.

A discharge can be taken from the battery one hour after it has been filled but, if time permits, it is advisable to first give the battery a four hour freshening charge at the normal recharge rate, i.e., 1·2 amperes for MLZ9E or 0·7 amperes for MKZ9E—2.

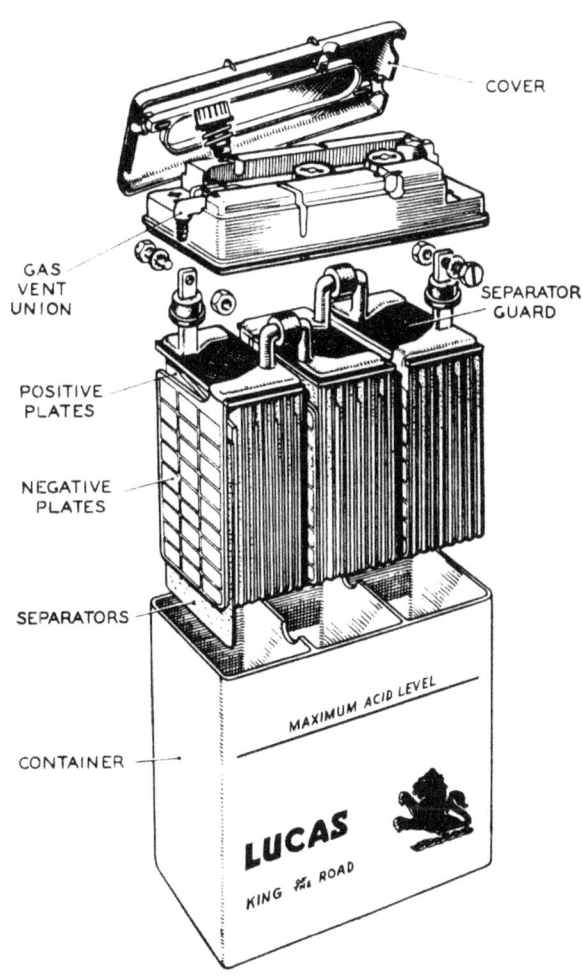

Fig. 25

Head and Tail Lamps

93. Headlamp

Various types of head lamp have been fitted to "Interceptor" models, depending on the date of manufacture, whether for the British or American market and whether or not an airflow fairing is fitted. All embody a Lucas "light unit" of the type shown in Fig. 26, with a "prefocus" bulb

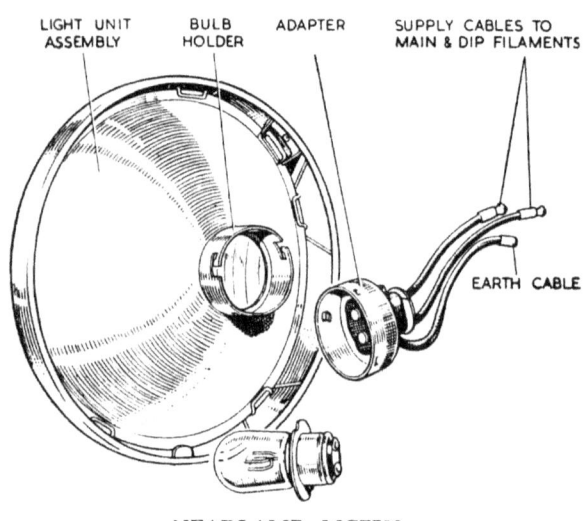

HEADLAMP MCF700

Fig. 26

with filaments for main and dipped beams. The earlier models for the British market had a casquette fork head fitted with a unit as shown in Fig. 26 with no pilot bulb, twin pilot lamps being provided in the casquette. Later British machines had a similar unit, MCF 700P, incorporating a pilot bulb in the lower part of the reflector, the pilot lamps being no longer in the casquette. All American models and the latest British models have a headlamp model SS700P consisting of the unit as used in MCF700P mounted in a separate shell carried on brackets attached to the fork tubes. All machines fitted with "airflow" fairings have a lamp, F700P, mounted on a flange attached to the fairing and provided with three spring-loaded screws for adjusting the vertical and horizontal aim of the beam. This also contains a pilot lamp and uses the same light unit as the MCF700P and SS700P lamps.

Machines with separate headlamps, type SS700P, have provision for adjusting the vertical aim by pivoting the lamp shell in the brackets which support it. Machines with casquette headlamps also have provision for adjusting the vertical aim. This is done by loosening the top screw securing the "fixing ring," LU/553267, to the casquette itself. The entire reflector, front rim and lens can then be inclined backwards or forwards as required before retightening the screw. Horizontal aim on these machines, and on those with SS700P lamps, is fixed and depends on the accuracy of machining of the fork head, etc. Correct vertical aim is most important and this should be adjusted with the machine carrying its normal load. A beam set too high not only fails to light the road but will also dazzle oncoming drivers even when the dipped beam is used. A beam set too low does not cause dazzle but fails to show up objects far enough ahead and is, therefore, not safe for fast driving.

94. Lucas Light Unit

The unit incorporates a combined reflector and front lens assembly (see Fig. 26). This construction ensures that the reflector and lenses are permanently protected, thus the unit keeps its high efficiency over a long period. A "prefocus" bulb is used, the filaments of which are accurately positioned with respect to the reflector, thus no focusing device is necessary.

The bulb has a large cap and a flange, which has been accurately positioned with relation to the bulb filaments during manufacture. A slot in the flange engages with a projection on the inside of the bulb holder positioned at the back of the reflector.

A bayonet-fitting adaptor with spring-loaded contacts secures the bulb firmly in position and carries the supply to the bulb contacts.

The outer surface of the lens is smooth to facilitate cleaning. The inner surface is formed of a series of lenses which determine the spread and pattern of the light beams.

In the event of damage to either the lens or reflector a replacement light unit must be fitted.

95. Replacing the Light Unit and Bulb

Slacken the securing screw at the top of the headlamp rim. Remove the front rim and Light Unit assembly.

Withdraw the adaptor from the Light Unit by twisting it in an anti-clockwise direction and pulling it off. Remove the bulb from its locating sleeve at the rear of the reflector.

Disengage the Light Unit securing springs from the rim and lift out the Light Unit.

Position the new unit in the rim so that the word "TOP" on the lens is correctly located when the assembly is mounted on the headlamp. Refit the securing springs ensuring that they are equally spaced around the rim.

Replace the bulb and adaptor. The main bulb must be the Lucas "prefocus" type—6 v. 30/24 watt Lucas No. 312 or 12 v. 50/40 watt Lucas No. 446. When a pilot bulb is fitted in the leadlamp this should be 6 v. 3 watt Lucas No. 988 or 12 v. 6 watt Lucas No. 989.

Locate the bottom of the Light Unit and front rim assembly in the headlamp shell or in the fixing rim attached to the casquette fork head. Press the front on and tighten the securing screw at the top of the headlamp.

96. Parking Lights (Early Models with Casquettes)

Access to the parking bulbs is obtained by removing the parking lamp rim (see Fig. 27). This is forced over the edge of the rubber lamp body and is additionally secured by means of a small fixing

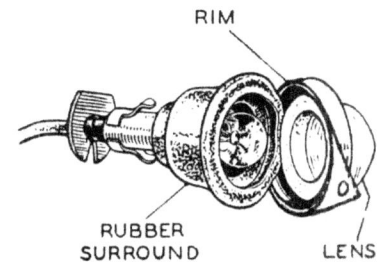

PARKING LIGHT EARLY U.K. MODELS
Fig. 27

screw. After removal of the lamp rim the parking lamp lens can be pulled out of the rubber body, after which the bulb will be accessible. Replace-

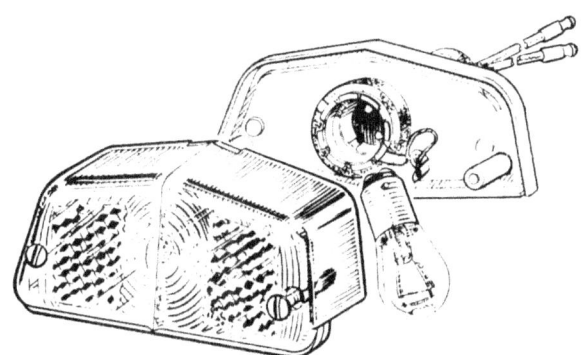

STOP-TAIL LAMP L.564
Fig. 28

ment bulbs should be 6 v. 3 watt Lucas No. 988 or 12 v. 6 watt Lucas No. 989.

97. Tail Light

The Lucas lamp, Type 564 (Fig. 28) is a combined stop and tail light and also incorporates a reflector.

Access to the bulb is obtained by removing the two screws which secure the plastic cover.

The correct bulb is Lucas No. 384 6 volt 6/18 watt. The 6 watt filament provides the normal tail light, while the 18 watt filament is illuminated on movement of the brake pedal. For 12 volt sets the bulb is Lucas No. 380, 12 volt, 6/21 watt.

(**Note.**—6 watt bulbs are now required by law in Great Britain on machines of more than 250 c.c. capacity.)

Care must be taken that the leads to the stop tail lamp are correctly connected, as the use of the 18 watt filament on the normal tail light will not only discharge the battery but could cause trouble from excessive heat affecting the plastic cover. At the same time, the 6 watt filament, if used as a stop-tail light, will be ineffective in bright sunlight or at night when the tail light filament is illuminated.

Frame

98. Description of Frame

The frame is built throughout of cold drawn weldless steel tubing with brazed or welded joints, liners being fitted where necessary for extra strength. All the main frame members are made of chrome-molybdenum alloy steel tubing which retains its strength and resistance to fatigue after brazing or welding.

The rear wheel is carried in a swinging arm unit which forms the chainstays. Two different lengths of swinging arm have been used, a shorter one, giving 54 in. wheelbase, on the earlier models for the English market and a longer one, giving 57 in. wheelbase for the American market and later models for the English market. Two types of pivot bearings have been used at the forward end of the swinging arm.

(a) Bronze bushes working on a steel tube secured to the main frame by a long bolt passing through the pivot lugs. Hardened steel thrust washers are provided to deal with side thrust. Two greasing points are provided and rubber sealing bands are fitted to exclude wet and dirt.

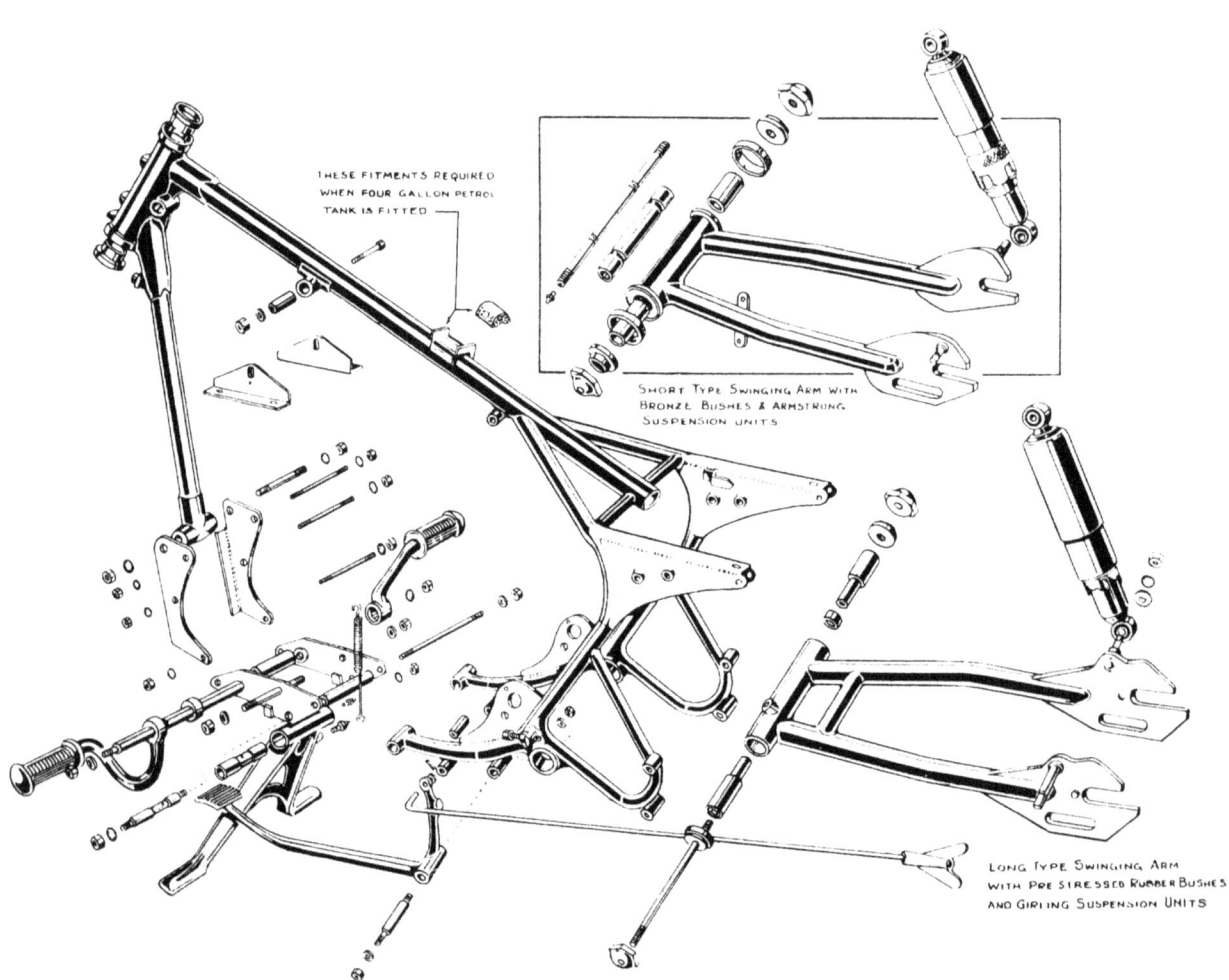

EXPLODED VIEW OF "INTERCEPTOR" FRAME

Fig. 29

(b) Pre-stressed rubber bushes with inner and outer metal sleeves. The inner sleeves are extended inwards and butt against a short distance piece fitted between them. The outer ends of the inner sleeves project beyond the ends of the rubber bushes and bear against steel thrust washers fitting into recesses in the main frame pivot lugs. A long steel bolt and nuts secure the whole assembly. No greasing is necessary with the rubber bushes.

99. Steering Head Races

The steering head races, 34085, are the same at the top and bottom of the head lug and are the same for all models. They are easily removed by knocking them out with a hammer and drift and new races can be fitted either under a press or by means of a hammer and a wooden drift.

100. Removal of Rear Suspension Unit

Place the machine on the centre stand and remove the dual seat and rear mudguard. (See Subsection 28.)

Remove the top pivot pin nut, drive out the pivot pin, then hinge the suspension unit back on the lower pivot pin. After removing the lower nut, the unit may be pushed off the pivot pin welded to the fork end.

101. Servicing Rear Suspension Units

The proprietary units fitted are sealed and servicing of the internal mechanism can be carried out only by the manufacturers.

The rubber bushes in the top and bottom eyes can easily be renewed and the spring can be removed by pushing down on the top spring cover so as to release the split collar above it. After removal of the split collar the top cover and spring can be lifted off. When reassembling, the spring should be greased to prevent rust and squeaking if it should come into contact with either of the covers (when fitted).

Early machines were fitted with Armstrong adjustable dampers, either $8\frac{1}{2}$ in. or $8\frac{3}{4}$ in. closed length. These have two springs each, a long one at the top and a shorter one at the bottom. By turning a knurled collar the lower spring can be made inoperative, giving a stiff suspension, or allowed to function, giving a softer action. The stiff suspension is suitable for pillion work or with a light sidecar; the softer suspension is for normal solo work. For heavy sidecar work a stiffer top spring can be supplied.

The part numbers of suitable springs for these dampers are:—

Bottom spring, common to all—AT6/521.

Top spring, $8\frac{1}{2}$ in. dampers, 130 lb./in.—AT6/452.

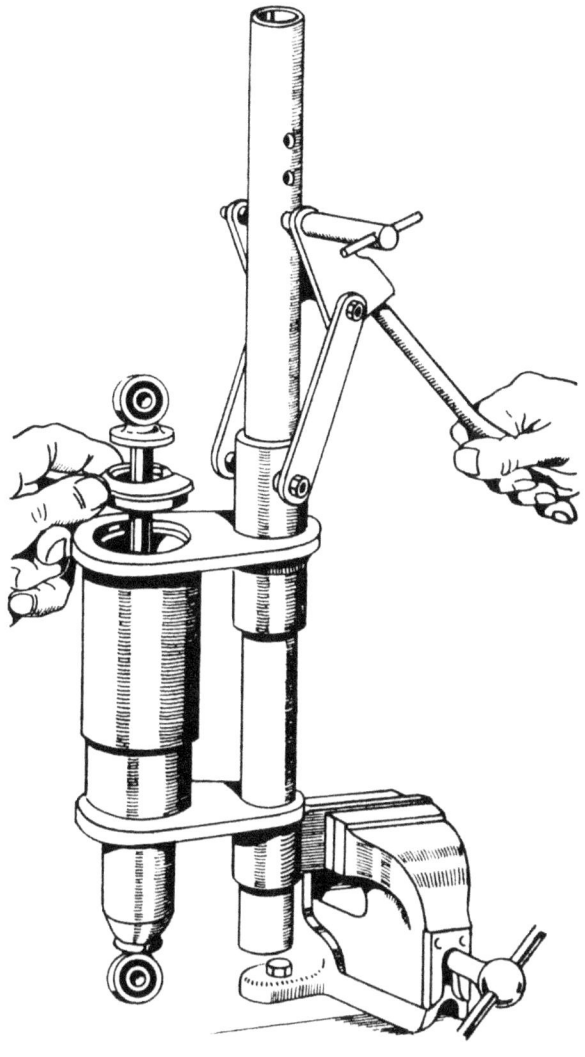

REAR SPRING COMPRESSOR

Fig. 30

Top spring, $8\frac{1}{2}$ in. dampers, 150 lb./in.—AT6/520.

Top spring, $8\frac{3}{4}$ in. dampers, 130 lb./in.—AT6/439.

Top spring, $8\frac{3}{4}$ in. dampers, 150 lb./in.—AT6/444 (W42358).

Later machines are fitted with Girling dampers which have only one spring but which can have the pre-load varied by turning the bottom spring cup by means of a "C" spanner (supplied in the tool kit) thus raising the rear of the machine and preventing bottoming on the bump stop under heavy loads. The lowest position is suitable for normal solo work, the middle position is for use with a pillion passenger and the top position is suitable for sidecar work. The part number for the spring for these dampers is 64539963, colour code Red/Orange, rating 132 lb./in.

When replacing a spring the use of a compressor, as shown in Fig. 30, is a great convenience. If one is not available, reduce the spring load as much as possible by setting Armstrong dampers to their "soft" position and Girling dampers to their lowest setting.

When the spring is removed it should be possible to push the plunger up and down *slowly* throughout the length of its stroke but it should resist *sudden* movements, particularly in the direction of the rebound. If it does not, or if there are signs of leakage of the hydraulic fluid, the complete damper unit should be exhanged for a service replacement. When making this test always hold the damper approximately upright so that the hydraulic fluid is at the lower end.

102. Removal of Swinging Arm Chain Stays

(a) With Bronze Bushes

First remove one of the pivot pin nuts and pull the pivot pin out from the other end. To release the pivot bearing it is necessary to spread the rear portion of the frame, using the frame expander E.5431, which will spread the frame sufficiently to enable the spigots on the thrust washers to clear the recesses in the pivot lugs forming part of the frame.

If it is necessary to remove the bronze bushes these can be driven out by means of a hammer and a suitable drift and new bushes can be fitted under a press without difficulty. After fitting the bushes they must be reamed to ·844/·843 in.

(b) With Rubber Bushes

The procedure is the same as above except that there is no need to spread the frame tubes.

If it is necessary to replace or remove the rubber bushes a press capable of exerting a load of 10/12 tons will be necessary. Support one end of the pivot tube on a piece of tube with a bore just large enough to accept the outside diameter of the outer metal sleeve of the rubber bush ($1\frac{1}{16}$ in.). Press one bush into the pivot tube, thus pushing out the other bush and the distance piece between them. Do this by means of a mandrel $1\frac{1}{32}$ in. diameter with one end stepped down to $\frac{31}{64}$ in. diameter to locate it in the inner sleeve of the bush.

Note.—This procedure will normally scrap one or both the rubber bushes which should not be removed unnecessarily. When fitting replacement bushes do not forget the distance piece between them.

103. Centre Stand

To remove the centre stand unscrew the nut from one end of the stand spindle, knock out the latter and withdraw the stand complete with its bearing sleeve after disconnecting one end of the stand spring.

104. Wheel Alignment

Note that it is not possible to guarantee that the wheels are correctly aligned when the same notch position is used on both adjuster cams. It is therefore not sufficient to count the notches and use the same position on both sides of the machine. The only way to guarantee that the wheels are in line is to check the alignment from front wheel to back using either a straight edge or a piece of taut string. The alignment should be checked on both sides of the machine and if the front and rear tyres are of different section allowance must be made for this.

It is usual to check the alignment of the wheels at a point about six inches above the ground but, if the alignment is checked also towards the top of the wheels, it will be possible to ascertain whether or not the frame is twisted so as to cause one wheel to be leaning while the other is vertical. To do this it is always necessary to remove the mudguards and, unless a straight edge cut away in its centre portion is available, it will be necessary also to remove the cylinders, toolboxes, battery, etc., in order to allow an unbroken straight edge or a piece of taut string to contact the front and rear tyres.

105. Lubrication

The steering head races, swinging arm pivot bearing and stand pivot bearing should be well greased on assembly. The swinging arm pivot on early models and stand pivot are provided with grease nipples but no nipples are provided for the steering head as experience has shown that the provision of nipples at this point causes trouble through chafing and cutting of control and lighting cables. If the steering head bearings are well packed they will last for several years or many thousands of miles.

Recommended greases are Shell Retinax A, Castrolease LM, Esso Multipurpose Grease H, Marfak Multipurpose 2, Mobilgrease MP, or Energrease L2.

Front Fork

106. Description

The telescopic fork consists of two legs each of which comprises a main tube of steel tubing. This may be either of chrome molybdenum alloy steel in 12 or 14 gauge or of 8 g. carbon steel. The outside diameter is the same in each case and the 12 g. alloy steel tube is at least as strong as the 8 g. carbon steel but, owing to the different wall thicknesses of the various tubes, different springs and other internal fittings have to be used with them. (See Subsection 109.) The 8 g. carbon steel main tubes were not fitted to machines for the U.S.A., nor to sidecar machines. The main tube is screwed into either the casquette fork head or into a fascia panel housing twin speedometer and revolution counters, and is securely clamped to the fork crown.

Fitted over the lower end of the main tube is the slider, or bottom tube, made of high strength aluminium alloy with an integral lug which carries the wheel spindle. The lower end of the main tube carries a steel bush held in place by a "valve port" which screws into the tube. This bush is a sliding fit in the bore of the bottom tube, the upper end of which carries a flanged bronze bush which is secured by means of a threaded steel housing containing an oil seal.

The spring, which is loaded in compression only, is fitted inside the upper end of the main tube with its upper end against the underside of the upper spring guide, which is brazed into the upper end of the tube. The lower end of the spring rests on top of the lower "spring guide," which is secured to a hollow spring stud held in the lower end of the fork slider, or bottom tube, and moving up and down with it. This spring stud passes through the "valve port" at the lower end of the main tube. Non-return disc valves are fitted on top of the "valve port" and underneath the lower "spring guide" so that the space between these, inside the main tube, becomes a damper chamber providing hydraulic control of the fork movement. (See Subsection 107.)

The lower ends of the main tubes and upper ends of the bottom tubes are protected either by a metal cover tube secured to the fork crown or by corrugated flexible gaiters. The upper ends of the main tubes are protected either by an extension of the casquette head or by cover tubes, carrying the lamp brackets, between the fascia panel and the fork crown.

A special fork is available for sidecar machines. This has bottom tubes with extended wheel lugs giving less trail and is fitted with stronger springs. A steering damper is standard on both solo and sidecar models.

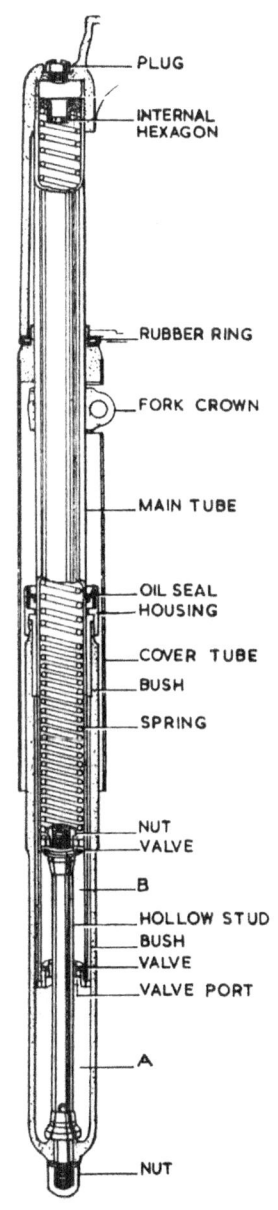

SECTION OF FORK LEG
Fig. 31

Three cross holes towards the lower end of the main tubes ensure lubrication of the upper bearing bushes.

107. Operation of the Fork

The fork provides a range of movement of 6 in. from the fully extended to the fully compressed position. The movement is controlled by the compression spring and by the hydraulic damping system. The hydraulic damping is light on the bump stroke and heavier on the rebound stroke, thus damping out any tendency to pitching or oscillation without interfering unduly with the free movement of the fork when the wheel encounters an obstacle.

The fork is filled with a light oil (S.A.E. 20) to a point above the lower end of the spring so that the damper chamber "B" is always kept full of oil. Upward movement of the wheel spindle forces oil from the lower chamber "A" through the annular space between the spring stud and the bore of the valve port into the damper chamber "B." During this stroke oil pressure on the underside of the disc valve on top of the valve port causes this to lift so that oil can also pass from "A" to "B" through the eight holes in the valve body. Since, however, the diameter of "B" is less than "A" there is not room in "B" to receive all the oil which must be displaced from "A" as the fork operates. The surplus oil passes through a cross hole towards the lower end of the spring stud and up the centre hole in the stud, spilling out through the nut which secures the lower spring guide to the spring stud. *The size of this cross hole has a considerable effect on the amount of damping both on the bump and rebound strokes.* The smaller the hole the heavier is the damping, in fact, if the hole were not there the forks would be solid. The usual size is $\frac{3}{16}$ in. diameter, which gives very light damping, but in some cases a $\frac{1}{8}$ in. hole has been used, giving more damping, and, for America a $\frac{3}{32}$ in. diameter hole giving very heavy damping. If the action of the fork is free for slow movements but too solid when a bump is encountered the $\frac{3}{32}$ in. or $\frac{1}{8}$ in. hole should be opened up, to $\frac{3}{16}$ in. With the larger sized hole it is possible that most of the oil will bypass the valve port, on the bump stroke, thus tending to cause cavitation in chamber "B." In this case the drop in pressure in "B" will cause the upper disc valve beneath the lower spring guide to open, thus admitting oil into chamber "B" from above and keeping it full.

On the rebound stroke the oil in the damper chamber "B" is forced through the annular space between the spring stud and the bore of the main tube valve port. During this stroke pressure in chamber "B" closes the two disc valves at the upper and lower ends of the chamber so that the only path through which the oil can escape is the annular space between the spring stud and the port. Damping on the rebound stroke is therefore heavier than on the bump stroke. At the extreme end of either bump or rebound stroke a small taper portion on the spring stud enters the bore of the valve port, thus restricting the annular space and increasing the amount of damping. At the extreme end of the bump stroke the larger diameter taper on the oil control collar enters the main counterbore of the valve port thus forming a hydraulic cushion to prevent metal to metal contact.

108. Dismantling the Fork to Replace Spring, Oil Seal or Bearing Bushes

Place the machine on the centre stand, disconnect the front brake control and remove the front wheel and mudguard complete with stays. Unscrew the bottom spring stud nut which will allow oil to run out of the fork down to the level

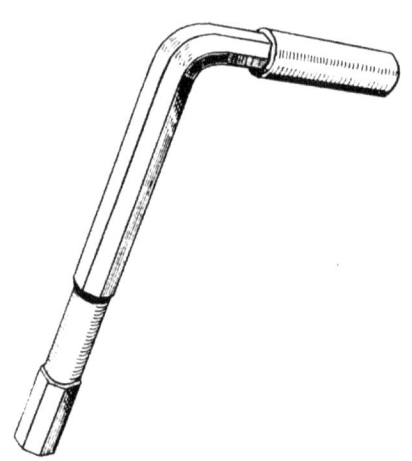

MAIN TUBE SPANNER
Fig. 32

of the cross hole in the spring stud. Now knock the spring stud upwards into the fork with a soft mallet, thus allowing the remainder of the oil to escape. Pull the fork bottom tube down as far as possible, thus exposing the oil seal housing. Unscrew this housing either by means of a spanner on the flats with which it is provided or by using the gland nut hand grips (E.5417). The bottom tube can now be withdrawn completely from the main tube, leaving the bottom tube bush, oil seal housing and oil seal in position on the main tube.

Now unscrew the main tube valve port using "C" spanner (E5418). The spring stud and spring can now be withdrawn from the lower end of the main tube.

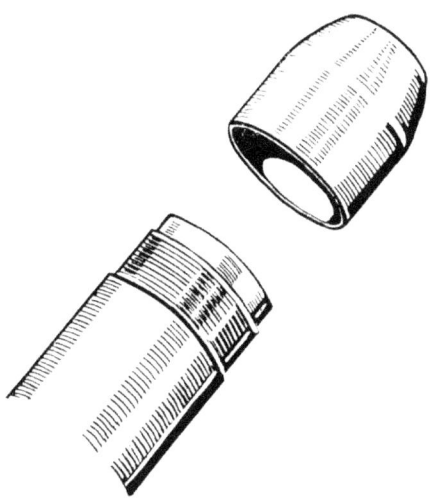

MAIN TUBE SEAL GUIDE
Fig. 33

The steel main tube bush (38156) can now be tapped off the lower end of the tube, if necessary using the bottom tube bush for this purpose. Before doing this, however, it is advisable to mark the position of the bush with a pencil line so as to ensure reassembling it in the same position on the main tube. The reason for this is that these bushes are finish ground to size after fitting on to the tubes so as to ensure concentricity. After removal of the main tube bush the bottom tube bush, oil seal housing and oil seal can be removed.

In case of difficulty in removing the main tube bush it is possible to withdraw the oil seal housing after loosening the crown clip bolt, removing the plug screw and unscrewing the main tube from the fork head by means of a hexagon bar ·500 in. across flats (Unbrako wrench W.11) or the special tool shown in Fig. 32.

109. Springs

The following table gives particulars of the springs which are available together with the gauge of main tube in which they can be fitted.

Part No.	Rate lb./in.	Total Coils	Wire Gauge	Outside Diam. ins.	Free Length ins.	Main Tube Gauge
40857	37/40	69	6	$1\frac{3}{16}$	$20\frac{3}{4}$	14
41569	40/50	68	$5\frac{1}{2}$	$1\frac{3}{16}$	$21\frac{1}{2}$	14
48228	30/35	$76\frac{1}{2}$	6	$1\frac{1}{4}$	$22\frac{1}{4}$	12
41952	45/50	67	$5\frac{1}{2}$	$1\frac{1}{8}$	$21\frac{1}{4}$	12
46615	30	89	7	$\frac{31}{32}$	21	8

Note that there is no spring suitable for heavy sidecar work that will fit in the 8 g. main tubes. For this class of work 12 gauge tubes W42695 with springs W41952 or 14 gauge tubes with springs W41569 should be used. These tubes, being of chrome molybdenum steel have ample strength for all ordinary road work with the heaviest sidecar.

110. Reassembly of Parts

When refitting the oil seal, or fitting a new one, great care must be exercised not to damage the synthetic rubber lip which forms the actual seal. If the seal has been removed from the upper end of the main tube and is refitted from this end a special nose piece (Fig. 33) must be fitted over the end of the tube to prevent the thread from damaging the oil seal.

The spring stud is a tight fit in the hole at the lower end of the bottom tube. Once the stud has been entered in the hole push the bottom tube up sharply against the spring until two or three threads on the stud project beneath the end of the bottom tube. Now fit the nut and washer and pull the stud into position by tightening the nut. If necessary fit the nut first without the washer until sufficient thread is projecting to enable the washer to be fitted.

111. Steering Head Races

The steering head bearing consists of two deep groove thrust races each containing nineteen

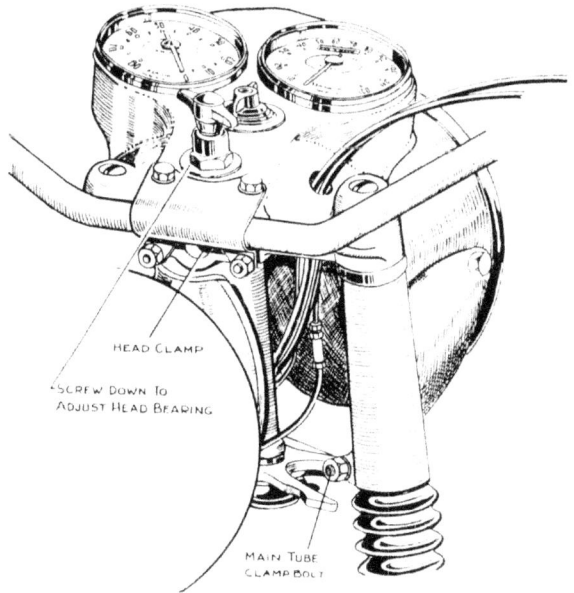

SHOWING THE POSITIONS OF THE CLAMP BOLTS SECURING THE STEERING STEM AND FORK TUBES

Fig. 34

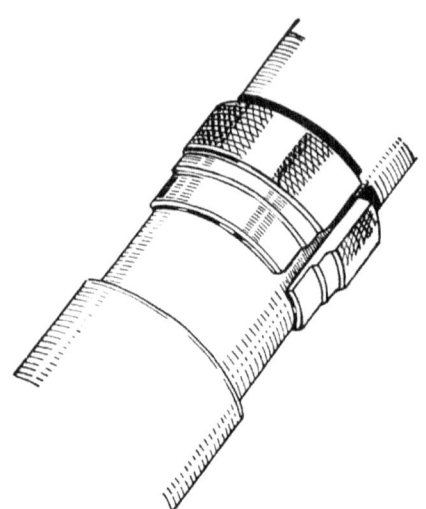

OUTER COVER CENTRALISING BUSHES

Fig. 35

¼ in. diameter balls. The bearing is adjusted by tightening the steering stem locknut after loosening the ball head clip screw and both the fork crown clamp bolts (Fig. 34.) The head should be adjusted so that, when the front wheel is lifted clear of the ground, a light tap on the handlebars will cause the steering to swing to full lock in either direction, while at the same time there should be only the slightest trace of play in the bearings. When testing for freedom of movement the steering damper should be disconnected by unscrewing the anchor plate pin. Do not forget to tighten the ball head clip screw and fork crown clamp bolts. Before tightening the latter make sure that the cover tubes (if fitted) are located centrally round the main tubes so that the bottom tube does not rub inside the cover tube. A pair of split bushes (Fig. 35) is useful to ensure centralisation of the cover tubes.

112. Removal of Complete Fork

The fork complete with front wheel and mudguard can be removed from the machine if necessary by adopting the following procedure.

Disconnect all electrical leads to the lighting switch and ammeter. Switches on all models are a push fit in a rubber bush in the casquette or fascia panel with the exception of early U.S.A. models which had the switch in the headlamp. The ammeter is a push fit in a rubber bush in the casquette head. On other models it is mounted in the headlamp, which can be removed complete. Recent models have switches containing a multipoint plug and socket connector, which can be pulled apart after removing the entire switch from the casquette or fascia panel. U.S.A. models have a plug and socket connector in the cable harness leading to the lamp (see Figs. 24a and 24b. In the case of early U.K. models with no plug and socket connector all leads should be disconnected at their lower ends rather than at the switch.

Disconnect the lighting leads and driving flexes from the speedometer and revolution counter (when fitted). Unscrew the steering damper knob and rod after removal of the split pin through the lower end of the rod. Undo the steering damper anchor plate pin so as to disconnect the damper from the frame of the machine.

Remove the two plug screws and loosen the steering head clip bolt and the two fork crown clamp bolts.

Now unscrew the fork main tubes from the fork head and the steering stem locknut from the top of the steering stem, turning each tube and the nut a turn or two at a time. When the nut has been removed from the steering stem and the main tubes have been completely unscrewed from the fork head the complete fork and wheel with steering stem can be lifted out of the head lug of the frame.

113. Lubrication

The lubrication of the fork bearings is effected by the oil which forms the hydraulic damping medium. All that is necessary is to keep sufficient oil in the fork to ensure that the top end of the bottom spring stud is never uncovered even in the full rebound position. The level of oil in the fork can be gauged by removing the top plug screw and inserting a long rod about ⅜ in. diameter. If slightly tilted this will ledge against the nut at the upper end of the bottom spring stud and indicate the level of oil above the stud. If the fork is empty to start with the quantity required is approximately 7½ fluid ounces in each leg. Recommended grades of oil are Shell X-100 20/20w, Castrolite, Essolube 20w, Mobiloil Arctic, Energol, S.A.E. 20w and Havoline 20/20w.

Front Wheel

With Single 7 in. Brake (U.S.A.) or Dual 6 in. Brake (U.K.)

114. Removal from Fork

To remove the front wheel from the fork place the machine on the centre stand with sufficient packing (about 2 in.) beneath each side of the stand to lift the wheel clear off the ground when tilted back on to the rear wheel. Slacken the brake cable adjustment(s) and disconnect the cable(s) from the handlebar lever and from the operating cam lever(s) on the hub. Unscrew the four nuts securing the fork leg caps and allow the wheel to drop forward out of the front fork. Make sure that the machine stands securely on the rear wheel and centre stand—if necessary place a weight on the saddle or a strut beneath the fork to ensure this.

115. Removal of Brake Cover Plate Assembly

Lock the brake "on" by pressure on the operating lever and unscrew the cover plate nut. The cover plate assembly can then be withdrawn from the brake drum.

116. Replacing Brake Linings

Brake linings are supplied either in pairs ready drilled complete with rivets or ready fitted to service replacement brake shoes.

Part Nos. are:—

Front, 7 in. × 1½ in.—43263 (lined shoe).
(U.S.A.)   —43264A/BX (lining and rivets).

Front, 6 in. × 1 in. —41342A (lined shoe).
(U.K.)   —41284A/BX (lining and rivets).

When riveting linings to shoes, secure the two centre rivets first then work towards each end in turn. This will ensure that the lining lies flat against the shoe. Standard linings are Ferodo AM2, which are drilled to receive cheese-headed rivets.

117. Removal of Brake Operating Cam(s)

To remove the operating cam unscrew the nut, 10314, which secures the operating lever to the splines on the cam. A sharp tap on the end of the cam spindle will now free the lever, after which the cam can be withdrawn from its housing.

To remove pivot pin, unscrew nut and tap out pin.

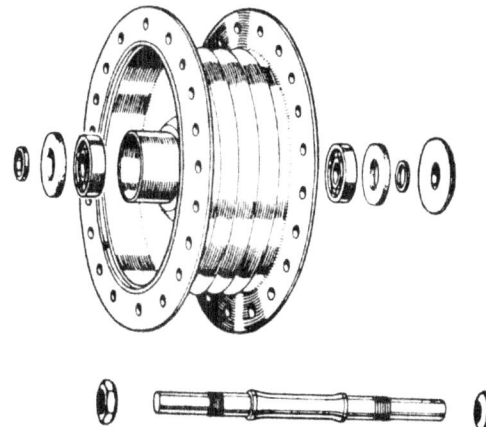

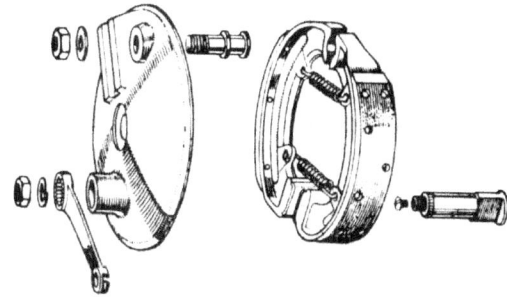

7 in. FRONT HUB AND BRAKE

Fig. 36

118. Removal of Hub Spindle and Bearings

To remove the hub spindle and bearings, having first removed the brake cover plate(s), unscrew the retaining nut and remove the dust excluder from the non-brake side of the hub. Now remove the felt washers and distance washers and hit one end of the spindle with a copper hammer or mallet, thus driving it out of the hub, bringing one bearing with it and leaving the other in position in the hub. Drive the bearing off the spindle and insert the latter once more in the hub at the end from which it was removed. Now drive the spindle through the hub the other way, when it will bring out the remaining bearing.

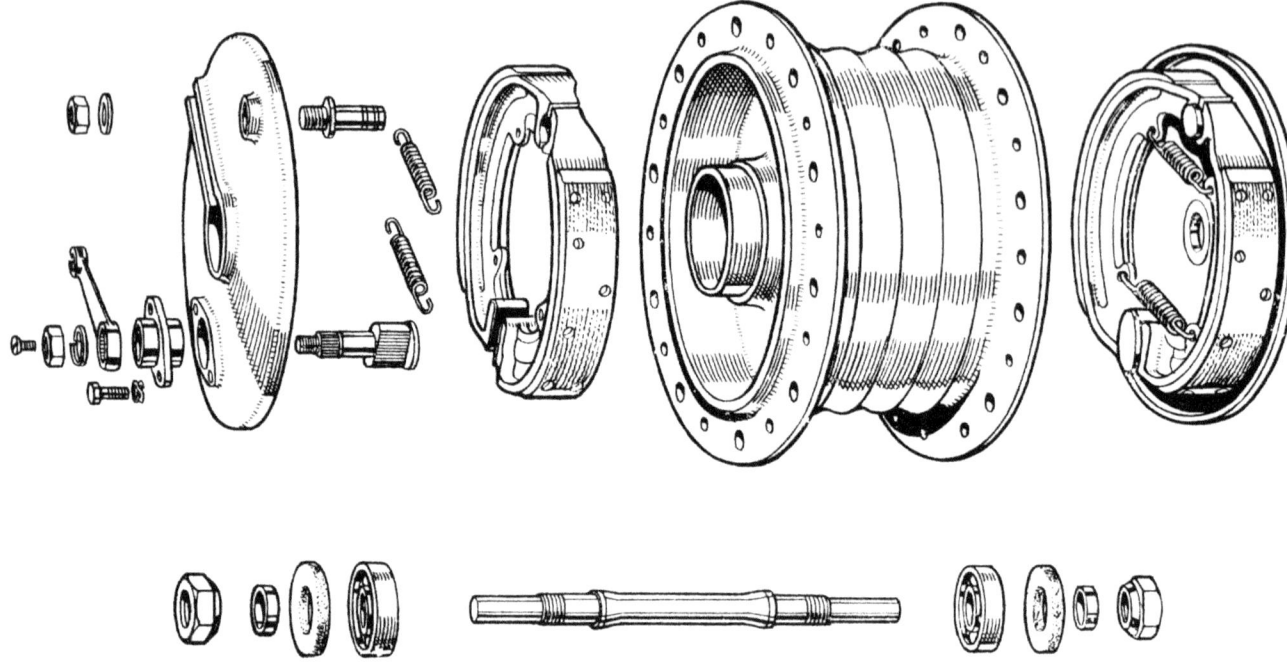

DUAL 6 in. FRONT HUB AND BRAKE
Fig. 36a

119. Hub Bearings

These are deep-groove single-row journal ball bearings, $\frac{5}{8}$ in. i/d by $1\frac{9}{16}$ in. o/d by $\frac{7}{16}$ in. wide. The Skefko Part No. is RLS5. Equivalent bearings of other makes are Hoffmann LS7, Ransome and Marles LJ $\frac{5}{8}$ in., Fafnir LS7. Bearings with slack fitting internal clearances marked "C3," "000" or "***" should be specified.

120. Fitting Limits for Bearings

The fit of the bearings in the hub barrel is important. The bearings are locked on the spindle between shoulders and the distance pieces, 30538, which in turn are held up by the nuts on the spindle. In order to prevent endways pre-loading of the bearings it is essential that there is a small clearance between the inner edge of the outer race of the bearing and the back of the recess in either end of the barrel. To prevent any possibility of sideways movement of the hub barrel on the bearings it is, therefore, necessary for the bearings to be a tight fit in the barrel, but this fit must not be so tight as to close down the outer race of the bearing and thus overload the balls. The following are the manufacturing tolerances which control the fit of the bearings. The figures for the bearings themselves are for SKF bearings, but other manufacturers' tolerances are similar.

Bearing o/d, 1·5622/1·5617 in.
Housing bore, 1·5620/1·5616 in.
Bearing bore, ·6252/·6248 in.
Shaft diameter, ·6252/·6248 in.

121. Refitting Ball Bearings

To refit the bearings in the hub, two hollow drifts are required, as shown in Fig. 37. One bearing is first fitted to one end of the spindle by means of the hollow drift; the spindle and bearing are then entered into one end of the hub barrel, which is then supported on one of the hollow drifts. The other bearing is then threaded over the upper end of the spindle and driven home by means of the second hollow drift either under a

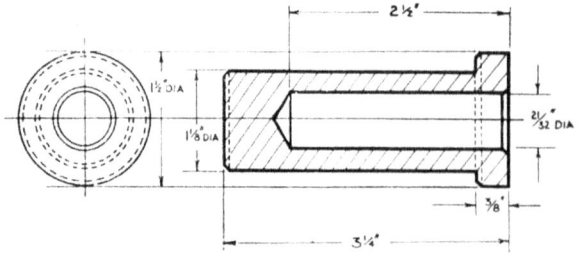

DRIFT FOR REFITTING RLS5 BEARINGS
Fig. 37

press, or by means of a hammer, which will thus drive both bearings into position simultaneously. In order to make quite sure that there is clearance between the inner faces of the outer bearing races and the bottom of the recesses, fit the distance washers, cover plate, dust excluder and the nuts on the spindle. Tightening the nuts should not have any effect on the ease with which the spindle can be turned. If tightening the nuts makes the spindle hard to turn this may be taken as proof that the bearings are bottoming in the recesses in the hub barrel before they are solid against the shoulders on the spindle. In this case, the bearing should be removed and a thin packing shim fitted between the inner race and the shoulder on the spindle.

122. Reassembly of Brake Shoes and Operating Cam into Cover Plate

No difficulty should be experienced in carrying out these operations. Put a smear of grease on the pivot pin and on the operating face of the cam; also on to the cylindrical bearing surface of the operating cam. Fit the operating lever on its splines in a position to suit the extent of wear on the linings and secure with the nut and washer. Note that the position of the operating lever may have to be corrected when adjusting the brake after refitting the wheel. The range of adjustment can be extended by moving this lever on to a different spline. Limit of wear is reached when the cam is turned through nearly 90° with the brake hard on, so that there is a danger that the springs cannot return the brake to the off position.

Note that the cams in the 6 in. dual brakes are fitted into housings bolted to the cover plates. The bolt holes in the flanges on the housings are slotted and double coil spring washers are fitted beneath the heads of the securing bolts. The housings are intended to be *free to be moved by hand* in the direction of the slots though not free enough to move by their own weight or under the influence of road shocks. The bolts are secured by locknuts inside the cover plate which should be centre punched as an additional precaution.

The use of floating cam housings makes the brake more powerful since the cam is free to move to follow up wear on the more efficient leading shoes, i.e., those towards the rear of the machine. At the same time the wear on the leading shoe linings will be greater than on the trailing shoes and in time the limit of float of the cam housings will be reached, after which the brake will continue to act as a fixed cam brake with some loss of efficiency. This can be restored by removing the shoes and refitting them in the opposite positions.

123. Final Assembly of Hub before Replacing Wheel

Before replacing the felt washers which form the grease seals, pack all bearings with grease. If new felt seals are fitted soak these in engine oil.

Recommended greases are:—Shell Retinax A, Castrolease LM, Esso Multipurpose Grease H, B.P. Energrease L2, Mobilgrease MP and Marfak Multipurpose Grease 2. These are all lithium soap greases and should not be mixed with lime, aluminium or soda soap greases.

Make sure that the inside of the brake drum is free from oil, grease, dust or damp. Replace the felt washers, distance collars and brake cover plate(s) and securely tighten the spindle nuts.

124. Wheel Rim

The wheel rim is WM2—19 in., plunged and pierced with forty holes for spoke nipples. The spoke holes are symmetrical, i.e., the rim can be assembled to the hub either way round. The rim diameter after building is 19·06 in., the tolerances on the circumference of the rim shoulders where the tyre fits being 59·925/59·865 in. The standard steel measuring tape for checking rims is $\frac{1}{4}$ in. wide, ·011 in. thick, and its length is 59·985/59·925 in.

125. Spokes

The spokes are of the single-butted type, 8-10 gauge, with 90° countersunk heads, and rolled threads ·144 in. diameter, 40 t.p.i., thread form British Standard Cycle. Spokes for use with 6 in. brakes are $6\frac{11}{16}$ in. long, Part No. 29205. Spokes for use with 7 in. brakes are $6\frac{5}{16}$ in. long, Part No. 44476. All spokes initially are bent to approximately 110° at the head end. Spokes threaded from the outside of the spoke flanges are hit with a hide hammer after lacing, but before truing the wheel, to make them fit close to the flange. This increases the bend to approximately 80°.

126. Wheel Building and Truing

The spokes are laced one over two, and the wheel rim must be built central in relation to the faces of the nuts on the spindle. The rim should be trued as accurately as possible, the maximum permissible run-out both sideways and radially being plus or minus $\frac{1}{32}$ in.

127. Tyre

The standard tyre is Dunlop 3·25—19 in., Ribbed. For the U.S.A. a 3·50—19 in. tyre is fitted. When removing the tyre always start close to the valve and see that the edge of the cover at the other side of the wheel is pushed down into the well of the rim.

When replacing the tyre fit the part by the valve last, also with the edge of the cover at the other side of the wheel pushed down into the well. Slightly inflate the tube and, if available, paint the rim and tyre with soapy water, or water containing a soapless detergent to assist the tyre in slipping over the edge of the rim.

If the correct method of fitting and removal of the tyre is adopted it will be found that the covers can be manipulated quite easily with the small levers supplied in the tool-kit. The use of long levers and/or excessive force is liable to damage the walls of the tyre. After inflation, make sure that the tyre is fitting evenly all the way round the rim. A line moulded on the wall of the tyre indicates whether or not the tyre is correctly fitted. If the tyre has a white mark indicating a balance point, this should be fitted near the valve.

128. Tyre Pressure

The recommended pressure for the front tyre for solo use is 18 lb. per sq. in. This is the same for both 3·25 in. and 3·50 in. section tyres. If a sidecar is fitted determine the load on the tyre and refer to the table in Subsection 148.

129. Lubrication

Grease the bearings by packing them with grease after removal of the brake cover plates, etc. as described in Subsection 115.

Note that the brake cam is drilled for a grease passage but the end of this is stopped up with a countersunk screw instead of being fitted with a grease nipple. This is done to prevent excessive greasing by over-enthusiastic owners. If the cam is smeared with grease on assembly it should require no further attention but, in case of necessity, it is possible to remove the screw, fit a grease nipple in its place and grease the cam by this means.

Rear Wheel

130. Description

This wheel is of the "detachable" type, which enables the main portion of the wheel to be removed from the machine without disturbing the chain or brake. The wheel incorporates the well-known Enfield cush drive and also a 7 in. internal expanding brake.

131. Removal and Replacement of Main Portion of Wheel for Tyre Repairs, etc.

Place the machine on the centre stand, if necessary putting packing pieces beneath the legs of the stand to lift the wheel clear of the ground. Unscrew the loose section of the spindle and withdraw this, together with the chain adjuster cam, preferably marking it to ensure that it is replaced in the same position. Now slide the distance collar out of the fork end and lift away the speedometer drive gearbox, which can be left attached to the driving cable. The spacing collar and the felt washer behind it may now be removed to prevent risk of them falling out when manipulating the tyre. If, however, these are too tight a fit in the hub to come out easily they may be left in place. The main body of the wheel can now be pulled across to the right-hand side of the machine, thus disengaging the six driving pins from the cush drive shell and enabling the wheel to be removed from the machine. (See Fig. 39.)

When replacing the main portion of the wheel, reverse the foregoing procedure. The cush drive shell can be prevented from rotating when turning the wheel to engage the six driving pins, if the machine is placed in gear or the rear brake is operated, taking care, when replacing the speedometer drive gearbox, that the driving dogs inside the gearbox engage with the slots in the end of the hub barrel. Before tightening the centre spindle make sure that the speedometer drive gearbox is correctly positioned so that there is no sharp bend in the driving cable.

132. Removal and Replacement of Complete Wheel for Access to Brake

Place the machine on the centre stand and remove the rear mudguard unit. Disconnect the rear driving chain at the spring link and remove the chain from the rear wheel sprocket. Unscrew the rear brake rod adjusting nut completely and depress the brake pedal so as to disengage the rod from the trunnion in the brake operating lever. Unscrew the brake cover plate anchor nut and remove this together with the washer behind it. Unscrew the loose section of the spindle two or three turns and the spindle nut by a similar amount. Mark the chain adjuster cams to ensure

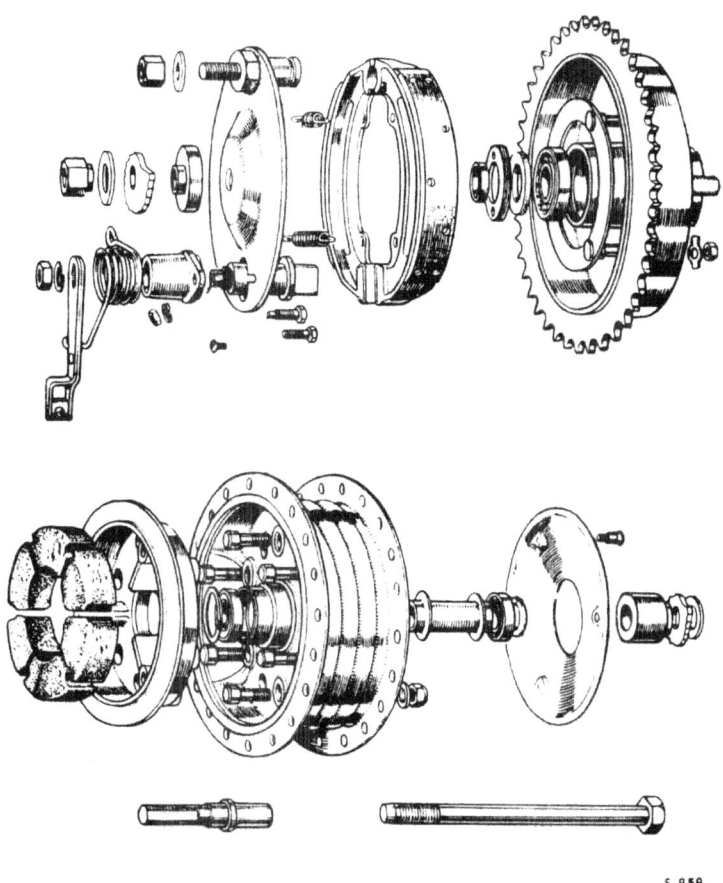

EXPLODED VIEW OF QUICKLY DETACHABLE REAR HUB

Fig. 38

replacing in the same position.* Disconnect the speedometer driving cable and slide the wheel out of the fork ends, tilting it so as to disengage the end of the brake shoe pivot pin from the slot in the fork end.

When replacing the wheel make sure that the dogs on the gear in the speedometer drive gearbox are engaged with the slots in the end of the hub barrel. Make sure also that the speedometer drive gearbox is correctly positioned so that there is no sudden bend in the driving cable. When replacing the connecting link in the driving chain, make sure that the closed end of the spring link points in the direction of travel of the chain. Replace the chain adjuster cams in their original

---

*Note that the wheel is not necessarily correctly lined up when the same notch position is used on both adjuster cams. Once the position of the cams which gives correct alignment has been found this alignment will, however, be maintained if both cams are moved the same number of notches. See also Subsection 104.

positions or, if necessary, turn each of them the same number of notches to tension the chain and maintain correct wheel alignment. The chain should have $\frac{1}{2}$ in. up and down minimum movement when the rear suspension is fully extended as it will be tighter in the normal laden position. Do not forget to refit the brake rod and adjust the brake so that the wheel turns freely when the brake is off, while at the same time only a small travel of the brake pedal is necessary to put the brake on.

133. Removal of Brake Shoes for Replacement, etc.

Remove the complete wheel as described above, then remove the spindle nut, chain adjuster and the distance collar, thus permitting the complete brake cover plate assembly, with operating cam, pivot pin, shoes and return springs, to be lifted off the hub spindle. The brake shoes can then be removed after detaching the return springs.

REMOVAL OF WHEEL (OFFSIDE VIEW)
Fig. 39

Brake linings are supplied either in pairs ready drilled complete with rivets (Part No. 41285A/BX) or ready fitted to service replacement brake shoes (Part No. 41343A). When riveting linings to shoes, secure the two centre rivets first so as to ensure that the lining lies flat against the shoe. Standard linings are Ferodo AM2, which are drilled to receive cheese-headed rivets.

134. Removal of Brake Operating Cam

To remove the operating cam unscrew the nut which secures the operating lever to the splines on the cam. A sharp tap on the end of the cam spindle will now free the lever, after which the cam can be withdrawn from its housing.

Do not try to remove the brake shoe pivot pin as this is cast into the cover plate.

135. Cush Drive

The sprocket/brake drum is free to rotate on the hub barrel. Three radial vanes are formed on the back of the brake drum and three similar vanes are formed on the cush drive shell. Six rubber blocks are fitted between the vanes on the brake drum and those on the cush drive shell, thus permitting only a small amount of angular movement of the sprocket/brake drum relative to the hub barrel and transmitting both driving and braking torques and smoothing out harshness and irregularity in the former.

If the cush drive rubbers become worn so that the amount of free movement measured at the tyre exceeds $\frac{1}{2}$ in. to 1 in., the rubbers should be replaced. To obtain access to them remove the complete wheel as described above; then unscrew

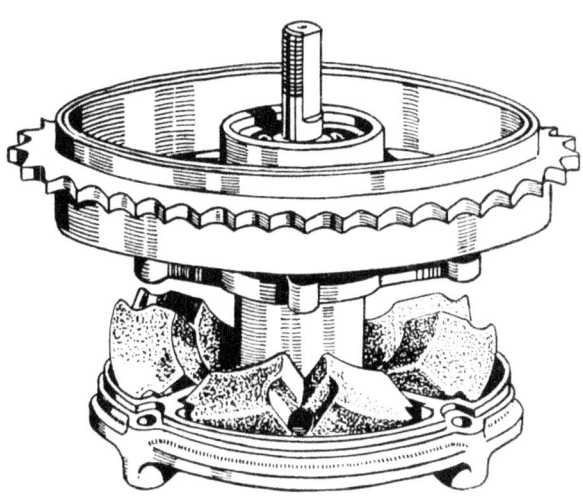

REASSEMBLY OF CUSH DRIVE
Fig. 40

the loose section of the spindle completely. The main portion of the wheel can then be lifted away from the assembly consisting of the fixed portion of the spindle, sprocket/brake drum complete with brake and the cush drive shell. Now remove the brake cover plate complete with brake shoes as described above, and unscrew the three nuts at the back of the cush drive shell after bending back the locking washers. The three studs are brazed to the lockring and should be driven out of the cush drive shell, each a little at a time to avoid distorting the lockring or bending the studs. The sprocket/brake drum can now be separated from the cush drive shell and the six cush drive rubbers lifted out.

When reassembling the cush drive the entry of the vanes between the rubbers will be facilitated if the latter are fitted into the driving shell first and then tilted. The rubbers should be liberally smeared with soapsuds to facilitate entry of the vanes. Grease the inner face of the lockring before assembling and tighten the three nuts down solid as there is a shoulder on the stud which prevents tightening of the nuts from locking the operation of the cush drive. Do not forget to bend up the tabs of the three locking washers.

When reassembling the cush drive, coat the inside of the bore of the sprocket/brake drum liberally with grease where it fits over the hub barrel.

136. Removal of Ball Bearings

To remove the ball bearings take the complete wheel out of the machine and separate the main portion of the wheel from the sprocket/brake drum cush drive shell assembly as described above. To remove the bearing from the sprocket/brake drum, first remove the brake cover plate complete with brake shoe assembly; then remove the distance collar and unscrew the bearing retaining ring with a peg spanner. Now screw the loose section of the spindle into the fixed section and drive out the bearing by hitting the hexagon-headed end of the loose section of the spindle.

To remove the bearings from the loose half of the hub barrel, first lift away the distance collar, speedometer drive gearbox, the spacing collar and the felt washer. Remove the bearing retaining circlip from the driving sprocket end of the barrel. Between the two bearings is a spacer, slotted at one end to enable a drift to be used on the bearing at that end. Remove this bearing first, then enter the loose section of the spindle into the spacer and drive out the remaining bearing by means of a hammer and drift applied to the hexagon-headed end of the spindle.

137. Hub Bearings

These are deep-groove single-row journal ball bearings. The sprocket/brake drum bearing is a Skefko RLS7, $\frac{7}{8}$ in. i/d, by 2 in. o/d, by $\frac{9}{16}$ in. wide. Equivalent bearings of other makes are Hoffmann LS9, Ransome & Marles LJ $\frac{7}{8}$ in., and Fafnir LS9. The two bearings in the hub barrel are Skefko RLS5, $\frac{5}{8}$ in. i/d, by $1\frac{9}{16}$ in. o/d, by $\frac{7}{16}$ in. wide. Equivalent bearings of other makes are Hoffmann LS7, Ransome & Marles LJ $\frac{5}{8}$ in. and Fafnir LS7. Bearings with slack fitting internal clearances marked "C3," "000" or "***" should be specified.

138. Fitting Limits for Bearings

The fit of the bearings in the hub barrel and sprocket/brake drum is important. The following are the manufacturing tolerances which control this and also the fits on the fixed and loose portions of the wheel spindle.

RLS5 Bearing o/d	1·5622/1·5617 in.
Hub Barrel bore	1·5620/1·5616 in.
RLS5 Bearing bore	·6252/·6248 in.
Loose Spindle dia.	·624/·622 in.
RLS7 Bearing o/d	1·9995/1·9990 in.
Sprocket bore	1·9994/1·9990 in.
RLS7 Bearing bore	·8752/·8748 in.
Fixed Spindle dia.	·8749/·8745 in.

All inner races are locked in position when the spindle nuts are tightened. The outer race of the RLS7 bearing is located by a screwed retaining ring and one of the RLS5 bearings is located by a circlip. Axial movement of the sprocket and/or barrel is therefore not possible. We recommend "Loctite" Sealant Grade C to secure any outer races which appear to have been rotating.

139. Removal of Hub Driving Pins

To remove the six driving pins from the aluminium full-width hub, first remove the hub cap after unscrewing the three screws attaching it to the hub. Unscrew the six Simmonds nuts and drive out the pins.

140. Refitting Ball Bearings

To refit the sprocket/brake drum bearing, use a hollow drift as shown in Fig. 41. The bearing is first fitted to the fixed section of the spindle; the spindle and bearing are then entered into the sprocket/brake drum and driven home, preferably under a press or using light hammer blows.

The two bearings in the hub barrel are pressed in, using the drift part of E.4823. First assemble

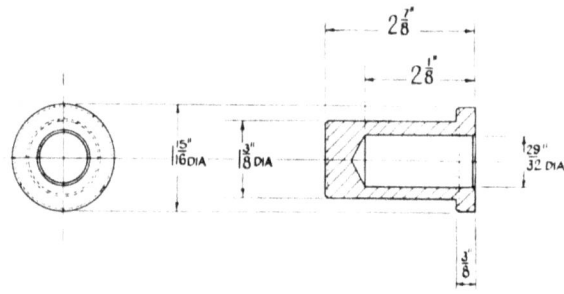

DRIFT FOR REFITTING RLS7 BEARING
Fig. 41

the bearing into the circlip grooved end of the barrel and fit the circlip. Replace the bearing spacer, the slot in the spacer can be at either end of the hub, and assemble the second bearing, supporting the hub on the inner race of the other bearing. If the drift part of E.4823 is not available it is essential that the last bearing is assembled by applying pressure to both inner and outer races simultaneously to avoid pre-loading the two hub barrel bearings.

141. Reassembly of Brake Shoes and Operating Cam into Cover Plate

No difficulty should be experienced in carrying out these operations. Put a smear of grease on the pivot pin and on the operating face of the cam; also on to the cylindrical bearing surface of the operating cam if this has been removed. Fit the operating lever and trunnion on its splines in a position to suit the extent of wear on the linings and secure with the nut. The range of adjustment can be extended by moving the lever on to a different spline.

142. Centring Cam Housing

Note that the bolt holes in the cam housing are slotted, thus enabling the brake shoe assembly to be centred in the drum. It is not intended that on rear brakes the cam housing should be left free to float but the shoes should be centred by leaving the screws just short of dead tight. The brake cover plate assembly with the shoes should then be fitted over the spindle into the brake drum and the brake applied as hard as possible by means of the operating lever. This will centre the shoes in the drum. The screws should then be tightened dead tight and secured with the locknuts. If the shoes are not correctly centred, the brake will be either ineffective or too fierce, depending on whether the trailing or leading shoe first makes contact with the drum. With the brake assembly correctly centred and the screws securing the cam housing correctly tightened wear on both linings should be approximately equal.

143. Final Reassembly of Hub Before Replacing Wheel

Before replacing the felt washers which form the grease seals, pack all bearings with grease. If new felt seals are fitted, soak these in engine oil.

Recommended greases are:—Shell Retinax A, Castrolease LM, Esso Multipurpose Grease H, B.P. Energrease L2, Mobilgrease MP and Marfak Multipurpose Grease 2. These are all lithium soap greases and should not be mixed with lime, aluminium or soda soap greases.

Make sure that the inside of the brake drum is free from oil, grease, dust or damp. Replace the felt washers, distance collars and brake cover plate and securely tighten the spindle nuts.

144. Wheel Rims

Machines for the U.K. are fitted with a WM2-19 in. rim, those for the U.S.A. with a WM3-18 in. rim. In both types the spoke holes are symmetrical, i.e., the rim can be assembled to the hub either way round. Rim diameters after building are 19·06 and 18·06 in. respectively. Tolerances on the circumference of the rim shoulders where the tyre fits are 59·925/59·865 in. for the 19 in. rim and 56·783/56·723 in. for the 18 in. rim. The standard steel measuring tape for checking rims is $\frac{1}{4}$ in. wide, ·011 in. thick, and its length is 59·985/59·925 in. for the 19 in. rim and 56·843/56·783 in. for the 18 in.

145. Spokes

The spokes are of the single-butted type, 8-10 gauge, with 90° countersunk heads and rolled threads, ·144 in. diameter, 40 t.p.i., thread form British Standard Cycle. Spokes for use with

19 in. rims are $6\frac{11}{16}$ in. long, Part No. 29205. Spokes for use with 18 in. rims are $6\frac{3}{16}$ in. long, Part No. 40636. All spokes initially are bent to approximately 110° at the head end. Spokes threaded from the outside of the spoke flanges are hit with a hide hammer after lacing, but before truing the wheel to make them fit close to the flange. This increases the bend to approximately 80°.

146. Wheel Building and Truing

The spokes are laced one over two and the wheel rim must be built central in relation to the outer faces of the distance collars. The rim should be trued as accurately as possible, the maximum permissible run-out both sideways and radially being plus or minus $\frac{1}{32}$ in.

147. Tyre

The standard tyre is Dunlop Gold Seal K70, 3·50 × 19 in. for the U.K., 4·00 × 18 in. for the U.S.A.

When removing the tyre always start close to the valve and see that the edge of the cover at the other side of the wheel is pushed down into the well in the rim.

When replacing the tyre fit the part by the valve last, also with the edge of the cover at the other side of the wheel pushed down into the well. Slightly inflate the tube and, if available, paint the rim and tyre with soapy water, or water containing a soapless detergent to assist the tyre in slipping over the edge of the rim.

If the correct method of fitting and removal of the tyre is adopted it will be found that the covers can be manipulated quite easily with the small levers supplied in the tool-kit. The use of long levers and/or excessive force is liable to damage the walls of the tyre. After inflation make sure that the tyre is fitting evenly all the way round the rim. A line moulded on the wall of the tyre indicates whether or not the tyre is correctly fitted. If the tyre has a white mark indicating a balance point, this should be fitted near the valve.

148. Tyre Pressures

With a solo rider of normal weight (150 lbs.) the correct tyre pressure is 20 lb. per sq. in. for 3·50-19 in. tyres and 16 lb. per sq. in. for 4·00-18 in. tyres. The addition of a pillion passenger of about the same weight increases these to 30 lb. per sq. in. and 22 lb. per sq. in. respectively.

With riders of unusual weight, or when carrying heavy luggage or when a sidecar is fitted the load on each tyre should be determined and the pressures increased in accordance with the following table.

Tyre Section ins.	Maximum Load lb. at Pressure of lbs. per sq. in.					
	16	18	20	24	28	32
3·25	200	230	260	320	380	440
3·50	280	310	335	390	450	500
4·00	360	395	430	500	570	640

149. Lubrication

Grease the bearings by packing them with grease after removal of the brake cover plate and speedometer drive gearbox as described above.

Note that the brake cam is drilled for a grease passage but the end of this is stopped up with a countersunk screw instead of being fitted with a grease nipple. This is done to prevent excessive greasing by over-enthusiastic owners. If the cam is smeared with grease on assembly it should require no further attention but in case of necessity it is possible to remove the screw, fit a grease nipple in its place and grease the cam by this means.

Special Tools

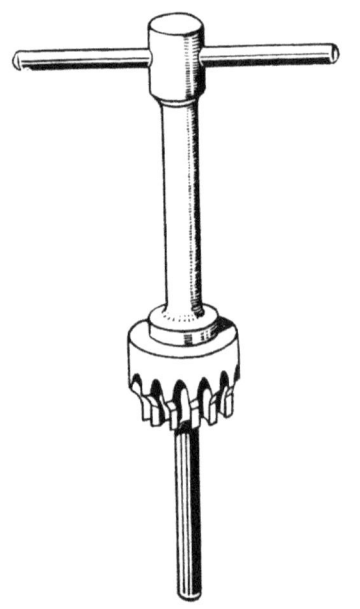

T.2053
INLET VALVE SEAT ARBOR

T.2054
INLET VALVE SEAT CUTTER

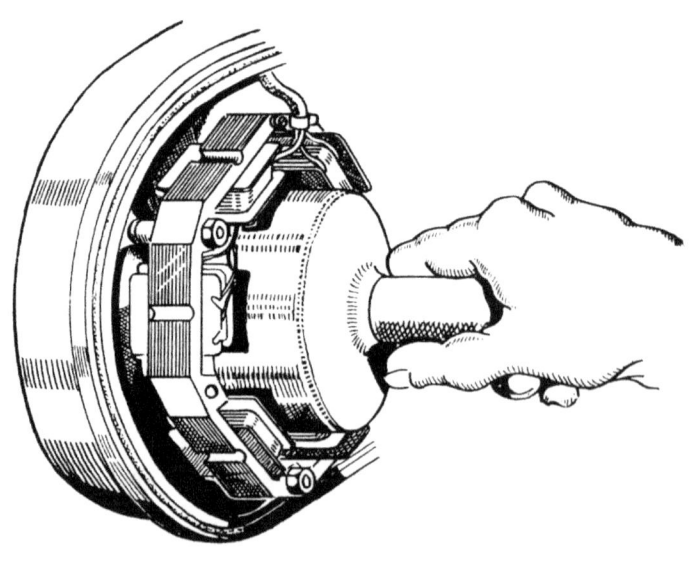

T.2055/19
ASSEMBLY GAUGE IN USE TO CENTRALISE ROTOR

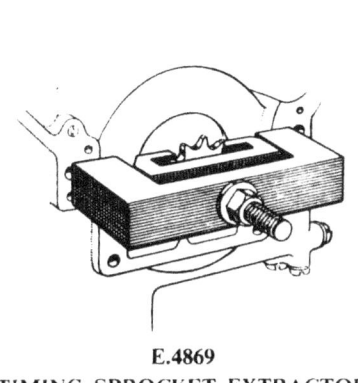

E.4869
TIMING SPROCKET EXTRACTOR

E.4871
CLUTCH HOLDING TOOL

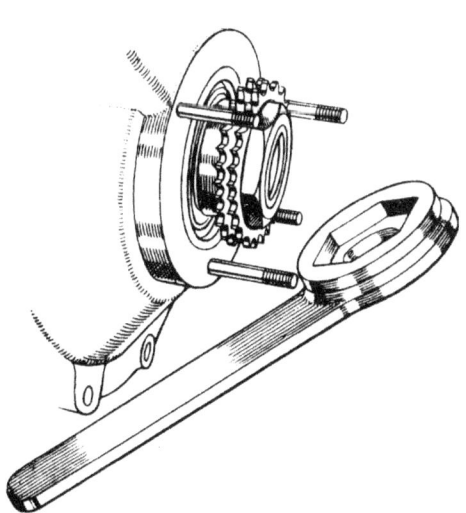

E.4877
ENGINE SPROCKET NUT SPANNER

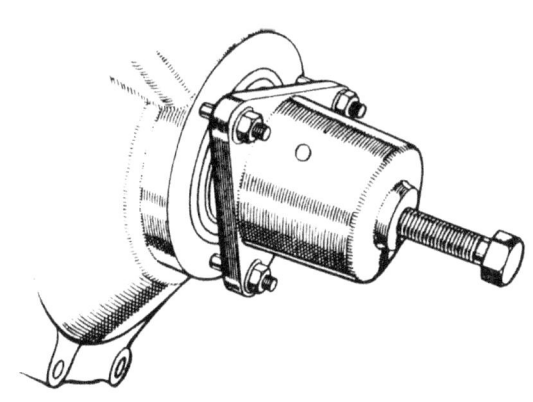

E.5121
CRANKSHAFT EXTRACTOR

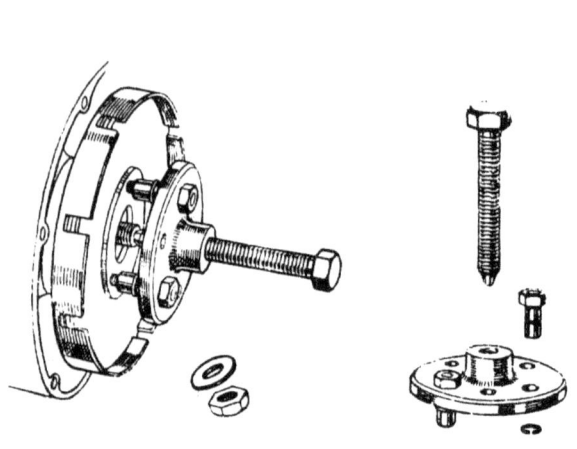

E.5414
CLUTCH HUB EXTRACTOR

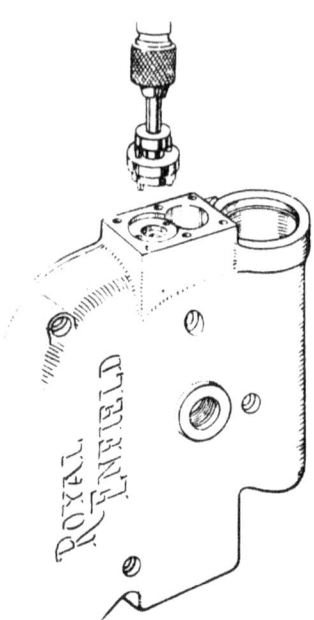

E.5425
PUMP DISC LAPPING TOOL

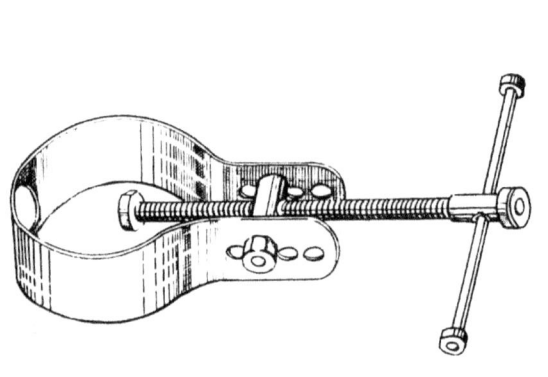

E.5477/T
GUDGEON PIN EXTRACTOR

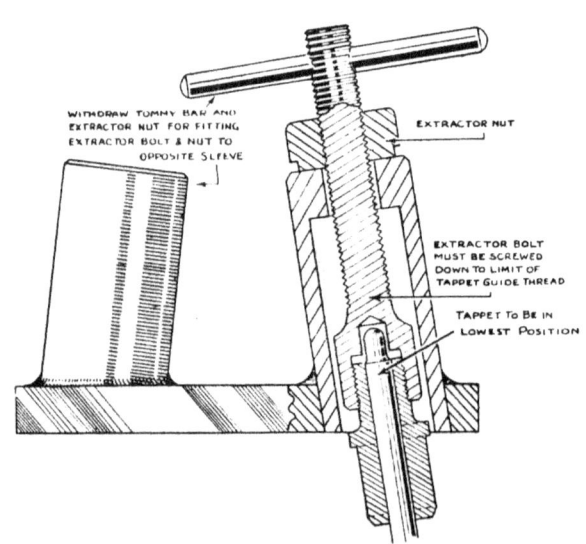

E.5790
TAPPET GUIDE EXTRACTOR

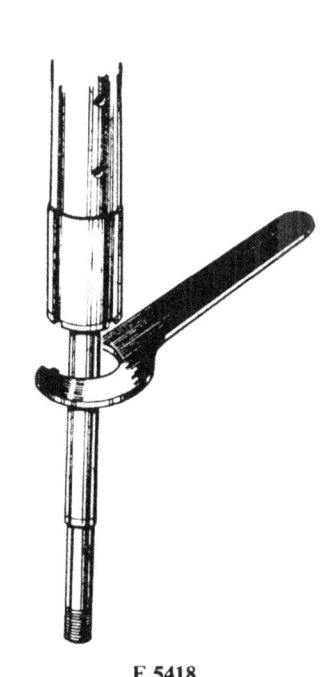

E.5418
VALVE PORT "C" SPANNER

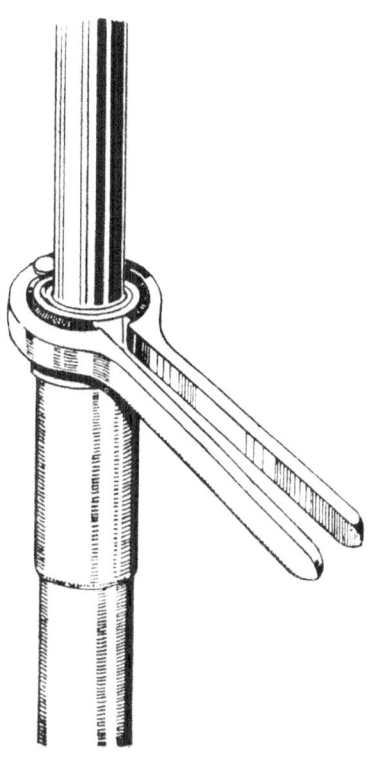

E.4912
OUTER TUBE HAND GRIPS

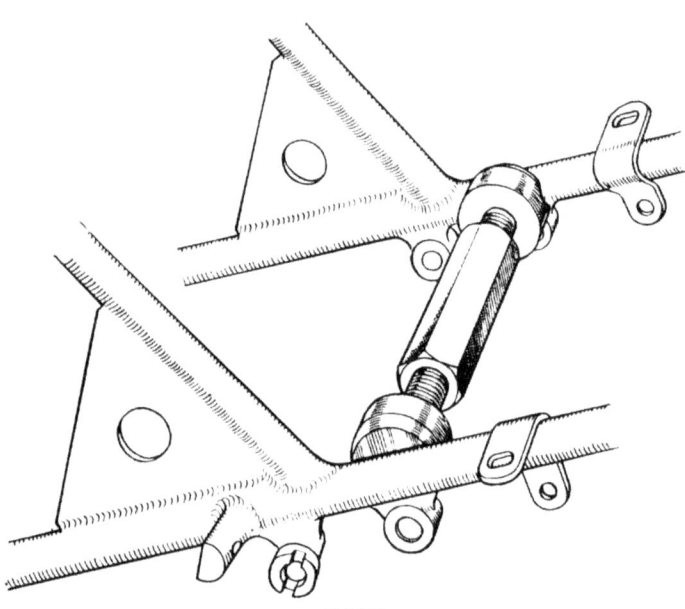

E.5431
FRAME EXPANDER

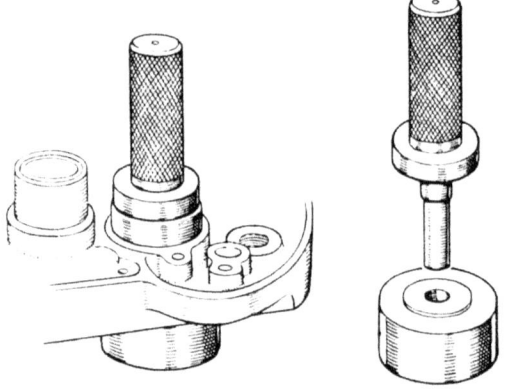

E.4823
GEARBOX COVER BALL BEARING
ASSEMBLY TOOL

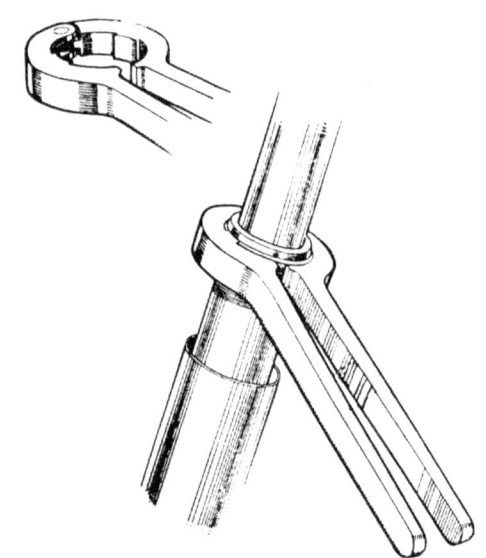

E.5417
GLAND NUT HAND GRIPS

WORKSHOP MAINTENANCE MANUAL for the

SEVEN-FIFTY INTERCEPTOR

SERIES II MOTOR CYCLE

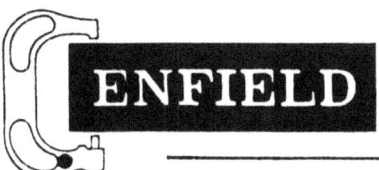 Enfield Precision Engineers Ltd.

UPPER WESTWOOD · BRADFORD-ON-AVON · WILTS
TELEPHONE BRADFORD-ON-AVON 2166-8
ENGLAND

1969 INTERCEPTOR 750 SERIES II U.K. MODEL

1969 INTERCEPTOR 750 SERIES II U.S.A. MODEL

Royal Enfield "Interceptor" 750 Series II Workshop Manual

LIST OF CONTENTS

	Page
TECHNICAL DATA	5
ENGINE SPECIFICATION	6–8
1. Engine	6
2. Cylinder Heads	6
3. Cylinders	6
4. Pistons	6
5. Connecting Rods	6
6. Crankcase	6
7. Crankshaft and Flywheel	6
8. Main Bearings	6
9. Camshafts	6
10. Valves	6
11. Valve Gear	6
12. Timing Drive	6
13. Ignition and Lighting System	7
14. Carburettors	7
15. Lubrication System	7
16. Breather	8
17. Gearbox	8
Oil Pump Diagrams	8
18. Clutch	8
SERVICE OPERATIONS WITH ENGINE IN FRAME	**9–18**
19. Removal of the Timing Cover	9
20. Valve Timing	9
21. Tappet Adjustment	10
22. Removal of the Camshafts	10
23. Ignition Timing	10
24. Primary Chain Adjustment	11
25. Timing Chain Adjustment	11
26. Removal of the Petrol Tank	12
27. Removal and Refitting of the Cylinder Head	12
28. Removal of the Valves	13
29. Removal of the Rockers	13
30. Removal of the Valve Guides	13
31. Removal of Sparking Plugs	13
32. Removal of the Cylinders	13
33. Removal of Pistons	14
34. Decarbonising	14
35. Grinding-in Valves	14
36. Reassembly after Decarbonising	15
37. Cleaning the Oil Filters	15
38. Overhaul of Oil Pumps	15
39. Removal of the Timing Chains	16
40. Removal of Pump Worm and Timing Sprocket	16
41. Removal of Camshaft Sprockets	16
42. Removal of the Engine and Clutch Sprockets	16
43. Removal of Tappets and Guides	16
44. Crankcase Breather	16
45. Removal of the Clutch	17
46. Removal of Final Drive Sprocket	17
47. Oil Seal Behind Engine Sprocket	17
48. Oil Pipe Unions	17
49. Rocker Oil Feed Relief Valve	18
50. Fitting the Alternator	18
SERVICE OPERATIONS WITH ENGINE REMOVED	**18–20**
51. Removal of the Engine Gearbox Unit from the Frame	18
52. Removal of the Gearbox	19
53. Dismantling the Crankcase	19
54. Main Bearings	19
55. Fitting the Connecting Rods	19
56. Reassembly of Crankcase	20
57. Crankshaft Plugs	20
GEARBOX AND CLUTCH	**20–25**
58. Description of the Clutch	20
59. Description of the Gearbox	21
60. Removal of the Gearbox	21
61. To Dismantle the Gearbox	21
62. Removal of the Ball Races	21

	Page
63. Change-Gear Mechanism	21
Operation of Gears	22
64. Reassembling the Gearbox	23
65. Dismantling and Reassembling the Clutch	23
66. Adjustment of Clutch Control	23
Exploded view of Gearbox	24
67. Adjustment of Neutral Finder	25
68. Gearbox Oil Level	25
AMAL MONOBLOC CARBURETTOR	**26–30**
69. General Description	26
70. Tuning the Carburettor(s)	27
71. Tuning Sequence with Two Carburettors	28
Exploded View of Monobloc Carburettor	29
72. Dismantling Carburettor	30
73. Causes of High Petrol Consumption	30
ELECTRICAL SYSTEM	**31–32**
74. Introduction	31
75. General	31
76. Routine Maintenance	31
77. Technical Data Specific Gravity of Electrolyte for Filling the Battery	32
COIL IGNITION SYSTEM	**32–35**
78. Description	32
79. Checking the Low Tension Circuit for Continuity	33
80. Fault Finding in the Low Tension Circuit	33
81. Ignition Coils	34
82. Bench Testing an Ignition Coil	34
83. Contact Breaker	34
84. Checking the High Tension Circuit	35
CAPACITOR IGNITION (Model 2MC)	
85. General	35
86. Identification of Capacitor Terminals	35
87. Storage Life of Model 2MC Capacitor	36
88. Testing	36
89. Wiring and Installation	36
90. Service Notes	36
CHARGING SYSTEM	**37–39**
91. Description	37
92. Checking the D.C. Input to Battery	37
93. Checking the Alternator Output	37
94. Rectifier Maintenance and Testing	37
95. Testing the Rectifier	38
96. Bench Testing the Rectifier	38
97. Checking the Charging Circuit for Continuity	38
98. Constructing a One-ohm Load Resistor	39
ZENER DIODE	**40–41**
99. Description	40
100. Maintenance	40
101. Test Procedure	40
102. Zener Diode Location	40
HORN	41
103. Description	41
104. Horn Adjustment	41
LAMP UNITS	**41–42**
105. Description	41
106. Beam Adjustment	41

	Page
107. Removing and Refitting the Headlamp	42
108. General	42
FUSES	42
109. Description	42
IGNITION and Headlamp Switches and Warning Lights	43
110. Description	43
111. General	43
Wiring Diagram	44
FRAME	**45–47**
112. Description of Frame	45
113. Steering Head Races	45
114. Removal of Rear Mudguard Assembly	45
115. Removal of Rear Suspension Unit	46
116. Servicing the Rear Suspension Units	46
117. Chain Stays	46
118. Centre Stand	47
119. Wheel Alignment	47
120. Lubrication	47
FRONT FORKS	**47–49**
121. Lubrication	47
122. To Drain the Fork	47
123. Filling Oil	47
124. Steering Head Adjustment	47
125. Dismantling the Forks	48
126. To Remove the Forks as a Unit	48
127. To Dismantle a Fork Slider	49
128. Assembling the Forks	49
FRONT WHEEL	**49–51**
129. To Remove the Front Wheel	49
130. To Refit the Front Wheel	49
131. To Dismantle the Hub	50
132. Assembling the Hub	50
133. Brake Adjustment	50
134. Brake Dismantling and Assembly	50
135. Brake Re-assembly	50
136. Balancing the Front Wheel	51
REAR WHEEL	**51–55**
137. Description	51
138. Removal and Replacement of Main Portion of Wheel for Tyre Repairs, etc.	51
139. Removal and Replacement of Complete Wheel for access to Brake	52
140. Removal of Brake Shoes for Replacement, etc.	52
141. Removal of Brake Operating Cam	52
142. Cush Drive	52
143. Removal of Ball Bearings	53
144. Hub Bearings	53
145. Fitting Limits for Bearings	53
146. Removal of Hub Driving Pins	54
147. Refitting Ball Bearings	54
148. Reassembly of Brake Shoes and Operating Cam into Cover Plate	54
149. Final Reassembly of Hub before Replacing Wheel	54
150. Wheel Rims	54
151. Spokes	54
152. Wheel Building and Truing	54
153. Tyre	55
154. Tyre Pressures	55
155. Lubrication	55
SPECIAL TOOLS	**56–58**

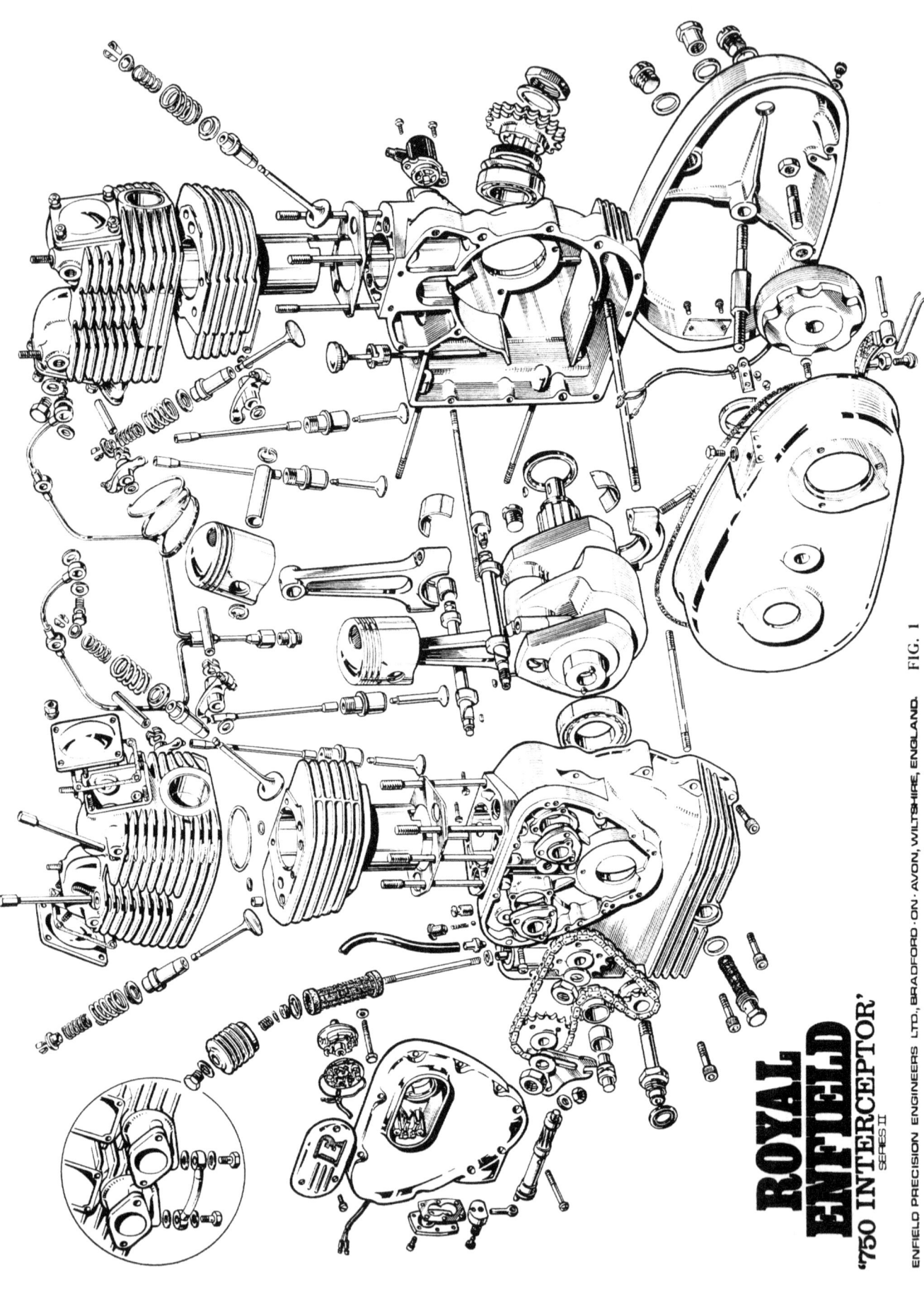

ROYAL ENFIELD "750 INTERCEPTOR" SERIES II
ENFIELD PRECISION ENGINEERS LTD., BRADFORD-ON-AVON, WILTSHIRE, ENGLAND. FIG. 1

Technical Data

"Interceptor" Series II Engine

Cubic Capacity	736 c.c.
Stroke ... Nominal	93 mm.
Bore ... Nominal	71 mm.
Actual	70.92 mm./2.792 in.
Rebore to .020 in. oversize when wear exceeds .0065 in.	
Compression Ratio	8.5 to 1
Piston Diameter:—	
Bottom of Skirt—	
Fore and Aft	2.788 in.
Top Lands	2.7675 in.
Skirt is tapered and oval turned.	
Piston Rings—	
Width—Plain Rings	.0625/.0635 in.
Scraper Ring Assembly	.1510/.1560 in.
Radial Thickness	2.883/3.085 mm.
Gap when in unworn Cylinder	.015/.020 in.
Clearance in grooves	.001/.003 in.
Renew Piston Rings when gap exceeds $\frac{1}{16}$ in.	
Oversize Pistons and Rings available	+.020 in.
Piston Boss Internal Diameter	.7498/.7500 in.
Gudgeon Pin Diameter	.7498/.7500 in.
Con. Rod Small End Internal Diameter	.7507/.7505 in.
Big End Internal Diameter Con. Rod	2.0190/2.0185 in.
Big End Internal Dia. Bearing Shells	1.8750/1.8755 in.*
Crank Pin Diameter, Timing Side	1.8744/1.8740 in.
Crank Pin Diameter, Driving Side	1.8741/1.8737 in.
Driving Side Main Ball Bearing—	
Type	Hoffman 145 or R and M—LJ45
Outside Diameter	85 mm.
Inside Diameter	45 mm.
Width	19 mm.
Timing Side Main Roller Bearing—	
Type	Hoffman R145 or R and M—LR45
Outside Diameter	85 mm.
Inside Diameter	45 mm.
Width	19 mm.
Rocker Inside Diameter	.5627/.5622 in.
Rocker Bearing Inside Diameter	.5622/.5617 in.
Rocker Spindle Diameter	.5617/.5615 in.
Inlet Valve Stem Diameter	.3430/.3425 in.
Exhaust Valve Stem Diameter	.3410/.3405 in.
Valve Guide Internal Diameter	.3437/.3447 in.
Valve Guide External Diameter	.6275/.6270 in.
Valve Guide Hole in Cylinder Head Dia.	.625/.626 in.
Tappet Stem Diameter	.3747/.3744 in.
Tappet Guide Internal Diameter	.3758/.3753 in.
Tappet Guide External Diameter	1.0125/1.0130 in.
Tappet Guide Hole in Crankcase Dia.	1.011/1.010 in.
Tappet Clearance with cold engine—	
Inlet	.006 in.
Exhaust	.007 in.

*Assumes .0005 in. "stretch" of eye of rod and cap due to interference fit of bearing shells.

Valve Spring Free Length—	
Inner	$1\frac{1}{2}$ in.
Outer	$1\frac{11}{16}$ in.
(Renew when reduced by $\frac{1}{16}$ in.)	
Valve Timing with .020 in. clearance. See Page 9.	
Camshaft Bearing Internal Diameters—	
Timing Side	.8135/.8125 in.
Driving Side	.750 in.
	(after assembly)
Camshaft Bearing Diameters—	
Timing Side	.8115/.8110 in.
Driving Side	.7490/.7485 in.
Cam Lift—	
Exhaust	.360 in.
Inlet	.360 in.
Valve Lift (approx.)—	
Exhaust	.350 in.
Inlet	.350 in.
Timing Sprocket	12 Teeth
Camshaft Sprockets	24 Teeth
Timing Chain—Type	Single No. 110038 endless
Length	66 Pitches
Width	.225 in.
Pitch	.375 in.
Roller	.250 in.
Contact Breaker	Half Engine Speed
Points	.015 in.
Timing—Advanced	.355 in. before T.D.C. (32°)
Engine Sprocket	29 Teeth
Clutch Sprocket	56 Teeth
Final Drive Sprocket	20 Teeth
Primary Chain—Type	Duplex No. 114038 endless
Length	92 Pitches
Width	.628 in.
Pitch	.375 in.
Roller	.250 in.
Feed Oil Pump—Speed	1/6 Engine Speed
Piston Diameter	.37500/.37475 in.
Stroke length	.5 in.

Sparking Plug—Lodge 2HLN. Champion N4 KLG FE 80, or Autolite AG2. For high speed running over long distances, use Lodge 3HLN, Champion N3, KLG FE.100, or Autolite AG 901.

Diameter	14 mm.
Reach	$\frac{3}{4}$ in.
Gap	.018/.022 in.

Engine Specification

1. Engine
The engine is an even-firing vertical twin-cylinder, having separate cylinders and heads and fully enclosed overhead valve gear. The oil is carried in a sump at the bottom of the crankcase and is pressure fed to big ends and valve rockers. A massive one-piece high-strength spheroidal graphite cast iron crankshaft is used.

2. Cylinder Heads
The cylinder heads are die-cast from light aluminium alloy with ample finning to ensure adequate cooling. The exhaust pipe inserts are cast-in and the valve inserts are of austenitic iron and are shrunk in so that they are replaceable. The large capacity induction ports are streamlined and blended to the valve seatings.

3. Cylinders
The separate cast-iron cylinders have a nominal bore of 71 mm, the stroke being 93 mm. The cubic capacity of the engine is 736 c.c. The cylinder heads are located on the cylinders by hollow dowels and the joint between head and barrel is made by a split, triangular section steel ring which seats on a chamfer at the top end of the cylinder barrel and stands about .005 in. proud of the joint face. The push rod tunnels are sealed by washers of special heat and oil resistant rubber bonded to metal and fitting in recesses in the cylinder head.

4. Pistons
The pistons are made of low expansion aluminium alloy, heat treated and form ground taper and oval. Each piston carries two taper faced compression rings and a special dual oil control ring.

One compression plate, .022 in. thick, is fitted below each cylinder barrel when the compression ratio is 8.5 to 1. With the plates removed the ratio is raised to 9 to 1.

5. Connecting Rods
The connecting rods are produced from stampings of Hiduminium RR56 light alloy. The little end bearings are of alloy direct on to the gudgeon pin. In case of wear after long service the little end can be bored out and fitted with a bush, but this is rarely necessary.

The big end bearings consist of white-metalled steel liners which are renewable. The detachable bearing caps are bolted to the connecting rods by means of high tensile socket screws, the heads of which are drilled for wiring.

6. Crankcase
The combined crankcase and oil tank is die-cast from light alloy in two halves, being split vertically.

7. Crankshaft and Flywheel
The crankshaft is cast in one piece, integral with the massive central flywheel, from high quality spheroidal graphitic cast iron. The total weight is approximately 24 lbs., and all crankshafts are dynamically balanced.

The main journals are ground, and the big end journals are ground and hand lapped.

8. Main Bearings
Heavy duty bearings are provided for the crankshaft, the driving side being ball and the timing side roller.

9. Camshafts
The camshafts are machined from drop forged steel stampings with the cams and bearings hardened and ground.

The camshafts are located in the crankcase and run in bronze bushes in the left hand case and in detachable aluminium housings which are bolted to the timing side crankcase. This enables the camshafts to be changed, if so desired for tuning purposes, without the necessity of dismantling the crankcase.

10. Valves
The inlet valves are machined from stampings of special Silicon-Chrome Valve Steel and the exhaust valves are of High-Nickel-Chromium-Tungsten Valve Steel with the stems Stellite-tipped.

11. Valve Gear
The valves are operated from the camshaft by means of large, flat-based, guided tappets, tubular alloy push rods with induction hardened steel ends and overhead rockers. Two compression springs are fitted to each valve secured by Bullock Type split collets locking in high strength aluminium collars. The springs are specially designed to give a variable rate on compression.

12. Timing Drive
The camshafts are driven by an endless chain from the timing sprocket on the crankshaft and the tightness of the chain can be adjusted by means of the chain tensioner in the timing chest.

An extension of the front camshaft drives the contact breaker housed in the timing cover.

A tachometer gearbox is mounted on the left hand crankcase and is driven by the front camshaft.

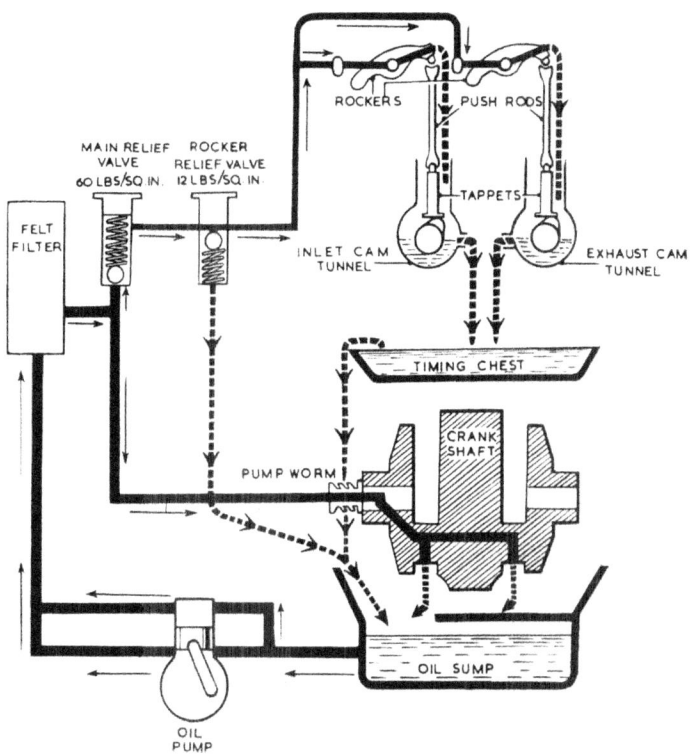

LUBRICATION SYSTEM. Diagrammatic Arrangement
Fig. 2

13. Ignition and Lighting System

This model is fitted with the Lucas capacitor system which has been developed to enable machines to be run with or without a battery. The rider, therefore, has the choice of running with normal battery operation or running without battery if desired, (e.g., competing in trials or other competitive events), and for emergency in case of battery failure.

Before running the machine with the battery disconnected it is essential that the battery negative lead be taped up to prevent it from shorting to earth (frame of machine). Otherwise, the capacitor will be ruined.

Machines can readily be started without the battery and run as normal with full use of **standard** lighting. When stationary, however, parking lights will not work unless the battery is connected.

The system incorporates an alternator and 12 volt battery coil ignition equipment with a zener diode charging regulator mounted on an efficient heat sink and a spring mounted high-capacity electrolytic capacitor.

Twin contact breakers with an automatic timing advance mechanism mounted on the end of the front camshaft, are housed in the timing cover.

14. Carburettors

Twin Amal Concentric carburettors with a bore of 30 mm are fitted as standard.

15. Lubrication System

Oil is carried in a sump cast integral with the crankcase, ensuring the full rate of circulation immediately the engine is started and rapid heating of the oil in cold weather.

The positively driven double acting piston type oil pump running at $\frac{1}{6}$ engine speed, at the rear of the timing cover pumps oil to the bearings under pressure. A gauze strainer, attached to the sump drain plug, protects the pump from foreign matter, and oil after leaving the pump, passes through a large capacity felt filter removable from the top of the crankcase. Pressure to the big ends is kept at 60 lbs./sq. in. by a relief valve situated in the top of the crankcase. This is the right hand of the two screws behind the right hand cylinder barrel.

The capacity of the pump is sufficient to ensure that there is always more oil available than required by the big ends and oil passing through the main relief valve is fed through external pipes to the overhead rocker gear. A secondary relief valve (the left hand screw behind the cylinder barrel) is set at 10 to 15 lbs./sq. in. and passes surplus oil back into the sump.

The oil from the rocker bearings is squirted through a small hole in each rocker on to the top ends of the push rods. It then flows down the push rod tunnels into the cam tunnels, where it lubricates the cams and tappets and overflows into the timing chest, where it lubricates the timing chains and then drains to the sump.

A small circular magnet is fitted over the fixing stud inside the oil filter for the purpose of collecting any ferrous particles which may be suspended in the oil.

16. Breather

The engine is ventilated to atmosphere by a long, large diameter plastic pipe extending to the rear of the machine and connected to a union screwed into the top of the crankcase.

17. Gearbox

The gearbox is bolted on to the back of the crankcase and has four speeds, which are foot controlled, and a patented neutral finder. All gears are in constant mesh, changes being affected by robust dog clutches. (See Subsection 64).

The standard gear ratios with 20T gearbox sprocket are as follows:—

Bottom Gear	12.40
Second Gear	8.19
Third Gear	6.05
Top Gear	4.44

18. Clutch

The clutch has six pressure plates and five friction plates, including the sprocket which is lined on both sides with a bonded cork based friction material.

A description of the operating mechanism is given in Subsection 63.

Oil Pump Diagram

Fig. 3

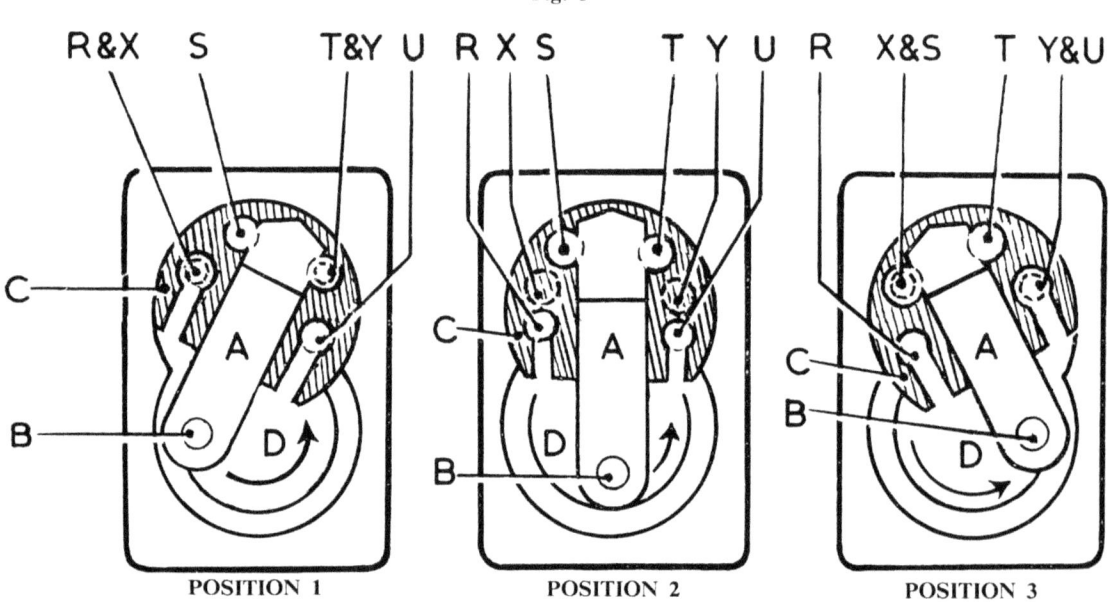

POSITION 1 POSITION 2 POSITION 3

The ports in the housing are connected as follows:—
X — delivery to big ends.   Y — suction from oil tank.

Position 1. The plunger A is being drawn out of the cylinder hole in the disc C by the action of the peg B on the shaft D. The port T in the disc C registers with the suction port Y in the housing, so that oil is drawn into the cylinder from the oil tank. At the same time port R in the disc registers with the delivery port X in the housing and oil below the disc is forced through X to the big ends.

Position 2. The disc is in the central position where the individual ports can be clearly seen.

Position 3. The plunger A is being pushed into the cylinder hole in the disc C. The port S in the disc now registers with the delivery port X in the housing, so that oil is forced out of the cylinder to the big ends. At the same time the suction port U in the disc registers with the suction port Y in the housing and oil is drawn into the housing below the disc from the oil tank.

Service operations with Engine in Frame

19. Removal of the Timing Cover

Before attempting to remove the timing cover it is first necessary to dismantle the contact breaker. Remove the oval cover retained by three screws and the contact breaker assembly will be revealed. Undo the hexagon nut and slotted headed screw retaining the contact breaker plate, pull the plate away from its recess, and leave suspended on the wiring harness. Remove the contact breaker centre screw and replace by the special extractor pin W.49622 included in the tool kit. Tightening this screw will force the unit from the taper on the end of the camshaft.

Place a tray under the engine to catch the oil which will escape when the timing cover is removed. Unscrew the timing cover fixing screws and draw off the cover, tapping it lightly if necessary.

Inspect both oil seals, particularly the crankshaft seal which is subjected to a high pressure. Any sign of a split in the rubber or of a fault in the bonding of the rubber to the casing means the seal must be replaced. Before the crankshaft seal can be changed, it is necessary to dismantle the oil pump as described in Sub-section 38. The new seal must be fitted carefully and a special tool Part No. W50011 is available for this purpose. Make certain the seal enters squarely into the housing and is fitted the right way round. The garter spring on the crankshaft seal faces into the recess and on the camshaft seal faces towards the engine.

In refitting the cover, make sure that the gasket is fitted the correct way round and that it is correctly located with no oil ways obstructed. Also see that the thrust washer is on the chain tensioner sprocket spindle.

Careful assembly of the timing cover is necessary to avoid damage to the oil seals. A special thimble Part No. W49994, fitted over the end of the exhaust camshaft, will ensure that the shaft enters the seal without causing damage to the sealing lip. Two studs can be screwed into the timing cover holes in the crankcase to act as temporary dowels to ensure that the seals line up with the shafts before entry.

The refitting of the cover will be facilitated if the engine is turned gently forwards while the cover is being put into place. This will help the engagement of the pump worm with the pump spindle and prevent damage to the gears.

Before refitting the contact breaker auto-advance unit, clean out the taper hole and also the mating taper on the end of the camshaft. If these are not clean and dry the unit may turn on the taper when the centre screw is tightened up. Assemble and time the ignition as described in Subsection 23.

To verify that the oil pump is working after replacing the timing cover, start the engine and slacken off the hexagon headed nut at the top of the finned oil cleaner cap.

20. Valve Timing

The camshaft sprockets are keyed to the camshafts so that the valve timing can only be incorrect if the timing chain is incorrectly fitted.

The correct setting is obtained with the marks stamped on the camshaft sprockets facing each other inwards on the centre line and the mark on the crankshaft sprocket pointing vertically downwards. (See Fig. 5). If it is necessary to remove the camshafts and sprockets see Subsections 22 and 41.

Remember that the camshaft sprocket nuts and the timing sprocket fixing bolt all have **Left-Hand Threads.** While tightening the camshaft nuts the sprockets should be held.

The correct valve timing at .020 in. tappet clearance is as follows:—

Exhaust opens 73° Before B.D.C.
Exhaust closes 33° After T.D.C.
Inlet opens 33° Before T.D.C.
Inlet closes 73° After B.D.C.

When checking opening and closing points do not expect precise agreement with the figures quoted. The figures obtained when checking will depend largely on the method used to decide when the valve opens or closes also, if using a dial gauge, whether this is reading the movement of the tappet or spring collar. It must be remembered, too, that the precise timing of each valve depends on the accurate position of *four* keyways and on whether the timing chain is new or worn. The figures in the table are intended as a guide to enable a check to be made that the timing marks are correctly lined up. If opening and closing points on the same shaft are early or late by about 30° the sprocket is fitted one tooth wrong.

21. Tappet Adjustment

The tappet clearance is adjusted by means of a screw in the outer end of the rocker. Access to the adjusting screws is obtained by removing the covers of the rocker boxes.

The correct clearances are:— Inlet .006 in., Exhaust .007 in.

These figures are for a COLD engine.

To adjust the clearance, loosen the locknut beneath the rocker arm, turn the screw and re-tighten the locknut.

The adjustment of each valve should be made with the corresponding valve in the other cylinder fully open. This ensures that the tappet is on the neutral position of the cam.

If the heads of the adjusting screws are worn they should be replaced.

22. Removal of the Camshafts

Remove the timing cover (Subsection 19).

Remove the timing chain (Subsection 39).

Remove the rocker box covers and screw the rocker adjusting screws right back.

Unscrew the three screws holding each of the timing side camshaft bearings. A hole is provided in the camshaft sprockets and this can be aligned with each screw in turn, for access with a hexagon wrench. The screws can be fully undone but will remain captive in the cast aluminium bearing.

Before removing the camshafts it is necessary to prevent the tappets falling through their guides when the shafts are no longer holding them up. If this happens, the push rods will come out of engagement with the rocker arms and make replacement difficult. This can be prevented by placing the motor cycle on its left side. With the machine in this position, rotate the camshaft until the timing marks on the sprockets are pointing at 2 o'clock for the inlet and 1 o'clock for the exhaust when they can be withdrawn upwards complete with sprockets and bearings. If the machine has to be moved before the shafts are replaced, it is essential that something is put into the camshaft tunnels to keep the tappets in place.

If it is necessary to remove the sprockets from the camshafts see Subsection 41.

23. Ignition Timing

The contact breakers are accessible after removing the small oval cover. Owing to the provision of automatic ignition advance, the contact breaker is always fully retarded when the engine is at rest or is being turned over slowly. The advance mechanism is situated behind the contact breaker and gives a range of approximately 12° on the half-speed shaft, corresponding to 24° on the engine shaft.

The optimum ignition timing is 32° advance, (.355 in. before T.D.C.), so that in the fully retarded position the contact points must open when the piston is 8° or .023 in. before T.D.C.

To obtain maximum performance and avoid possible damage to the engine, it is vitally important that the ignition timing is set accurately and also identical on both cylinders. It is easier to obtain the necessary accuracy by timing with the ignition cam in the advanced position and, to hold the cam in this position, a special recessed washer is included in the tool kit.

As a further aid to ignition timing, an indicator has been incorporated to show the correct position of the piston when the points are just beginning to open. Inside the primary chaincase, a line engraved on the alternator rotor lines up with a second line engraved on a fixed plate when the pistons are 32° before T.D.C. These lines are visible after removing the large screwed plug situated towards the front end of the chaincase.

To check the ignition timing, proceed as follows:

Switch off and check the maximum opening of the points, on both sets of contacts; this should be .014 in. to .016 in. The gap must always be checked with the line on face of the cam pointing towards the appropriate contact heel. To adjust the gap, slacken off the slotted screw, marked "A" in Fig. 4, and pivot the small contact plate by turning the eccentric headed screw marked "B" (clockwise to increase the gap). Re-tighten screw "A".

Unscrew and remove the centre screw and washer securing the contact breaker cam centre to the shaft, replace the washer by the special recessed one, Part No. W.49717, included in the tool kit, and refit the centre screw with the recess on the washer pointing towards the engine. Before tightening the centre screw, rotate the cam clock-

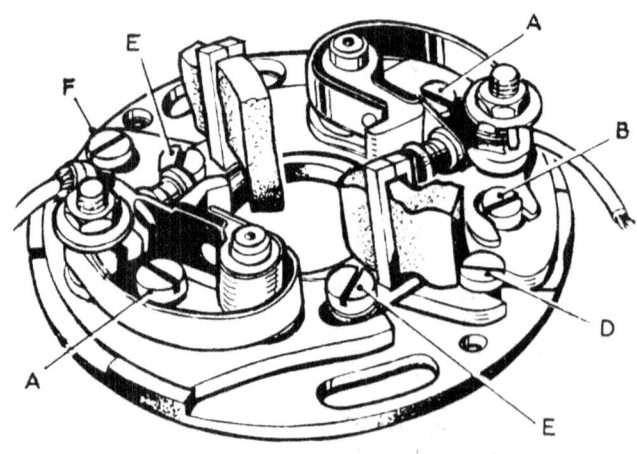

CONTACT BREAKER ASSEMBLY
Fig. 4

wise into the advanced position by means of a screwdriver located in the end slot and hold in this position as the screw is tightened. On removing the screwdriver the ignition cam will now stay locked in the advanced position.

Place the machine on the centre stand and remove both sparking plugs. Switch on the ignition, engage top gear and turn the engine by rotating the back wheel forward until the top set of contacts are closed. Continue to rotate the wheel until the ammeter needle flicks to zero, indicating that the points have opened.

Remove the screwed plug, at the front end of the primary chaincase, and the timing marks, now visible through the hole in the chaincase, should be in line.

If the timing is incorrect, adjust by slackening the two screws marked "C" in Fig. 4 and rotating the top contact breaker plate by turning the eccentric headed screw marked "D" (anti-clockwise to advance) Re-tighten screws "C" and again go through the procedure of rotating the back wheel and checking the alignment of the timing marks.

When the timing is correct for the top set of points, carry out a similar check for the bottom set and make any necessary adjustment using screws "E" and "F".

When satisfied that both contact sets are adjusted correctly, remove the centre screw, replace the original plain washer, and re-tighten the screw. Check that the cam is moving freely on the centre.

If the engine has been dismantled or the timing has slipped it will first be necessary to re-time the contact breaker cam centre before making any adjustments on the contact breaker plate. To do this, first unscrew and remove the centre screw securing the contact breaker cam centre to the shaft. Screw the extractor, provided in the tool kit, into the centre of the cam and tighten. A light tap on the head of the extractor will free the cam centre from the driving shaft. Remove the extractor and refit the cam centre loosely on to the shaft with the correct centre screw and washer. Loosen the two screws which secure the circular contact breaker back plate and set the plate central in its slots. Tighten the screws.

Rotate the top and bottom contact breaker plates into their extreme clockwise positions by means of screws "C", "D", "E", and "F", as previously described. With the machine on the centre stand and both sparking plugs removed, engage top gear and turn the engine by rotating the back wheel forward until the timing side (R.H.) piston is on T.D.C. of the compression stroke (both valves closed).

Switch on the ignition and rotate the cam centre in a clockwise direction until the top set of contacts are closed. Continue turning until the ammeter needle flicks to zero. Give the cam centre a sharp tap endways to secure it on the shaft and lock up with the centre screw. The cam centre is now locked in a position where correct timing can be obtained by close adjustment of the small separate contact breaker plates and to do this, follow the procedure given previously for checking the ignition timing. After the correct timing has been obtained, check that the cam is moving freely on the centre.

If a Timing Light is available, this can be used on the timing marks, visible through the hole in the chaincase. The engine must be run at 3,000 r.p.m. to ensure that the ignition is in the fully advanced position, and, if the timing is correct, the two marks will appear to be in line. Make this test on both cylinders.

Occasionally apply two drops of clean engine oil to the rear end of the felt pads bearing against the contact breaker cam and apply a smear of grease to the moving contact pivot post.

24. Primary Chain Adjustment

The tension of the primary chain can be checked through the inspection cover in the primary chain case and, should it require adjustment, access to the adjuster is gained by removing the chain case cover, which is held in position by a single nut. Before removing the nut, place a tray under the engine to catch the oil from the chaincase.

Beneath the bottom run of the chain is a curved slipper on which the chain rests and which may be raised or lowered by turning the adjusting screw after having first slackened the locknut.

A rubber button is fitted to the end of the adjusting screw to prevent the transmission of chain noise to the chaincase and this is held against the chaincase by a hairpin spring, which prevents it from bouncing.

Do not adjust the chain to be dead tight but rotate the engine slowly and, while doing so, test the tension of the top run of the chain by pressing it up and down with the fingers. Adjust the tension so that there is $\frac{1}{4}$ in. up and down movement at the tightest spot.

Re-tighten the locknut on the adjusting screw, replace the chain cover and replenish with oil to the height of the level plug.

25. Timing Chain Adjustment

Before adjusting the tension of the timing chain, turn the engine until the chain is in its tightest position, checking the chain between all sprockets.

Adjust the tension so that there is $\frac{1}{4}$ in. movement of the chain.

The tension of the timing chain is altered by moving the quadrant after slackening the nut A which secures it (see Fig. 6). This rotates the eccentric spindle on which the chain tensioner jockey sprocket is mounted. Tightening of the chain is effected by moving the quadrant to the left.

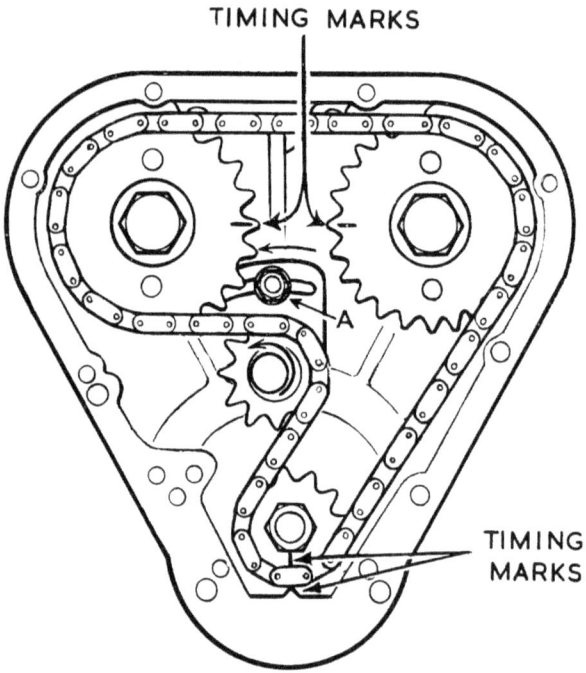

TIMING CHAIN ADJUSTMENT SHOWING TIMING MARKS
Fig. 5

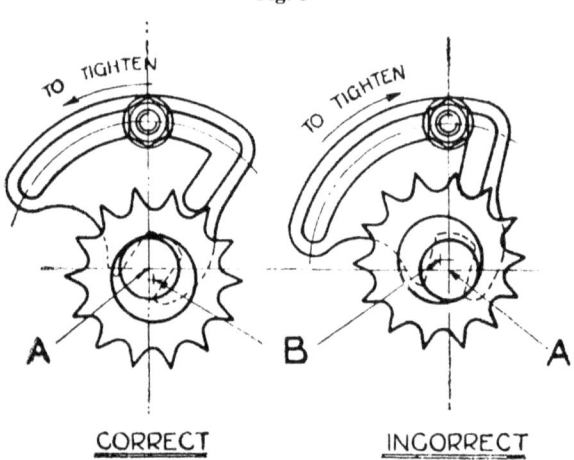

TIMING CHAIN ADJUSTMENT
Fig. 6

It is imperative that the quadrant is fitted the right way round and that the eccentric spindle is fitted correctly in the quadrant fork. If the chain tightens when the quadrant is moved to the right, the tensioner has been wrongly assembled and may cause damage to the quadrant (see Fig. 6).

In making the adjustment, care must be taken to see that any backlash in the quadrant is taken up in the "tightening" direction, i.e. do not make the chain too tight and then move the quadrant back slightly, but tighten the chain progressively until the correct tension is obtained and then lock the quadrant. If the chain becomes too tight during adjustment, slacken it right back and make the adjustment again.

If the chain is too slack it may give rise to a loud noise which can be mistaken for a faulty bearing. If it is too tight the result will be a high pitched howl. If such noises are heard, therefore, first check the adjustment of the timing chain.

26. Removal of the Petrol Tank

The petrol tank is rubber mounted front and rear. The front attachment is by means of a horizontal stud passing through a rubber sleeve housed in a lug across the frame immediately behind the steering head. The rear fixing is a rubber lined metal clip secured by two $\frac{1}{4}$ in. diameter bolts and nuts.

To remove the tank, first disconnect the petrol pipes, then remove the nut from one end of the front attachment stud and knock out the stud. Then unscrew the nuts and bolts securing the rear end of the tank and lift it away, taking care not to damage the paintwork on top at the front end where it may come into contact with the handlebar clamp.

27. Removal and Refitting of the Cylinder Head

First remove the petrol tank and petrol pipe. (Subsection 26).

Remove head steady brackets.

Disconnect the oil pipes and plug leads.

Remove the exhaust pipes and carburettors.

Remove the rocker box covers.

Turn the engine until both valves in one head are closed.

Remove the five cylinder head nuts from the head, hit it smartly with a hide mallet beneath the exhaust and inlet ports (not the fins) and lift it off.

Turn the engine through one revolution and repeat with the other head.

When replacing the heads, see that the dowels are in position in the cylinder barrels and that the push rods are the right way up (shallow cups upwards).

See that the taper section "Cross" sealing ring and its seatings are perfectly clean and that the rubber seals for the push rod tunnels are in good condition and correctly fitted. With the head upside down on the bench drop the seal with the metal side downwards into the recess. A little jointing compound should be applied to both sides of the "Cross" sealing ring and the rubber push rod tunnel seals.

Lower the cylinder heads over the push rods making sure that the rockers locate in the cups.

Fit the head nuts *and washers* and tighten down lightly. Do not overtighten the nuts—20 lbs. ft. is the recommended figure. Tighten each nut a little at a time in turn. Begin with the two inside nuts and the one by the spark plug, leaving the final tightening of the corners to the last.

28. Removal of the Valves

Having removed the cylinder head, remove the rocker-box covers, each held by four nuts, and swing the rocker clear of the valve. Using a suitable valve spring compressing tool, compress the valve springs and remove the split collets from the end of the valve stem. Slacken back the compressing tool and release the springs. Withdraw the valve and place its springs, top spring collar (and bottom collar if it is loose) and split collets together in order that they may be reassembled with the valve from which they were removed.

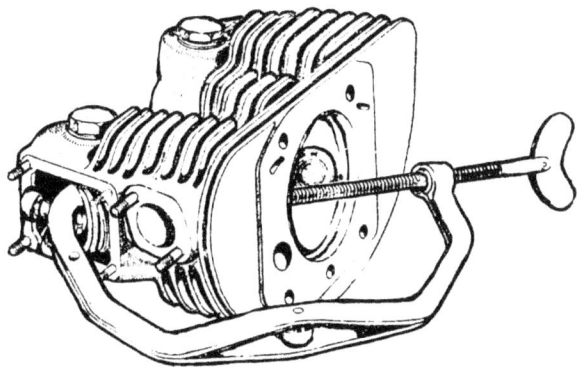

REMOVAL OF VALVES
Fig. 7

Deal similarly with the other valves in the heads.

If the valve will not slide easily through the valve guide, remove any slight burrs on the end of the valve stem with a carborundum stone. If the burrs are not removed and the valve is forced out, the guide may be damaged.

29. Removal of the Rockers

To remove the rocker, first take off the cylinder head. Remove the hexagon plug on the inner side and the rocker spindle may be drawn out by means of a bolt screwed into the rocker spindle, which is tapped $\frac{5}{16}$ in. B.S.F.

On reassembling make sure that the spring washers are fitted on the sides of the rockers nearest the centre of the engine and the plain thrust washers on the outer sides.

30. Removal of the Valve Guides

To remove the valve guides from the heads two special tools are required which can easily be made.

The first is a piece of tube with an internal bore of not less than $\frac{7}{8}$ in.

The second is a mandrel about 4 in. long made from $\frac{9}{16}$ in. diameter bar with the end turned down to about $\frac{5}{16}$ in. diameter for $\frac{1}{2}$ in.

Support the cylinder head on the tube which fits over the collar of the valve guide. Using the mandrel force the guide out of the head with a hand press or by using a hammer.

To fit a new guide, support the head at the correct angle and use a hand press and the same mandrel. If a hand press is not available and the guide is replaced by a hammer, use a piece of tube of $\frac{9}{16}$ in. internal diameter to prevent damage to the bore of the guide. If a valve guide is removed for any reason, an oversize one should be fitted in order to maintain the interference. It is necessary to re-cut the valve seat and grind in the valve after a a guide has been replaced. (See Subsection 35).

A worn exhaust valve guide may give rise to slight smoking from the exhaust pipe due to oil passing down the valve stem on to the hot valve head. This may also be caused or increased by faulty operation of the breather.

31. Removal of the Sparking Plugs

Care must be taken when removing and replacing the sparking plugs not to damage the threads in the cylinder heads.

If the threads do become damaged, they can be tapped out to a larger size and steel wire inserts fitted.

Special tools are available for tapping and inserting the steel wire inserts. The latter tool consists of a piece of $\frac{7}{16}$ in. diameter tube or rod with a slot cut in the end.

The insert is placed over the tool with the tag engaging in the slot and it is screwed into the plug hole in the cylinder head from the outside until the last coil is 1 to $1\frac{1}{2}$ threads below the top face. A reverse twist of the tool will then break off the tag.

If the cylinder head has been removed, the fitting of the insert will be facilitated if the tool is put through the hole from the inside and the insert screwed back from the outside.

If the cylinder head has not been removed, care must be taken not to drop the end of the tag into the cylinder and in such a case it is better to break off the tag with a pair of long-nosed pliers.

32. Removal of the Cylinders

When the cylinder heads have been removed the cylinders can be lifted clear of the studs. This should be done with the pistons at top dead centre.

It is advisable to put a clean cloth over the mouth of the crankcase to prevent anything, such as a piece of broken piston ring, from falling in.

When replacing the cylinders, clean off the joint faces and fit new paper joints, two to each cylinder, one each side of the compression plate.

33. Removal of Pistons

Remove the cylinder heads and cylinders.

With a tang of a file remove the two outer circlips retaining the gudgeon pins. Remove the long central cylinder studs which come opposite the gudgeon pins.

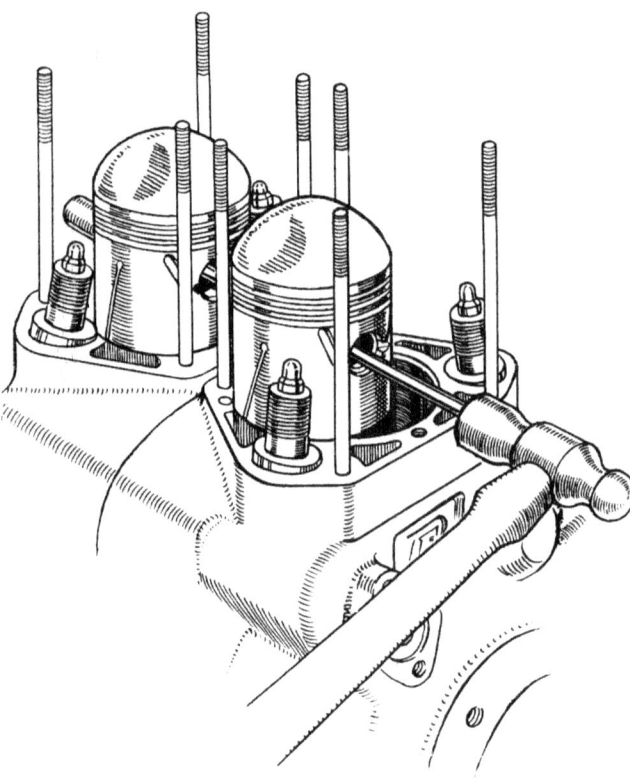

REMOVAL OF PISTONS
Fig. 8

Use Special Tool No. E.5477/T to extract the gudgeon pin or using a rod about $\frac{1}{4}$ in. in diameter insert this right through one gudgeon pin and drive the other pin out of its piston, supporting the connecting rod substantially meanwhile to prevent distortion.

Having lifted the first piston away, the other one may be readily removed in the same manner. Mark the pistons and gudgeon pins so that they go back into the same pistons the same way round and so that the pistons go back into the same barrels the same way round.

Take care not to drop the gudgeon pin circlip into the crankcase. A clean cloth should be put over the mouths of the crankcase to prevent this.

34. Decarbonising

Having removed the cylinder heads as described in Subsection 27, scrape away all carbon, bearing in mind that you are dealing with aluminium which is easily damaged. Scrape gently and avoid scoring the combustion chamber or the valve seats which are of austenitic iron shrunk into the head. Be careful while performing this work not to injure the joint faces which bed down on to the head gaskets.

Do not, in any circumstances, use caustic soda or potash for the removal of carbon from aluminium alloy.

Scrape away all carbon from the valve heads and beneath the heads, being very careful not to cause any damage to the valve faces.

If the piston rings are removed the grooves should be cleaned out and new rings fitted. For cleaning the grooves, a piece of discarded ring thrust into a wooden handle and filed to a chisel point is a useful tool.

If the piston ring gaps exceed $\frac{1}{16}$ in. when the rings are in position in the barrel, new rings should be fitted. The correct gap for new rings is .015—.020 in. The gap should be measured in the least worn part of the cylinder, which will be found to be the extreme top or bottom of the bore.

While the cylinders and pistons are not in position on the engine, cover the crankcase with a clean cloth to prevent the ingress of dust and dirt of all kinds. Do not, of course, attempt to scrape the carbon from the pistons when the mouths of the crankcase are open.

35. Grinding-in Valves

To grind a valve, smear the seating with a little grinding-in compound, place a light, short coil spring over the valve stem and beneath the head, insert the valve into its appropriate guide, press it on to the seat using a tool with a suction cup and with a backwards and forwards rotary motion, grind it on to its seat. Alternatively, a tool which pulls on the valve stem can be used. Frequently lift the valve and move it round so that an even and true seating is obtained. If no light spring is available, the lifting will have to be done by hand. Continue grinding until a bright ring is visible on both valve and seating.

The faces and seats of the exhaust valves are cut at 45 degrees but the profiles of the inlet valves are of a special streamlined design which eliminates pockets and sharp edges and allows a smooth flow of gas without eddies.

If the inlet valves or their seats are pitted and require re-cutting, care must be taken to reproduce the correct profile as shown in Fig. 9.

The cylinder heads should preferably be returned to the Works for the inlet valve seats to be re-cut but, if this is not possible, a special tool consisting of an arbor No. T.2053 and cutter No. T.2054 is available. Great care must be exercised in using this tool as it is located off the valve guides and these may be damaged if suitable apparatus is not employed.

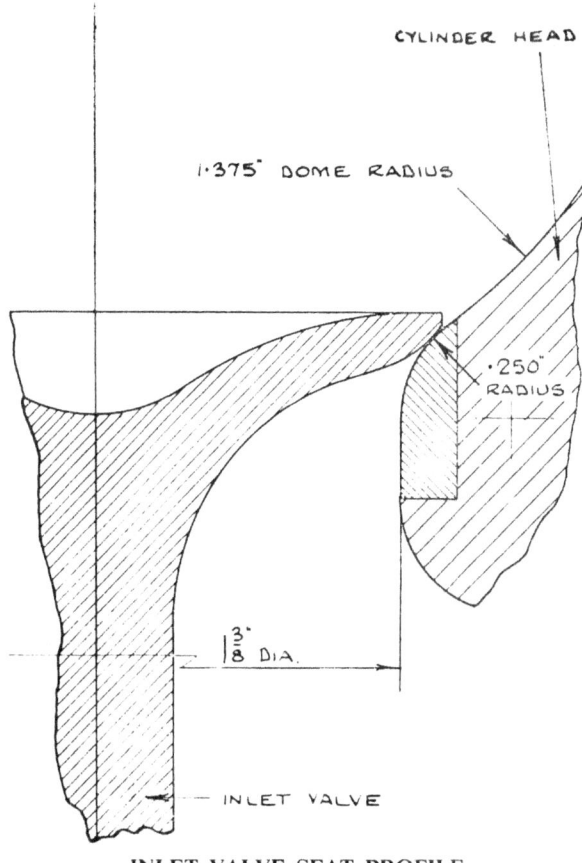

INLET VALVE SEAT PROFILE
Fig. 9

The inlet valve faces and seats can be cut at 45 degrees in cases of emergency but this may have a deleterious effect on the performance of the engine.

36. Reassembly after Decarbonising

Before building up the engine, see that all parts are scrupulously clean and place them conveniently to hand on a clean sheet of brown paper.

Check the piston ring gaps to find out whether excessive wear has taken place (see Subsection 34).

It is advisable to fit new gaskets to the cylinder base and cylinder head. Two paper gaskets are fitted to the base of each cylinder, one each side of the compression plate.

Smear clean oil over the pistons, having replaced the rings if these have been removed, lower the piston over the connecting rod and insert the gudgeon pin from the outer side. Fit the circlip and then fit the second piston in a similar manner.

Oil the cylinder bores and lower the barrels over the pistons and seat them gently on their gaskets.

Drop the push rods down their tunnels on to the tappet heads, shallow cups upwards.

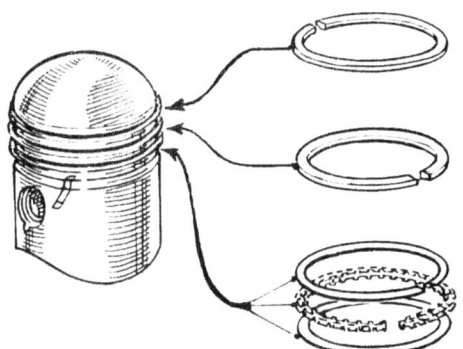

CORRECT ASSEMBLY OF APEX OIL CONTROL RINGS
Fig. 10

Replace the cylinder heads as described in Subsection 27.

After the engine has been assembled, run it for a brief period at a speed which will ensure that the ignition has been advanced by the automatic advance device. If it is run too slowly "blueing" of the exhaust pipes may take place.

After the engine has been run for some time and has become thoroughly hot, go over **all** the cylinder head and other nuts to ensure that they are tight.

37. Cleaning the oil Filters

The oil filter is located at the top of the crankcase and is in the feed circuit to the big ends. (See Fig. 11).

The filter element is removed by unscrewing the nut holding the end cap in position. A small circular magnet supported on a short distance piece is also fitted over the fixing stud inside the filter for the purpose of collecting any ferrous particles which may be suspended in the oil. When reassembling the filter after cleaning, take care that no grit or other foreign matter is sticking to it. After replacing or renewing the felt filter, fill the filter housing with oil, level with the top of the finned cap, before fitting the hexagon sleeve nut.

The felt element should be taken out and washed in petrol after the first 500 miles and after every subsequent 2,000 miles. Fit a new element every 5,000 miles.

38. Overhaul of Oil Pump

Remove the timing cover as described in Subsection 19.

Remove the pump end plate followed by the pump disc, spring and plunger.

The spindle can be pulled out from the pump housing after undoing the nut on the forward end. This nut has a LEFT HAND thread. A hole is provided in the spindle and timing cover through which a $\frac{3}{16}$ in. dia. tommy bar can be fitted to prevent the spindle turning whilst the nut is undone.

The bar must be pushed through the spindle and right to the bottom of the hole in the cover or the spindle boss may fracture.

Check the fit of the plunger in the pump disc which should have a minimum of clearance but should be able to be moved in and out by hand.

If, when fitting a new disc or plunger, the plunger is found to be too tight a fit, carefully lap with metal polish until it is just free. If the pump disc is not seating properly or if a new pump disc is being fitted, it should be lapped to the seating with Special Tool No. E.5425, using Carborundum 360 Fine Paste or liquid metal polish until an even grey surface is obtained.

Wash all passages, etc., thoroughly with petrol after lapping to remove all traces of grinding paste.

Check the pump disc spring for fatigue by assembling in the timing cover and placing the pump cover in position. If the spring is correct, the pump cover should be held ¼ in. off the timing cover by the pump spring.

The pump spindle must be a good fit in the timing cover and should be renewed if the clearance is such that oil can escape from the pump. Check the gear teeth for excessive wear.

Reassemble the oil pump, replacing the paper cover gasket if necessary. Before fitting the cover fill the pump chamber with clean oil.

Having assembled the pump lay the timing cover flat and fill the oil ports by means of an oilcan. Turn the pump spindle with a screwdriver in a clockwise direction looking on the front and it can then be seen whether the pump is operating correctly.

Refit the timing cover as described in Subsection 19 and time the ignition as described in Subsection 23.

39. Removal of the Timing Chain

Remove the timing cover (Subsection 19).

Loosen the chain tensioner locknut and stud.

Lift the adjusting plate clear of the chain tensioner spindle.

Remove the chain tensioner spindle and sprocket.

Lift the chain off the sprockets.

40. Removal of Pump Worm and Timing Sprocket

Remove the timing chain (Subsection 39).

Unscrew the oil pump worm by means of the hexagon head behind it. This is a **Left-Hand Thread.**

Withdraw the timing sprocket.

41. Removal of the Camshaft and Sprockets

Remove the camshaft together with sprocket as described in Subsection 22.

Hold the timing side cam between soft vice jaws and unscrew the sprocket nut (L.H. thread). The sprockets can now be extracted using the special extractor Part No. 49907. The special plug must be used in the end of the exhaust camshaft to protect the contact breaker driving taper.

When assembling the sprockets great care must be taken to prevent the key from tipping in the keyway on the shaft otherwise it will be wedged against the end of the bearing causing damage. The sprocket must be fitted with the timing mark facing outwards. The sprocket nut should be tightened to 50 ft. lbs. torque.

42. Removal of the Engine and Clutch Sprockets

The primary chain is endless so that it is necessary to remove both the engine and clutch sprocket simultaneously.

The alternator stator is removed by undoing the three fixing nuts, after which the stator can be pulled off the three studs on which it is located.

Remove the central hexagon nut and washer securing the alternator rotor, which can then be drawn off, taking care not to lose the key.

Unscrew the engine sprocket nut, using Special Tool No. 49908. The engine sprocket is mounted on splines and can then be removed with the clutch sprocket.

To remove the clutch sprocket, unscrew the three pressure plate pins and remove the pressure plate assembly, the centre retaining plate and the assembly of driving and driven clutch plates. The clutch sprocket can then be withdrawn from the centre after the removal of the large circlip which secures it.

43. Removal of the Tappets and Guides

It is only necessary to remove the tappets and guides if they have become worn.

Remove the cylinder heads and barrels. (Subsections 27 and 32).

Extract the tappet guides, using Special Tool No. 49925, having heated the case first.

The guides are made from Nickel Chrome Alloy Iron and if a guide should break while removing it, it can be withdrawn with a pair of pliers if the crankcase is heated locally with a blowlamp. Otherwise it is necessary to dismantle the crankcase and drive the tappet and guide out from underneath using a heavy bar in the cam tunnel.

The guide should have an interference of .0015 to .0025 in. in the crankcase and can be driven in with a bronze drift, care being taken when the guide is nearly home to avoid breaking the collar.

If a tappet guide is taken out it should be replaced by an oversize one.

44. Crankcase Breather

The crankcase breather is in the form of a long plastic tube attached by a hose clip to an adaptor on the top of the case.

There are no moving parts and nothing to go wrong. Check that the plastic tube is not pinched anywhere causing a restriction.

45. Removal of the Clutch

Remove the engine sprocket and clutch sprocket together as described in Subsection 42.

To remove the clutch hub, hold the clutch with Special Tool No. 49919 and remove the centre retaining nut and washer with a box spanner.

The hub can then be withdrawn from the shaft with Special Tool No. 49909.

46. Removal of the Final Drive Sprocket

Remove the clutch as described in Subsection 45. Remove the primary chain tensioner.

Remove the rear half of the primary chain case by taking out three socket screws and the centre stud.

Remove the splined collar from the gearbox mainshaft using special extractor No. 49926.

Remove the grub screw locking the final drive sprocket nut.

Hold the sprocket and remove the nut (**Right-Hand Thread**). The sprocket can then be withdrawn.

47. Oil Seal Behind Engine Sprocket

This consists of a neoprene oil seal, with a garter spring, backed up by one steel washer. The correct order of assembly is as follows:—

(1) Press the oil seal W43382 into the chain case from the front with the garter spring facing the inside of the case. The seal should be pressed in till its outer face is flush with the inner surface of its housing in the back half of the chain case.

(2) Into the recess thus formed at the back of the chaincase fit the washer W34069.

(3) Fit the back half of the chain case to the engine and tighten the three socket screws. Engines numbered 1B1001 to 1B2001 require C.E.1 threaded screws Part No. 38027, engines numbered 1B2002 and later require B.S.F. threaded screws Part No. 49918. Tightening the screws should result in the oil seal being pushed in to the chain case so that its face stands slightly proud of the inner surface of its housing.

(4) Fit the engine sprocket, taking great care not to damage the lip of the seal when pushing the sprocket through it.

48. Oil Pipe Unions

The oil feed to the rocker gear is through pipes from a union at the back of the crankcase below the cylinder base to unions on the cylinder heads.

The tapped holes into which the unions screw into the aluminium cylinder heads are fitted with steel wire inserts to prevent the threads in the aluminium from stripping.

The method of fitting the thread inserts is the same as that used for the sparking plug inserts described in Subsection 31.

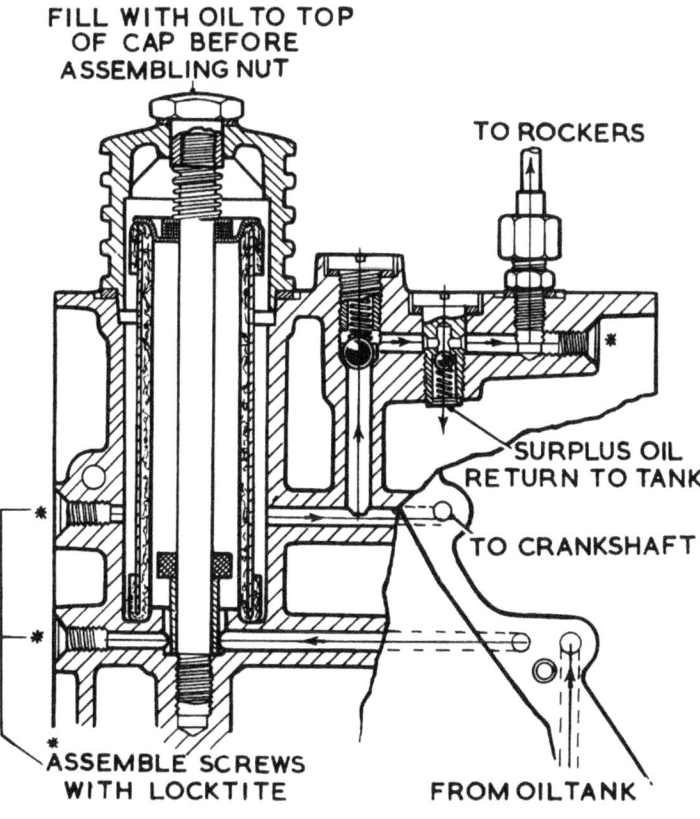

OIL RELEASE VALVES AND OIL FILTER
Fig. 11

49. Oil Feed Relief Valves

There are two pressure relief valves in the oiling system, both are located at the top of the crankcase, behind the right hand cylinder barrel. (See Fig. 11).

The right hand screw holds a $\frac{5}{16}$ dia. ball and spring in position, forming the main relief valve holding a pressure of 60 lbs./sq. in. in the oil supply line to the big-ends. It is important that the correct washer is used under the head of the screw, a thinner washer or no washer at all will give a higher pressure and a thicker washer will give a lower pressure than intended. Too high a pressure in this part of the system could cause damage to the crankshaft seal in the timing cover and leakage at this point will reduce the amount of oil passing the main release valve. This could cause oil starvation at the rockers and lead to excessive wear of cams and tappets and poor lubrication of camshaft bearings. If the pressure in the main system is too low, the amount of oil reaching the big-ends will be reduced.

The second screw forms a pressure relief valve for the oil supply to the overhead rockers. The unit is pre-set at the Works to release at 10-15 lbs./sq. in. and cannot be adjusted.

50. Fitting the Alternator

The alternator consists of two parts, the stator and the rotor.

The stator is mounted on to the primary chaincase with three studs and distance pieces.

The rotor, which contains the permanent magnets, is mounted on the end of the crankshaft and is located by a key and secured by a stud, nut and washer.

The radial air gap between the rotor and the poles of the stator should be .020 in. in all positions and care must be taken when refitting to see that it is not less than .010 in. at any point.

Fit the rotor first, making sure that it is located concentrically on the end of the crankshaft. Attention must be given to the seating of the key because a badly-fitting key may cause the rotor to run unevenly. Finally secure the rotor with the appropriate nut and washer.

Place the three distance pieces over the three chaincase studs. The stator can then be fitted, with the coil connections facing outwards.

Replace the nuts and shakeproof washers only fingertight, and insert six strips (preferably of non-magnetic material) .015 in. thick and about $\frac{1}{8}$ in. wide between the rotor and each pole piece.

Tighten the stator nuts and withdraw the strips.

Check the air gap with narrow feelers and, if less than .010 in. at any point, remove the stator and set the three studs carefully until the correct gap is obtained.

An alternative, and more satisfactory, method of assembling the alternator requires the use of Special Tool No. T2055/19.

This is a gauge .015 in. greater in radius than the rotor and fits over the adaptor on the end of the crankshaft in the rotor's place.

The stator is then put in position on the studs in the chaincase and the nuts tightened up.

Remove the gauge and fit the rotor, then check the air gap.

Service operations with Engine Removed

51. Removal of the Engine Gearbox Unit from the Frame

Remove battery cover and disconnect the battery leads.

Remove the petrol tank (Subsection 26).

Remove the cylinder head steady plates.

Remove the exhaust pipes.

Loosen the rectifier bracket and swing the rectifier clear.

Disconnect the contact breaker leads and alternator leads.

Remove the sparking plug caps.

Loosen the breather tube clip and disconnect the tube from the adaptor.

Remove fixed portion of rear chainguard and remove rear chain.

Remove air intake tubes from carburettors.

Remove screws holding mixing chamber tops to carburettors and withdraw slides.

Disconnect the clutch cable.

Disconnect the tachometer drive cable.

Remove the footrest bar.

Slacken off the nuts holding the prop stand cross bar to the frame.

Remove the bottom rear engine bolt and the bolt securing the gearbox bracket to the frame. Loosen the nuts on the chainstay pivot bolt.

Support the engine on a suitable box or wood block.

Raise the centre stand and remove the spring.

Loosen the bottom gearbox nuts and swing the lower engine plates down.

Remove the front engine plates, and stand.

Lift the engine out of the frame.

52. Removal of the Gearbox

Remove the engine sprocket and clutch (Sub-sections 42 and 45).

Remove the rear half of the primary chaincase by removing three socket screws and the centre stud.

The gearbox and gearbox bracket can now be withdrawn from the back of the crankcase after unscrewing the four nuts which secure them.

53. Dismantling the Crankcase

Drain the oil tank by removing the drain plug.

Having removed the engine from the frame as described in Subsection 51, dismantle the heads, barrels, pistons, timing gear and camshafts, as described in Subsections 19, 22, 27, 32, 33, 39, and 40.

Remove the gearbox as described in Subsection 52.

Remove the two screws holding the crankcases together at the top. Holes are provided in the timing-side case to provide access for the screwdriver (See Fig. 12).

Remove three nuts in the timing chest, two loose studs through the rear of the crankcase and four screws through the bottom of the oil tank. (The other studs have already been removed to take the engine out of the frame).

Turn the crankshaft until the connecting rods are at bottom dead centre and the two halves of the crankcase can then be separated, tapping the crankcase with a soft mallet.

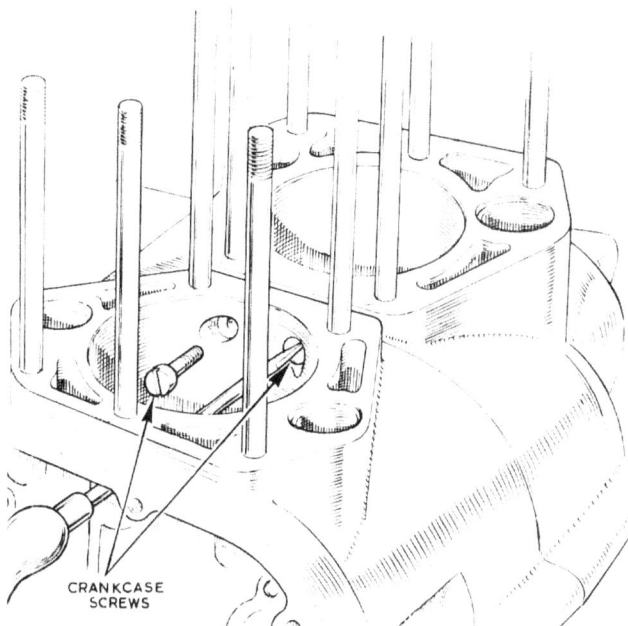

REMOVAL OF SCREWS IN CRANKCASE
Fig. 12

The inner race of the roller bearings on the timing side will remain on the crankshaft bringing with it the cage and rollers and leaving the outer race fixed to the crankcase.

The inner race of the ball bearing on the driving side is a tight fit on the shaft and can be removed with Special Tool No. W49910. If this is not available, the shaft can be driven out with a hide mallet or a soft metal drift.

To avoid damage to the ball bearing the case should be heated to about 100°C. before doing this.

54. Main Bearings

To remove the ball bearing from the driving side crankcase, heat the crankcase to about 100 degrees C. by immersion in hot water or in an oven after which the bearing can be driven out using a drift **which applies pressure to the outside race only.**

When refitting a new ball bearing, heat the crankcase in the same way and use the same drift taking great care to keep the bearing square with the bore.

To remove the outer roller race from the timing side crankcase, first heat the crankcase then drive the race out using a small punch through the three holes provided.

The inner race and rollers can be withdrawn from the crankshaft using a claw type extractor.

When refitting the inner race drive it on to the shaft until the shaft projects $\frac{1}{16}$ in. from the face of the bearing.

55. Fitting the Connecting Rods

To remove the connecting rods from the crankshaft, unscrew the socket screws in the connecting rods, having first removed the security wires through the heads.

If the big end bearing caps are removed to examine the condition of the bearings, *make sure that the caps are refitted the same way round on the same rods and that the rods themselves are refitted the same way round on the same crank pins.*

In refitting the connecting rods, the socket screws should be tightened with a torque wrench set at 275 in. lb. (23 ft. lb.)

No cotter pins or other locking devices are fitted. If the socket screws are correctly tightened they will never come loose. If they are *not* adequately tightened they are liable to fatigue failures. Use only genuine big end screws, Part No. 47876 These have a very high fatigue strength due to the use of a special steel and the fact that the threads are rolled *after* heat treatment.

Wire the heads using .024" diameter stainless steel wire.

If it is necessary to replace the big ends, a service crankshaft can be supplied with connecting rods fitted.

56. Reassembly of Crankcase

If the main bearings have been removed fit the replacement ball bearing in the driving side crankcase and the outer roller race in the timing side as described in Subsection 54. The outer race should be pressed home and then secured by making four equally spaced centre punch marks in the case so as to spread the aluminium over the radiused edge of the race.

Assembly of the two halves of the crankcase on to the crankshaft is easier if the crankcase is warmed while the crankshaft is cold. First fit the crankshaft assembly into the drive side crankcase, pulling the shaft right through the ball race and fitting the engine sprocket and nut. The nut must be tightened right home before the timing side crankcase is fitted otherwise the roller bearing inner race may be inadvertently moved along the shaft through the crankshaft entering too far into the timing side case. This can also happen, or a roller can be dislodged, if the rollers tilt out of the inner race and make assembly difficult. Wrapping a piece of string round the rollers will keep them in place and ensure their easy entry into the outer race. The string must be long enough to be easily pulled free after assembly.

Before assembly make sure that all parts are scrupulously clean, put clean oil on bearings, remove all traces of old jointing compound and any protruding pieces of metal from the joint face by means of a scraper and put fresh jointing compound on the face between the two halves of the crankcase. Do not forget the distance piece W34062 between the driving side ball bearing and the crank web.

Bolt the two halves of the crankcase together before the jointing compound has set. Do not forget the two screws between the cylinder barrels (see Fig. 12).

57. Crankshaft Plugs

The oil passage through the big ends is sealed by two screwed aluminium plugs locked by a centre punch.

If the crankcase is taken out of the engine for any reason, the plugs should be removed and the oil passage cleared of sludge.

Gearbox and Clutch

58. Description of the Clutch

The clutch is built into the clutch sprocket and is mounted on the gearbox mainshaft which projects through into the primary chaincase.

There are six driven plates which are plain and five driving plates, giving ten friction surfaces.

The driven plates comprise the clutch centre back plate, two dished and two flat steel plates on splines on the clutch centre drum, and the clutch front plate (see Fig. 14).

The driving plates include the clutch sprocket itself, which has a ring of friction material bonded to it and is located on the clutch centre drum by a ring of low friction material. There are four loose friction plates, having bonded-on segments of "J.17" synthetic cork based material, splined to the clutch outer drum, which is riveted to the clutch sprocket.

Pressure is applied to the clutch plates by six springs fitted between the outside of the clutch front plate and the inside of a star-shaped pressure plate.

The clutch operating mechanism consists of a lever mounted on the inside of the outer cover of the gearbox and operated by the control cable and handlebar lever. When the control is operated the clutch front plate is caused to move to the left,

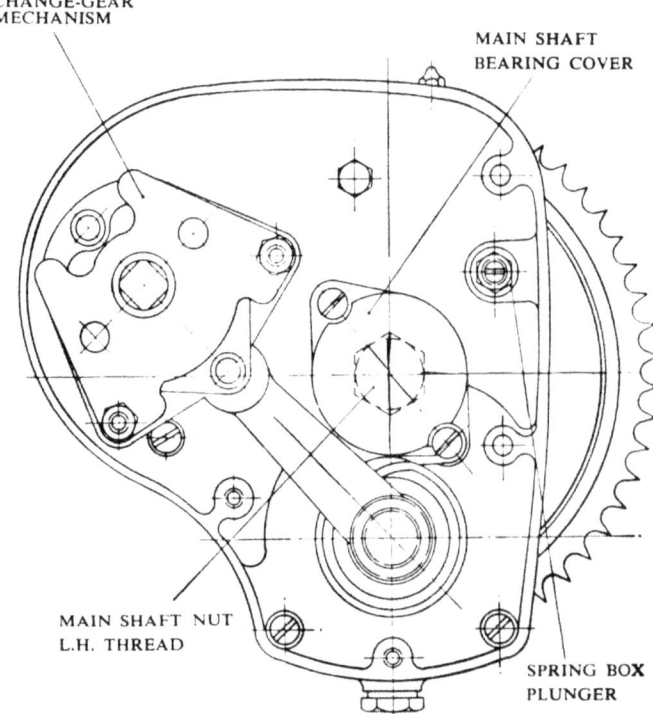

GEARBOX WITH OUTER COVER REMOVED
Fig. 13

against the pressure of the springs, by means of a pad pushed by a rod passing through the gearbox mainshaft and operated by the lever in the outer cover through an adjusting screw and ball.

The clutch centre drum drives the mainshaft through a cush drive with six rubber blocks.

59. Description of the Gearbox

The operation of the gearbox is shown diagrammatically in Fig. 15.

The clutch sprocket A is mounted on the end of the mainshaft B which passes through the mainshaft sleeve C on the end of which is the final drive sprocket D.

At the other end of the mainshaft B is a pinion E which engages with a pinion F on the layshaft G. At the other end of the layshaft G is a pinion H engaging with a pinion J which runs free on the mainshaft sleeve C.

The mainshaft sleeve C has splines on which slides a double pinion KL. This double pinion KL engages with two pinions M and N which are free to rotate or slide on the layshaft G.

The double pinion KL has dogs at each end which can engage with dogs on the pinion E or on the pinion J.

The pinions M and N have internal dogs which can engage or slide over projecting dogs P and Q on the layshaft G.

The double pinion KL and the pinions M and N all slide together and are moved by the operator fork R and are located by a spring plunger S which engages with a notched plate which is part of the operator arm R.

The kickstart lever is connected to the pinion F on the layshaft by a ratchet mechanism which automatically disengages when the lever is released.

60. Removal of the Gearbox

This is described in Subsection 52.

The gearbox can, however, be completely dismantled with the engine in the frame except for the removal of the inside operator and the bearings in the gearbox shell.

61. To Dismantle the Gearbox

First remove the kickstart crank, the change-gear lever and the neutral finder and pointer.

Remove four screws and the gearbox outer cover can then be detached.

Remove the change-gear mechanism, by taking off the two nuts securing it.

Remove the mainshaft bearing cover which is attached by two screws.

Remove four cheese-headed screws and one hexagon bolt.

Remove the spring box locating plunger nut and washer.

Remove the mainshaft nut **(left-hand thread)**.

The gearbox inner cover can then be removed.

The mainshaft can be drawn straight out if the clutch has been removed, which, however, should be done before taking off the gearbox inner cover. (See Subsection 45). The top gear pinion and dog will come away with the mainshaft.

The layshaft can then be removed and the 2nd and 3rd gears drawn off the final drive sleeve together with the operator fork.

To take out the final drive sleeve, the final drive sprocket must be removed and this is preferably done before removing the inner cover. (See Subsection 46).

62. Removal of the Ball Races

The mainshaft ball bearings can be removed by using a stepped drift $1\frac{7}{16} - 1\frac{11}{64}$ in. diameter for the bearing in the box and $\frac{13}{16} - \frac{39}{64}$ in. diameter for the bearing in the cover.

When refitting the bearings stepped drifts of $2\frac{5}{16} - 1\frac{11}{64}$ in. diameter and $1\frac{11}{16} - \frac{39}{64}$ in. diameter must be used for the bearings in the box and cover respectively.

Note the oil seal in the recess behind the larger mainshaft bearing.

63. Change-Gear Mechanism

If the two nuts securing the change-gear ratchet mechanism are slackened the adjuster plate

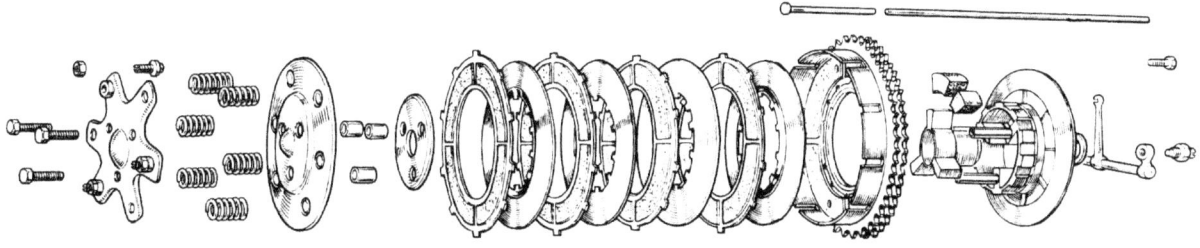

EXPLODED VIEW OF CLUTCH
Fig. 14

Page 22 *Royal Enfield "Interceptor" 750 Series II Workshop Manual*

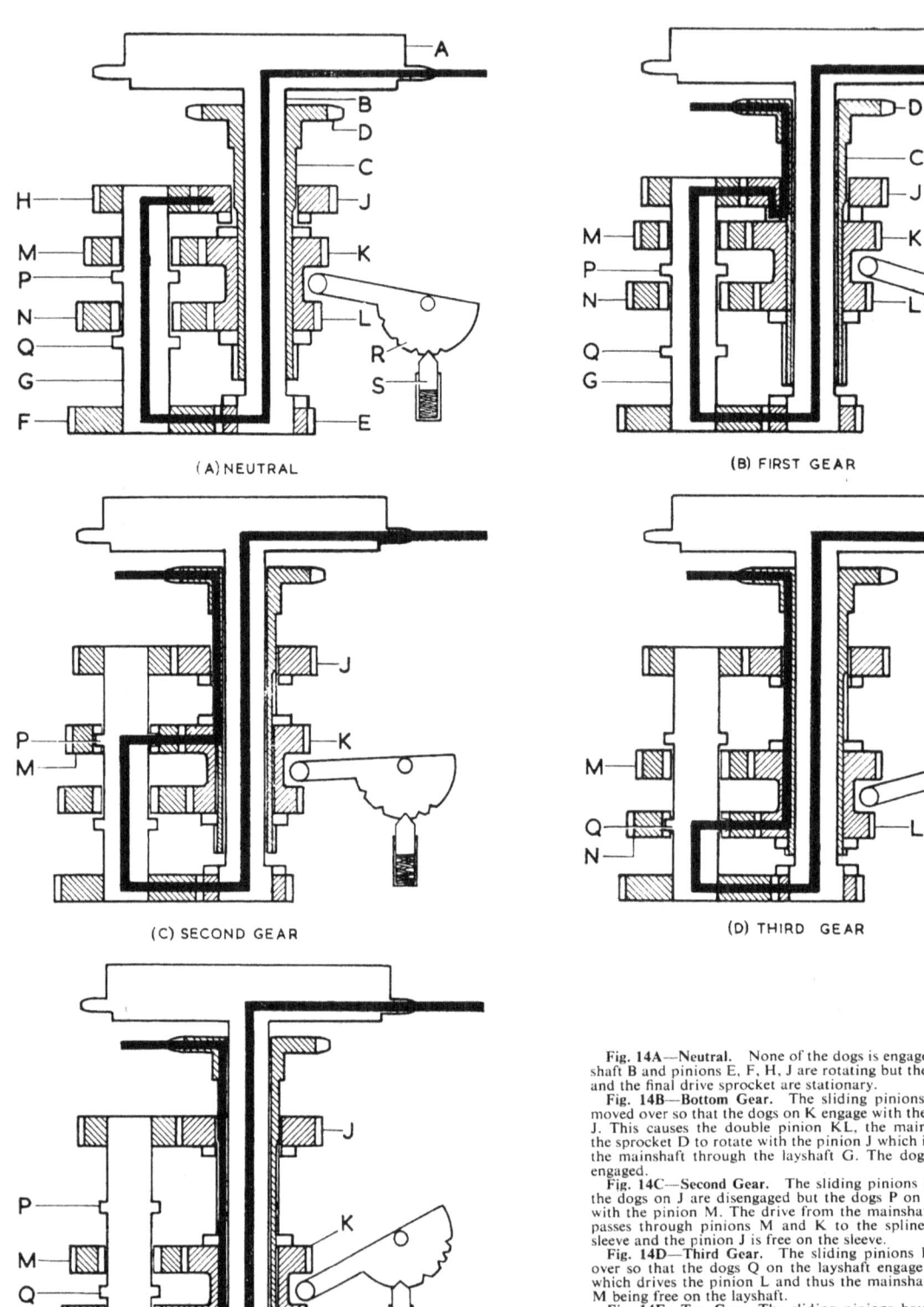

Fig. 14A—**Neutral.** None of the dogs is engaged so that the mainshaft B and pinions E, F, H, J are rotating but the mainshaft sleeve C and the final drive sprocket are stationary.

Fig. 14B—**Bottom Gear.** The sliding pinions K, L, M, N have moved over so that the dogs on K engage with the dogs on the pinion J. This causes the double pinion KL, the mainshaft sleeve C and the sprocket D to rotate with the pinion J which is being driven from the mainshaft through the layshaft G. The dogs P and Q are not engaged.

Fig. 14C—**Second Gear.** The sliding pinions have moved so that the dogs on J are disengaged but the dogs P on the layshaft engage with the pinion M. The drive from the mainshaft and layshaft then passes through pinions M and K to the splines on the mainshaft sleeve and the pinion J is free on the sleeve.

Fig. 14D—**Third Gear.** The sliding pinions have moved further over so that the dogs Q on the layshaft engage with the pinion N which drives the pinion L and thus the mainshaft sleeve, the pinion M being free on the layshaft.

Fig. 14E—**Top Gear.** The sliding pinions have now moved right over so that both sets of dogs P and Q on the layshaft have disengaged but the dogs on the double pinion KL have engaged with those on the pinion E and the mainshaft and sleeve rotate together giving a one to one drive through the gearbox from the clutch sprocket to the output sprocket, the pinions M, N, J being free to rotate.

OPERATION OF GEARS
Fig. 15

82

can be set in the correct position. In this position the movement of the gear lever necessary to engage the ratchet teeth will be approximately the same in each direction.

If the plate is incorrectly adjusted, it may be found that, after moving from top to third or from bottom to second gear, the outer ratchets do not engage the teeth on the inner ratchets correctly.

If, when fitting new parts, it is found that the gears do not engage properly, ascertain whether a little more movement is required or whether there is too much movement so that the gear slips right through second or third gear into neutral. If more movement is required, this can be obtained by filing the adjuster plate very slightly at the points of contact with the pegs on the ratchet ring.

If too much movement is already present, a new adjuster plate giving less movement must be fitted.

64. Reassembling the Gearbox

The procedure is the reverse of that given in Subsection 61, but the following points should be noted:—

If the mainshaft top gear pinion and dog have been removed, make sure that the dog is replaced the right way round or third and top gears can be engaged simultaneously.

Make sure that the trunnions on the operator fork engage with the slots in the inside operator.

See that the mainshaft is pushed right home. It may tighten in the felt washer inside the final drive shaft nut.

The layshaft top gear and kickstarter pinion should be assembled on the layshaft and the kickstarter shaft and ratchet assembled on to it before fitting the end cover. Do not forget the washer on the layshaft between the kickstarter pinion and the kickstarter shaft.

The joint between the gearbox and the inner cover should be made with gold size, shellac or a similar jointing compound.

Make sure that all parts are clean before commencing assembly. In normal climates the recesses in the gearbox should be packed with soft grease and the box should be filled up to the correct level with engine oil. (See Subsection 68). **On no account must heavy yellow grease be used.**

65. Dismantling and Reassembling the Clutch

The method of removing the clutch is described in Subsection 42.

When reassembling the clutch, the following sequence must be adhered to, after first securing the clutch sprocket with the large circlip.

Fit the cush rubbers, retaining plate and three distance tubes, and follow with the pressure plate assembly as follows:—

Plain dished plate (dish projecting outwards).
Friction plate (with bonded facings).
Plain flat plate.
Friction plate (with bonded facings).
Plain flat plate.
Friction plate (with bonded facings).
Plain dished plate (dish projecting inwards).
Friction plate (with bonded facings).
Front plate.
Pressure plate and springs.

When reassembling the pressure and front plates, see that the three distance pieces are fitted over the pins securing the pressure plate to the clutch centre drum. These must pass through the holes in the front plate into the three recesses in the clutch centre retaining plate. Note that three strong (13g) and three weak (14g) springs are used. These *must* be fitted alternately and, the 14g springs *must* be fitted behind the adjusting screws. The three pressure plate pins must be locked up tight.

If the clutch lifts unevenly adjust one or, if necessary, two of the adjusting screws in the pressure plate. These screws can also be used to increase the spring pressure when wear has taken place on the friction surfaces but care must be taken not to screw them in too far. This could reduce the lift of the clutch by causing some of the springs to become coil bound, thus causing clutch drag.

66. Adjustment of Clutch Control

It is essential that there is about $\frac{1}{32}$ in. free movement in the clutch cable, to ensure that all the spring pressure is exerted on the plates.

There are three points of adjustment for the clutch control. The first is in the clutch operating lever in the gearbox and is accessible after removing the lower inspection cover in the front cover of the gearbox (see Fig. 17). The clutch cable should be slacked right off or, preferably, disconnected when making this adjustment. Slacken the locknut and adjust the centre screw in or out until it is as nearly as possible in line with the clutch push rod. Tighten the locknut and check that no part of the lever is hard against the inside of the gear box front cover or either of the inspection covers.

The second and third adjustments are in the outer casing of the clutch control cable. There is an adjustable sleeve with a locknut forming the abutment for the outer casing at the gearbox end and also a finger-operated sleeve and locknut at the handlebar end.

To adjust the control cable, having first set the adjuster in the gearbox clutch operating lever correctly, couple up the control cable, screw the adjusting sleeve at the handlebar end of the casing in as far as possible then unscrew it two turns.

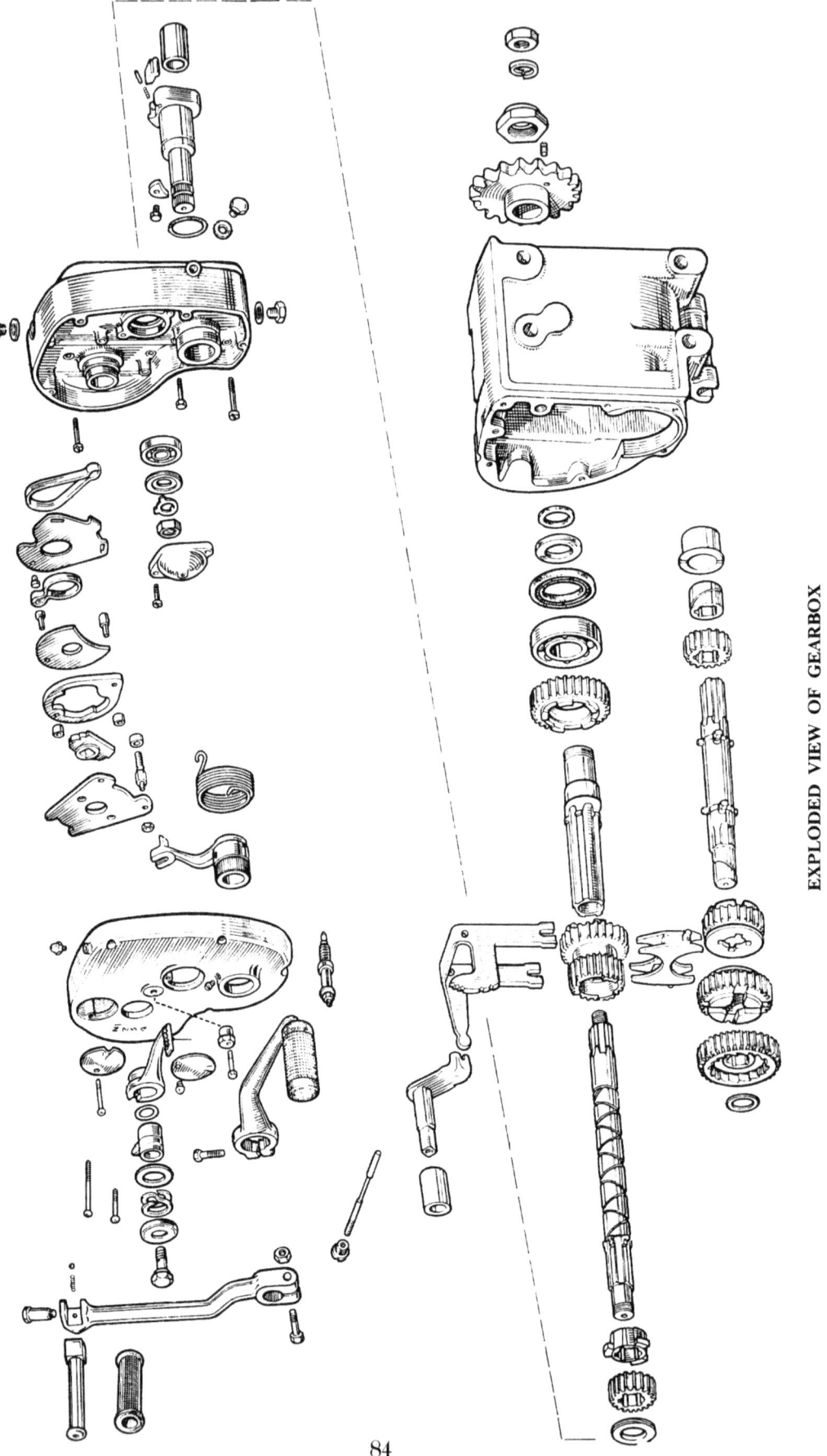

EXPLODED VIEW OF GEARBOX
Fig. 16

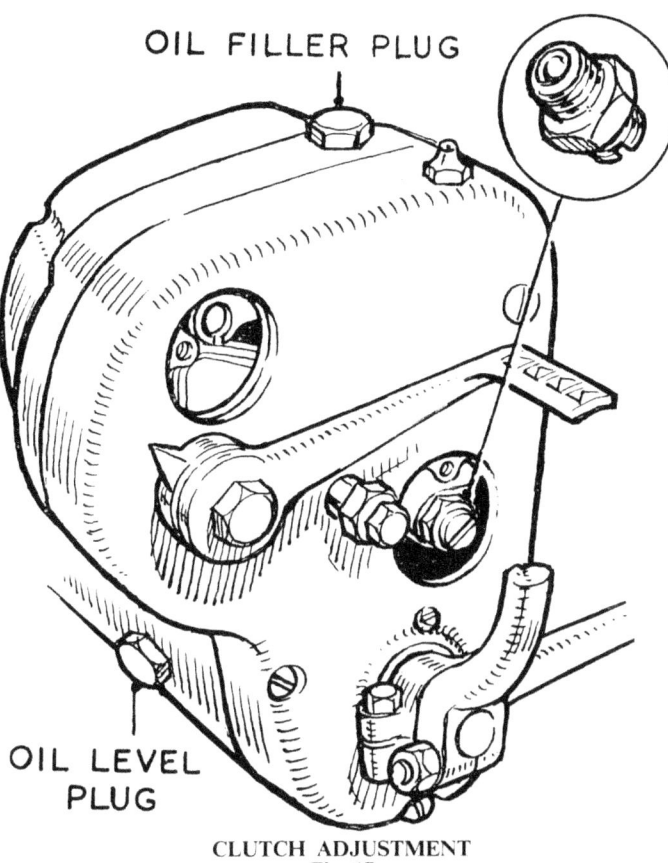

CLUTCH ADJUSTMENT
Fig. 17

Now adjust the sleeve at the gearbox end of the casing until there is $\frac{1}{32}$ in. to $\frac{1}{16}$ in. slack in the control. If the control is adjusted in this manner the finger adjustment at the handlebar end can be used to take up any slack which may appear temporarily as the result of the friction material swelling due to heat if the clutch has to be slipped a great deal in traffic. This adjustment can also be used to give more clearance temporarily if this is necessary as a result of wear of the friction linings. This, however, should be corrected finally by adjusting the centre screw in the gearbox clutch operating lever.

67. Adjustment of the Neutral Finder

The neutral finder is adjusted by means of an eccentric stop secured to the front of the gearbox cover by a bolt which limits the travel of the operating pedal. Slacken the bolt and turn the eccentric until the correct movement of the pedal is obtained.

68. Gearbox Oil Level

The gearbox is filled with oil by removing a plug in the top and the correct level can be checked by removing a second plug lower down on the left-hand side looking at the cover. (See Fig. 17).

Recommended Lubricants

	B.P.	CASTROL	DUCKHAMS	ESSO	MOBIL	REGENT or Caltex/Texaco	SHELL
Engine Below 20°F	Energol SAE 20W	Castrolite	Q.20/50	Extra 20W/30	Arctic or Mobiloil Super (10W/50)	Havoline 20/20W	X-100 20/20W
Engine 20°F-50°F (British Winter)	Energol SAE 30	Castrolite or XL	Q.20/50	Extra 20W/30	A or Mobiloil Super (10W/50)	Havoline 30	X-100 30
Engine 50°F-90°F (British Summer) Gearbox top up Rear Chain	Energol SAE 40	XXL	Q.20/50	Extra 40/50	AF or BB or Mobiloil Super (10W/50)	Havoline 40	X-100 40
Engine Above 90°F	Energol SAE 50	Grand Prix	Q.20/50	Extra 40/50	BB or D or Mobiloil Super (10W/50)	Havoline 50	X-100 50
Front Fork	Energol SAE 20W	Castrolite	Q.20/50	Extra 20W/30	Arctic	Havoline 20/20W	X-100 20/20W
Grease Gun Wheel hubs (Re pack)	Energrease L2	Castrolease LM	LB.10	Esso Multipurpose grease H	Mobilgrease MP	Marfak Multipurpose 2	Retinax A

MULTIGRADE OILS—Several of the above suppliers offer "Multigrade" oils. Those rated at S.A.E. 10W/30 are approved for use at ambient temperatures up to 50°F. Oils rated at S.A.E. 20W/40, 20/50 and 10W/50 are approved for use at all ambient temperatures.

Amal Concentric Carburettor
750 Series I & II

69. General Description

Two of the well-known AMAL Concentric carburettors are fitted direct on to the inlet ports. A sectioned view of the carburettor is shown in Figs. 18 & 19 and an "exploded" view in Fig. 22. Each carburettor is self contained with its own float chamber fed from a tap in the fuel tank. The float chambers are connected together by a short flexible tube joining the two banjos and both fuel taps must always be turned on to ensure an ample supply of fuel at high revs. Each float chamber contains a plastic float operating on a kemetal fuel needle with a powerful lever action which ensures a positive cut-off unless there is dirt on the seating.

The supply of air to the engine is controlled by a throttle slide which carries a taper needle operating in the needle jet. The needle is secured to the throttle slide by a spring clip fitting in one of three grooves and the mixture strength throughout a large proportion of the throttle range is controlled by the position of this needle in the slide and by the size of the jet in which it works. There is, however, a restricting or main jet at the bottom of the needle jet and the size of this controls the mixture strength at the largest throttle openings. At very small throttle openings petrol and air are fed to the engine through a separate pilot system, which has an outlet at the engine side of the throttle. The air supply to this pilot system is controlled by the pilot air screw and the slow running of the engine can be adjusted by means of this screw and a stop which holds the throttle open a very small amount. The throttle slide is cut away at the back and the shape of this cut-away controls the mixture at throttle openings slightly wider than that required for slow running. There is a compensating system to prevent undue enriching of the mixture with increasing engine speed, this system consisting of a primary choke surrounding the upper end of the needle jet through which air is drawn in increasing quantities as the depression in the main choke increases. This air supply and the supply to the pilot system are taken from two separate ducts in the main air intake to the carburettor so that all the air passing to the engine can be filtered by fitting an air cleaner to the main carburettor air intake.

Two small cross holes in the needle jet, at a level just below the static level in the float chamber, permit petrol to flow into the primary choke when the engine is not running or when it is running at very low speeds, thus forming a well of petrol which will be drawn into the engine on starting or accelerating from low speeds. At moderately high engine speeds the level of petrol in the float chamber falls slightly and in consequence no more fuel flows through the cross holes in the needle jet so that the petrol well remains empty until the engine slows down or stops.

A handlebar controlled air slide is provided to enrich the mixture temporarily when required.

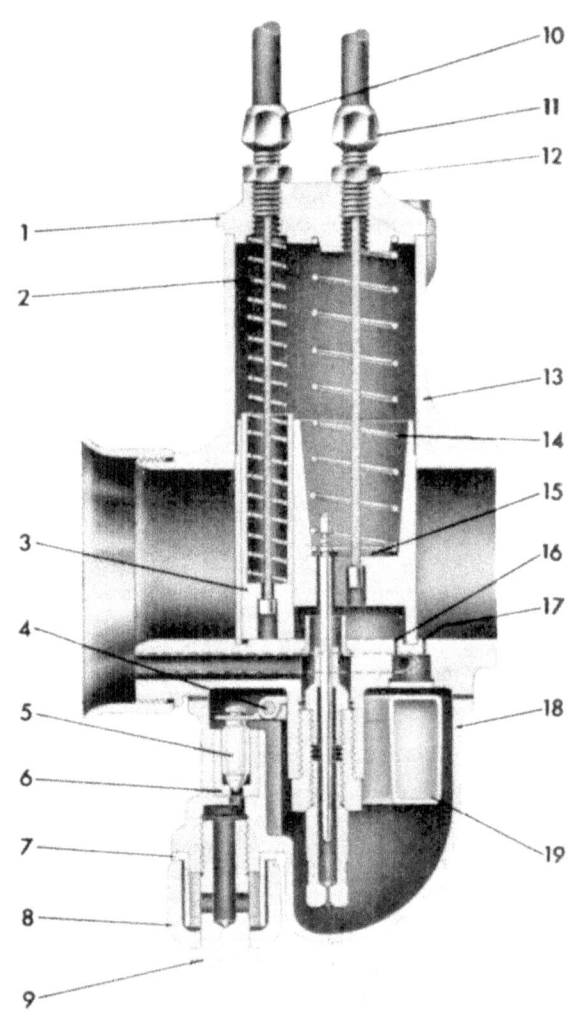

SECTION THROUGH MIXING CHAMBER, SHOWING AIR VALVE AND THROTTLE CLOSED
Fig. 18

1. Mixing Chamber Top.
2. Air Valve Spring.
3. Air Valve.
4. Float Spindle.
5. Float Needle.
6. Needle Seating.
7. Filter Gauze.
8. Banjo.
9. Banjo Bolt.
10. Cable Adjuster (Air).
11. Cable Adjuster (Throttle).
12. Cable Adjuster Locknuts.
13. Carburettor Body.
14. Throttle Valve Spring.
15. Jet Needle Clip.
16. Pilot By-pass.
17. Pilot Outlet.
18. Float Chamber Body.
19. Float.
20. Mixing Chamber Top Screws.
21. Throttle Valve.
22. Jet Needle.
23. Choke Tube.
24. Needle Jet.
25. Tickler.
26. Throttle Adjusting Screw.
27. Float Chamber Washer.
28. Jet Holder.
29. Main Jet.
30. Pilot Jet.
31. Pilot Jet Feed Passages.
32. Feed Passage from Pilot Jet.
33. Pilot Air Feed Passage.
34. Pilot Air Adjusting Screw.

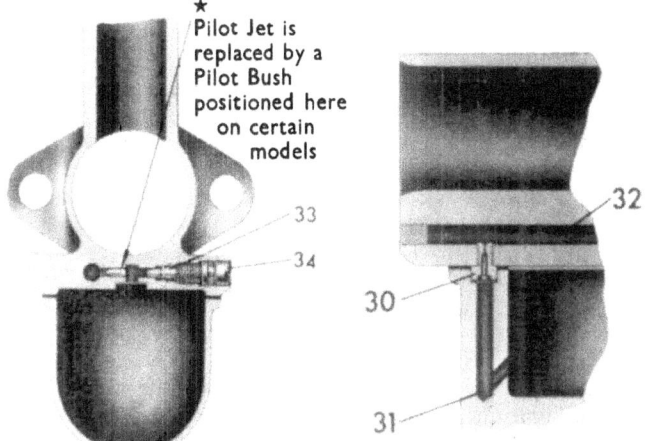

Pilot Jet is replaced by a Pilot Bush positioned here on certain models

SECTION SHOWING PILOT JET AND PILOT JET FEED PASSAGES

Fig. 20

70. Tuning the Carburettors

The throttle opening at which each tuning point is most effective is shown in Fig. 21. It should be remembered, however, that a change of setting at any point will have some effect on the setting required at other points; for instance, a change of main jet will have some effect on the mixture strength at half throttle which, however, is mainly controlled by the needle position. Similarly an alteration to the throttle cut-away may affect both the needle position required and the adjustment of the pilot air screw. For this reason it is necessary to tune the carburettor in a definite sequence, which is as follows:

First—Main Jet. The size should be chosen which gives maximum speed at full throttle with the air control wide open. If two different sizes of jet give the same speed the larger should be chosen for safety as it is dangerous to run with too weak a mixture at full throttle.

Second—The pilot air screw should be set to give good idling. On Series I and early Series II machines the pilot jet is detachable.

Third—The throttle valve should be selected with the largest amount of cut-away which will prevent spitting or misfiring when opening the throttle slowly from the idling position.

Fourth—The lowest position of the taper needle should be found consistent with good acceleration with the air slide wide open.

Fifth—The pilot air screw should be checked to improve the idling if possible. When setting the adjustment of the pilot air screw this should be done in conjunction with the throttle stop. Note that the correct setting of the air screw is the one which gives the fastest idling speed for a given position of the throttle stop. If the idling speed is then undesirably fast it can be slowed down by unscrewing the throttle stop a fraction of a turn.

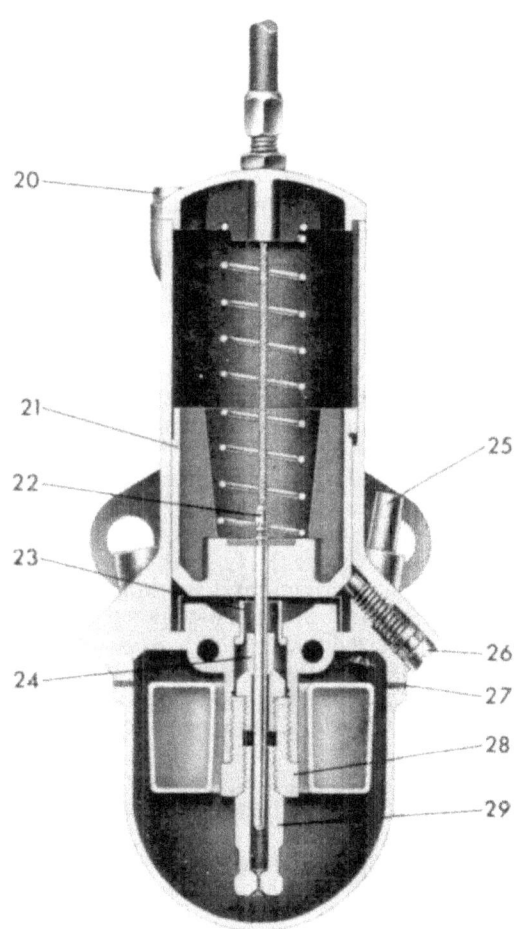

SECTION THROUGH FLOAT CHAMBER

Fig. 19

It will be noted that of the four points at which adjustments are normally made, i.e., pilot air screw, throttle cut-away, needle position and main jet size, the first and third do not require changing of any parts of the carburettor. Assuming that the carburettor has the standard setting to suit the particular type of engine any small adjustments occasioned by atmospheric conditions, changes in quality of fuel, etc., can usually be covered by adjustment of the pilot air screw and raising or lowering the taper needle one notch. If, however, the machine is used at very high altitudes or with a very restricted air cleaner a smaller main jet will be necessary. The following table gives the reduction in main jet size required at different altitudes:

Altitude, ft.	Reduction, %
3,000	5
6,000	9
9,000	13
12,000	17

When using alcohol fuels the following new components are necessary. A metallic double feed banjo, banjo bolt washer 13/163, needle jet 622/100, jet needle 928/099, filter gauze 376/093B and banjo washer 14/175 are required for each carburettor. The main jets must be increased for straight alcohol by approximately 150%. The final setting must be a question of trial and error according to the nature of fuel used. When using alcohol fuels it is advisable to err on the rich side to avoid engine overheating.

If the engine is run on fuel containing a small proportion of alcohol added to the petrol, a rough and ready guide is that the main jet should be increased by 1% for every 1% of alcohol in the fuel. In most cases alcohol blends available from petrol pumps do not contain sufficient alcohol to require any alteration to the carburettor setting.

The range of adjustment of the taper needle and the pilot air screw are determined by the size of the needle jet and of the pilot outlet respectively. Standard needle jets have a bore at the smallest point of .1065 in. and are marked 106. Alternative needle jets. 1055 in., .1075 in., .109 in. and .113 in. bore are available and are marked 105, 107, 109 and 113 respectively.

The standard pilot outlet bore is .025 in. but in some cases larger size pilot outlets are used. Since the pilot outlet is actually drilled in the body of the carburettor it is necessary to have a carburettor with the correct size pilot outlet if the best results are to be obtained.

The accompanying table shows the standard settings for Amal Concentric Carburettors used on Royal Enfield "Interceptor" Series I & II motor cycles.

These may be taken as correct for all normal conditions and for practical purposes carburettor

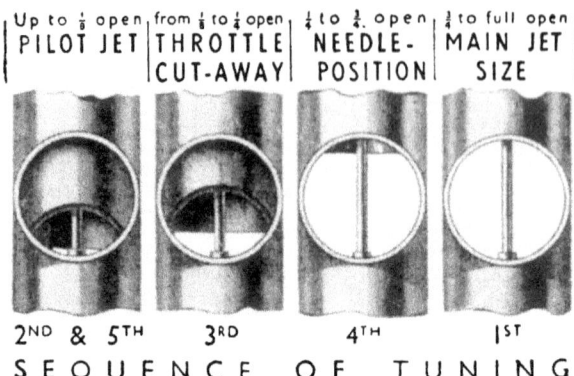

PHASES OF AMAL CONCENTRIC CARBURETTOR
THROTTLE OPENINGS
SEQUENCE OF TUNING
Fig. 21

tuning consists only of setting the pilot air screw and throttle stop.

71. Tuning Sequence with Two Carburettors

When setting the slow running on machines fitted with two carburettors the following procedure is recommended:—

(1) See that both throttle slides are open the same amount for any given position of the twist grip. This is most easily checked by looking into the air intakes while slowly opening and closing the throttles with the air slides wide open. Make sure that the highest point of the cut-away on the throttle valve reaches the top of the bore simultaneously in both carburettors. If necessary adjust one or both mid-cable adjusters in the throttle cables.

(2) Repeat this procedure for the air slides.

(3) Start the engine and let it run at a fast idle till thoroughly warm. Open the air slides fully and remove the H.T. lead and waterproof plug cap from the right-hand sparking plug, opening the throttle if necessary to keep the engine running on one cylinder.

(4) Adjust the throttle stop on the left-hand carburettor to hold the throttle just wide enough open to keep the engine running with the twist grip shut.

(5) Adjust the pilot air screw on the left-hand carburettor to give the maximum speed for this throttle position.

(6) Slow down the engine as far as possible by adjusting the throttle stop and reset the pilot air screw if necessary to give the maximum speed for the new throttle position. Repeat till the engine is running as fast as possible on the smallest possible throttle opening.

(7) Replace the right-hand plug cap and lead and remove the left-hand ones.

(8) Repeat (4), (5) and (6) on the right-hand carburettor.

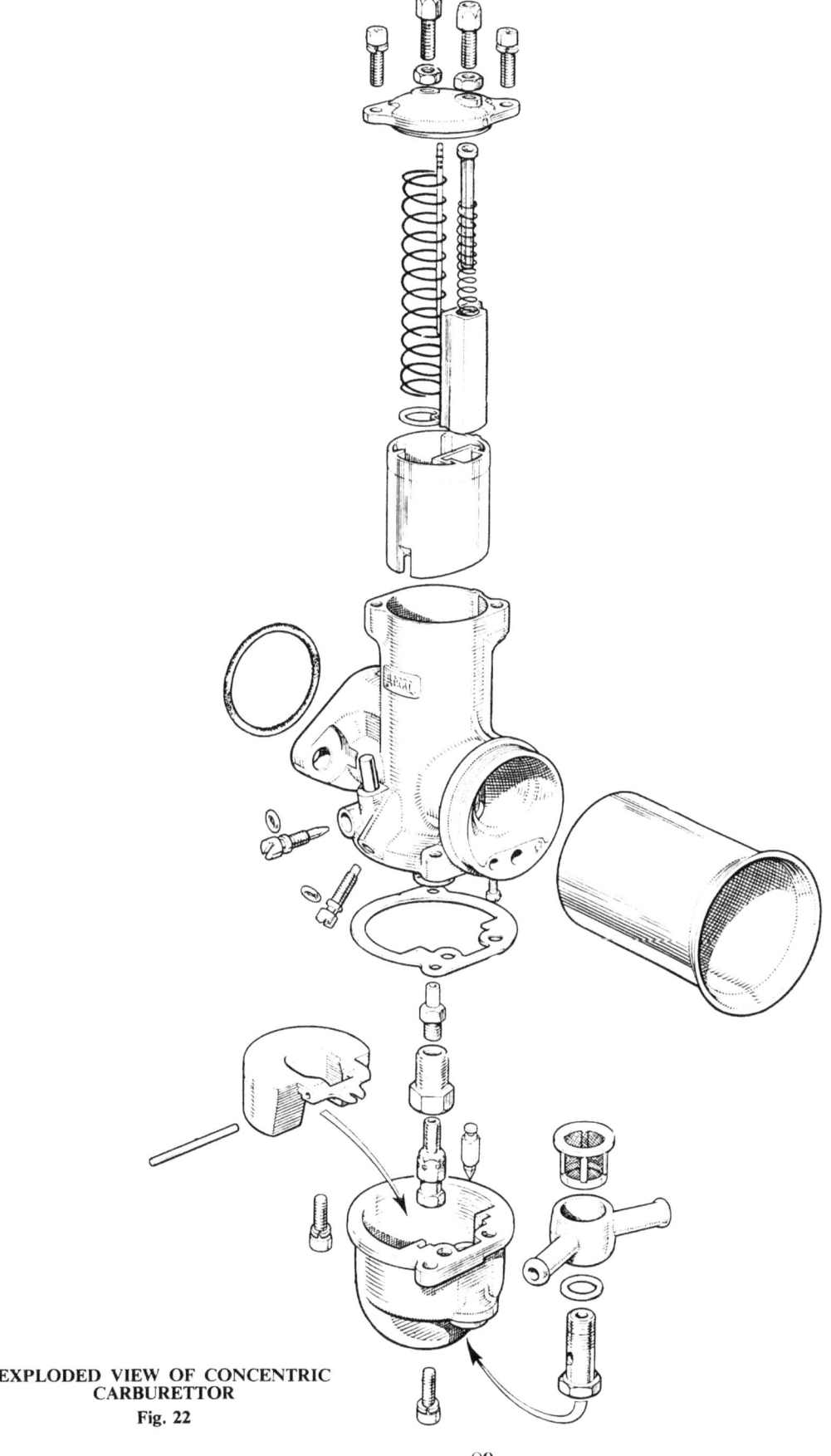

EXPLODED VIEW OF CONCENTRIC CARBURETTOR
Fig. 22

(9) Replace the left-hand plug cap and lead. The engine should now be running steadily at a fast idle.

(10) Slow the engine down by unscrewing each throttle stop equally. If running becomes lumpy adjust each pilot air screw an equal amount. If necessary, slow engine down further by unscrewing each throttle stop equally but do not try to get *too* slow an idle with a hot engine otherwise it will be liable to stop when only partly warmed up.

72. Dismantling Carburettor

The construction of the carburettor is clearly shown in Fig. 22.

If the float chamber floods, first make sure that there is no dirt on the fuel needle seating. Owing to the use of a Kemetal needle and the leverage ratio between float and needle, flooding is very unlikely with this type of carburettor unless dirt is present or, of course, the float is punctured.

73. Causes of High Petrol Consumption

If the petrol consumption is excessive first look for leaks either from the carburettor, petrol pipes, petrol taps or tank. If coloured petrol is in use this will readily indicate the presence of any small leaks which otherwise might pass unnoticed. If the petrol system is free from leaks, carefully set the pilot adjusting screw as described in Subsections 70 and 71 to give the correct mixture when idling. Running with the pilot adjusting screw too far in is a common cause of excessive petrol consumption. If the consumption is still heavy try the effect of lowering the taper needle in the throttle slide by one notch. Do not fit a smaller main jet as this will not affect consumption except when driving on nearly full throttle and may make the mixture too weak at large throttle openings, thus causing overheating. Remember that faults in other parts of the machine can have a marked effect on petrol consumption. Examples of this are binding brakes, chains too tight or out of line and, in particular, under-inflated tyres.

Settings for AMAL Concentric Carburettors on Royal Enfield "Interceptor" 750 Series I and II Motor Cycles

Carburettor Type No.	Choke Bore m.m.	Main Jet c.c.	Needle Jet in.	Needle Position	Throttle Valve	Pilot Jet	Remarks
L/H L930/4 R/H R930/3	30	220	.107	2	3	25 c.c.	Series I & early Series II engines.
L/H L930/33 R/H R930/32	30	220	.107	2	$3\frac{1}{2}$	622/107	Pilot jets are not removable.

Notes: Needle positions:—No. 1=clip in top groove. No. 3=clip in bottom groove.
L930/4 and R930/3 carburettors fitted to Series II engines have different throttle needles, needle jets and jet holders from the carburettors fitted on Series I engines, and these three items are only interchangeable as sets.

Electrical System

74. Introduction

The electrical system is supplied from an alternating current generator contained in the primary chaincase and driven from the crankshaft. The generator output is then converted into direct current by a silicon diode rectifier. The direct current is supplied to a 12 volt 8 ampere/hour battery with a Zener diode in circuit to regulate the battery current.

The current is then supplied to the ignition system which is controlled by a double contact breaker driven direct from the exhaust camshaft.

The contact breaker feeds two ignition coils, one for each cylinder.

Current from the alternator is also stored in a high capacity electrolytic capacitor which ensures that the engine can be started and run with a discharged battery or without a battery in the circuit.

The routine maintenance needed by the various components is set out in the following sections. All electrical components and connections including the earthing points to the frame of the machine must be clean and tight.

BATTERY INSPECTION AND MAINTENANCE

75. General

The battery containers are moulded in translucent polystyrene through which the acid level can be seen. The battery top is so designed that when the cover is in position, the special anti-spill filler plugs are sealed in a common venting chamber. Gas from the filler plugs leaves this chamber through a vent pipe union at the side of the top. The vent at the other side of the top is sealed off. Polythene tubing is attached to the vent pipe union to lead corrosive fumes away from parts of the machine which may otherwise suffer damage.

To prepare a dry-charged battery for service, first discard the vent hole sealing tape and then pour into each cell pure dilute sulphuric acid of appropriate specific gravity to THE COLOURED LINE. (See table). Give the battery an initial charge of 1 ampere for 2—3 hours and allow the battery to stand for at least one hour for the electrolyte to settle down, thereafter maintain the acid level at the coloured line by adding distilled water.

76. Routine Maintenance

Every week examine the level of the electrolyte in each cell. Lift off the battery cover so that the coloured filling line can be seen. Add distilled water until the electrolyte level reaches this line.

Note—On no account should batteries be topped up to the separator guard but only to the coloured line.

With this type of battery, the acid can only be reached by a miniature hydrometer, which would indicate the state of charge.

Great care should be taken when carrying out these operations not to spill any acid or allow a naked flame near the electrolyte. The mixture of

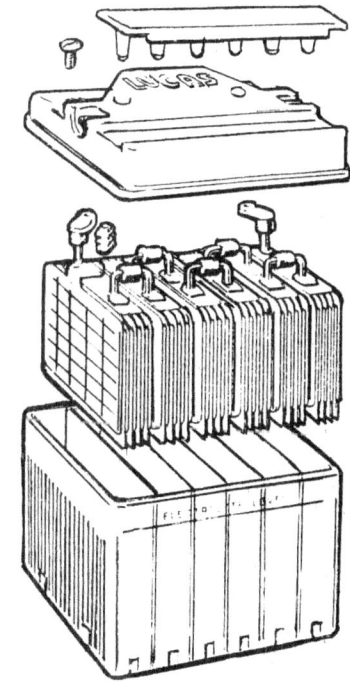

EXPLODED VIEW OF BATTERY PUZ5A
Fig. 23

oxygen and hydrogen given off by a battery on charge, and to a lesser extent when standing idle, can be dangerously explosive.

The readings obtained from the battery electrolyte should be compared with those given in table. If a battery is suspected to be faulty it is advisable to have it checked by a Lucas Service Centre or Agent.

77. Technical Data

Specific gravity of electrolyte for filling the battery.

U.K. and Climates normally below 90°F (32.2°C)		Tropical Climates over 90°F (32.2°C)	
Filling	Fully charged	Filling	Fully charged
1.260	1.280/1.300	1.210	1.220/1.240

Every 1,000 miles (1,500 k.m.) or monthly, or more regularly in hot climates the battery should be cleaned as follows. Remove the battery manifold (cell cover) and clean the battery top. Examine the terminals: if they are corroded scrape them clean and smear them with a film of petroleum jelly, such as vaseline. Check that the vent holes are clear.

Maximum permissible electrolyte temperature during charge

Climates normally Below 80°F (27°C)	Climates between 80-100°F (27-38°C)	Climates frequently above 100°F (38°C)
100°F (38°C)	110°F (43°C)	120°F (49°C)

Notes

The specific gravity of the electrolyte varies with the temperature. For convenience in comparing specific gravities, they are always corrected to 60°F., which is adopted as a reference temperature. The method of correction is as follows:

For every 5°F. below 60°F. deduct .020 from the observed reading to obtain the true specific gravity at 60°F. For every 5°F. above 60°F., add .020 to the observed reading to obtain the true specific gravity at 60°F.

The temperature must be indicated by a thermometer having its bulb actually immersed in the electrolyte and not the ambient temperature. To take a temperature reading tilt the battery sideways and then insert into the electrolyte.

It is extremely important that the battery is correctly connected into the circuit to avoid damage to the electrical equipment. All machines use a positive (+ve) earth system. Refer to Fig. 24 which shows the correct method of connecting the battery.

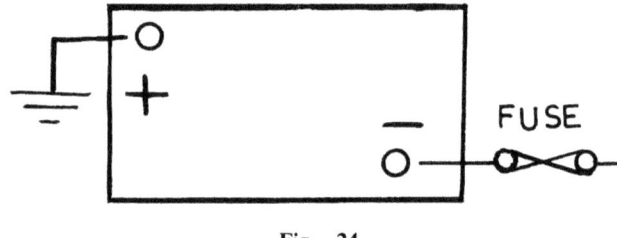

Fig. 24

COIL IGNITION SYSTEM

78. Description

The coil ignition system comprises two ignition coils and a contact breaker fitted in the timing cover and driven by the exhaust camshaft. The ignition coils are mounted to the rear of the vertical partition behind the battery. To gain access to the coils it is first necessary to remove the rear mudguard carrier assembly (Subsection 114) the coil cover can now be removed after undoing the two fixing bolts. It may first be necessary to slacken off the two bolts clamping the top of the partition to the frame. The cover must first be moved to the left to clear the frame before lifting off. Apart from cleaning the coils, in between the terminals and checking the low tension and high tension connections, the coils will not require any other attention. Testing the ignition coils is amply covered in Subsection 81 below whilst testing the contact breaker is described in Subsection 83. The 6CA type of contact breaker is used, with the two capacitors mounted on a separate bracket in the same compartment. Access to the capacitors is gained by removing the contact breaker cover and detaching them from the supporting bracket.

The best method of approach to a faulty ignition system, is that of first checking the low tension circuit for continuity as shown in Subsection 79, and then following the procedure laid out in Subsection 80 to locate the fault(s).

Failure to locate a fault in the low tension circuit indicates that the high tension circuit or sparking plugs are faulty, and the procedure detailed in Subsection 84 must be followed. Before commencing any of the following tests, however, the contact breaker and sparking plugs must be cleaned and adjusted to eliminate this possible source of fault.

79. Checking the Low Tension Circuit for Continuity

To check whether there is a fault in the low tension circuit and to locate its position, the following tests should be carried out:

Remove the white lead which connects the "SW" terminals of the left and right ignition coils. Then, with the wiring harness white lead connected to the SW terminal of the left ignition coil only, turn the ignition switch to the "IGN" position. Slowly crank the engine and at the same time observe the ammeter needle, which should fluctuate between zero and a slight discharge, as the contacts open and close respectively.

Disconnect the wiring harness white lead from the left ignition coil and connect it to the SW terminal of the right ignition coil and then repeat the test. If the ammeter needle does not fluctuate in the described way then a fault in the low tension circuit is indicated.

First, examine the contact breaker contacts for pitting, piling or presence of oxidation, oil or dirt etc. Clean and ensure that the gap is set correctly to .014 in.–.016 in. (.35–.40 m.m.) as described in Subsection 23.

80. Fault Finding in the Low Tension Circuit

To trace a fault in the low tension wiring, turn the ignition switch to "IGN" position and then crank the engine until both sets of contacts are opened, or alternatively, place a piece of insulating material between both sets of contacts whilst the following test is carried out.

Disconnect the Zener Diode. To do this remove the white lead from the Diode centre terminal.

For this test, it is assumed that the wiring is fully connected as shown in the appropriate wiring diagram. With the aid of a D.C. voltmeter and 2 test-prods (Voltmeter 0–15 volts) make a point to check along the low tension circuit starting at the battery and working right through to the ignition coils, stage by stage, in the following manner, referring to the wiring diagram.

(1) First, establish that the battery is earthed correctly by connecting the volt meter across the battery negative terminal and the machine frame earth. No voltage reading indicates that the red earthing lead is faulty (or the fuse has blown, in —ve lead). Also, a low reading would indicate a poor battery earth connection.

(2) Connect the voltmeter between the left ignition coil SW terminal and earth and then the right ignition coil SW terminal and earth. No voltage reading indicates a breakdown between the battery and the coil SW terminal, or that the switch connections or ammeter connections are faulty.

(3) Connect the voltmeter between both of the ammeter terminals in turn and earth. No reading on the "feed" side indicates that either the ammeter is faulty or there is a bad connection along the brown and blue lead from the battery, and a reading on the "battery" side only indicates a faulty ammeter.

(4) Connect the voltmeter between ignition switch input terminal and earth. No reading indicates that the brown and white lead has faulty connections. Check for voltage at the brown/white lead connections at rectifier and ammeter.

(5) Connect the voltmeter across ignition switch output terminal and earth. No reading indicates that the ignition switch is faulty and should be replaced. Battery voltage reading at this point but not at the ignition coil SW terminals indicates that the white lead has become "open circuit" or become disconnected.

(6) Disconnect the black/white, and black/yellow leads from the C.B. terminals of each ignition coil. Connect the voltmeter across the CB terminal of the left coil and earth and then the CB terminal of the right coil and earth. No reading on the voltmeter in either case indicates that the coil primary winding is faulty and a replacement ignition coil should be fitted.

(7) With both sets of contacts open reconnect the ignition coil leads and then connect the voltmeter across both sets of contacts in turn. No reading in either case indicates that there is a faulty connection or the internal insulation has broken down in one of the capacitors.

If a capacitor is suspected then a substitution should be made and a re-test carried out.

(8) Finally, reconnect the Zener Diode white lead and then connect the volt meter between the Zener Diode centre terminal and earth (with ignition "ON"). The volt meter should read battery volts. If it does not the Zener Diode is faulty and a substitution should be made. Refer to Subsection 101 for the correct procedure for testing a Zener Diode on the machine. Ignition coil check procedure is given in Subsection 81.

81. Ignition Coils

The ignition coils consist of primary and secondary windings wound concentrically about a laminated soft iron core, the secondary winding being next to the core. The primary winding usually consists of some 300 turns of enamel covered wire and the secondary some 17,000–26,000 turns of much finer wire—also enamel covered. Each layer is paper insulated from the next in both primary and secondary windings.

To test the ignition coil on the machine, first ensure that the low tension circuit is in order as described in Subsection 79 then disconnect the high tension leads from the left and right sparking plugs. Turn the ignition switch to the "IGN" position and crank the engine until the contacts (those with the black/yellow lead from the ignition coil) for the right cylinder are closed. Flick the contact breaker lever open a number of times whilst the high tension lead from the right ignition coil is held about $\frac{3}{16}$ in. away from the cylinder head. If the ignition coil is in good condition a strong spark should be obtained. If no spark occurs this indicates the ignition coil to be faulty.

Repeat this test for the left high tension lead and coil by cranking the engine until the contacts with the black/white lead from the left ignition coil are closed.

Before a fault can be attributed to an ignition coil it must be ascertained that the high tension cables are not cracked or showing signs of deterioration, as this may often be the cause of mis-firing etc. It should also be checked that the ignition points are actually making good electrical contact when closed and that the moving contact is insulated from earth (ground) when open. It is advisable to remove the ignition coils and test them by the method described below.

82. Bench Testing an Ignition Coil

Connect the ignition coil into the circuit shown in Fig. 25 and set the adjustable gap to 9 mm. for the MA12 Type and 8 mm. for the 17M12 Type.

With the contact breaker running at 600 r.p.m. for a single lobe cam and the coil in good condition, not more than 5% missing should occur at the spark gap over a period of 15 seconds. The primary winding can be checked for short-circuit coils by connecting an ohmeter across the low tension terminals. The reading obtained should be within the figures quoted below (at 20°C.)

Coil	Primary Resistance	
	Min.	Max.
MA12	3.0 ohms.	3.4 ohms.
17M12	3.3 ohms.	3.8 ohms.

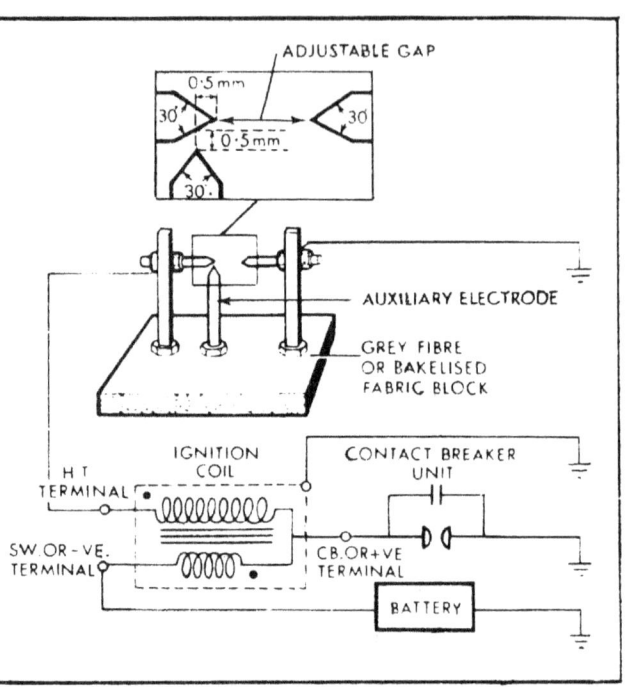

IGNITION COIL TEST RIG
Fig. 25

83. Contact Breaker

Faults occurring at the contact breaker are in the main due to, incorrect adjustment of the contacts or the efficiency being impaired by piling, pitting or oxidation of the contacts due to oil etc. Therefore, always ensure that the points are clean and that the gap is adjusted to the correct working clearance.

To test for a faulty capacitor, first turn the ignition switch to "IGN" position and then take voltage readings across each set of contacts with the contacts open. No reading indicates that the capacitor internal insulation has broken down. Should the fault be due to a capacitor having a reduction in capacity, indicated by excessive arcing when in use, and overheating of the contact faces, a check should be made by substitution.

Particular attention is called to the periodic lubrication procedure for the contact breaker. When lubricating the parts ensure that no oil or grease gets onto the contacts.

Note—Under no circumstances should the shaft and action plate and the cam shaft be lubricated.

If it is felt that the contacts require surface grinding then the complete contact breaker unit should be removed and the moving contacts disconnected by unscrewing the securing nuts from the capacitor terminals. Grinding is best achieved by using a fine carborundum stone or very fine emery cloth, afterwards wiping away any trace of dirt or metal dust with a clean petrol (gasoline) moistened cloth. The contact faces should be slightly domed to ensure point contact. There is no need to remove the pitting from the fixed contact. When re-fitting the moving contacts do not forget to refit the insulating shields to the capacitor terminals. Apply two drops of clean engine oil to the rear end of the C.B. cam. felt pads. Also apply a smear of grease to the moving contact pivot post.

Key
A—Cable Eyelet
B—Fixed Contact Securing Screw
C—Fixed Contact Eccentric Adjustment Screw
D—Angular Adjustment Plate Fixing Screw
E—Angular Adjustment Plate Eccentric Screw

84. Checking the High Tension Circuit

If ignition failure or mis-firing occurs, and the fault is not in the low tension circuit, then check the ignition coils as described in Subsection 81. If the coils prove satisfactory, ensure that the high tension cables are not the cause of the fault.

If a good spark is available at the high tension cable, then the sparking plug suppressor cap or the sparking plug itself may be the cause of the fault. Clean the sparking plug and adjust the electrodes to the required setting, and then re-test the engine for running performance. If the fault recurs then it is likely the suppressor caps are faulty and these should be renewed.

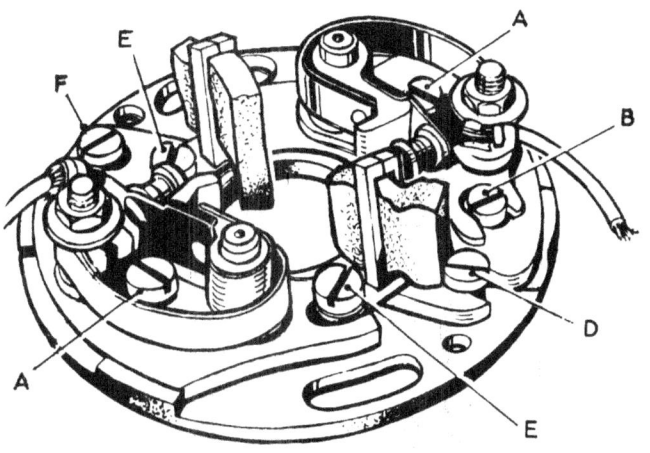

CONTACT BREAKER—TYPE 6CA
Fig. 26

CAPACITOR IGNITION (MODEL 2MC)

85. General

The Lucas motor cycle capacitor system has been developed to enable machines to be run with or without a battery. The rider therefore has the choice of running with normal battery operation or running without battery if desired (e.g. competing in trials or other competitive events) and for emergency operation in case of battery failure.

Machines can readily be started without the battery and run as normal with full use of standard lighting. When stationary, however, parking lights will not work unless the battery is connected. The capacitor system also has the advantage of being much less critical with regard to alternator timing.

The system utilises the standard 12 volt battery-coil ignition equipment with the Zener diode charging regulator mounted on an efficient heat sink, plus a spring mounted high capacity electrolytic capacitor (Model 2MC), of a special shock-resistant type.

The energy pulses from the alternator are stored by the capacitor to ensure that sufficient current flows through the ignition coil at the moment of contact opening, thus producing an adequate spark for starting. When running, the capacitor also helps to reduce the D.C. voltage ripple.

Also with this system alternator timing is much less critical. Provided the centres of the rotor and stator poles are roughly in line in the fully retarded position satisfactory starting will be obtained. Furthermore any auto-advance angle and speed characteristics may be used and perfect running ignition performance achieved.

86. Identification of Capacitor Terminals

The 2MC capacitor is an electrolytic (polarised) type and care must be taken to see that the correct wiring connections are made when fitting. Spare Lucar connectors are supplied to assist in connecting up. Looking at the terminal end of the unit it will be seen that there are two sizes of Lucar connector. The small $\frac{3}{16}$ in. Lucar is the *positive* (earth) terminal the rivet of which is marked with a spot of red paint. The double $\frac{1}{4}$ in. Lucar forms the *negative* terminal.

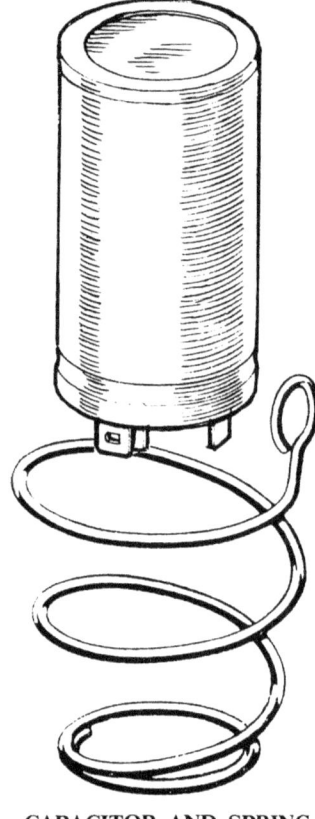

CAPACITOR AND SPRING
Fig. 27

The illustration shows the spring and capacitor. The capacitor should be positioned with its terminals pointing downwards. When fitting the spring to the capacitor, insert the capacitor at the widest end of the spring and push it down until the small coil locates in the groove on the capacitor body.

87. Storage Life of Model 2MC Capacitor

The life of the 2MC is very much affected by storage in high temperatures. The higher the temperature the shorter its shelf life. At normal temperature i.e. 20°C. (68°F.) it will have a shelf life of about 18 months. At 40°C. (86°F.) about 9 to 12 months. Therefore, storing in a cool place will maintain their efficiency.

88. Testing

The efficiency of a stored capacitor can be determined fairly accurately with the aid of a voltmeter (scale 0–12 volts) connected to the terminals of a charged capacitor and the instantaneous reading on the meter noted. The procedure is as follows:—

(1) Connect the capacitor to a 12 volt supply and leave connected for 5 *minutes*. Observe carefully the polarity of connections, otherwise the capacitor may be ruined.

(2) When charging time has been completed, disconnect the supply leads and allow the charged capacitor to stand for at least 5 *minutes*.

(3) Then connect the voltmeter leads to the capacitor and note the instantaneous reading. This should not be less than 8.0 volts for a serviceable unit.

If a voltmeter is not available a rough check can be made by following the procedures in (1) and (2) and using a single strand of copper wire instead of the voltmeter to short-circuit the capacitor terminals. A good spark will be obtained from a serviceable capacitor at the instant the terminals are shorted together.

89. Wiring and Installation

The capacitor is fitted into the spring and is mounted with its terminals downwards. The capacitor negative terminal *and* Zener diode is connected to the rectifier centre (D.C.) terminal (brown/white), and the positive terminal must be connected to the centre bolt earthing terminal (see capacitor ignition terminal on diagram).

90. Service Notes

Before running a 2MC equipped machine with the battery disconnected it is essential that the *battery negative lead be insulated* to prevent it from re-connecting and shorting to earth (frame of machine). Otherwise, the capacitor will be ruined. This can be done by removing the fuse from its holder and replacing it with a length of $\frac{1}{4}$ in. dia. dowel rod or other insulating medium.

A faulty capacitor may not be apparent when used with a battery system. To prevent any inconvenience arising, periodically check that the capacitor is serviceable by disconnecting the battery to see if the machine will continue to run in the normal manner, with full lighting also available.

CHARGING SYSTEM

91. Description

The charging current is supplied by the two lead alternator, but due to the characteristics of alternating current the battery cannot be charged direct from the alternator. To convert the alternating current to direct current a full wave bridge rectifier is connected into the circuit. The alternator gives full output, all the alternator coils being permanently connected across the rectifier.

Excessive charge is absorbed by the Zener Diode which is connected across the battery. Always ensure that the ignition switch is in the "OFF" position whilst the machine is not in use, to prevent overheating of the ignition coils, and discharging the battery.

To locate a fault in the charging circuit, first test the alternator as described in Subsection 93. If the alternator is satisfactory, the fault must lie in the charging circuit, hence the rectifier must be checked as given in Subsection 94 and then the wiring and connections as shown in Subsection 97.

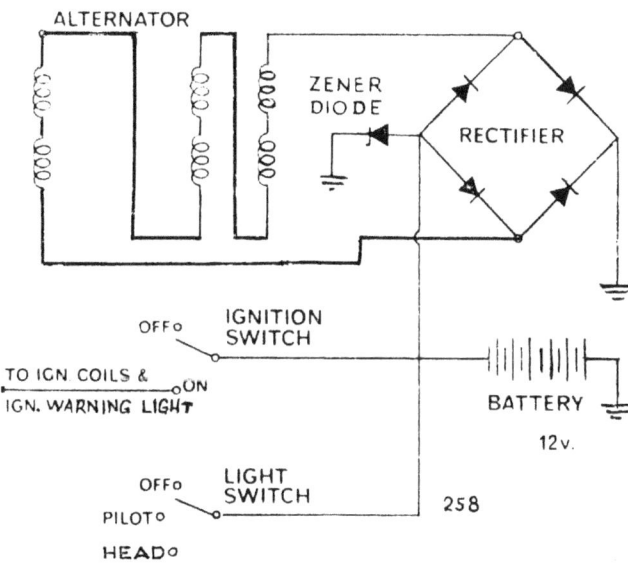

SCHEMATIC DIAGRAM OF 12 VOLT CHARGING CIRCUIT WITH SINGLE CHARGE RATE, ZENER DIODES
Fig. 28

92. Checking the D.C. Input to Battery

For this test the battery must be in good condition and a good state of charge, therefore before conducting the test ensure that the battery is up to the required standard, or alternatively fit a good replacement battery.

Disconnect the Zener Diode battery connection.

Connect D.C. ammeter (0–15 amp.) in series between the battery main lead (brown/blue) and battery negative terminal and then start the engine and run it at approximately 3,000 r.p.m.

Note—Ensure that the ammeter is well insulated from the surrounding earth points otherwise a short circuit may occur.

With the Zener Diode disconnected the minimum reading on the ammeter should be 8 amperes.

Caution—Do not run machine for more than 15 seconds under these conditions.

Reduce engine speed and reconnect the Zener Diode. Increase engine speed to 3,000 r.p.m. and note reduction of input to the battery. No reduction of input to the battery will indicate faulty Zener Diode or associated wiring—see Zener Diode test, Subsection 101. If the reading is lower than quoted, then the alternator must be tested as described in Subsection 93 below.

93. Checking the Alternator Output

Disconnect the two alternator output cables coming from the engine and run the engine at 3,000 r.p.m.

Connect an A.C. voltmeter (0–15 volts) with 1 ohm load resistor in parallel with the two alternator leads. The minimum reading on the voltmeter should be 9 volts.

A suitable 1 ohm load resistor can be made from a piece of nichrome wire as shown in Subsection 98.

From the results obtained, the following deductions can be made:—

(1) If the reading is equal to or higher than quoted then the alternator is satisfactory.

(2) A low reading indicates that some turns of the coils are short circuited, or that the rotor has become partially demagnetised. If the latter case applies, check that this has not been caused by a faulty rectifier or that the battery is of incorrect polarity, and only then fit a new rotor.

(3) A zero reading indicates that a coil has become disconnected, is open circuit, or is earthed.

(4) A reading obtained between any one lead and earth indicates that coil windings or connections have become earthed.

94. Rectifier Maintenance and Testing

The silicon bridge rectifier requires no maintenance beyond checking that the connections are clean and tight, and that the nut securing the rectifier to the frame is tight. It should always be kept clean and dry to ensure good cooling, and spilt oil washed off immediately with hot water.

Note—The nuts clamping the rectifier plates together must not be disturbed or slackened in any way.

When tightening the rectifier securing nut, hold the spanners as shown in Fig. 29, for if the plates are twisted, the internal connections will be broken. Note that the circles marked on the fixing bolt and nut indicate that the thread form is ¼ in. U.N.F.

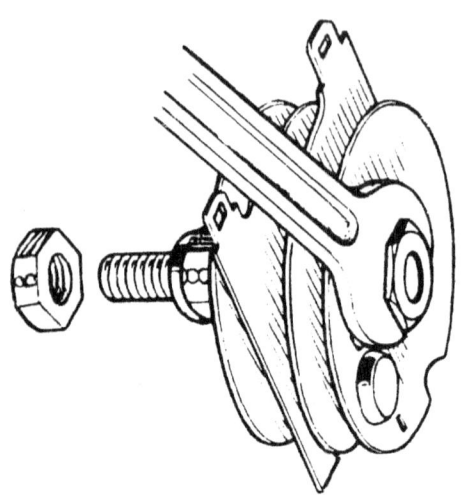

REFITTING THE RECTIFIER
Fig. 29

95. Testing the Rectifier

For test purposes disregard the end earth (ground) terminal.

To test the rectifier, first disconnect the brown/white lead from the rectifier centre terminal and insulate the end of the lead to prevent any possibility of a short circuit occurring, and then connect a D.C. voltmeter (with 1 ohm load resistor in parallel) between the rectifier centre terminal and earth.

Note—Voltmeter positive terminal to frame earth (ground) and negative terminal to centre terminal on rectifier.

With the engine running at approximately 3,000 r.p.m. observe the voltmeter reading. The reading obtained should be at least 7.5V minimum.

(1) If the reading is equal to or slightly greater than that quoted, then the rectifier elements in the forward direction are satisfactory.

(2) If the reading is excessively higher than the figures given, then check the rectifier earthing bolt connection. If the connection is good then a replacement rectifier should be fitted.

(3) If the reading is lower than the figure quoted or zero readings are obtained, then the rectifier or the charging circuit wiring is faulty and the rectifier should be disconnected and bench tested so that the fault can be located.

Note that all of the above conclusions assume that the alternator A.C. output figures were satisfactory. Any fault at the alternator will, of course, reflect on the rectifier test results. Similarly any fault in the charging circuit wiring may indicate that the rectifier is faulty. The best method of locating a fault is to disconnect the rectifier and bench-test it as shown below:

96. Bench Testing the Rectifier

For this test the rectifier should be disconnected and removed. Before removing the rectifier, disconnect the leads from the battery terminals to avoid the possibility of a short circuit occurring.

Connect the rectifier to a 12 volt battery and 1 ohm load resistor, and then connect the D.C. voltmeter in the V2 position, as shown in Fig. 30. Note the battery voltage (should be 12V) and then connect the voltmeter in V1 position whilst the following tests are conducted.

A voltmeter in position V1 will measure the volt drop across the rectifier plate. In position V2 it will measure the supply voltage to check that it is the recommended 12 volts on load.

Test 1. With the test leads, make the following connectings but keep the testing time as short as possible to avoid overheating the rectifier cell: (a) 1 and 2, (b) 1 and 4, (c) 3 and 4, (d) 3 and 2. Each reading should not be greater than 2.5 volts with the battery polarity as shown.

Test 2. Reverse the leads or battery polarity and repeat Test 1. The readings obtained should not be more than 1.5 volts below battery voltage (V2) (i.e. 10.5 volts minimum).

If the readings obtained are not within the figures given, then the rectifier internal connections are shorting or aged and the rectifier should be renewed.

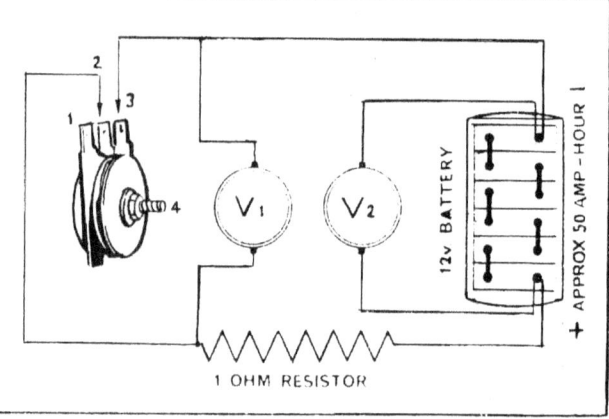

BENCH TESTING THE RECTIFIER
Fig. 30

97. Checking the Charging Circuit for Continuity

First check that there is voltage at the battery and that it is correctly connected into the circuit +ve earth (ground). Ensure that the fuse has not blown in the negative line.

(1) First, check that there is voltage at the rectifier centre terminal by connecting a D.C. voltmeter, with 1 ohm load resistor in parallel, between the rectifier centre terminal (not the end terminal on latest rectifiers) and earth (remember (+ve) positive earth (ground)). The voltmeter should read battery volts. If it does not, disconnect the alternator leads (green/white and green/yellow) at the snap connectors.

(a) Fit a jumper lead across the brown/white and green/yellow connections at the rectifier, and check the voltage at the snap connector. This test will indicate whether the harness alternator lead is open circuit.

TEST 1 CHECKING FORWARD RESISTANCE
TEST 2 CHECKING BACK LEAKAGE

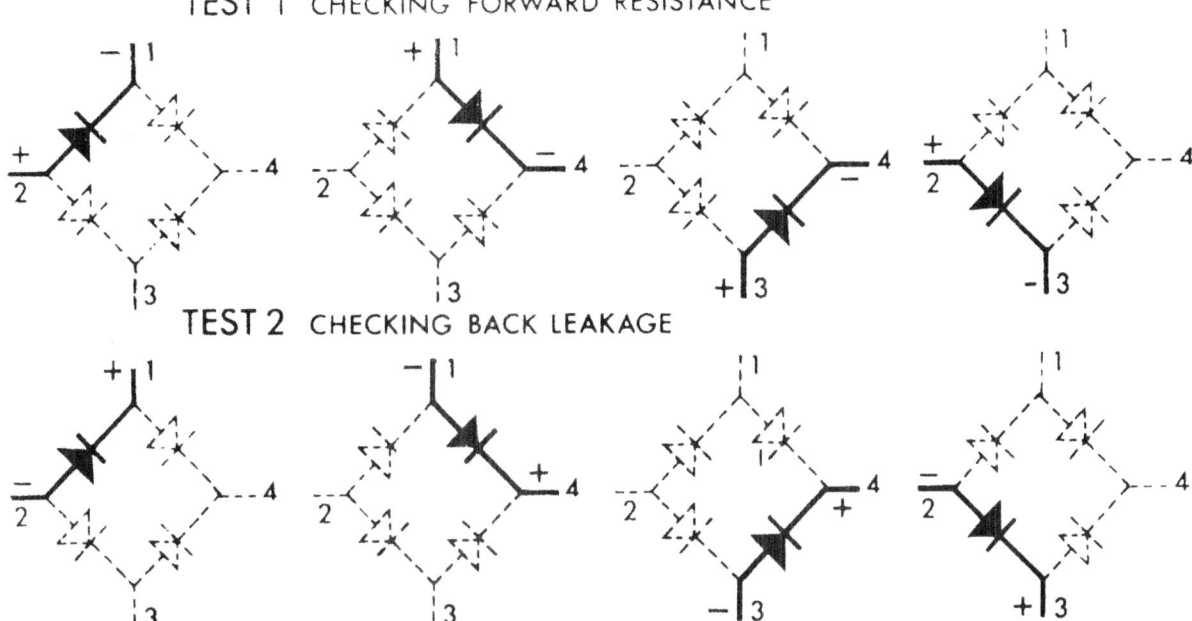

RECTIFIER TEST SEQUENCE FOR CHECKING FORWARD RESISTANCE AND BACK LEAKAGE
Fig. 31

(b) Repeat this test at the rectifier for the white/green lead.

(2) If no voltage is present at the rectifier central terminal (brown/white), check the voltage at the ammeter terminal. If satisfactory, it indicates that the brown/white wire is open circuit. If not, the ammeter is open circuit.

(3) If no voltage is present at either ammeter terminal, then the brown/blue wire from the battery (—ve) is open circuit, or the fuse has blown.

98. Constructing a One-ohm Load Resistor

The resistor used in the following tests must be accurate and constructed so that it will not overheat otherwise the correct values of current or voltage will not be obtained.

A suitable resistor can be made from 4 yards (3¾ metres) of 18 S.W.G. (.048 in. (i.e. 1.2 m.m.) dia.) NICHROME wire by bending it into two equal parts and calibrating it as follows:—

(1) Fix a heavy gauge flexible lead to the folded end of the wire and connect this lead to the positive terminal of a 6 volt battery.

(2) Connect a D.C. voltmeter (0–10V) across the battery terminals and an ammeter (0–10 amp) between the battery negative terminal and the free ends of the wire resistance, using a crocodile clip to make the connection.

(3) Move the clip along the wires, making contact with both wires until the ammeter reading is numerically equal to the number of volts shown in the voltmeter. The resistance is then 1 ohm. Cut the wire at this point, twist the two ends together and wind the wire on an asbestos former approximately 2 inches (5 cm.) dia. so that each turn does not contact the one next to it.

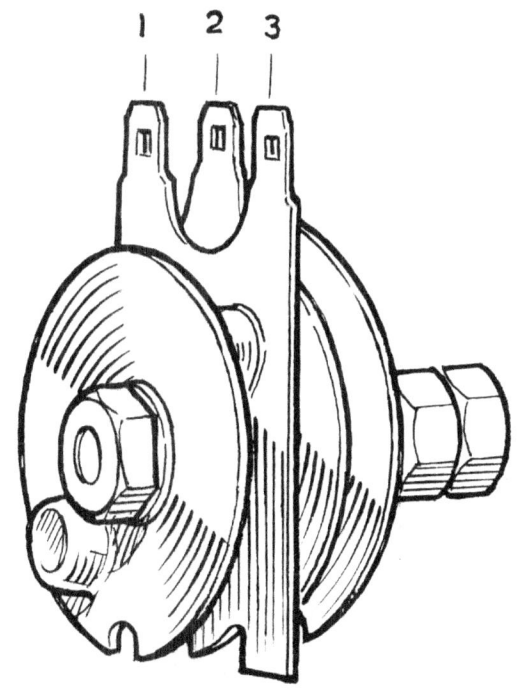

RECTIFIER—SHOWING TERMINAL CONNECTIONS FOR BENCH TESTS 1 AND 2
Fig. 32

ZENER DIODE

99. Description

The Zener Diode output regulating system uses all the coils of the 6-coil alternator connected permanently across the rectifier, provides automatic control of the charging current. It will only operate successfully on a 12 volt system where it is connected in parallel with the battery as shown in the wiring diagram. The Diode may be connected through the ignition switch or direct to the centre terminal of the rectifier.

Assuming the battery is in a low state of charge its terminal voltage (the same voltage is across the Diode) will also be low, therefore the maximum charging current will flow into the battery from the alternator. At first none of the current is by-passed by the Diode because of it being non-conducting due to the low battery terminal volts. However, as the battery is quickly restored to a full state of charge, the system voltage rises until at 13.5 volts the Zener Diode becomes partially conducting, thereby providing an alternative path for a small part of the charging current. Small increases in battery voltage result in large increases in Zener conductivity until, at approximately 15 volts about 5 amperes of the alternator output is by-passing the battery. The battery will continue to receive only a portion of the alternator output as long as the system voltage is relatively high.

Depression of the system voltage, due to the use of headlamp or other lighting equipment, causes the Zener Diode current to decrease and the balance to be diverted and consumed by the component in use.

If the electrical loading is sufficient to cause the system voltage to fall to 13.5 volts, the Zener Diode will revert to a high resistance state of non-conductivity and the full generated output will go to meet the demands of the battery.

100. Maintenance

The Zener Diode is mounted on an aluminium heat sink. Providing the Diode and the heat sink are kept clean, and provided with an adequate airflow, to ensure maximum efficiency, and provided a firm flat "metal to metal" contact is maintained between the base of the Diode and the surface of the heat sink, to ensure adequate heat flow, no maintenance will be necessary.

101. Test Procedure

(Procedure for testing on the Machine)

The test procedure given below can be used when it is required to check the performance of the Zener Diode type ZD715 whilst it is in position on the machine.

Good quality moving coil meters should be used when testing. The voltmeter should have a scale 0–18, and the ammeter 0–5 amps min. The test procedure is as follows:—

(1) Disconnect the cable from the Zener Diode and connect ammeter (in series) between the Diode Lucar terminal and cable previously disconnected. The ammeter red or positive lead must connect to the Diode Lucar terminal.

(2) Connect voltmeter across Zener Diode and heat sink. The red or positive lead must connect to the heat sink which is earthed to the frame of the machine by its fixing bolts and a separate earth lead. The black lead connects to the Zener Lucar terminal.

(3) Start the engine, ensure that all lights are off, and gradually increase engine speed while at the same time observing both meters:—

(a) the series connected ammeter must indicate zero amps, up to 12.75 volts, which will be indicated on the shunt connected voltmeter as engine speed is slowly increased.

(b) increase engine speed still further, until Zener current indicated on ammeter is 2.0 amp. At this value the Zener voltage should be 13.5 volts to 15.3 volts.

TEST CONCLUSIONS:—

If the ammeter in test (a) registers any current at all before the voltmeter indicates 13.0 volts, then a replacement Zener Diode must be fitted.

If test (a) is satisfactory but in test (b) a higher voltage than that stated is registered on the voltmeter, before the ammeter indicates 2.0 amp., then a replacement Zener Diode must be fitted.

102. Zener Diode Location

The Zener Diode is mounted in front of the right hand rear suspension unit. The aluminium heat sink is finned to assist cooling and is secured to the frame by a bracket and bolt. See Fig. 37.

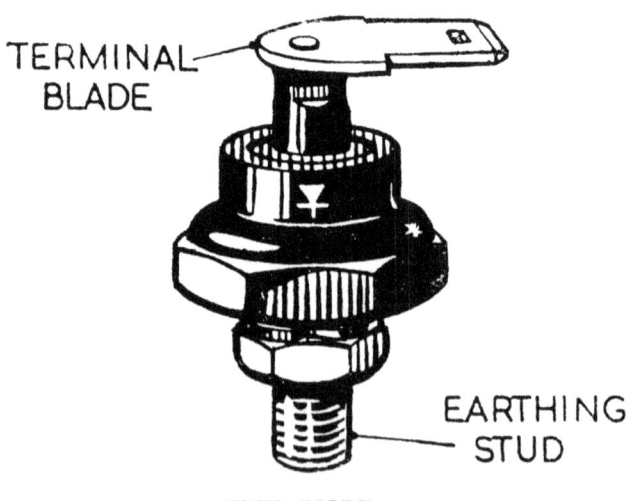

ZENER DIODE
Fig. 33

To remove Diode only, disconnect the brown/white double "Lucar" connector from the Diode. Unscrew the nut which secures the Diode (see Fig. 33). When refitting, the Diode nut must be tightened with extreme care. The correct torque is 24-28 lbs. in. To remove the finned heat sink, remove the front bolt from the retaining bracket. A double red earth (ground) wire is attached at this point.

NOTE—The earth wire must NOT be placed between the Zener body and heat sink as this could cause a heat build up possibly resulting in a Zener Diode failure.

HORN

103. Description

The 6H horn is of a high frequency single note type and is operated by direct current from the battery. The method of operation is that of a magnetically operated armature, which impacts on the cone face, and causes the tone disc of the horn to vibrate. The magnetic circuit is made self interrupting by contacts which can be adjusted externally.

If the horn fails to work, check the mounting bolts etc., and horn connection wiring. Check the battery for state of charge. A low supply voltage at the horn will adversely effect horn performance. If the above checks are made and the fault is not remedied, then adjust the horn as follows.

104. Horn Adjustment

When adjusting and testing the horn, do not depress the horn push for more than a fraction of

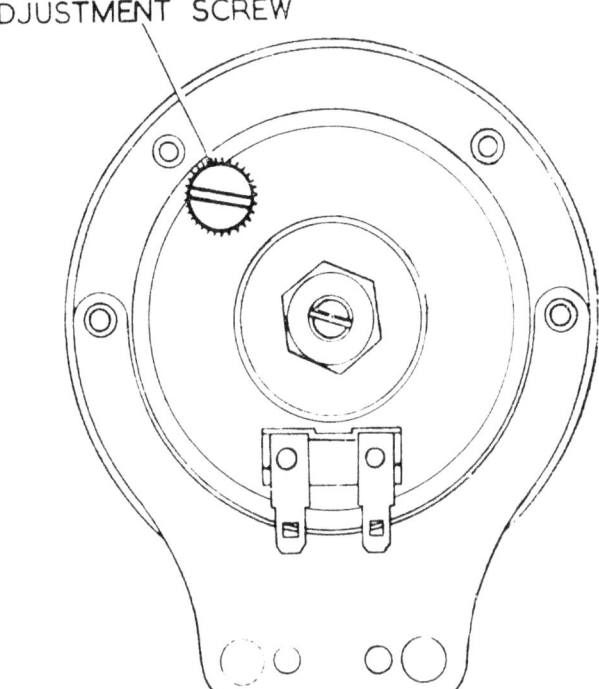

HORN ADJUSTMENT SCREW
Fig. 34

a second or the circuit wiring may be overloaded.

A small serrated adjustment screw situated near the terminals (see Fig. 34), is provided to take up wear in the internal moving parts of the horn. To adjust, turn this crew anticlockwise until the horn just fails to sound, and then turn it back (clockwise) about one quarter to half a turn.

LAMP UNITS

105. Description

The headlamp is of sealed beam unit type and access is gained to the bulb and bulb holder by withdrawing the rim and beam unit assembly. To do so slacken the screw at the top of the headlamp and prise off the rim and beam unit assembly.

The bulb can be removed by first pressing the cylindrical cap inwards and turning it anticlockwise. The cap can then be withdrawn and the bulb is free to be removed.

When fitting a new bulb, note that it locates by means of a cutaway and projection arrangement. Also note that the cap can only be replaced one way, the tabs being staggered to prevent incorrect reassembly. Check the replacement bulb voltage and wattage specification and type before fitting. Focusing with this type of beam unit is unnecessary and there is no provision for such.

106. Beam Adjustments

The beam must in all cases be adjusted as specified by local lighting regulations. In the United Kingdom the Transport Lighting Regulations reads as follows:—

A lighting system must be arranged so that it can give a light which is incapable of dazzling any person standing on the same horizontal plane as the vehicle at a greater distance than twenty-five feet from the lamp, whose eye level is not less than three feet-six inches above that plane.

The headlamp must therefore be set so that the main beam is directed straight ahead and parallel with the road when the motor cycle is fully loaded. To achieve this, place the machine on a level road pointing towards a wall at a distance of twenty-five feet away with a rider and passenger, on the machine, slacken the two pivot bolts at either side of the headlamp and tilt the headlamp until the beam is focused at approximately two feet six inches from the base of the wall. Do not forget that the headlamp should be on "full beam" lighting during this operation.

107. Removing and Refitting the Headlamp

Disconnect the leads from the battery terminals then slacken the light unit securing screw at the top of the headlamp. Prise the top of the light unit free.

Detach the pilot bulbholder from the light unit and disconnect the main bulbholder leads at the snap connector. Disconnect the 4 spade terminals from the lighting switch and the terminals from the ammeter. The red leads for the warning lights should be parted at the snap connectors and then the harness complete with warning light bulbholders can be withdrawn with the grommet from the back of the headlamp shell. Finally remove the pivot bolts to release the shell and collect the spacers.

Refitting is the reversal of the above instruction but reference should be made to the wiring diagram. Finally, set the headlamp main beam as explained previously.

Do not tighten the headlamp pivot bolts over the torque setting of 10 lb. ft. (1.4 kg.M).

108. General

Access to the bulbs in the tail and stop lamp unit is achieved by unscrewing the two slotted screws which secure the lens. The bulb is of the double-filament offset pin type and when a replacement is carried out, ensure that the bulb is fitted correctly.

Check that the two supply leads are connected correctly and check the earth (ground) lead to the bulb holder is in satisfactory condition.

When refitting the lens, do not overtighten the fixing screws or the lens may fracture as a result.

Fuses

109. Description

The fuse is to be found on the brown/blue live lead from the battery negative terminal. It is housed in a quickly detachable shell and is of 35 amp fuse rating.

Before following any fault location procedure always check that the fuse is not the source of the fault. A new fuse-cartridge should be fitted if there is any doubt about the old one.

The fuse rating must not under any circumstances be below 35 amp rating.

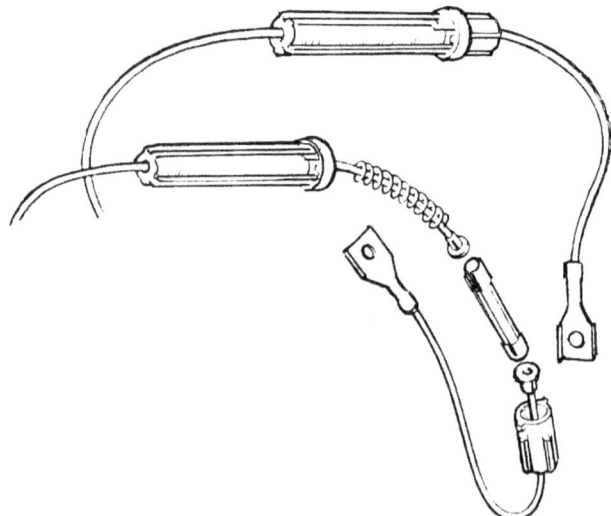

EXPLODED VIEW OF FUSEHOLDER ASSEMBLY
Fig. 35

IGNITION AND HEADLAMP SWITCHES AND WARNING LIGHTS

110. Description

The ignition switch incorporates a "barrel" type lock, having individual "Yale" type keys rendering the ignition circuit inoperative when the switch is turned off and the key removed. It is advisable for the owner to note the number stamped on the key to ensure a correct replacement in the event of the key being lost.

Three Lucar connectors are incorporated in the switch and these should be checked from time to time to ensure good electrical contact. The switch body can be released from the switch panel by removing the large retaining nut and pushing the switch out. The battery leads should be removed before attempting to remove the switch to avoid a short circuit.

The lock is retained in the body of the switch by a spring loaded plunger. This can be depressed with a pointed instrument through a small hole in the side of the switch body and the lock assembly withdrawn after the lock and switch together have been detached from the machine.

111. General

A headlamp main beam (red) warning light is incorporated in the headlamp shell.

Bulb replacement is simple and only requires extraction by normal hand pressure of the bulb adaptor from its location.

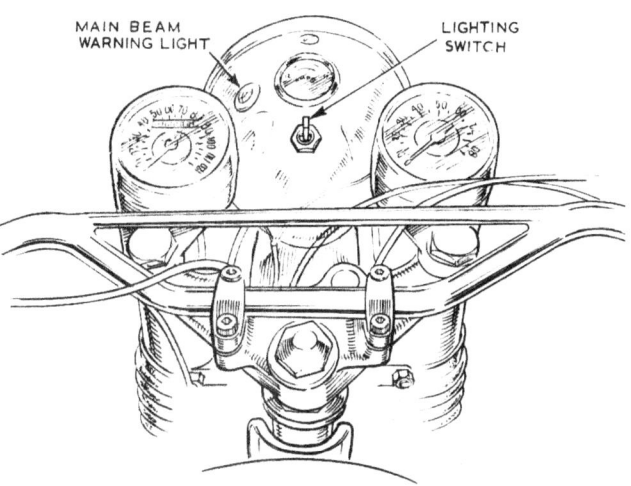

LOCATION OF MAIN BEAM WARNING
Fig. 36

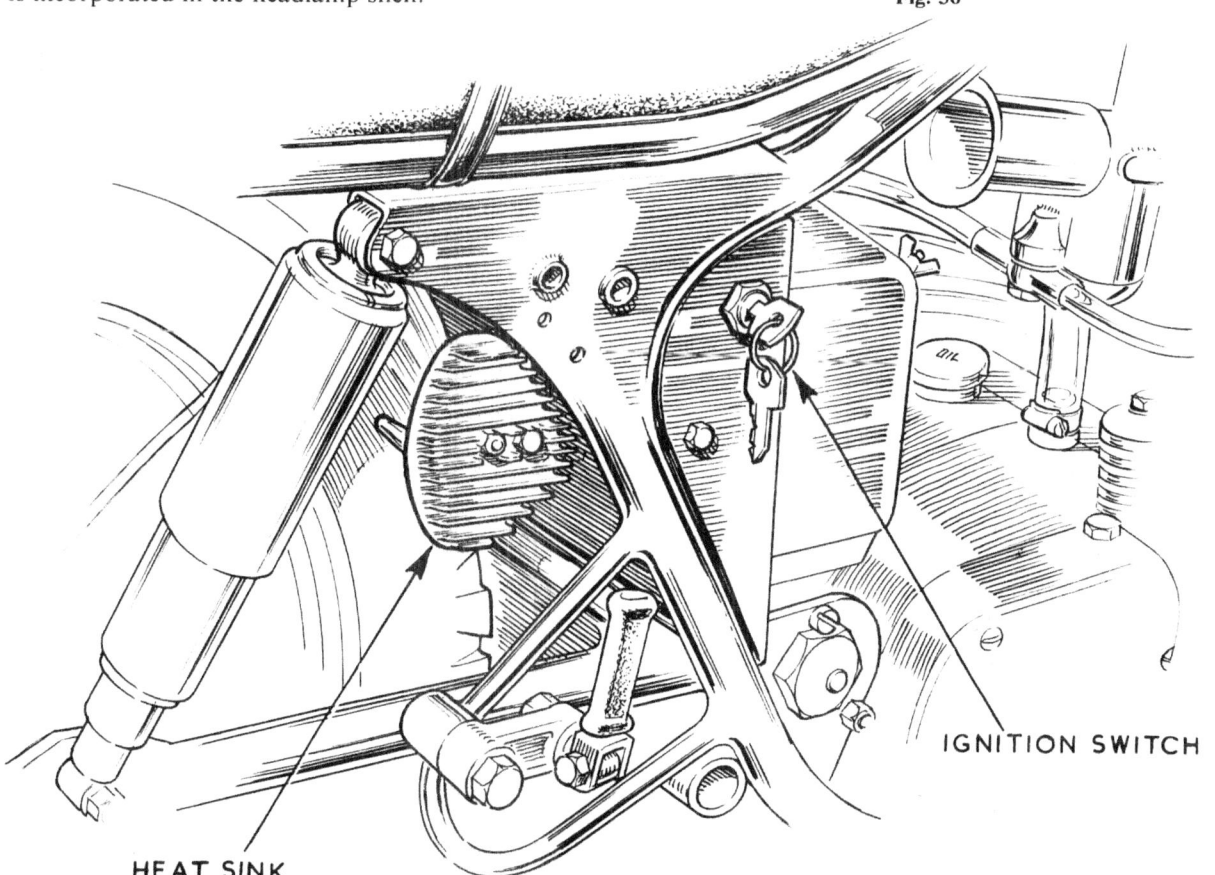

SHOWING THE IGNITION SWITCH   FINNED HEATSINK   ZENER DIODE LOCATION
Fig. 37

Page 44   Royal Enfield "Interceptor" 750 Series II Workshop Manual

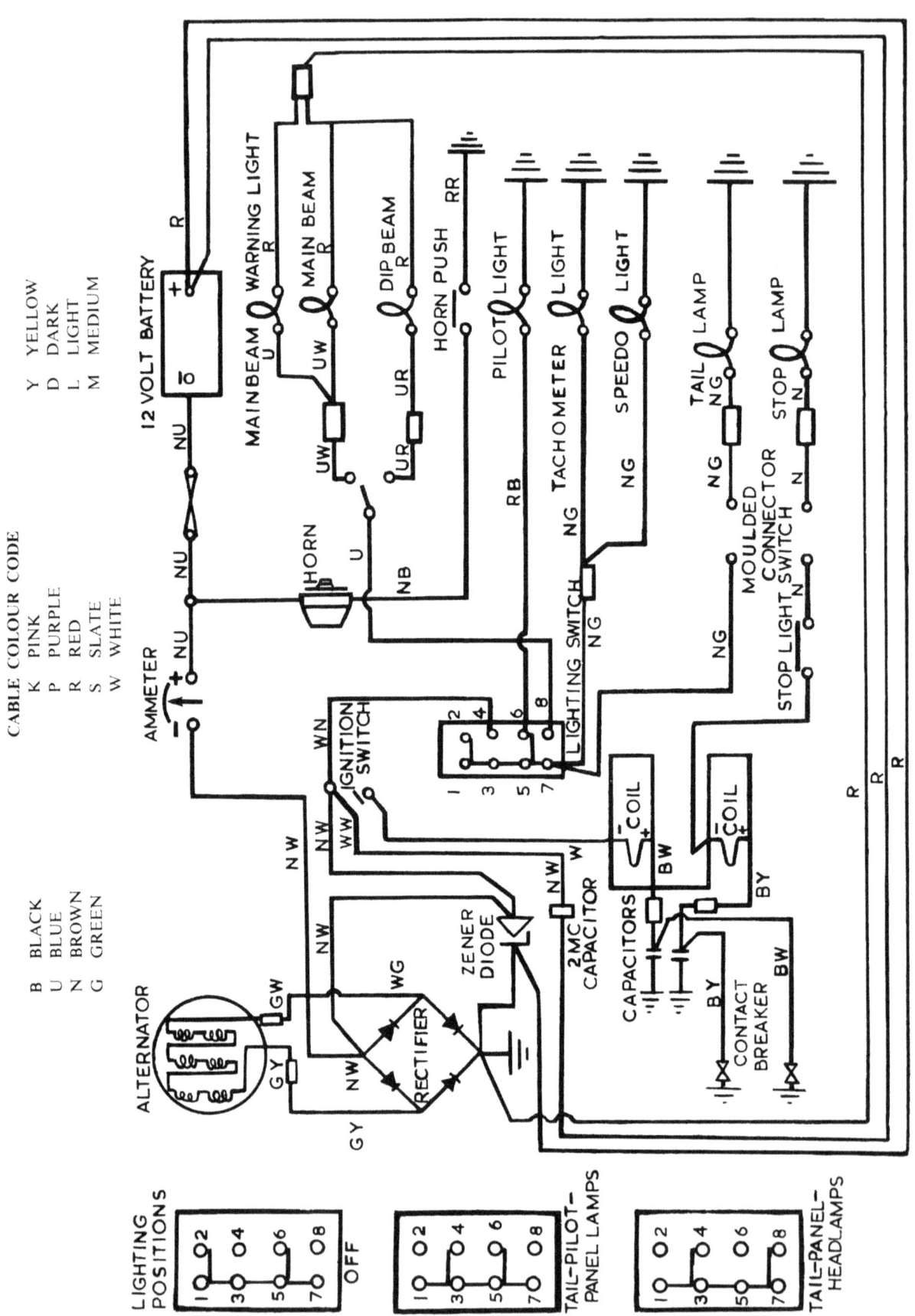

Fig. 38   2MC CAPACITOR IGNITION SYSTEM

Frame

112. Description of Frame

The frame is built throughout of cold drawn weldless steel tubing with brazed or welded joints, liners being fitted where necessary for extra strength. All the main frame members are made of chrome-molybdenum alloy steel tubing which retains its strength and resistance to fatigue after brazing or welding.

The rear wheel is carried in a swinging arm unit which forms the chainstays.

This unit pivots on pre-stressed rubber bushes with inner and outer metal sleeves. The inner sleeves are extended inwards and butt against a short distance piece fitted between them. The outer ends of the inner sleeves project beyond the ends of the rubber bushes and bear against steel thrust washers fitting into recesses in the main frame pivot lugs. A long steel bolt and nuts secure the whole assembly. No greasing is necessary.

113. Steering Head Races

The steering head races, 34085, are the same at the top and bottom of the head lug. They are easily removed by knocking them out with a hammer and drift and new races can be fitted either under a press or by means of a hammer and a wooden drift.

114. Removal of Rear Mudguard Assembly

With the machine on the centre stand, slacken off the two top rear suspension pivot nuts to free them from the recesses in the mudguard carrier plates. The mudguard assembly can now be lifted upwards and backwards sufficiently to gain access to the rear lamp wiring connectors. When these are disconnected and the breather tube straps undone the assembly is free to be removed leaving the breather tube in position in the main frame.

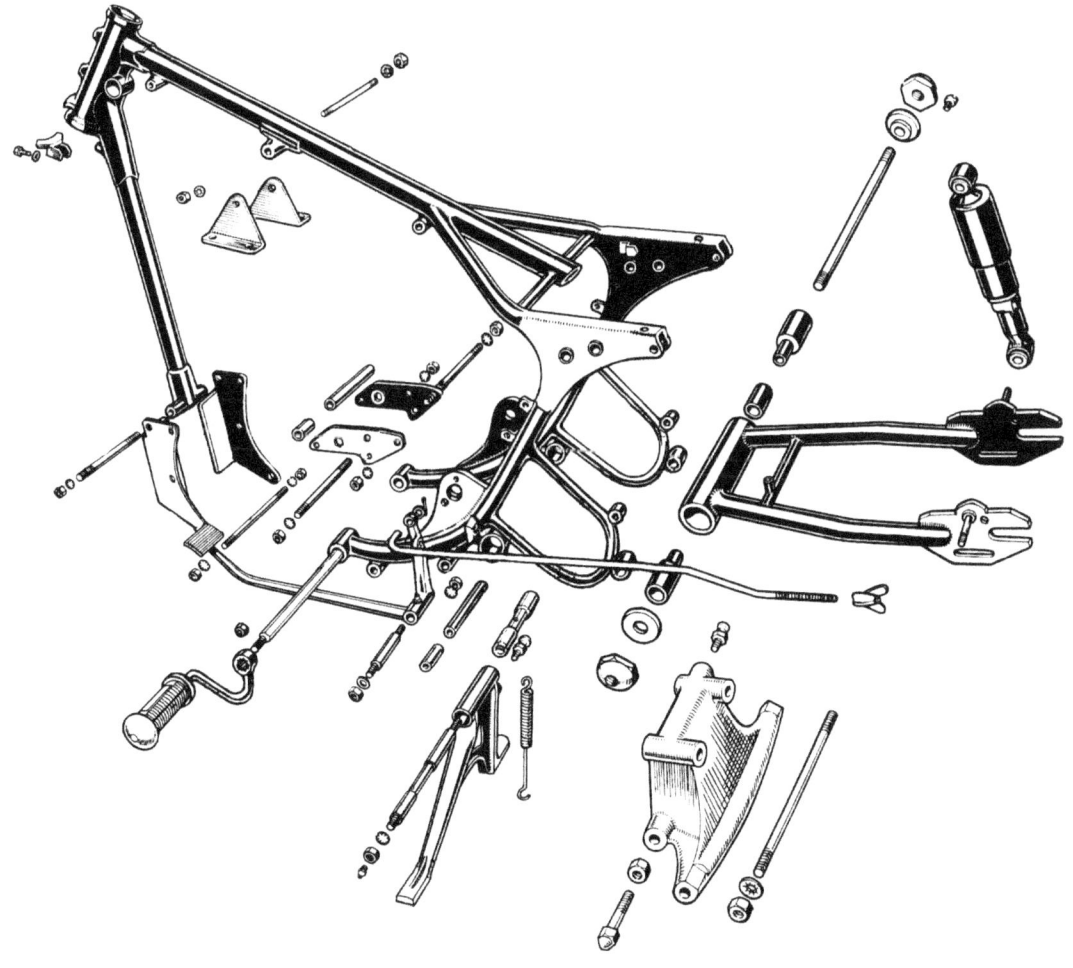

EXPLODED VIEW OF "INTERCEPTOR" FRAME
Fig. 39

When reassembling the unit make certain that the clips at the front of the carrier are located on the cross bar of the frame and that the carrier side plates are fully home on the suspension top pivot pins before tightening the nuts. Do not forget to re-connect the rear lamp wiring harness.

115. Removal of Rear Suspension Unit

Place the machine on the centre stand and remove the dual seat and rear mudguard. (See Subsection 114).

Remove the top pivot pin nut, drive out the pivot pin, then hinge the suspension unit back on the lower pivot pin. After removing the lower nut, the unit may be pushed off the pivot pin welded to the fork end.

116. Servicing Rear Suspension Units

The proprietary units fitted are sealed and servicing of the internal mechanism can be carried out only by the manufacturers.

The rubber bushes in the top and bottom eyes can easily be renewed and the spring can be removed by pushing down on the top spring cover so as to release the split collar above it. After removal of the split collar the top cover and spring can be lifted off. When reassembling, the spring should be greased to prevent rust and squeaking if it should come into contact with either of the covers (when fitted).

The Girling dampers have only one spring but the pre-load can be varied by turning the bottom spring cup by means of a "C" spanner thus raising the rear of the machine and preventing bottoming on the bump stop under heavy loads. The lowest position is suitable for normal solo work, the middle position is for use with a pillion passenger and the top position is suitable for sidecar work. The part number for the spring for these dampers is 64539963, colour code red/orange, rating 132 lb./in.

When replacing a spring the use of a compressor, as shown in Fig. 00, is a great convenience. If one is not available, reduce the spring load as much as possible by setting the dampers to their lowest setting.

When the spring is removed it should be possible to push the plunger up and down *slowly* throughout the length of its stroke but it should resist *sudden* movements, particularly in the direction of the rebound. If it does not, or if there are signs of leakage of the hydraulic fluid, the complete damper unit should be exchanged for a service replacement. When making this test always hold the damper approximately upright so that the hydraulic fluid is at the lower end.

REAR SPRING COMPRESSOR
Fig. 40

117. Removal of Swinging Arm Chain Stays

First remove one of the pivot pin nuts and pull the pivot pin out from the other end. The swinging arm can now be withdrawn from between the pivot plates.

If it is necessary to replace or remove the rubber bushes a press capable of exerting a load of 10/12 tons will be necessary. Support one end of the pivot tube on a piece of tube with a bore just large enough to accept the outside diameter of the outer metal sleeve of the rubber bush ($1\frac{1}{16}$ in.). Press one bush into the pivot tube, thus pushing out the other bush and the distance piece between them.

Do this by means of a mandrel $1\frac{1}{32}$ in. diameter with one end stepped down to $\frac{3}{4}$ in. diameter to locate it in the inner sleeve of the bush.

Note—This procedure will normally scrap one or both the rubber bushes which should not be removed unnecessarily. When fitting replacement bushes do not forget the distance piece between them.

118. Centre Stand

To remove the centre stand unscrew the nut from one end of the stand spindle, knock out the latter and withdraw the stand complete with its bearing sleeve after disconnecting one end of the stand spring.

119. Wheel Alignment

Note that it is not possible to guarantee that the wheels are correctly aligned when the same notch position is used on both adjuster cams. It is therefore not sufficient to count the notches and use the same position on both sides of the machine. The only way to guarantee that the wheels are in line is to check the alignment from front wheel to back using either a straight edge or a piece of taut string. The alignment should be checked on both sides of the machine and if the front and rear tyres are of different section allowance must be made for this.

It is usual to check the alignment of the wheels at a point about six inches above the ground but, if the alignment is checked also towards the top of the wheels, it will be possible to ascertain whether or not the frame is twisted so as to cause one wheel to be leaning while the other is vertical. To do this it is always necessary to remove the mudguards and, unless a straight edge cut away in its centre portion is available, it will be necessary also to remove the cylinders, battery, etc., in order to allow an unbroken straight edge or a piece of taut string to contact the front and rear tyres.

120. Lubrication

The steering head races, and stand pivot bearing should be well greased on assembly. The stand pivot is provided with a grease nipple but no nipples are provided for the steering head as experience has shown that the provision of nipples at this point causes trouble through chafing and cutting of control and lighting cables. If the steering head bearings are well packed they will last for several years or many thousands of miles.

Recommended greases are Shell Retinax A, Castrolease LM, Esso Multipurpose Grease H, Marfak Multipurpose 2, Mobilgrease MP, or Energrease L2.

Front Forks

121. Lubrication

Use one of the grades of oil, S.A.E. 20 as shown in the table of lubricants. The normal oil content is $6\frac{1}{2}$ fluid ozs. (170.4 cc.) Attention is only necessary at the first 1,000 miles and again at 10,000 miles when the oil should be changed by draining. An exploded drawing of the front forks is shown in Fig. 00 from which it will readily be seen that the fork springs abut against the filler plugs (34), before removing these plugs weight must be taken off the front wheel, by placing the machine on its central stand to avoid the forks collapsing.

122. To Drain the Forks

With the machine on the central stand: Unscrew the two filler plugs (34). Have available a container to catch oil drained, then remove the drain plug screw (7) with its washer, with the container under the fork leg. If the wheel is inclined to one side, draining will be more complete. Deal with the other fork leg in a similar manner.

123. Filling Oil

It will be seen the air space between the fork spring, and the inside of the tube is very close: therefore fresh oil must be filled with extreme care, to avoid losses by spilling. Use a measured container for the correct content of $6\frac{1}{2}$ ozs. Replace the drain plugs before filling, also firmly tighten the filler plugs after.

124. Steering Head Adjustment

On a new machine the filler plugs (34) should be checked for tightness due to settling down, check as well the steering head bearings at the first 100 miles, and then occasionally, as the mileage increases. Using the machine with movement in these bearings will damage the races. Movement in these bearings can usually be detected when the front brake is applied. To check, raise the front wheel well clear of the ground with a box under the crankcase. Try to raise or lower the front wheel with one hand and use the fingers of the other hand encircling the handle bar lug where it meets the frame, when movement can be felt. To adjust bearings a thin open ended spanner $1\frac{3}{8}$ in. across the flats is needed. First release the tube clamping stud nut (28), unscrew the stem nut (37) slightly. Use the thin spanner on the sleeve nut (30) and manipulate as necessary. The bearing should be devoid of play with free movements. Retighten the column nut, also the clamping stud nuts.

The steering head bearing consists of two deep groove thrust races each containing 19 ¼ in. dia. balls. See Subsection 113 for removal of races from frame head lug. Use an old screwdriver, or taper wedge to take off the cone on the fork column.

125. Dismantling the Forks

The forks can be removed as a unit, or the fork legs can be removed individually. To take out one one fork leg remove the front wheel as described elsewhere. Take off the front mudguard with stays. Release nut for pinch bolt (28), and pull top end of rubber gaiter from cover tube. Remove filler cap plug (34), disconnect it from the damper rod, by using two spanners.

The fork inner tube can now be drawn downwards clear of the handlebar lug and fork crown. If the tube resists removal fit back the filler plug without being connected to the damper rod, screw in a few turns, then give it a few sharp blows with a soft faced mallet to separate the tube from its taper fixing in the handlebar lug.

Front Fork Assembly
1. Fork main tube.
2. Main tube bush.
3. Main tube bottom bush.
4. Main tube bottom bush circlip.
5. Fork end left hand.
6. Fork end right hand.
7. Fork end drain plug.
8. Washer for plug.
9. Oil damper tube.
10. Oil damper rod.
11. Oil damper tube bolt.
12. Washer for bolt.
13. Washer for tube.
14. Nut for rod top.
15. Nut for rod bottom.
16. Damper tube cap.
17. Piston locating peg.
18. Oil damper valve cup.
19. Oil damper valve cup slotted ring.
20. Main tube lock ring with cup.
21. Main spring.
22. Main spring locating bushes.
23. Spring cover tube.
24. Spring top cover tube securing plate.
25. Screws securing plate.
26. Crown lug complete with column.
27. Pinch stud for crown lug.
28. Nut for stud.
29. Rubber gaiter.
30. Fork head race adjuster nut.
31. Top cover left hand.
32. Top cover right hand.
33. Main tube top cover ring.
34. Fork main tube filler and retaining plug.
35. Washer for plug.
36. Fork head clip.
37. Fork crown and column lock nut.
38. Fork spring locating bush.
39. Main fork tube oil seal.
40. Main fork tube oil seal washer.
41. Bottom cover tube seal.

126. To Remove the Forks as a Unit

Follow the instructions given for removing a fork leg, as far as disconnecting the filler plugs from the damper rods. Proceed by taking off the headlamp leaving it suspended by the loom. Separate the control cables from the levers, and remove handlebars. Remove the column nut (37) then

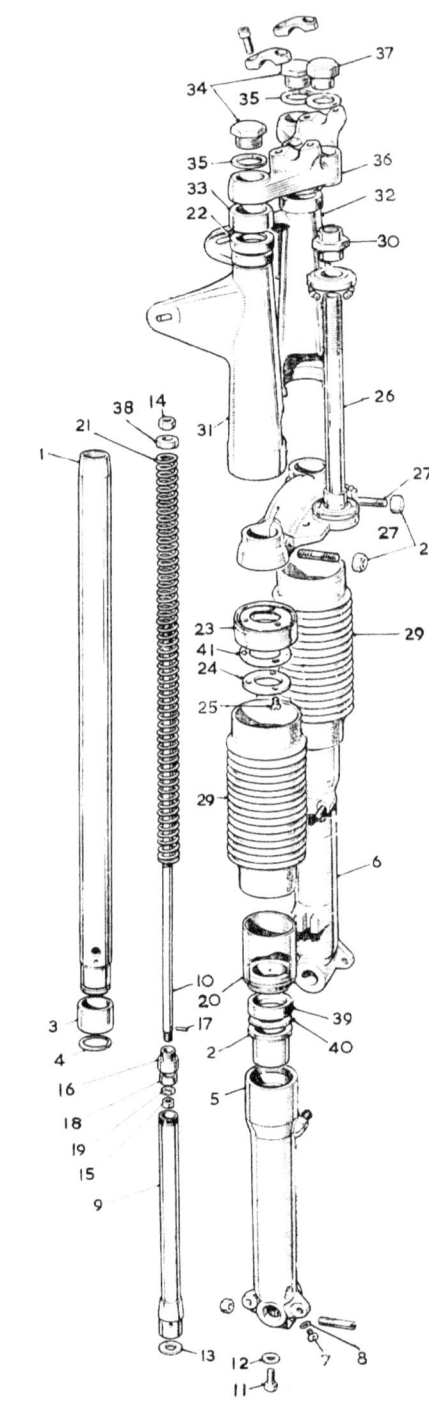

FRONT FORKS
Fig. 41

give the underside of the handlebar lug one or two blows with a mallet until it is clear of the fork tubes. At this stage support the ends of the forks, for after removing the sleeve nut (30) the forks will drop out. Watch for the steel balls for the races, there are 19 in each race (38 in all), if a steering damper is fitted detach the fixed plate from the frame.

127. To Dismantle a Fork Slider

Remove from the fork slider the bolt fixing damper tube (11). Unscrew the bottom cover (23), and take away the fork slider (5).

The damper tube with the fork spring can be extracted from the tube. To dismantle further, take off nut securing fork spring, unscrew the damper tubecap (16) with a tommy bar through the holes in the damper tube, for if this is held in a vice it will distort and become useless. The damper assembly sequence is clearly depicted in Fig. 41.

Note—When removing the oil seal, sealing washer and flanged bush pass them along the fork tube and take off from the top end past the taper end, if the oil seal is to be used again.

128. Assembling the Forks

It will be apparent from the dismantling instructions given that there is nothing complicated in the fork assembly and if the reverse sequence is used, no difficulty should occur with the following precautions.

The fork tube, where the oil seal operates, must have a smooth finish and free from blemish.

The oil seal is fitted from the top of the tube, with the visible spring facing downwards against the flange for the bush.

The damper tube cap also the damper tube fixing bolt must be properly tightened.

Finally tighten the bottom cover (23) when the front wheel has been put back.

Fill 6½ ozs. of S.A.E. 20 oil to each fork leg.

Front Wheel

129. To Remove the Front Wheel

With the machine on the central stand: Detach the brake cable from the expander lever. Detach the brake cable adjuster from the brake plate. Detach the right hand spindle nut. Release the pinch stud in left fork slider end. Take the weight of the wheel by the left hand, pull out the wheel spindle. The wheel can be taken out of the forks.

130. To Refit the Wheel

Reverse the procedure described for removal, with the following precautions. Remove traces of rust from the spindle and grease. Exercise care to correctly locate brake plate in the fork slider. Do not tighten unduly the slider pinch bolt, overtightening can cause a fracture.

Note—If the fork motion is stiff after refitting the wheel, slack off the spindle nut and work the forks up and down (the fork tubes will take up alignment), then retighten the spindle nut.

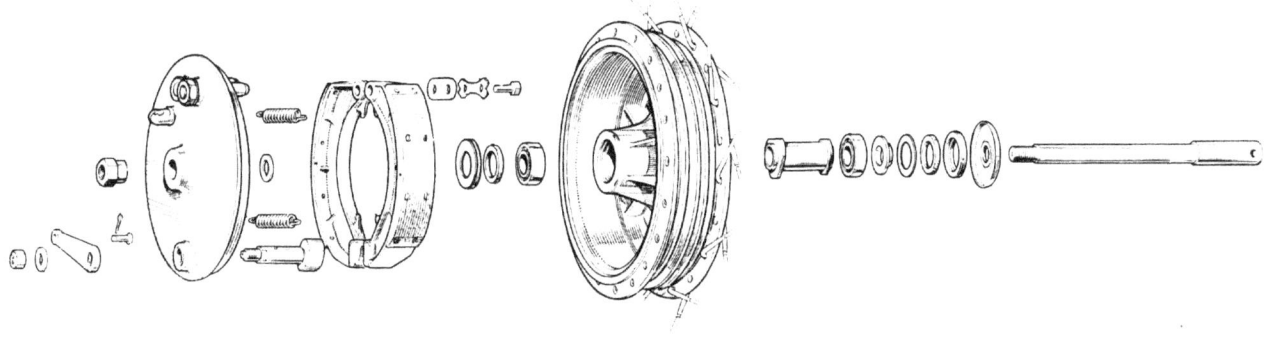

FRONT HUB
Fig. 42

131. To Dismantle the Hub

The wheel hub is packed with grease during initial assembly, and should not need further lubrication for at least 10,000 miles when the hub should be dismantled for cleaning and fresh grease used. To dismantle the hub, with the wheel removed take away the brake plate with brake shoes.

Unscrew bearing lock plate on left side of hub, holes are provided for a peg spanner or use a punch. If the plate resists removal use a little heat which will facilitate removal, take out felt sealing washer and distance piece.

To eject the bearing use a drift through the brake side (the front wheel spindle can be used for this purpose) when a few light blows from a mallet will drive out the bearing until it is clear of the hub, and no more, as the other bearing goes into the hub during this process.

Take out the spindle, or drift, invert the wheel and repeat the process to eject the double bearing which will bring with it the large steel washer, the felt washer, also the thin steel washer.

BALANCING THE ROAD WHEELS
Fig. 43

132. Assembling the Hub

Clean and repack both bearings with fresh grease (see table of lubricants). Press into the left side of the hub the single bearing, fit the distance washer (flat side against the bearing), then the felt washer and secure with the lock plate.

Invert the hub, insert the distance tube (small end first) against the bearing.

Enter the double bearing square with the hub, use the drift through both bearings and drive home until the bearing abuts against the distance tube.

Fit the smallest of the two washers, the felt washer, then the large steel washer.

With a suitable punch peen the hub material, where it joins the washer in three equidistant positions to retain the washer.

133. Brake Adjustment

Clearance between the brake shoes and drum can be reduced by unscrewing the adjusters on the cable and handlebar lever. Continual adjustment causes the expander lever to occupy a position with lost leverage. To restore leverage, take off the cable and reverse the expander lever.

To improve brake efficiency, release the spindle nut a few turns, hold the brake hard on, retighten the spindle nut at the same time. The brake shoes will then centralise.

134. Brake Dismantling and Assembly

Remove brake plate from drum. Remove nut and washer from cam spindle. Remove cam lever.

Remove springs from shoes. This is best done with a screwdriver placed against one of the spring hooks and held in position with one hand, now knock the screwdriver with the palm of the other hand to push the spring off the lug on the shoe. The spring may fly off so care should be taken that it is not lost.

Turn back the tabwasher and unscrew the two hexagon headed set screws which secure the shoes to the pivot pins. Lift off the pivot pin tie plate and remove the brake shoes.

The cam can now be withdrawn. It may be tight in its bush if the cam lever nut has been overtight as this causes the end of the spindle to become swelled. When this happens the end immediately behind the flats should be eased down with emery tape.

If the cam will pass through the bush but is tight, it can be eased down more easily after removal.

135. Brake Re-assembly

Remove all traces of rust and dirt from the expander cam and pivot pins, apply a slight smear of grease. For ease in working the brake plate can be held in a smooth jaw vice, clamping it by the torque stop. Fit the brake shoes, tie plate and tab washer and set screws. If the tab washer has been used on more than one occasion discard it and use a new one. Fit the shoe springs, by anchoring the end farthest away from the operator, use a length of stout string in the free end of the spring, stretch the spring with one hand and guide the spring onto its anchorage with the other hand. Alternatively use a narrow blade screwdriver. Finally fit the expander lever with its nut and washer.

136. Balancing the Front Wheel

At high speeds, if the tyres are out of balance, the steering can be affected and in extreme cases the front forks can "flap" at maximum speed. As oil seals are used on the wheel spindle, the wheel cannot be accurately balanced until the friction caused by the seals is removed.

The courses open are:
(1) Remove the oil seals.
(2) Obtain two ball races with an internal diameter sufficiently large enough to take the wheel spindle, mount the wheel on two boxes as shown in Fig. 43.

If the wheel is correctly balanced, it should remain stationary in any position in which the wheel is placed. The most likely out of balance position will be where the valve is situated or where a security bolt is fitted. The heaviest part will of course come to rest at 180° or 6 o'clock. To counterbalance, use thin strips of lead twisted round the spoke. Special weights for this purpose are supplied by the tyre makers. When the wheel is in perfect balance, secure the strips of lead with insulating tape which should be painted with jointing compound. The effect of a balanced wheel has to be tried to be appreciated if continued high speeds are permissible.

Rear Hub

137. Description

This wheel is of the "detachable" type, which enables the main portion of the wheel to be removed from the machine without disturbing the chain or brake. The wheel incorporates the well-known Enfield cush drive and also a 7 in. internal expanding brake.

138. Removal and Replacement of Main Portion of Wheel for Tyre Repairs, etc.

Place the machine on the centre stand, if necessary putting packing pieces beneath the legs of the stand to lift the wheel clear of the ground. Unscrew the loose section of the spindle and withdraw this, together with the chain adjuster cam, preferably marking it to ensure that it is replaced in the same position. Now slide the distance collar out of the fork end and lift away the speedometer drive gearbox, which can be left attached to the driving cable. The spacing collar and the felt washer behind it may now be removed to prevent risk of them falling out when manipulating the tyre. If, however, these are too tight a fit in the hub to come out easily they may be left in place. The main body of the wheel can

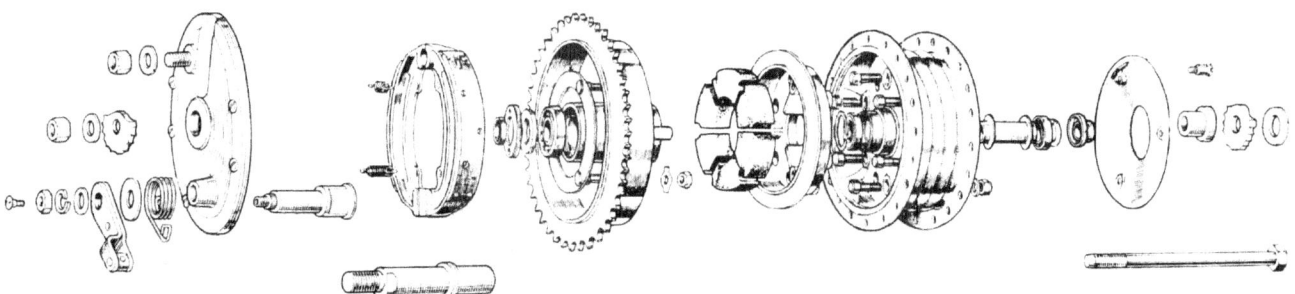

EXPLODED VIEW OF QUICKLY DETACHABLE REAR HUB
Fig. 44

now be pulled across to the right-hand side of the machine, thus disengaging the six driving pins from the cush drive shell and enabling the wheel to be removed from the machine. (See Fig. 45).

When replacing the main portion of the wheel, reverse the foregoing procedure. The cush drive shell can be prevented from rotating when turning the wheel to engage the six driving pins, if the machine is placed in gear or the rear brake is operated, taking care, when replacing the speedometer drive gearbox, that the driving dogs inside the gearbox engage with the slots in the end of the hub barrel. Before tightening the centre spindle make sure that the speedometer drive gearbox is correctly positioned so that there is no sharp bend in the driving cable.

139. Removal and Replacement of Complete Wheel for Access to Brake

Place the machine on the centre stand and remove the rear mudguard unit. Disconnect the rear driving chain at the spring link and remove the chain from the rear wheel sprocket. Unscrew the rear brake rod adjusting nut completely and depress the brake pedal so as to disengage the rod from the trunnion in the brake operating lever. Unscrew the brake cover plate anchor nut and remove this together with the washer behind it. Unscrew the loose section of the spindle two or three turns and the spindle nut by a similar amount. Mark the chain adjuster cams to ensure replacing in the same position.* Disconnect the

*Note that the wheel is not necessarily correctly lined up when the same notch position is used on both adjuster cams. Once the position of the cams which gives correct alignment has been found this alignment will, however, be maintained if both cams are moved the same number of notches. See also Subsection 119.

REMOVAL OF WHEEL (OFFSIDE VIEW)
Fig. 45

speedometer driving cable and slide the wheel out of the fork ends, tilting it so as to disengage the end of the brake shoe pivot from the slot in the fork end.

When replacing the wheel make sure that the dogs on the gear in the speedometer drive gearbox are engaged with the slots in the end of the hub barrel. Make sure also that the speedometer drive gearbox is correctly positioned so that there is no sudden bend in the driving cable. When replacing the connecting link in the driving chain, make sure that the closed end of the spring link points in the direction of travel of the chain. Replace the chain adjuster cams in their original positions or, if necessary, turn each of them the same number of notches to tension the chain and maintain correct wheel alignment. The chain should have $\frac{1}{2}$ in. up and down minimum movement when the rear suspension is fully extended as it will be tighter in the normal laden position. Do not forget to refit the brake rod and adjust the brake so that the wheel turns freely when the brake is off, while at the same time only a small travel of the brake pedal is necessary to put the brake on.

140. Removal of Brake Shoes for Replacement, etc.

Remove the complete wheel as described above, then remove the spindle nut, chain adjuster and the distance collar, thus permitting the complete brake cover plate assembly, with operating cam, pivot pin, shoes and return springs, to be lifted off the hub spindle. The brake shoes can then be removed after detaching the return springs. Brake linings are supplied either in pairs ready drilled complete with rivets (Part No. 41285A/BX) or ready fitted to service replacement brake shoes (Part No. 41343A). When riveting linings to shoes, secure the two centre rivets first so as to ensure that the lining lies flat against the shoe. Standard linings are Ferodo AM2, which are drilled to receive cheese-headed rivets.

141. Removal of Brake Operating Cam

To remove the operating cam unscrew the nut which secures the operating lever to the splines on the cam. A sharp tap on the end of the cam spindle will now free the lever, after which the cam can be withdrawn from its housing.

Do not try to remove the brake shoe pivot pin as this is cast into the cover plate.

142. Cush Drive

The sprocket/brake drum is free to rotate on the hub barrel. Three radial vanes are formed on the back of the brake drum and three similar vanes are formed on the cush drive shell. Six rubber blocks are fitted between the vanes on the brake drum and those on the cush drive shell, thus permitting only a small amount of angular movement of the sprocket/brake drum relative to the hub barrel and transmitting both driving and braking torques and smoothing out harshness and irregularity in the former.

If the cush drive rubbers become worn so that the amount of free movement measured at the tyre exceeds ½ in. to 1 in., the rubbers should be replaced. To obtain access to them remove the complete wheel as described above; then unscrew the loose section of the spindle completely. The main portion of the wheel can then be lifted away from the assembly consisting of the fixed portion of the spindle, sprocket/brake drum complete with brake and the cush drive shell. Now remove the brake cover plate complete with brake shoes as described above, and unscrew the three nuts at the back of the cush drive shell after bending back the locking washers. The three studs are brazed to the lockring and should be driven out of the cush drive shell, each a little at a time to avoid distorting the lockring or bending the studs. The sprocket/brake drum can now be separated from the cush drive shell and the six such drive rubbers lifted out.

When reassembling the cush drive the entry of the vanes between the rubbers will be facilitated if the latter are fitted into the driving shell first and then tilted. The rubbers should be liberally smeared with soapsuds to facilitate entry of the vanes. Grease the inner face of the lockring before assembling and tighten the three nuts down solid as there is a shoulder on the stud which prevents tightening of the nuts from locking the operation of the cush drive. Do not forget to bend up the tabs of the three locking washers.

When reassembling the cush drive, coat the inside of the bore of the sprocket/brake drum liberally with grease where it fits over the hub barrel.

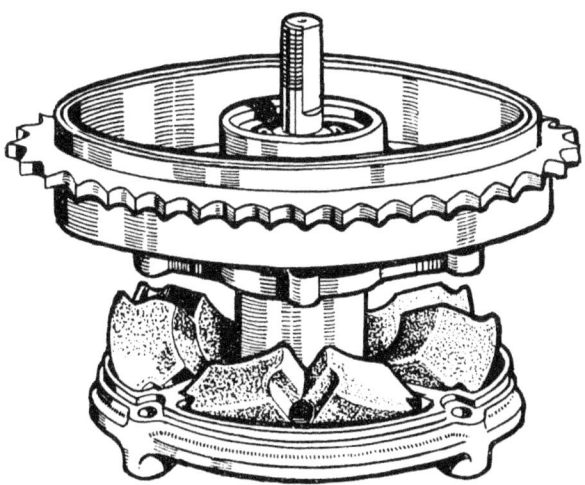

REASSEMBLY OF CUSH DRIVE
Fig. 46

143. Removal of Ball Bearings

To remove the ball bearings take the complete wheel out of the machine and separate the main portion of the wheel from the sprocket/brake drum cush drive shell assembly as described above. To remove the bearing from the sprocket/brake drum, first remove the brake cover plate complete with brake shoe assembly; then remove the distance collar and unscrew the bearing retaining ring with a peg spanner. Now screw the loose section of the spindle into the fixed section and drive out the bearing by hitting the hexagon-headed end of the loose section of the spindle.

To remove the bearings from the loose half of the hub barrel, first lift away the distance collar, speedometer drive gearbox, the spacing collar and the felt washer. Remove the bearing retaining circlip from the driving sprocket end of the barrel. Between the two bearings is a spacer, slotted at one end to enable a drift to be used on the bearing at that end. Remove this bearing first, then enter the loose section of the spindle into the spacer and drive out the remaining bearing by means of a hammer and drift applied to the hexagon-headed end of the spindle.

144. Hub Bearings

These are deep-groove single-row journal ball bearings. The sprocket/brake drum bearing is a Skefko RLS7, ⅞ in. i/d, by 2 in. o/d, by 9/16 in. wide. Equivalent bearings of other makes are Hoffmann LS9, Ransome & Marles LJ ⅞ in., and Fafnir LS9. The two bearings in the hub barrel are Skefko RLS5, ⅝ in. i/d, by 1 9/16 in. o/d, by 7/16 in. wide. Equivalent bearings of other makes are Hoffman LS7, Ransome & Marles LJ ⅝ in. and Fafnir LS7. Bearings with slack fitting internal clearances marked "C3," "000" or "***" should be specified.

145. Fitting Limits for Bearings

The fit of the bearings in the hub barrel and sprocket/brake drum is important. The following are the manufacturing tolerances which control this and also the fits on the fixed and loose portions of the wheel spindle.

RLS5 Bearing o/d	1.5622/1.5617 in.
Hub Barrel bore	1.5620/1.5616 in.
RLS5 Bearing bore	.6252/.6248 in.
Loose Spindle dia.	.624/.622 in.
RLS7 Bearing o/d	1.9995/1.9990 in.
Sprocket bore	1.9994/1.9990 in.
RLS7 Bearing bore	.8752/.8748 in.
Fixed Spindle dia.	.8749/.8745 in.

All inner races are locked in position when the spindle nuts are tightened. The outer race of the RLS7 bearing is located by a screwed retaining ring and one of the RLS5 bearings is located by a circlip. Axial movement of the sprocket and/or barrel is therefore not possible. We recommend "Loctite" Sealant Grade C to secure any outer races which appear to have been rotating.

146. Removal of Hub Driving Pins

To remove the six driving pins from the aluminium full-width hub, first remove the hub cap after unscrewing the three screws attaching it to the hub. Unscrew the six Simmonds nuts and drive out the pins.

147. Refitting Ball Bearings

To refit the sprocket/brake drum bearing, use a hollow drift as shown in Fig. 47. The bearing is first fitted to the fixed section of the spindle; the spindle and bearing are then entered into the sprocket/brake drum and driven home, preferably under a press or using light hammer blows.

The two bearings in the hub barrel are pressed in, using the drift part of E.4823. First assemble the bearing into the circlip grooved end of the barrel and fit the circlip. Replace the bearing spacer, the slot in the spacer can be at either end of the hub, and assemble the second bearing, supporting the hub on the inner race of the other bearing. If the drift part of E.4823 is not available it is essential that the last bearing is assembled by applying pressure to both inner and outer races simultaneously to avoid pre-loading the two hub barrel bearings.

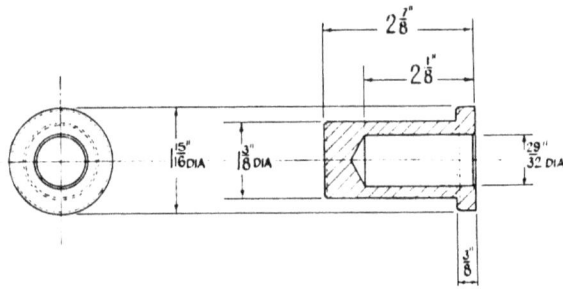

DRIFT FOR REFITTING RLS7 BEARING
Fig. 47

148. Reassembly of Brake Shoes and Operating Cam into Cover Plate

No difficulty should be experienced in carrying out these operations. Put a smear of grease on the pivot pin and on the operating face of the cam; also on to the cylindrical bearing surface of the operating cam if this has been removed. Fit the operating lever and trunnion on its splines in a position to suit the extent of wear on the linings and secure with the nut. The range of adjustment can be extended by moving the lever on to a different spline.

149. Final Reassembly of Hub Before Replacing Wheel

Before replacing the felt washers which form the grease seals, pack all bearings with grease. If new felt seals are fitted, soak these in engine oil.

Recommended greases are:— Shell Retinax A, Castrolease LM, Esso Multipurpose Grease H, B.P. Energrease L2, Mobilgrease MP and Marfak Multipurpose Grease 2. These are all lithium soap greases and should not be mixed with lime, aluminium or soda soap greases.

Make sure that the inside of the brake drum is free from oil, grease, dust or damp. Replace the felt washers, distance collars and brake cover plate and securely tighten the spindle nuts.

150. Wheel Rim

The wheel rim is WM3-18 in. plunged and pierced with forty holes for spoke nipples. The spoke holes are symmetrical, i.e., the rim can be assembled to the hub either way round. The rim diameter after building is 18.06 in. the tolerances on the circumference of the rim shoulders where the tyre fits being 56.783/56.723 in. The standard steel measuring tape for checking rims is $\frac{1}{4}$ in. wide, .011 in. thick, and its length is 56.843/56.783 in.

151. Spokes

The spokes, Part No. 40636, are of the single-butted type, 8-10 gauge, with 90° countersunk heads and rolled threads, .144 in. diameter, 40 t.p.i., thread form British Standard Cycle, $6\frac{3}{16}$ in. long. All spokes initially are bent to approximately 110° at the head end. Spokes threaded from the outside of the spoke flanges are hit with a hide hammer after lacing, but before truing the wheel to make them fit close to the flange. This increases the bend to approximately 80°.

152. Wheel Building and Truing

The spokes are laced one over two and the wheel rim must be built central in relation to the outer faces of the distance collars. The rim should be trued as accurately as possible, the maximum permissible run-out both sideways and radially being plus or minus $\frac{1}{32}$ in.

153. Tyre

The standard tyre is Dunlop Gold Seal K70, 4.00 × 18 in.

When removing the tyre always start close to the valve and see that the edge of the cover at the other side of the wheel is pushed down into the well in the rim.

When replacing the tyre fit the part by the valve last, also with the edge of the cover at the other side of the wheel pushed down into the well. Slightly inflate the tube and, if available, paint the rim and tyre with soapy water, or water containing a soapless detergent to assist the tyre in slipping over the edge of the rim.

If the correct method of fitting and removal of the tyre is adopted it will be found that the covers can be manipulated quite easily with the small levers supplied in the tool-kit. The use of long levers and/or excessive force is liable to damage the walls of the tyre. After inflation make sure that the tyre is fitting evenly all the way round the rim. A line moulded on the wall of the tyre indicates whether or not the tyre is correctly fitted. If the tyre has a white mark indicating a balance point, this should be fitted near the valve.

154. Tyre Pressures

With a solo rider of normal weight (154 lbs.) the correct tyre pressure is 21 lb. per sq. in. for 4.00-18 in. tyres. If the rider's weight exceeds 154 lbs. increase the pressure by 1 lb. per sq. in. for every 14 lb. increase in weight above 154 lb.

If additional load is carried in the form of a pillion passenger or luggage, the actual load bearing upon the tyre should be determined and the pressure increased in accordance with the following table.

Tyre Section ins.	Maximum Load lb. at Pressure of lbs. per sq. in.					
	16	18	20	24	28	32
3.25	200	230	260	320	380	440
3.50	280	310	335	390	450	500
4.00	360	395	430	500	570	640

155. Lubrication

Grease the bearings by packing them with grease after removal of the brake cover plate and speedometer drive gearbox as described above.

Note that the brake cam is drilled for a grease passage but the end of this is stopped up with a countersunk screw instead of being fitted with a grease nipple. This is done to prevent excessive greasing by over-enthusiastic owners. If the cam is smeared with grease on assembly it should require no further attention but in case of necessity it is possible to remove the screw, fit a grease nipple in its place and grease the cam by this means.

Special Tools

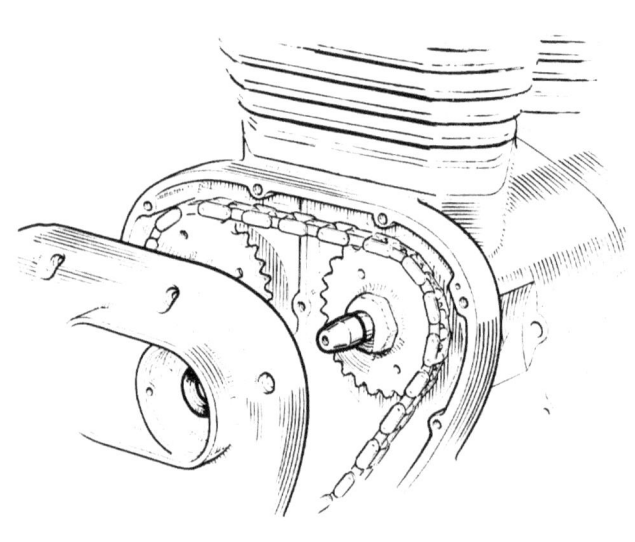

W.49994
CAMSHAFT SEAL ASSEMBLY THIMBLE

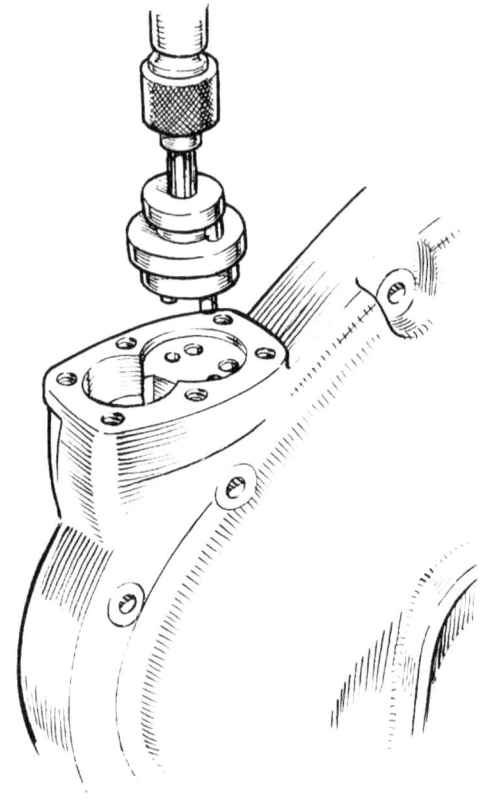

E.5425
PUMP DISC LAPPING TOOL

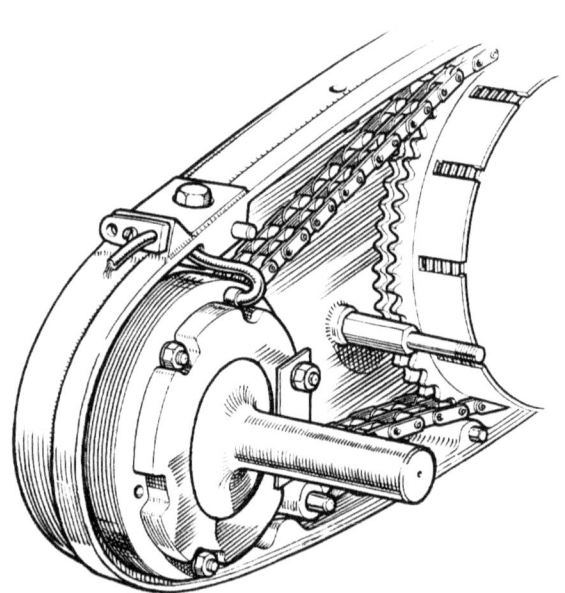

T.2055/19
ASSEMBLY GAUGE IN USE TO
CENTRALISE ROTOR

W.49926
GEARBOX COLLAR (SPLINED) EXTRACTOR

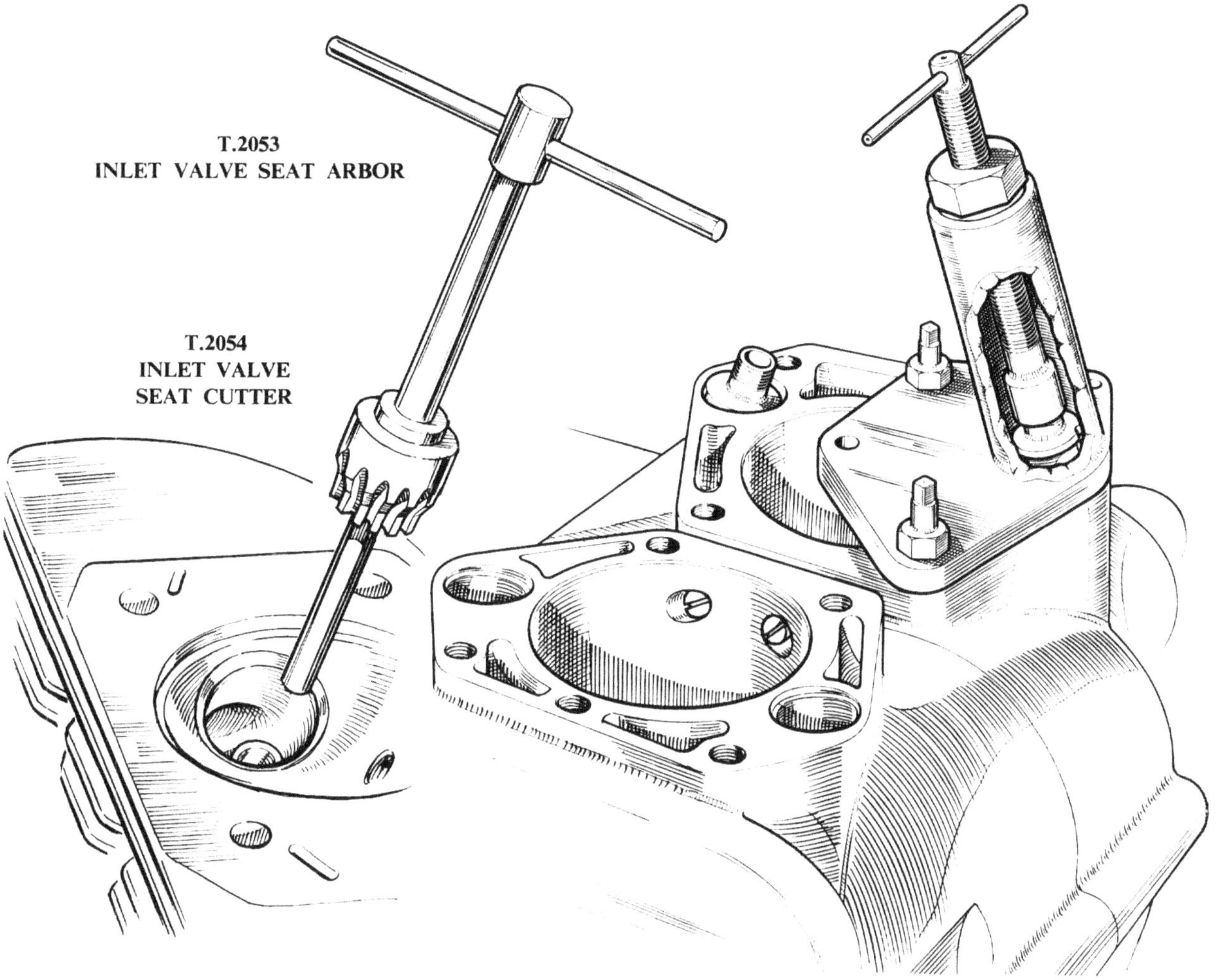

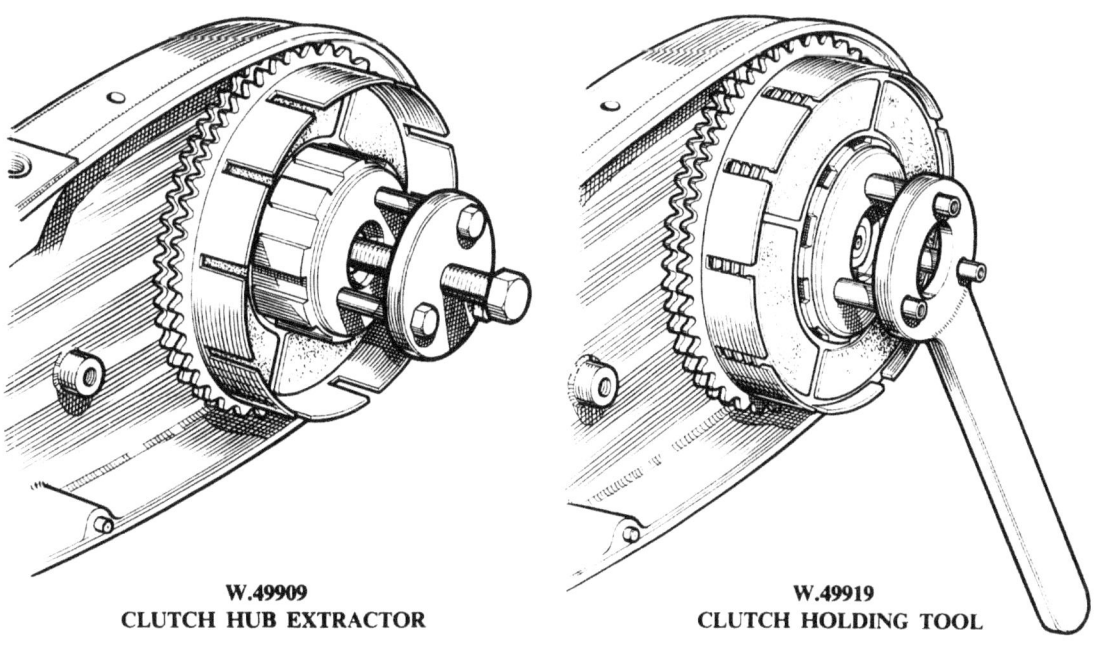

T.2053 INLET VALVE SEAT ARBOR

T.2054 INLET VALVE SEAT CUTTER

W.49925 TAPPET GUIDE EXTRACTOR

W.49909 CLUTCH HUB EXTRACTOR

W.49919 CLUTCH HOLDING TOOL

W.49907
CAMSHAFT SPROCKET EXTRACTOR

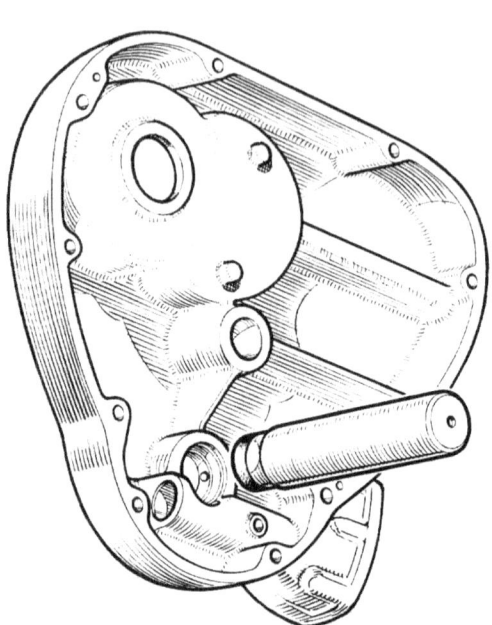

W.50011
DRIFT FOR ASSEMBLY OF TIMING COVER SEALS

W.49910
CRANKSHAFT EXTRACTOR

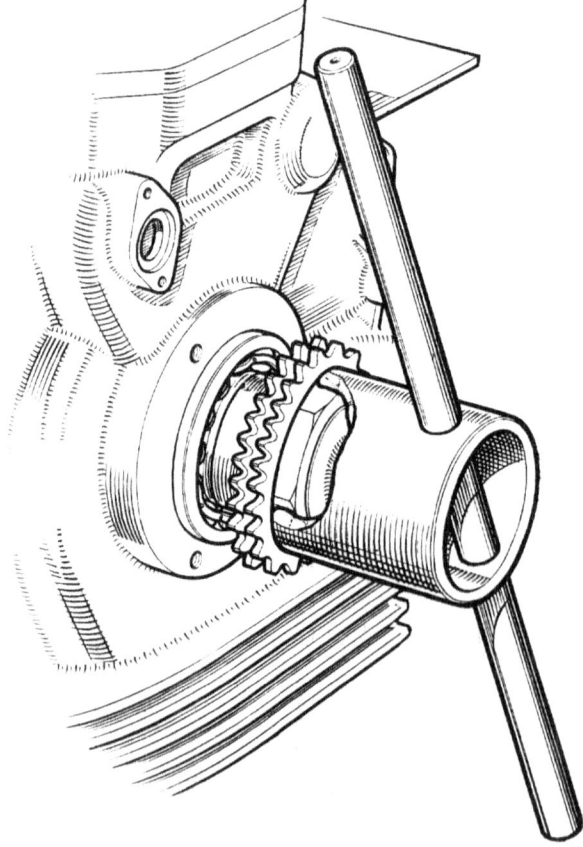

W.49908
ENGINE SPROCKET NUT SPANNER

NOTES

IMPORTANT

Each of the 5 individual manuals included in this publication have their own specific index and corresponding page numbers.

The numbers to the bottom center of the page is the page number within each 'Section' as referenced in the 'Section' index below.

SECTION 2 - ILLUSTRATED PARTS MANUALS – INDEX

MK1/Series I - Parts Manual	Pages 1-56
MK1A/Series IA - Parts Manual	Pages 57-112
MK2/Series II - Parts Manual	Pages 113-166
1970 MK2/Series II - Supplement	Pages 167-173

Price 2/-

A List of
SPARE & REPLACEMENT PARTS
for the
1963 - 1966
Royal Enfield
'Made like a Gun'

"INTERCEPTOR"
MOTOR CYCLE

●

THE
ENFIELD CYCLE COMPANY LIMITED
Head Office & Works:
REDDITCH, WORCESTERSHIRE
ENGLAND

Telegrams:
"*Cycles, Redditch.*"

Telephone:
Redditch 4222 (9 lines)

INDEX

	Page
Alternator	52
Battery	48
Brake Control, Rear	46
Carburettor	24, 24A
Chains & Covers	14, 44
Clutch	22
Colour Key	28
Crankcase	4
Crankshaft	8
Cylinder	6
" Head	6
Dual Seat	48
Electrical Equipment	52–54
Engine	4-12
Estimates and Quotations	3
Exhaust Pipes	46
Footrests	46
Frame	40
Front Fork	30, 32
Gearbox	16-20
" Bracket	40
Guarantee	56
Handlebar	26
" Controls	26
" Control Cables	28
Lamps	54
Magneto	52
Mudguard, Front, and Number Plate	34
" Rear, and Number Plate	42
Oil Filter	12
" Pump	12
Pannier Fittings	48
Petrol Tank	34
Pillion Footrests	44
Piston	8
Rectifier	52
Revolution counter	32
Silencer	46
Speedometer	50
Stand, Centre	40
" Front	34
" Prop	44
Suspension, Rear	42
Terms of Business	3
Timing Cover	10
" Gear	10
Toolbox	48
Toolkit	50
Wheel & Brake, Front	36
" " Rear	36, 38

Shakeproof Washers. To avoid unnecessary repetition, these washers are listed separately on page 20.

State Colour when ordering enamelled parts. - See Page 28

TERMS OF BUSINESS

All prices of Spare and Replacement Parts are subject to revision or modification, at our discretion, without notice.

Our terms are STRICTLY NET CASH WITH ORDER, or cash on receipt of PRO-FORMA INVOICE. Repairs and sundries items cannot be booked. Prices do not include cost of carriage or postage which will be covered by a percentage surcharge on the nett invoice value. C.O.D. fees and the cost of packing cases or crates are additional to the fixed surcharge.

Any part or complete motor cycle sent for repair should be consigned CARRIAGE PAID and the sender's name and address should be given in full on the address tally. Parts sent to us carriage forward are liable to be refused, and to lie with the carriers at sender's risk and expense.

Full instructions regarding the necessary repairs to be done, with advice as to the mode of despatch of the machine (or part), should be posted the same day.

When forwarding motor cycles for repair it is advisable to remove all accessories and easily detached fittings, such as badges, mascots, tools, tyre inflator, etc. Besides facilitating the work of repair, it will also prevent any loss during transit.

Order all parts by the name of the article and the No. of Part, also state the number of the engine or machine for which they are intended. The engine number will be found stamped on the driving side of the crankcase below the cylinder barrel and the machine number at the top of the front down tube or head lug.

ESTIMATES AND QUOTATIONS

When customers send complete Motor Cycles or parts thereof to us for repairs, we are always prepared to furnish estimates before proceeding with the necessary work. At the same time, it must be distinctly understood that we can only give approximate quotations. Frequently, when the actual work is in progress, it is found necessary to replace parts other than those specified in the estimate, as we make a practice of including in such estimates only those items and parts which at the time we consider really essential to put the machine (or parts) in a thoroughly satisfactory condition.

If any estimate prepared in this way is not accepted, we reserve the right to make a nominal charge for taking down and re-assembling any parts necessary in preparing it.

We cannot hold ourselves responsible for loss of, or damage to, any parts lying at our Works for repairs, unless instructions to proceed with same are given within twenty-one days of our estimate for the said repairs having been rendered.

All welded repairs to crankcases and other aluminium parts are carried out with extreme care, but we cannot give any guarantee with or accept responsibility for, any parts so treated.

When forwarding a complete Motor Cycle, Engine, or other Assembly with the request that we overhaul the same, we understand by the term "Overhaul" that it is to be entirely dismantled, thoroughly renovated, any worn parts renewed, and put in perfect working order. In case a customer desires only certain parts attended to, full instructions should be given to that effect, otherwise the cost may be in excess of that anticipated.

GUARANTEE

We respectfully refer customers to the terms of guarantee on page 56.

ENGINE UNIT & CRANKCASE ASSEMBLY

Illus. No.	No. of part.	Description.	No. per set
	46155	Interceptor engine unit c/w carburettor, magneto sparking plugs and sprocket	1
8	46164	Crankcase assy. with main and camshaft bearings, tappets and guides and fixed studs	
9	45451	Stud, cylinder and head, $\frac{3}{8}''$ B.S.F. $\times 5''$	10
10	34968	" nut, shouldered $\frac{3}{8}'' \times \frac{3}{8}''$	2
	45448	" " shouldered $\frac{3}{8}'' \times 3\frac{3}{8}''$	4
11	45449	" " $\frac{3}{8}'' \times 4\frac{1}{8}''$ o'all	4
	1437	" washer	10
12 & 13	47208	Stud, gearbox, $\frac{3}{8}'' \times 6\frac{5}{3}'' \times 26$ (C.E.I.)	4
	29854	" nut	4
	15641	" washer	2
16	34368	Stud, crankcase, top, $\frac{5}{16}'' \times 4\frac{1}{2}'' \times 22$ (B.S.F.)	3
17	35589	" " rear, $\frac{5}{16}'' \times 4\frac{3}{8}'' \times 22$ (B.S.F.)	2
18	35595	" " " $\frac{1}{4}'' \times 6\frac{1}{4}'' \times 26$ (B.S.F.)	2
19	36079	" " front, $\frac{5}{16}'' \times 4\frac{1}{2}'' \times 26$ (C.E.I.)	3
20	44360	" " rear engine plate, $\frac{5}{16}'' \times 5'' \times 22$	1
21	34378	" " bottom, $\frac{1}{4}'' \times 8\frac{3}{8}'' \times 26$ (B.S.F.)	1
22	46167	" " " $\frac{1}{4}'' \times 7\frac{3}{8}'' \times 26$ (B.S.F.)	1
	27620	" nut, $\frac{1}{4}'' \times 26$ (B.S.F.)	8
	82	" washer, $\frac{1}{4}''$	8
	27621	" nut, $\frac{5}{16}'' \times 22$ (B.S.F.)	4
	8633	" " $\frac{5}{16}'' \times 26$ (C.E.I.)	6
	36221	" " $\frac{5}{16}'' \times 22$ (B.S.F.) Simmonds "Spinloc"	3
	8634	" washer, $\frac{5}{16}''$	5
	45370	Dowel for timing cover	1
27	40383	Oil filler extension	1
28	34365	" " " gasket	1
29	18275	" " " collar	1
30	35591	" " " screw, $\frac{1}{4}'' \times 1\frac{5}{8}'' \times 26$ (B.S.F.)	2
31	35592	" " " " $\frac{1}{4}'' \times \frac{5}{8}'' \times 26$ (B.S.F.)	1
32	42636	" " cap and dipstick	1
35	37884	Drain plug and filter assy.	1
35A	17024	" " " " washer	1
	26127	Drain plug	1
	46141	" " washer	1
	46181	Camshaft Tunnel Sealing Ring	2
	45452	Crankcase blanking screw	2
	5662	" " " washer	2
36	46152	Oil shield T/S crankcase	1
	46151	" " D/S "	1
	35636	" " screw, Parker Kalon, Type Z No. 4,	8
38	16476	Oil plug screw, $\frac{1}{4}'' \times \frac{7}{32}'' \times 26$ (B.S.F.)	2
39	34375	" " " $\frac{1}{4}'' \times \frac{1}{4}'' \times 26$ (B.S.F.)	2
40	34374	" " " $\frac{5}{16}'' \times \frac{1}{4}'' \times 22$ (B.S.F.)	1
42	34373	" " " $\frac{5}{16}'' \times \frac{9}{32}'' \times 22$ (B.S.F.)	1
	26177	" " " C'sk. head, $\frac{1}{4}'' \times \frac{3}{16}'' \times 26$	1
43	30394	" " " fibre washer, $\frac{1}{4}''$ dia.	2
44	36136	" " " " " $\frac{5}{16}''$ dia.	1
45	34381	" " " " " two hole	1
46	37724	Crankcase bridge screw	2
	34690	" " " washer	2
47	43359	" plug	2

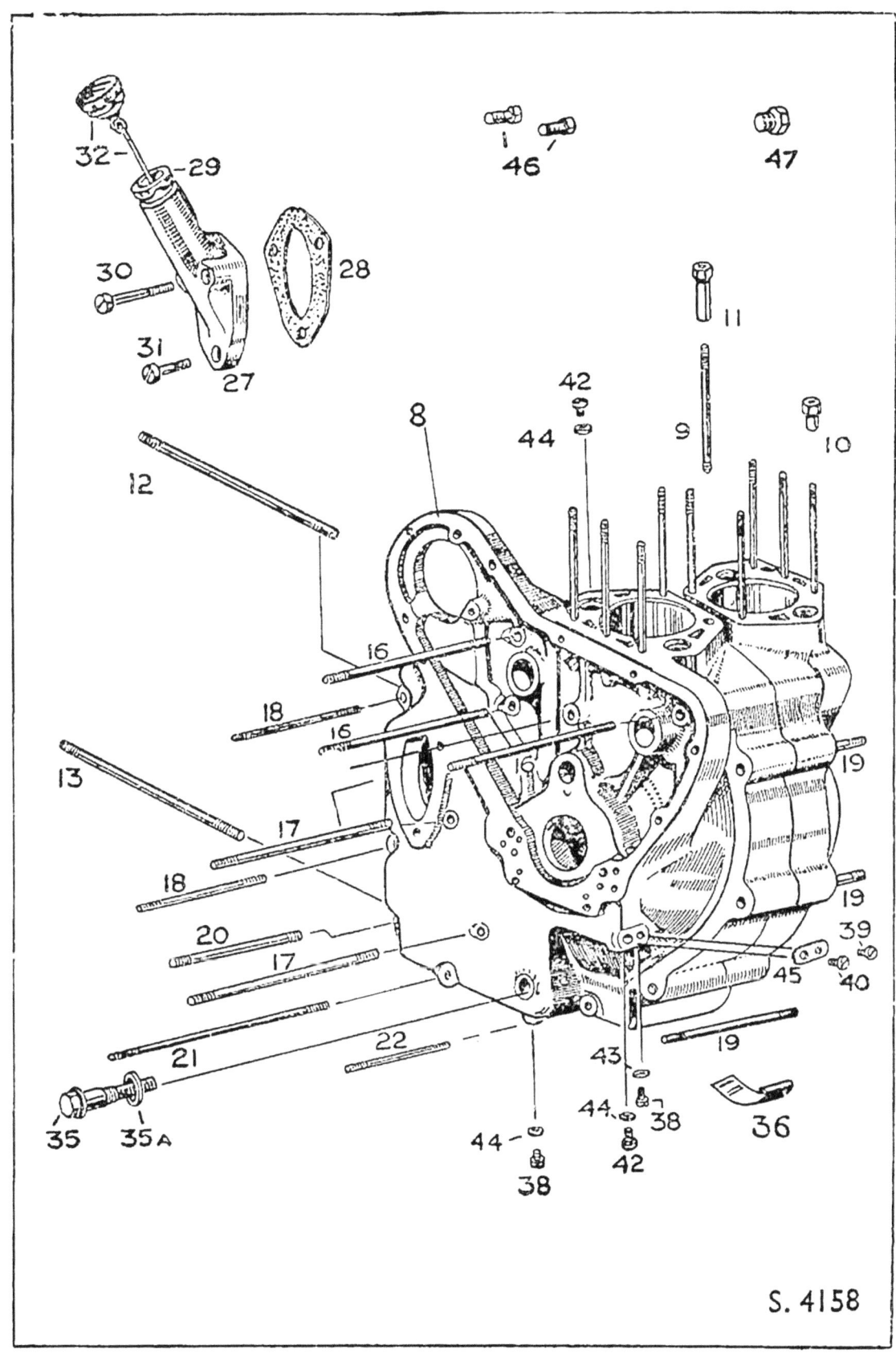

CYLINDER AND HEAD ASSEMBLY

Illus. No.	No. of part.	Description.	No. per set
3	42518	Carburettor gasket	2
8	42835	" flange screw, $\frac{5}{16}'' \times \frac{5}{8}'' \times 22$ (B.S.F.)— up to Engine No. YA15077	4
	46192	" flange screw, $\frac{5}{16}'' \times \frac{13}{16}'' \times 22$ (B.S.F.) } from Engine No. YA15078	4
	46191	" heat insulator washer	2
	46156	Cylinder head, R.H. } Fitted with valve guides and fixed studs	1
11	46153	" " L.H.	1
	45447	" " dowel	4
	46184	" " sealing ring	2
13	85780	" " engine steady stud, $\frac{5}{16}'' \times \frac{13}{16}''$ BSF.	4
	27621	" " " " " nut	4
	8634	" " " " " washer	4
14	82552	Rocker box cover	4
15	32553	" " " gasket	4
16	31262	" " " stud $\frac{1}{4}'' \times \frac{7}{8}'' \times 26$ (B.S.F.)	16
	87852	" " " " nut, $\frac{1}{4}''$ B.S.F.	16
	82	" " " " washer	16
19	89735	Rocker (Inlet R.H., Exhaust L.H.)	2
	89736	" (Inlet L.H., Exhaust R.H.)	2
20	32550	" adjusting screw	4
21	32549	" " locknut	4
22	38644	Rocker spindle	4
23	88985	" " end plug	4
25	89468	" " " " washer (copper)	4
26	32554	" " thrust washer	4
27	85904	" " spring washer	4
28	43521	Valve, exhaust	2
	42661	" inlet	2
29	42660	" guide	4
30	42693	Valve spring, inner	4
31	42692	" " outer	4
32	42651	" collar, top	4
33	42652	" " bottom	4
34	42492	" split cotter	8
36	46129	Cylinder barrel	2
37	45450	" base gasket	4
	46150	Push rod tunnel oil seals	4
	46189	" " " " " shims, $\cdot 015''$	4
	ST239	Gasket set, decarbonisation only	1
	ST240	" " complete engine and chaincase	1

In. 6. 63

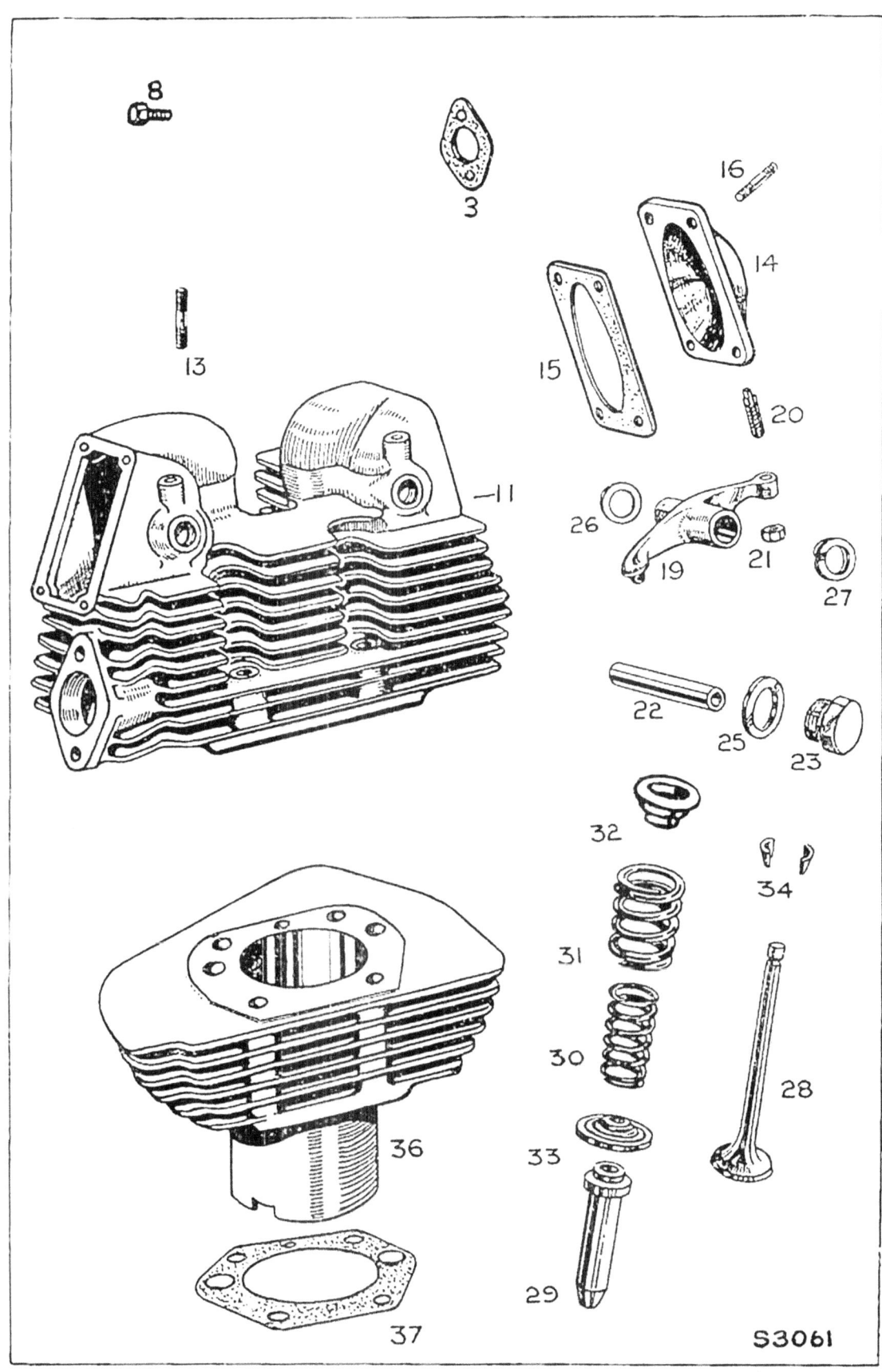

PISTONS AND CRANKSHAFT ASSEMBLY

Illus. No.	No. of part.	Description.	No. per set
1	*46160	Piston c/w rings, gudgeon pin, and circlips, ratio 8:1	2
2	46161	Piston ring, (top, chrome plated)	2
3	46162	" " (lower, compression)	2
4	46163	" " (twin segment scraper)	2
5	47178	Gudgeon pin	2
6	38771	" " circlip	4
7	‡41719/B	Connecting rod assy. c/w B.E. screws and shells	2
8	47876	" " B.E. screw	4
10	14691	" " " " washer	4
	45444	" " inserts	4
	36017	" " S.E. bush (for Service use)	2
11	‡41722	" " B.E. bearing shell (one half)	4
14	SK/N209	Crankshaft timing-side roller bearing, 45 × 85 × 19 m.m.	1
15	36275/A	" timing-side roller bearing steel washer	1
16	SK/6209	" drive side bearing, 45 × 85 × 19 m.m.	1
17	34062	" " bearing distance collar	1
18	41965A	Engine sprocket 29T.	1
19	34076	" " washer	1
20	34064	" " locknut	1
	46168	Crankshaft assy. c/w connecting rods	1
21	46169	" only	1
22	44510	" oil plug	2
24	45403	" bolt and breather	1
	42030	" " washer	1
25	41327	Oil return pipe and adaptor	1
	29781	Adaptor screw	2

*Pistons and piston rings are available ·020″ oversize. To order, suffix /20 to the part number. Thus: 46160/20 piston complete ·020″ oversize.

‡Connecting rods, either new or service, can be supplied with B.E. bearing shells ·010″ or ·020″ undersize to suit ground down crankshafts; suffix /10 or /20 to the part number thus: 41719B/10 and 41719B/20.

†Service crankshafts are available ·010″ and ·020″ undersize on the B.E. journal and are numbered 46169/10 and 46169/20, respectively.

In. 8. 63

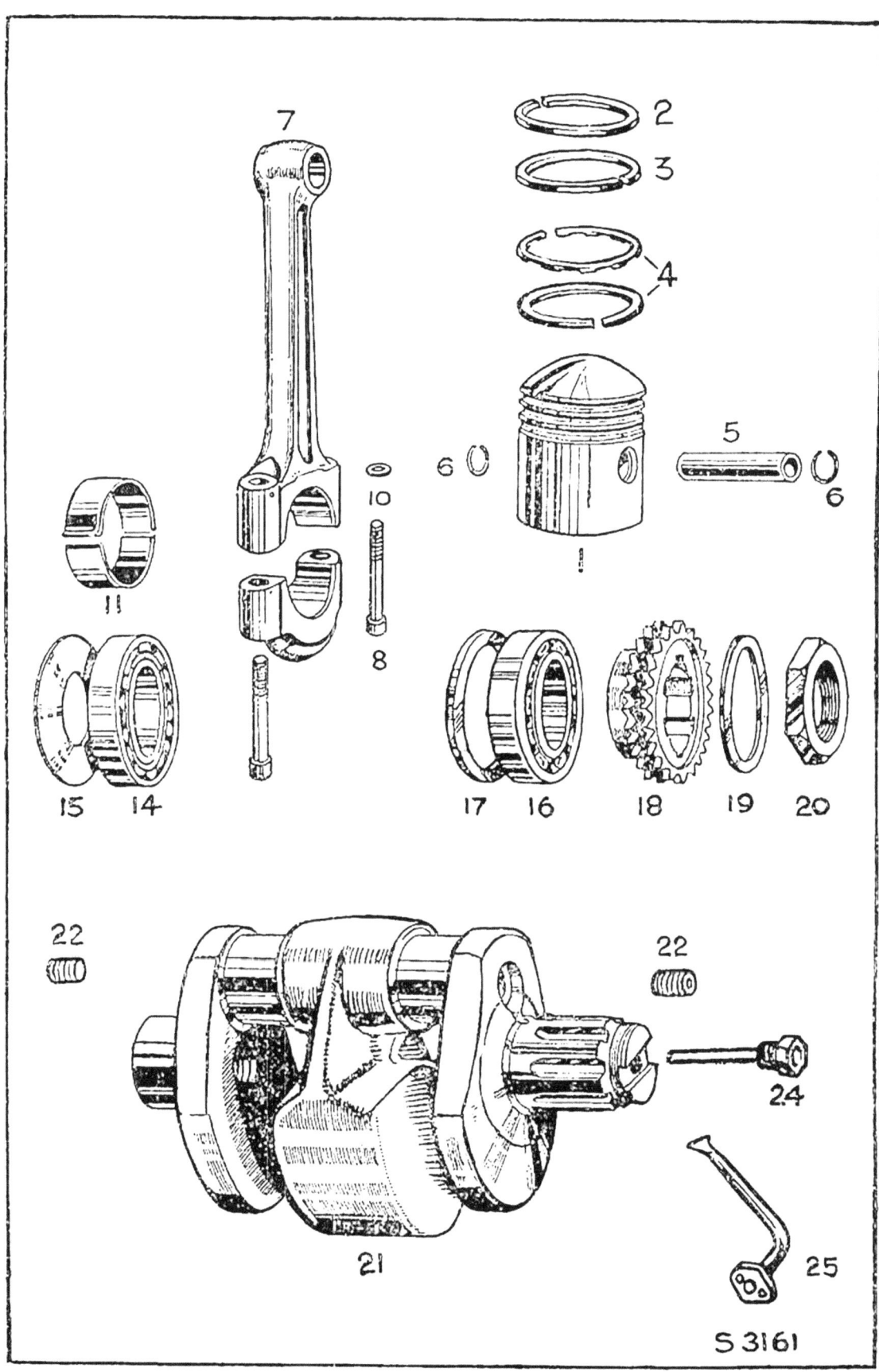

TIMING COVER & TIMING GEAR ASSEMBLY

Illus. No.	No. of part.	Description.	No. per set
1	46127/B	Timing cover	1
2	46170	" " gasket	1
3	42133	" " screw $\frac{1}{4}'' \times 1\frac{13}{16}'' \times 26$ (B.S.F.)	2
	42139	" " " $\frac{1}{4}'' \times 1\frac{1}{4}'' \times 26$ (B.S.F.)	5
	42140	" " " $\frac{1}{4}'' \times 1\frac{7}{16}'' \times 26$ (B.S.F.)	2
	42136	" " " $\frac{1}{4}'' \times 2'' \times 26$ (B.S.F.)	3
4	34690	" " " washer	12
	28858	" " oil passage screw, $\frac{3}{16}'' \times \frac{1}{4}'' \times 32$	4
5	42458	Tachometer drive cover	1
6	42504	" " " gasket	1
	45411	" " " screw	2
7	46185	Push rod assy. (alloy)	4
8	38052	" " end, top	4
9	37839	" " " bottom	4
10	23480	Tappet	4
11	34360	" guide	4
12	32705/A	Camshaft	2
16	32709	" bearing (timing side)	2
17	32710	" " (L.H. side)	2
18	35894	" thrust washer	2
	42528	" shim	-
19	43348	" bearing housing c/w bearing	2
	43345	" " " only	2
19A	43346	" " " gasket	4
	45385	" " " screw Unbrako, $\frac{3}{16}'' \times \frac{1}{2}''$	6
20	RN/114500/44	Magneto duplex chain, endless, 8 mm. × 44 pitches	1
21	38602	" sprocket	1
	14538	" " nut	1
22	35735	Timing sprocket 12T	1
23	35724	" " peg	1
24	34350	Camshaft sprocket, exhaust	1
25	36140	" " inlet.	1
26	9410	Sprocket key	2
27	41534	" securing bolt, exhaust $\frac{1}{2}'' \times \frac{7}{8}'' \times 26$ L.H.	1
28	36142	" " " inlet $\frac{1}{2}'' \times 1\frac{1}{4}'' \times 26$ L.H.	1
29	15380	" " " washer	2
30	34372	Chain tensioning sprocket and bush	1
31	34354	" " " bush only	1
32	34353	" " " thrust washer	1
33	38552	" " " spindle	1
34	34351	" " plate	1
35	29314	" " " stud, $\frac{1}{4}'' \times \frac{7}{8}'' \times 26$	1
	36222	" " " " nut	1
	82	" " " " washer	1
36	RN/110038/66	Timing chain, endless, 66 pitches	1

In. 10. 63.

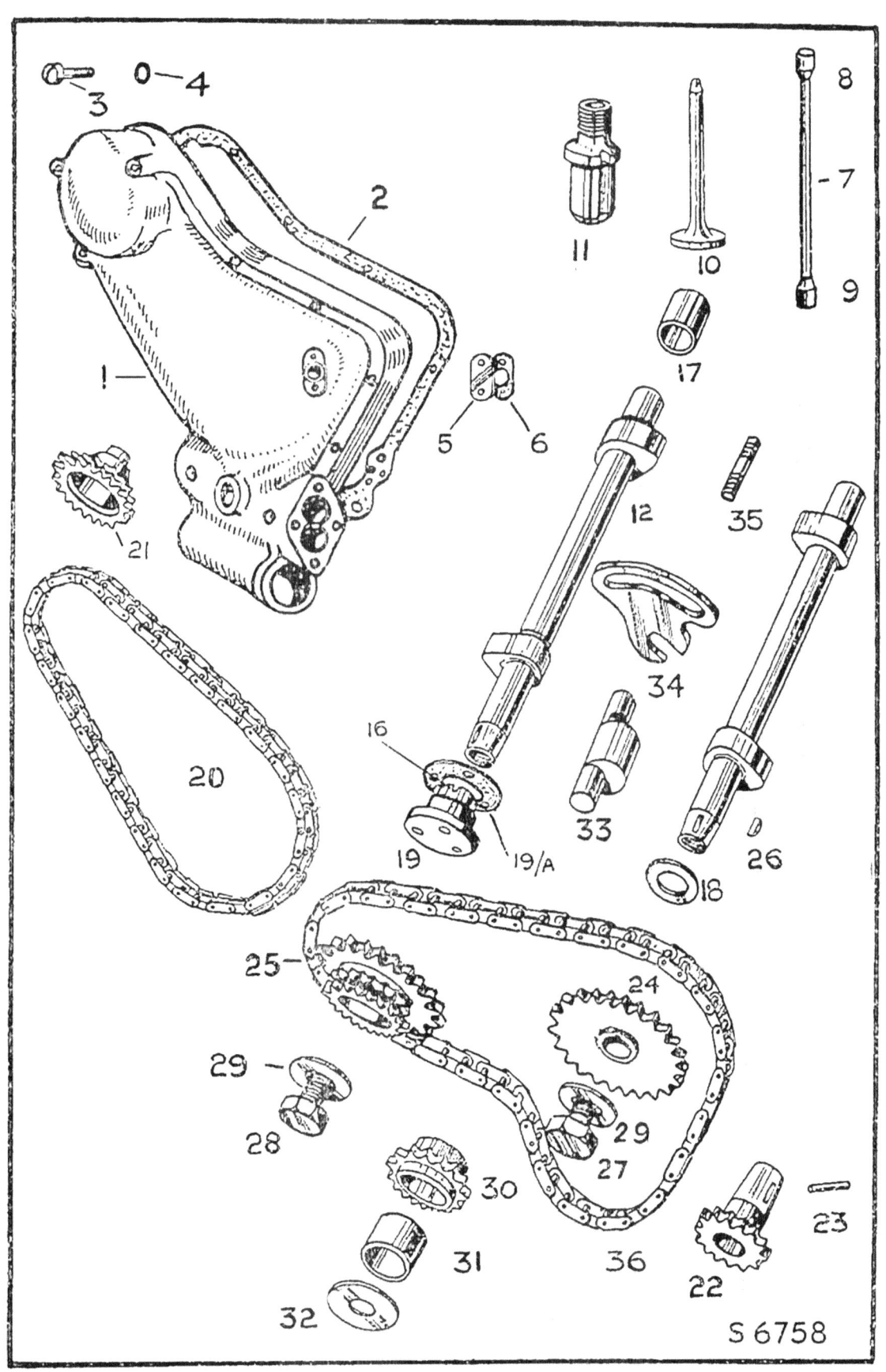

OIL PUMP, FILTER ASSEMBLY AND CRANKCASE BREATHER

Illus. No.	No. of part.	Description.	No. per set
1	42113	Oil feed plug	1
2	24177	" " " fibre washer	1
3	38622	Oil pump worm (2 start)	1
4	42114	" " " rubber seal	1
6	38623	" " spindle	1
7	37665A	" " disc (feed)	1
8	37666A	" " " (return)	1
9	41851	" " " spring	2
9A	37669	" " " " end pad	2
10	34346	" " plunger (feed)	1
11	34347	" " " (return)	1
11A	46142	" " spindle loc. screw	1
12	45382	" " cover	2
13	45383	" " " gasket	2
13A	45385	" " " screw, $\frac{3}{16}'' \times \frac{1}{2}'' \times 32$	12
14	40792	Oil cleaner element	1
15	40684	" " " filling piece	1
16	28254	" " spring cup	1
17	18793	" " " " felt washer	1
18	8894	" " " thrust washer	1
19	28255	" " stud, $\frac{3}{8}'' \times 6\frac{1}{4}''$	1
	13785	" " " washer	1
	26996	" " " locknut	1
20	28259	" " spring	1
21	28256	" " cap	1
22	28258	" " " washer	1
23	23748	" " " nut	1
	8894	" " " " washer	3
24	42505	" " magnet	1
26	47702	" feed pipe complete R.H.	1
27	47705	" " " " L.H.	1
28	32389	" " union body	6
29	39469	" " " " washer (copper)	12
30	38621	Union body wire insert (in crankcase & heads)	6
31	46197	Oil release valve plug ⎫ In timing	1
32	39974	" " " spring ⎬ cover joint	1
33	32017	" " " ball ⎭ face	1
34	47672	Crankcase breather body & pipe	1
35	39879	" " disc	2
36	39880	" " backplate	1
	26648	" " screw, $\frac{3}{16}'' \times \frac{11}{16}''$	2
	26664	" " " $\frac{3}{16}'' \times \frac{3}{8}''$	1
37	46195	" " pipe connector	1
38	13785	" " fibre washer	1
	47674	" " tube	1

In. 12. 63.

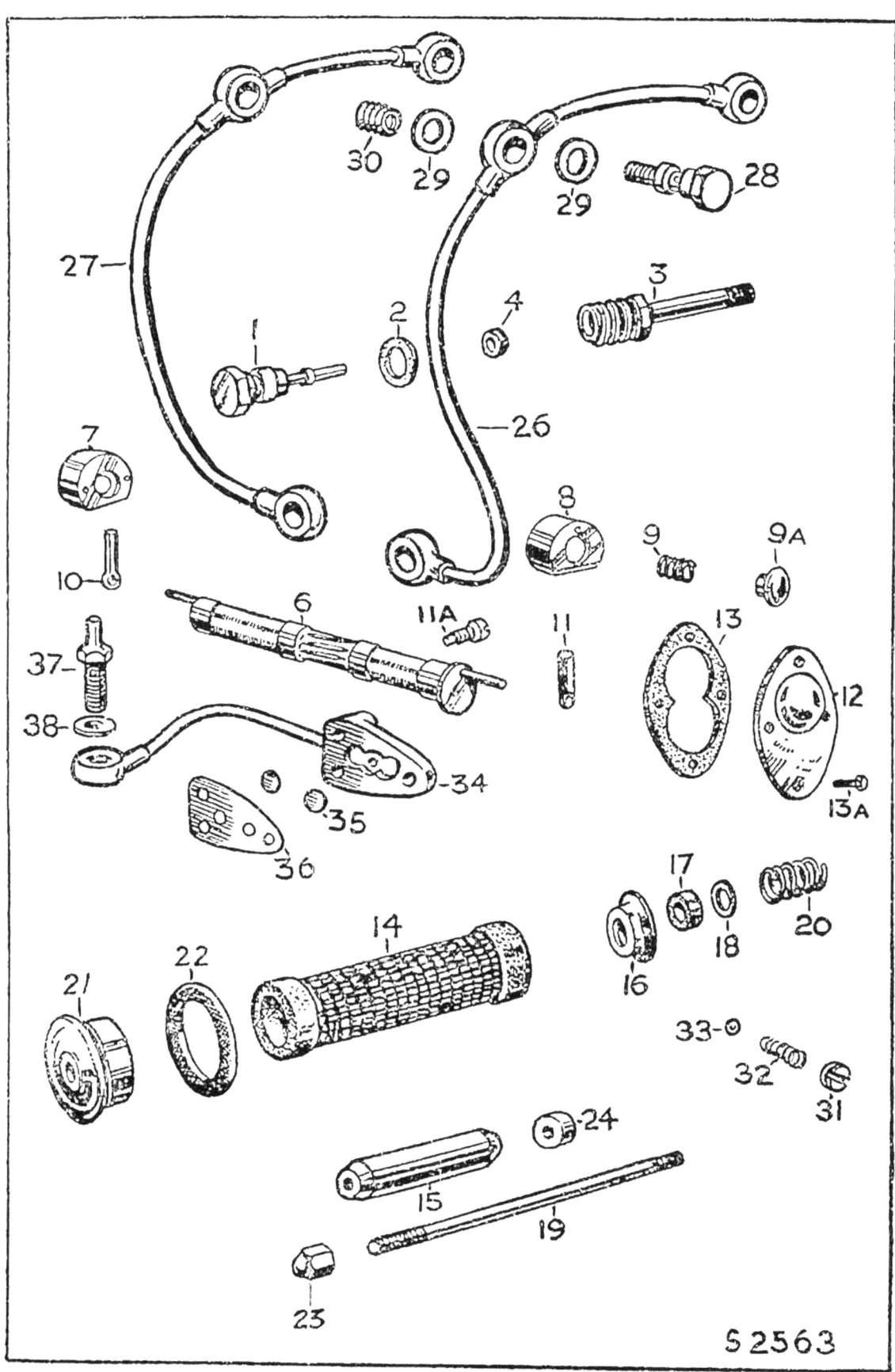

PRIMARY CHAINCASE

Illus. No.	No. of part.	Description.	No. per set
1	45372	Chaincase (back)	1
2	43405	" (front)	1
3	40097	Chaincase rubber joint	1
4	38027	" (back) fixing screw $\frac{5}{16}'' \times 1''$ o'all $\times 26$	3
5	45373	" dowel	2
6	43565	Oil seal (gearbox mainshaft)	1
10	45386	Chain tensioner	1
12	36911	" " spindle	1
13	45367/1/2/3	" " adjusting screw with buffer	1
14	15771	" " " " locknut	1
16	39664	" " spring	1
17	45387	Chaincase (front) fixing stud	1
18	35032	" stud nut	1
18A	1580	" " washer	1
19	40640	" inspection cover	2
20	40641	" " " washer	2
21	35704	Oil level plug	1
22	31497	" " " fibre washer	1
24	43382	Oil seal	1
25	34069	" " washer (outer) $3\frac{21}{64}'' \times 2\frac{9}{32}'' \times .024''$	2
26	34068	" " " (inner) $3\frac{21}{64}'' \times 2\frac{7}{8}'' \times .007''$	1
27	42268	Chaincase cable grommet	1
28	42269	" " " housing	1
	31172	" " " " screw	1
30	45404	" breather pipe assy.	1
31	36999	" " banjo	1
32	37000	" " " union	1
	30395	" " " fibre washer $\frac{3}{8}'' \times \frac{5}{8}'' \times \frac{3}{64}''$	1
	13785	" " " " $\frac{25}{64}'' \times \frac{11}{16}'' \times \frac{1}{16}''$	1
	45443	Stator fixing stud	3
	27944	" " nut	3
	45388	" " distance collar	3
	42834	Cable hole plug	1

In. 14. 63

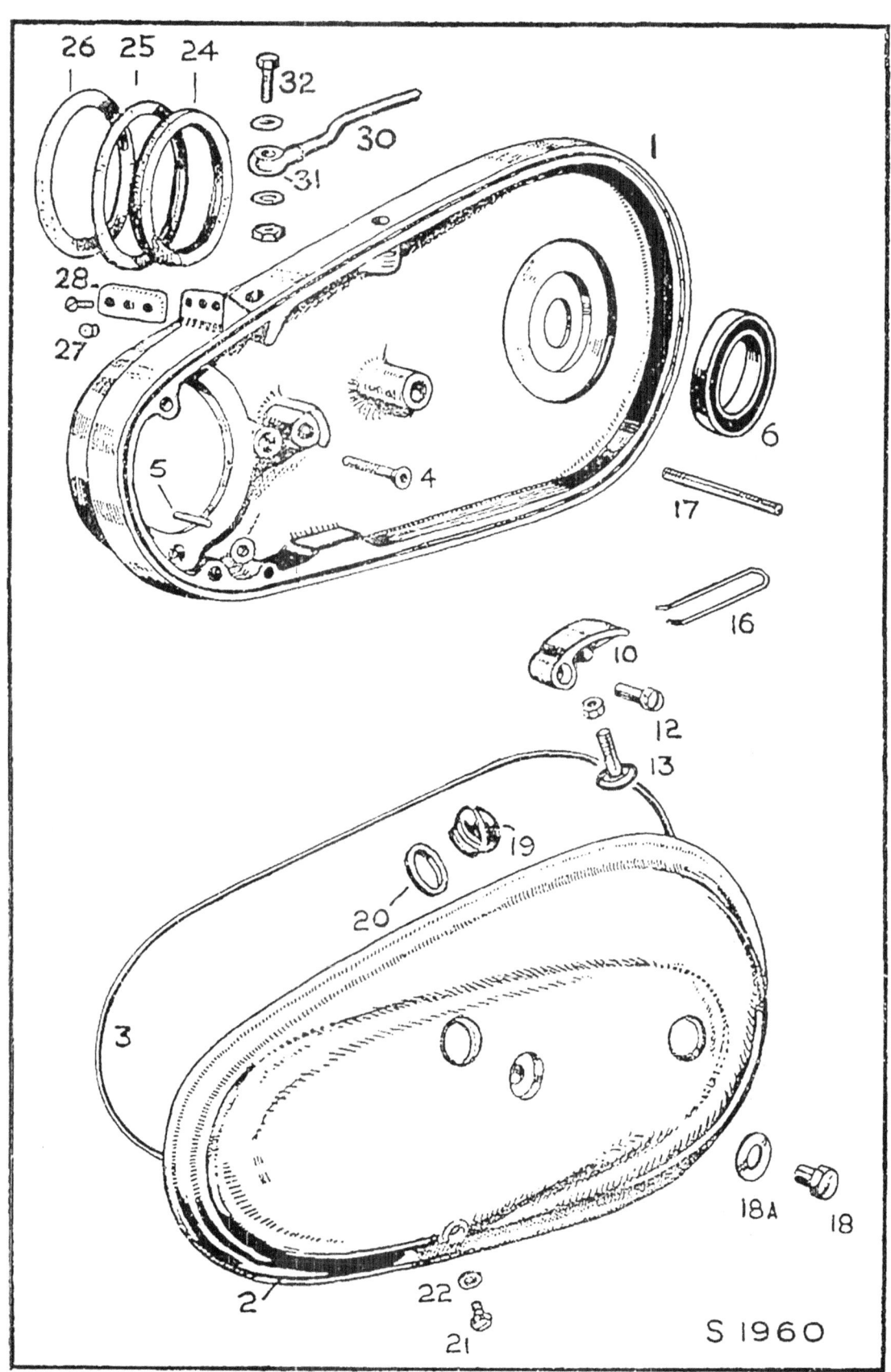

GEAR BOX

Illus. No.	No. of part.	Description.	No. per set
	46135	Gearbox c/w Clutch, 21T sprocket	1
1	33885/1	″ case c/w seal	1
2	37518A	″ ″ end cover	1
3	FC/57/107	″ ″ cover screw ch/hd. $\frac{1}{4}''\times1\frac{7}{16}''\times20$	2
	FC/57/103	″ ″ ″ ″ $\frac{1}{4}''\times1\frac{3}{16}''\times20$	2
4	H54/103	″ ″ bolt, $\frac{1}{4}''\times1\frac{3}{16}''\times20$	1
	G2/14	Oil hole screw, ch/hd. $\frac{1}{4}''\times\frac{3}{16}''\times24$	1
5	HJ73	End cover inspection cap	2
6	H60/1	Inspection cap pin, $\frac{3}{16}''\times\frac{3}{8}''$ B.S.F.	1
	H60/1A	″ ″ ″ $\frac{3}{16}''\times1\frac{1}{4}''$ B.S.F.	1
7	E140	Oil filler plug or drain plug	2
	E140A	″ ″ ″ ″ ″ ″ washer	2
8	BJ23	″ level plug	1
	BJ23A	″ ″ ″ washer	1
9	G2/7/TA	Mainshaft	1
10	H5	″ ball race (large) SK/6206	1
11	H3/2	″ ″ oil seal	1
13	31966	″ ″ ″ (small) M.S.7.	1
14	H71	″ ″ ″ oil thrower (outer)	1
15	H52	″ ″ ″ ″ ″ (inner)	1
16	H40/1	″ ″ ″ ″ ″ cap	1
17	FC57/009	″ ″ ″ ″ ″ pin, ch/hd. $\frac{1}{4}''\times\frac{9}{16}''$	2
18	G2/8B	″ sleeve (bushed)	1
19	HG9/15	″ high gear 15T	1
20	H10A	″ ″ ″ dog	1
21	HG11/21/18	″ sliding gear 21T and 18T	1
22	HG12/25	″ low gear 25T	1
23	H55	″ nut (R.H. thread), clutch end	1
24	H56	″ ″ (L.H. ″), K.S. end	1
25	H57	″ spring washer	1
	H91	″ (L.H.T.) nut locking washer	1

In. 16. 63

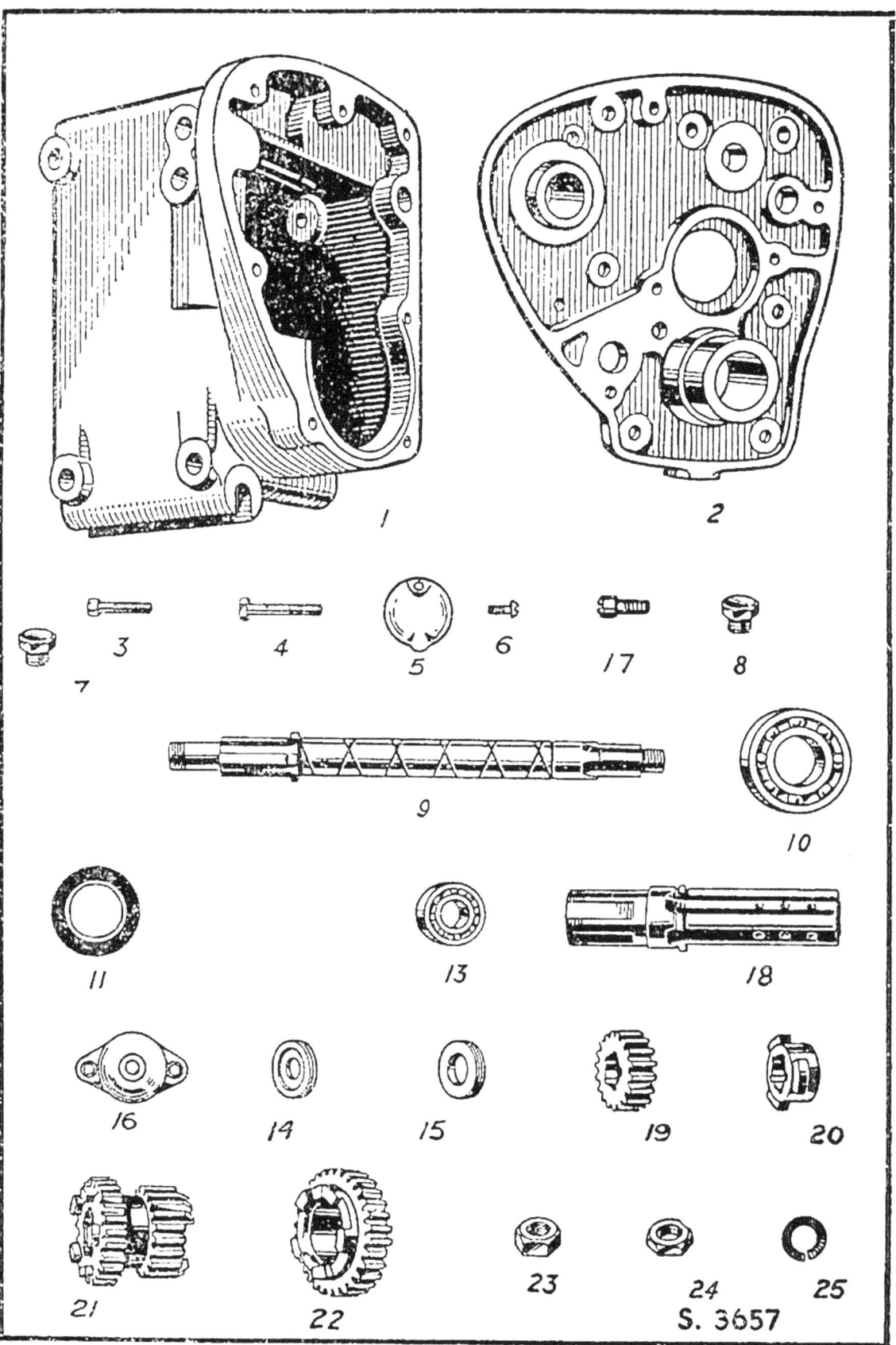

GEAR BOX—Contd. (I)

Illus. No.	No. of part	Description	No. per set
1	M13	Layshaft	1
2	H14	" bush (case end)	1
3	H15	" " (kickstart end)	1
4	H16	" splined bush	1
5	HG17/15	" low gear 15T	1
6	HG18/19	" second gear 19T	1
7	HG19/22	" third gear 22T	1
8	HG20/25	" high gear and kickstart wheel 25T	1
9	H21/4	Footstarter spindle	1
10	H77	" " oil seal	1
	H15A	" " washer	1
11	37355	" pawl	1
12	H22A	" " plunger	1
13	H23	" " " spring	1
14	37356	" " stop plate	1
15	37357	" " " " bolt	2
16	E137/5	" return spring	1
17	H42/42A/6	Folding F/S crank assy.	1
18	H42/4	F/S pedal	1
19	H42B	" " bolt	1
20	H42C	" " lock spring	1
21	32018	" " " " ball	1
22	H43S	" crank bolt and nut	1
23	G46KS	" pedal rubber	1
24	H33	Gear operator (inside)	1
25	H34	" " fork	1
26	G2/36/1	" " pin	1
27	G2/37	" " bush	1
28	H67Ass.	" " selector box assembly	1
	H67B	" " " nut	1
	H67C	" " " washer	1
29	H49/21	Drive sprocket 21T solo	1
	G2/53	" " distance piece	1
31	45428	" " locknut	1
32	H121	" " " felt washer	1
33	H122	" " " screw	1

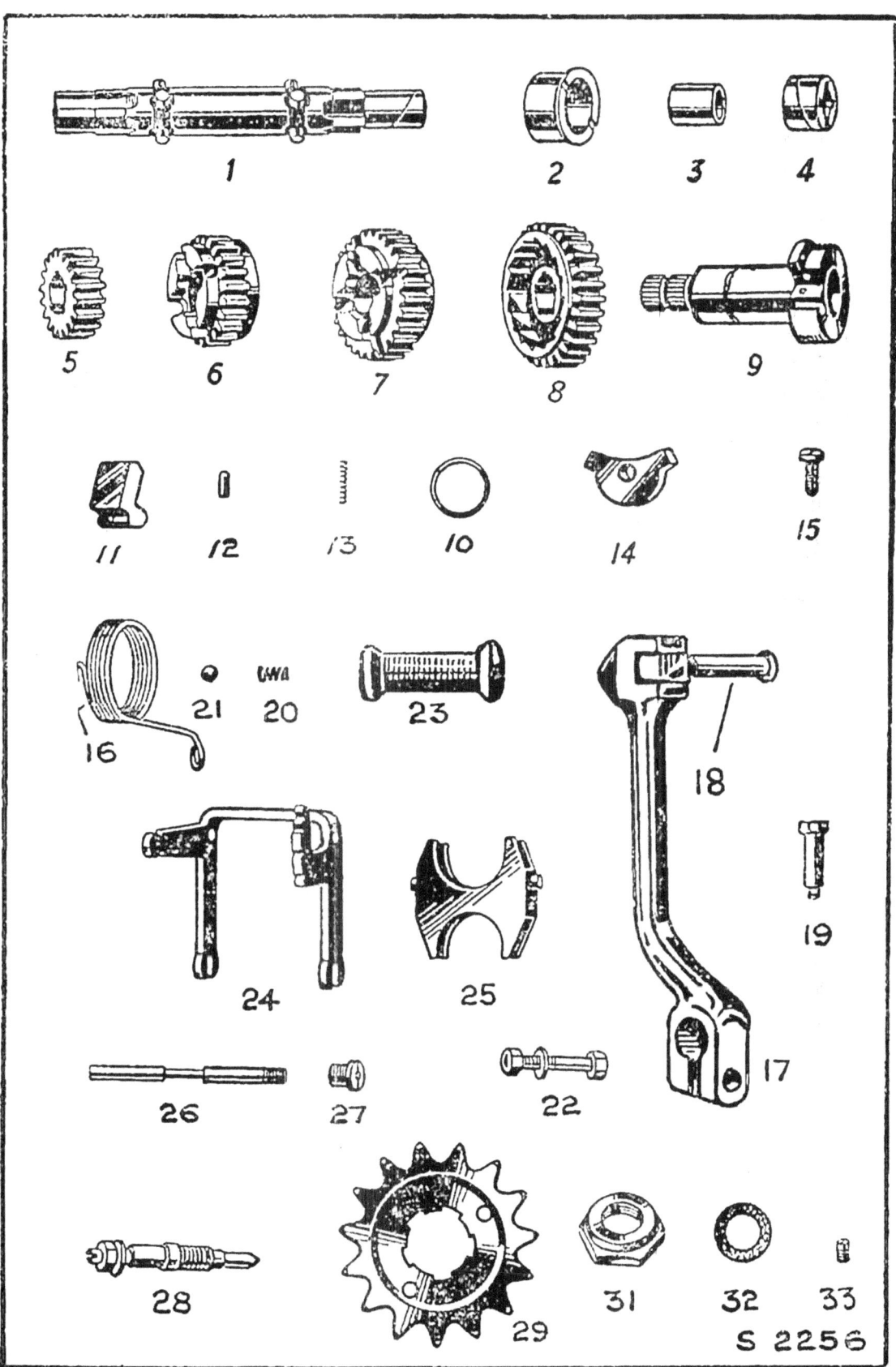

GEAR BOX—Contd. (2)

Illus. No.	No. of part	Description	No. per set
1	G2/1A/1	Foot control cover	1
2	FC57/212	F/C cover screw, ch/hd. $\frac{1}{4}'' \times 2\frac{3}{4}'' \times 20$	2
	FC57/103	" " " " $\frac{1}{4}'' \times 1\frac{3}{16}'' \times 20$	2
	G2/14	" " oil hole screw, ch/hd. $\frac{1}{4}'' \times \frac{3}{16}'' \times 24$	1
3	HFC4	" ratchet (inner)	1
4	FC1/35/1	" " (outer)	1
5	FC44	" " pin	1
7	FC51	" " spring	1
8	FC41/1	" adjuster plate	1
9	FC43	" " " pin	2
10	FC58	" " " " bush	2
11	H113	" " " nut	2
12	FC45	" " " spring stop	1
13	FC53	" plate	1
14	FC54	" " pin bush	2
	FC46	" " spring stop	1
16	FC42/1	" stop plate and spring retainer	1
17	FC47/E	" operator shaft with lever	1
	FC6E	" " " bush	1
18	FC/30F	" lever	1
19	FC/30/A	" " pinch bolt	1
20	FC/48F	" " (short, inside)	1
21	FC/52/1	" " return spring	1
22	NS1/1	" neutral lever	1
23	NS2	" " " spring	1
24	NS3	" " " " cap	1
25	NS4	" " " " washer	1
26	NS6	" " " " eccentric bush	1
27	NS5	" " " " stop pin	1
28	NS8	" " " " securing pin	1
29	NS7/1	" gear indicator	1
30	NS9	" " " washer	1

Standard Shakeproof Washers

No. of part	Dia.	No. of part	Dia.
29058	$\frac{3}{16}''$	27918	$\frac{3}{8}''$
27916	$\frac{1}{4}''$	27919	$\frac{7}{16}''$
27917	$\frac{5}{16}''$	27920	$\frac{1}{2}''$

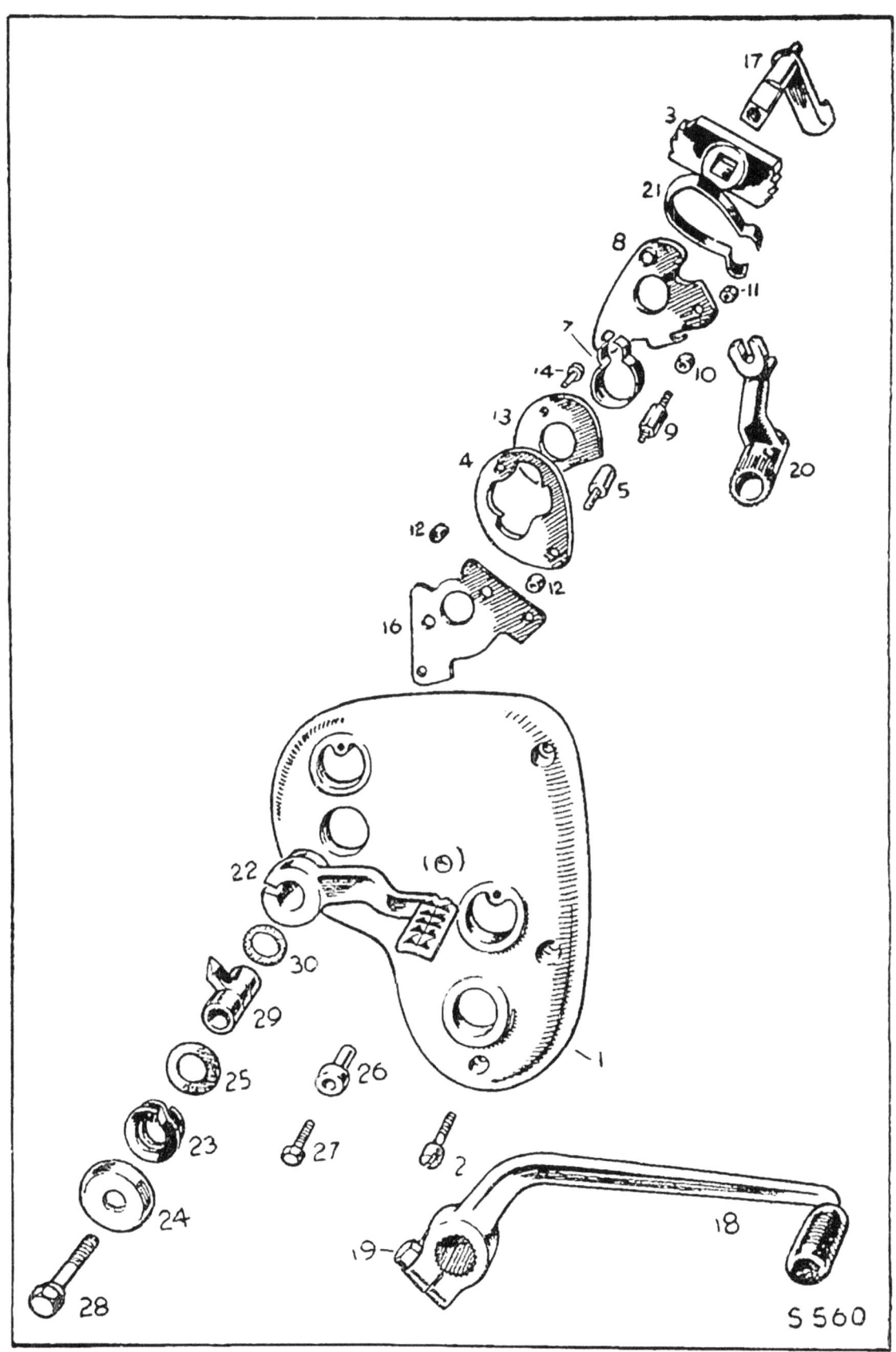

CLUTCH

Illus. No.	No. of part.	Description.	No. per set
	28433/5/2	Clutch assembly	1
1	27535/G2/5K	,, sprocket 56T. and drum assembly	1
2	H81/5	,, ,, drum	1
	G74A	,, ,, ,, rivets	15
3	H82K	,, ,, friction disc	2
	C10	,, ,, ,, ,, rivet	7
4	G74	,, ,, ball cage	2
	G66	,, ,, ,, ,, rivet	15
	32017	,, ,, balls, $\frac{3}{16}''$ dia.	54
5	H72	,, retaining spring	1
6	VR68/5	,, centre drum and back plate assembly	1
7	H89K	,, plate with Klinger inserts	1
7A	G67K	,, ,, Klinger insert	24
8	H89CB	,, ,, cork bonded	3
9	VR72/1	,, stud distance tube	3
10	G69/5	,, centre	1
11	G70/5	,, ,, cush rubber (large)	3
12	G70A/5	,, ,, ,, ,, (small)	3
13	G71	,, centre retaining plate	1
14	G78/13½	,, spring, 13½G.	6
15	G80	,, ,, screw	3
16	TR77	,, front plate	1
17	G75	,, intermediate plate (flat)	2
18	G75A	,, ,, ,, (dished)	2
19	TR79	,, steel pressure plate	1
20	G2/41/1	,, lever	1
21	G2/13	,, ,, bearing block pin ¼" × ⅝" W.	2
22	H44/1	,, adjuster, nut and ball	1
23	H66/1008	,, rod, 10½" long	1
24	H66B	,, ,, pad	1
25	TC/PZ6	Grease nipple	1

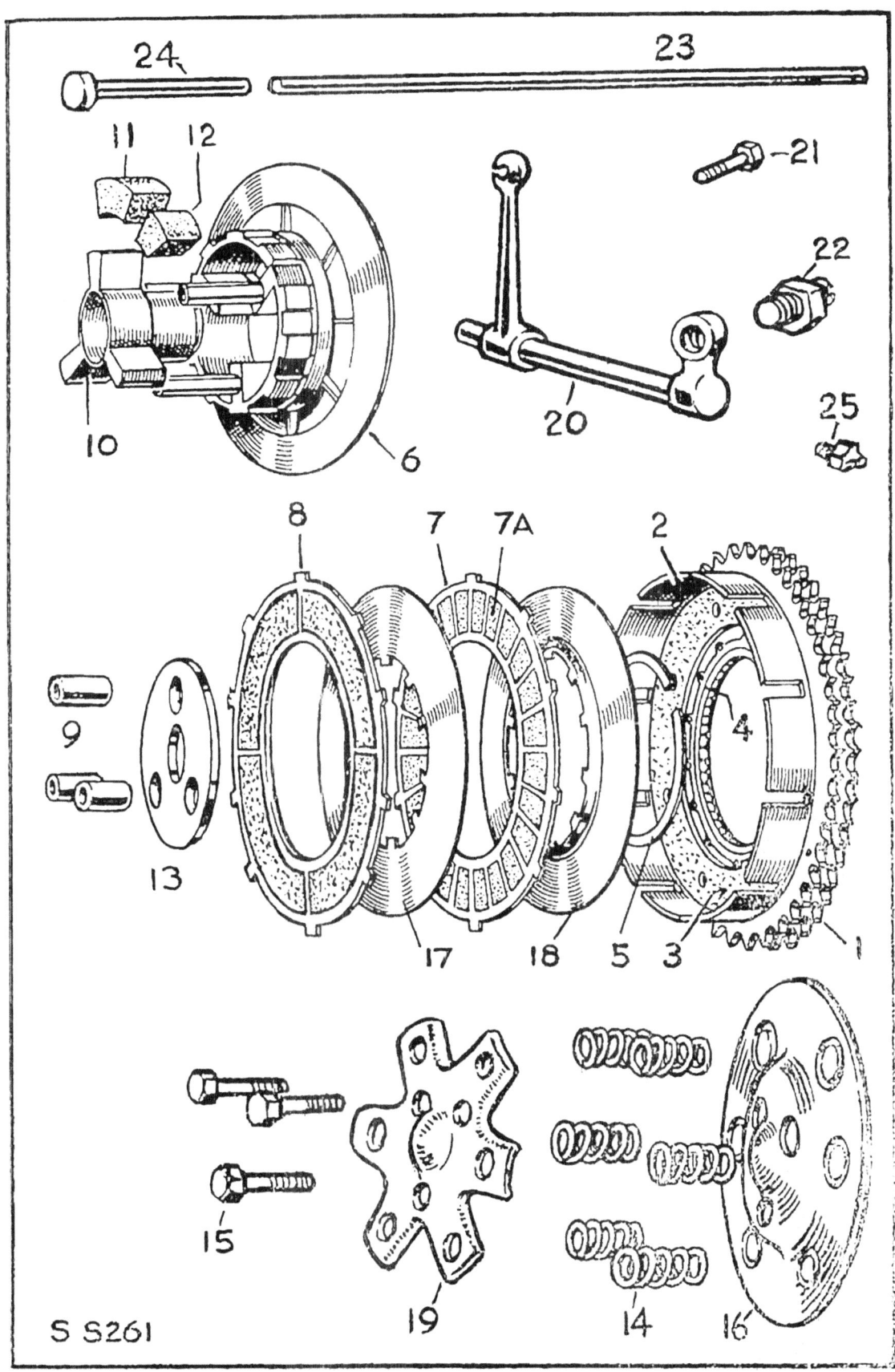

AMAL "MONOBLOC" CARBURETTOR

Illus. No.	No. of part.	Description.	No. per set
	AM/389/85	Carburettor c/w float chamber } less controls	1
	AM/389/86	" less " " } and cables	1
1	AM/389/004	Mixing chamber body with float chamber	1
	AM/389/025	" " " less " "	1
	AM/244/1048	" " flange sealing ring	2
2	AM/389/058	Jet block	2
3	AM/376/070	" " locating peg	2
4	AM/376/067	" " washer	2
5	AM/389/064	Mixing chamber top	2
6	AM/389/065	" " " cap ring	2
7	AM/29/301	" " " " spring	2
8	AM/4/241	Cap spring screw	2
9	AM/6/132A	Cable ferrule (throttle)	2
9A	AM/4/035	" " (air)	2
10	AM/389/060/3½	Throttle valve, No. 3½	2
11	AM/389/092	" " spring	2
12	AM/389/063	Taper needle	2
13	AM/4/230	" " clip	2
14	AM/389/062	Air valve	2
15	AM/29/057	" " guide	2
16	AM/4/046	" " spring	2
17	AM/376/072/1065	Needle jet	2
18	AM/376/100/380	Main jet, Std. No. 380	2
19	AM/376/140	" " holder	2
19A	AM/376/141	" " " banjo	2
20	AM/376/074	" " " and banjo washer	4
21	AM/376/075	" " cover nut	2
22	AM/376/076/25	Pilot jet, Std. No. 25	2
23	AM/376/095	" " cover nut	2
24	AM/116/162	" " " " washer	2
25	AM/332/017	Air adjusting screw	2
26	AM/4/148	" " " spring	2
27	AM/376/068	Throttle stop screw	2
28	AM/376/069	" " spring	2
29	AM/389/066	Air intake ring	2
30	AM/376/083	Float, complete	1
31	AM/376/085	" hinge spindle	1
32	AM/376/094	" spindle bush	1
33	AM/376/089	" needle	1
34	AM/376/088	" " seating	1
36	AM/376/097	Banjo	1
37	AM/14/175	" washer	1
38	AM/376/091	" bolt	1
39	AM/376/092	" " washer	1
40	AM/376/093	" filter gauze	1
41	AM/376/086	Tickler	1
42	AM/343/011	" body	1
43	AM/376/087	" spring	1
44	AM/376/077	Float chamber cover	1
45	AM/376/078	" " " joint	1
46	AM/376/079	" " " screw	3
47	45433	Connecting petrol pipe, 3½" long	1
48	45415	" " " clip	2
	AM/244/1037	Monobloc servicing spanner	1

In. 24. 63

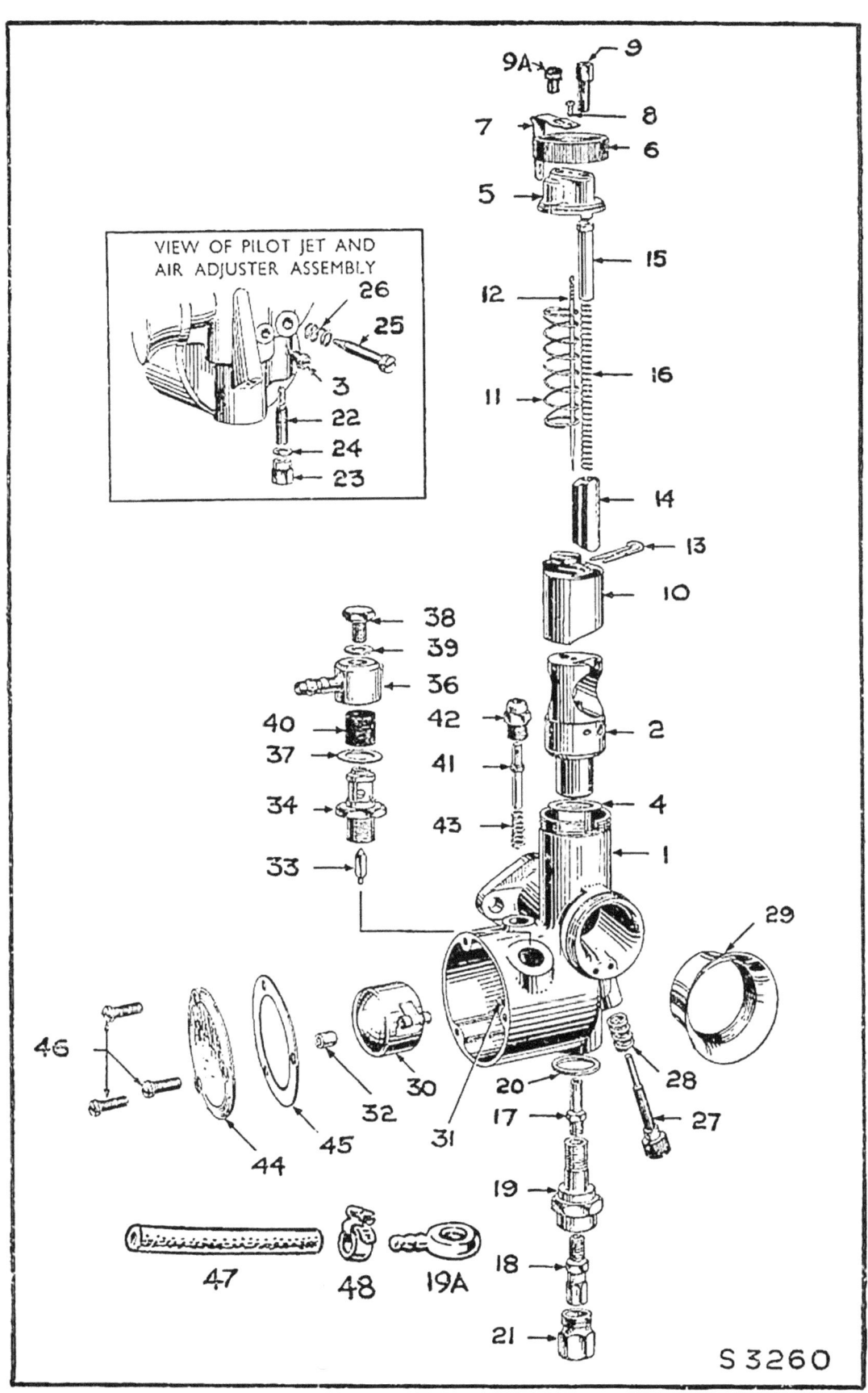

HANDLEBAR & CONTROLS

Illus. No.	No. of part.	Description.	No. per set
	46710	H'bar c/w controls less cables	1
1	44780	" bend only	1
	DH/107PA/LH	Clutch control assy.	1
2	DH/1078	" control body	1
3	DH/1008	" " " clip	1
4	DH/1009	" " " " screw	2
5	DH/2071	" " adjuster	1
6	DH/2072	" " " locknut	1
7	DH/1070LH	" lever	1
8	DH/5066	" " pivot pin	1
9	DH/1102	" " " " nut	1
	DH/100LH	Ignition control assy.	1
12	DH/1001LH	" " body	1
13	DH/1008	" " " clip	1
14	DH/1009	" " " " screw	2
15	DH/1002LH	" lever	1
16	DH/1005	" " cap	1
17	DH/1006	" " " screw	1
18	DH/1007	" " spring washer	1
	DH/311P	Brake control assy.	1
21	DH/3111	" " body	1
22	DH/1008	" " " clip	1
23	DH/1009	" " " " screw	2
24	DH/3114	" " swivel plate	1
25	DH/3117	" " " " pin	1
20	DH/3115	" " " " nut	1
26	DH/3112	" lever	1
27	DH/5066	" " pivot pin	1
28	DH/1102	" " " " nut	1
29	DH/3113	" " nipple swivel	1
	AM/194/013	" " swivel cotter	1
	DH/100RH	Air control assy.	1
32	DH/1001RH	" " body	1
33	DH/1008	" " " clip	1
34	DH/1009	" " " " screw	2
35	DH/1002RH	" lever	1
36	DH/1005	Air lever cap	1
37	DH/1006	" " " screw	1
38	DH/1007	" " spring	1
	DH/77	Twist grip control assy.	1
41	DH/07713	" " rotor	1
42	DH/07193	" " " rubber	1
43	DH/07723	" " clip, top	1
44	DH/07733	" " " bottom	1
45	DH/07770	" " " screw	2
46	DH/07140	" " adjuster screw	1
47	DH/07150	" " " " nut	1
48	DH/07760	" " " spring	1
49	DH/07180	" " cable stop	2
50	DH/U4	Dummy grip rubber	1

In. 26. 63

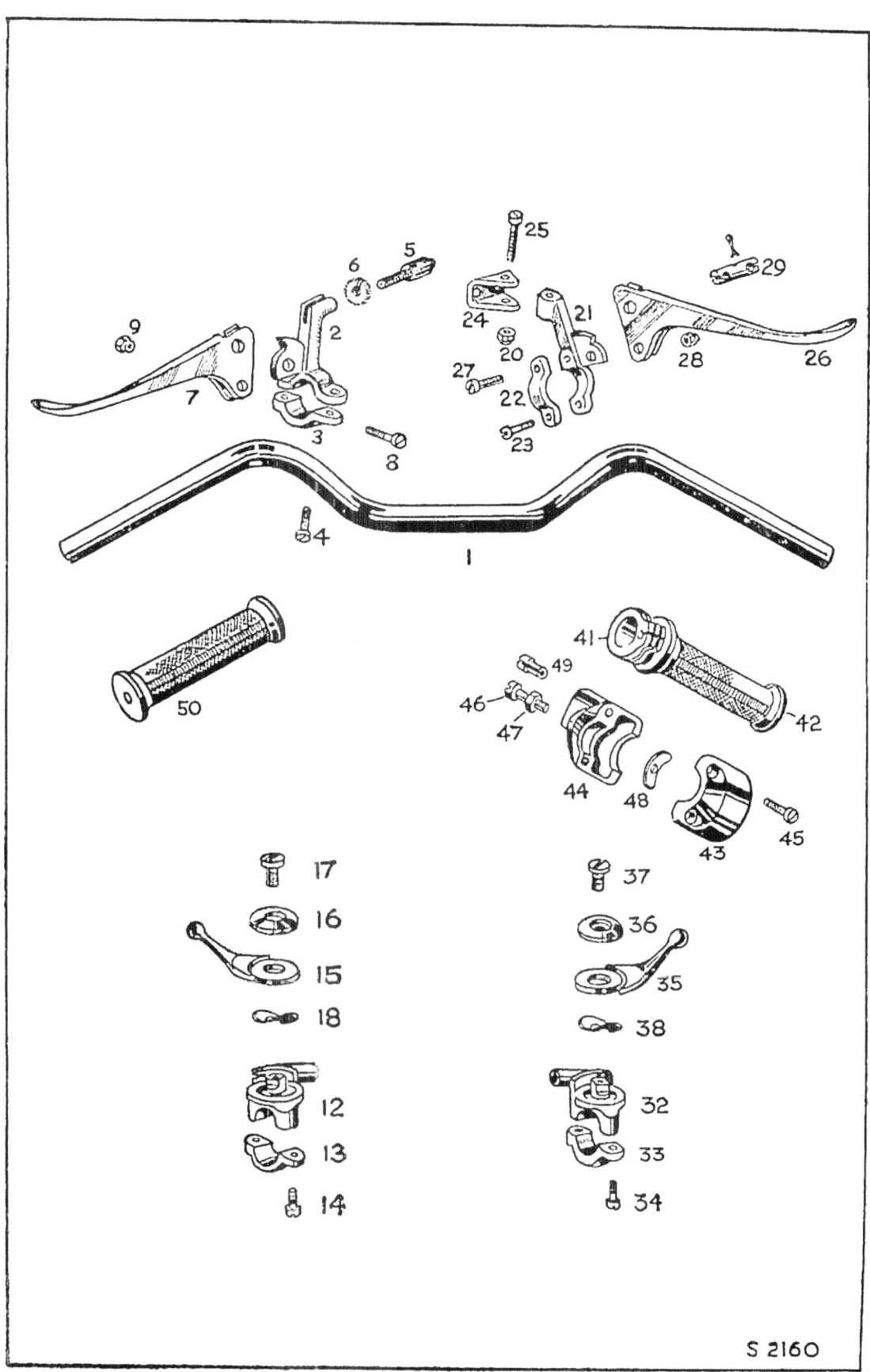

HANDLEBAR CONTROL CABLES

Illus. No.	No. of part.	Description.	No. per set
1	44940..	Clutch cable assembly	1
2	DHJ ..	" " nipple, handlebar end	1
3	40112..	" " " gearbox end	1
	37100..	" " adjusting screw	1
	3257..	" " " " locknut	1
12	40960..	Magneto cable assembly	1
13	DH/A	" " nipple, handlebar end	1
14	LU/463952	" " " magneto end	1
15	LU/463107	" advance/retard set	1
16	LU/454475	" A/R set rubber sleeve	1
17	38702..	Brake cable assembly	2
18	DH/J	" " nipple, handlebar end	2
19	38031..	" " " brake end	2
20	AM/18/680	" " stop	2
23	38032..	" " adjusting screw	2
24	14980..	" " " " locknut	2
25	45760A	Throttle cable assy.	2
26	AM/12/034	" " nipple, handlebar end	2
27	AM/1482	" " " carburettor end	2
	46374..	Air cable assy. c/w junction box	1
29	46372..	" " " handlebar end	1
30	46373..	" " " carburettor end	2
31	AM/12/034	" " nipple, handlebar end	1
32	AM/1482	" " " carburettor end and junction box	5
33	45719..	" " junction box	1
	46386..	" " " " clip	1
	45229..	" " " " " screw	1
35	33613..	Cable midway adjuster, throttle or air	3
36	35605..	" strap, rubber, 4" long	3
37	29609..	" " leather, 5" "	1
	29610 .	" " " 7" "	4

COLOURS

Most enamelled parts are available in different colours according to the model and year of manufacture, and it is essential to state the colour required if the part is to be supplied correctly.

If no colour is specified the part will normally be supplied in black or the standard colour applicable to the machine.

For the 1963 Interceptor the following 2-colour finishes are available:

    Black: Polychromatic Blaze
    Black: Polychromatic Gold

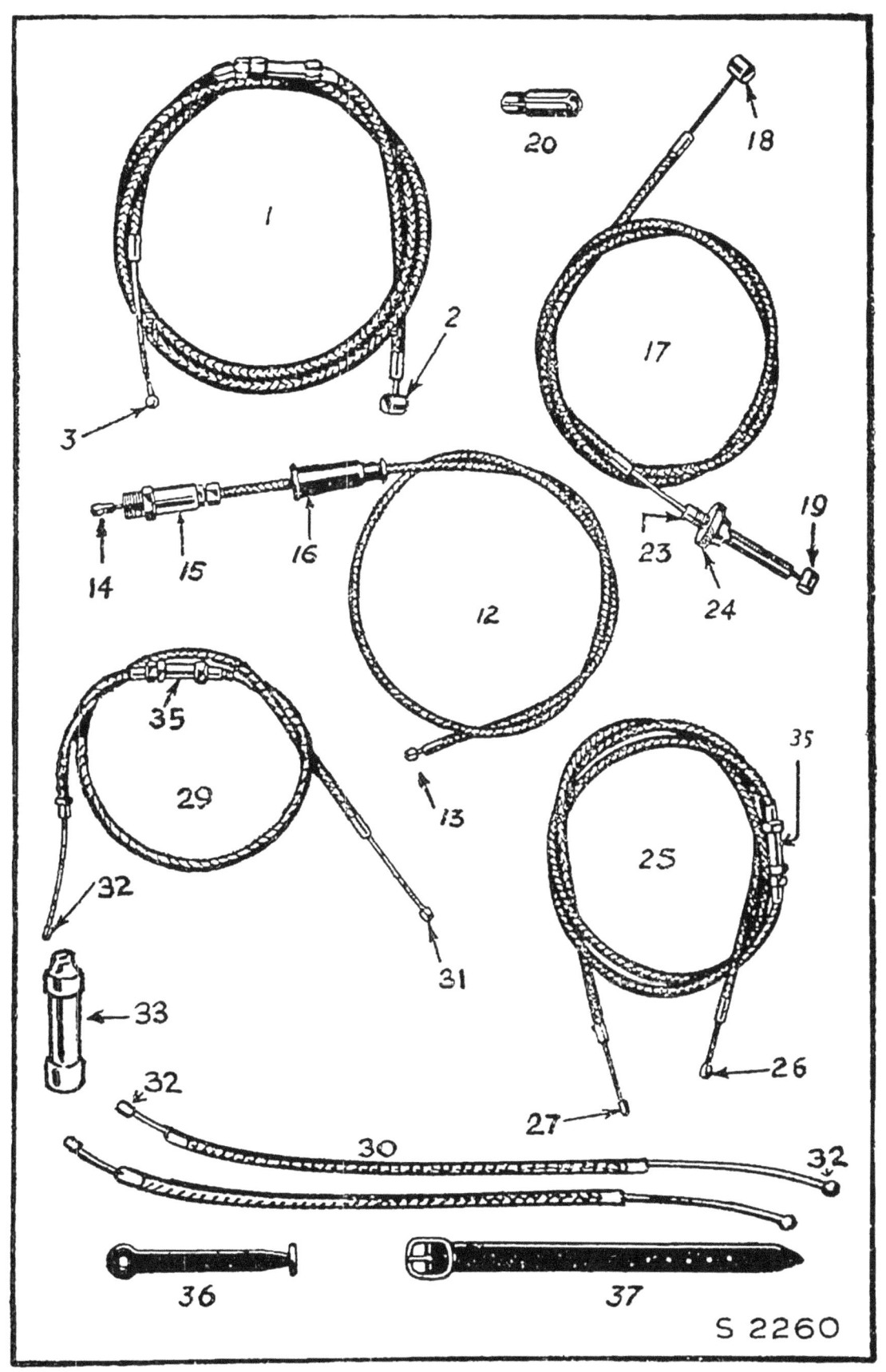

TELESCOPIC FRONT FORK

Illus. No.	No. of part.	Description.	No. per set
	46613..	Fork assy. c/w steering stem	1
	44797..	Steering stem c/w cover tubes and clamp bolts	1
1	41545..	,, ,, less ,, ,, ,, ,, ,,	1
3	*44798..	Steering stem locknut	1
4	36095..	,, ,, ,, washer	1
5	39038..	,, crown clamp bolt	2
6	27944..	,, ,, ,, ,, nut	2
7	27917..	,, ,, ,, ,, shakeproof washer	2
8	43604..	,, ,, cover plate	1
9	38881..	Steering stem cover tube	2
10	38844..	,, ,, ,, ,, bush	2
11	38877..	,, ,, ,, ,, rubber washer	2
12	43610..	Fork head headlamp casing c/w ball race and handlebar studs	1
13	43611..	Steering lock c/w key	1
	43034..	,, ,, grub screw	1
14	45675..	,, ,, hole rubber plug	1
15	88888..	Clip bolt	1
16	88886..	,, ,, sleeve (tapped)	1
17	88887..	,, ,, ,, (plain)	1
18	*88968..	Fork plug screw	1 or 2
19	27248..	Ball race (fork head)	1
20	27249..	,, ,, (crown)	1
21	32018..	Ball, ¼" diameter	38
22	42910..	Handlebar clip	2
24	43004..	,, ,, stud, 6/16"×1¼"×26	4
25	DE110	,, ,, ,, nut	4
		STEERING DAMPER	
27	45087..	Damper knob and rod	1
28	15248..	,, friction disc	2
29	35499..	,, anchor plate	1
30	41418..	,, pressure plate	1
31	30602..	,, spring washer	1
33	41929..	,, coupling peg circlip	2
34	241..	,, anchor plate pin	1
35	45896..	,, ,, ,, clip	1
36	36821..	Front fork stop—on frame	1

* Special parts required if revolution counter fitted: see page 32.

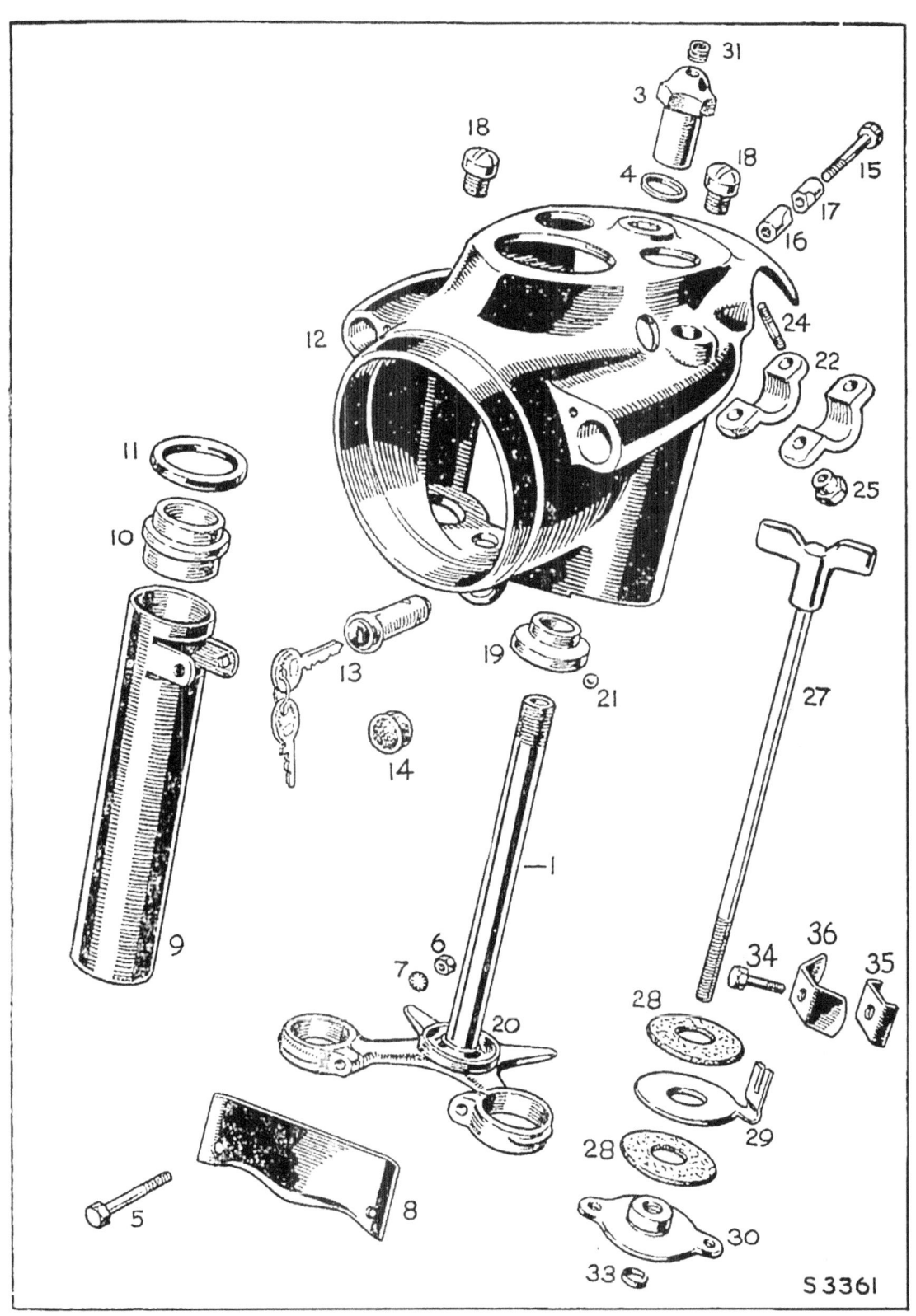

TELESCOPIC FRONT FORK—Contd.
AND REVOLUTION COUNTER

Illus. No.	No. of part.	Description.	No. per set
1	47032	Main tube with valve port and bush	2
2	38156	" " bush	2
3	38138	" " valve port	2
4	38073	" " " plate	2
5	40058	" " " circlip	2
6	46375	Bottom tube and lug R.H.	1
	46376	" " " " L.H.	1
7	38593	" " lug cap	2
8	38063	" " " stud $\tfrac{5}{16}'' \times 1\tfrac{3}{8}'' \times 22$	4
9	34705	" " " " nut	4
11	36176	" " bush	2
12	45297	" " oil seal assy.	2
13	37923	" " " " washer	2
14	46615	Fork spring	2
15	46616	" " guide (bottom, bronze)	2
16	46620	" " " retaining screw	2
17	46661	" " valve plate	2
18	37886	" " " circlip	2
19	46618	" " stud	2
21	38080	" " " nut (bottom of stud)	2
22	34790	" " " washer	2
20	46617	Oil control collar (on stud)	2
24	39711	Licence holder bracket	1
		REVOLUTION COUNTER	
30	SM/RC/184	Revolution counter head	1
31	SM/BG1506/01	" " gearbox	1
32	SM/DF1111/15/43	Driving cable, 43″	1
33	45738	Head bracket	1
	45739	" " nut, $\tfrac{5}{8}'' \times 26$	1
34	44995	" " stud	1
34A	44992	" " " tube	1
	7916	" " " nut, $\tfrac{1}{4}'' \times 26$	1
35	*45740	Steering stem locknut	1
36	*44991	Fork plug screw	1
37	44011	Head fixing grommet	2
	44994	" " nut, $\tfrac{1}{4}'' \times 26$ shouldered	2
	15641	" " washer	2
38	20199	" spacer "	2

* When a revolution counter is fitted:
45740 locknut replaces 44798; 1 off 44991 plug screw replaces 38968.

12
13
24
11
16
15
17
18
19
5
4
1
14
3
6
8
7
9
22
21
2
20
S 2460

30
33
34
32
34A
31
37
35
38
36
S 3160

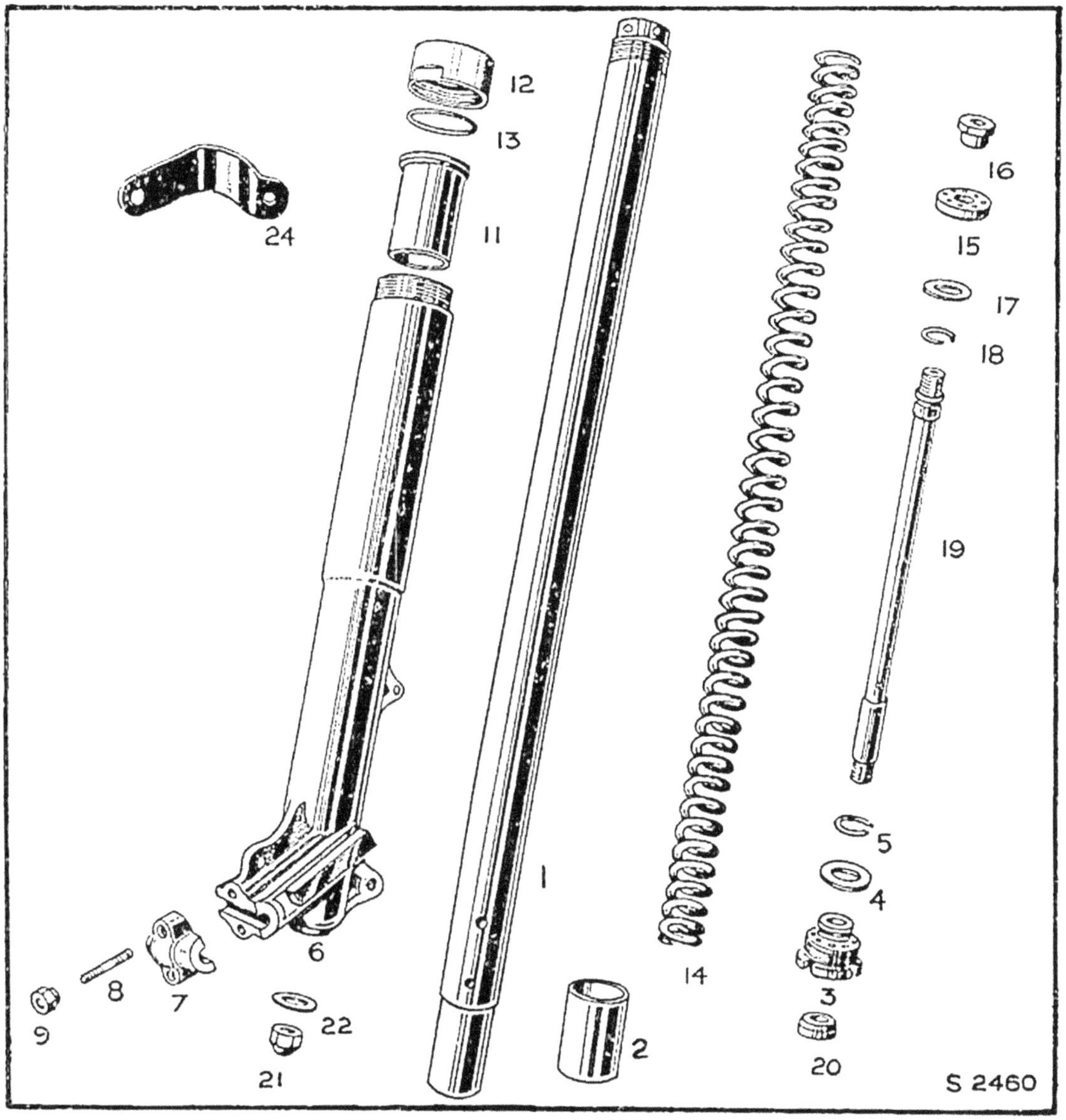

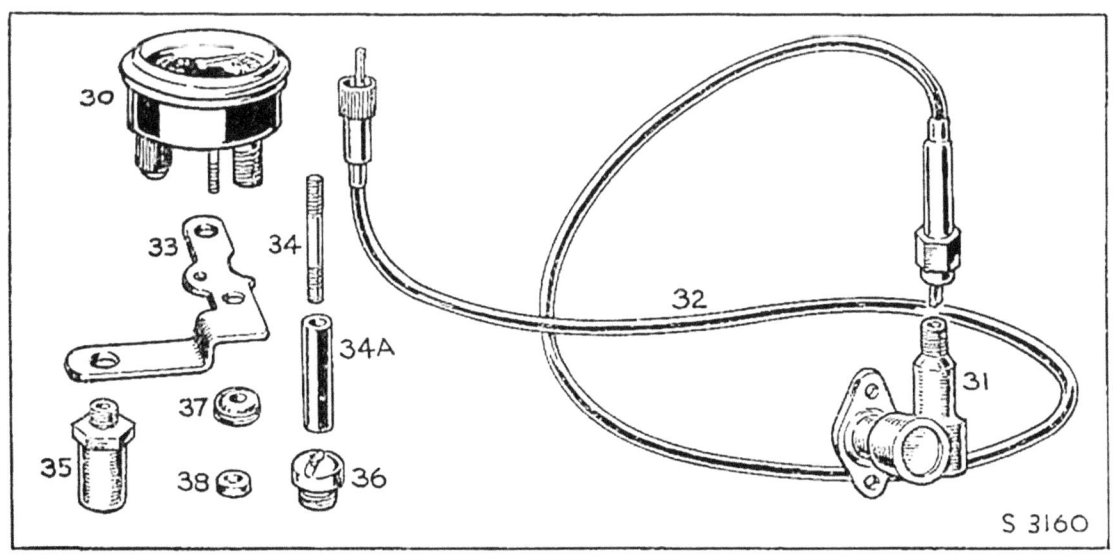

PETROL TANK, FRONT MUDGUARD, NUMBER PLATE AND FRONT STAND

Illus. No.	No. of part.	Description.	No. per set
1	47061	Petrol tank, chrome, with knee grips only	1
2	45305	Badge, "Royal Enfield"	2
3	41307	" rubber mount	2
	42195	" screw	4
4	15941	Tank filler cap	1
5	45177	" buffer sleeve	1
6	45176	" fixing bolt Front	1
	27621	" " " nut fixing	1
7	41644	" steady buffer	2
8	45174	" bracket Rear	1
	36174	" " screw fixing	2
9	46061	" " rubber block	1
10	46063	" " buffer	1
11	46895	Petrol tap and strainer	1
	5662	" " fibre washer	1
12	41361	" pipe complete	1
	41522	Knee grip, R.H.	1
13	41521	" " L.H.	1
14	46349	Mudguard	1
15	45491	" stay (front)	1
16	38767	" bolt (to stay)	2
	26998	" " nut	2
17	39792	" stay stud, $\frac{5}{16}'' \times \frac{3}{4}'' \times 22$ (B.S.F.)	2
18	45347	" " " $\frac{5}{16}'' \times 1'' \times 22$ (B.S.F.)	2
	27944	" " " nut	6
19	38387	Brake cable adjuster carrier	2
20	45495	Number plate	1
21	5171	" " screw	3
22	14904	" " clip	3
	26999	" " " nut	3
23	25226	" " " washer	3
24	44959	Front stand	1
	46367	" " pivot bolt	2
	15641	" " " " washer	2
25	46242	" " clip stud	1
26	22937	" " " " plain washer	1
27	27001	" " " " nut	1
28	6148	" " securing nut	1

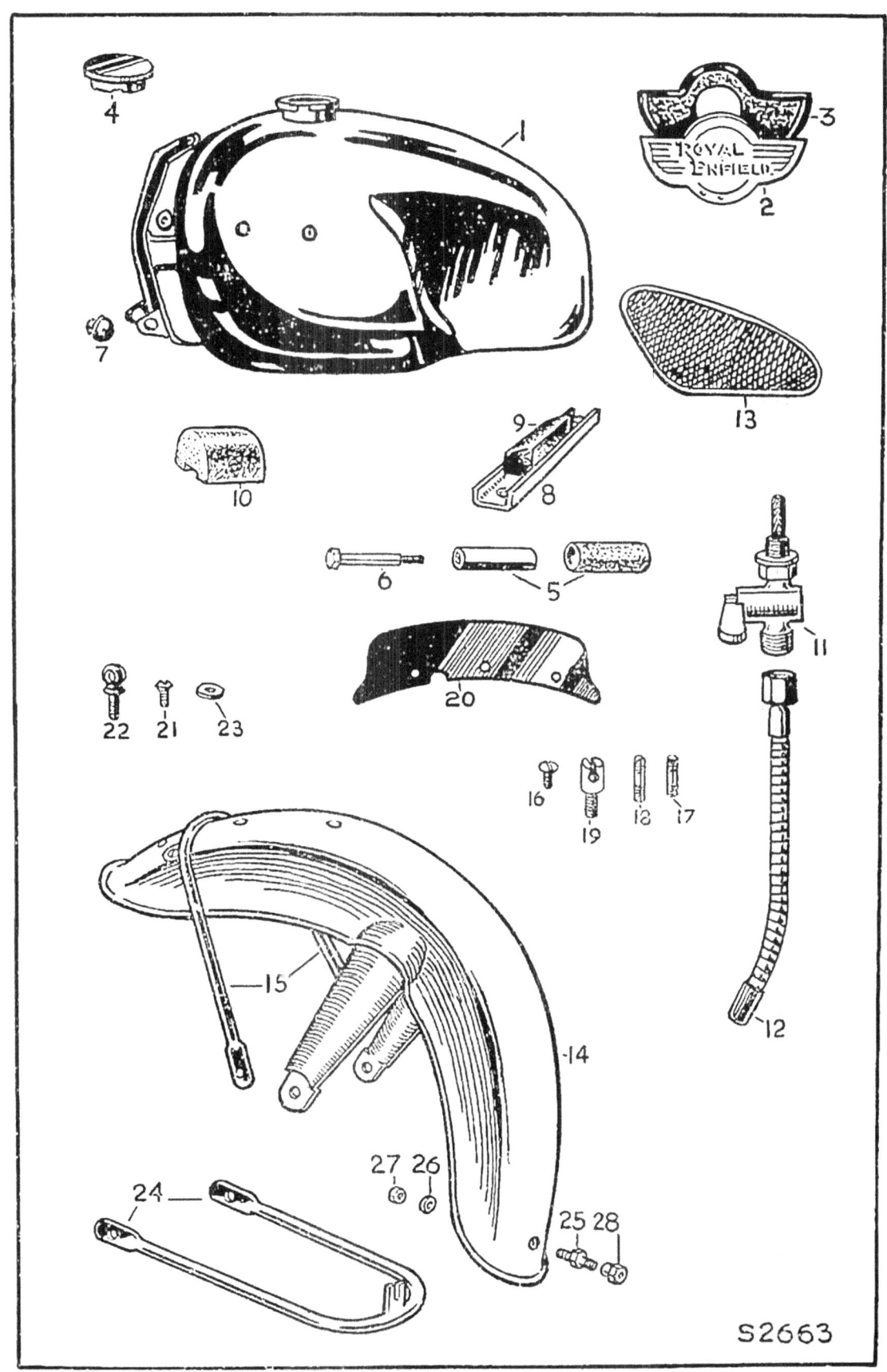

FRONT WHEEL AND BRAKE

Illus. No.	No. of part.	Description.	No. per set
	42960..	Wheel c/w brake assy., less tyre, (WM 2-19 rim)	1
1	42961..	,, rim WM 2-19	1
	28264..	,, ,, security bolt	1
3	*29205..	,, spoke $6\frac{5}{8}" \times 10G.$ B8G	40
4	*29206..	,, ,, nipple	40
	44589..	Balance weight	2
	44590..	,, ,, screw	2
5	37320..	Hub and brake drums	1
7	36468..	,, spindle	1
8	SKF/RLS5	,, journal bearing, $\frac{5}{8}" \times 1\frac{9}{16}" \times \frac{7}{16}"$	2
9	30538..	,, ,, ,, distance collar	2
10	21466..	,, felt washer	2
11	41342A	Brake shoe with lining	4
12	41284A/BX	,, ,, lining (1 pair, c/w rivets)	2
16	26033..	,, ,, return spring (pivot side)	2
	45298..	,, ,, ,, ,, (cam side)	2
18	38386..	,, ,, pivot pin	2
19	17551..	,, ,, ,, ,, washer	2
20	28715..	,, ,, ,, ,, locknut, $\frac{3}{8}" \times 26$	2
	36469..	,, cover plate, R.H.	1
21	84906..	,, ,, ,, L.H.	1
22	81347..	,, ,, ,, nut	2
23	27067..	,, operating cam	2
24	14472..	,, ,, ,, plug screw	2
25	26836..	,, ,, ,, bush	2
26	252..	,, ,, ,, ,, pin, $\frac{1}{4}" \times \frac{3}{4}" \times 26$	4
27	7916..	,, ,, ,, ,, ,, nut	4
28	87906..	,, ,, ,, ,, ,, spring washer	4
	38905..	,, ,, lever, R.H.	1
29	38906..	,, ,, ,, L.H.	1
30	10314..	,, ,, ,, nut, $\frac{7}{16}"$ dia.	2
	14613..	,, ,, ,, spring washer	2

DETACHABLE REAR WHEEL & BRAKE.

Illustrations on page 39.

Illus. No.	No. of part.	Description.	No. per set
	44809A	Wheel c/w cush drive & brake assy. less tyre	1
	44954..	Wheel (detachable) only	1
1	42766..	,, rim, WM 2-19	1
	28264..	,, ,, security bolt	2
2	*29205..	,, spoke $6\frac{5}{8}" \times 10G.$ B8G	20
	*41084..	,, ,, $6\frac{1}{4}" \times 10G.$ B8G	20
3	*29206..	,, ,, nipple	40

*Spokes and nipples screwed .140" dia. × 40 T.P.I.

S.3857

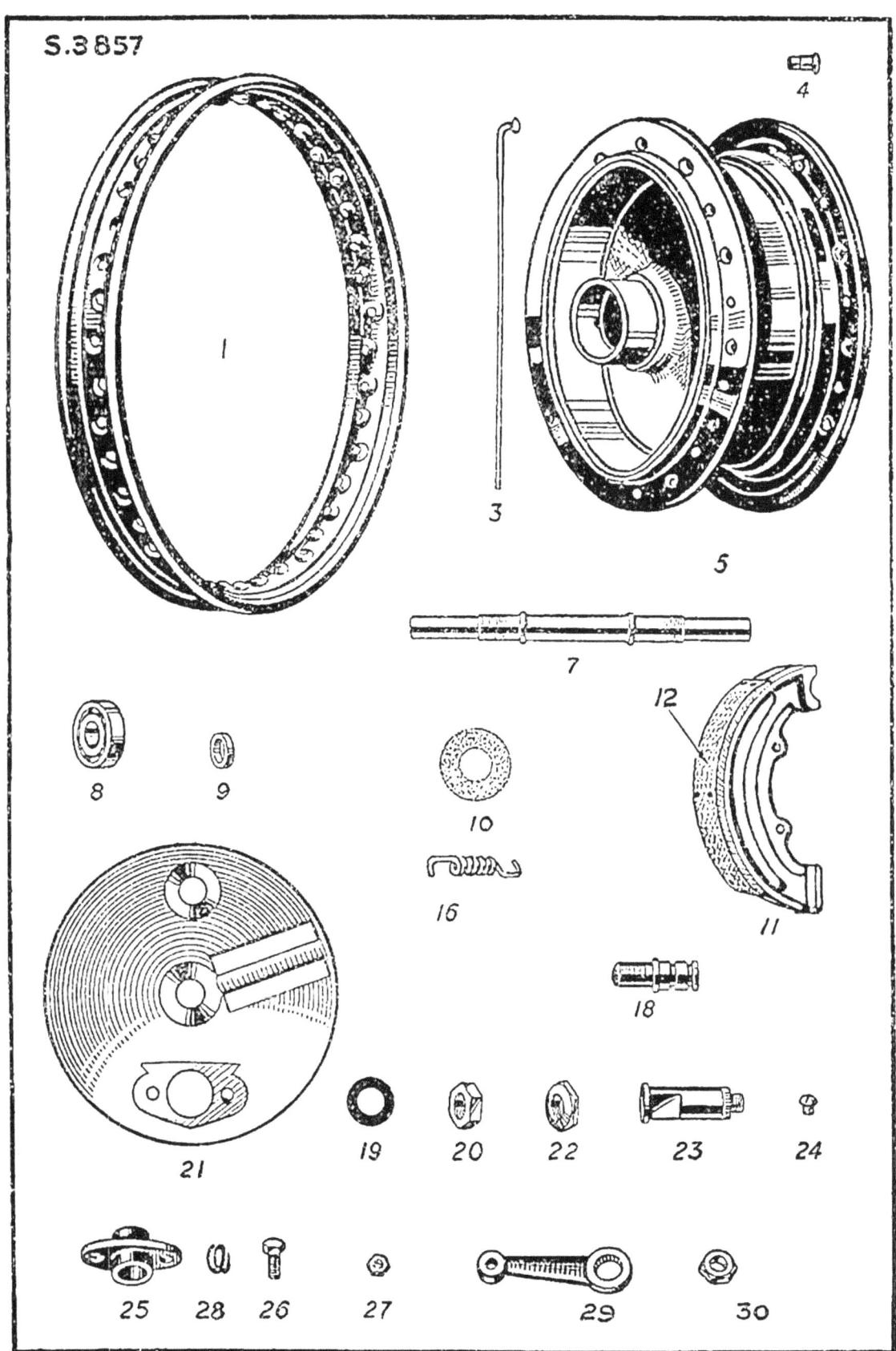

DETACHABLE REAR WHEEL & BRAKE—Contd.

Illus. No.	No. of part.	Description.	No. per set
4	47639	Hub only	1
5	41000	" drive pin	6
6	27918	" " " washer	6
7	DE394	" " " nut	6
8	40981	" cap	1
9	40983	" " screw	3
10	41233	Brake drum and sprocket, 46T	1
11	40967	Cush drive shell	1
12	26193	" " rubber	6
13	41003	" " lockring assy.	1
14	41001	" " " stud washer	3
15	19870	" " " " nut	3
16	41369	Wheel spindle (detachable)	1
17	41371	" " (fixed)	1
18	41185	" " " washer	1
19	28832	" " " nut	1
20	SK/RLS5	Ball bearing (hub) $\frac{5}{8}'' \times 1\frac{9}{16}'' \times \frac{7}{16}''$	2
21	SK/RLS7	" " (drum) $\frac{7}{8}'' \times 2'' \times \frac{9}{16}''$	1
22	41108	Bearing (drum) retaining ring	1
23	41006	Bearing felt washer (hub) R.H.	1
24	41106	" " " (drum) L.H.	1
25	40995	Hub bearing spacer tube	1
26	41032	" " circlip	1
27	40990	" distance collar, R.H.	1
28	44364	" " " L.H.	1
30	41343A	Brake shoe with lining	2
31	41285A/BX	" " lining, (one pair c/w rivets)	1
32	26033	" " spring, long	1
33	42267	" " " short	1
35	44844	Brake cover plate	1
36	7598	" " " anchor nut	1
37	20112	" " " " " washer	1
38	41105	" " " distance washer (behind plate)	1
40	46326	Brake cam	1
41	14472	" " plug screw	1
42	44362	" " bush	1
43	26309	" " " pin, $\frac{1}{4}'' \times \frac{9}{16}'' \times 26$	1
44	35140	" " " " $\frac{1}{4}'' \times \frac{13}{16}'' \times 26$	1
44A	4395	" " " " nut	2
45	23371A	" lever and trunnion	1
46	10314	" " nut, $\frac{7}{16}''$ dia.	1
46A	14613	" " washer	1
	46325	" " "	1
48	36904	" return spring	1
49	36649	Rear hub adjuster	2

In. 38. 63

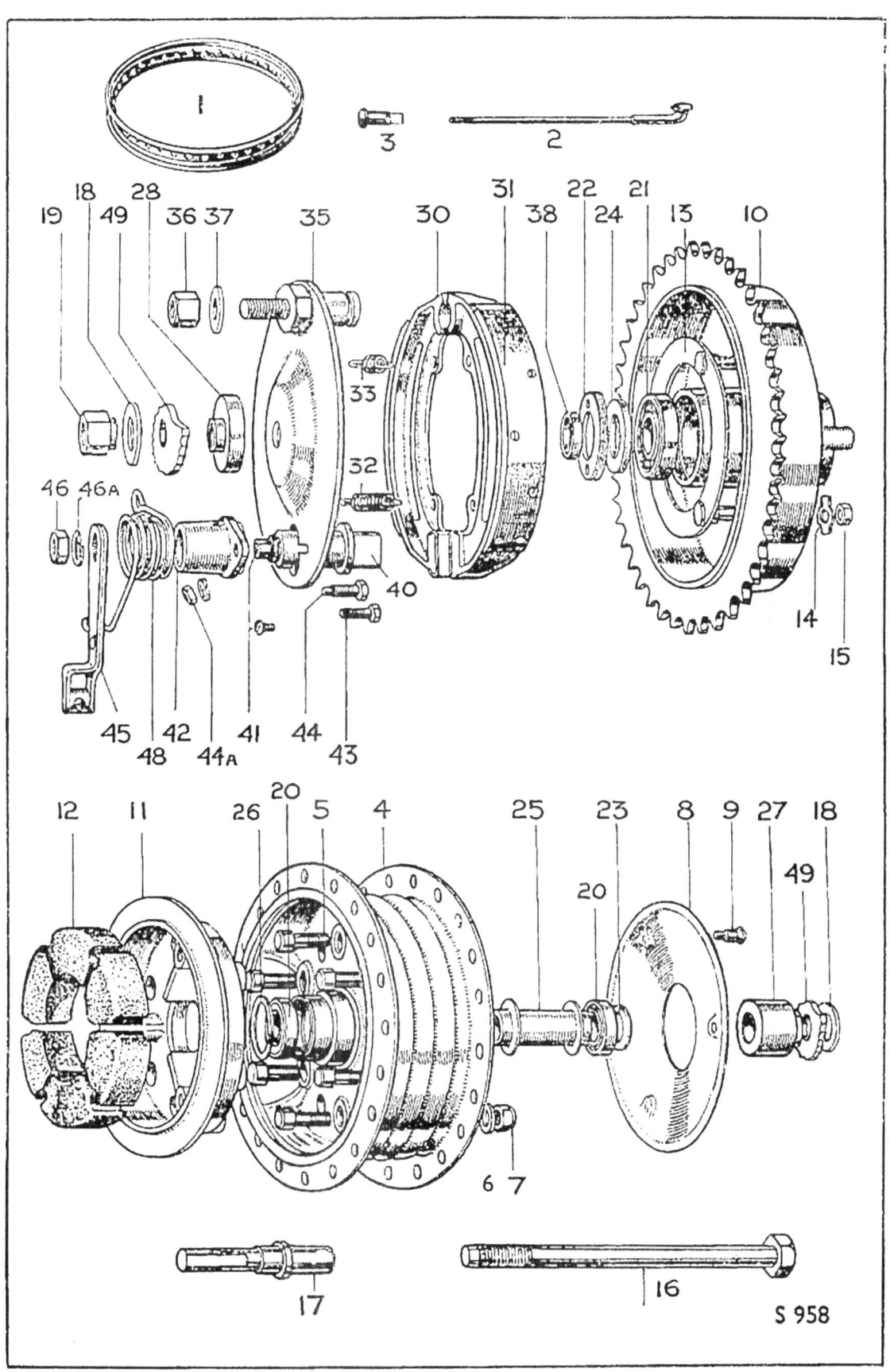

FRAME ASSEMBLY, GEARBOX BRACKET AND CENTRE STAND

Illus. No.	No. of part.	Description.	No. per set
1	46077	Frame assy. with head races, less all other loose fittings	1
2	34085	Head ball race	2
4	47307	Front engine plate, R.H.	1
5	47308	" " " L.H.	1
6	35948	" " " stud (frame), $\frac{1}{2}'' \times 5\frac{1}{4}'' \times 26$	1
	402	" " " " nut	2
7	43542	Rear engine plate, R.H.	1
8	43544	" " " L.H.	1
9	40558	" " " distance tube $1\frac{1}{4}''$ long L.H.	1
10	34099	" " " " " $4''$ " centre	1
11	44948	" " " stud (frame), $\frac{3}{8}'' \times 10\frac{9}{16}'' \times 26$	1
	26995	" " " " nut	2
12	35948	" " " " (gearbox) $\frac{1}{2}'' \times 5\frac{3}{16}'' \times 26$	1
	402	" " " " nut	2
13	42834	Rubber plug for spring box bracket	2
14	41937	" " " sidecar att. boss	2
15	45337A	Engine steady bracket	2
16	41331	" " " stud, $\frac{7}{16}'' \times 1\frac{7}{8}'' \times 26$	1
	10314	" " " " nut	2
	38151	Centre stand with spring post	1
17	38152	Centre stand only	1
18	36861	" " spring post	1
19	33824	" " bearing sleeve	1
20	43551	" " " spindle	1
	27819	" " " " s'proof washer	2
	1898	" " " " nut, $\frac{7}{16}'' \times 26$	2
	TC/PZ6	" " " " grease nipple	1
21	37891	" " spring	1
22	47207	Gearbox bracket	1
23	47292	Centre stand spring post	1
	47204	Chaincase steady bolt	1
	26995	" " " nut	1
	38960	Gearbox bracket stud	1
	26995	" " " nut	2

In. 40. 63

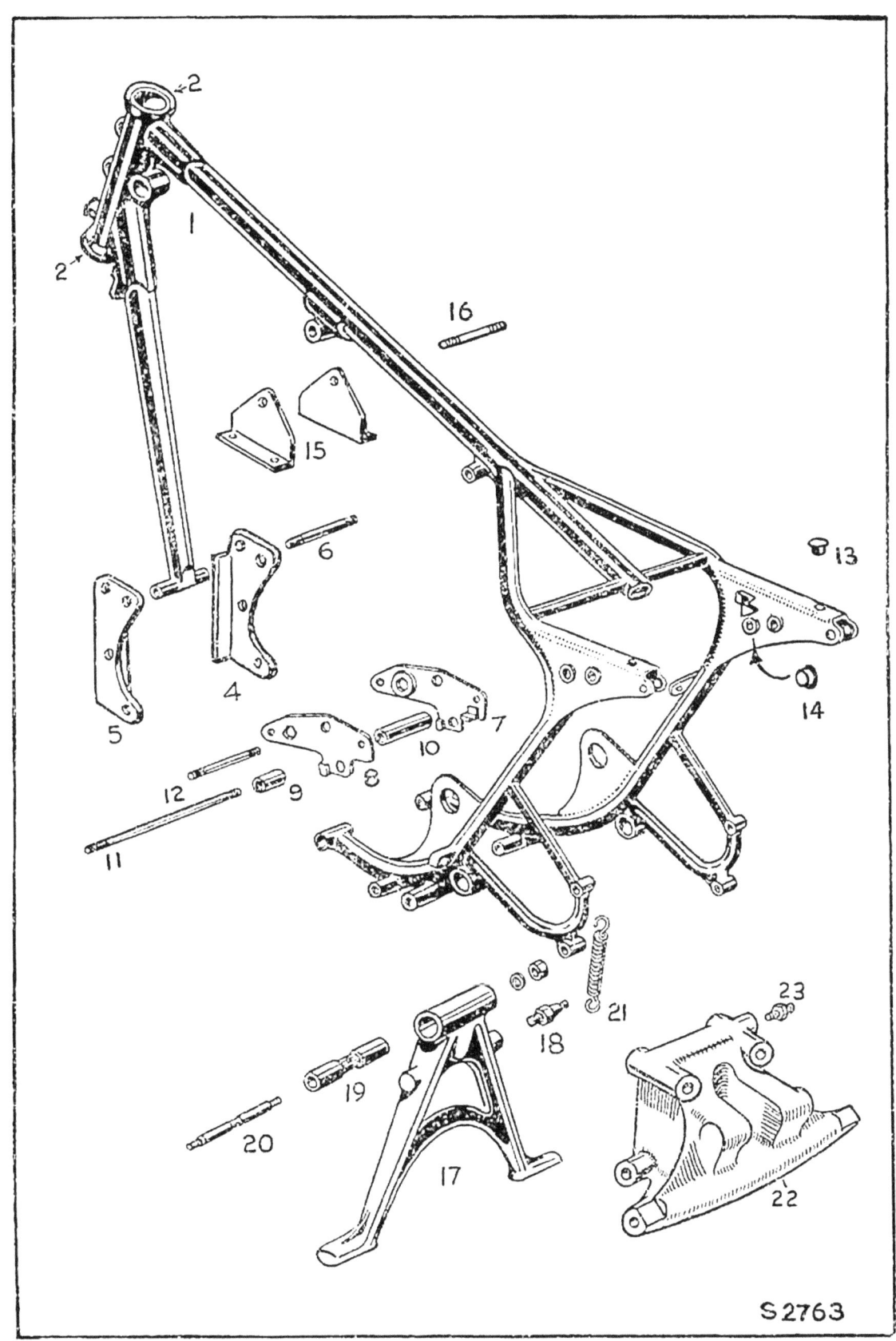

REAR SUSPENSION, MUDGUARD AND NUMBER PLATE

Illus. No.	No. of part	Description.	No. per set
1	46807..	Chainstay assy. with bearings	1
2	46262..	,, bearing	2
3	46266..	,, ,, distance piece	1
4	46263..	,, ,, stud	1
5	46264..	,, ,, ,, nut	2
6	46265..	,, ,, ,, collar	2
7	45703..	,, nut locking screw	1
9	AR/AT6-7/S 6070/1	Suspension unit	2
10	AR/AT6/452	Upper spring	2
11	AR/AT6/521	Lower ,,	2
12	AR/AT6/522	Outer shroud	2
13	AR/AT6/523	Inner ,,	2
14	AR/AT6/518	Lower ,,	2
15	AR/AT6/534	Spring cover	2
16	AR/AT6/450	Pivot pin rubber	4
17	AR/AT6/456	,, ,, ,, bush	4
18	AR/AT6/333	Top spring abutment	2
19	42002..	Spring box pivot pin, top, $\frac{3}{8}'' \times 1\frac{5}{8}'' \times 20$	2
20	33783..	,, ,, ,, ,, lock washer..	2
	DE394	,, ,, ,, ,, nut (bottom)	2
	26374..	,, ,, ,, ,, ,, (top)	2
21	45654..	Mudguard	1
22	38767..	,, bolt, rd/hd. $\frac{1}{4}'' \times \frac{1}{2}'' \times 26$	4
	26998..	,, ,, nut	4
23	45660..	,, carrier	1
24	39767..	,, ,, end cover, plastic	2
25	41196..	,, ,, ,, ,, stiffener	2
26	40053..	,, ,, bridge	2
	10142..	,, ,, ,, screw	4
27	20199..	,, ,, ,, spacer	4
28	41039..	Number plate	1
29	41087..	,, ,, beading	1
30	22655..	,, ,, fixing pin	1

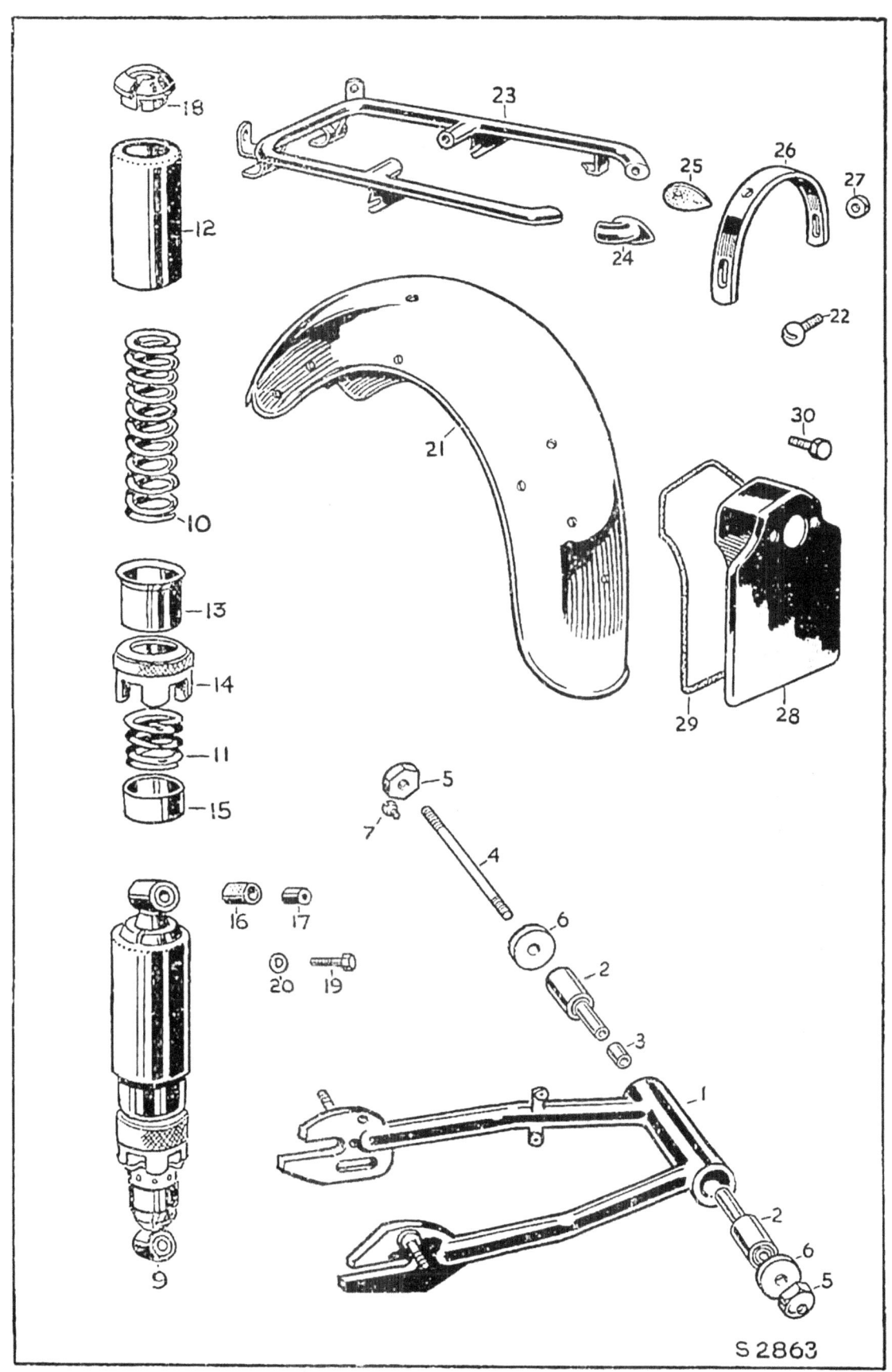

PROP STAND, PILLION FOOTRESTS, CHAINGUARD AND CHAINS

Illus. No.	No. of part.	Description.	No. per set
1	47191	Prop stand leg	1
2	47194	" " " pivot bolt	1
3	47188	" " plate c/w spring post	1
4	47195	" " "U" bolt	2
5	27621	" " " " nut	4
6	34908	" " spring	1
7	41526	Pillion footrest	2
8	26324	" " rubber	2
9	41523	P/rest pivot block	2
10	41499	" " " pin, $\frac{5}{16}'' \times 1\frac{3}{16}'' \times 26$	2
	3257	" " " " nut	2
11	37207	" " " stud, $\frac{7}{16}'' \times 2\frac{9}{16}'' \times 26$	2
	30807	" " " " nut	2
12	43253	" " " distance tube, L.H.	1
13	44819A	Chainguard	1
	14447	" bolt, rear $\frac{5}{16}'' \times \frac{3}{8}'' \times 26$	1
	251	" " front, $\frac{1}{4}'' \times \frac{1}{2}'' \times 26$	2
	82	" " plain washer	2
14	46073	Gearbox sprocket cover	1
15	46075	" " " bracket	2
	46482	" " " " att. screw	2
	25226	" " " " " washer	2
	46481	" " " " " nut	2
	20689	" " " " stud, $\frac{5}{16}'' \times 4\frac{5}{8}'' \times 26$	2
	26997	" " " " nut	4
17	RN/114038/92	Front chain, $\frac{3}{8}''$ duplex $\times$ 92 pitches	1
18	RN/110056/101	Rear chain $\frac{5}{8}'' \times \frac{3}{8}'' \times$ 101 pitches	1

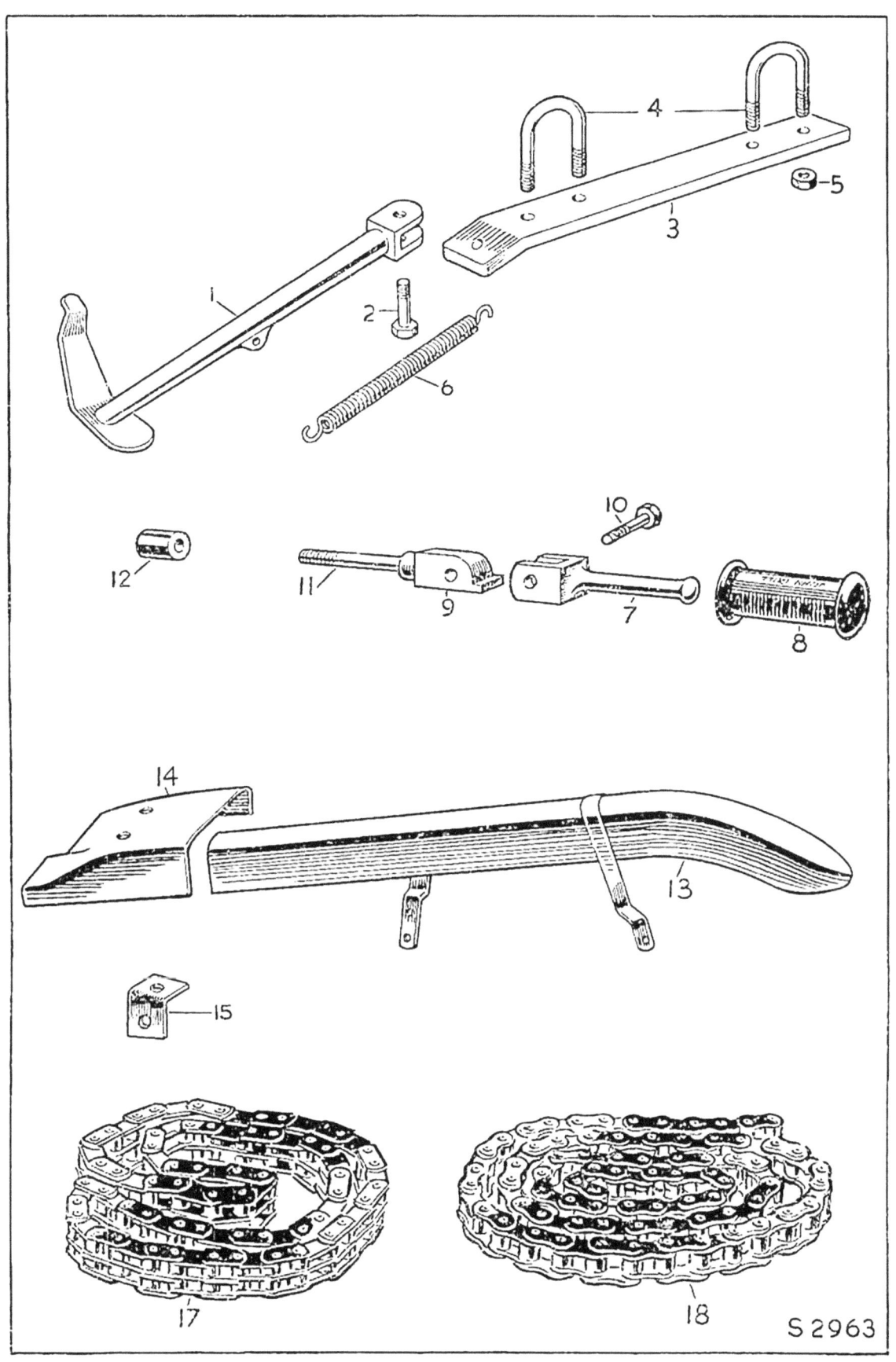

REAR BRAKE CONTROL, EXHAUST SYSTEM AND FOOTRESTS

Illus. No.	No. of part.	Description.	No. per set
1	41183A	Brake pedal	1
	26995	" " securing nut $\frac{3}{8}"\times 26$	1
	15641	" " " " washer	1
2	40339	" " fulcrum stud	1
	10314	" " " " nut $\frac{7}{16}"\times 26$	1
3	252	" " stop pin, $\frac{1}{4}"\times\frac{3}{4}"\times 26$	1
	27000	" " " " locknut	1
	TC/PZ6	" " grease nipple	1
4	38600	" rod	1
	14691	" " washer	1
	30779	" " split pin, $\frac{1}{16}"\times\frac{3}{4}"$	1
5	17691	" " adjusting nut	1
	46589	Silencer complete	1
13	46634	" taper section	1
14	46590	" barrel centre	1
15	46635	" stud & baffle assy.	1
16	46336	" barrel seal	1
	27001	" " attachment nut	1
	46740	" " " washer	1
17	46203	" outlet end	1
	46776	" tab washer	1
23	41341	" clip (to exhaust pipe)	1
	4860	" " bolt, $\frac{1}{4}"\times 1\frac{1}{16}"\times 26$	1
	12881	" " " nut	1
18	46247	Exhaust pipe R.H.	1
19	46249	" " L.H.	1
20	41044	" " clip (head)	2
	19555	" " " screw	2
	26998	" " " " nut	2
21	44442	" " (cross over pipe)	1
22	44964	" " tie rod	1
	14691	" " " " washer	2
	26168	" " " " nut, sleeved	2
	27001	" " " " " standard	2
6	38959A	Footrest bar	1
	1898	" " nut $\frac{7}{16}"\times 26$	2
	20018	" " washer	2
7	39197	Footrest distance tube, centre, $3\frac{3}{4}"$ long	1
8	41017	" " " L.H., $\frac{5}{8}"$ long	1
10	43233	" arm, L.H.	1
9	43232	" " R.H.	1
11	25838	" " rubber	2

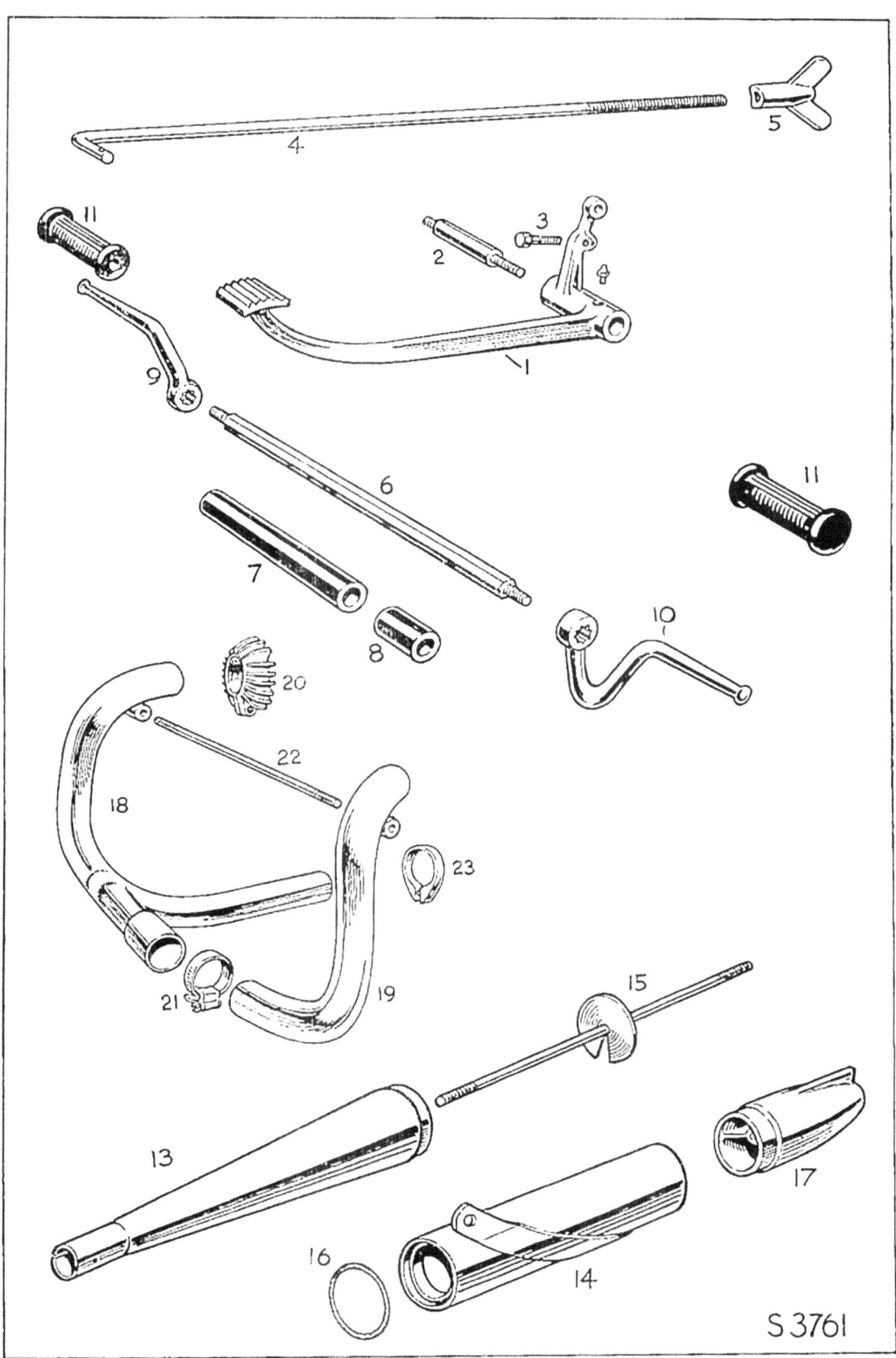

TOOLBOX, BATTERY & DUAL SEAT

Illus. No.	No. of part.	Description	No. per set
	46404	Toolbox with lids	1
1	46405	" less "	1
2	45682	" lid R.H.	1
3	45684	" " L.H.	1
4	41860	" " screw	2
5	38803	" " " keeper washer, rubber	2
6	41479	" clip	1
7	44374	" packing strip	1
	7201	" " bolt, $\frac{1}{4}'' \times \frac{21}{32}'' \times 26$	2
	29419	" bolt, rear, $\frac{1}{4}'' \times \frac{15}{16}'' \times 26$	2
7A	25586	" " collar	2
	26998	" " nut	4
8	LU/MLZ9E	Battery, 6v., 12 amp.hr. (dry charged)	1
9	LU/54280790	Cover	1
10	46409	Battery clip	1
	46346	" " nut	1
	45229	" " screw	2
	10480	" " washer	2
	46319	" cushion	1
11	46410	Toolbox lid attachment post	1
12	45815	Dual seat	1
13	45661	" " brackets (front)	2
14	45822	" " " (rear)	1
	12659	" " bolt, $\frac{5}{16}'' \times \frac{1}{2}'' \times 26$ (seat to bracket)	4
	8634	" " " washer	2
	10142	" " " $\frac{5}{16}'' \times \frac{11}{16}'' \times 26$ (bracket to carrier)	2
	26997	" " " nut	2
	251	" " " $\frac{1}{4}'' \times \frac{1}{2}'' \times 26$ (rear, to guard)	2
	26998	" " " nut	2
	82	" " " washer	2

PANNIERS

Illus. No.	No. of part.	Description	No. per set
15	41634	Pannier carrier R.H.	1
	41635	" " L.H.	1
16	46622	" " stud	4
17	20356	" " " nut shouldered	4
18	38559	" bag	2
19	46623	" support tube	1
20	46633	" " stud, $\frac{3}{8}'' \times 12\frac{7}{8}'' \times 26$	1
	26995	" " " nut	2

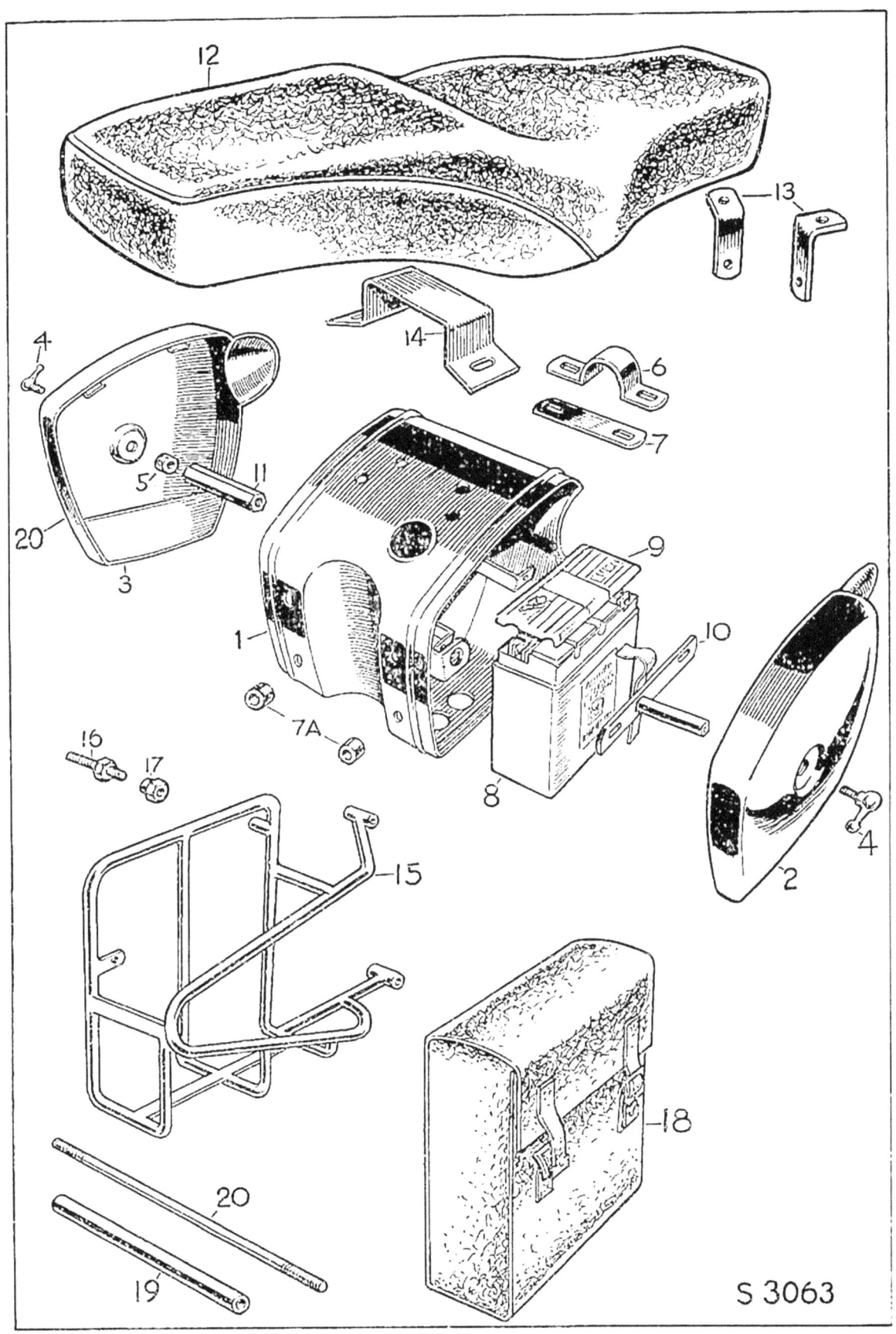

TOOL KIT*

Illus. No.	No. of part.	Description.	No. per set
1	35634	Tubular spanner, $\frac{1}{4}'' \times \frac{5}{16}''$ Whit.	1
2	44710	" " sparking plug	1
3	24095	" " $\frac{1}{2}''$ Whit.	1
4	35635	" " $\frac{9}{16}''$ Whit.	1
5	24094	" " $\frac{11}{16}''$ Whit.	1
6	29042	Tommy bar $\frac{2}{10}''$ dia.	1
7	24092	Spanner, $.343'' \times .380''$ Hex.	1
8	27896	" $\frac{3}{16}'' \times \frac{1}{4}''$ Whit.	1
9	29044	" $\frac{1}{4}'' \times \frac{5}{16}''$ Whit.	1
10	ST78	Allen key $\frac{5}{16}''$ hex.	1
	ST79	" " $\frac{1}{2}''$ hex.	1
	43449	Valve rocker adjusting spanner	1
12	6406	Combination spanner	1
13	4272	Tyre lever	2
14	3482	Screwdriver flat blade	1
15	16014	Grease gun	1
16	16026	Inflator, $12\frac{1}{4}''$	1
17	DWU-05	Screwdriver star blade	1
18	ST73	Adjustable spanner, 7"	1
19	TE/1124	Valve spring compressor	1
20	TE/1167	" grinding tool	1
	16007	Tool roll, canvas	1
	ST71	Leather strap, $42'' \times 1''$	1

*These tools are available but are not necessarily supplied with new machines.

SMITH'S SPEEDOMETER

Illus. No.	No. of part.	Description.	No. per set
1	SM/SC3303/01	Speedometer head 150 m.p.h. trip, illuminated	1
	SM/SC3303/11	" " 240 k.p.h. trip, illuminated	1
	SM/53205	Speedometer light bulb	1
2	38896	Bracket for head	1
3	SM/N1253	Nut (fixing bracket to head)	2
4	SM/W7216	Spring washer	2
5	SM/53395/4/54	Flexible drive complete, 54 inches	1
	SM/53398/4/54	" " outer cable assembly	1
	SM/52108/1/54	" " inner " "	1
6	SM/BG5331/247	Gear box (self-contained) complete	1
7	46868	" " spacing collar	1

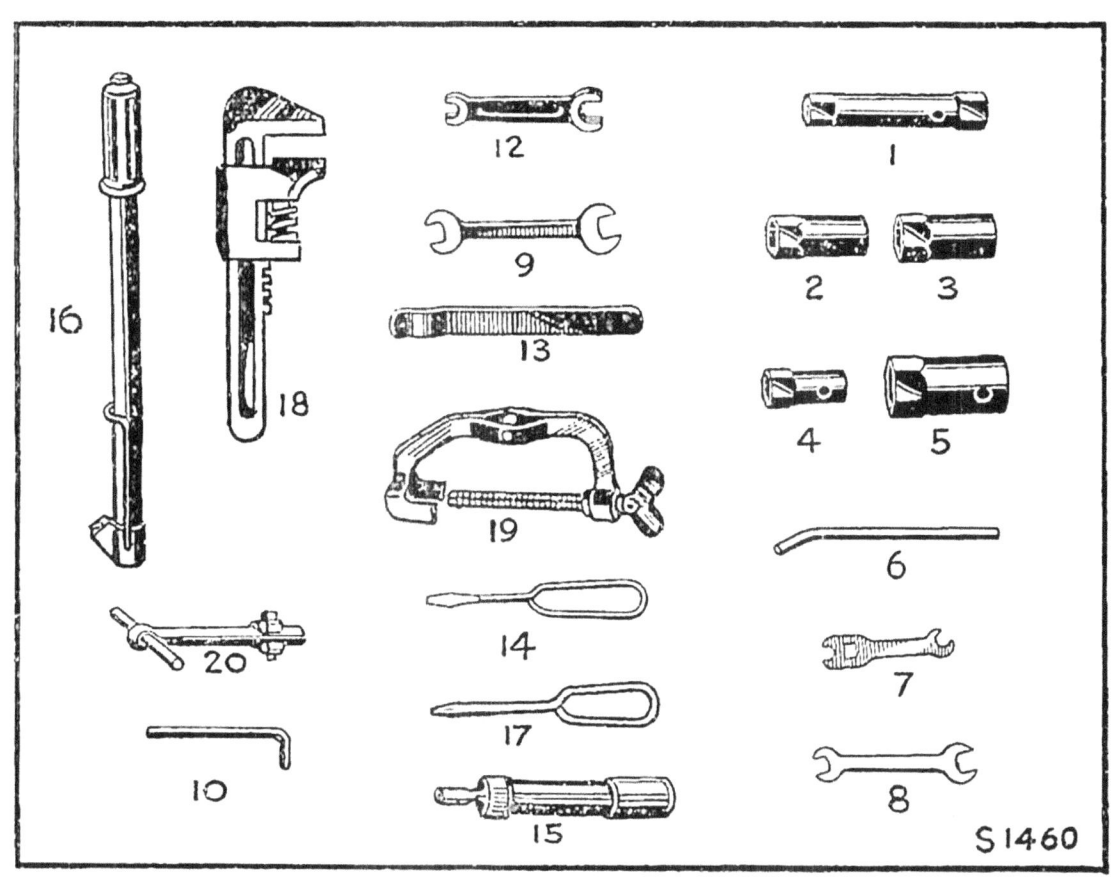

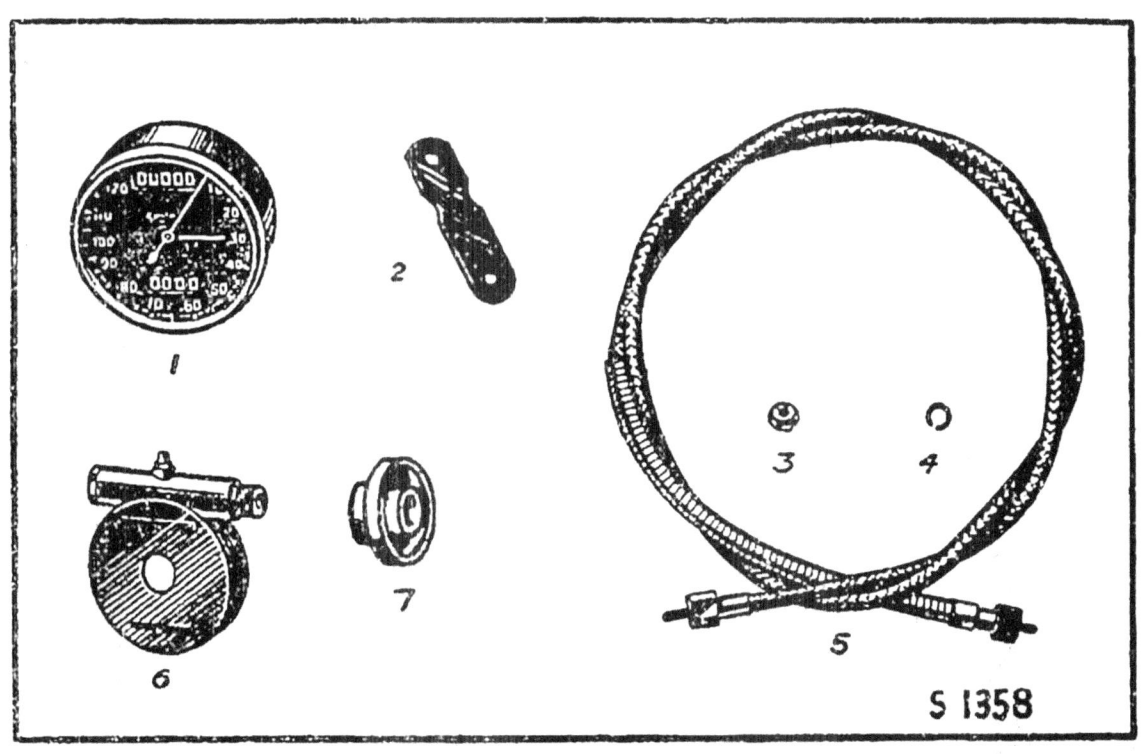

LUCAS MAGNETO, ALTERNATOR, RECTIFIER AND HORN

Illus. No.	No. of part.	Description.	No. per set
	LU/42369B	Magneto, K2F.	1
1	LU/458367	Pick up assy. R.H.	1
	LU/458368	" " " L.H.	1
2	LU/451260	" " brush & spring	2
3	LU/410600	H.T. Cable nut	2
4	LU/493836	Contact breaker	1
5	LU/458619	" " cover	1
6	LU/455190	" breaker earthing brush & spring	1
7	LU/463107	" " adv/ret. control set	1
8	LU/454475	" " control set rubber sleeve	1
9	LU/458855	" " cam	1
10 & 11	LU/54440887	Contact set	1
12	LU/455190	Earthing brush & spring	1
	42448	Magneto adaptor mounting complete	1
15	42449	" " body only	1
	11554	" " stud	3
	19870	" " " nut	3
	26379	" " screw	3
	40377	" " gasket	1
	LU/047531	Alternator stator & rotor assy. RM15 ⎱ Early fitting	1
16	LU/469427	Stator	1
17	LU/423506	Rotor	1
	LU/54021023	Alternator stator & rotor assy. RM19 ⎱ Later fitting	1
	LU/54213901	Rotor	1
	LU/47164	Stator	1
18	43385	Rotor sleeve	1
19	43386	" key	1
22	LU/47132B	Rectifier	1
	LU/132469	" screw ⎱ Early fitting	3
	LU/154409	" washer	3
	LU/166094	" nut	3
	LU/49072A	Rectifier—Later fitting	1
23	39621	Clip	1
	16320	" pin	1
	26995	" " nut	1
	27944	Nut on rectifier spindle	1
25	LU/069424	Horn, H.F. 1234	1
26	LU/700168	Bracket	1
27	45549	" locating plate	1
28	35949	" packing collar	1
29	LU/76204D	Horn or cut-out switch	2
30	LU/31549B	Dipper switch	1
	LU/838481	Cable harness	1

In. 52. 63

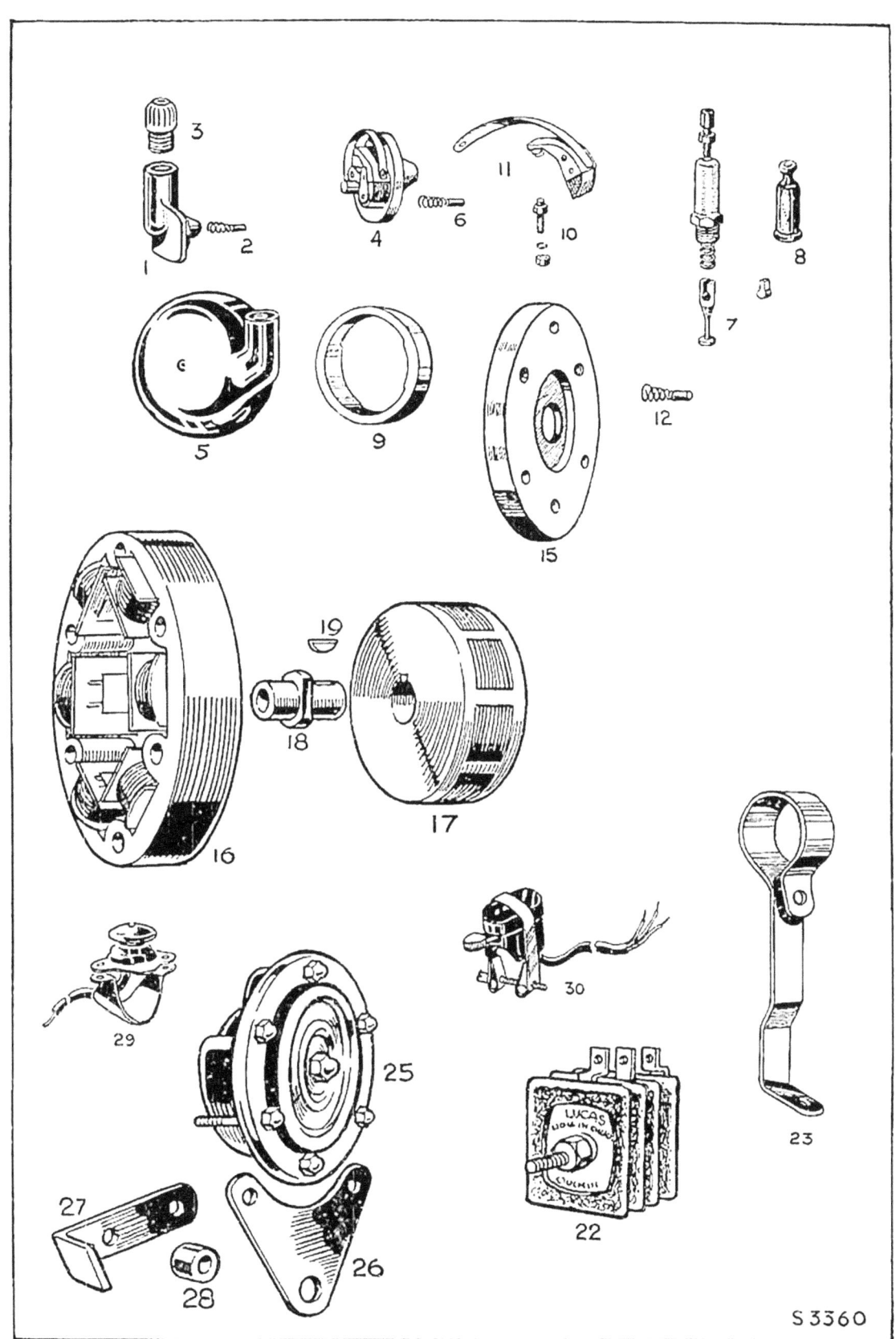

LUCAS LAMPS AND STOPLIGHT

Illus. No.	No. of part.	Description.	No. per set
	LU/50943E	Headlamp MCF 700P comprising unit light with front and fixing rims	1
1	LU/553248	Front rim	1
2	LU/553267	Fixing ring	1
3	39218	Rim fixing screw	2
4	LU/144921	" adjusting screw	1
5	LU/553925	Unit light	1
6	LU/504665	" " fixing wire	4
7	LU/554602	Bulb holder	1
8	LU/312	Main bulb, 6v., 30 × 24w.	1
9	LU/36084F	Ammeter	1
10	LU/31491A	Lighting switch	1
	LU/351567	Handle and fixing screw	1
11	LU/365408	Rubber ring, ammeter or switch	2
	LU/52234A	Pilot lamp complete, L550	2
12	LU/526496	Rim	2
	39218	" screw	2
13	LU/573615	Lens	2
15	LU/553780	Interior (bulb holder)	2
16	LU/526493	Rubber mounting	2
17	LU/988	Bulb, 6v. 3w.	2
	LU/53432B	Stop tail lamp No. 564	1
	LU/166014	Lamp securing nut	2
	LU/188327	" " " washer	2
22	LU/573839	Ruby lens	1
23	LU/575200	Clear window	1
24	LU/575208	Lens gasket	1
	LU/575219	" securing nut	2
26	LU/575209	Bulb holder	1
27	LU/575207	" " rubber cap	1
28	LU/573828	Contact assy.	1
29	LU/384	Bulb, 6v., 6 × 18w.	1
30	LU/573825	Cable grommet	1
	LU/199001	" grommet in mudguard	1
31	LU/31688	Stoplight switch	1
32	42701	" " distance tube	1
33	45702	" " attachment stud	1
	27944	" " " nut	1
	35605	" cable band	3

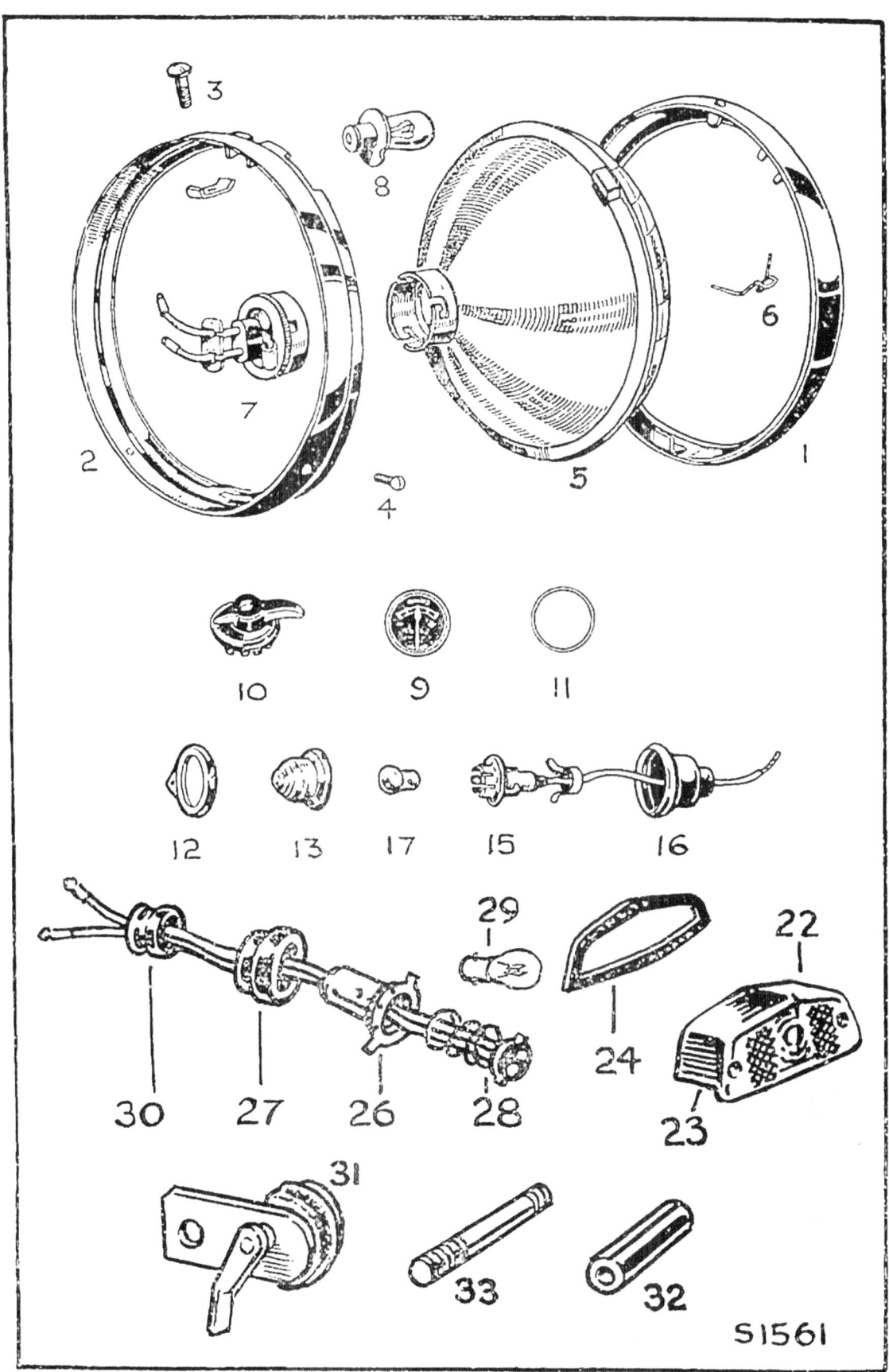

Guarantee

TERMS AND CONDITIONS OF SALE AND GUARANTEE

1. In this Guarantee the word "machine" refers to the new motor cycle, scooter, motor cycle combination or sidecar, as the case may be, purchased by the Purchaser.
2. In order to obtain the benefit of this Guarantee, the Purchaser must correctly complete the registration form and return it to us within fourteen days of the purchase.
3. We will supply, free of charge, a new part in exchange for, or, if we consider repair sufficient, will repair free of charge any part proved within six months of the date of purchase of any new machine, or within three months of its renewal or repair in the case of a part already renewed or repaired, to be defective by reason of our faulty workmanship or materials. We do not undertake to bear the cost of fitting such new or repaired part or accessory.
4. Any part considered to be defective must be sent to our Works, carriage paid, accompanied by the following information:—
   (a) Name of Purchaser and his address.
   (b) Date of purchase of machine.
   (c) Name of dealer from whom the purchase was made.
   (d) Engine and frame numbers of machine.
5. This Guarantee shall not extend to defects or damage appearing after misuse, neglect, abnormal stress or strain, or the incorporation or affixing of unsuitable attachments or parts and in particular:—
   (a) Hiring out.
   (b) Racing and competitions.
   (c) Adaptation or alteration of any part or parts after leaving our Works.
   (d) The attaching of a sidecar in a manner not approved by us or to an unsuitable motor cycle.
   This Guarantee shall not extend to machines whose trade mark, name, or manufacturing number has been altered or removed, or in which has been used any part not supplied or approved by us, or to tyres, saddles, chains, speedometers, revolution counters, and electrical equipment or to parts supplied to the order of the Purchaser and different from our standard specification.
6. Our liability and that of our dealer who sells the machine shall be limited to that set out in paragraph 3 and no other claims including claims for consequential damage or injury to person or property, shall be admissible.
   All other conditions and warranties statutory or otherwise and whether express or implied are hereby excluded and no guarantee other than that expressly herein contained applies to the machine to which this Guarantee relates or any accessory or part thereof.

REPAIRS GUARANTEE

1. While the highest standard of workmanship and materials is aimed at, we cannot accept liability for any defects appearing more than three months after the machine, assembly or component, has left our Works after being repaired.
2. We will repair or replace at our option free of charge any defective work, materials or parts relating to the repairs carried out by us appearing within that time but shall not be under any further or other liability for any other loss or damage whether direct or consequential and our liability shall be limited to the cost of so making good.
3. We do not accept liability in respect of parts of proprietary manufacture, e.g. tyres, saddles, chains, speedometers, revolution counters and electrical equipment which may be used by us in effecting a repair. All other conditions and warranties statutory or otherwise express or implied are hereby excluded.

NOTICE

We do not appoint Agents for the sale on our behalf of our Motor Cycles or other goods but we assign to Motor Cycle Dealers areas in which we supply to such Dealers exclusively for re-sale in such areas. No such Dealer is authorised to transact any business, give any warranty, make any representations or incur any liability on our behalf.

SPARE AND REPLACEMENT PARTS

for the 1967-1968

INTERCEPTOR

ROAD SCRAMBLER T.T. 7

and

ROAD RACER G.P. 7

MOTOR CYCLES

IMPORTANT

In order to avoid confusion or delay, engine or frame numbers and colour of enamelled parts MUST be quoted when ordering parts, along with the part number and description of the article required.

The engine number will be found stamped on the driving side of the crankcase below the cylinder barrel and the frame number on the head lug.

**THE ENFIELD CYCLE COMPANY LTD.,
MARSTON ROAD, WOLVERHAMPTON, STAFFORDSHIRE, ENGLAND.**

INDEX

	Page
Engine Unit and Crankcase Assembly	2
Cylinder and Head Assembly	4
Pistons and Crankshaft Assembly	6
Timing Gear and Timing Gear Assembly	8
Oil Pump, Filter Assembly, Oil Return Pipe and Crankcase Breather	10
Primary Chaincase	12
Gearbox: Cases and Kickstarter Mechanism	14
Gearbox: Running Gear	16
Gearbox: Gear Selector Mechanism	18
Clutch/Standard Shakeproof Washers	20
Frame Assembly, Gearbox Bracket and Centre Stand	22
Telescopic Front Fork	24
Handlebar, Controls and Control Cables	26
Front Wheel and Brake	28
Detachable Rear Wheel and Brake	30
Petrol Tank, Front Mudguard and Front Stand	32
Rear Suspension, Mudguard and Number Plate	34
Prop Stand, Pillion Footrests, Chainguard and Chains	36
Rear Brake Control, Exhaust System and Footrests	38
Tool Kit	40
Smiths Speedometer, Revolution Counter and Mounting	42
Amal "Monobloc" Carburettor	44
Amal "Concentric" Carburettor	46
Contact Breaker, Alternator, Rectifier, Heat Sink and Diode-Zener	48
Battery and Mounting, Coil and Cover, Electrolytic Capacitor and Ignition Switch	50
Lamps, Stoplight and Switches, Ammeter, Horn and Horn Push and Dipper Switch	52

Page 1

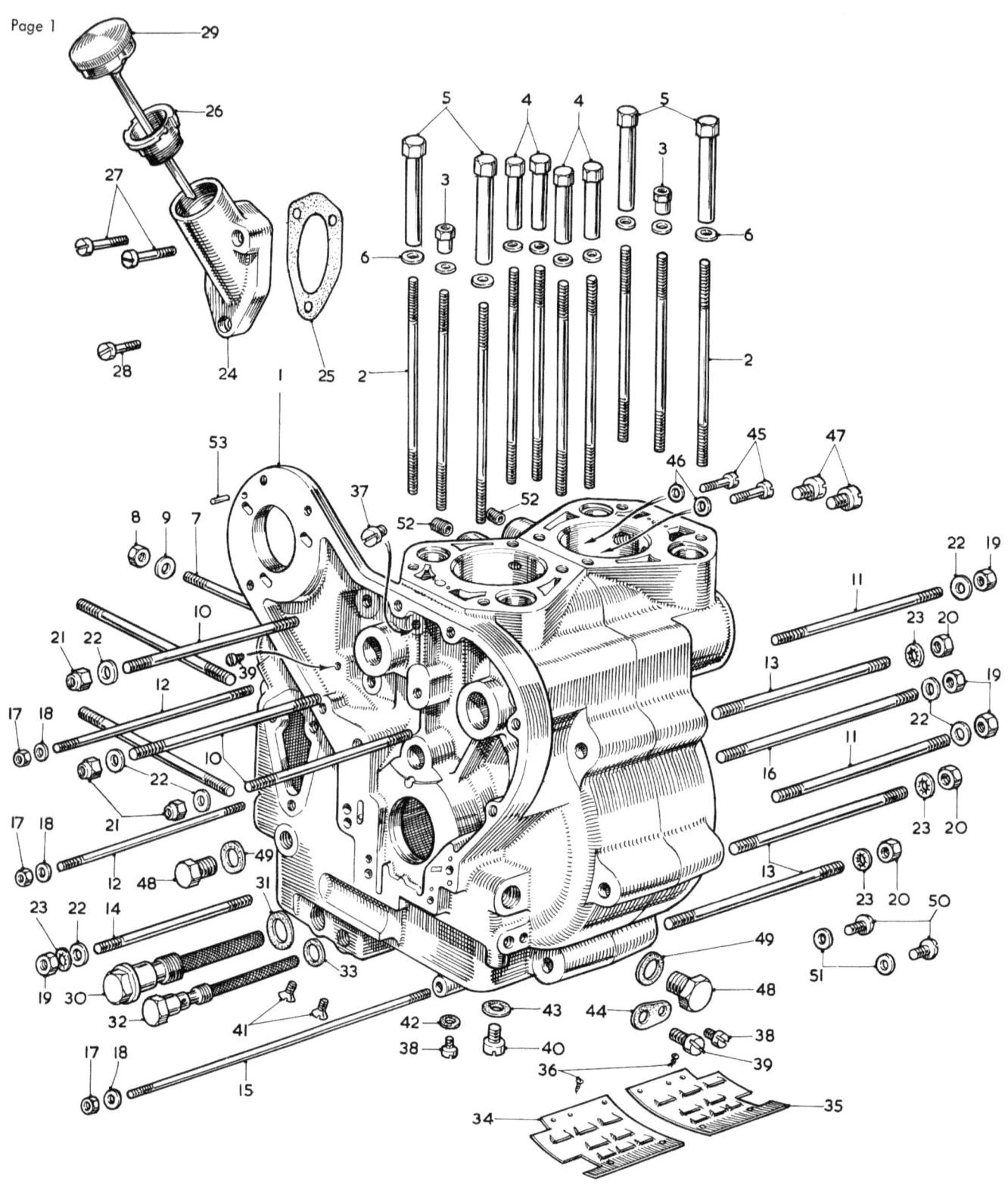

ENGINE UNIT AND CRANKCASE ASSEMBLY

Illustration No.	Part No.	Description	No. per Set
	41655	Interceptor engine unit, complete with carburettors contact breaker unit, sparking plugs and sprocket	1
1	46164	Crankcase assembly with main and camshaft bearings, tappets and guides and fixed studs) Earlier models	1
	49687	Crankcase assembly with main and camshaft bearings tappets and guides and fixed studs) Later models	1
2	45451	Stud, cylinder and head, 5/16" x 5" x 22 (BSF)	10
3	34968	Stud nut, 5/16" x 1/2" shouldered	2
4	45449	Stud nut, 5/16" x 3.1/4" shouldered	4
5	45448	Stud nut, 5/16" x 4.1/8" overall	4
6	1437	Stud washer	10
7	47208	Stud, gearbox, 3/8" x 6.5/8" x 26	4
8	29854	Stud nut	4
9	15641	Stud washer	4
10	34368	Stud, crankcase, top, 5/16" x 4.1/2" x 22 (BSF)	3
11	35589	Stud, crankcase, rear, 5/16" x 4.3/8" x 22 (BSF)	2
12	35595	Stud, crankcase, rear, 1/4" x 6.1/4" x 26 (BSF)	2
13	36079	Stud, crankcase, front, 5/16" x 4.1/2" x 26 (CEI)	3
14	44360	Stud, crankcase rear engine plate, 5/16" x 5" x 22	1
15	46167	Stud, crankcase bottom, 1/4" x 7.3/8" x 26 (BSF)	1
16	49026	Stud, crankcase bottom, 5/16" x 4.15/16" x 26 (BSF)	1
17	27620	Stud nut, 1/4" x 26 (BSF)	6
18	82	Stud washer, 1/4" (plain)	6
19	27621	Stud nut, 5/16" x 22 (BSF)	5
20	8633	Stud nut, 5/16" x 26 (CEI)	6
21	36221	Stud nut, 5/16" x 22 (BSF) nylock	3
22	8634	Stud washer, 5/16" (plain)	13
23	27917	Stud washer, 5/16" (shakeproof)	8
24	48016	Oil filler extension	1
25	34365	Oil filler extension gasket	1
26	18275	Oil filler extension collar	1
27	35591	Oil filler extension screw, 1/4" x 1.5/8" x 26 (BSF)	2
28	35592	Oil filler extension screw, 1/4" x 5/8" x 26 (BSF)	1
29	48017	Oil filler cap and dipstick	1
30	37884	Drain plug and filter assembly)	1
31	17024	Drain plug and filter washer) Earlier models	1
32	48022/A	Scavenge feed plug (complete))	1
33	5662	Scavenge feed plug fibre washer)	1
32	48022/A	Scavenge feed plug (complete)) Later models	2
33	5662	Scavenge feed plug fibre washer)	2
34	46152	Oil shield T/S crankcase	1
35	46151	Oil shield D/S crankcase	1
36	35636	Oil shield screw, Parker Kalon, type Z No. 4	8
37	16476	Oil plug screw, 1/4" x 7/32" x 26 (BSF)	1
38	34375	Oil plug screw, 1/4" x 3/4" x 26 (BSF)	2
39	34374	Oil plug screw, 5/16" x 1/4" x 22 (BSF), omitted when oil cooler is fitted	1
40	34373	Oil plug screw, 5/16" x 9/32" x 22 (BSF)	1
41	26177	Oil plug screw countersunk head, 1/4" x 3/16" x 26	2
42	30394	Oil plug screw fibre washer, 1/4" dia.	1
43	36136	Oil plug screw fibre washer, 5/16" dia.	1
44	34381	Oil plug screw fibre washer two hole	1
45	37724	Crankcase bridge screw	2
46	34690	Crankcase bridge screw washer	2
47	43359	Crankcase plug	2
48	45452	Crankcase blanking screw (oil cooler port)	2
49	5662	Crankcase blanking screw washer	2
50	35704	Oil drain plug	2
51	46141	Oil drain plug washer	2
52	38621	"Cross" wire insert	2
53	45370	Timing cover dowel	1

Always quote Engine or Frame Number

Page 3

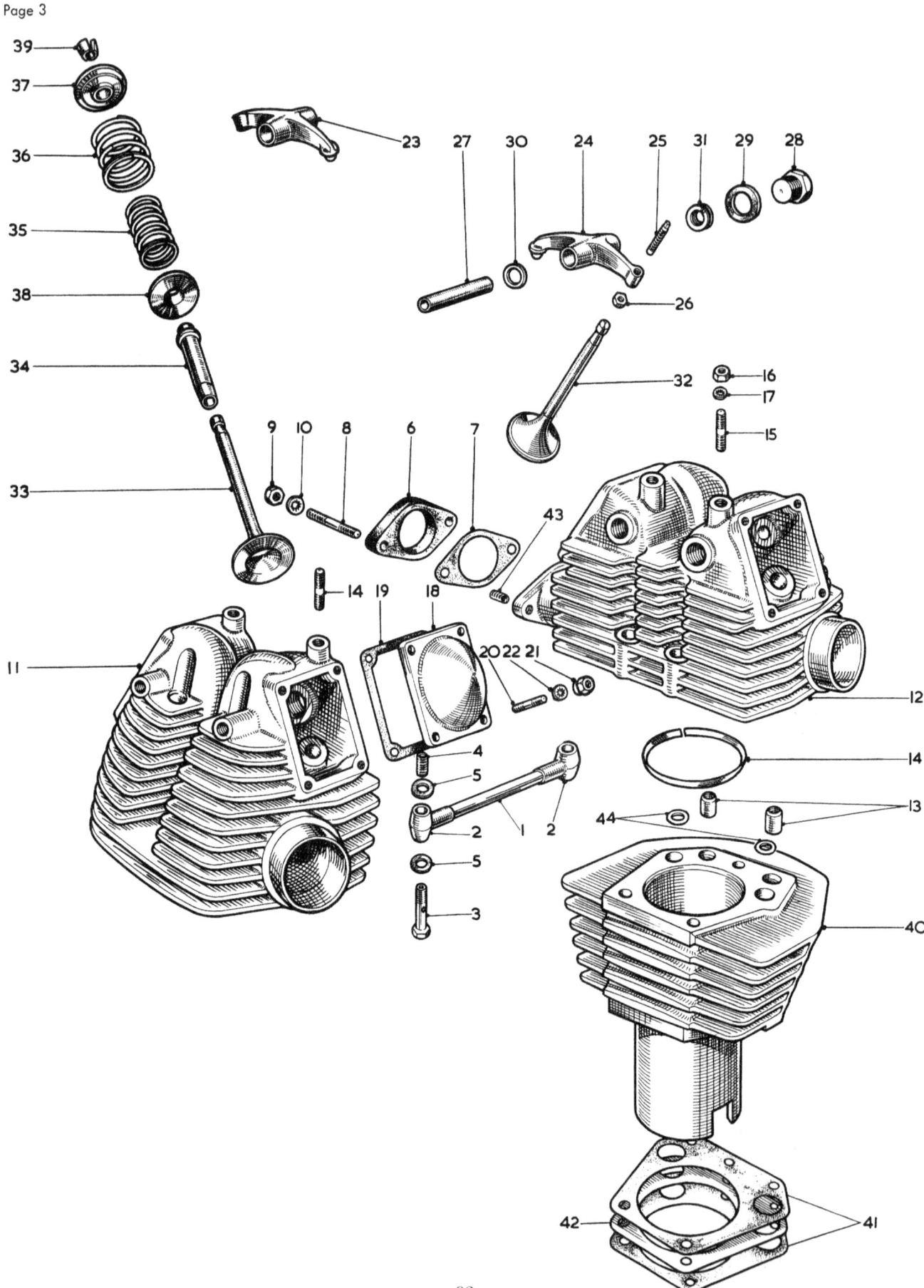

CYLINDER AND HEAD ASSEMBLY

Illustration No.	Part No.	Description	No. per Set
	48007	Induction balance pipe complete	1
1	48009	Induction balance pipe	1
2	D5254	Induction balance pipe banjo	2
3	48012	Induction balance pipe banjo bolt	2
4	48010	Induction balance pipe cross wire inserts	2
5	46191	Heat insulation washer	2
6	42518	Carburettor flange gasket	2
7	32363	Carburettor flange stud, 1/4" x 1.3/16" x 26 (BSF)	4
8	27944	Carburettor flange stud nut, 1/4" (BSF)	4
9	27917	Carburettor flange stud washer	4
10	46156	Cylinder head, R.H.) fitted with valve guides and fixed studs	1
11	46158	Cylinder head, L.H.)	1
12	45447	Cylinder head dowel	4
13	46184	Cross gasket ring	2
14	35780	Cylinder head engine steady stud, 5/16" x 13/16" (BSF)	4
15	27944	Cylinder head engine steady stud nut	4
16	8634	Cylinder head engine steady stud washer	4
17	32552	Rocker box cover	4
18	32553	Rocker box cover gasket	4
19	48011	Rocker box cover stud, 1/4" x 7/8" x 26 (BSF)	16
20	37852	Rocker box cover stud nut, 1/4" (BSF)	16
21	82	Rocker box cover stud washer	16
22	39735	Rocker (inlet R.H., Exhaust L.H.)	2
23	39736	Rocker (inlet L.H., exhaust R.H.)	2
24	32550	Rocker adjusting screw	4
25	32549	Rocker adjusting locknut	4
26	38644	Rocker spindle	4
27	36985	Rocker spindle end plug	4
28	39468	Rocker spindle end plug washer (copper)	4
29	32554	Rocker spindle thrust washer	4
30	35904	Rocker spindle spring washer	4
31	43521	Valve, exhaust	2
32	42661	Valve, inlet	2
33	42660	Valve, guide	2
34	42693	Valve spring, inner	4
35	42692	Valve spring, outer	4
36	42651	Valve collar, top	4
37	42652	Valve collar, bottom	4
38	42492	Valve split collar	4
39	46129	Cylinder barrel	2
40	45450	Cylinder base gasket	4
41	46193	Compression plate	2
	239	Gasket set, decarbonisation only	1
	240	Gasket set, complete engine and chaincase	1
42	38621	Cross wire insert	4
43	46150/A	Push rod tunnel oil seal (complete)	4

Always quote Engine or Frame Number

Page 5

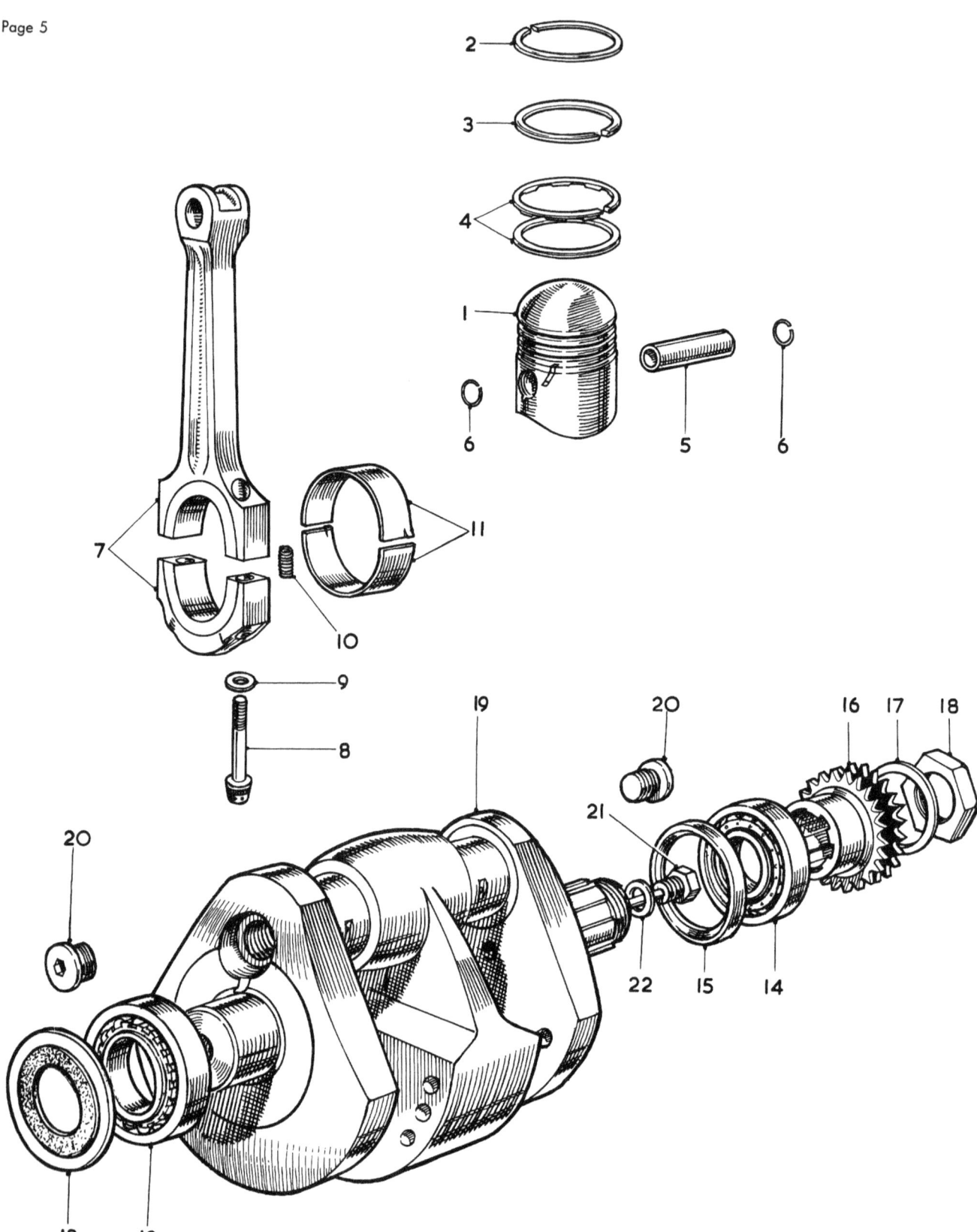

PISTONS AND CRANKSHAFT ASSEMBLY

Page 6

Illustration No.	Part No.	Description	No. per Set
	46160	Piston, complete with rings, gudgeon pin and circlips, ratio 8 to 1 } up to Engine No. 17076	2
1	46160/A	Piston, complete with rings, gudgeon pin and circlips, ratio 8.5 to 1 } after Engine No. 17077	2
2	46161	Piston ring (top, chrome plated)	2
3	46162	Piston ring (lower, compression)	2
4	46163	Piston ring (twin segment scraper)	2
5	47178	Gudgeon pin	2
6	38771	Gudgeon pin circlip	4
7	41719/B	Connecting rod assembly, complete with B.E. screws and shells	2
8	47876	Connecting rof B.E. screw	4
9	14691	Connecting rod B.E. screw washer	4
10	45444	Connecting rod inserts	4
	36017	Connecting rod S.E. bush (for Service use)	2
11	41722	Connecting rod B.E. bearing shell (one half)	4
12	SK/N209 Hoffman R.145 or R & M.LRJ45	Crankshaft timing side roller bearing, 45 x 85 x 19 mm	1
13	462001	Crankshaft timing side steel and rubber oil seal	1
14	SK/6209 Hoffman 145 or R & M.LJ.45	Crankshaft drive side bearing, 45 x 85 x 19 mm	1
15	34062	Crankshaft drive bearing distance collar	1
16	41965/A	Engine sprocket 29T	1
17	34076	Engine sprocket washer	1
18	34064	Engine sprocket locknut	1
	46168	Crankshaft assembly, complete with connecting rods	1
19	46153	Crankshaft only	1
20	44510	Crankshaft oil plug	2
21	48025	Crankshaft bolt	1
22	42030	Crankshaft bolt washer	1

Always quote Engine or Frame Number

Page 7

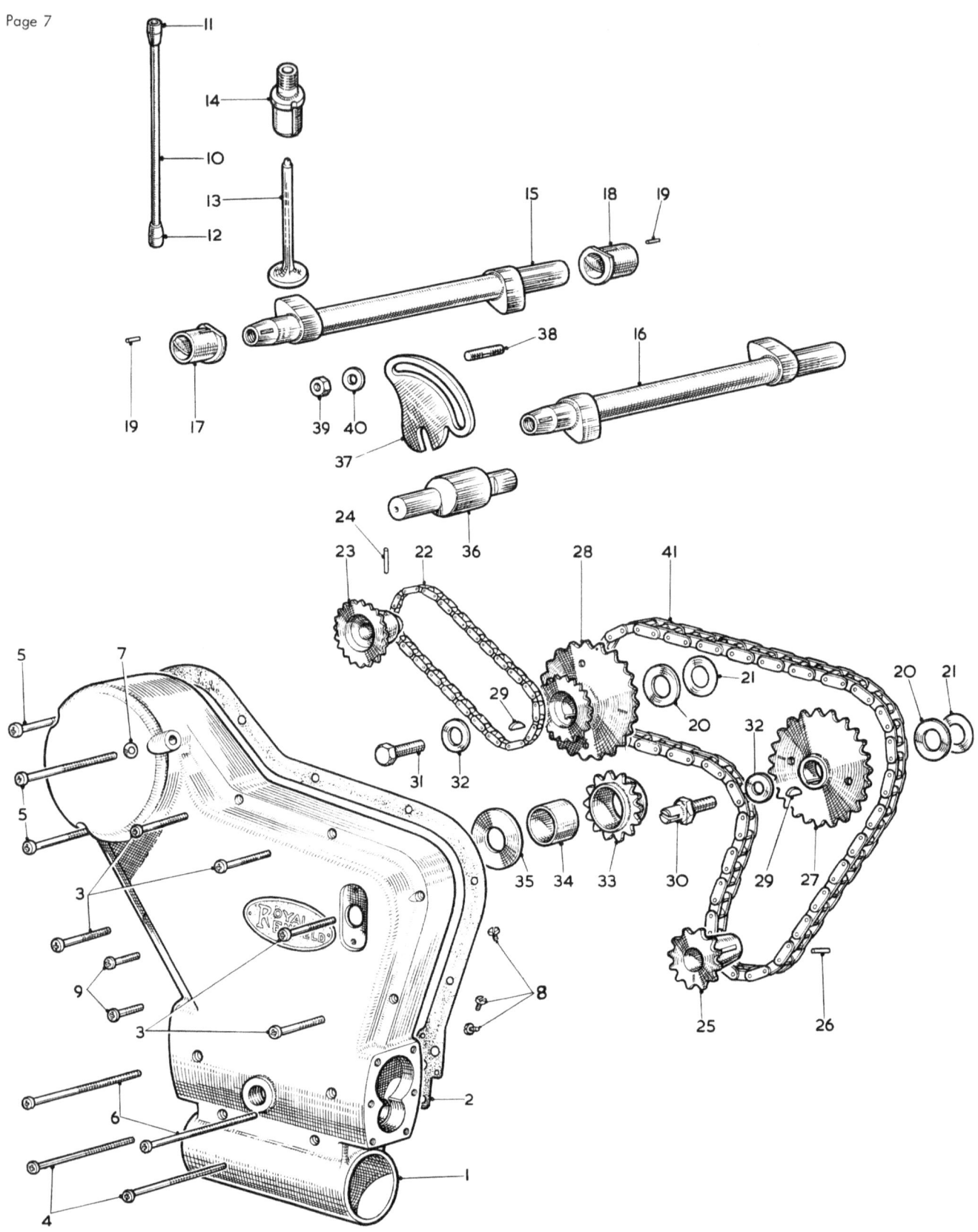

TIMING GEAR AND TIMING GEAR ASSEMBLY

Illustration No.	Part No.	Description	No. per Set
1	46127/B	Timing cover	1
2	46170	Timing cover gasket	1
3	42139	Timing cover screw, 1/4" x 1.1/4" x 26 (B.S.F.)	5
4	42140	Timing cover screw, 1/4" x 1.7/16" x 26 (B.S.F.)	2
5	42136	Timing cover screw, 1/4" x 2" x 26 (B.S.F.)	3
6	42133	Timing cover screw 1/4" x 1.13/16" x 26 (B.S.F.)	2
7	34690	Timing cover screw washer	12
8	28858	Timing cover oil passage screw, 3/16" x 1/4" x 32	4
	42458	Tachometer drive cover	1
	42504	Tachometer drive cover gasket	1
9	45411	Tachometer drive cover screw 1/4" x 13/16" x 26 (B.S.F.)	2
10	48028	Push rod assembly (alloy)	4
11	38052	Push rod end top	4
12	37839	Push rod end bottom	4
13	23480	Tappet	4
14	34360	Tappet guide	4
15	W35344	Camshaft (inlet)	1
16	W35345	Camshaft (exhaust)	1
17	32709	Camshaft bearing (timing side)	2
18	32710	Camshaft bearing (L.H. side)	2
19	48015	Mills pin	2
20	35894	Camshaft thrust washer	2
21	42528	Camshaft shim	
22	RN/110500/40	Contact breaker duplex chain, endless, 8 m.m. x 5 m.m. x 40 pitches	1
23	41936	Contact breaker sprocket	1
24	4821	Contact breaker sprocket bolt peg	1
25	35735	Timing sprocket, 12T	1
26	35724	Timing sprocket peg	1
27	34350	Camshaft sprocket exhaust	1
28	48027	Camshaft sprocket inlet	1
29	9410	Sprocket key	2
30	41534	Sprocket securing bolt, exhaust, 1/2" x 7/8" x 26 L.H.	1
31	41968	Sprocket securing bolt, inlet, 1/2" x 1.1/4" x 26 L.H.	1
32	15380	Sprocket securing washer	2
33	34372	Chain tensioning sprocket and bush	1
34	34354	Chain tensioning sprocket bush only	1
35	34353	Chain tensioning sprocket thrust washer	1
36	38552	Chain tensioning sprocket spindle	1
37	34351	Chain tensioning plate	1
38	29314	Chain tensioning plate stud, 1/4" x 7/8" x 26	1
39	36222	Chain tensioning plate stud nut	1
40	82	Chain tensioning plate stud washer	1
41	RN/110038/66	Timing chain, endless, 66 pitches	1

Always quote Engine or Frame Number

Page 9

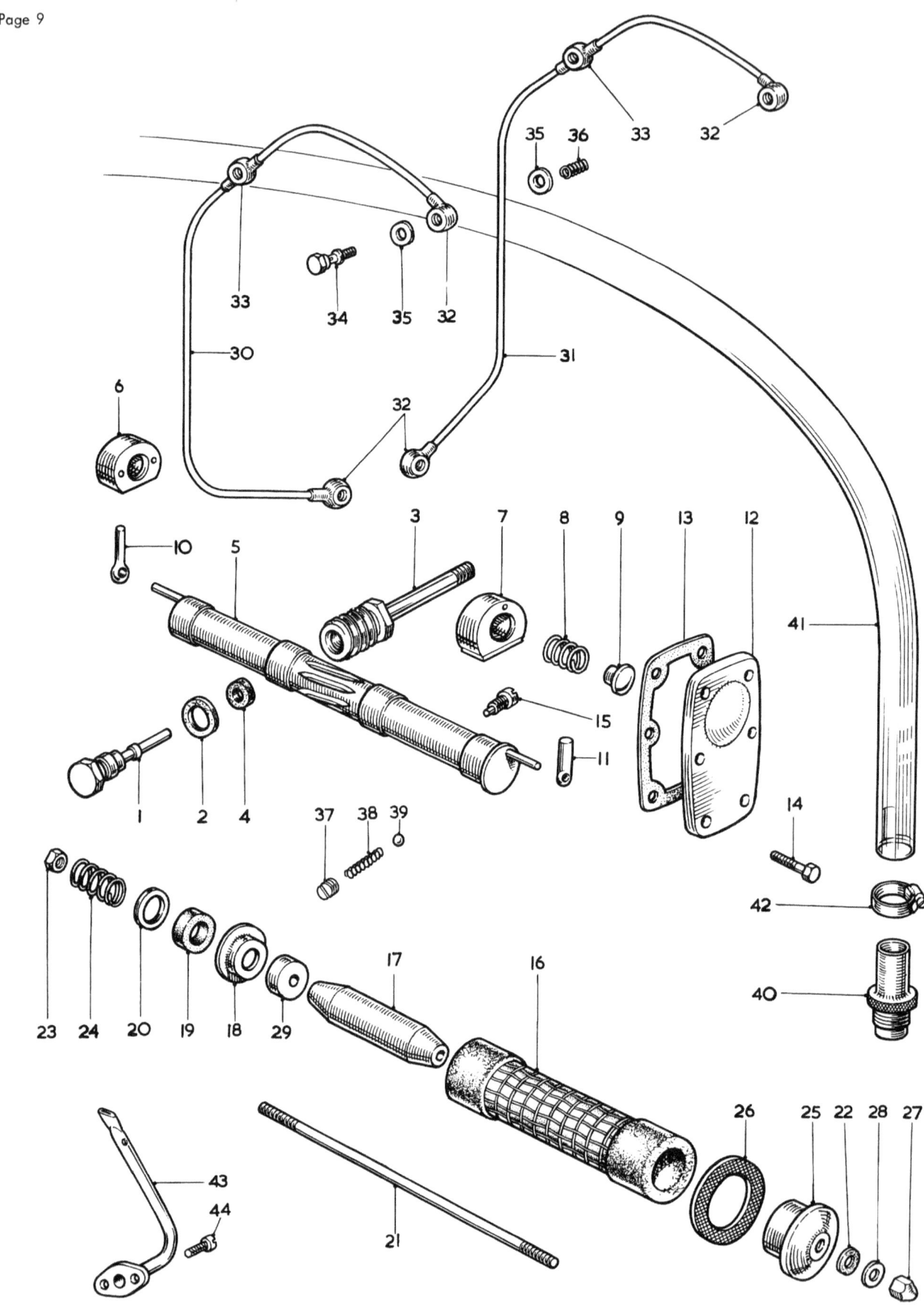

OIL PUMP, FILTER ASSEMBLY, OIL RETURN PIPE AND CRANKCASE BREATHER

Page 10

Illustration No.	Part No.	Description	No. per Set
1	42113	Oil feed plug	1
2	24177	Oil feed plug fibre washer	1
3	38622	Oil pump worm (2 start)	1
4	42114	Oil pump worm rubber seal	1
5	38623/A	Oil pump spindle	1
6	37665A	Oil pump disc (feed)	1
7	37666A	Oil pump disc (return)	1
8	41851	Oil pump disc spring	2
9	37669	Oil pump disc spring end pad	2
10	34346	Oil pump plunger (feed)	1
11	34347	Oil pump plunger (return)	1
12	45382	Oil pump cover	2
13	45383	Oil pump cover gasket	2
14	45385	Oil pump cover screw, 3/16" x 1/2" x 32	12
15	46142	Oil pump locating screw	1
16	40792	Oil cleaner element	1
17	40684	Oil cleaner element filling piece	1
18	28254	Oil cleaner spring cup	1
19	18793	Oil cleaner spring cup felt washer	1
20	8894	Oil cleaner spring thrust washer	1
21	28255	Oil cleaner stud, 3/8" x 6.1/4"	1
22	13785	Oil cleaner stud fibre washer	1
23	26996	Oil cleaner stud locknut	1
24	28259	Oil cleaner spring	1
25	28256	Oil cleaner cap	1
26	28258	Oil cleaner cap washer	1
27	23748	Oil cleaner cap nut	1
28	8894	Oil cleaner cap nut washer	4
29	42505	Oil cleaner magnet	1
30	47702	Oil feed pipe, complete R.H.	1
31	47705	Oil feed pipe, complete L.H.	1
32	32388	Oil feed pipe banjo	4
33	39152	Oil feed pipe banjo	2
34	32389	Oil feed union body	6
35	39469	Oil feed union body washer (copper)	12
36	38621	Union body wire insert (in crankcase and heads)	6
37	46197	Oil release valve plug)	1
38	39974	Oil release valve spring) In timing cover joint face	1
39	32017	Oil release valve ball)	1
40	48764	Breather union	1
41	48785	Breather tube	1
42	43965	Breather tube clip	1
43	41327	Oil return pipe and adaptor assembly	1
44	29781	Oil return pipe and adaptor screw	2

Always quote Engine or Frame Number

Page 11

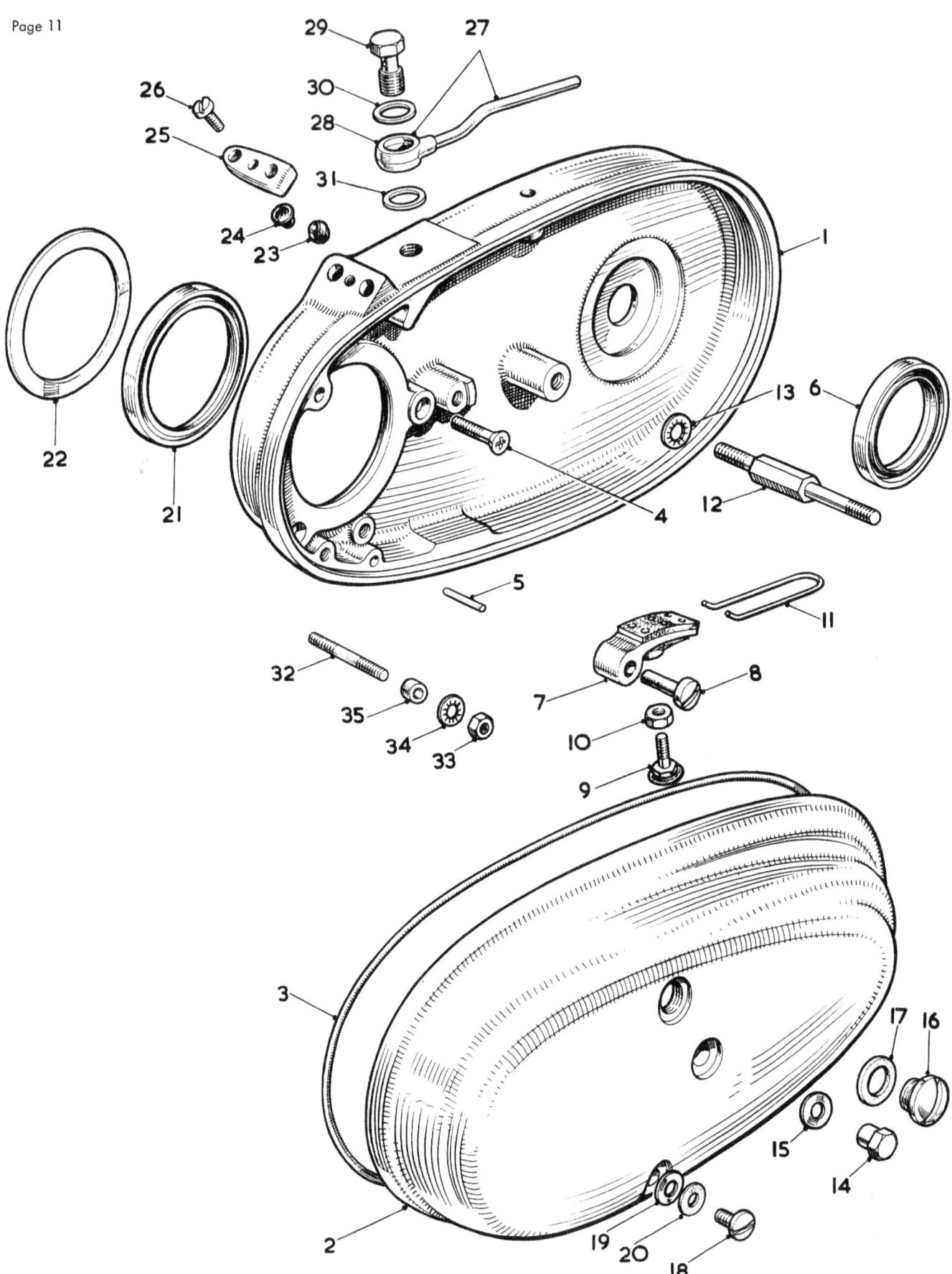

PRIMARY CHAINCASE

Illustration No.	Part No.	Description	No. per Set
1	45372	Chaincase (back)	1
2	48008	Chaincase (front)	1
3	40097	Chaincase rubber joint	1
4	38027	Chaincase (back) fixing screw 5/16" x 1" overall x 26	3
5	45373	Chaincase dowel	2
6	43565	Oil seal (gearbox mainshaft)	1
7	45386	Chain tensioner	1
8	36911	Chain tensioner spindle	1
9	45367	Chain tensioner adjusting screw with buffer	1
10	15771	Chain tensioner adjusting screw locknut	1
11	39664	Chain tensioner spring	1
12	45387	Chaincase (front) fixing stud	1
13	27918	Chaincase (front) fixing stud washer	1
14	35032	Chaincase stud nut	1
15	1580	Chaincase stud washer	1
16	40640	Chaincase inspection cover	2
17	40641	Chaincase inspection cover washer	2
18	35704	Oil level plug	1
19	46141	Oil level plug washer	1
20		Oil level plug fibre washers	1
21	43382	Oil seal	1
22	34069	Oil seal washer (outer) 3.21/64" x 2.9/32" x .024"	1
23	42268	Chaincase cable grommet	1
24	42834	Cable hole plug	1
25	42269	Cable hole plug housing	1
26	31172	Cable hole plug housing screw	1
27	45404	Breather pipe assembly	1
28	36999	Breather banjo	1
29	37000/A	Breather banjo union	1
30	30395	Breather fibre washer 3/8" x 5/8" x 3/64"	1
31	13785	Breather fibre washer 25/64" x 11/16" x 1/16"	1
32	46199	Stator fixing stud (5/16" x 1.7/8" x 22) RM 19 (B)	3
33	27944	Stator fixing stud nut	3
34	27917	Stator fixing stud nut washer	3
35	45388	Stator fixing distance collar	3

OIL COOLER

Part No.	Description	No. per Set
45441	Oil cooler complete	1
45436	Oil cooler body	1
45438	Oil cooler body end cap (R.H.)	1
45439	Oil cooler body end cap (L.H.)	1
45440	Oil cooler body end cap gasket	2
45385	Oil cooler body end cap screws	12
34370	Oil cooler body stud	2
27620	Oil cooler body nut	2
27916	Oil cooler body washer	4
45454	Union body	4
5664	Union	1
45456	Feed pipe assembly	1
45451	Feed pipe	1
45455	Feed pipe banjo	2
45458	Return pipe assembly	1
45459	Feed pipe	1
45455	Feed pipe banjo	2
5662	Fibre washer	
45442	Mounting bracket	2
45453	Oil plug plug screw 3/8"	1

Always quote Engine or Frame Number

Page 13

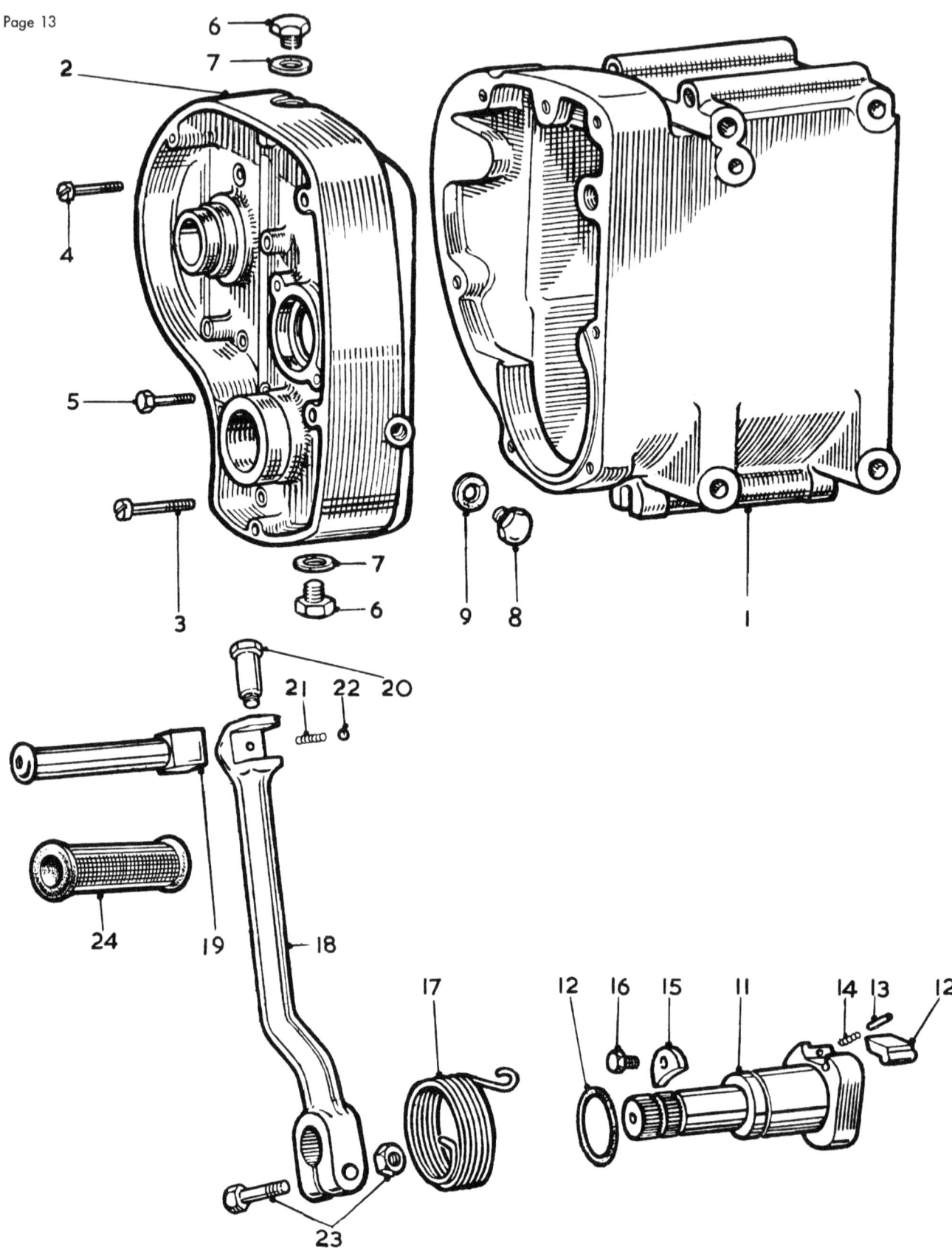

GEARBOX: CASES AND KICKSTARTER MECHANISM

Page 14

Illustration No.	Part No.	Description	No. per Set
	46135/A	Gearbox, complete with clutch, 20T sprocket	1
1	33885/1	Gearbox case, complete with seal	1
2	37518/A	Gearbox case end cover	1
3	FC/57/107	Gearbox cover screw, cheese head, 1/4" x 1.7/16" x 20	2
4	FC/57/103	Gearbox cover screw, cheese head, 1/4" x 1.3/16" x 20	2
5	H54/103	Gearbox cover bolt, 1/4" x 1.3/16" x 20	1
6	E140	Oil filler plug or drain plug	2
7	E140A	Oil filler plug or drain plug washer	2
8	BJ23	Oil level plug	1
9	BJ23A	Oil level plug washer	1
10	H21/4	Footstarter spindle	1
11	H77	Footstarter spindle oil seal	1
12	37355	Footstarter pawl	1
13	H22A	Footstarter pawl plunger	1
14	H23	Footstarter pawl plunger spring	1
15	37356	Footstarter pawl stop plate	1
16	37357	Footstarter pawl stop plate bolt	2
17	E137/5	Footstarter return spring	1
18	H42/42A/6	Folding footstarter crank assembly	1
19	H42/4	Footstarter pedal	1
20	H42B	Footstarter pedal bolt	1
21	H42C	Footstarter pedal lock spring	1
22	32018	Footstarter pedal lock spring ball	1
23	H43S	Footstarter crank bolt and nut	1
24	G46KS	Footstarter pedal rubber	1

Always quote Engine or Frame Number

Page 15

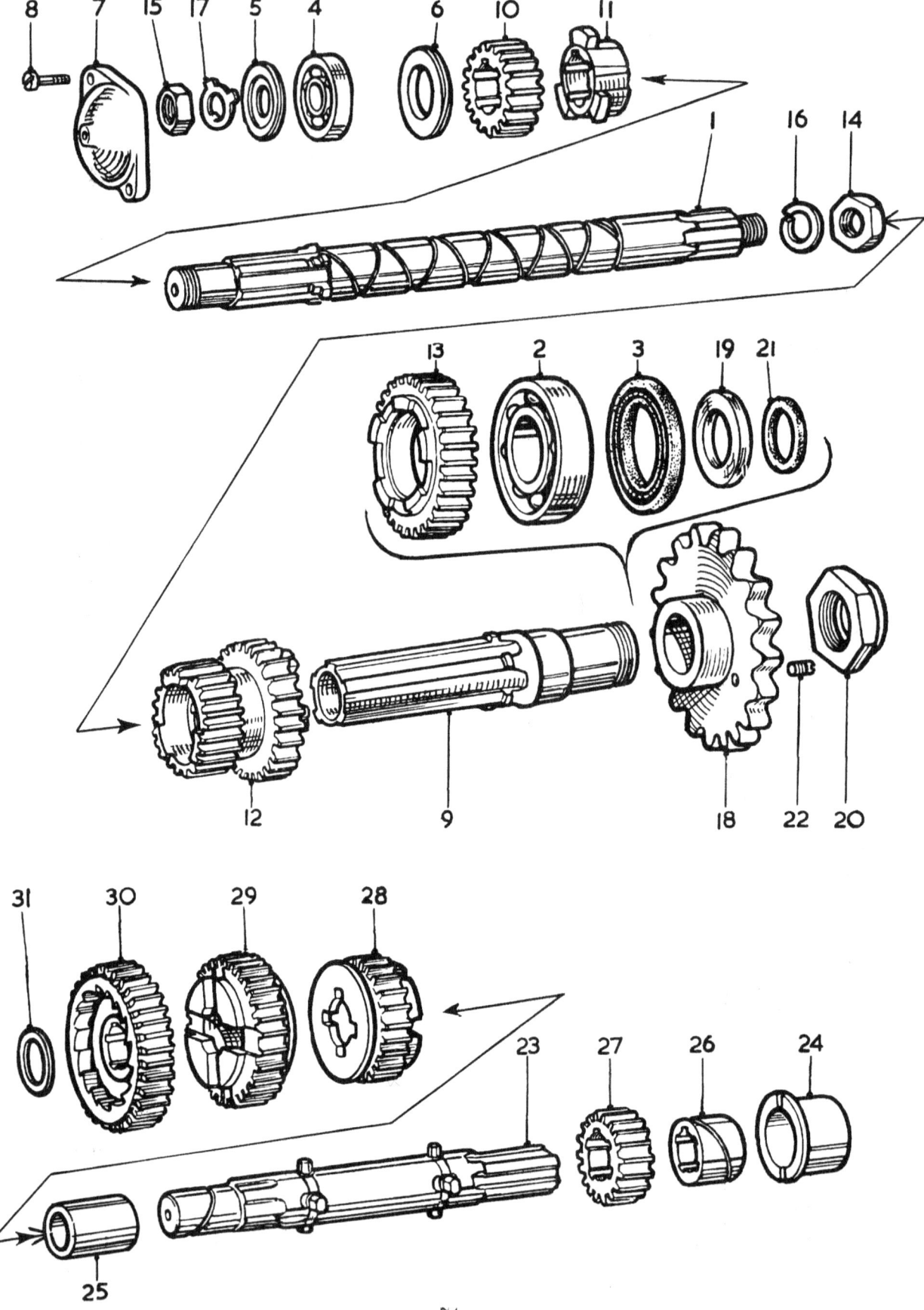

GEARBOX: RUNNING GEAR

Illustration No.	Part No.	Description	No. per Set
1	G2/7/TA	Mainshaft	1
2	H5	Mainshaft ball race (large) SK/6206	1
3	H3/2	Mainshaft ball race oil seal	1
4	31966	Mainshaft ball race (small) M.S.7	1
5	H71	Mainshaft ball race oil thrower (outer)	1
6	H52	Mainshaft ball race oil thrower (inner)	1
7	H40/1	Mainshaft ball race oil thrower cap	1
8	FC57/009	Mainshaft ball race oil thrower pin, cheese head, 1/4" x 9/16"	2
9	G2/8B	Mainshaft sleeve (bushed)	1
10	HG9/15	Mainshaft high gear 15T	1
11	H10A	Mainshaft high gear dog	1
12	HG11/21/18	Mainshaft sliding gear 21T and 18T	1
13	HG12/25	Mainshaft low gear 25T	1
14	H55	Mainshaft nut (R.H. thread), clutch end	1
15	H56	Mainshaft nut (L.H. thread), kickstart end	1
16	H57	Mainshaft spring washer	1
17	H91	Mainshaft (L.H. thread) nut locking washer	1
18	H49/20T	Drive sprocket 20T solo	1
19	G2/53	Drive sprocket distance piece	1
20	45428	Drive sprocket locknut	1
21	H121	Drive sprocket locknut felt washer	1
22	H122	Drive sprocket locknut screw	1
23	M13	Layshaft	1
24	H14	Layshaft bush (case end)	1
25	H15	Layshaft bush (kickstart end)	1
26	H16	Layshaft splined bush	1
27	HG17/15	Layshaft low gear 15T	1
28	HG18/19	Layshaft second gear 19T	1
29	HG19/22	Layshaft third gear 22T	1
30	HG20/25	Layshaft gear and kickstart wheel 25T	1
31	H15A	Foot starter spindle washer	1

Always quote Engine or Frame Number

Page 17

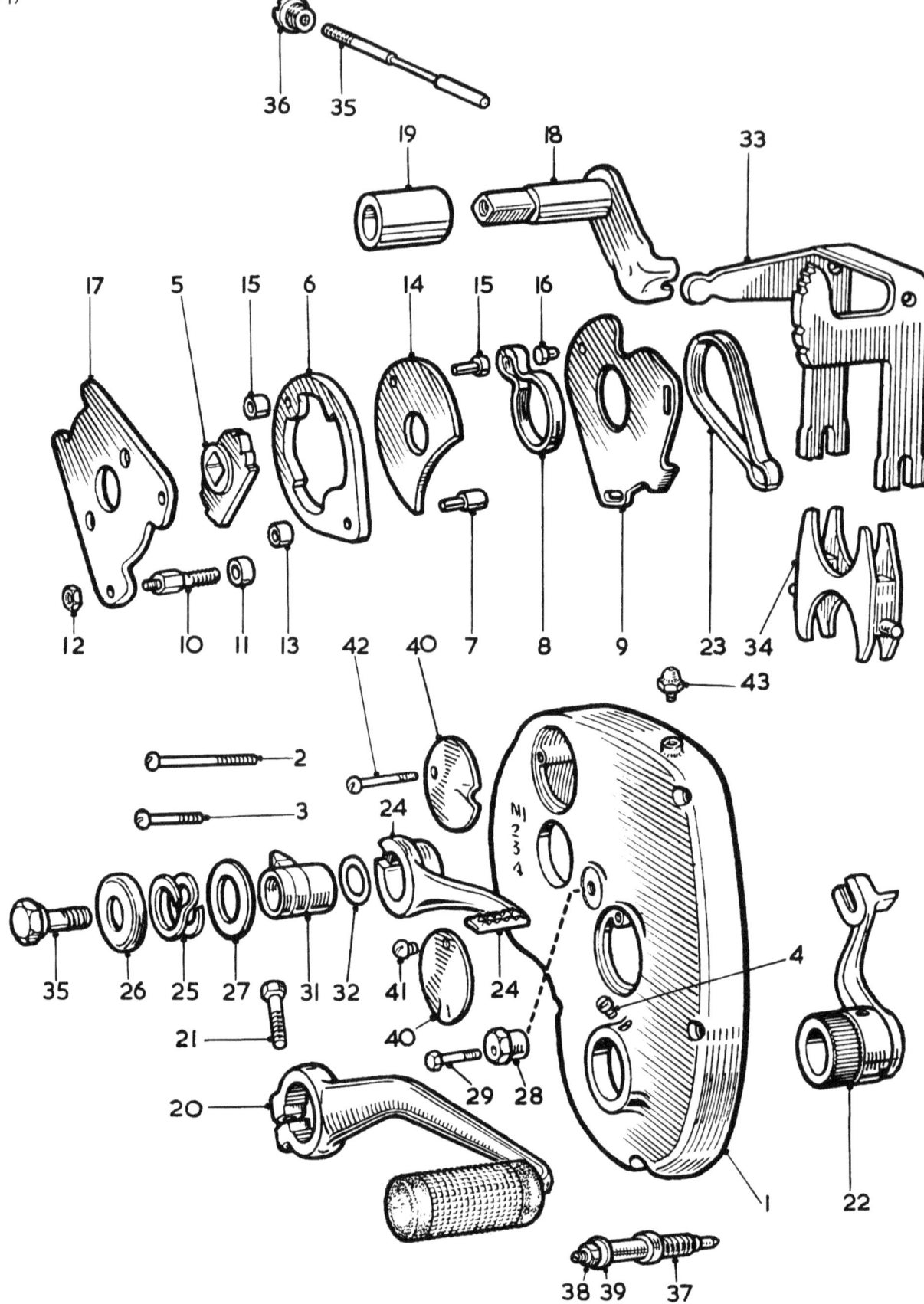

GEARBOX: GEAR SELECTOR MECHANISM

Illustration No.	Part No.	Description	No. per Set
1	G2/1A/1	Foot control cover	1
2	FC57/212	Foot control cover screw, cheese head, 1/4" x 2.3/4" x 20	2
3	FC57/103	Foot control cover screw, cheese head, 1/4" x 1.3/16" x 20	2
4	G2/14	Foot control cover oil hole screw, cheese head, 1/4" x 3/16" x 24	1
5	HFC4	Foot control ratchet (inner)	1
6	FC1/35/1	Foot control ratchet (outer)	1
7	FC44	Foot control ratchet pin	1
8	FC51	Foot control ratchet spring	1
9	FC41/1	Foot control adjuster plate	1
10	FC43	Foot control adjuster plate pin	2
11	FC58	Foot control adjuster plate pin bush	2
12	H113	Foot control adjuster plate nut	2
13	FC45	Foot control adjuster plate spring stop	1
14	FC53	Foot control plate	1
15	FC54	Foot control plate pin bush	2
16	FC46	Foot control plate spring stop	1
17	FC42/1	Foot control stop plate and spring retainer	1
18	FC47/E	Foot control operator shaft with lever	1
19	FC6E	Foot control operator shaft bush	1
20	FC/30F	Foot control lever	1
21	FC/30/A	Foot control lever pinch bolt	1
22	FC/48F	Foot control lever (short, inside)	1
23	FC/52/1	Foot control lever return spring	1
24	NS1/1	Foot control neutral lever	1
25	NS2	Foot control neutral lever spring	1
26	NS3	Foot control neutral lever spring cap	1
27	NS4	Foot control neutral lever spring washer	1
28	NS6	Foot control neutral lever eccentric bush	1
29	NS5	Foot control neutral lever stop pin	1
30	NS8	Foot control neutral lever securing pin	1
31	NS7/1	Foot control gear indicator	1
32	NS9	Foot control gear indicator washer	1
33	H33	Gear operator (inside)	1
34	H34	Gear operator fork	1
35	G2/36/1	Gear operator pin	1
36	G2/37	Gear operator pin bush	1
37	H67Ass.	Gear operator selector box assembly	1
38	H67B	Gear operator selector nut	1
39	H67C	Gear operator selector washer	1
40	HJ73	End cover inspection cap	2
41	H60/1	Inspection cap pin, 3/16" x 3/8" B.S.F.	1
42	H60/1A	Inspection cap pin, 3/16" x 1.1/4" B.S.F.	1
43	TC/PZ6	Grease nipple	1

Always quote Engine or Frame Number

Page 19

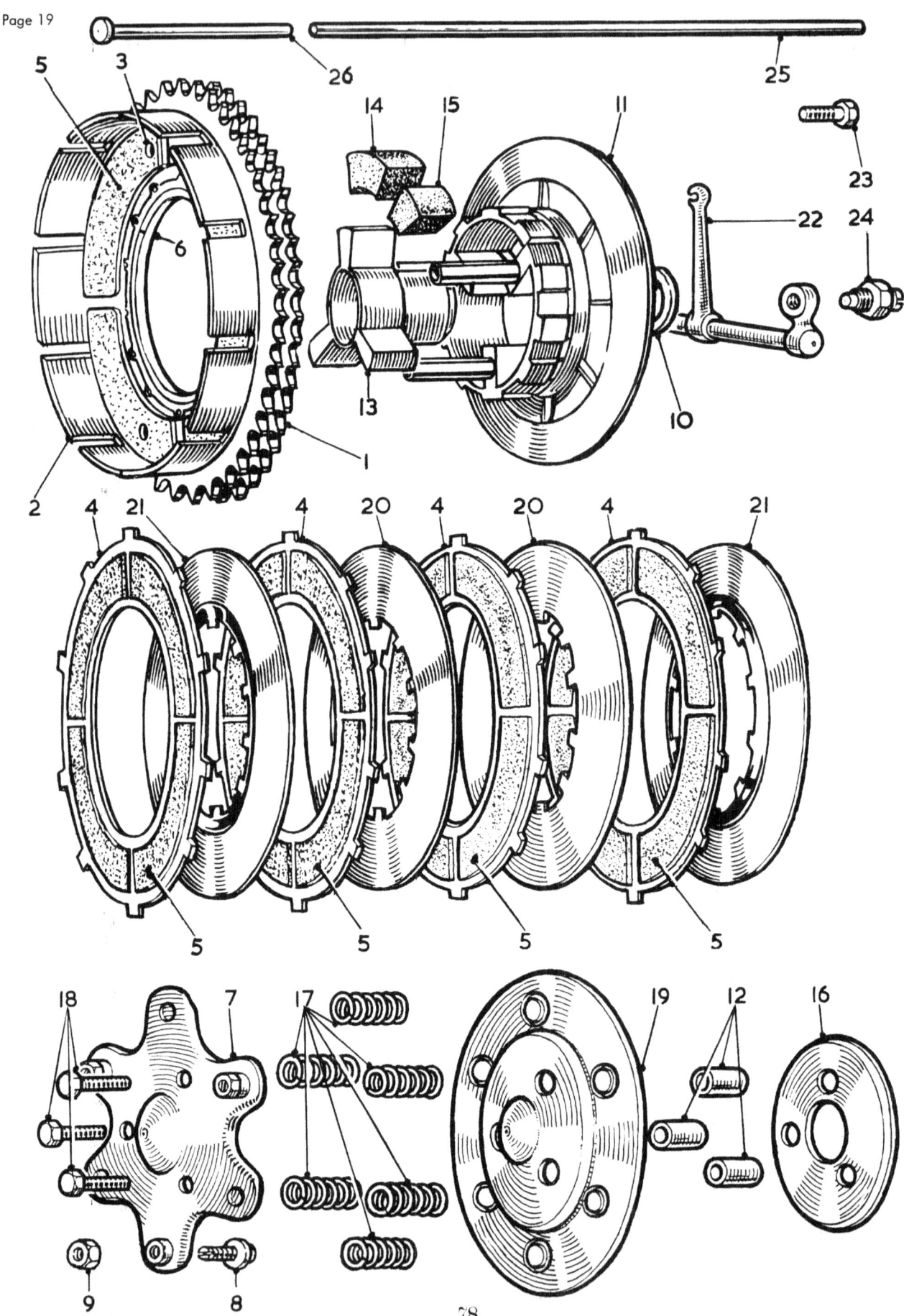

CLUTCH

Illustration No.	Part No.	Description	No. per Set
	28433/5/2	Clutch assembly	1
1	27535/6	Clutch sprocket 56T and drum assembly	1
2	H81/5	Clutch sprocket drum	1
3	G74A	Clutch sprocket drum rivets	15
4	H89CB	Clutch plate, cork bonded	4
5	H89/CB/2	Clutch plate, cork segments	32
6	GPG235/4	Clutch sprocket bearing ring	1
7	TR91	Clutch pressure plate, complete with adjuster collar	1
8	TR92	Clutch pressure plate adjuster screw	3
9	TR93	Clutch pressure plate adjuster nut	3
10	VR73/6	Clutch hardened distance piece	1
11	VR68/5	Clutch centre drum and back plate assembly	1
12	VR72/1	Clutch stud distance tube	3
13	G69/6	Clutch centre	1
14	G70/5	Clutch centre cush rubber (large)	3
15	G70A/5	Clutch centre cush rubber (small)	3
16	G71	Clutch centre retaining plate	1
17	G78/13½	Clutch spring, 13½G	6
18	G80	Clutch spring screw	3
19	TR77	Clutch front plate	1
20	G75	Clutch intermediate plate (flat)	2
21	G75A	Clutch intermediate plate (dished)	2
22	TR79	Clutch steel pressure plate	1
23	G2/41/1	Clutch lever	1
24	G2/13	Clutch lever bearing block pin 1/4" x 5/8" W	2
25	H44/1	Clutch adjuster, nut and ball	1
26	H66/1008	Clutch rod, 10.1/2" long	1
27	H66B	Clutch rod pad	1

STANDARD SHAKEPROOF WASHERS

Part Number	Diameter	Part Number	Diameter
29058	3/16"	27918	3/8"
27916	1/4"	27919	7/16"
27917	5/16"	27920	1/2"

Always quote Engine or Frame Number

Page 21

FRAME ASSEMBLY, GEARBOX BRACKET AND CENTRE STAND

Illustration No.	Part No.	Description	No. per Set
1	49515	Frame assembly with head races, less all other loose fittings	1
2	34085	Head ball race	2
3	47307	Front engine plate, R.H.	1
4	47308	Front engine plate, L.H.	1
5	20946	Front engine plate stud (frame) 1/2" x 5.1/4" x 26	1
6	402	Front engine plate stud nut	2
7	27920	Front engine plate stud washer	2
8	39209	Rear engine plate R.H.	1
9	39210	Rear engine plate L.H.	1
10	40558	Rear engine plate distance tube 1.1/4" long L.H.	1
11	34099	Rear engine plate distance tube 4" long centre	1
12	43550	Rear engine plate stud (frame) 3/8" x 10.9/16" x 26	1
13	26995	Rear engine plate stud nut	2
14	6740	Rear engine plate stud washer	2
15	14176	Rear engine plate stud (gearbox) 1/2" x 5.3/16" x 26	1
16	402	Rear engine plate stud nut	2
17	27920	Rear engine plate stud washer	2
18	42834	Rubber plug for spring box bracket	2
19	45337A	Engine steady bracket	2
20	41331	Engine steady bracket stud, 7/16" x 1.7/8" x 26	1
21	10314	Engine steady bracket stud nut	2
22	27919	Engine steady bracket stud washer	2
	40786	Centre stand with spring post	1
23	40787	Centre stand only	1
24	36861	Centre stand spring post	1
25	33824	Centre stand bearing sleeve	1
26	34113	Centre stand bearing spindle	1
27	27919	Centre stand bearing spindle shakeproof washer	2
28	1898	Centre stand bearing spindle nut 7/16" x 26	2
29	NA/5700/-	Centre stand bearing spindle grease nipple	1
30	34908	Centre stand spring	1
31	47209	Gearbox bracket	1
32	47204	Chaincase steady bolt	1
33	26995	Chaincase steady bolt nut	1
34	38960	Gearbox bracket stud	1
35	27918	Gearbox bracket stud washer	2
36	26995	Gearbox bracket stud nut	2
37	20689	Gearbox bracket stud (top)	2
38	26997	Gearbox bracket stud nut	4
39	27917	Gearbox bracket stud washer	4
40	47292	Gearbox bracket spring post	1
41	49529	Dual seat	1
42	10142	Dual seat bolt 5/16" x 1/2" x 26	4
43	7915	Dual seat bolt washer	4

Always quote Engine or Frame Number

Page 23

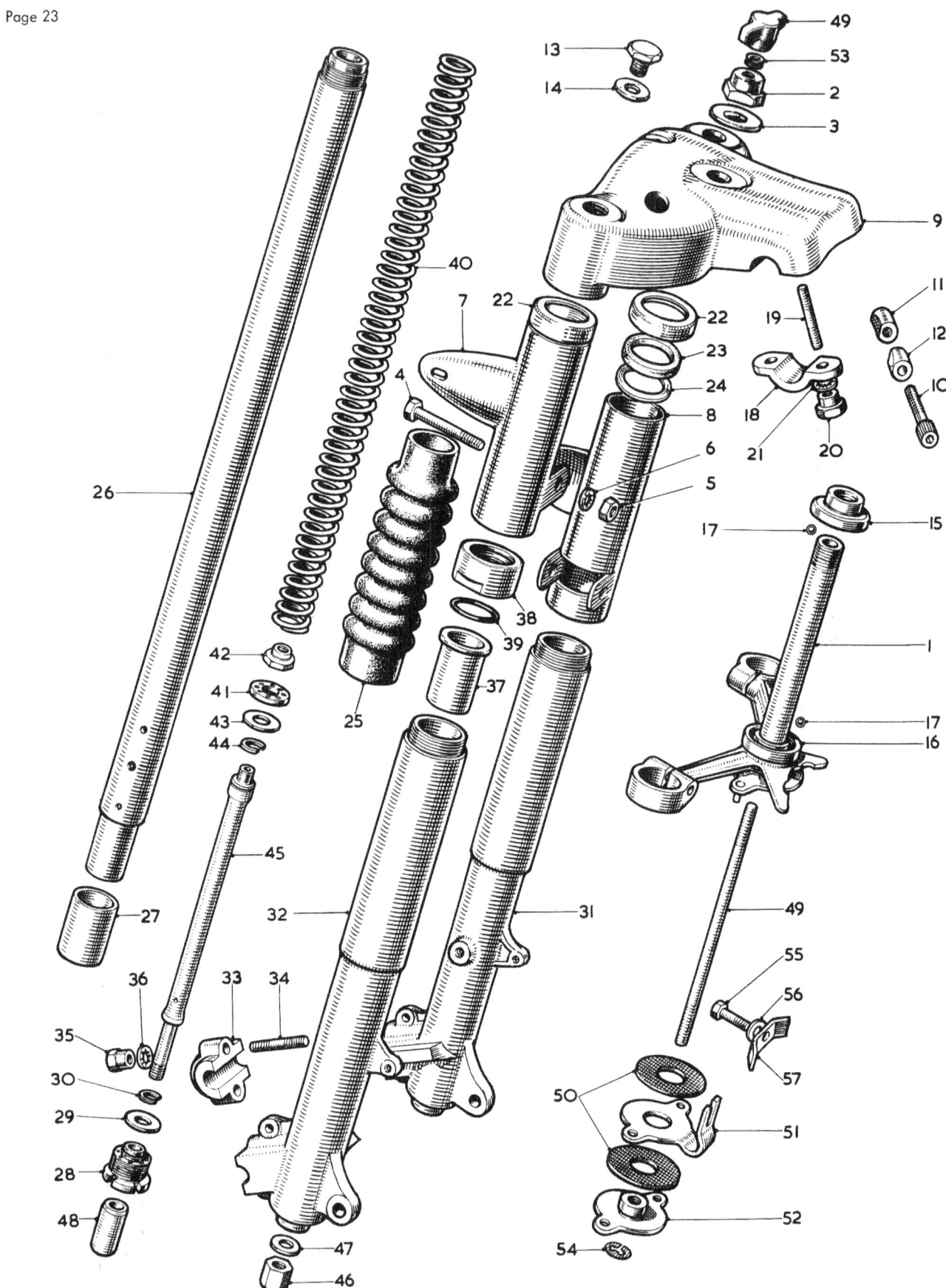

TELESCOPIC FRONT FORK

Illustration No.	Part No.	Description	No. per Set
	49530	Fork assembly, complete with steering stem	1
	47247	Steering stem, complete with cover tubes and clamp bolts	1
1	45992	Steering stem less cover tubes and clamp bolts	1
2	36163	Steering stem locknut	1
3	36095	Steering stem locknut washer	1
4	43989	Steering crown clamp bolt	2
5	27944	Steering crown clamp bolt nut	2
6	27917	Steering crown clamp bolt shakeproof washer	2
7	49525	Fork cover tube, complete with lamp bracket L.H.	1
8	49526	Fork cover tube, complete with lamp bracket R.H.	1
9	49527	Fork head, complete with ballrace and handlebar studs	1
10	38888	Clip bolt	1
11	38886	Clip bolt sleeve (tapped)	1
12	38887	Clip bolt sleeve (plain)	1
13	49559	Fork plug screw	2
14	46325	Fork plug screw washer	2
15	27248	Ball race (fork head)	1
16	27249	Ball race (crown)	1
17	32018	Ball 1/4" diameter	38
18	42910	Handlebar clip	2
19	43004	Handlebar clip stud 5/16" x 1.1/4" x 26	4
20	DE110	Handlebar clip stud nut	4
21	27917	Handlebar clip stud washer	4
22	35113	Lamp bracket collar	2
23	36318	Lamp bracket packing collar	2
24	35974	Lamp bracket washer	2
25	49228	Fork gaiter	2
26	42695	Main tube with valve port and bush	2
27	38156	Main tube bush	2
28	38138	Main tube valve port	2
29	38073	Main tube valve plate	2
30	40058	Main tube valve circlip	2
31	46375	Bottom tube and lug R.H.	1
32	46376	Bottom tube and lug L.H.	1
33	46347	Bottom tube lug cap	2
34	38063	Bottom tube lug stud 5/16" x 1.3/8" x 22	4
35	34705	Bottom tube lug stud nut	4
36	27917	Bottom tube lug stud washer	2
37	36176	Bottom tube bush	2
38	45297	Bottom tube oil seal assembly	2
39	37923	Bottom tube oil seal washer	2
40	49587	Fork spring	2
41	41824	Fork spring guide (bottom, bronze)	2
42	41828	Fork spring guide nut	2
43	41827	Fork spring valve plate	2
44	37886	Fork spring valve circlip	2
45	38067	Fork spring stud	2
46	38080	Fork spring stud nut (bottom of stud)	2
47	34790	Fork spring stud washer	2
48	41624	Oil control collar (on stud)	2
		STEERING DAMPER	
49	45087	Damper knob and rod	1
50	15248	Damper friction disc	2
51	35499	Damper anchor plate	1
52	41418	Damper pressure plate	1
53	30602	Damper spring washer	1
54	41929	Damper coupling peg circlip	2
55	44935	Damper anchor plate pin	1
56	7674	Damper anchor plate pin washer	1
57	45896	Damper anchor plate clip	1

Always quote Engine or Frame Number

Page 25

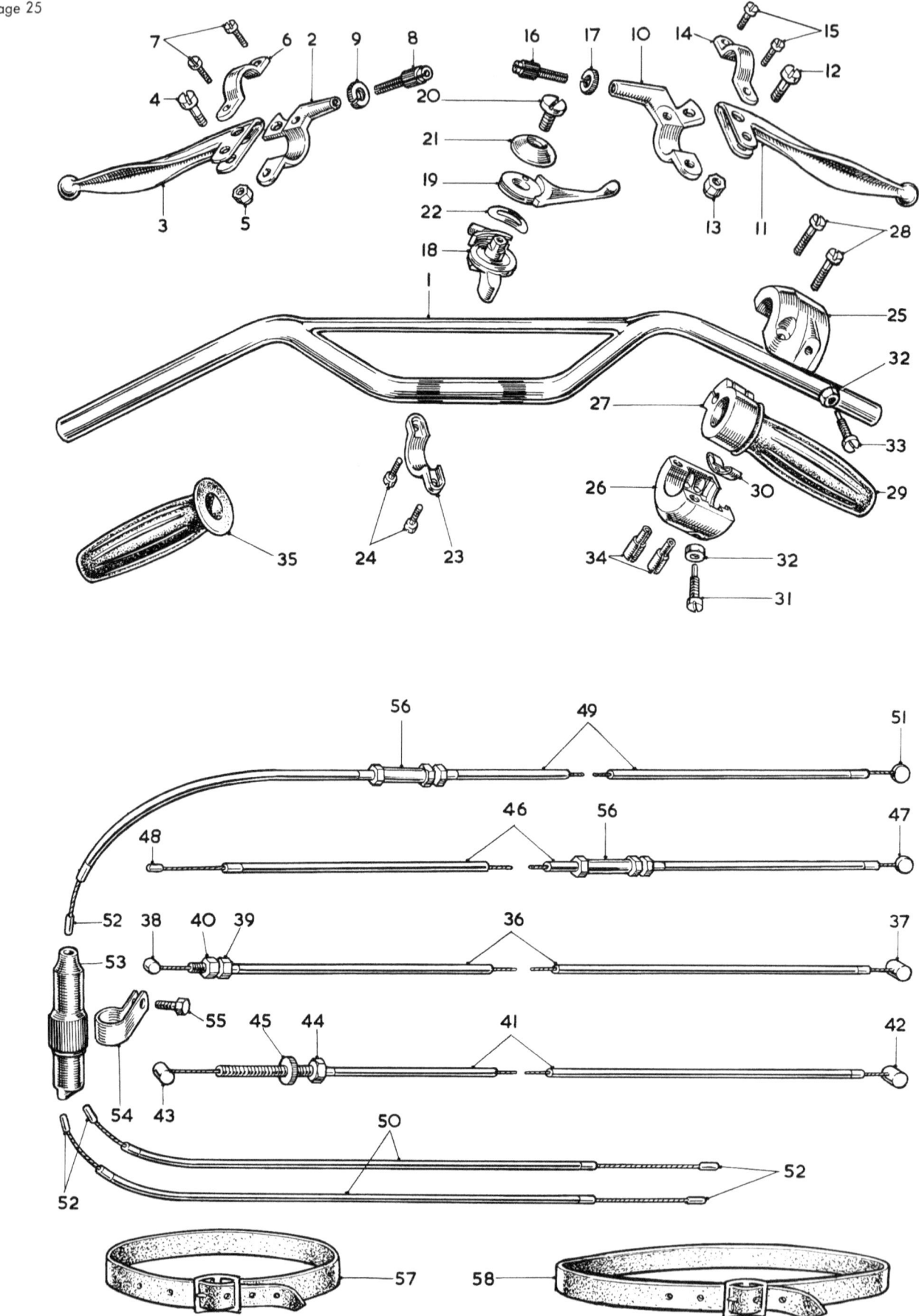

HANDLEBAR, CONTROLS AND CONTROL CABLES

Illustration No.	Part No.	Description	No. per Set
	106/1850	Handlebar, complete with controls, less cables	1
1	91/371	Handlebar bend only	1
	18/1074	Clutch control assembly	1
2	18/1007	Clutch control bracket	1
3	18/753	Clutch control lever	1
4	18/087	Clutch control fulcrum pin	1
5	18/053	Clutch control fulcrum pin nut	1
6	12/595	Clutch control clip	1
7	11/014	Clutch control clip screw	2
8	18/1005	Clutch control cable adjuster	1
9	18/1006	Clutch control cable adjuster locknut	1
	18/1065	Brake control assembly	1
10	18/1013	Brake control bracket	1
11	18/754	Brake control lever	1
12	18/087	Brake control fulcrum pin	1
13	18/053	Brake control fulcrum pin nut	1
14	12/595	Brake control clip	1
15	11/014	Brake control clip screw	2
16	18/1005	Brake control cable adjuster	1
17	18/1006	Brake control cable adjuster locknut	1
	12/608	Air control assembly	1
18	12/619	Air control body	1
19	12/556	Air control lever	1
20	12/607	Air control bolt	1
21	12/606	Air control cap	1
22	12/033	Air control spring washer	1
23	12/595	Air control clip	1
24	11/014	Air control clip screw	2
	313/14	Twist grip control assembly	1
25	313/020	Twist grip control body - top half	1
26	313/021	Twist grip control body - bottom half	1
27	313/004	Twist grip control rotor	1
28	18/084	Twist grip control clamp bolts	2
29	366/012	Twist grip control grip	1
30	16/008	Twist grip control friction spring	1
31	210/007	Twist grip control spring adjuster	1
32	5/077	Twist grip control locknut for spring adjuster and rotor stop	2
33	210/008	Twist grip control rotor stop	1
34	16/011	Twist grip control cable stop	2
35	366/011	Dummy grip rubber	1
36	47735	Clutch cable assembly	1
37	18/073	Clutch cable nipple, handlebar end	1
38	40112	Clutch cable nipple, gearbox end	1
39	37100	Clutch cable adjusting screw	1
40	3257	Clutch cable adjusting screw locknut	1
41	45696	Brake cable assembly	1
42	18/088	Brake cable nipple, handlebar end	1
43	38031	Brake cable nipple, brake end	1
44	38032	Brake cable adjusting screw	1
45	14980	Brake cable adjusting screw locknut	1
46	49576	Throttle cable assembly	2
47	121034	Throttle cable nipple, handlebar end	2
48	1482	Throttle cable nipple, carburettor end	2
	49577	Air cable assembly, complete with junction box	1
49	46008	Air cable assembly, handlebar end	1
50	49578	Air cable assembly, carburettor end	2
51	121034	Air cable nipple, handlebar end	1
52	1482	Air cable nipple, carburettor end and junction box	5
53	45719	Air cable junction box	1
54	46386	Air cable junction box clip	1
55	45229	Air cable junction box clip screw	1
56	33613	Cable midway adjuster, throttle or air	3
57	29609	Cable strap leather, 5"	1
58	29610	Cable strap leather, 7"	4

Always quote Engine or Frame Number

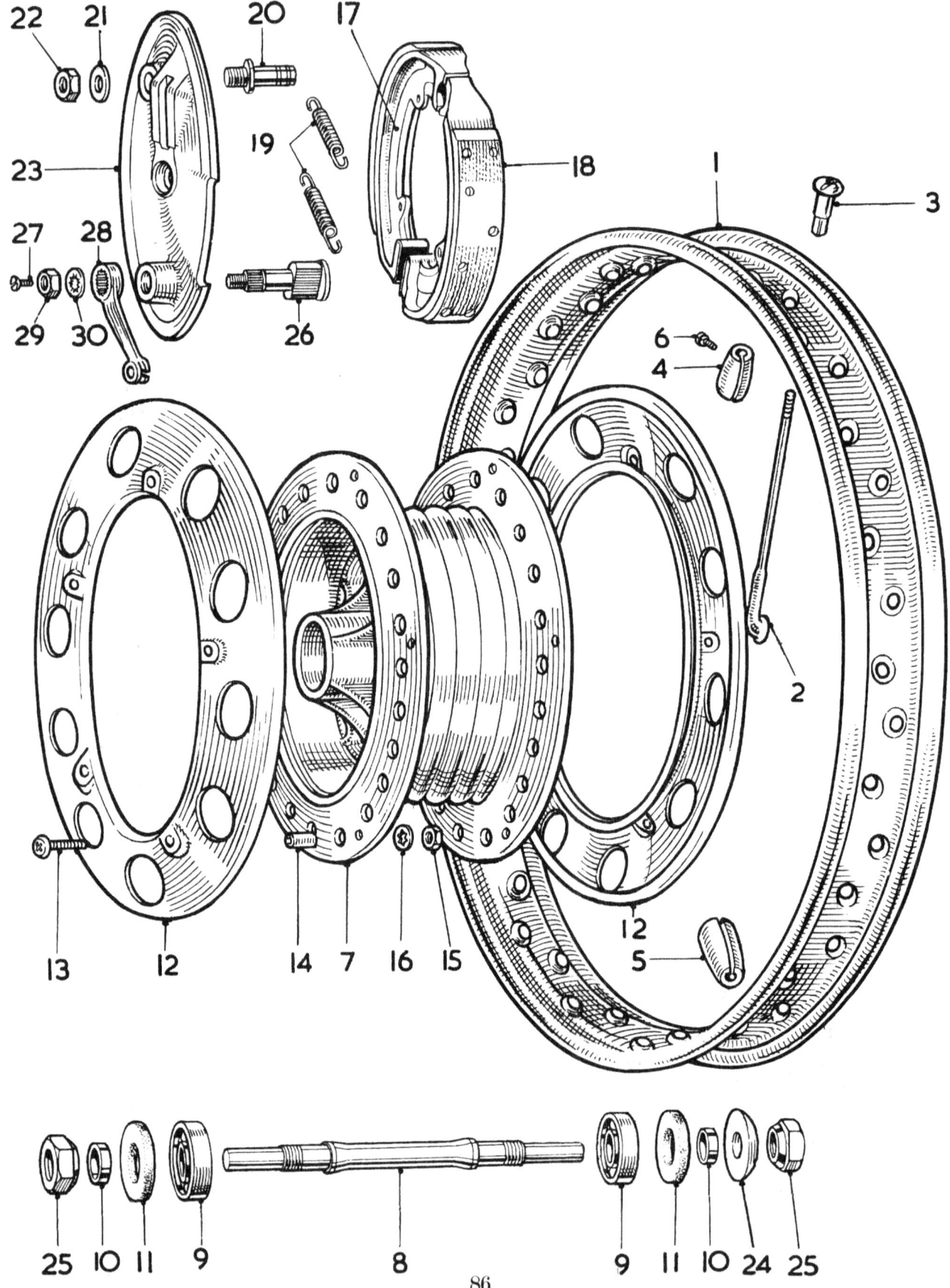

FRONT WHEEL AND BRAKE

Illustration No.	Part No.	Description	No. per Set
	49390	Wheel, complete with assembly, less tyre (WM 2-19 rim)	1
1	37639	Wheel rim WM 2-19	1
2	44476	Wheel spoke 6.5/8" x 10G B8G	40
3	29206	Wheel spoke nipple	40
4	44589	Balance weight - weight 9.6 oz.) as required	
5	44287	Balance weight - weight 13.2 oz.)	
6	44590	Balance weight screw	
	49391	Hub and brake drum, complete with shoes, etc.	1
7	48879	Hub and brake drum only	1
8	36468	Hub spindle	1
9	SKF/RLS5	Hub journal bearing, 5/8" x 1.9/16" x 7/16"	2
10	30538	Hub journal bearing distance collar	2
11	21466	Hub felt washer	2
12	48656	Hub flange	2
13	48799	Hub flange screw	10
14	48800	Hub flange distance piece	10
15	30204	Hub flange nut	10
16	29058	Hub flange washer	10
17	43263/A	Brake shoe with lining	2
18	43264/A	Brake shoe lining (1 pair, complete with rivets)	1
19	26033	Brake shoe return spring	2
20	43215	Brake shoe pivot pin	2
21	17551	Brake shoe pivot pin washer	2
22	28715	Brake shoe pivot pin locknut, 5/8" x 26	2
23	43525	Brake cover plate	1
24	40982	Hub centre	1
25	31347	Brake cover plate nut	2
26	43720	Brake operating cam	1
27	14472	Brake operating cam plug screw	2
28	38906	Brake operating lever	1
29	10314	Brake operating lever nut, 7/16" dia.	2
30	14613	Brake operating lever spring washer	2

Always quote Engine or Frame Number

Page 29

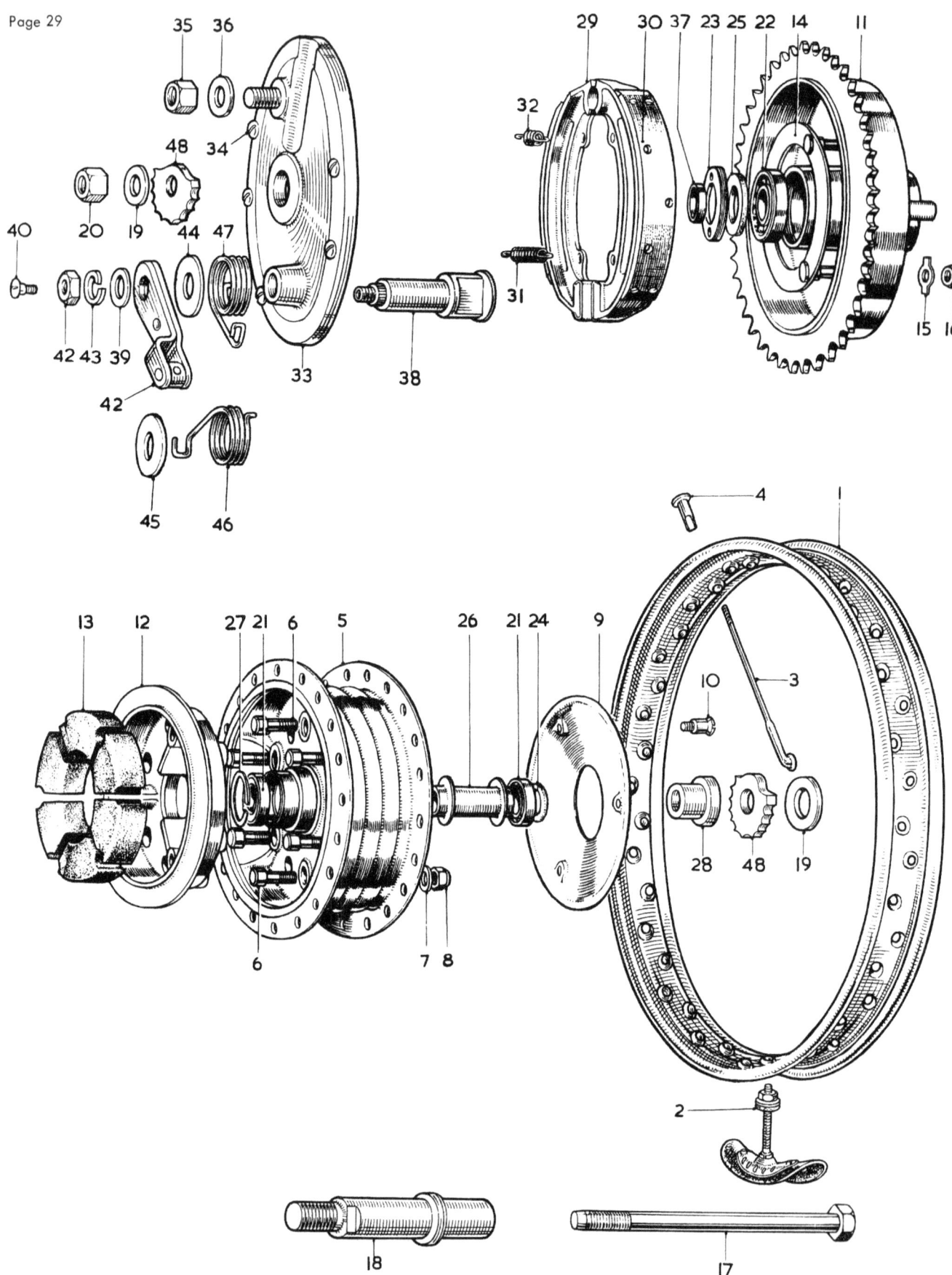

DETACHABLE REAR WHEEL AND BRAKE

Page 30

Illustration No.	Part No.	Description	No. per Set
	48094	Wheel, complete with cush drive & brake assembly, less tyre	1
	49640	Wheel (detachable) only	1
1	45638	Wheel rim, WM 2-19	1
2	35643	Wheel rim security bolt	2
3	40636	Wheel spoke, 6.3/16" x 10G. B8G	40
4	29206	Wheel spoke nipple	40
5	40950	Hub only	1
	46681A	Hub complete	1
6	41000	Hub drive pin	6
7	27918	Hub drive pin washer	6
8	DE394	Hub drive pin nut	6
9	40981	Hub cap	1
10	40983	Hub cap screw	3
11	41233	Brake drum and sprocket, 46T	1
12	40967	Cush drive shell	1
13	26193	Cush drive rubber	6
14	41003	Cush drive lockring assembly	1
15	41001	Cush drive lockring stud washer	3
16	19870	Cush drive lockring stud nut	3
17	41369	Wheel spindle (detachable)	1
18	46385	Wheel spindle (fixed)	1
19	41185	Wheel spindle (fixed) washer	1
20	28832	Wheel spindle (fixed) nut	1
21	SK/RL85	Ball bearing (hub) 5/8" x 1.9/16" x 7/16"	2
22	SK/RLS7	Ball bearing (drum) 7/8" x 2" x 9/16"	1
23	41108	Bearing (drum) retaining ring	1
24	41006	Bearing felt washer (hub) R.H.	1
25	41106	Bearing felt washer (drum) L.H.	1
26	40995	Hub bearing spacer tube	1
27	41032	Hub bearing circlip	1
28	40990	Hub distance collar, R.H.	1
29	41343A	Brake shoe, with lining	2
30	41285A	Brake shoe lining (one pair complete with rivets)	1
31	26033	Brake shoe spring, long	1
32	42267	Brake shoe spring, short	1
33	46382	Brake cover plate	1
34	44359	Brake cover plate screw	5
35	7598	Brake cover plate anchor nut	1
36	20112	Brake cover plate anchor nut washer	1
37	41105	Brake cover plate distance washer (behind plate)	1
38	46326	Brake cam	1
39	4964	Brake cam washer	1
40	14472	Brake cam plug screw	1
41	23371A	Brake lever and trunnion	1
42	10314	Brake lever nut, 7/16" dia.	1
43	14613	Brake lever spring washer	1
44	49599	Brake lever plain washer (Road Scrambler TT7)	1
45	46325	Brake lever plain washer (Road Racer GP7)	1
46	46384	Brake return spring (Road Racer GP7)	1
47	49562	Brake return spring (Road Scrambler TT7)	1
48	36649	Hub adjuster	2

Always quote Engine or Frame Number

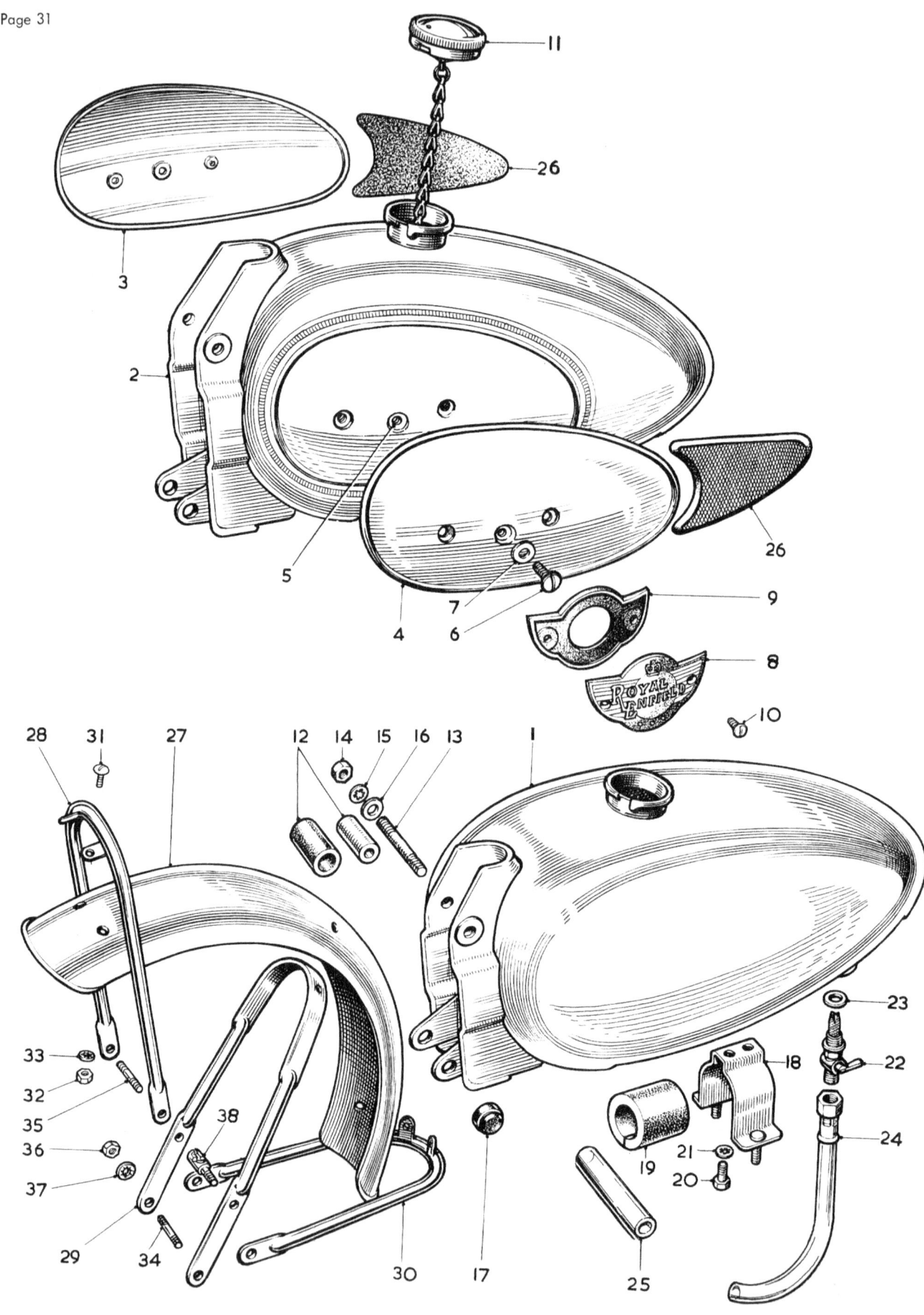

PETROL TANK, FRONT MUDGUARD AND FRONT STAND

Illustration No.	Part No.	Description	No. per Set
1	49555	Petrol tank, assembled (Road Scrambler TT7)	1
2	48087	Petrol tank, assembled with panels, etc. (Road Racer GP7)	1
3	41355	Petrol tank panel, R.H.)	1
4	41354	Petrol tank panel, L.H.)	1
5	41627	Petrol tank badge bush)	4
6	5171	Petrol tank panel attachment screw) Road Racer GP7	2
7	27916	Petrol tank panel attachment washer)	2
8	45305	Badge "Royal Enfield")	2
9	41307	Badge rubber mount)	2
10	42195	Badge screw)	4
11	P521	Tank filler cap	1
12	41602	Tank buffer sleeve	1
13	25336	Tank fixing stud)	1
14	26521	Tank fixing stud nut)	2
15	27918	Tank fixing stud washer) Front fixing	2
16	26995	Tank fixing stud washer)	2
17	41644	Tank steady buffer)	2
18	44702	Tank attachment clip set	1
19	41562	Tank attachment clip sleeve	1
20	253	Tank attachment clip pin	2
21	29058	Tank attachment clip washer	2
22	46895	Petrol tap and strainer	2
23	5662	Petrol tap fibre washer	2
24	49570	Petrol pipe complete	2
25	49696	Float chamber balance pipe	1
26	41207	Knee grip	2
27	49522	Mudguard, chrome	1
28	49320	Mudguard stay (front)	1
29	48509	Mudguard stay (centre)	1
30	49532	Mudguard stay (rear)	1
31	1083	Mudguard bolt (to stay)	6
32	26998	Mudguard bolt nut	6
33	27916	Mudguard bolt washer	6
34	38149	Mudguard stay stud, 5/16" x 7/8" x 22 (B.S.F.)	2
35	38150	Mudguard stay stud, 5/16" x 1" x 22 (B.S.F.)	4
36	27944	Mudguard stay stud nut	6
37	27917	Mudguard stay stud washer	6
38	38904	Brake cable adjuster carrier	1

Always quote Engine or Frame Number

Page 33

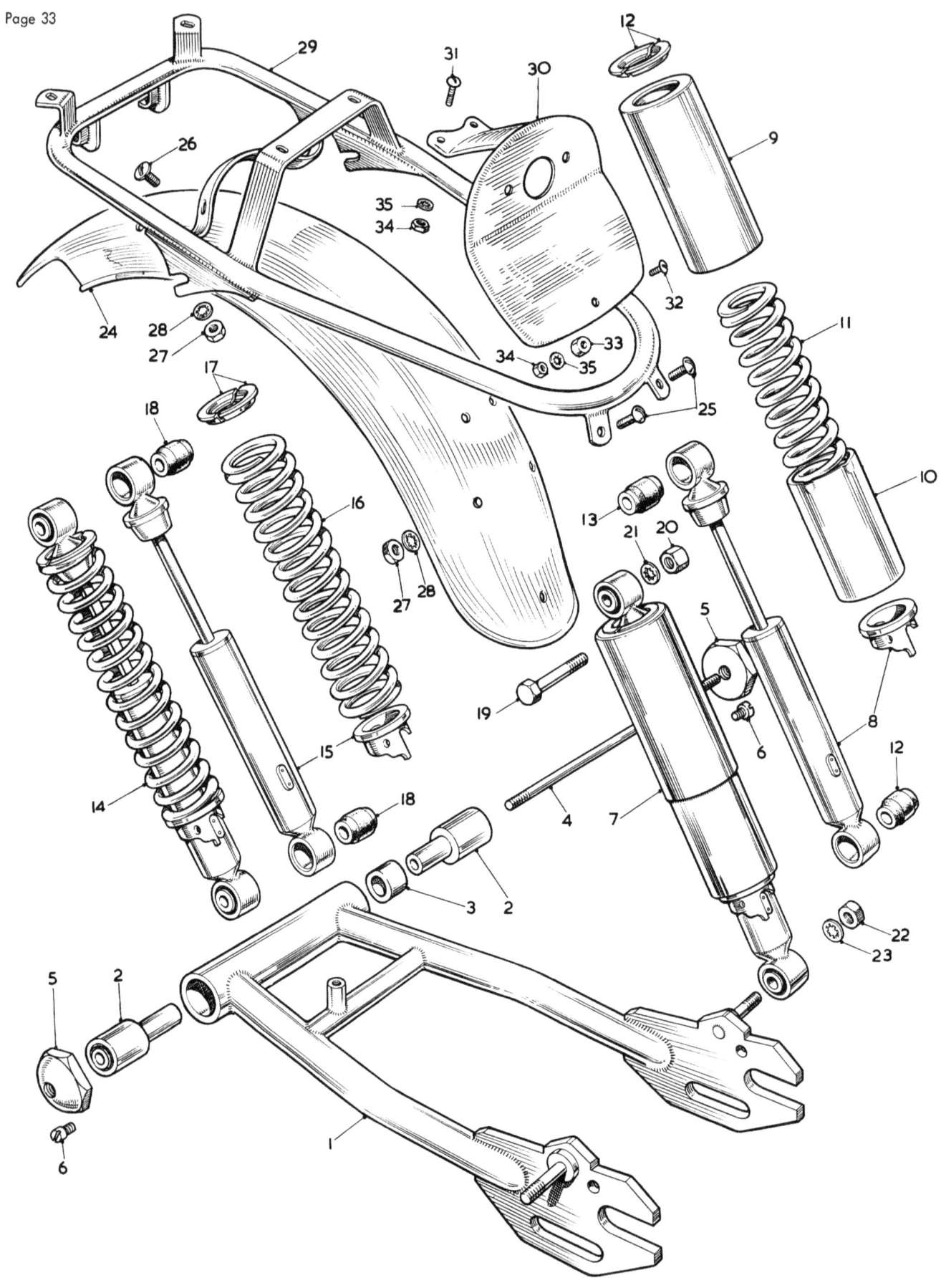

REAR SUSPENSION, MUDGUARD AND NUMBER PLATE

Illustration No.	Part No.	Description	No. per Set
1	49524	Chainstay assembly with bearings	1
2	46262	Chainstay bearing	2
3	46266	Chainstay bearing distance piece	1
4	46263	Chainstay bearing stud	1
5	46264	Chainstay bearing stud nut	2
6	45703	Chainstay nut locking screw	1
7	W49557	Suspension unit (Road Racer GP90) (64054968 Girling No.)	2
8	S64054646	Damper unit (Road Racer GP90)	2
9	64533032	Outer dirt shield (Road Racer GP90)	2
10	64532778	Inner dirt shield	2
11	64539963	Suspension spring (Road Racer GP90)	2
12	9054/171	Spring retaining clip	4
13	64533652	Metalastik bush	4
14	W49558	Suspension unit (Road Scrambler GT90) (64054969 Girling No.)	2
15	S64054646	Damper unit (Road Scrambler GT90)	2
16	64543764	Suspension spring (Road Scrambler GT90)	2
17	9054/171	Spring retaining clip	4
18	64533652	Metalastik bush	4
19	42002	Spring box pivot pin, top, 3/8" x 1.5/8" x 20	2
20	26374	Spring box pivot pin nut (top)	2
21	27918	Spring box pivot pin lockwasher (top)	2
22	DE394	Spring box pivot pin nut (bottom)	2
23	33783	Spring box pivot pin lockwasher (bottom)	2
	49550	Mudguard (Road Scrambler TT7)	1
24	49584	Mudguard (Road Racer GP7)	1
25	251	Mudguard bold rh/hd, 1/4" x 1/2" x 26	2
26	38767	Mudguard bolt	2
27	26998	Mudguard bolt nut	4
28	27916	Mudguard bolt washer	4
29	49551	Mudguard carrier	1
30	49586	Number plate	1
31	1083	Number plate attachment pin (top)	2
32	18446	Number plate attachment pin (bottom)	1
33	18229	Number plate attachment pin collar	2
34	26998	Number plate attachment pin nut	3
35	27916	Number plate attachment pin washer	3

Always quote Engine or Frame Number

Page 35

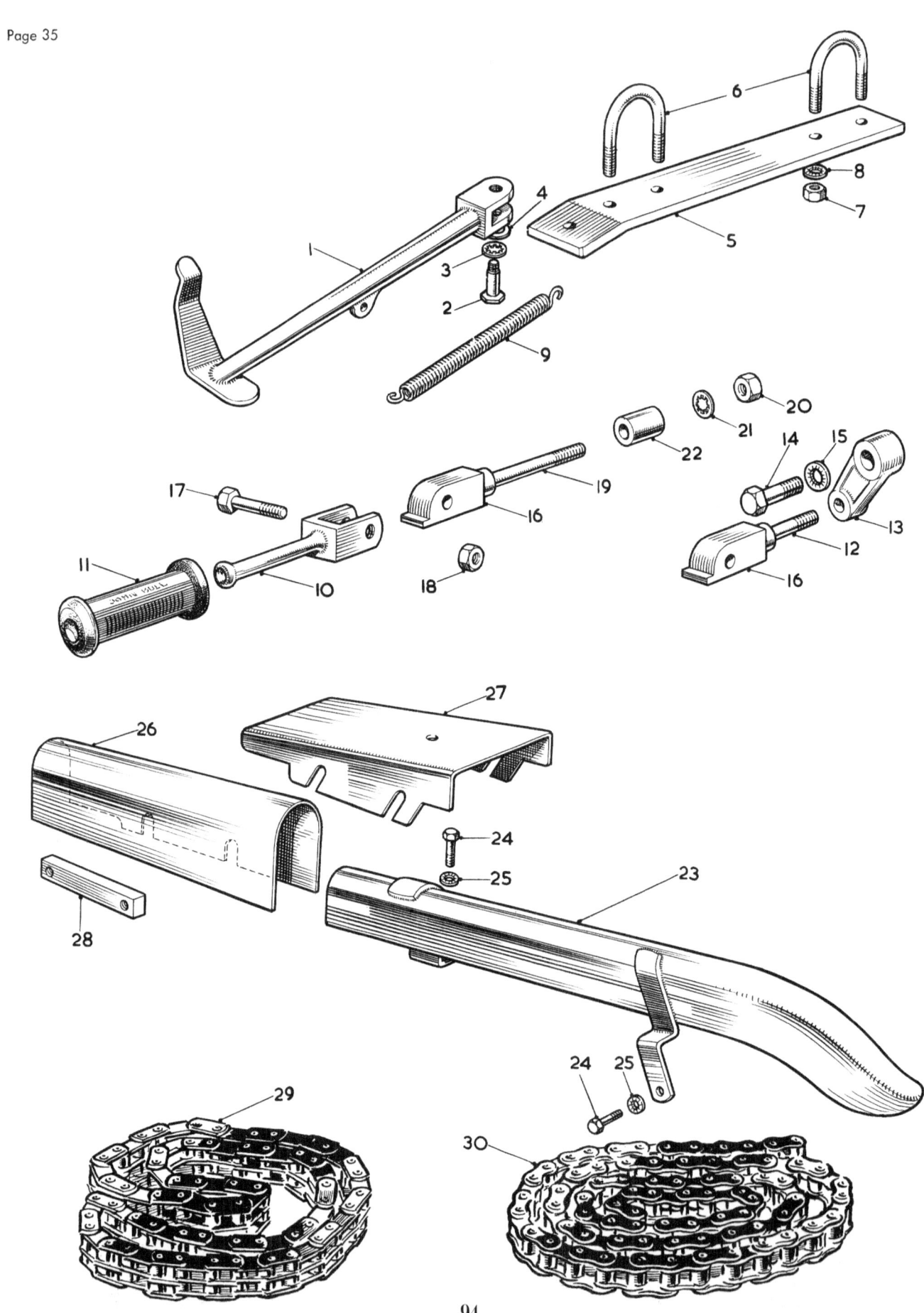

PROP. STAND, PILLION FOOTRESTS, CHAINGUARD AND CHAINS

Illustration No.	Part No.	Description	No. per Set
1	47191	Prop. stand leg	1
2	47194	Prop. stand leg pivot bolt	1
3	27919	Prop. stand leg spring washer	1
4	37258	Prop. stand leg plain washer	1
5	47188	Prop. stand plate, complete with spring post	1
6	47195	Prop. stand "U" bolt	2
7	27621	Prop. stand "U" bolt nut	4
8	27917	Prop. stand "U" bolt washer	4
9	34908	Prop. stand spring	1
10	48749	Pillion footrest	2
11	42691	Pillion footrest rubber	2
12	41680	Pillion footrest stud)	2
13	41636	Pillion footrest bracket) Road Scrambler TT7	2
14	49583	Pillion footrest bracket bolt)	2
15	27920	Pillion footrest bracket washer)	2
16	41523	Pillion footrest pivot block	2
17	41499	Pillion footrest pivot block pin, 5/16" x 1.3/16" x 26	2
18	3257	Pillion footrest pivot block pin nut	2
19	37207	Pillion footrest pivot block stud, 7/16" x 2.9/16" x 26 (Road Racer GP7)	2
20	30807	Pillion footrest pivot block stud nut	2
21	27919	Pillion footrest pivot block stud washer	2
22	43253	Pillion footrest pivot block distance tube (Road Racer GP7)	2
23	49523	Chainguard	1
24	14447	Chainguard bolt, rear 5/16" x 3/8" x 26	2
25	27917	Chainguard bolt washer (shakeproof)	2
26	49512	Chainguard (fixed)	1
27	49517	Gearbox cover	1
28	49533	Gearbox cover clamping strip	1
29	RN/114038/92	Front chain, 3/8" duplex x 92 pitches	1
30	RN/110056/110	Rear chain, 5/8" x 3/8" x 110 pitches	1

Always quote Engine or Frame Number

Page 37

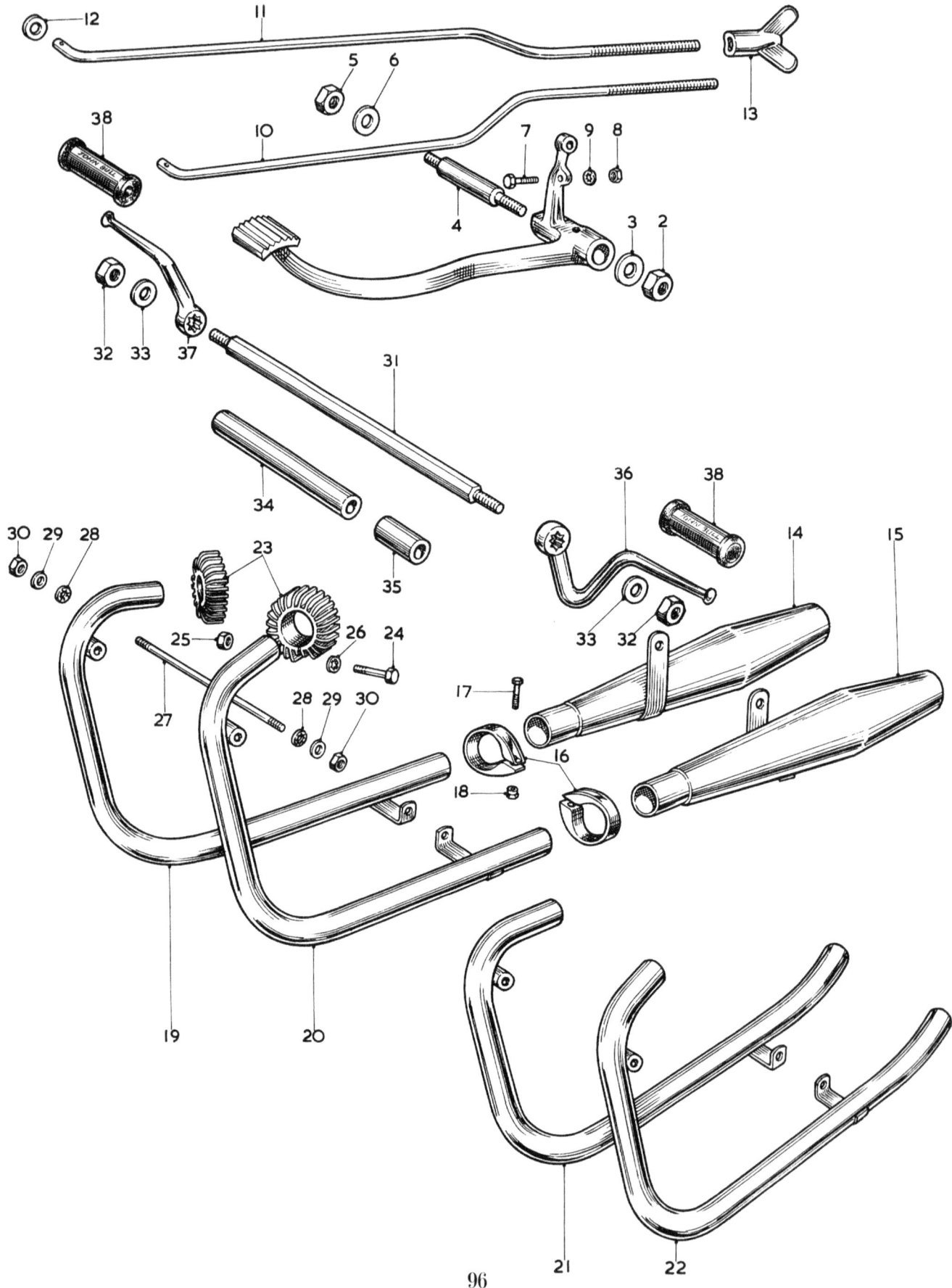

REAR BRAKE CONTROL, EXHAUST SYSTEM AND FOOTRESTS

Illustration No.	Part No.	Description	No. per Set
	49549	Brake control, complete (Road Racer G.P.7)	1
	49561	Brake control, complete (Road Scrambler T.T.7)	1
1	41183/A	Brake pedal	1
2	26995	Brake pedal securing nut, 3/8" x 26	1
3	15641	Brake pedal securing nut washer	1
4	40339	Brake pedal fulcrum stud	1
5	10314	Brake pedal fulcrum stud nut 7/16" x 26	1
6	27919	Brake pedal fulcrum stud nut washer	1
7	252	Brake pedal stop pin, 1/4" x 3/4" x 26	1
8	27000	Brake pedal stop pin locknut	1
9	NA5700/1	Brake pedal grease nipple	1
10	49548	Brake rod (Road Racer G.P.7)	1
11	49560	Brake rod (Road Scrambler T.T.7)	1
12	14691	Brake rod washer	1
	30779	Brake rod split pin, 1/16" x 3/4"	1
13	17691	Brake rod adjusting nut	1
14	49538	Silencer, complete (R.H.)	1
15	49537	Silencer, complete (L.H.)	1
16	41341	Silencer clip (to exhaust pipe)	2
17	4860	Silencer clip bolt, 1/4" x 1.1/16" x 26	2
18	12881	Silencer clip bolt nut	2
19	49563	Exhaust pipe (R.H.) Road Racer G.P.7	1
20	49565	Exhaust pipe (L.H.) Road Racer G.P.7	1
21	49579	Exhaust pipe (R.H.) Road Scrambler T.T.7	1
22	49581	Exhaust pipe (L.H.) Road Scrambler T.T.7	1
23	41044	Exhaust pipe clip (head)	2
24	19555	Exhaust pipe clip screw	2
25	26998	Exhaust pipe clip screw nut	2
26	27916	Exhaust pipe clip screw nut washer	2
27	44964	Exhaust pipe tie rod	1
28	14691	Exhaust pipe tie rod washer	2
29	26168	Exhaust pipe tie rod nut, sleeved	2
30	27001	Exhaust pipe tie rod nut, standard	2
31	20769/A	Footrest bar	1
32	10315	Footrest bar nut, 7/16" x 26	2
33	37315	Footrest bar washer	2
34	39197	Footrest distance tube, centre, 3.3/4" long	1
35	48136	Footrest distance tube, 5/8" long	2
36	35020	Footrest arm (L.H.)	1
37	33162	Footrest arm (R.H.)	1
38	25838	Footrest arm rubber	2

Always quote Engine or Frame Number

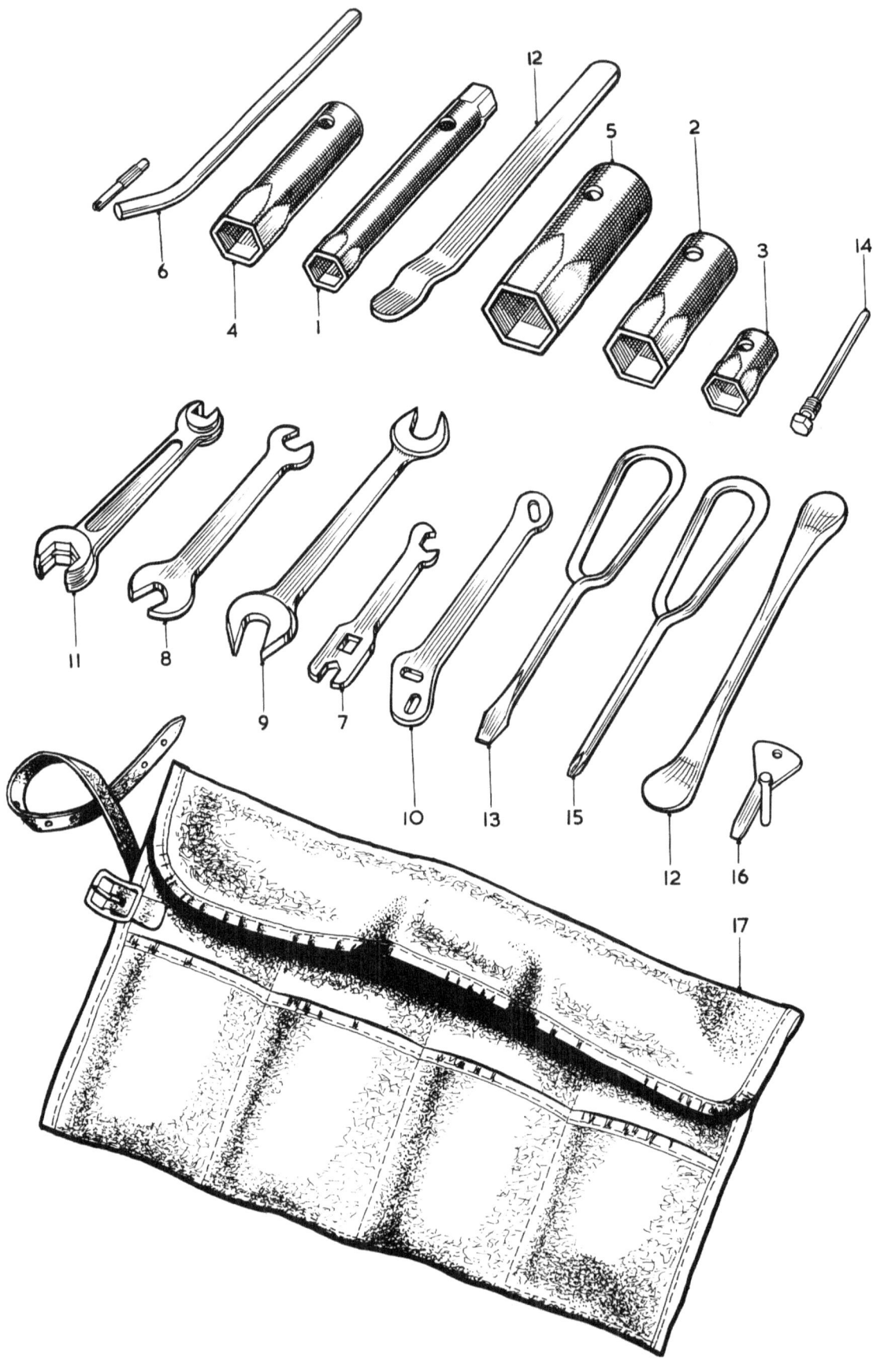

TOOL KIT

Illustration No.	Part No.	Description	No. per Set
1	35634	Tubular spanner, 1/4" x 5/16" Whit.	1
2	44710	Tubular spanner sparking plug	1
3	24095	Tubular spanner, 1/2" Whit.	1
4	35635	Tubular spanner, 9/16" Whit.	1
5	24094	Tubular spanner, 11/16" Whit.	1
6	29042	Tommy bar, 5/16" dia.	1
7	24092	Spanner, .343" x .380" Hex.	1
8	27896	Spanner, 3/16" x 1/4" Whit.	1
9	29044	Spanner, 1/4" x 5/16" Whit.	1
10	43449	Valve rocker adjusting spanner	1
11	6406	Combination spanner	1
12	4272	Tyre lever	2
13	3482	Screwdriver flat blade	1
14	49622	Contact breaker extractor	1
15	DWU-05	Screwdriver	1
16	400935	Contact breaker screwdriver	1
17	16007	Tool roll	1

Always quote Engine or Frame Number

Page 41

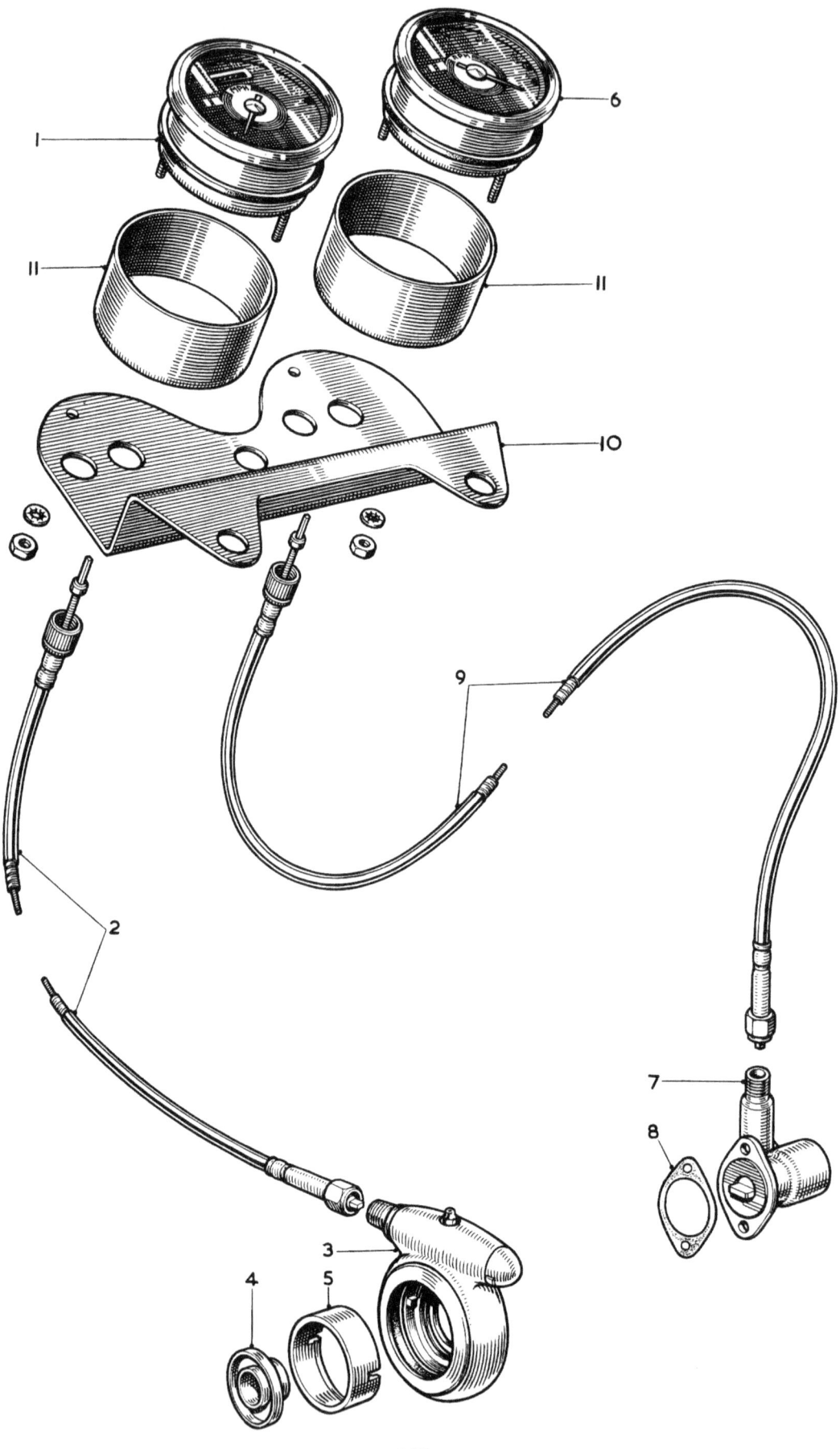

SMITHS' SPEEDOMETER, REVOLUTION COUNTER AND MOUNTING

Illustration No.	Part No.	Description	No. per Set
1	SSM/3002/00	Speedometer head 125 m.p.h. trip, illuminated	1
2	DF9110/00	Flexible drive complete, 58 inches	1
3	46879	Gearbox (self-contained) complete	1
4	46868	Gearbox spacing collar	1
5	46869	Gearbox drive coupling	1
6	RSM3004/02	Revolution counter head	1
7	BG1506/01	Revolution counter gearbox	1
8	47673	Revolution counter gearbox gasket	1
9	DF9111/00	Driving cable, 34"	1
10	49591	Head bracket (speedometer and revolution counter)	1
11	48479	Head bracket tube	2

Always quote Engine or Frame Number

Page 43

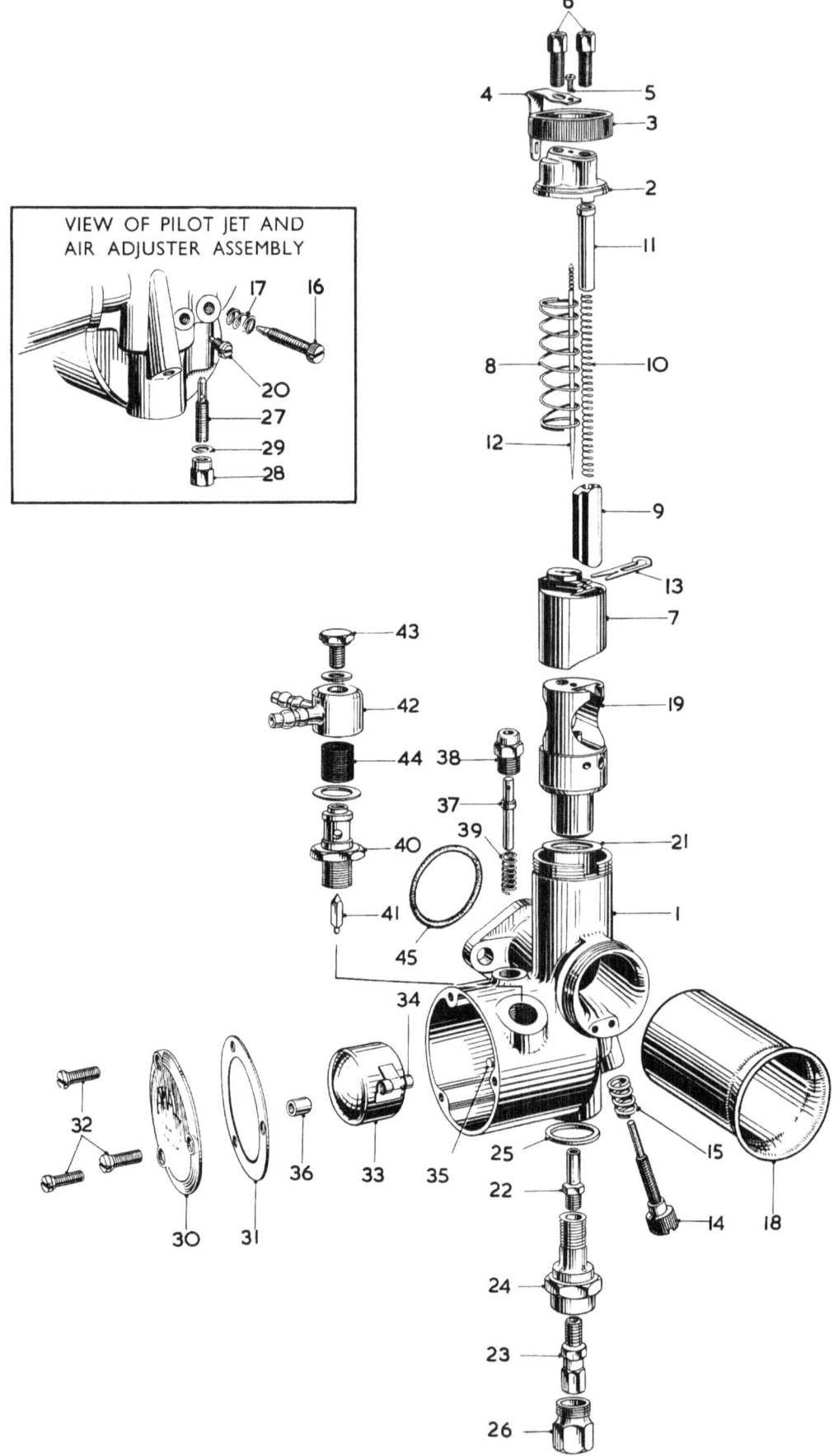

VIEW OF PILOT JET AND AIR ADJUSTER ASSEMBLY

AMAL "MONOBLOC" CARBURETTOR

Illustration No.	Part No.	Description	No. per Set
	689/225	Carburettor, complete with float chamber) less controls and cables	1
	389/225	Carburettor, complete with float chamber)	1
1	689/005	Carburettor body	1
	389/035	Carburettor body	1
2	389/107	Carburettor mixing chamber top	1
3	389/065	Carburettor mixing chamber cap	1
4	29/301	Carburettor mixing chamber cap spring	1
5	4/241	Carburettor mixing chamber cap spring screw	1
6	4/035	Carburettor cable adjusters	2
7	689/060	Carburettor throttle valve	1
8	389/061	Carburettor throttle valve spring	1
9	389/062	Carburettor air valve	1
10	4/046	Carburettor air valve spring	1
11	29/057	Carburettor air valve guide	1
12	389/063	Carburettor jet needle	1
13	4/230	Carburettor jet needle clip	1
14	376/068	Carburettor throttle adjusting screw	1
15	376/069	Carburettor throttle adjusting screw spring	1
16	332/017	Carburettor pilot air adjusting screw	1
17	4/148	Carburettor pilot air adjusting screw spring	1
18	389/066	Carburettor air intake tube	1
19	689/058	Carburettor jet block complete	1
20	376/070	Carburettor locating peg for jet block	1
21	376/067	Carburettor jet block washer	1
22	376/072	Carburettor needle jet	1
23	376/100	Carburettor main jet	1
24	376/073	Carburettor jet holder	1
25	376/074	Carburettor jet holder washer	1
26	376/075	Carburettor main jet cover	1
27	376/076	Carburettor pilot jet	1
28	376/095	Carburettor pilot jet cover nut	1
29	116/162	Carburettor pilot jet cover nut washer	1
30	376/077	Carburettor side cover	1
31	376/078	Carburettor side cover washer	1
32	376/079	Carburettor side cover screws	3
33	376/083	Carburettor float complete with hinge	1
34	376/411	Carburettor float hinge	1
35	376/085	Carburettor float hinge spindle	1
36	376/094	Carburettor float spindle bush	1
37	376/086	Carburettor tickler	1
38	343/011	Carburettor tickler body	1
39	376/087	Carburettor tickler spring	1
40	376/118	Carburettor needle seating	1
41	376/089	Carburettor needle	1
42	376/097	Carburettor banjo	1
43	376/091	Carburettor banjo bolt	1
44	376/093	Carburettor filter gauze	1
45	244/1048	Carburettor sealing ring	1

Always quote Engine or Frame Number

Page 45

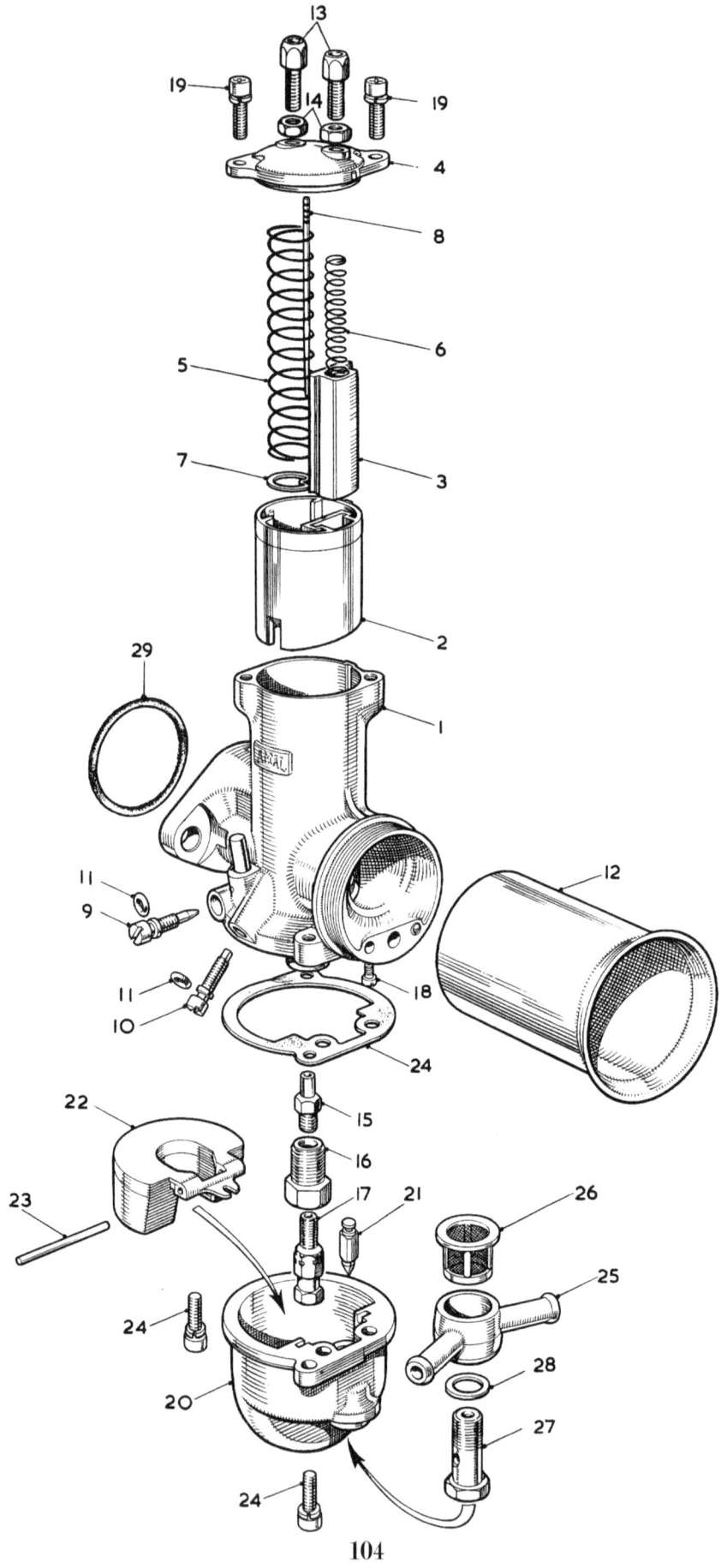

AMAL 'CONCENTRIC' CARBURETTOR

Illustration No.	Part No.	Description	No. per Set
	R930/3	Carburettor, complete with float chamber) less controls and cables	1
	R930/4	Carburettor, complete with float chamber)	1
1	R930	Carburettor body and tickler assembly	1
2	928/060	Carburettor throttle valve	1
3	928/062	Carburettor air valve	1
4	928/097	Carburettor mixing chamber top	1
5	622/061	Carburettor throttle valve spring	1
6	622/065	Carburettor air valve spring	1
7	622/067	Carburettor needle clip	1
8	928/063	Carburettor throttle needle	1
9	622/076	Carburettor pilot air adjuster screw	1
10	622/077	Carburettor throttle stop	1
11	622/082	Carburettor 'O' ring	2
12	928/069	Carburettor air funnel	1
13	4/035	Carburettor cable adjuster	2
14	5/077	Carburettor cable adjuster locknut	2
15	622/079	Carburettor needle jet	1
16	622/080	Carburettor jet holder	1
17	376/100	Carburettor main jet	1
18	124/026	Carburettor pilot jet	1
19	622/086	Carburettor screws for float chamber and mixing chamber top	4
20	622/050	Carburettor float chamber body	1
21	622/068	Carburettor float chamber needle	1
22	622/069	Carburettor float chamber float	1
23	622/071	Carburettor float chamber float spindle	1
24	622/073	Carburettor float chamber washer	1
25	376/139	Carburettor banjo	1
26	376/093	Carburettor filter	1
27	622/078	Carburettor banjo bolt	1
28	13/163	Carburettor banjo bolt washer	1
29	622/101	Carburettor 'O' ring for flange	1

Always quote Engine or Frame Number

Page 47

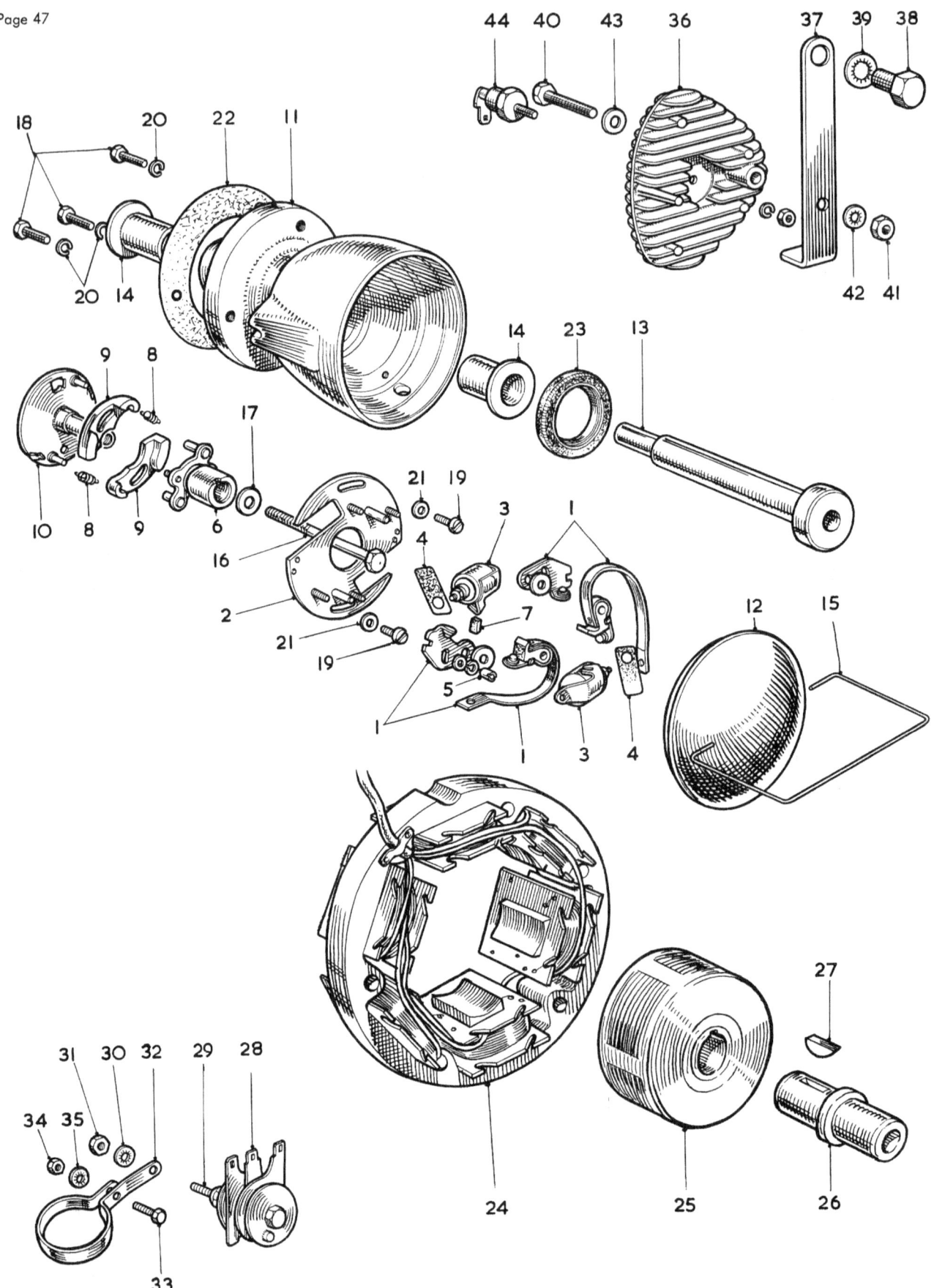

CONTACT BREAKER, ALTERNATOR, RECTIFIER, HEAT SINK AND DIODE-ZENER

Page 48

Illustration No.	Part No.	Description	No. per Set
	48006	Contact breaker unit, 4CA	1
		LU/425379 & LU/54419167	
1	LU/54415803	Contact set	2
2	LU/425370	Base plate, contact breaker	1
3	LU/425377	Condenser	2
4	LU/425382	Condenser terminal insulating plate	2
5	LU/169194	Condenser mounting plate nut	2
6	LU/54440029	Cam	1
7	LU/425378	Cam lubricating felt	2
	LU/54440028	Auto advance unit	1
8	LU/54413020	Auto advance spring	2
9	LU/54440031	Auto advance weight	2
10	LU/54415655	Auto advance sleeve and action plate	1
11	48001	Contact breaker body	1
12	48005	Contact breaker cover	1
13	48002	Contact breaker spindle	1
14	48003	Contact breaker bush	2
15	48004	Spring clip	1
16	48021	Bolt	1
17	82	Washer	1
18	26379	Screw	3
19	29781	Screw	2
20	27916	Washer	3
21	7047	Washer	2
22	40377	Gasket	1
23	43565	Oil seal	1
	LU/54021027	Alternator stator and rotor assembly, RM19	1
24	LU/47162A	Stator	1
25	LU/54213901	Rotor	1
26	46188	Rotor adaptor	1
27	43386	Rotor key	1
	LU/54210167	Cable clip	1
	LU/131023	Cable clip washer	1
28	LU/49072A	Rectifier 2DS506	1
29	LU/132469	Rectifier screw	3
30	LU/154409	Rectifier washer	3
31	LU/156594	Rectifier nut	3
32	49554	Clip	1
33	42835	Clip pin	1
34	27944	Clip pin nut	1
35	27917	Clip pin washer	1
36	49605	Heat sink	1
37	49604	Heat sink bracket	1
38	41567	Heat sink bracket attachment pin	1
39	27920	Heat sink bracket washer	1
40	15253	Heat sink attachment pin	1
41	19870	Heat sink attachment nut	1
42	27917	Heat sink attachment washer	1
43	27976	Heat sink attachment washer	1
44	LU/49345	Diode-Zener ZD715	1
	LU/54951688	Cable harness	1

Always quote Engine or Frame Number.

Page 49

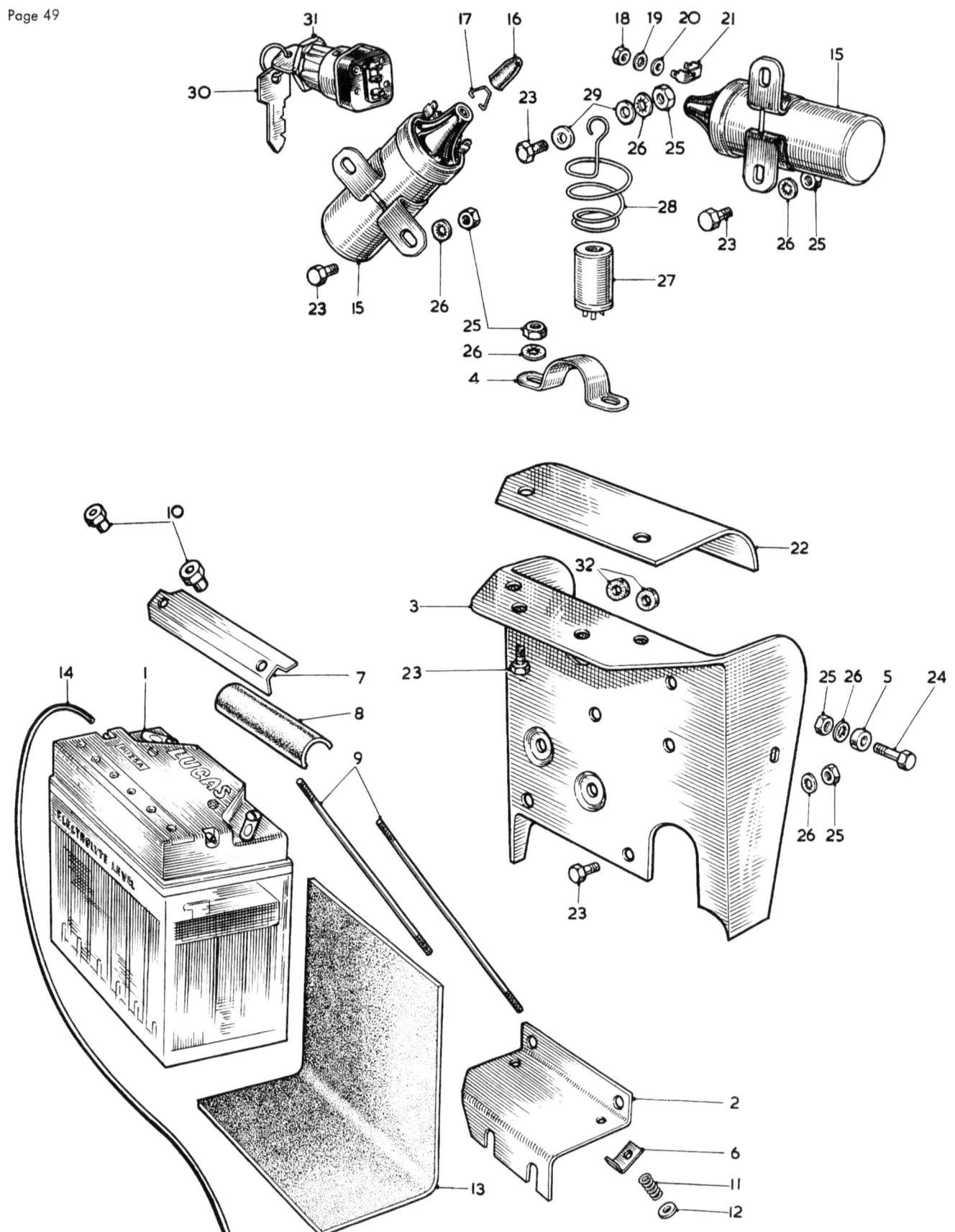

BATTERY AND MOUNTING, COIL AND COVER, ELECTROLYTIC CAPACITOR AND IGNITION SWITCH

Page 50

Illustration No.	Part No.	Description	No. per Set
1	54027029	Battery 12 volt PUZ5A	1
2	49504	Battery platform	1
3	49508	Battery back plate	1
4	41479	Battery back plate clip	1
5	46731	Battery back plate spacer	2
6	49594	Battery rod bracket	2
7	49505	Battery retaining strap	1
8	49567	Battery retaining rubber strip	1
9	49506	Battery securing rod	2
10	49507	Battery securing rod nut	2
11	49593	Battery securing rod spring	2
12	351	Battery securing rod washer	2
13	49510	Battery pad	1
14	49606	Battery vent tube	1
15	LU/45110D	Coil MA12	2
16	LU/421554	Rubber grommet	2
17	LU/421863	Clip, contact cable	
18	LU/166043	Terminal nut	8
19	LU/188330	Terminal shakeproof washer	8
20	LU/131023	Terminal plain washer	8
21	LU/54190108	Lucas connector	4
22	49509	Coil cover	1
23	251	Attachment bolt	9
24	7201	Attachment bolt	4
25	26998	Attachment nut	13
26	27916	Attachment washer	13
27	LU/54170009	Electrolytic capacitor	1
28	LU/54483156	Electrolytic spring	1
29	82	Electrolytic capacitor attachment plain washer	2
30	LU/31899B	Ignition switch S45	1
31	LU/54130041	Ignition switch nut	
	LU/54140331	Warning light washer	1
	LU/54937974	High tension lead	2
32	LU/199001	Rubber grommet	4

Always quote Engine or Frame Number

Page 51

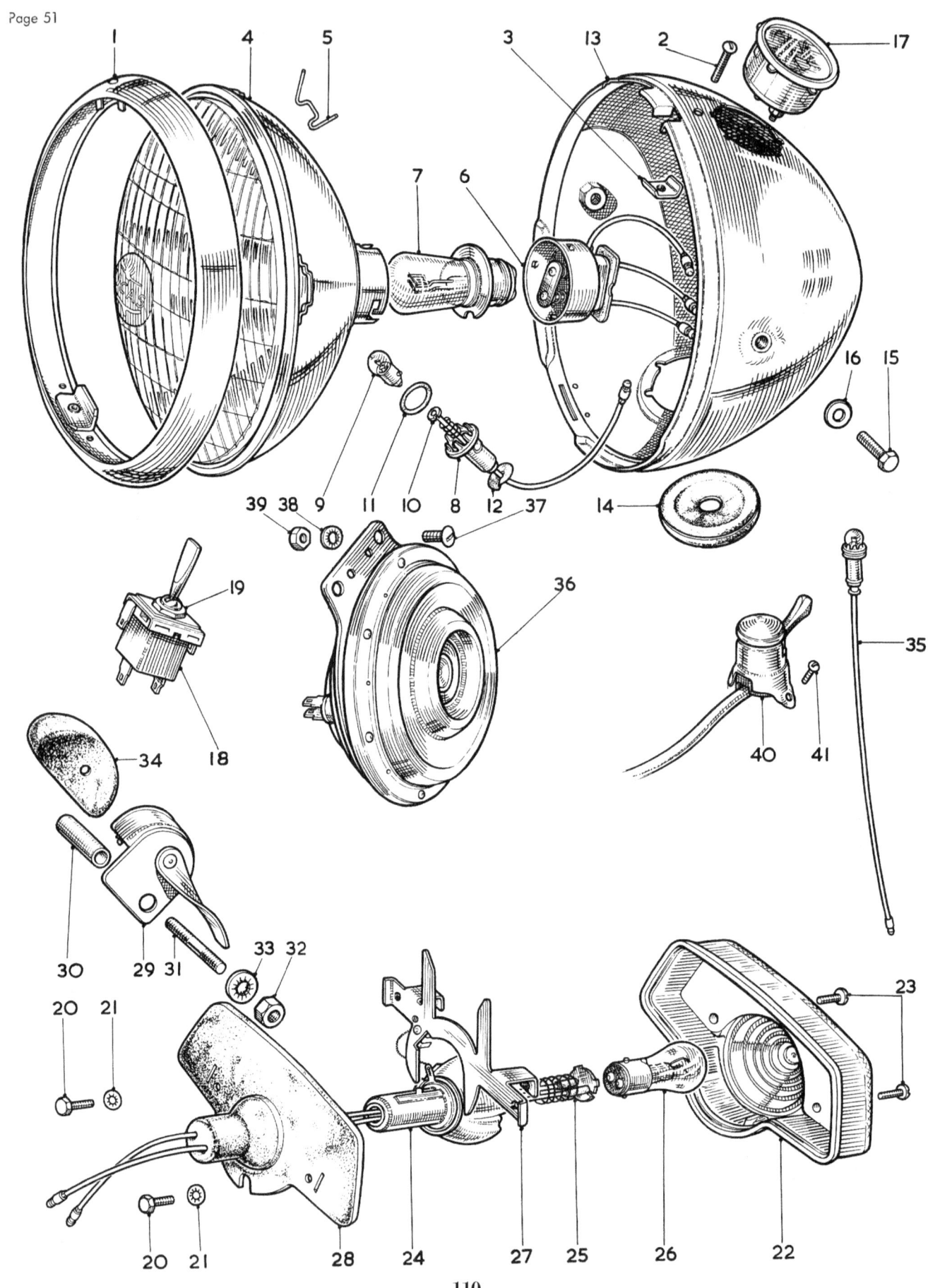

LAMPS, STOPLIGHT AND SWITCHES, AMMETER, HORN AND HORN PUSH AND DIPPER SWITCH

Illustration No.	Part No.	Description	No. per Set
	LU/59529A	Headlamp SS700P comprising unit light with front and fixing rims	1
1	LU/553248	Front rim	1
2	LU/144921	Front rim attachment screw	1
3	LU/534296	Front rim attachment plate	1
4	LU/516798	Light unit	1
5	LU/504665	Light unit attachment wire	
6	LU/554602	Main bulb holder	
7	LU/446	Main bulb	
	LU/54360102	Main beam warning light	1
	LU/555910	Terminal sleeve	1
8	LU/554710	Pilot bulb holder	1
9	LU/989	Pilot bulb	1
10	LU/553780	Pilot interior	1
11	LU/454354	Pilot bulb holder seating ring	
12	LU/516285	Pilot cable grip washer	
13	LU/54523022	Headlamp body	1
14	199002	Headlamp body grommet	1
15	LU/112201	Headlamp body attachment screw	2
16	LU/137498	Headlamp body attachment screw washer	2
17	LU/36296A	Ammeter 2AR	1
18	LU/31788D	Lighting switch 57SA	1
19	LU/153630	Lighting switch attachment nut	
	LU/53973D	Stop tail lamp 679	1
20	LU/110714	Stop tail lamp attachment screw	2
21	LU/188330	Stop tail light attachment screw washer	2
22	LU/54577109	Lens	1
23	LU/144921	Lens attachment screw	2
24	LU/54574348	Bulb holder with reflector	1
25	LU/573828	Bulb holder interior	1
26	LU/380	Bulb	1
27	LU/54577139	Baseplate	1
28	LU/5451677	Lamp seating gasket	1
29	LU/31688B	Stop lamp switch 6SA	1
30	45701	Stop lamp switch distance tube	1
31	45702	Stop lamp switch attachment stud	1
32	27944	Stop lamp switch attachment nut	1
33	27917	Stop lamp switch attachment washer	1
	35605	Stop lamp cable band type B	3
34	LU/360363	Stop lamp rubber terminal cover	
	LU/188818	Stop lamp terminal sleeve	
	LU/864892	Stop lamp tail lead	1
35	LU/54934904	Speedometer and Revolution counter lead	2
36	LU/70183	Horn 6H	1
37	38767	Horn attachment pin	2
38	27916	Horn attachment pin washer	2
39	26998	Horn attachment pin nut	2
40	LU/31563D	Horn push and dipper switch 25SA	1
41	136291	Horn push attachment screw	2

Always quote Engine or Frame Number

NOTES

SPARE AND REPLACEMENT PARTS

for the 1969-1970

SEVEN-FIFTY INTERCEPTOR

SERIES II

MOTOR CYCLE

INDEX

	Page
Engine Unit and Crankcase Assembly	2
Cylinder and Head Assembly	4
Pistons and Crankshaft Assembly	6
Timing Cover and Timing Gear Assembly	8
Oil Pump, Filter, Rocker Oil Feed and Crankcase Breather	10
Primary Chaincase	12
Gearbox: Cases and Kickstart Mechanism	14
Gearbox: Running Gear	16
Gearbox: Gear Selector Mechanism	18
Clutch/Standard Shakeproof Washers	20
Frame Assembly, Gearbox Bracket and Centre Stand	22
Telescopic Front Fork	24
Handlebar, Controls and Control Cables	26
Front Wheel and Brake	28
Detachable Rear Wheel and Brake	30
Petrol Tank, Front Mudguard and Front Stand	32
Rear Suspension, Mudguard and Number Plate	34
Prop Stand, Pillion Footrests, Chainguard and Chains	36
Rear Brake Control, Exhaust System and Footrests	38
Tool Kit	40
Smiths Speedometer, Revolution Counter and Mounting	42
Amal "Concentric" Carburettor	44
Contact Breaker, Alternator, Rectifier, Heat Sink and Zener-Diode	46
Battery and Mounting, Coil and Cover, Electrolytic Capacitor and Ignition Switch	48
Lamps, Stoplight and Switches, Ammeter, Horn and Horn Push, Dipper Switch and Side Reflectors	50

Page 1

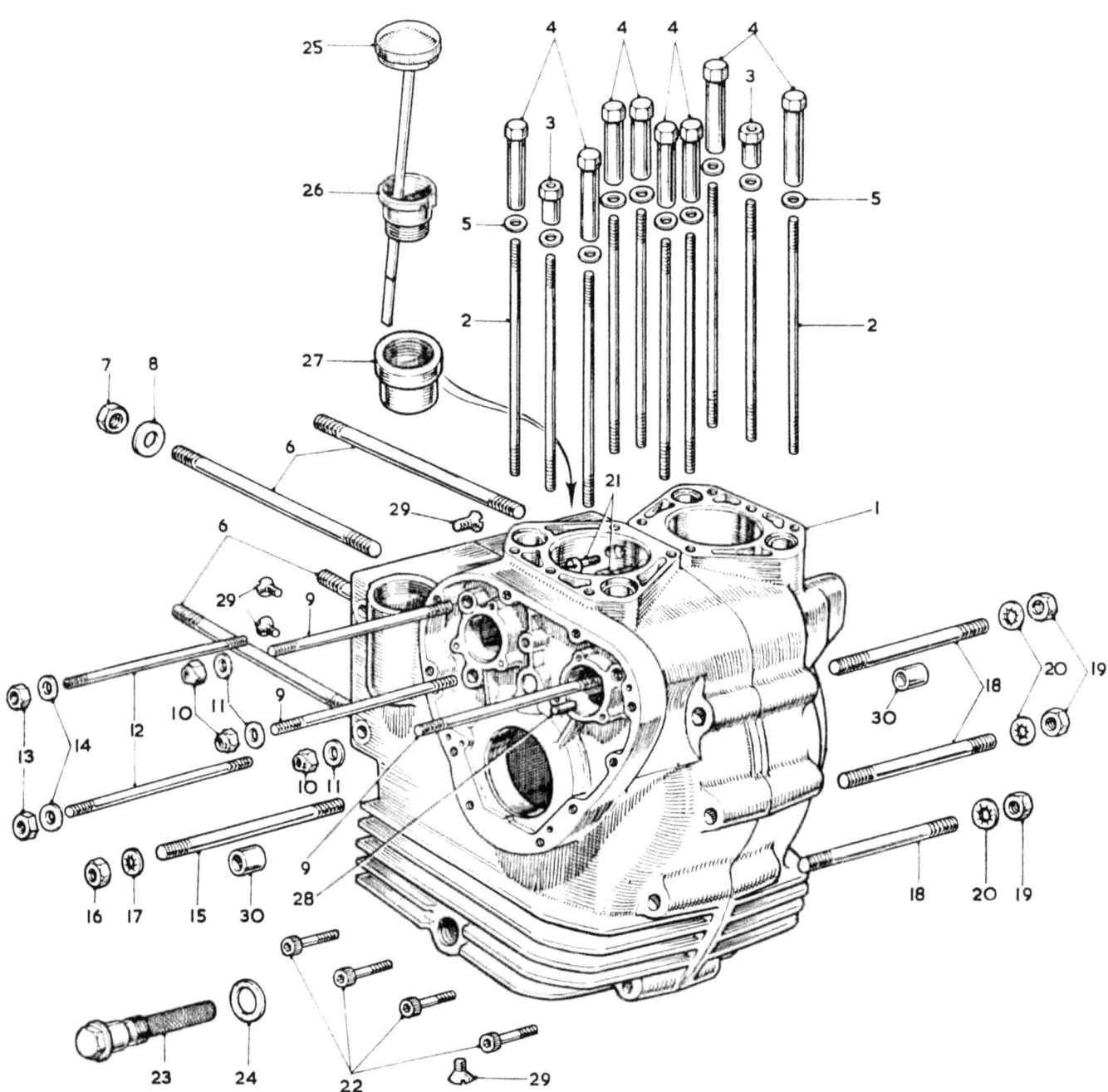

ENGINE UNIT AND CRANKCASE ASSEMBLY

Page 2

Illustration No.	Part No.	Description	No. per Set
	49659	Interceptor engine unit, 736 c.c. twin cylinder, complete with gearbox, chaincase and carburettors	1
	49660	Interceptor engine unit only, less gearbox, chaincase and carburettors	1
1	49661	Crankcase assembly, complete with main and camshaft bearings, tappets and guides, and fixed studs (from engine No. 1B1001 to No. 1B1001)	1
	49917	Crankcase assembly complete with main and camshaft bearings, tappets and guides, and fixed studs (from engine No. 1B2002 onwards)	1
2	45451	Stud, cylinder and head securing	10
3	34968	Nut (short shoulder), cylinder and head securing	2
4	45449	Nut (long shoulder), cylinder and head securing	8
5	1437	Washer, cylinder and head securing nut	10
6	47208	Stud, gearbox attachment	4
7	29854	Nut, gearbox attachment stud	4
8	15641	Washer, stud nut	4
9	49643	Stud, crankcase top (5/16" dia.)	3
10	36221	Locknut, top stud	3
11	8634	Washer, top stud locknut	3
12	35595	Stud, crankcase, rear (1/4" dia.)	2
13	27620	Nut, rear stud	4
14	82	Washer, rear stud nut	4
15	44360	Stud, crankcase, rear engine plate (5/16" dia.)	1
16	27621	Nut, rear engine plate stud	2
17	27917	Lockwasher, rear engine plate stud nut	2
18	36079	Stud, crankcase, front (5/16"dia.)	3
19	8633	Nut, front stud	6
20	27917	Lockwasher, front stud nut	6
21	37724	Bridge screw, crankcase top	2
22	39382/A	Cap screw, crankcase bottom	4
23	37884/A	Oil drain plug, with gauge filter	1
24	17024	Fibre washer, oil drain plug	1
25	49613	Oil filler cap, with dipstick	1
26	18275	Collar, oil filler cap	1
27	49751	Adaptor, oil filler collar (from engine No. 1B1001 to No. 1B1333)	1
28	45370	Dowel, timing cover locating	1
29	48718	Oil plug screw (from engine No. 1B1001 to No. 1B1200)	4
	48718	Oil plug screw (from engine No. 1B1201 onwards)	3
30	26709	Dowel, crankcase	2

Always quote Engine or Frame Number

Page 3

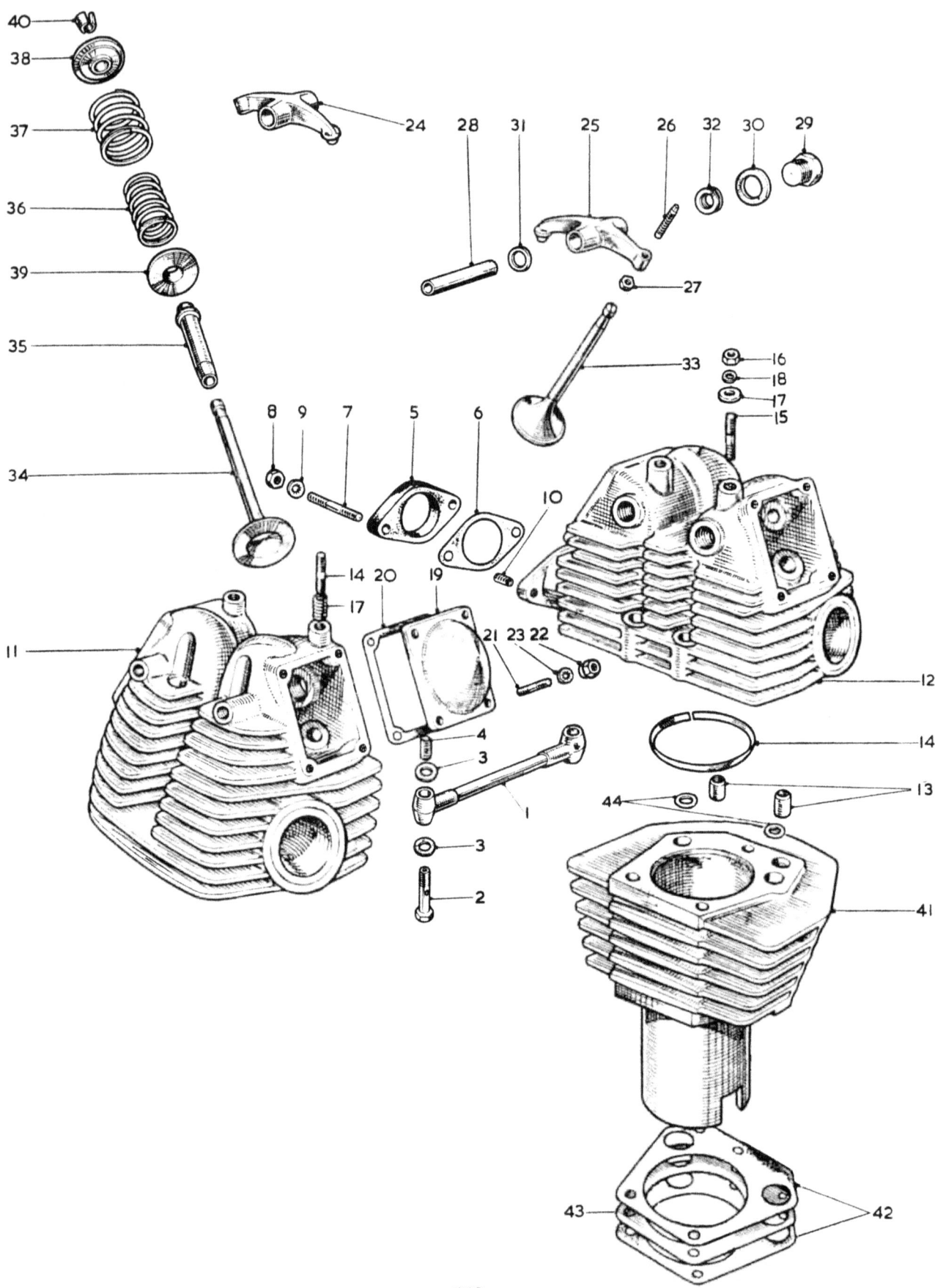

118

CYLINDER AND HEAD ASSEMBLY

Illustration No.	Part No.	Description	No. per Set
1	48007	Induction balance pipe complete	1
2	37000/A	Induction balance pipe banjo bolt	2
3	30395	Fibre washer, banjo bolt	4
4	48010	Induction balance pipe cross wire inserts	2
5	46191	Heat insulation washer	2
6	42518	Carburettor flange gasket	2
7	32363	Carburettor flange stud, 1/4" x 1.3/16" x 26 (BSF)	4
8	27944	Carburettor flange stud nut, .1/4" (BSF)	4
9	27917	Carburettor flange stud washer	4
10	38621	Cross wire insert	4
11	46156	Cylinder head, R.H.) fitted with valve guides and fixed studs	1
12	46158	Cylinder head, L.H.)	1
13	45447	Cylinder head dowel	4
14	46184	Cross gasket ring	2
15	49684	Cylinder head engine steady stud, 5/16" x 13/16" (BSF)	4
16	27621	Cylinder head engine steady stud nut	4
17	8634	Cylinder head engine steady stud washer	4
18		Cylinder head engine steady stud washer	4
19	32552	Rocker box cover	4
20	32553	Rocker box cover gasket	4
21	48011	Rocker box cover stud, 1/4" x 7/8" x 26 (BSF)	16
22	37852	Rocker box cover stud nut, 1/4" (BSF)	16
23	82	Rocker box cover stud washer	16
24	39735	Rocker (inlet R.H., Exhaust L.H.)	2
25	39376	Rocker (inlet L.H., Exhaust R.H.)	2
26	32550	Rocker adjusting screw	4
27	32549	Rocker adjusting locknut	4
28	38644	Rocker spindle	4
29	36985	Rocker spindle end plug	4
30	39468	Rocker spindle end plug washer (copper)	4
31	32554	Rocker spindle thrust washer	4
32	35904	Rocker spindle spring washer	4
33	43521	Valve, exhaust	2
34	42661	Valve, inlet	2
35	42660/A	Valve, guide	2
36	42693	Valve spring, inner	4
37	42692	Valve spring, outer	4
38	42651	Valve collar, top	4
39	42652	Valve collar, bottom	4
40	42492	Valve split collar	4
41	46129	Cylinder barrel	2
42	45450	Cylinder base gasket	4
43	46193	Compression plate	2
44	46150/A	Push rod tunnel oil seal (complete)	4
	239	Gasket set, decarbonisation only	1
	240	Gasket set, complete engine and chaincase	1

Always quote Engine or Frame Number

Details of thread inserts for repair work will be found on page 40

Page 5

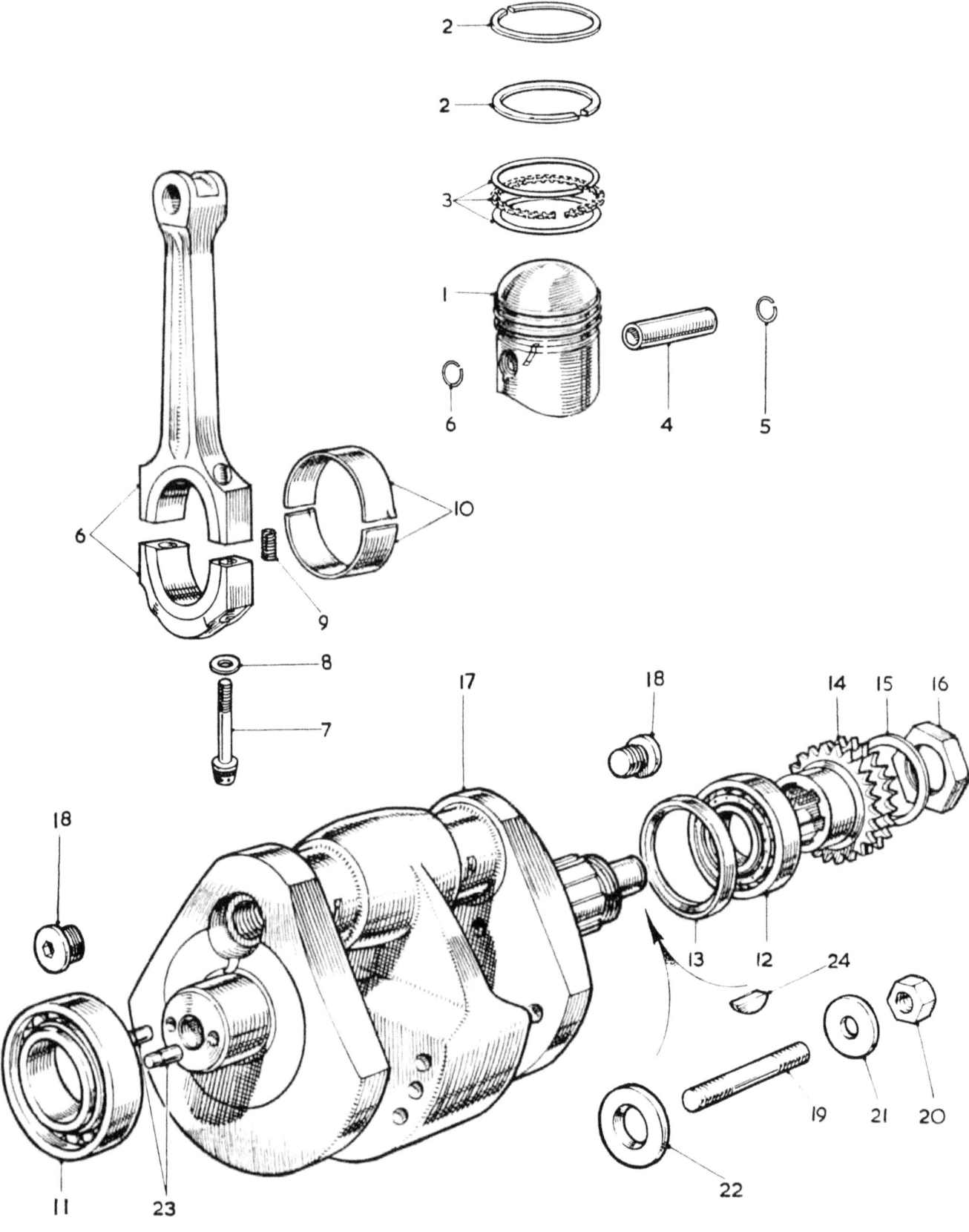

120

PISTONS AND CRANKSHAFT ASSEMBLY

Illustration No.	Part No.	Description	No. per Set
1	49886/A	Piston, complete with rings, gudgeon pin and circlips, ratio 8.5 to 1) after Engine No. 17077	2
2	49883	Piston ring (tapered compression, top and middle)	4
3	49955	Piston ring (appex oil control, lower)	2
4	47178	Gudgeon pin	2
5	38771	Gudgeon pin circlip	4
6	41719/B	Connecting rod assembly, complete with B.E. screws and shells	2
7	47876	Connecting rod B.E. screw	4
8	14691	Connecting rod B.E. screw washer	4
9	45444	Connecting rod inserts	4
	36017	Connecting rod S.E. bush (for Service use)	2
10	41722	Connecting rod B.E. bearing shell (one half)	4
11	SK/N209 Hoffman R.145 or R & M. LRJ45	Crankshaft timing side roller bearing, 45 x 85 x 19 mm	1
12	SK/6209 Hoffman 145 or R & M.LJ.45	Crankshaft drive side bearing, 45 x 85 x 19 mm	1
13	34062	Crankshaft drive bearing distance collar	1
14	41965/A	Engine sprocket 29T	1
15	34076	Engine sprocket washer	1
16	34064	Engine sprocket locknut	1
	49715	Crankshaft assembly, complete with connecting rods	1
17	49670	Crankshaft only	1
18	44510	Crankshaft oil plug	2
19	49673	Stud, alternator rotor attachment	1
20	DE394	Nut, attachment stud	1
21	41134	Washer, attachment stud nut	1
22	41133	Distance washer, alternator rotor	1
23	49672	Peg, timing sprocket	2
24	43386	Key, alternator	1

Always quote Engine or Frame Number

Page 7

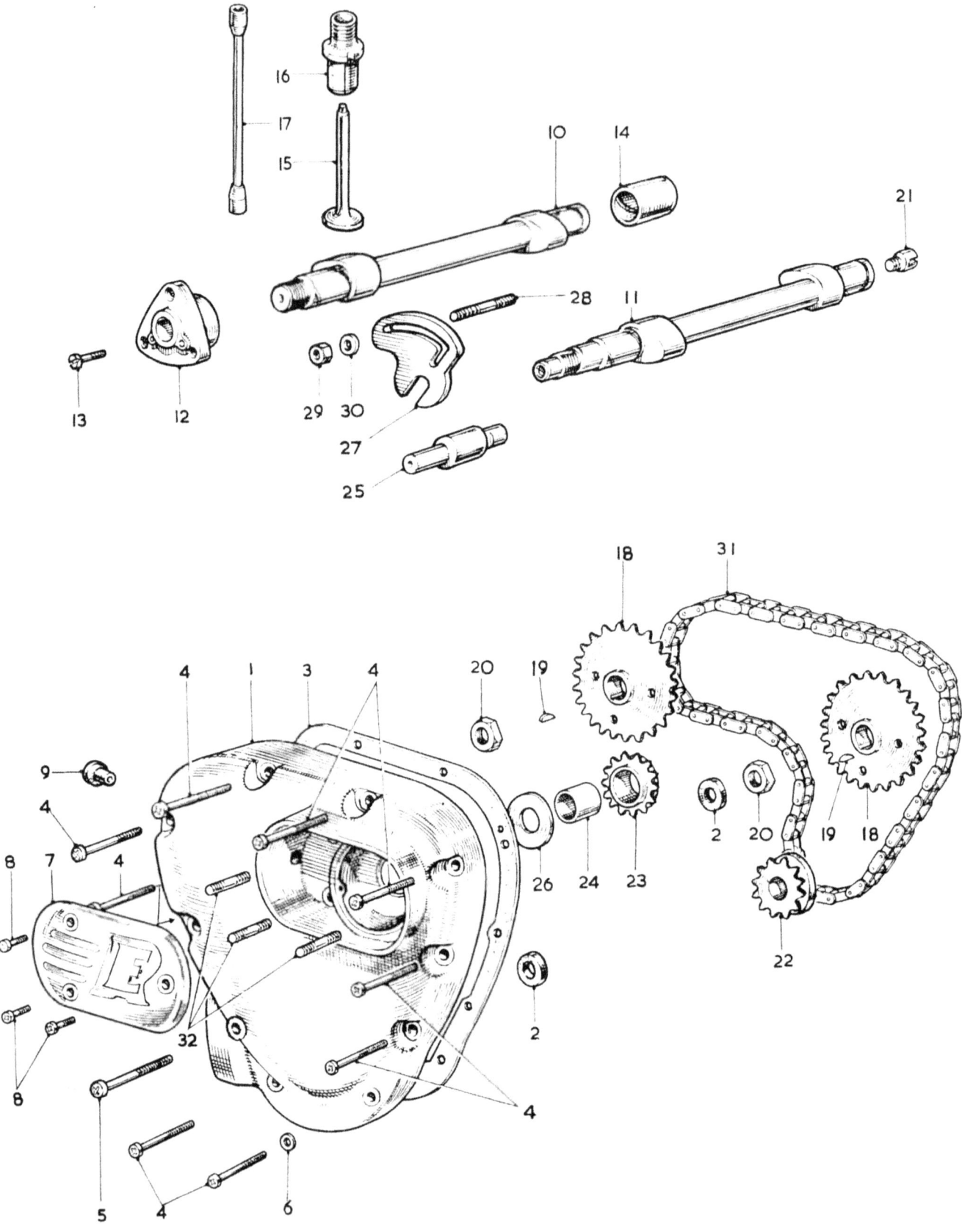

TIMING COVER AND TIMING GEAR ASSEMBLY

Illustration No.	Part No.	Description	Qty. per Set
	49668	Timing cover, complete with oil seals	1
1	49595	Timing cover, bare	1
2	49724	Oil seal, timing cover (contact breaker unit and oil pump worm)	2
3	49639	Gasket, timing cover	1
4	42135	Screw, short, timing cover securing	9
5	42140	Screw, long, timing cover securing	1
6	34690	Washer, timing cover securing screw	10
7	49632	Contact breaker cover	1
8	35869	Screw, contact breaker cover securing	3
9	49725	Rubber grommet, contact breaker cable	1
10	49637	Inlet camshaft	1
11	49638	Exhaust camshaft	1
12	49635	Bearing, camshaft (timing side)	2
13	49722	Screw, camshaft bearing locking	6
14	49646	Bearing, camshaft (drive side)	2
15	23480	Tappet, timing side and drive side	4
16	34360	Tappet guide, timing side and drive side	4
17	49720	Push rod	4
18	49636	Drive sprocket, camshaft	2
19	49723	Key, drive sprocket	2
20	49647	Nut, drive sprocket securing	2
21	49642	Driving screw, tachometer	1
22	49671	Timing sprocket, 12T	1
23	34372	Tensioner sprocket, timing chain, bushed	1
24	34354	Bush, tensioner sprocket	1
25	38552	Tensioner spindle, timing chain	1
26	34353	Thrust washer, tensioner spindle	1
27	34351	Tensioner locating plate, timing chain	1
28	29314	Stud, locating plate	1
29	36222	Locknut, locating plate stud	1
30	82	Washer, locating plate stud locknut	1
31	34396	Timing chain, 3/8" pitch x 0.25" dia. roller x 0.225" wide. Chain No. 110038 x 66 pitches, endless	1
32	47332	Contact breaker plate and condenser clip stud	3

Always quote Engine or Frame Number

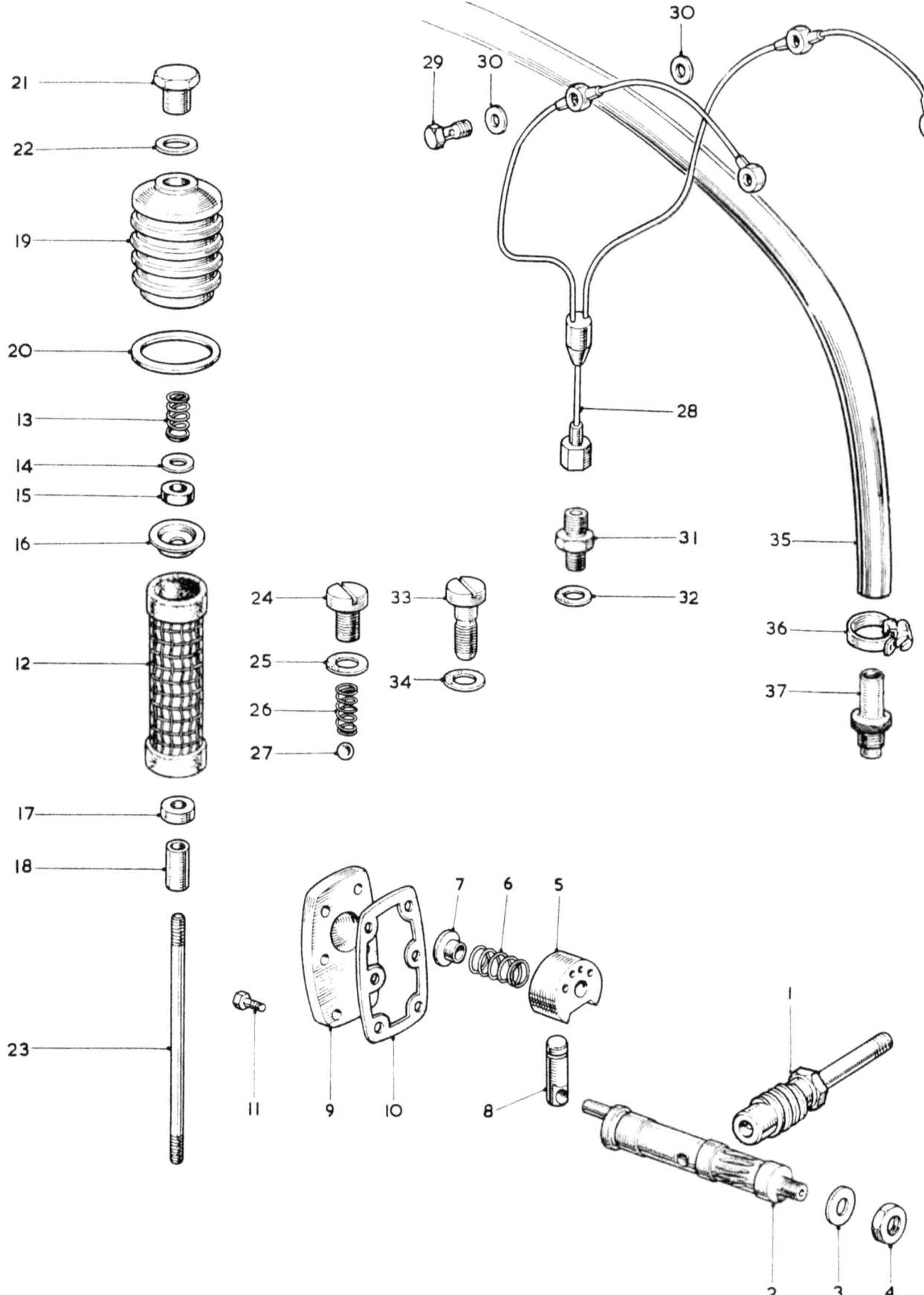

OIL PUMP, FILTER, ROCKER OIL FEED PIPE AND CRANKCASE BREATHER

Page 10

Illustration No.	Part No.	Description	No. per Set
1	49674	Oil pump worm	1
2	49614	Oil pump spindle	1
3	37315	Thrust washer, oil pump spindle	1
4	49650	Nut, oil pump spindle	1
5	49617	Oil pump disc	1
6	41851	Spring, oil pump disc	1
7	37669	End pad, oil pump disc spring	1
8	34347	Plunger, oil pump	1
9	45382	Oil pump cover	1
10	45383	Gasket, oil pump cover	1
11	45385	Cap screw, oil pump cover	6
12	40792	Oil cleaner element	1
13	28259	Spring, oil cleaner	1
14	8894	Thrust, washer, oil cleaner	1
15	18793	Felt washer, oil cleaner	1
16	28254	Spring cup, oil cleaner	1
17	42505	Magnet, oil cleaner	1
18	49645	Distance piece, oil cleaner	1
19	49601	Oil cleaner cap	1
20	49654	Sealing washer, oil cleaner cap	1
21	43773	Nut, oil cleaner cap securing	1
22	9732	Fibre washer, securing nut	1
23	37128	Stud, oil cleaner	1
24	47457	Oil Release valve plug	1
25	15034	Fibre washer, oil release valve plug	1
26	47458	Spring, oil release valve	1
27	32019	Steel ball, oil release valve	1
28	49664	Rocker oil feed pipe assembly complete	1
29	32389	Union body, rocker oil feed pipe assembly	4
30	39469	Copper washer, union body	8
31	29065	Union, rocker oil feed pipe assembly	1
32	5566	Fibre washer, union	1
33	49602	Rocker release valve complete	1
34	15034	Fibre washer, rocker release valve	1
35	48785	Breather tube (black nylon)	1
36	43965	Hose clip, size 'O'	1
37	48764	Union breather tube	1

Always quote Engine or Frame Number.

Page 11

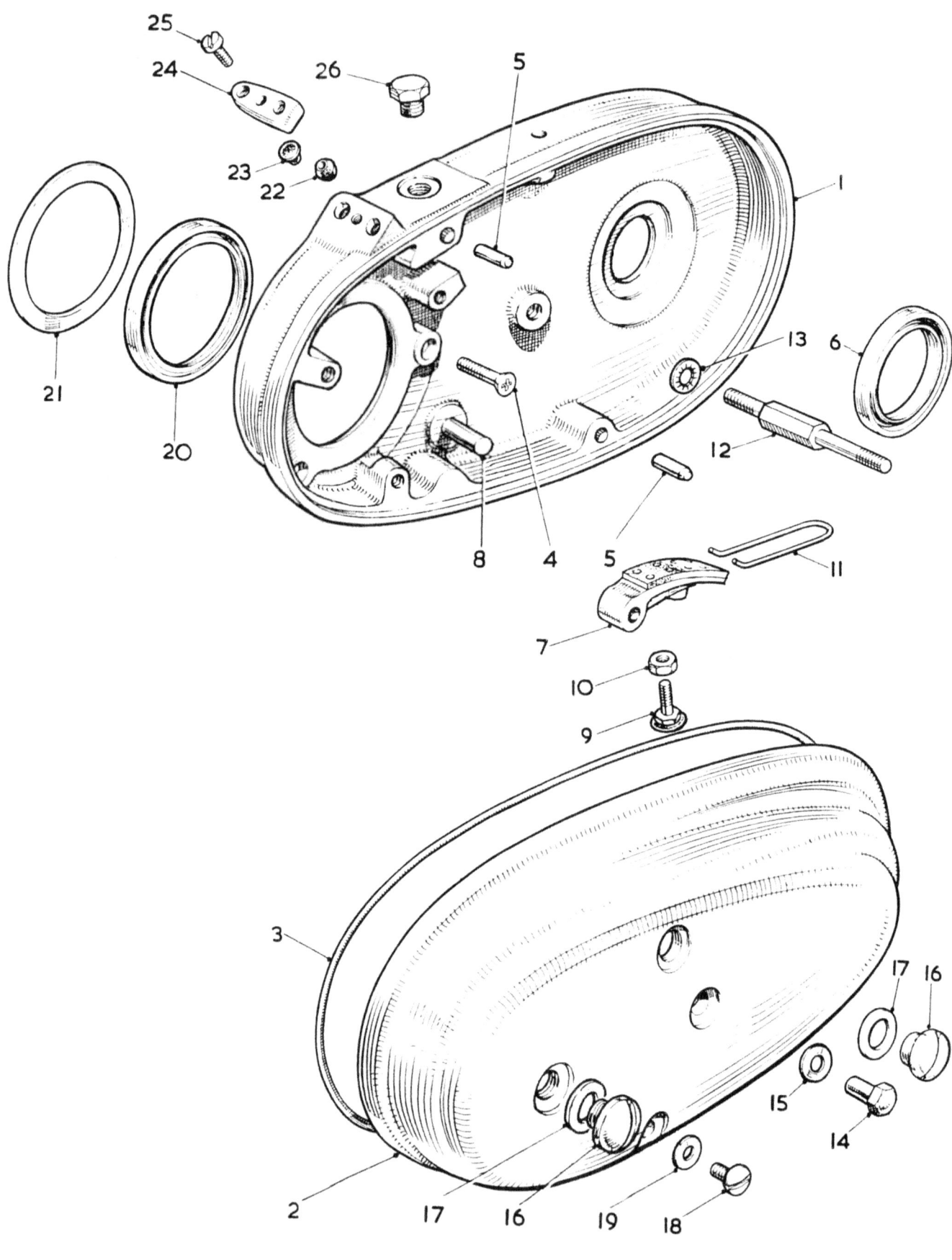

PRIMARY CHAINCASE

Illustration No.	Part No.	Description	No. per Set
1	45372	Chaincase (back)	1
2	49721	Chaincase (front)	1
3	40097	Chaincase rubber joint	1
4	38027	Chaincase (back) fixing screw 5/16" x 1" overall x 26 (from engine No. 1B1001 to 1B2001)	3
	49918	Chaincase (back) fixing screw (from engine No. 1B2002 onwards)	3
5	45373	Chaincase dowel	2
6	43565	Oil seal (gearbox mainshaft)	1
7	45386	Chain tensioner	1
8	36911	Chain tensioner spindle	1
9	45367	Chain tensioner adjusting screw with buffer	1
10	15771	Chain tensioner adjusting screw locknut	1
11	39664	Chain tensioner spring	1
12	45387	Chaincase (front) fixing stud	1
13	27918	Chaincase (front) fixing stud washer	1
14	35032	Chaincase stud nut	1
15	1580	Chaincase stud washer	1
16	40640	Chaincase inspection cover	2
17	40641	Chaincase inspection cover washer	2
18	35704	Oil level plug	1
19	46141	Oil level plug washer	1
20	43382	Oil seal	1
21	34069	Oil seal washer (outer) 3.21/64" x 2.9/32" x .024"	1
22	42268	Chaincase cable grommet	1
23	42834	Cable hole plug	1
24	42269	Cable hole plug housing	1
25	31172	Cable hole plug housing screw	1
26	49669	Breather screw	1

Always quote Engine or Frame Number

Page 13

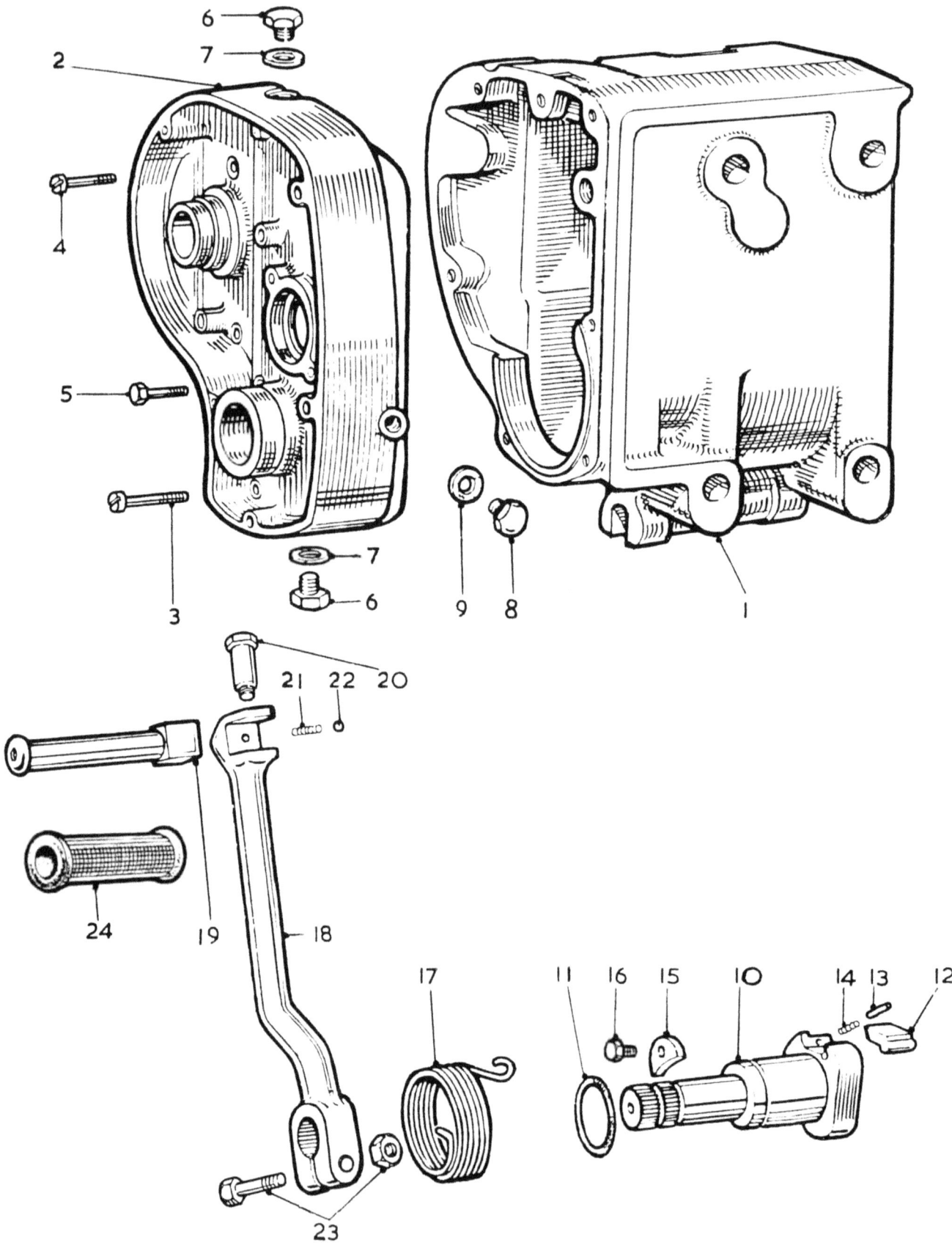

GEARBOX: CASES AND KICKSTARTER MECHANISM

Illustration No.	Part No.	Description	No. per Set
	49644	Gearbox, complete with clutch, 20T sprocket	1
1	33885/1	Gearbox case, complete with seal	1
2	37518/A	Gearbox case end cover	1
3	FC/57/107	Gearbox cover screw, cheese head, 1/4" x 1.7/16" x 20	2
4	FC/57/103	Gearbox cover screw, cheese head, 1/4" x 1.3/16" x 20	2
5	H54/103	Gearbox cover bolt, 1/4" x 1.3/16" x 20	1
6	E140	Oil filler plug or drain plug	2
7	E140A	Oil filler plug or drain plug washer	2
8	BJ23	Oil level plug	1
9	BJ23A	Oil level plug washer	1
10	H21/4	Footstarter spindle	1
11	H77	Footstarter spindle oil seal	1
12	37355	Footstarter pawl	1
13	H22A	Footstarter pawl plunger	1
14	H23	Footstarter pawl plunger spring	1
15	37356	Footstarter pawl stop plate	1
16	37357	Footstarter pawl stop plate bolt	2
17	E137/5	Footstarter return spring	1
18	H42/42A/6	Folding footstarter crank assembly	1
19	H42/4	Footstarter pedal	1
20	H42B	Footstarter pedal bolt	1
21	H42C	Footstarter pedal lock spring	1
22	32018	Footstarter pedal lock spring ball	1
23	H43S	Footstarter crank bolt and nut	1
24	G46KS	Footstarter pedal rubber	1

Always quote Engine or Frame Number

Page 15

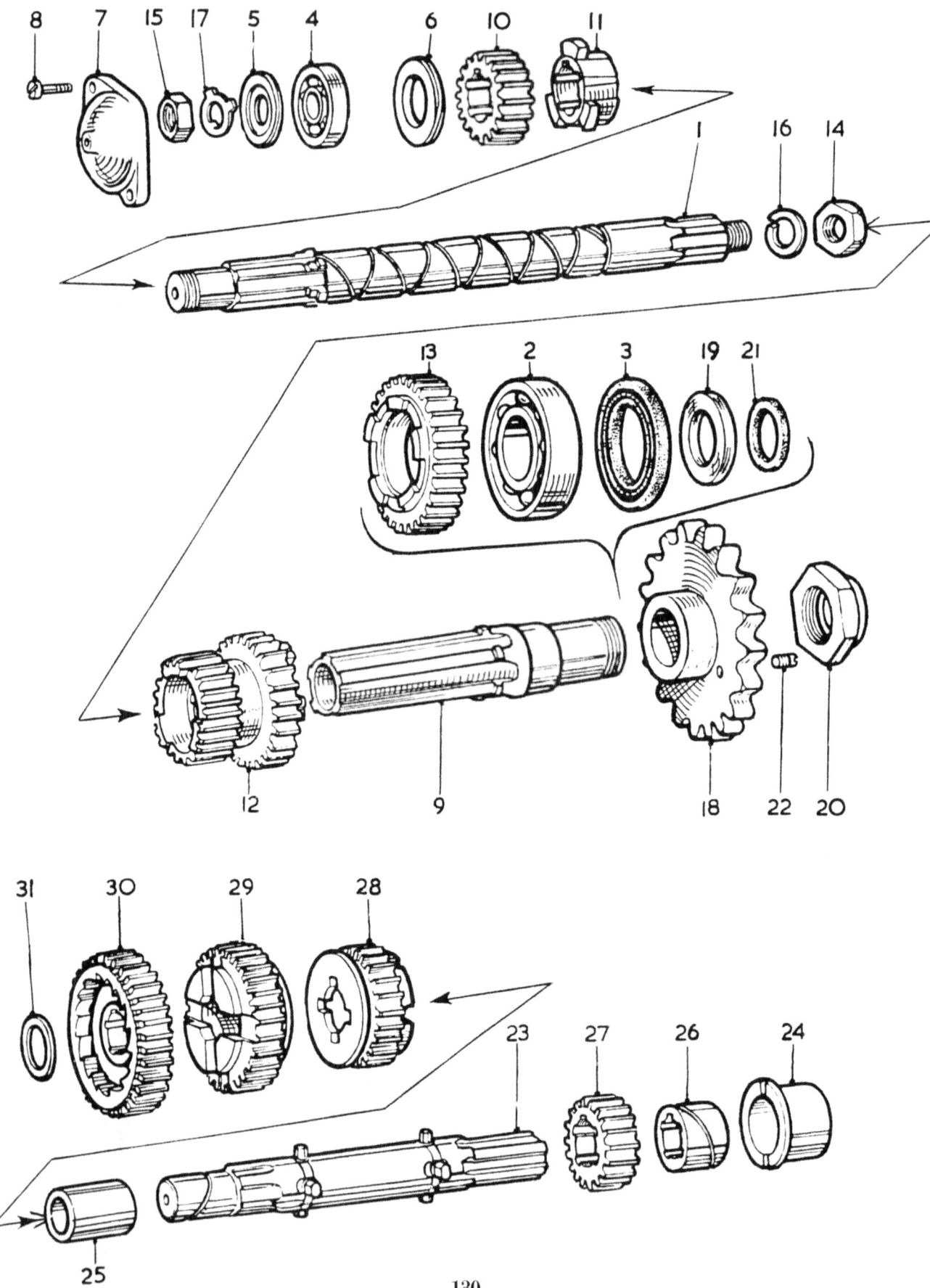

GEARBOX: RUNNING GEAR

Illustration No.	Part No.	Description	No. per Set
1	G2/7/TA	Mainshaft	1
2	H5	Ball journal bearing, SK/6206 (large)	1
3	H3/2	Oil seal, ball journal bearing	1
4	31966	Ball journal bearing, MS7 (small)	1
5	H71	Oil thrower (outer), ball journal bearing	1
6	H52	Oil thrower (inner), ball journal bearing	1
7	H40/1	Cap, oil thrower	1
8	FC57/009	Pin, oil thrower cap securing	2
9	G2/8B	Bushed sleeve, mainshaft	1
10	HG9/15	High gear 15T, mainshaft	1
11	H10A	High gear DOG, mainshaft	1
12	HG11/21/18	Sliding gear 21T and 18T, mainshaft	1
13	HG12/25	Low gear 25T, mainshaft	1
14	H55	Nut, mainshaft, clutch end (R.H. thread)	1
15	H56	Nut, mainshaft, kickstart end (L.H. thread)	1
16	H57	Springwwasher, mainshaft, clutch end	1
17	H91	Locking washer, mainshaft nut, clutch end	1
18	H49/20T	Drive sprocket 20T (Solo)	1
19	G2/53	Distance piece, drive sprocket	1
20	45428	Locknut, drive sprocket	1
21	H121	Felt washer, drive sprocket locknut	1
22	H122	Screw, drive sprocket locknut securing	1
23	M13	Layshaft	1
24	H14	Bush, layshaft, case end	1
25	H15	Bush, layshaft, kickstart end	1
26	H16	Splined bush, layshaft	1
27	HG17/15	Layshaft low gear 15T	1
28	HG18/19	Layshaft second gear 19T	1
29	HG19/22	Layshaft third gear 22T	1
30	HG20/25	Layshaft gear and kickstart wheel 25T	1
31	H15A	Washer, kickstart spindle	1

Always quote Engine or Frame Number.

Page 17

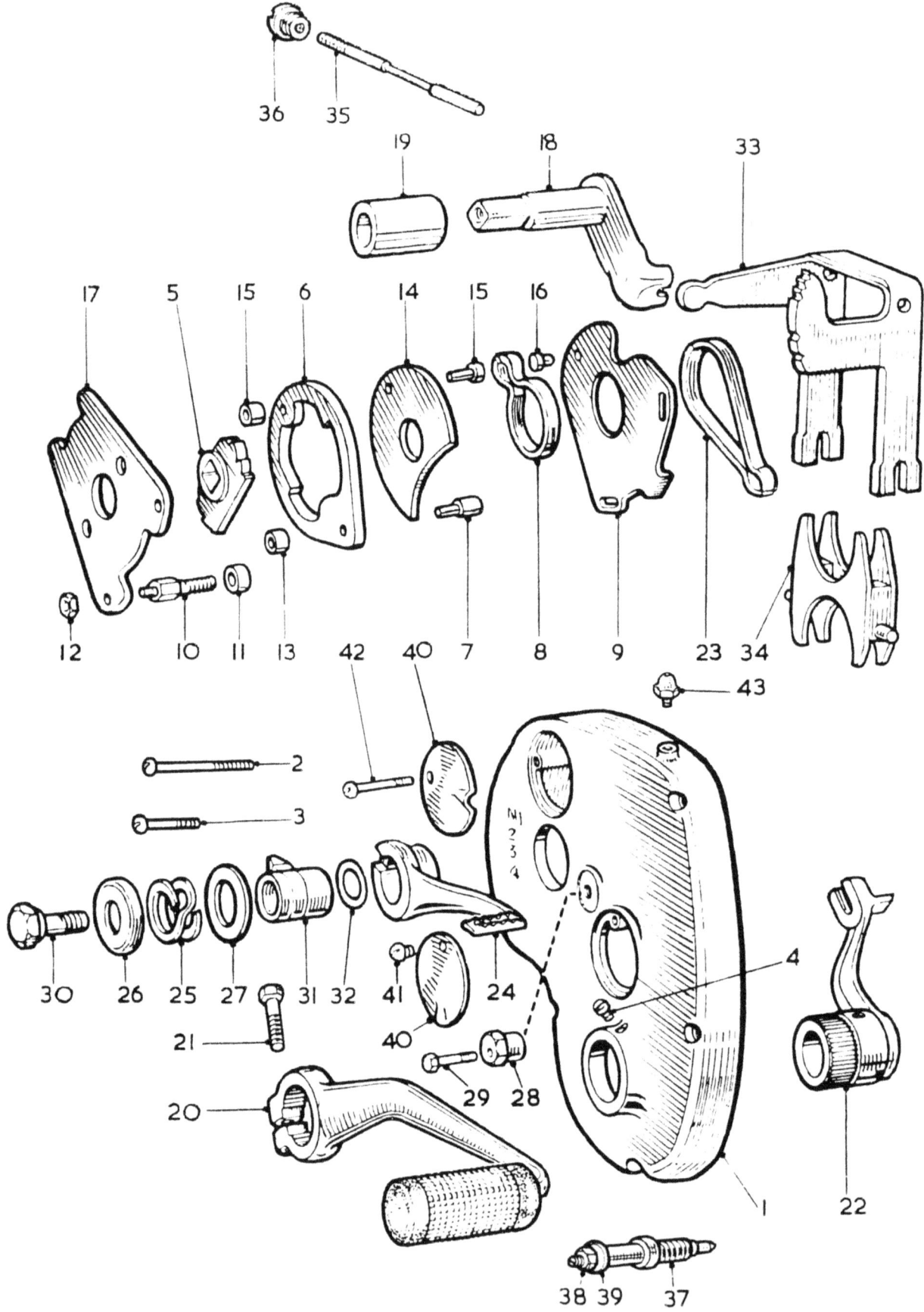

GEARBOX: GEAR SELECTOR MECHANISM

Illustration No.	Part No.	Description	No. per Set
1	G2/1A/1	Foot control cover	1
2	FC57/212	Foot control cover screw, cheese head, 1/4" x 2.3/4" x 20	2
3	FC57/103	Foot control cover screw, cheese head, 1/4" x 1.3/16" x 20	2
4	G2/14	Foot control cover oil hole screw, cheese head, 1/4" x 3/16" x 24	1
5	HFC4	Foot control ratchet (inner)	1
6	FC1/35/1	Foot control ratchet (outer)	1
7	FC44	Foot control ratchet pin	1
8	FC51	Foot control ratchet spring	1
9	FC41/1	Foot control adjuster plate	1
10	FC43	Foot control adjuster plate pin	2
11	FC58	Foot control adjuster plate pin bush	2
12	H113	Foot control adjuster plate nut	2
13	FC45	Foot control adjuster plate spring stop	1
14	FC53	Foot control plate	1
15	FC54	Foot control plate pin bush	2
16	FC46	Foot control plate spring stop	1
17	FC42/1	Foot control stop plate and spring retainer	1
18	FC47/E	Foot control operator shaft with lever	1
19	FC6E	Foot control operator shaft bush	1
20	FC/30F	Foot control lever	1
21	FC/30/A	Foot control lever pinch bolt	1
22	FC/48F	Foot control lever (short, inside)	1
23	FC/52/1	Foot control lever return spring	1
24	NS1/1	Foot control neutral lever	1
25	NS2	Foot control neutral lever spring	1
26	NS3	Foot control neutral lever spring cap	1
27	NS4	Foot control neutral lever spring washer	1
28	NS6	Foot control neutral lever eccentric bush	1
29	NS5	Foot control neutral lever stop pin	1
30	NS8	Foot control neutral lever securing pin	1
31	NS7/1	Foot control gear indicator	1
32	NS9	Foot control gear indicator washer	1
33	H33	Gear operator (inside)	1
34	H34	Gear operator fork	1
35	G2/36/1	Gear operator pin	1
36	G2/37	Gear operator pin bush	1
37	H67Ass.	Gear operator selector box assembly	1
38	H67B	Gear operator selector nut	1
39	H67C	Gear operator selector washer	1
40	HJ73	End cover inspection cap	2
41	H60/1	Inspection cap pin, 3/16" x 3/8" B.S.F.	1
42	H60/1A	Inspection cap pin, 3/16" x 1.1/4" B.S.F.	1
43	TC/PZ6	Grease nipple	1

Always quote Engine or Frame Number

Page 19

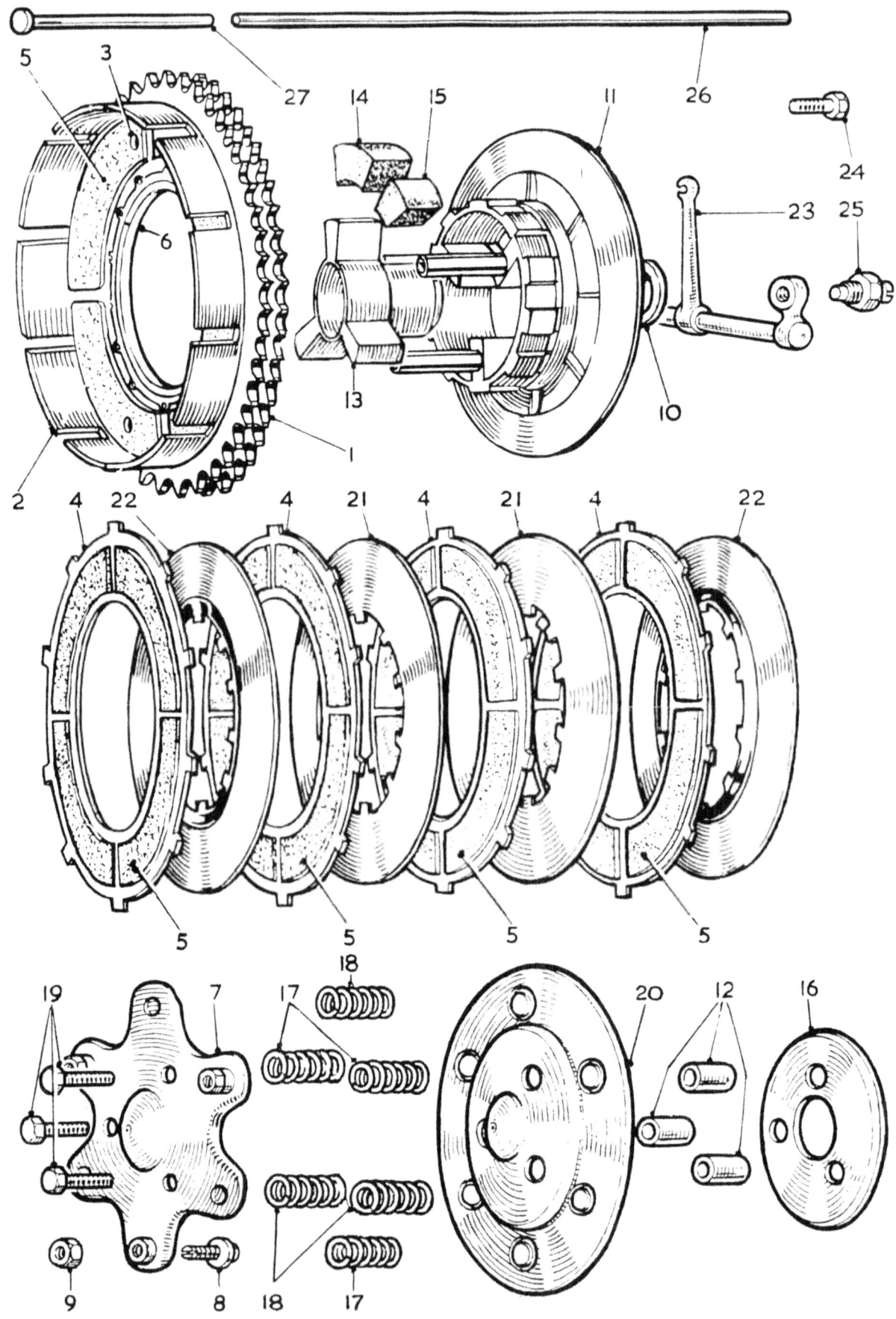

CLUTCH

Illustration No.	Part No.	Description	No. per Set
	28433/5/2	Clutch assembly	1
1	27535/6	Clutch sprocket 56T and drum assembly	1
2	H81/5	Clutch sprocket drum	1
3	G74/A	Clutch sprocket drum rivets	15
4	H89/CB	Clutch plate, cork bonded	4
5	H89/CB/2	Clutch plate, cork segments	36
6	GPG235/4	Clutch sprocket bearing ring	1
7	TR91	Clutch pressure plate, complete with adjuster collar	1
8	TR92	Clutch pressure plate adjuster screw	3
9	TR93	Clutch pressure plate adjuster nut	3
10	VR73/6	Clutch hardened distance piece	1
11	VR68/6	Clutch centre drum and back plate assembly	1
12	VR72/1	Clutch stud distance tube	3
13	G69/6	Clutch centre	1
14	G70/5	Clutch centre cush rubber (large)	3
15	G70A/5	Clutch centre cush rubber (small)	3
16	G71	Clutch centre retaining plate	1
17	G78/13	Clutch spring, 13G	3
18	G78/14	Clutch spring, 14G	3
19	G80	Clutch spring screw	3
20	TR77	Clutch front plate	1
21	G75	Clutch intermediate plate (flat)	2
22	G75A	Clutch intermediate plate (dished)	2
23	G2/41/1	Clutch lever	1
24	G2/13	Clutch lever bearing block pin 1/4" x 5/8" W	2
25	H44/1	Clutch adjuster, nut and ball	1
26	H66/1008	Clutch rod, 10.1/2" long	1
27	H66B	Clutch rod pad	1

STANDARD SHAKEPROOF WASHERS

Part Number	Diameter	Part Number	Diameter
29058	3/16"	27918	3/8"
27916	1/4"	27919	7/16"
27917	5/16"	27920	1/2"

Always quote Engine or Frame Number

Page 21

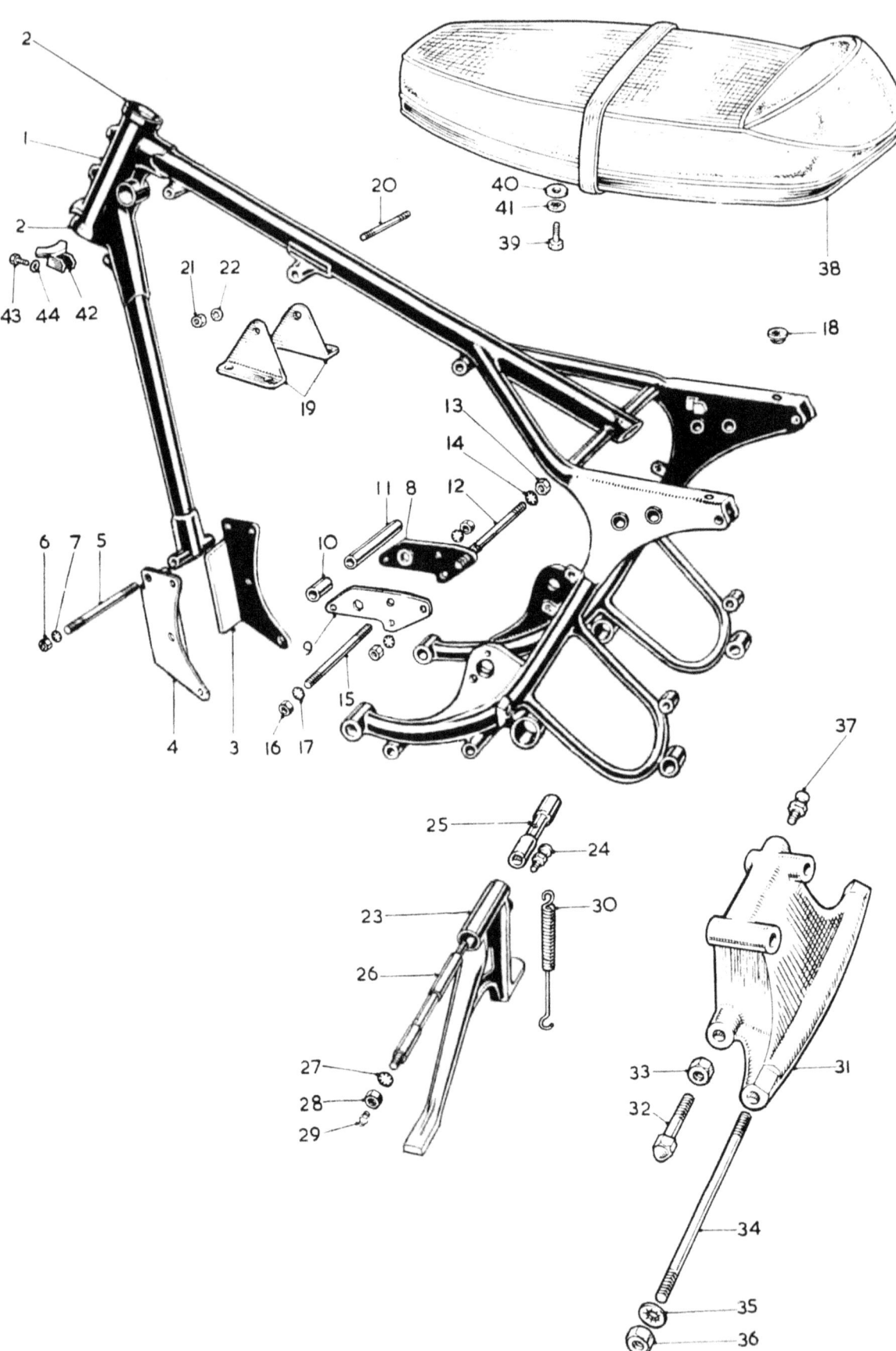

FRAME ASSEMBLY, GEAR BOX BRACKET AND CENTRE STAND

Illustration No.	Part No.	Description	No. per Set
1	49515	Frame assembly with head races, less all other loose fittings (from Frame No. F1001 to F1501)	1
	49912	Frame assembly with head races, less all other loose fittings (from Frame No. F1502 onwards)	1
2	34085	Head ball race	2
3	49655	Front engine plate, R.H.	1
4	49656	Front engine plate, L.H.	1
5	20946	Front engine plate stud (frame) 1/2" x 5.1/4" x 26	1
6	402	Front engine plate stud nut	2
7	27920	Front engine plate stud washer	2
8	39209	Rear engine plate R.H.	1
9	39210	Rear engine plate L.H.	1
10	40558	Rear engine plate distance tube 1.1/4" long L.H.	1
11	34099	Rear engine plate distance tube 4" long centre	1
12	43550	Rear engine plate stud (frame) 3/8" x 10.9/16" x 26	1
13	26995	Rear engine plate stud nut	2
14	6740	Rear engine plate stud washer	2
15	14176	Rear engine plate stud (gearbox) 1/2" x 5.3/16" x 26	1
16	402	Rear engine plate stud nut	2
17	27920	Rear engine plate stud washer	2
18	42834	Rubber plug for spring box bracket	2
19	45337A	Engine steady bracket	2
20	41331	Engine steady bracket stud, 7/16" x 1.7/8" x 26	1
21	10314	Engine steady bracket stud nut	2
22	27919	Engine steady bracket stud washer	2
	40786	Centre stand with spring post	1
23	40787	Centre stand only	1
24	47292	Centre stand spring post	1
25	33824	Centre stand bearing sleeve	1
26	34113	Centre stand bearing spindle	1
27	27919	Centre stand bearing spindle shakeproof washer	2
28	1898	Centre stand bearing spindle nut 7/16" x 26	2
29	NC.6050	Centre stand bearing spindle grease nipple	1
30	34908	Centre stand spring	1
	47209	Gearbox bracket with chaincase steady bolt and spring post	1
31	47207	Gearbox bracket only	1
32	47204	Chaincase steady bolt	1
33	26995	Chaincase steady bolt nut	1
34	38960	Gearbox bracket stud	1
35	27918	Gearbox bracket stud washer	2
36	26995	Gearbox bracket stud nut	2
37	47292	Gearbox bracket spring post	1
38	49529/A	Dual seat	1
39	49757	Dual seat bolt	4
40	7915	Dual seat washer	4
41	27917	Dual seat lockwasher	4
42	49681	Steering stop) From Frame No. F1001 to No. F1501 only.	1
43	44935	Steering stop screw)	1
44	27916	Steering stop lockwasher)	1

Always quote Engine or Frame Number

Page 23

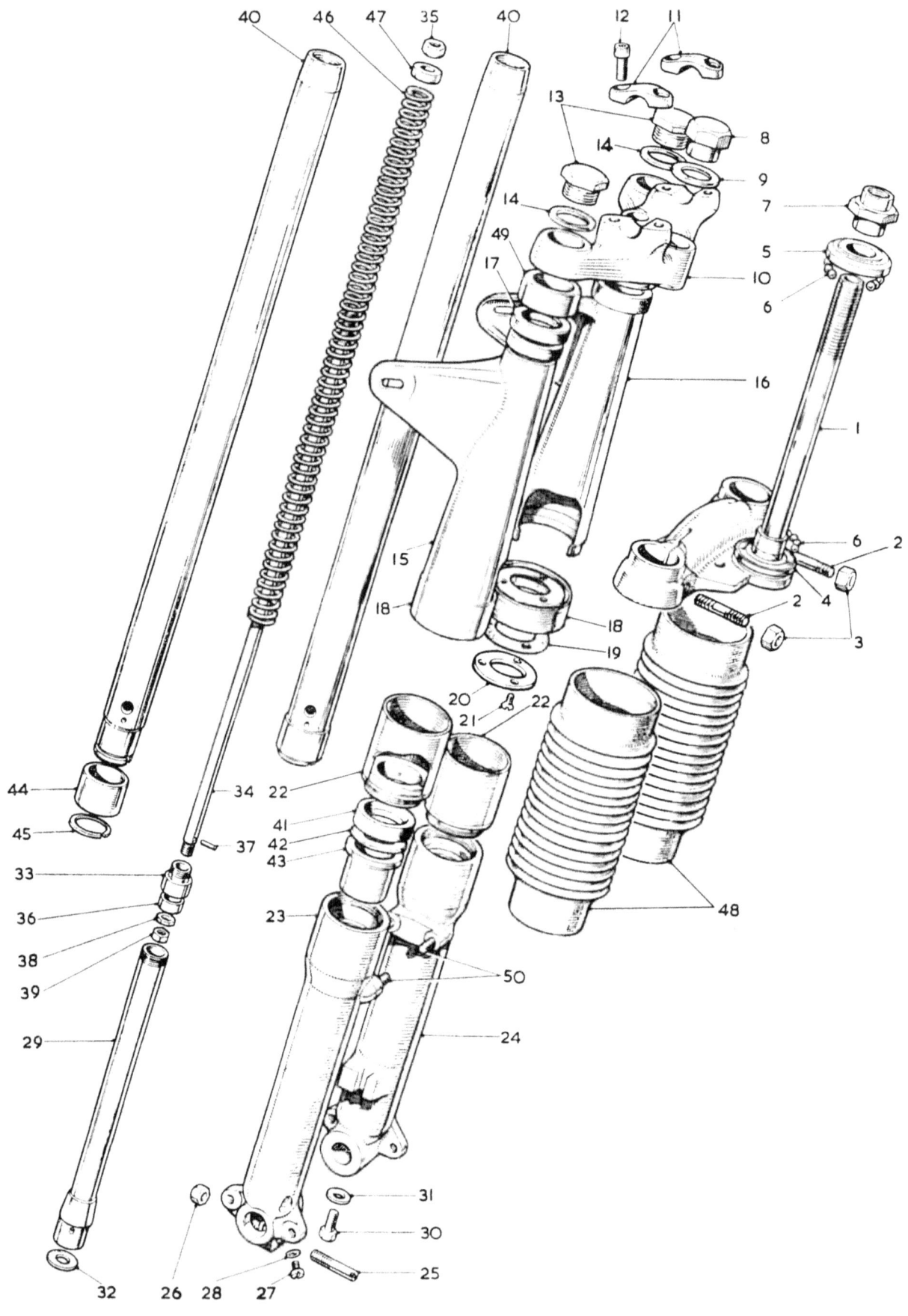

TELESCOPIC FRONT FORK

Illustration No.	Part No.	Description	No. per Set
	49707	Telescopic front fork assembly complete	1
1	49680	Fork crown assembly	1
2	49773	Pinch stud, fork crown	2
3	49774	Nut, fork crown pinch stud	2
4	49677	Ball race, fork crown	1
5	49678	Ball race, fork head	1
6	32018	Steel ball, 1/4" dia.	38
7	49770	Head nut	1
8	49772	Head nut top	1
9	49771	Head nut top washer	1
10	49765	Handlebar lug	1
11	49766	Clip, handlebar	2
12	49767	Cap screw, handlebar clip	4
13	49775	Top bolt, inner tube	2
14	49776	Washer, top bolt	2
15	49777	Top cover tube assembly L.H.	1
16	49778	Top cover tube assembly R.H.	1
17	49779	Spigot rubber, top cover tube	2
18	49780	Bottom cover tube assembly	2
19	49781	Seal, bottom cover tube	2
20	49782	Washer, bottom cover tube	2
21	49783	Screw, bottom cover tube	6
22	49784	Slider extension assembly	2
23	49785	Slider, L.H.	1
24	49786	Slider, R.H.	1
25	49789	Pinch stud, slider	1
26	49790	Nut, slider pinch stud	1
27	49787	Drain plug, slider	2
28	49788	Washer, slider drain plug	2
29	49791	Damper tube assembly	2
30	49792	Anchor bolt, damper tube	2
31	49793	Washer, damper tube anchor bolt	2
32	49794	Washer, damper tube anchor bolt	2
33	49795	Cap, damper tube	2
34	49796	Damper rod	2
35	49797	Locknut, damper rod	2
36	49798	Damper valve	2
37	49799	Stop pin, damper valve	2
38	49800	Seat, damper valve	2
39	49801	Nut, damper valve seat	2
40	49802	Main fork tube	2
41	49803	Oil seal, main fork tube	2
42	49804	Oil seal, washer, main fork tube	2
43	49805	Guide bush, main fork tube	2
44	49806	Bottom bush, main fork tube	2
45	49807	Circlip, bottom bush retaining	2
46	49808	Fork spring	2
47	49809	Locating bush, fork spring	2
48	49810	Fork gaiter	2
49	49679	Cover tube, top collar	2
50	49843	Mudguard bridge, stud	4

Always quote Engine or Frame Number.

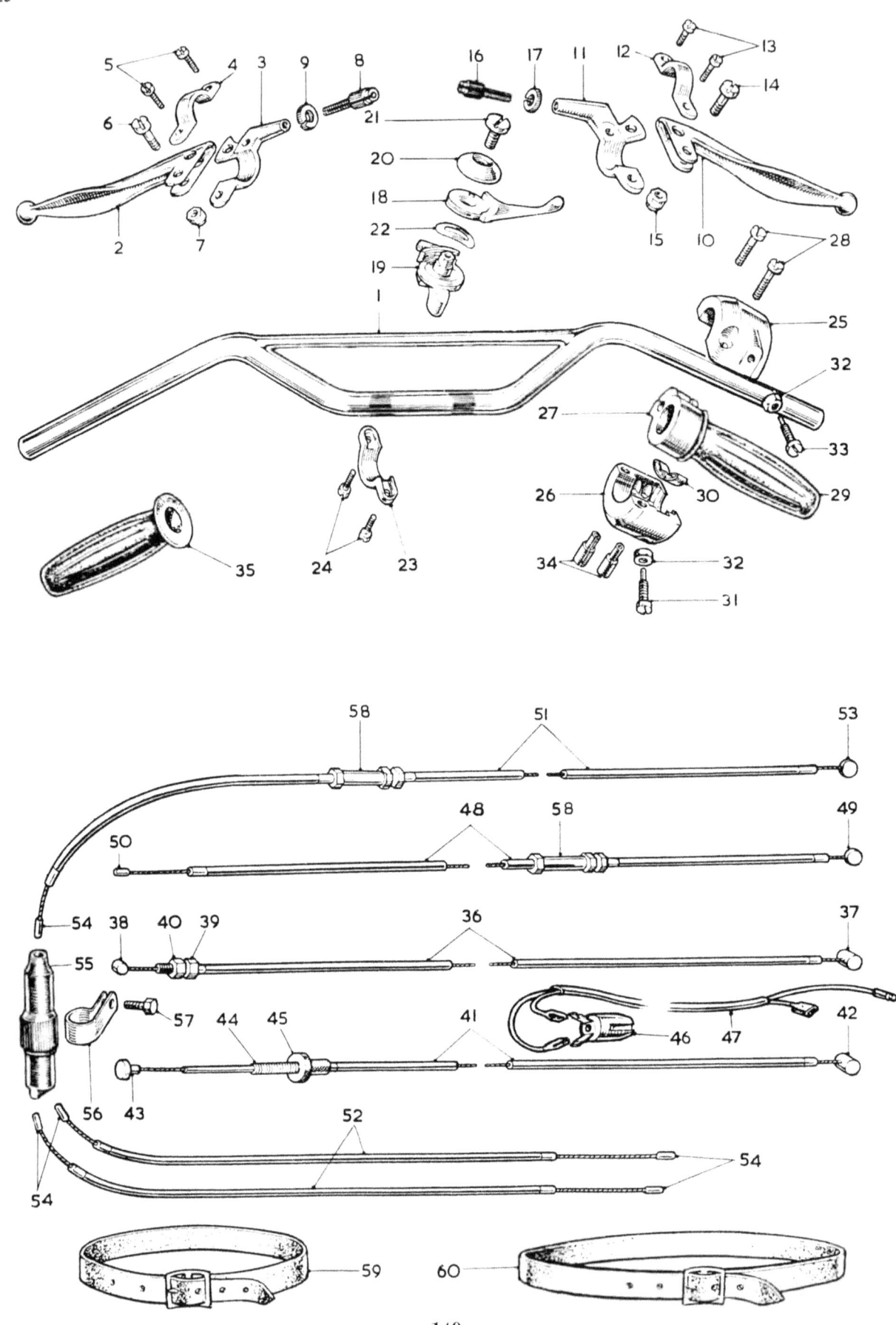

HANDLEBAR, CONTROLS AND CONTROL CABLES

Illustration No.	Part No.	Description	No. per Set
1	49708	Handle bend, based pattern	1
	207PA/LH	Clutch control lever, and cable adjuster	1
2	2070	Clutch control lever	1
3	1078	Clutch control lever body	1
4	10/1	Clutch control lever clip	1
5	71/7	Clutch control lever, clip screw ch. hd.	2
6	10/2	Clutch control lever pivot pin	1
7	10/3	Clutch control lever pivot pin nut	1
8	10/4	Clutch control lever adjuster	1
9	10/5	Clutch control lever adjuster nut	1
	207PA/RH	Front brake control lever assembly complete	1
10	2070	Brake control lever	1
11	1078	Brake control lever body	1
12	10/1	Brake control lever clip	1
13	71/7	Brake control lever clip screw	2
14	10/2	Brake control lever pivot pin	1
15	10/3	Brake control lever pivot pin nut	1
16	10/4	Brake control lever adjuster	1
17	10/5	Brake control lever adjuster nut	1
	12/608	Air control lever assembly complete	1
18	12/556	Air control lever	1
19	12/619	Air control body	1
20	12/606	Air control top cap	1
21	12/625	Air control centre screw	1
22	12/033	Air control spring washer	1
23	12/595	Air control clip	1
24	11/014	Air control clip screw	2
	313/9	Twist grip control complete	1
25	313/020	Twist grip control body (top half)	1
26	313/021	Twist grip control body (bottom half)	1
27	313/004	Twist grip control rotor	1
28	18/084	Twist grip control clamp bolt	2
29	366/012	Twist grip control grip rubber	1
30	16/008	Twist grip control friction spring	1
31	210/007	Twist grip control spring adjuster	1
32	5/077	Twist grip control locknut for spring adjuster and rotor stop	2
33	210/008	Twist grip control rotor stop	1
34	16/011	Twist grip control cable stop	2
35	366/011	Dummy grip rubber	1
36	47735/A	Clutch cable assembly complete	1
37	18/073	Clutch cable nipple, handlebar end	1
38	40112	Clutch cable nipple, gear box end	1
39	37100	Clutch cable adjusting screw	1
40	3257	Clutch cable adjusting screw locknut	1
41	49906	Front brake cable assembly complete with brake stop switch	1
42	18/088	Brake cable nipple, handlebar end	1
43	38031	Brake cable nipple, brake end	1
44	38032	Brake cable adjusting screw	1
45	14980	Brake cable adjusting screw locknut	1
46	49931	Brake cable stop switch	1
47	LU/54956181	Brake cable stop switch lead	1
48	49576	Throttle cable assembly	2
49	121034	Throttle cable nipple, handlebar end	2
50	1482	Throttle cable nipple, carburettor end	2
	49577	Air cable assembly complete with junction box	1
51	46008	Air cable assembly, handlebar end	1
52	49578	Air cable assembly, carburettor end	2
53	121034	Air cable nipple, handlebar end	1
54	1482	Air cable nipple, carburettor end and junction box	5
55	45719	Air cable junction box	1
56	46386	Air cable junction box clip	1
57	45229	Air cable junction box clip screw	1
58	33613	Cable midway adjuster, throttle and air	3
59	29609	Cable strap, leather 5"	1
60	29610	Cable strap, leather 7"	4

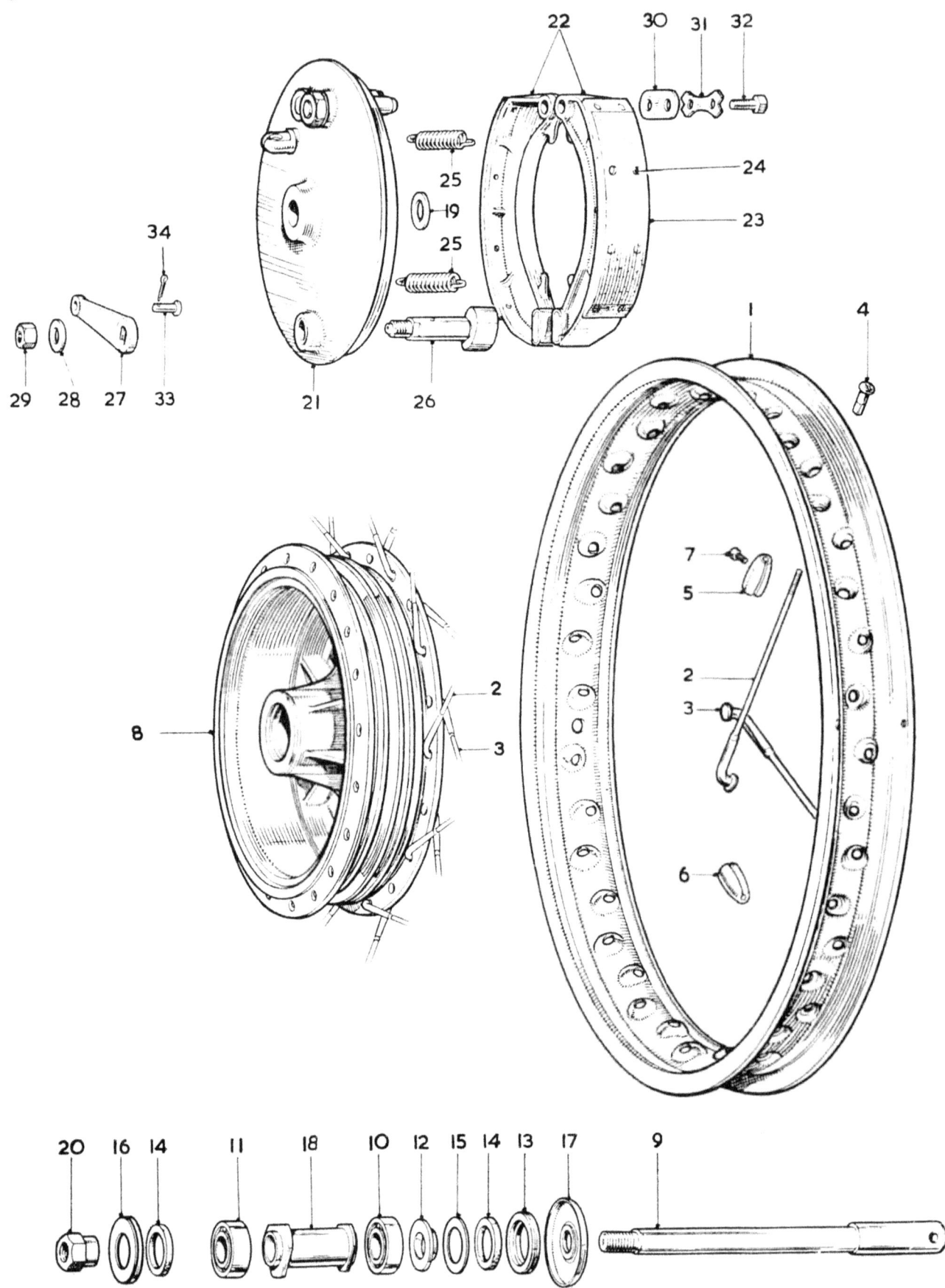

FRONT WHEEL AND BRAKE

Illustration No.	Part No.	Description	No. per Set
	49710	Front wheel assembly, complete with brake assembly, less tyre	1
1	49813	Wheel rim, type WM2-19	1
2	49814	Wheel spoke	20
3	49815	Wheel spoke	20
4	49816	Nipple, wheel spoke	40
5	44589	Balance weight, heavy)	
6	48287	Balance weight, light) fit as required	
7	44590	Screw, balance weight)	
	49859	Front hub assembly, complete with brake assembly	1
8	49817	Front hub only	1
9	49818	Wheel spindle	1
10	49819	Journal bearing, L.H.	1
11	49820	Journal bearing, R.H.	1
12	49821	Bearing spacer	1
13	49822	Bearing lockring	1
14	49823	Felt washer	2
15	49824	Washer, felt washer retaining	1
16	49825	Washer, oil retaining	1
17	49826	Dust cover	1
18	49827	Bearing spacer	1
19	49828	Spacer washer, brake cover plate (fit as required)	
20	49829	Nut, wheel spindle	1
21	49830	Brake cover plate complete	1
22	49958	Brake shoe, complete with lining and rivets	2
23	49956	Brake lining	2
24	49957	Brake lining rivet	16
25	49832	Brake shoe spring	2
26	49833	Brake cam	1
27	49834	Brake cam lever	1
28	49835	Washer, brake cam lever	1
29	49836	Nut, brake cam lever attachment	1
30	49837	Retaining plate, pivot pin	1
31	49838	Washer, retaining plate	1
32	49839	Bolt, retaining plate	2
33	49840	Yoke pin, front brake cable	1
34	49841	Split pin, yoke pin retaining	1

Always quote Engine or Frame Number

Page 29

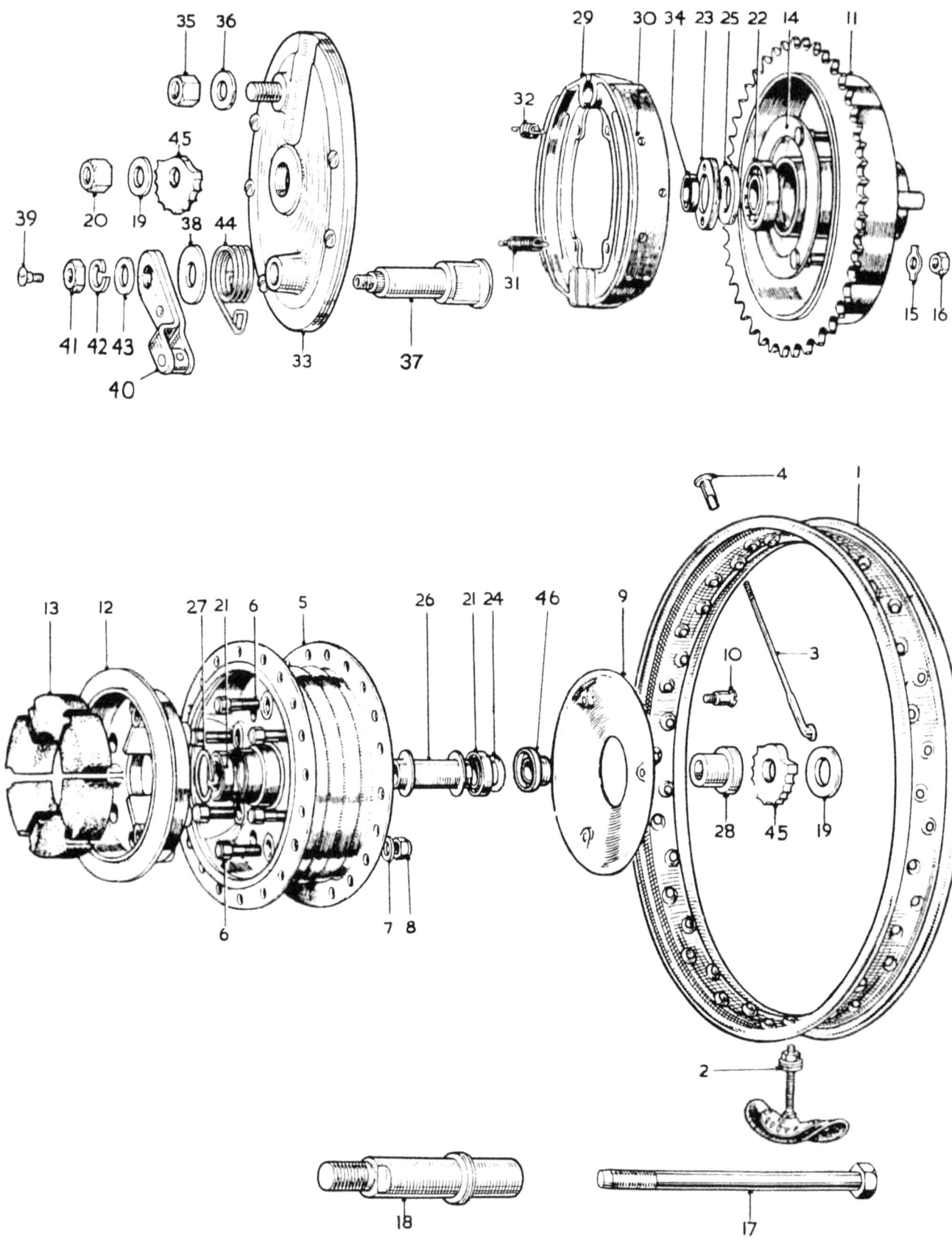

DETACHABLE REAR WHEEL AND BRAKE

Illustration No.	Part No.	Description	No. per Set
	48094	Rear wheel assembly, complete with cush drive and brake assembly, less tyre	1
	49640	Wheel detachable only	1
1	45638	Wheel rim, type WM3-18 with security bolt holes	1
2	35643	Security bolt, tyre (WM3 type)	2
3	40636	Wheel spoke, butted - 6.3/16" lg x 10G-Butted 8G	40
4	29206	Nipple, wheel spoke	40
	49695	Rear hub assembly, complete with cush drive and brake assembly	1
5	47639	Rear hub and barrel assembly only, complete with speedometer drive coupling	1
6	41000	Driving pin, rear hub	6
7	27918	Washer, driving pin	6
8	DE394	Nut, driving pin	6
9	40981	Rear hub cap, aluminium	1
10	40983	Screw, rear hub cap	3
11	41233	Brake drum and sprocket, 46T	1
12	40967	Cush drive shell	1
13	26193	Rubber block, cush drive	6
14	41003	Cush drive lockring	1
15	41001	Locking washer, lockring attachment	3
16	19870	Nut, lockring attachment	3
17	41369	Wheel spindle, detachable for wheel removal	1
18	46385	Hub spindle, fixed	1
19	41185	Washer, spindle	2
20	28832	Nut, spindle	1
21	27922	Journal bearing, hub, SKF.RLS5 Type 000	2
22	41110	Journal bearing, brake drum, SKF.RLS7 Type 000	1
23	41108	Retaining ring, brake drum journal	1
24	41006	Felt washer, R.H. hub journal	1
25	41106	Felt washer, L.H. (brake drum)	1
26	40995	Bearing spacer	1
27	41032	Internal circlip, L.H. hub journal retaining	1
28	40990	Distance collar, R.H.	1
29	41343/A	Brake shoe, complete with brake shoe lining	2
30	41285/A	Lining, brake shoe (one pair with rivets)	1
31	26033	Brake shoe spring (long)	1
32	42267	Brake shoe spring (short)	1
33	49694	Brake cover plate	1
34	41105	Distance collar, brake cover plate	1
35	7598	Anchor nut, brake cover plate	1
36	20112	Washer, anchor nut	1
37	46326	Brake cam	1
38	4964	Washer, brake cam	1
39	14472	Plug screw, brake cam	1
40	23371/A	Rear brake lever, complete with trunnion	1
41	10314	Nut, rear brake lever attachment	1
42	14613	Spring washer, attachment nut	1
43	49599	Washer, rear brake lever	1
44	49562	Return spring, rear brake lever	1
45	36649	Adjuster cam, rear hub	2
46	46868	Speedo drive spacing collar	1

Always quote Engine or Frame Number.

Page 31

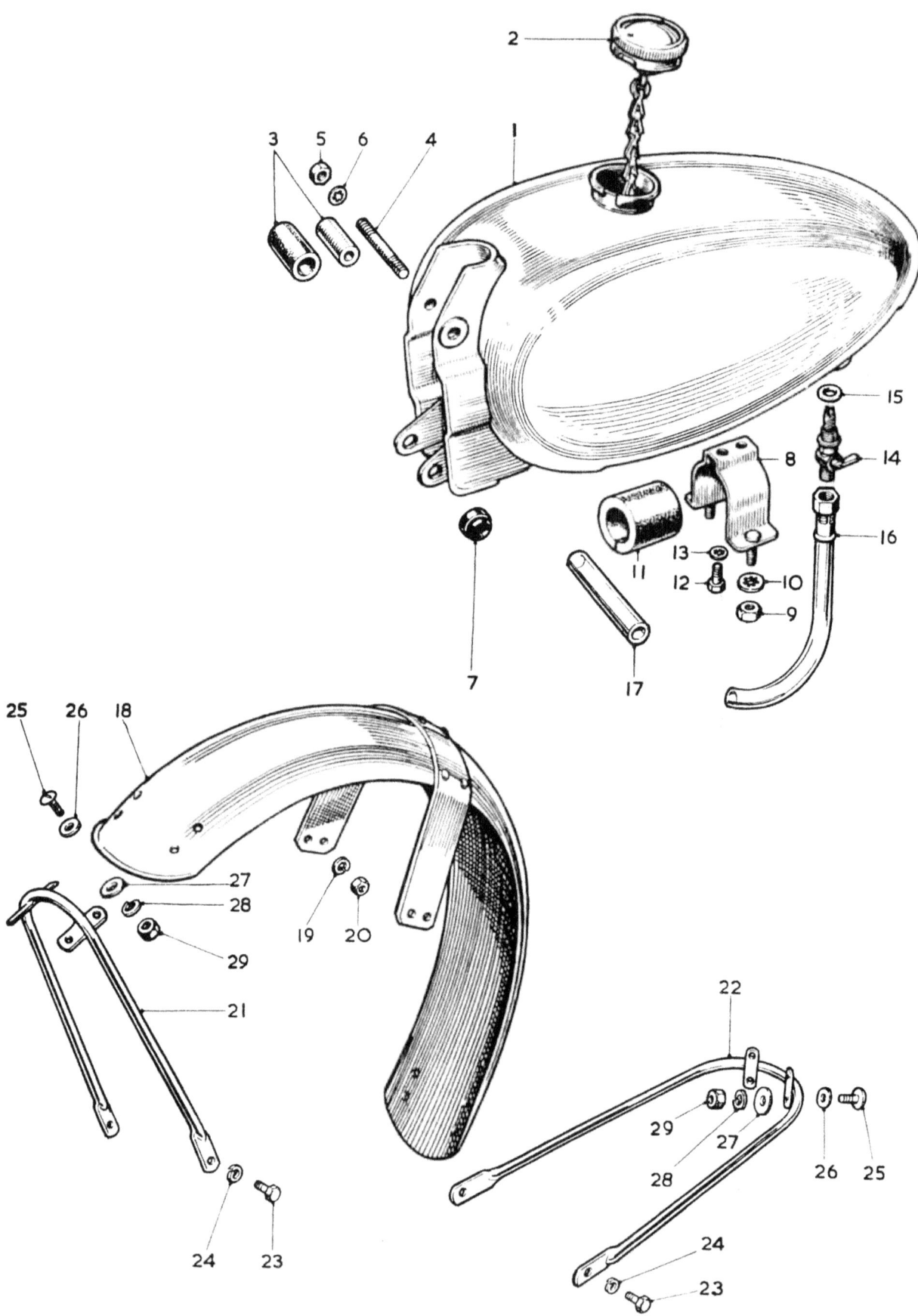

PETROL TANK, FRONT MUDGUARD AND FRONT STAND

Illustration No.	Part No.	Description	No. per Set
1	49555	Petrol tank, complete with filler cap and chain	1
2	P521	Tank filler cap	1
3	41602	Tank buffer sleeve	1
4	25336	Tank fixing stud)	1
5	26995	Tank fixing stud nut) Front fixing	2
6	27918	Tank fixing stud washer)	2
7	41644	Tank steady buffer)	2
8	44702	Tank attachment clip set	1
9	26998	Petrol tank clip nut	2
10	27916	Petrol tank clip nut washer	2
11	41562	Tank attachment clip sleeve	1
12	253	Tank attachment clip pin	2
13	29058	Tank attachment clip washer	2
14	46895	Petrol tap and strainer	2
15	5662	Petrol tap fibre washer	2
16	49570	Petrol pipe complete	2
17	49696	Float chamber balance pipe	1
	49749	Petrol tank centre strip transfer	1
18	49711	Mudguard, chrome	1
19	49844	Slider stud washer	4
20	49845	Slider stud nut	4
21	49846	Mudguard stay (front)	1
22	49847	Mudguard stay (rear)	1
23	49848	Slider bolt, stay attachment	4
24	49849	Slider bolt, washer	4
25	49850	Mudguard bolt, stay attachment	8
26	49851	Mudguard bolt washer	8
27	49852	Mudguard bolt washer	8
28	49853	Mudguard bolt washer	8
29	49854	Mudguard bolt nut	8

Always quote Engine or Frame Number

Page 33

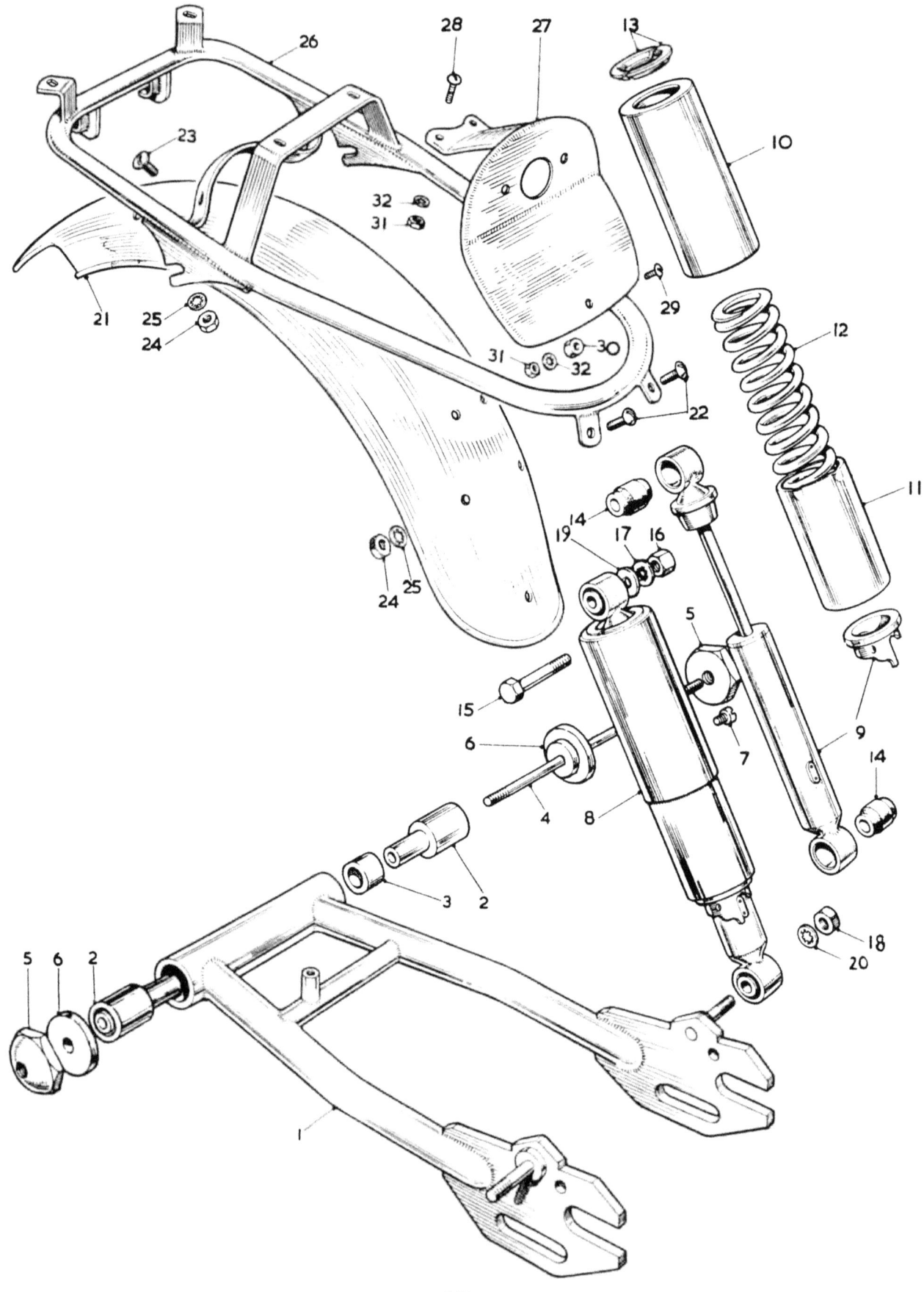

148

REAR SUSPENSION, MUDGUARD AND NUMBER PLATE

Illustration No.	Part No.	Description	No. per Set
1	49524	Chainstay assembly less bearings	1
2	46262	Chainstay bearing	2
3	46266	Chainstay bearing distance piece	1
4	46263	Chainstay bearing stud	1
5	46264	Chainstay bearing stud nut	2
6	46265	Chainstay bearing stud collar	2
7	45703	Chainstay nut locking screw	1
8	49557	Suspension unit (64054968 Girling No.)	2
9	564564646	Damper unit	2
10	64533032	Outer dirt shield	2
11	64532778	Inner dirt shield	2
12	64539963	Suspension spring	2
13	9054/171	Spring retaining clip	4
14	64533652	Metalastik bush	4
15	42002	Spring box pivot pin, top, 3/8" x 1.5/8" x 20	2
16	26374	Spring box pivot pin nut (top)	2
17	27918	Spring box pivot pin lockwasher (top)	2
18	DE394	Spring box pivot pin nut (bottom)	2
19	33783	Spring box pivot pin washer (top)	2
20	27918	Lockwasher, bottom pivot pin	2
21	49584	Mudguard	1
22	251	Mudguard bolt rh/hd, 1/4" x 1/2" x 26	2
23	38767	Mudguard bolt	2
24	26998	Mudguard bolt nut	4
25	27916	Mudguard bolt washer	4
26	49551	Mudguard carrier	1
27	49586	Number plate	1
28	1083	Number plate attachment pin (top)	2
29	18446	Number plate attachment pin (bottom)	1
30	18229	Number plate attachment pin collar	2
31	26998	Number plate attachment pin nut	3
32	27916	Number plate attachment pin washer	3

Always quote Engine or Frame Number

Page 35

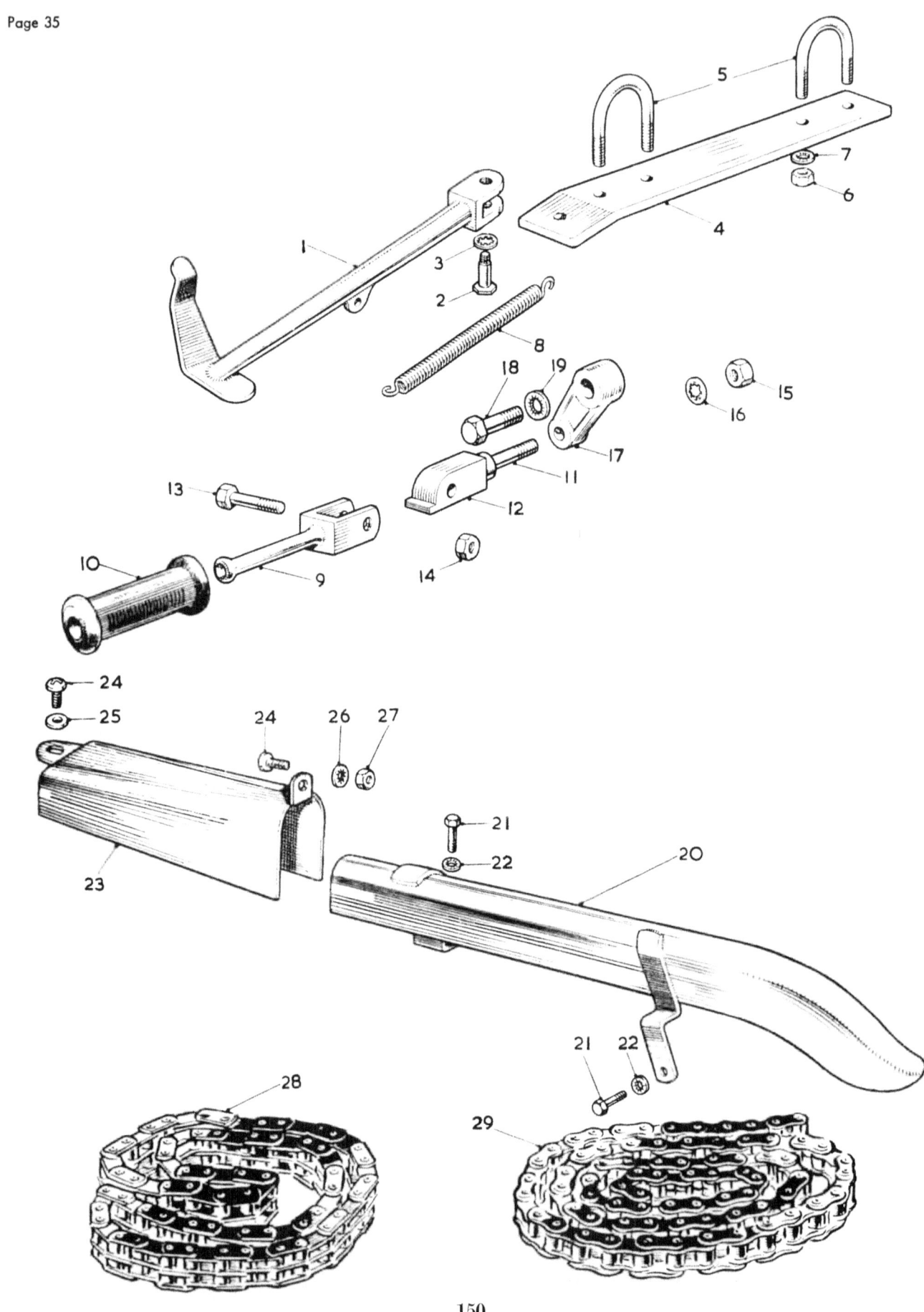

PROP. STAND, PILLION FOOTRESTS, CHAINGUARD AND CHAINS

Illustration No.	Part No.	Description	No. per Set
1	47191	Prop. stand leg	1
2	47194	Prop. stand leg pivot bolt	1
3	27919	Prop. stand leg spring washer	1
4	47188	Prop. stand plate, complete with spring post	1
5	47195	Prop. stand "U" bolt	2
6	27621	Prop. stand "U" bolt nut	4
7	27917	Prop. stand "U" bolt washer	4
8	34908	Prop. stand spring	1
9	48749	Pillion footrest	2
10	42691	Pillion footrest rubber	2
11	41680	Pillion footrest stud	2
12	41523	Pillion footrest pivot block	2
13	41499	Pillion footrest pivot block pin, 5/16" x 1.3/16" x 26	2
14	3257	Pillion footrest pivot block pin nut	2
15	30807	Pillion footrest pivot block stud nut	2
16	27919	Pillion footrest pivot block stud washer	2
17	41636	Pillion footrest bracket	2
18	49583	Pillion footrest bracket bolt	2
19	27920	Pillion footrest bracket washer	2
20	49523	Chainguard, rear	1
21	14447	Chainguard bolt, rear 5/16" x 3/8" x 26	2
22	27917	Chainguard bolt washer (shakeproof)	2
23	49657	Chainguard (fixed)	1
24	49685	Screw, fixed chainguard attachment	2
25	7674	Washer, attachment screw	1
26	27916	Lockwasher, attachment screw	1
27	27620	Nut, attachment screw	1
28	RN/114038/92	Front chain, 3/8" duplex x 92 pitches	1
29	RN/110056/110	Rear chain, 5/8" x 3/8" x 110 pitches	1

Always quote Engine or Frame Number

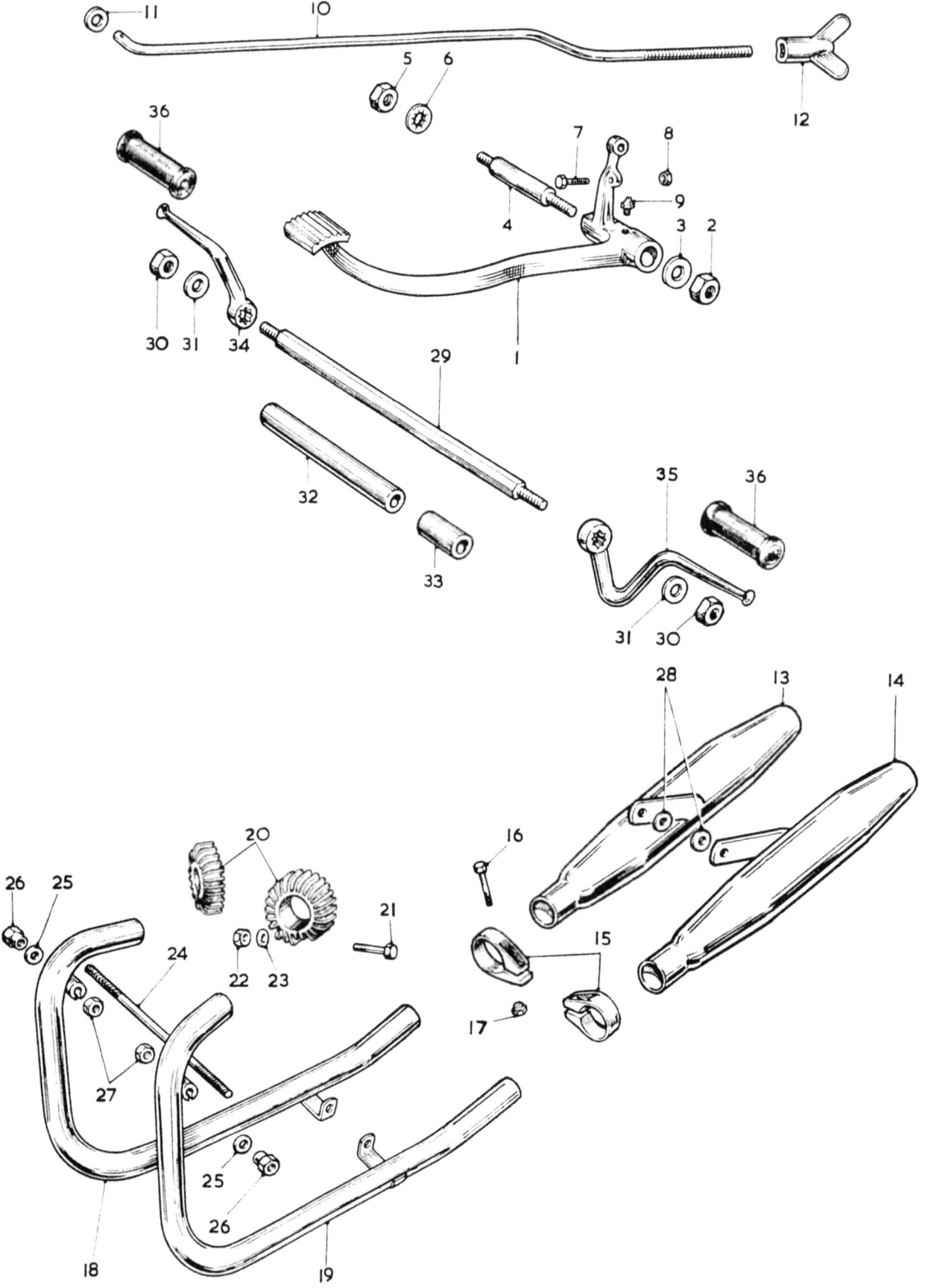

REAR BRAKE CONTROL, EXHAUST SYSTEM AND FOOTRESTS

Illustration No.	Part No.	Description	No. per Set
1	41183/A	Brake pedal	1
2	26995	Brake pedal securing nut, 3/8" x 26	1
3	15641	Brake pedal securing nut washer	1
4	40339	Brake pedal fulcrum stud	1
5	10314	Brake pedal fulcrum stud nut 7/16" x 26	1
6	27919	Brake pedal fulcrum stud nut washer	1
7	252	Brake pedal stop pin, 1/4" x 3/4" x 26	1
8	27000	Brake pedal stop pin locknut	1
9	NA5700/1	Brake pedal grease nipple	1
10	49560	Brake rod (Road Scrambler)	1
11	14691	Brake rod washer	1
	30779	Brake rod split pin, 1/16" x 3/4"	1
12	17691	Brake rod adjusting nut	1
13	49704	Silencer, complete (R.H.)	1
14	49705	Silencer, complete (L.H.)	1
15	41341	Silencer clip (to exhaust pipe)	2
16	4860	Silencer clip bolt, 1/4" x 1.1/16" x 26	2
17	12881	Silencer clip bolt nut	2
18	49753	Exhaust pipe (R.H.)	1
19	49581	Exhaust pipe (L.H.)	1
20	41044	Exhaust pipe clip (head)	2
21	19555	Exhaust pipe clip screw	2
22	26998	Exhaust pipe clip screw nut	2
23	27916	Exhaust pipe clip screw nut washer	2
24	44964	Exhaust pipe tie rod	1
25	14691	Exhaust pipe tie rod washer	2
26	26168	Exhaust pipe tie rod nut, sleeved	2
27	27001	Exhaust pipe tie rod nut, standard	2
28	6740	Exhaust pipe distance piece	2
29	20769/A	Footrest bar	1
30	10315	Footrest bar nut, 7/16" x 26	2
31	37315	Footrest bar washer	2
32	39197	Footrest distance tube, centre 3.3/4" long	1
33	48136	Footrest distance tube, 5/8" long	2
34	35020	Footrest arm (L.H.)	1
35	33162	Footrest arm (R.H.)	1
36	25838	Footrest arm rubber	2

Always quote Engine or Frame Number

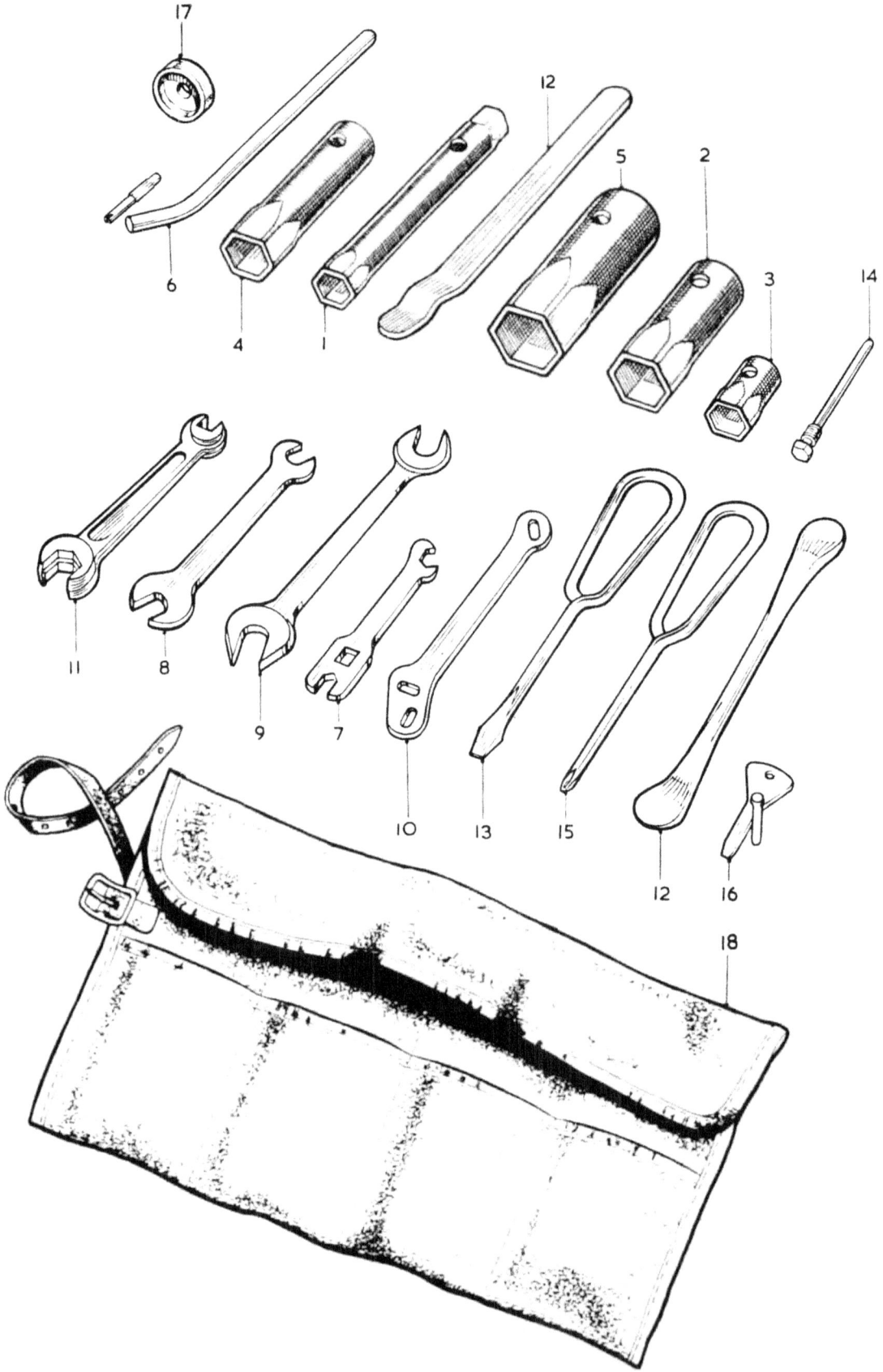

TOOL KIT

Illustration No.	Part No.	Description	No. per Set
1	35634	Tubular spanner, 1/4" x 5/16" Whit.	1
2	44710	Tubular spanner sparking plug	1
3	24095	Tubular spanner, 1/2" Whit.	1
4	35635	Tubular spanner, 9/16" Whit.	1
5	24094	Tubular spanner, 11/16" Whit.	1
6	29042	Tommy bar, 5/16" dia.	1
7	24092	Spanner, .343" x .380" Hex.	1
8	27896	Spanner, 3/16" x 1/4" Whit.	1
9	29044	Spanner, 1/4" x 5/16" Whit.	1
10	43449	Valve rocker adjusting spanner	1
11	6406	Combination spanner	1
12	4272	Tyre lever	2
13	3482	Screwdriver flat blade	1
14	49622	Contact breaker extractor	1
15	DWU-05	Screwdriver	1
16	400935	Contact breaker screwdriver	1
17	49717	Advance washer, contact breaker	1
18	16007	Tool roll	1

THREAD INSERTS

The following cross wire thread inserts are available for repairing stripped threads in crankcases, covers and cylinder heads. The appropriate insert tap and a special assembly tool are necessary for each size of thread.

Part No.	Size	Qty	Application
49959	3/16" B.S.F. x 7/32"	6-off	Oil pump cover studs
49960	3/16" Whit. x 7/32"	4-off	C'breaker cover & condenser clip studs
		2-off	Rev. counter gearbox screws
49961	1/4" B.S.F. x 3/8"	2-off	Crankcase bridge screws
		1-off	Timing chain tensioner stud
		6-off	Camshaft bearing screws
		4-off	Crankcase screw (bottom)
		10-off	Timing cover screws
49962	1/4" Whit. x 3/8"	16-off	Rocker Cover studs
49963	5/16" B.S.F. x 15/32"	3-off	Crankcase studs
		4-off	Carburettor flange studs
		4-off	Cylinder hd. steady studs
		3-off	Chaincase screws
38621	5/16" CEI x 5/16"	4-off	Oil feed union, cyl. hd. (std. fitting)
49964	3/8" BSF x 9/16"	10-off	Cylinder studs
		1-off	Chaincase, centre stud
		1-off	Oil filter hsg. stud
48010	3/8" BSF x 5/16"	2-off	Balance pipe union, cyl.hd. (std. fitting)
49965	3/8" CEI x 3/4"	4-off	Gearbox attachment studs
49966	5/8" CEI x 5/16"	4-off	Rocker spindle end plug
49967	14 mm x 5/8"	2-off	Sparking plug

Always quote Engine or Frame Number

Page 41

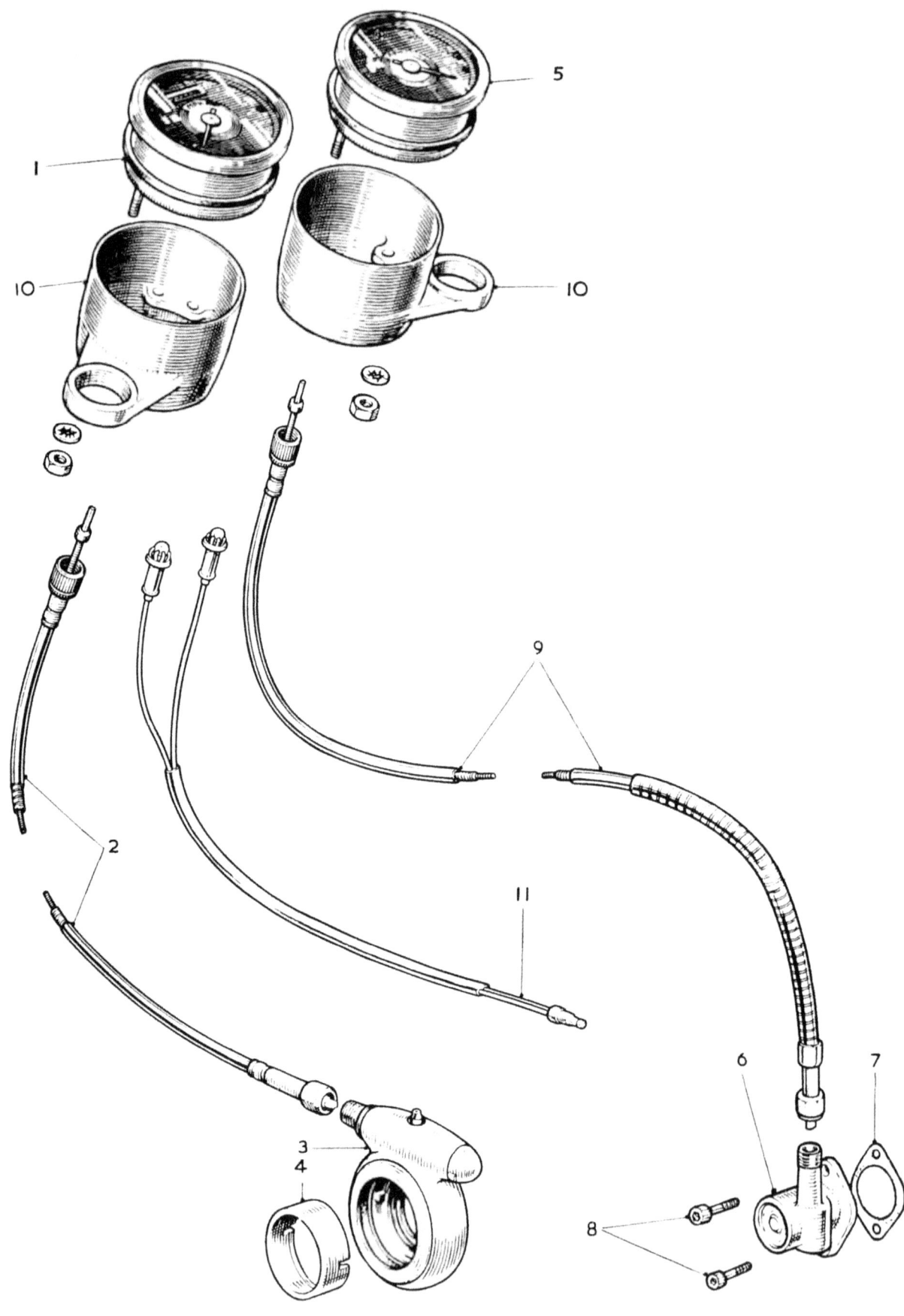

SMITHS' SPEEDOMETER, REVOLUTION COUNTER AND MOUNTING

Illustration No.	Part No.	Description	No. per Set
1	SSM/3001/00	Speedometer head 125 m.p.h. trip, illuminated complete with attachment nuts and lockwashers	1
2	DF9110/00	Flexible drive complete, 58 inches	1
3	49727	Gearbox (self-contained) complete	1
4	46869	Gearbox drive coupling	1
5	RSM3003/03	Revolution counter head complete with attachment nuts and lockwashers	1
6	BG1508/01	Revolution counter gearbox	1
7	47673	Revolution counter gearbox gasket	1
8	49726	Revolution counter gearbox cap screw	2
9	DF911/03	Driving cable, 29.5" long	1
10	49712	Instrument case	2
11	LU/54953387/B	Speedometer and revolution counter light lead	1

Always quote Engine or Frame Number

Page 43

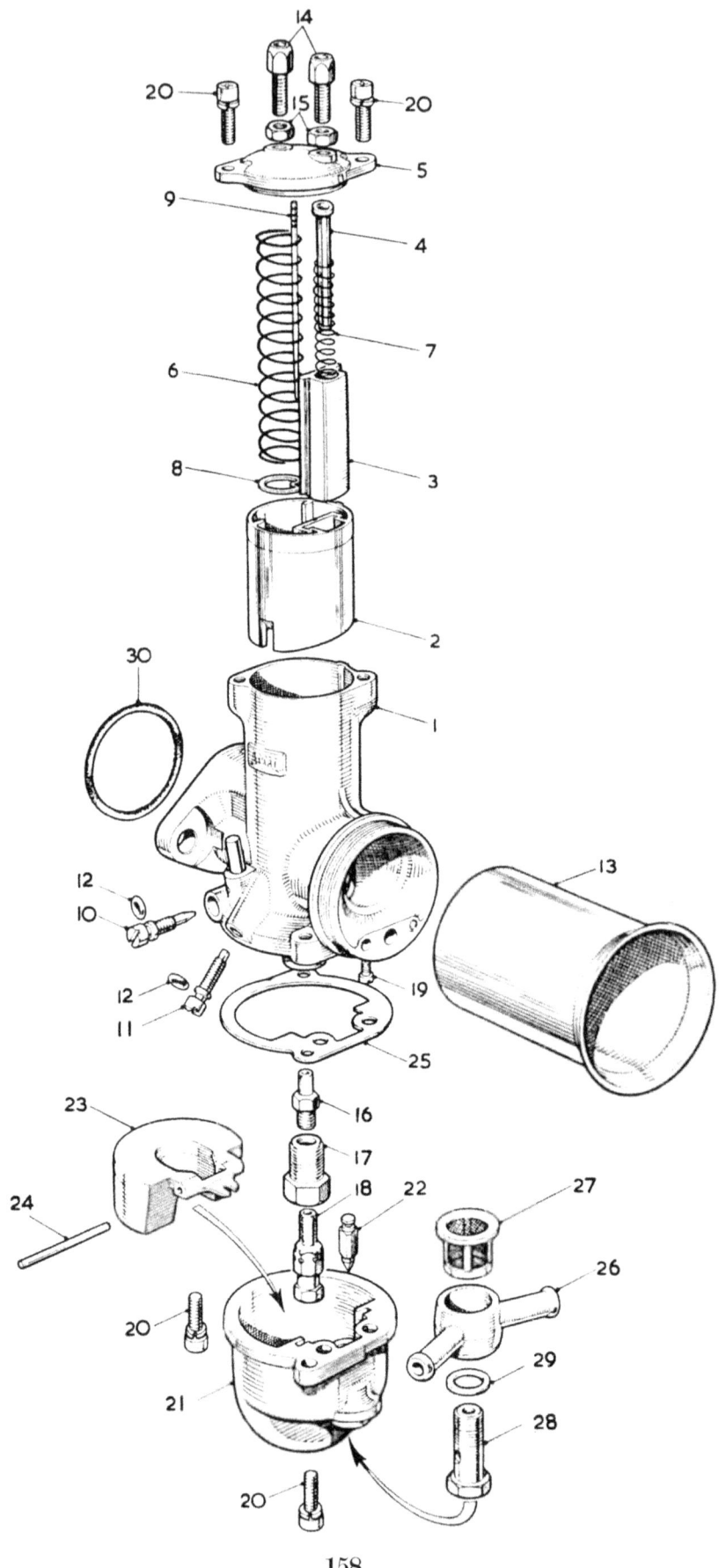

AMAL 'CONCENTRIC' CARBURETTOR

Illustration No.	Part No.	Description	No. per Set
	R930/3	Carburettor, complete with float chamber right hand) less controls and cables	1
	L930/4	Carburettor, complete with float chamber left hand)	1
1	R930/001	Carburettor body complete right hand	1
	L930/001	Carburettor body complete left hand	1
2	928/060	Carburettor throttle valve	1
3	928/062	Carburettor air valve	1
4	928/103	Carburettor air slide guide	1
5	928/097	Carburettor mixing chamber top	1
6	622/131	Carburettor throttle valve spring	1
7	622/129	Carburettor air valve spring	1
8	622/067	Carburettor needle clip	1
9	622/124	Carburettor throttle needle	1
10	622/076	Carburettor pilot air adjuster screw	1
11	622/077	Carburettor throttle stop	1
12	622/082	Carburettor 'O' ring	2
13	928/069	Carburettor air funnel	1
14	4/035	Carburettor cable adjuster	2
15	5/077	Carburettor cable adjuster locknut	2
16	622/122	Carburettor needle jet	1
17	622/128	Carburettor jet holder	1
18	376/100	Carburettor main jet	1
19	124/026	Carburettor pilot jet	1
20	622/086	Carburettor screws for float chamber and mixing chamber top	4
21	622/050	Carburettor float chamber body	1
22	622/068	Carburettor float chamber needle	1
23	622/069	Carburettor float chamber float	1
24	622/071	Carburettor float chamber float spindle	1
25	622/073	Carburettor float chamber washer	1
26	376/139	Carburettor banjo	1
27	376/093	Carburettor filter	1
28	622/078	Carburettor banjo bolt	1
29	13/163	Carburettor banjo bolt washer	1
30	622/101	Carburettor 'O' ring for flange	1

Always quote Engine or Frame Number

Page 45

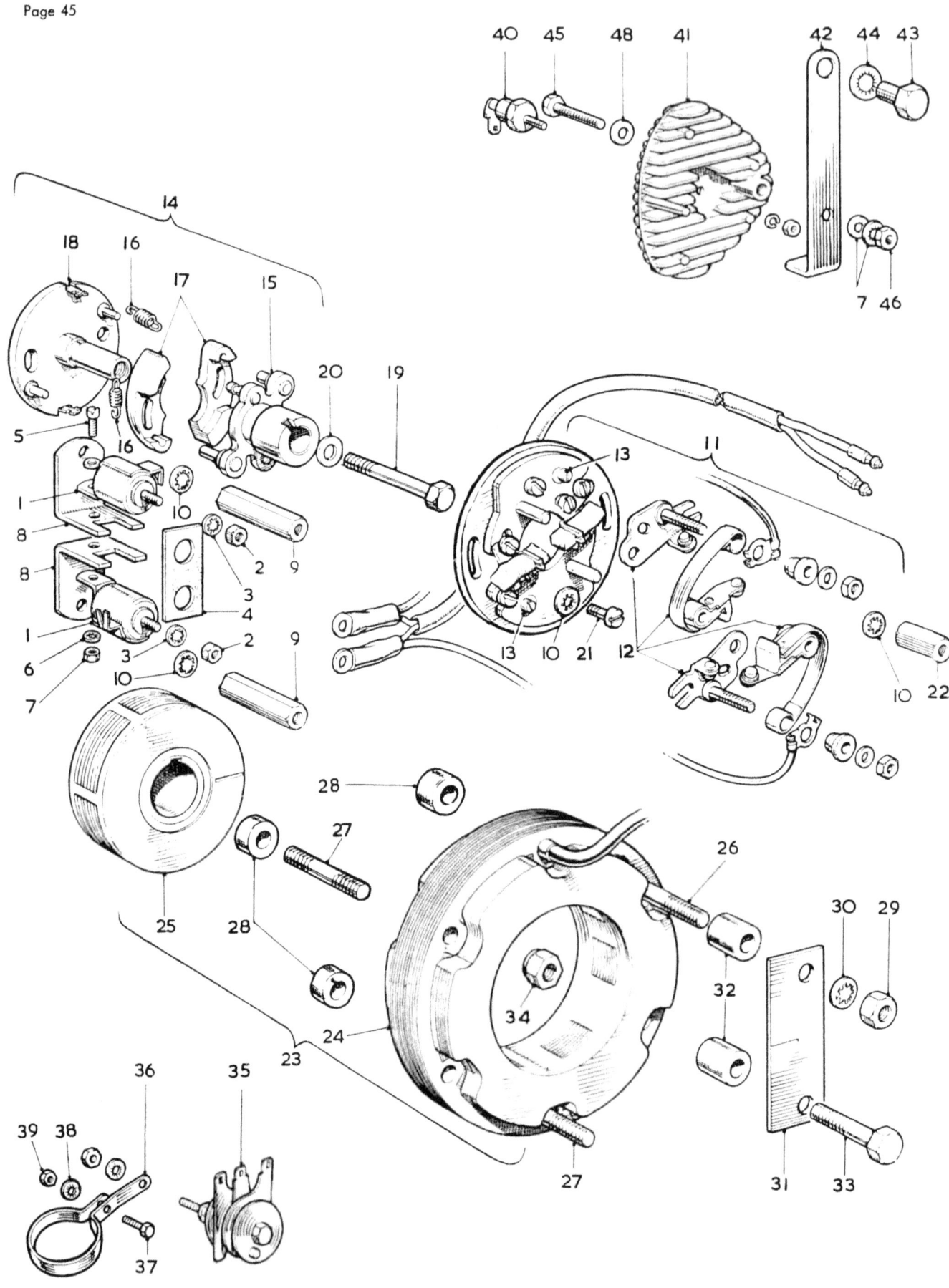

CONTACT BREAKER, ALTERNATOR, RECTIFIER, HEAT SINK AND ZENER-DIODE

Illustration No.	Part No.	Description	No. per Set
	54041144B	Contact breaker assembly, Lucas type 6CA	1
1	LU/425377	Condenser	2
2	LU/166074	Condenser nut	2
3	LU/185006	Condenser washer	2
4	49634	Condenser fibre strip	1
5	49652	Condenser clip screw	1
6	29950	Condenser clip lockwasher	1
7	49653	Condenser clip nut	1
8	49633	Condenser clip	2
9	49714	Condenser clip nut	2
10	31579	Condenser clip lockwasher	4
11	LU/54419097	Contact breaker unit	1
12	LU/54419827	Contact set	2
13	LU/54419220	Contact breaker adjustment pin	2
14	LU/54420472	Automatic advance unit	1
15	LU/54419338	Contact breaker cam	1
16	LU/54413020	Automatic advance springs (set of 2)	1
17	LU/425359	Automatic advance weights	2
18	LU/54420000	Automatic advance shaft plate and pins assembly	1
19	48021	Contact breaker centre screw	1
20	82	Contact breaker centre screw washer	1
21	49651	Contact breaker plate screw	1
22	49713	Contact breaker plate nut	1
23	LU/54021167	Alternator, Lucas type RM21	1
24	LU/47205	Alternator stator	1
25	LU/54213901	Alternator rotor	1
26	49700	Alternator stator attachment stud (long)	1
27	46199	Alternator stator attachment stud	2
28	45388	Alternator stator distance collar	3
29	27944	Alternator stator attachment stud nut	3
30	27917	Alternator stator attachment stud lockwasher	3
31	49699	Ignition timing plate	1
32	49718	Ignition timing plate distance piece	2
33	37119	Ignition timing plate bolt	1
34	36222	Ignition timing plate nut	1
35	LU/54048008/B	Rectifier, Lucas type 2DS5, complete	1
36	49554	Rectifier clip	1
37	42835	Rectifier clip pin	1
38	27917	Rectifier clip washer	1
39	27944	Rectifier clip nut	1
40	LU/54048288	Zener diode, Lucas type ZD715	1
41	49605	Zener diode, heat sink	1
42	41604	Heat sink bracket	1
43	41567	Heat sink bracket attachment pin	1
44	27920	Heat sink bracket attachment lockwasher	1
45	33566	Heat sink attachment pin	1
46	19870	Heat sink attachment nut	1
47	27917	Heat sink attachment lockwasher	2
48	76	Heat sink attachment washer	1

Always quote Engine or Frame Number

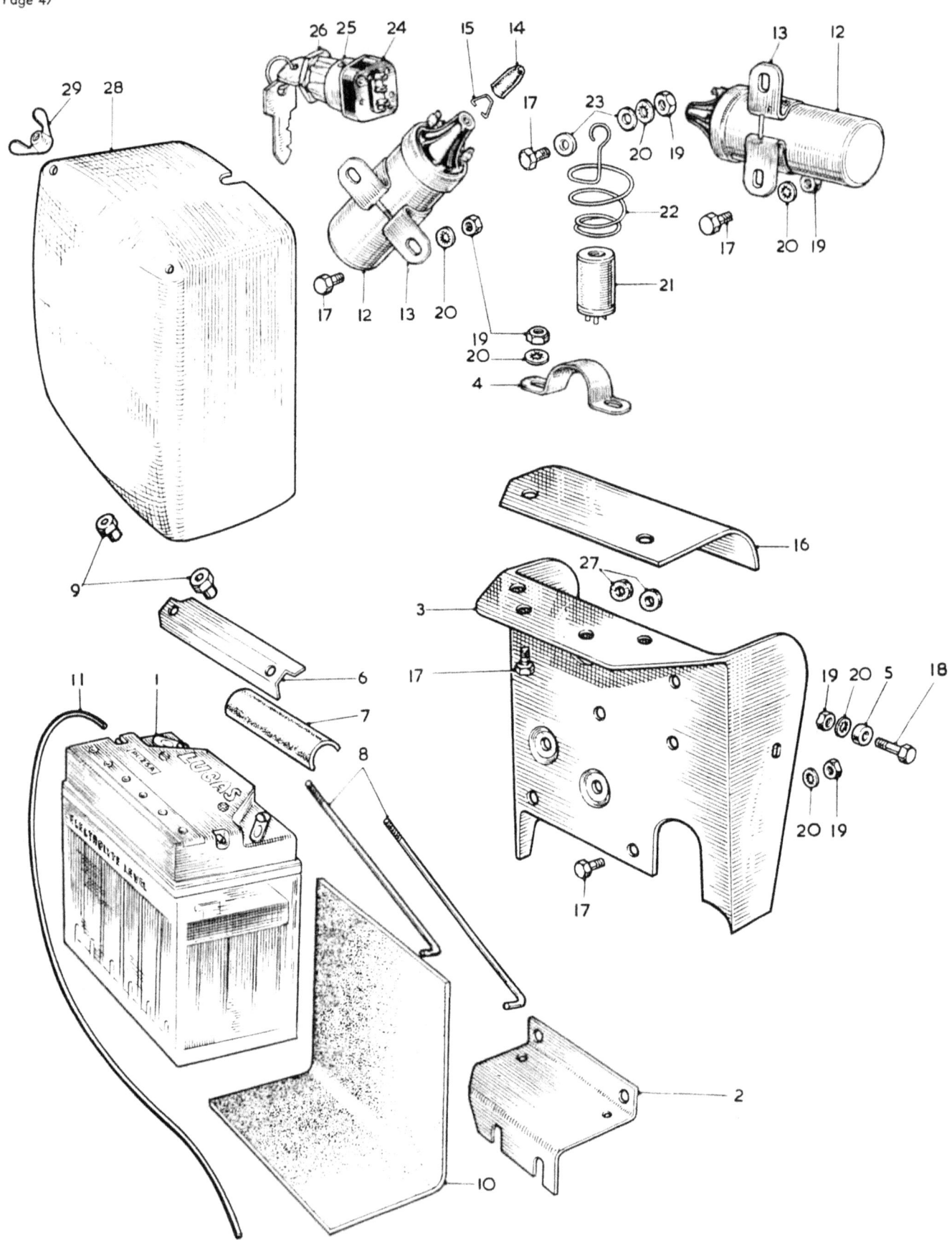

BATTERY AND MOUNTING, COIL AND COVER, ELECTROLYTIC Capacitor AND IGNITION SWITCH

Page 48

Illustration No.	Part No.	Description	No. per Set
1	54027029	Battery 12 volt PUZ5A	1
2	49504	Battery platform	1
3	49508/A	Battery back plate	1
4	41479	Battery back plate clip	1
5	46731	Battery back plate spacer	2
6	49505	Battery retaining strap	1
7	49567	Battery retaining rubber strip	1
8	49701	Battery securing rod	2
9	49507	Battery securing rod nut	2
10	49510	Battery pad	1
11	49606	Battery vent tube	1
	LU/54041149	Coil and saddle bracket assembly, Lucas type 17M12	2
12	LU/45221	Coil type 17M12	2
13	LU/54420641	Coil saddle bracket assembly	2
14	LU/421554	Rubber grommet	2
15	LU/421863	Clip, contact cable	
16	49509	Coil cover	1
17	251	Attachment bolt	9
18	7201	Attachment bolt	4
19	26998	Attachment nut	13
20	27916	Attachment washer	13
21	LU/54170009	Electrolytic capacitor	1
22	LU/54483156	Electrolytic spring	1
23	82	Electrolytic capacitor attachment plain washer	2
24	LU/31899/B	Ignition switch S45	1
25	S45	Ignition switch barrel lock with keys	1
26	LU/54130041	Ignition switch nut	1
27	LU/199001	Rubber grommet	4
28	49697	Battery cover	1
29	49702	Battery cover wing nut	2
	LU/54937974	High tension lead	2

Always quote Engine or Frame Number

Page 49

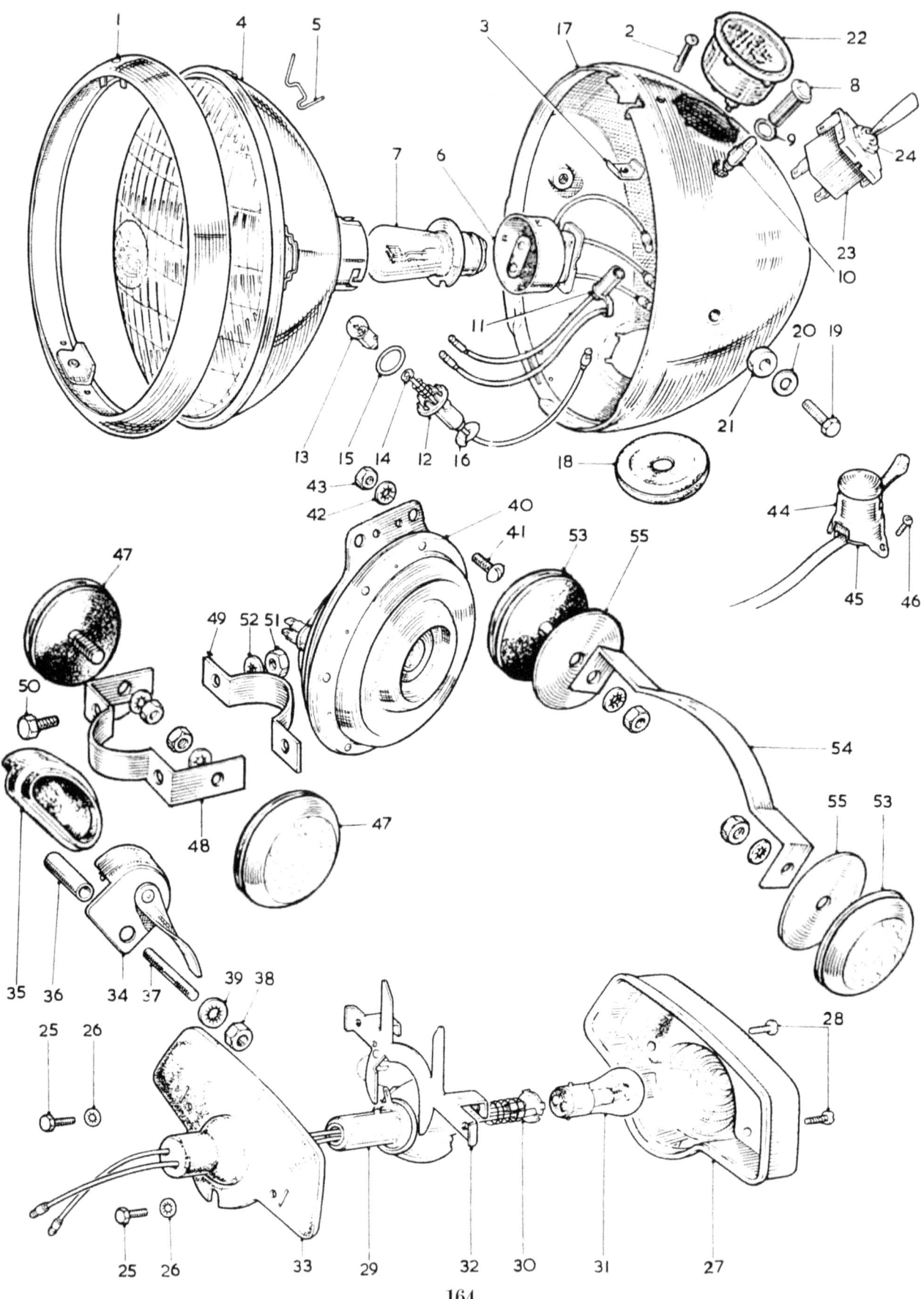

164

LAMPS, STOPLIGHT AND SWITCHES, AMMETER, HORN AND HORN PUSH AND DIPPER SWITCH

Illustration No.	Part No.	Description	No. per Set
	LU/54052875	Headlamp and harness assembly, complete with horn push and dip switch	1
	LU/59872/A	Headlamp, Lucas type SS700P, complete with light unit and rim, 12 volt	1
1	LU/553248	Front rim	1
2	LU/144921	Screw, front rim attachment	1
3	LU/534296	Plate, front rim attachment	1
4	LU/516798	Light unit	1
5	LU/504665	Spring wire, light unit attachment	1
6	LU/554602	Main bulb holder	1
	LU/555910	Terminal sleeve	1
7	LU/446	Main bulb, 12 volt, 50/40 watt	1
8	LU/54360102	Warning light, main beam, body assembly	1
9	LU/54140331	Warning light sealing washer	1
10	LU/281	Warning light bulb, 12 volt, 2 watt	1
11	LU/54945043	Warning light bulb holder	1
12	LU/54573590	Pilot bulb holder	1
13	LU/989	Pilot bulb, 12 volt, 6 watt	1
14	LU/553780	Interior parts, pilot bulb holder	1
15	LU/554354	Seating ring, pilot bulb holder	1
16	LU/516285	Grip washer, for pilot cable	1
17	LU/54523999	Headlamp body	1
18	LU/199002	Grommet, headlamp body	1
19	LU/112201	Screw, headlamp attachment	2
20	LU/137498	Washer, headlamp attachment screw	2
21	LU/54522706	Spacer washer, headlamp	2
22	LU/36403	Ammeter Lucas type 2AR	1
23	LU/31788/D	Lighting switch 57SA	1
24	LU/153630	Lighting switch attachment unit	1
	LU/53973/D	Stop tail lamp, Lucas type 679	1
25	LU/110714	Screw, stop tail lamp attachment	1
26	LU/188330	Washer, stop tail lamp attachment screw	2
27	LU/54577109	Lens	1
28	LU/144921	Screw, lens attachment	2
29	LU/54578213	Bulb holder with reflector	1
30	LU/573828	Interior parts, bulb holder	1
31	LU/380	Stop tail bulb, 12 volt, 21/6 watt	1
32	LU/54578212	Baseplate	1
33	LU/54571677	Gasket, lamp seating	1
34	LU/31688/B	Stop lamp switch, Lucas type 6SA	1
35	LU/360363	Stop lamp switch rubber terminal cover	1
	LU/188818	Stop lamp switch terminal sleeve	2
36	42701	Distance tube, stop lamp switch	1
37	45702	Stud, stop lamp switch attachment	1
38	27944	Nut, stop lamp switch attachment stud	1
39	27917	Lockwasher, stop lamp switch attachment stud	1
	LU/35605	Cable band type S, stop lamp switch	3
	LU/54953386	Lead, stop tail lamp	1
40	LU/70197/D	Horn, Lucas type 6H	1
41	251	Pin, horn attachment	2
42	27916	Lockwasher, horn attachment pins	2
43	26998	Nut, horn attachment pin	2
44	LU/31563/D	Horn, push and dipper switch 25SA	1
45	LU/380459	Horn push and dipper switch pad	1
46	DE572	Horn push attachment screw	2
47	LU/57162/A	Front side reflector (Amber)	2
48	49706	Front side reflector bracket	1
49	41869	Front side reflector clip	1
50	42835	Front side reflector bolt	2
51	47944	Front side reflector nut	2
52	27917	Front side reflector washer	2
53	LU/57110/A	Rear side reflector (Red)	2
54	49728	Rear side reflector bracket	1
55	49729	Rear side reflector washer	2

Always quote Engine or Frame Number

NOTES

SUPPLEMENT TO THE 1969

SPARE AND REPLACEMENT PARTS LIST

COVERING THE

1970 ROYAL ENFIELD 750 INTERCEPTOR SERIES II MOTOR CYCLE

THIS SUPPLEMENT LISTS ONLY THOSE ITEMS THAT ARE DIFFERENT OR ADDITIONAL TO THOSE USED ON THE 1969 MODEL

ENFIELD PRECISION ENGINEERS LTD.

UPPER WESTWOOD . BRADFORD-ON-AVON . WILTS.
TELEPHONE: BRADFORD-ON-AVON 2166
ENGLAND.

FEBRUARY 1970

Illus. No.	Part No.	Description.	No. per set.
		Page 2:	
15	49979	Stud, crankcase, rear engine plate (5/16BSF x 5¼). Replaces 44360.	1
18	36079	Stud, crankcase, front (5/16CEI x 4½). 1 off in place of 3 off.	1
		Page 4:	
44	49740	Push rod tunnel oil seal. Replaces 46150/A.	4
	50114	Gasket set, complete engine and chaincase. Replaces 240	1
		Page 8:	
2	49724	Oil seal, timing cover (oil pump worm) 1 off in place of 2 off.	1
New item.	50137	Oil seal, timing cover (contact breaker unit)	1
New item.	50026	Contact breaker cover gasket	1
		Page 10:	
13	49871	Spring, oil cleaner. Replaces 28259	1
14	50035	Thrust washer, oil cleaner " 8894	1
15	49881	Felt " , " " " 18793	1
16	49880	Spring cup, " " " 28254	1
18	49870	Distance piece, " " " 49645	1
19	50039	Oil Cleaner cap (complete) " 49601	1
21	49874	Nut, oil cleaner cap securing " 43773	1
22	50036	Fibre washer, securing nut " 9732	1
23	49866	Stud, oil cleaner " 37128	1
New item.	5029	Washer, oil cleaner stud	1
27	49995	Oil release valve plunger " 32019	1
		Page 12:	
New item.	50122	Chain tensioner re-lining set.	1
		Page 14:	
1	50115	Gearbox case, complete with seal. Replaces 33885/1.	1
16	37357	Footstarter pawl stop plate bolt. In place of 2 off.	1
		Page 22:	
38	49924	Dual seat. Replaces 49529/A	1

Illus. No.	Part No.	Description.		No. per set.
		Page 24:		
		Frame No. F.1001 to F.1949 as 1969 list.		
		Frame No. F.1950 onwards as below:		
	49707/A	Telescopic front fork assembly complete. Replaces 49707		1
1	50043	Fork Crown assembly	Replaces 49680	1
2	50063	Pinch stud, fork crown	" 49773	2
3	50064	Nut, fork crown pinch stud	" 49774	2
7	50061	Head nut	" 49770	1
8	50062	Head nut top	" 49772	1
10	50059	Handlebar lug	" 49765	1
12	50060	Cap screw, handlebar clip	" 49767	4
20	50055	Washer, bottom cover tube	" 49782	2
21	50056	Screw, " " "	" 49783	6
New item.	50057	Washer, bottom cover tube screw		6
22	50065	Slider extension assembly	" 49784	2
23	50066	Slider, L.H.	" 49785	1
24	50067	" R.H.	" 49786	1
25	50069	Pinch stud, slider	" 49789	1
26	50070	Nut, slider pinch stud	" 49790	1
27	50068	Drain plug, slider	" 49787	2
29	50071	Damper tube assembly	" 49791	2
30	50072	Anchor bolt, damper tube	" 49792	2
33	50073	Cap, damper tube	" 49795	2
34	50074	Damper rod	" 49796	2
35	50075	Locknut, damper rod	" 49797	2
36	50058	Damper valve	" 49798	2
39	50070	Nut, damper valve seat	" 50070	2
50	50053	Stud, mudguard bridge	" 49843	4
New item.	50054	Spring top post		2
		Page 26:		
		Frame No. R.1001 to F.1949 as 1969 list.		
		Frame No. F.1950 onwards as below:		
41	50102	Front brake cable assembly complete. Replaces 49906		1
44	50103	Brake cable adjusting screw	Replaces 38032	1
45	50104	Brake cable adjusting screw locknut	" 49931	1
		Page 30:		
38	49599	Washer, brake cam. Replaces 4964		1

Illus. No.	Part No.	Description.	No. per set.
		Page 32:	
8	43617	Tank attachment clip. Replaces 44702	1
9	26998	Not required.	
10	27916	" "	
19	82	Slider stud washer. Replaces 49844	4
20	49845	Slider stud nut (from Frame no. F.1001 to F.1949)	4
20	50051	Slider stud nut (from frame No. F.1950 onwards)	4
23	49848	Slider bolt, stay attachment (from frame No. F.1001 to F.1949)	4
23	50052	Slider bolt, stay attachment (from frame No. F.1950 onwards)	4
24	8634	Slider bolt, washer. Replaces 49849.	4
28	31579	Mudguard bolt washer. Replaces 49853	8
		Page 42:	
		Frame No. F.1001 to F.1820 as 1969 list. Frame No. F.1821 onwards as below:	
1	SSM/3001/05	Speedometer head 150 m.p.h. Replaces SSM/3001/00.	1
3	50016	Gearbox complete. Replaces 49727	1
		Optional fittings:	
1	SSM/3001/01A	Speedometer head 200 K.P.H. (frame No. F.1001 to F.1820)	1
1	SSM/3001/06	Speedometer head 240 K.P.H. (frame No. F.1821 onwards)	1
		Page 44:	
	R930/3	Carburettor, complete R.H.) Frame No. F.1001	1
	L930/4	" " L.H.) to F.1910.	1
	R930/32	" " R.H.) Frame No. F.1911	1
	L930/43	" " L.H.) onwards.	1
13	928/069	Not required.	
		Page 46:	
15	LU/54419338)		
17	LU/425359)	No longer supplied.	
18	LU/54420000)		
35	LU/49072	Rectifier, Lucas type 2DS5, complete. Replaces LU/54048008/B.	1
40	LU/49345	Zener diode, Lucas type ZD715. Replaces LU/54048288.	1

Illus. No.	Part No.	Description.		No. per set.
		Page 48:		
12	LU/45223	Coil type 17M12	Replaces LU/45221	2
17	251	Attachment bolt	In place of 9 off	11
18	7201	" "	In place of 4 off	2
		Page 50:		
	LU/59969/A	Headlamp, Lucas type SS700P. Replaces LU/59872/A.		1
New item.	LU/54956914	Lighting harness, including front brake stop switch wires		1
8	LU/38189	Warning light, main beam, body assembly. Replaces LU/54360102.		1
		NEW ITEMS:		
	49970	Skid plate		1
	45436	Oil cooler body		1
	45438	End cap R.H., oil cooler body		1
	45439	End cap L.H., oil cooler body		1
	45440	End cap gasket, oil cooler body		2
	45385	End cap screw, oil cooler body		12
	16476	Oil bleed screw - cleaner cap		1
	30394	Washer, oil bleed screw		1
	50037/A	Feed pipe, oil cleaner		1
	49928	Banjo bolt, oil cooler feed pipe		2
	27642	Fibre washer, banjo bolt. 11/16 O/dia x 1/16 thick.		4
	50038/A	Return pipe, oil cleaner		1
	27642	Fibre washer, oil cooler return pipe. 11/16 O/dia x 1/16 thick.		1
	49932	Adaptor, oil cooler return pipe		1
	47341	Fibre washer, adaptor, 5/8 O/dia x 1/16 thick		1
	50105	Upper fixing plate, oil cooler		2
	50106	Lower " " " "		2
	12405	Packing washer, lower fixing plates. 3/4 O/dia x 1/8 thick.		2
	34370	Stud, upper, oil cooler. 1/4 BSP x 4 7/16		1
	50108	Stud, lower, " " 1/4 BSP x 4 11/16		1
	27620	Nut, oil cooler stud. 1/4 B.S.P.		4
	27916	Washer, oil cooler stud. 1/4 dia. shakeproof		4
	50034	Stud, middle, front engine plate. 5/16 CEI x 4 5/8		1
	50107	Stud, lower, front engine plate. 5/16 CEI x 4 7/8		1
	49885	Rear handrail		1
	49905	Clip, rear handrail		2
	49757	Bolt, " "		2
	27621	Nut, " "		2
	27917	Washer, " "		2

Illus. No.	Part No.	Description.		No. per set.
		NEW ITEMS: cont.		
	49946	Air Filter, complete with element		1
	49947	Air Filter, cover, front		1
	49948	Air filter, cover, rear		1
	49949	Air filter cartridge		1
	49940	Washer, air filter cover		2
	49914	Retaining ring-air filter		2
	49951	Bolt, air filter		1
	7673	Nut, " "		2
	82	Washer," "		2
	49950	Wingnut, air filter		1
	50010	Shield, " "		1
		OPTIONAL EQUIPMENT:		
		Front wheel and two leading shoe brake.		
		As 1969 list, page 28, with the following exceptions:		
	50078	Front wheel assembly complete. Replaces	49710	1
	50080	Front hub assembly "	49859	1
8	50081	Front hub only "	49817	1
9	50082	Wheel spindle "	49818	1
13	50083	Bearing retainer "	49822	1
20	50084	Nut, wheel spindle "	49829	1
21	50085	Brake cover plate, complete "	49830	1
22	50086	Brake shoe c/w lining and rivets "	49958	2
23	50158	Brake lining "	49956	2
24	50159	Brake lining rivet "	49957	16
25	50087	Brake show spring "	49832	2
New item	50088	Brake shoe slipper		2
26	50089	Brake cam "	49833 (1 off)	2
27	50090	Brake cam lever, long "	49834	1
New item.	50091	Brake cam lever, short		1
28	50092	Washer, brake cam lever "	49835 (1 off)	2
29	50093	Nut, brake cam lever attachment "	49836 (1 off)	2
30	50094	Washer, pivot pin "	49837 (1 off)	2
31	50095	Circlip, pivot pin "	49838 (1 off)	2
32	49839	Not required		
33	50096	Yoke pin, front brake cable "	49840 (1 off)	3
34	50097	Circlip, yoke pin retaining "	49841 (1 off)	3

Illus. No.	Part No.	Description.	No. per set.
		OPTIONAL EQUIPMENT: cont.	
New item.	50098	Tie rod complete	1
"	50099	Locknut, tie rod	1
"	50100	Yoke, L.H. thread	1
"	50101	Yoke, R.H. "	1
	50151	Petrol tank, complete, 4 gallon glass fibre	1
	50150	Front buffer sleeve, petrol tank	1
	50149	Front buffer sleeve centre	1
	50156	Front attachment screw	2
	50145	Bracket, petrol tank mounting	1
	50148	Strap, petrol tank	1
	50156	Screw, petrol tank strap	2
	43617	Clip, petrol tank	1
	41562	Clip rubber sleeve (1 extra to standard required)	2
	50155	Bolt, petrol tank attachment	2
	27918	Washer, " " "	2
	50015	Rubber washer, petrol tank attachment	2
	44650	Handlebar bend -- English pattern	1
	50000	Front brake cable complete - to suit English pattern bend	1
	50002	Front number plate	1
	5171	Screw, front number plate	3
	14904	Clip, " " "	3
	29508	Washer, " " "	3
	26999	Nut, " " "	3
	25226	Washer, " " "	3
	50160	Gearbox complete with splined clutch	1
	A11370	Clutch assembly, splined type	1
	A11329	Clutch sprocket and drum splined type	1
	A10847	Clutch plate, cork bonded, " "	4
	A11330	Clutch centre drum and back plate assembly, splined type	1
	A10579	Clutch intermediate plate (flat) splined type (dished plates not required)	4

VELOCEPRESS MANUALS – MOTORCYCLE BY MAKE

AJS 1932-1948 SINGLES & TWINS 250cc THRU 1000cc (BOOK OF)
AJS 1945-1960 SINGLES 350cc & 500cc MODELS 16 & 18 (BOOK OF)
AJS 1955-1965 SINGLES 350cc & 500cc (BOOK OF)
AJS 1957-1966 FACTORY WSM - ALL SINGLES & TWINS
ARIEL UP TO 1932 (BOOK OF)
ARIEL 1932-1939 PREWAR MODELS (BOOK OF)
ARIEL 1933-1951 (WORKSHOP MANUAL)
ARIEL 1939-1960 4 STROKE SINGLES (BOOK OF)
ARIEL 1958-1964 LEADER & ARROW (BOOK OF)
BMW R26 R27 (1956-1967) FACTORY WORKSHOP MANUAL
BMW R50 R50S R60 R69S (1955-1969) FACTORY WORKSHOP MANUAL
BRIDGESTONE 90 SERIES FACTORY WSM & PARTS CATALOGUE
BRIDGESTONE 175 SERIES FACTORY WSM & PARTS CATALOGUE
BRIDGESTONE 350 SERIES FACTORY WSM & PARTS CATALOGUES
BSA SERVICE SHEETS MASTER CATALOGUE ALL MODELS 1945-1967
BSA BANTAM D1 TO D7 1948-1966 FACTORY SERVICE SHEETS MANUAL
BSA BANTAM ALL MODELS FROM 1948 ONWARDS (BOOK OF)
BSA DANDY FACTORY WORKSHOP MANUAL (COMPILATION)
BSA SINGLES & V-TWINS UP TO 1927 (BOOK OF)
BSA SINGLES & V-TWINS UP TO 1930 (BOOK OF)
BSA SINGLES & V-TWINS UP TO 1935 (BOOK OF)
BSA SINGLES & V-TWINS 1936-1939 (BOOK OF)
BSA C10, C11 & C12 1945-1958 FACTORY SERVICE SHEETS MANUAL
BSA OHV & SV SINGLES 250-600cc 1945-1959 (BOOK OF)
BSA C15 & B40 1958-1967 FACTORY SERVICE SHEETS MANUAL
BSA OHV & SV SINGLES 250cc (ONLY) 1954-1970 (BOOK OF)
BSA B31, B32, B33 & B34 1945-60 FACTORY SERVICE SHEETS MANUAL
BSA OHV SINGLES 350 & 500cc 1955-1967 (BOOK OF)
BSA M20, M21 & M33 1945-1963 FACTORY SERVICE SHEETS MANUAL
BSA TWINS A7 & A10 1948-1962 FACTORY SERVICE SHEETS MANUAL
BSA TWINS A7 & A10 1948-1962 (BOOK OF)
BSA TWINS A50 & A65 1962-1965 FACTORY WORKSHOP MANUAL
BSA TWINS A50 & A65 1962-1969 (SECOND BOOK OF)
DOUGLAS 1929-1939 PREWAR ALL MODELS (BOOK OF)
DOUGLAS 1948-1957 POSTWAR ALL MODELS FACTORY SHOP MANUAL
DUCATI 160cc, 250cc & 350cc OHC MODELS FACTORY SHOP MANUAL
HONDA 50cc ALL MODELS UP TO 1970 INC MONKEY & TRAIL (BOOK OF)
HONDA 90cc ALL MODELS UP TO 1966 (BOOK OF)
HONDA 50-65-70-90cc OHC SINGLES 1959-1983 FACTORY WSM
HONDA 100-125cc SINGLES CB/CD/CL/SL/TL 1970-1984 FACTORY WSM
HONDA 125-150cc TWINS C/CS/CB/CA FACTORY WORKSHOP MANUAL
HONDA 125-160-175-200cc TWINS 1965-1978 WORKSHOP MANUAL
HONDA 250-305cc TWINS C/CS/CB 1959-1967 FACTORY WSM
HOHDA 250-350cc TWINS CB/CL/SL 1968-1973 FACTORY WSM
HONDA 450CC CB/CL 1965-1974 K0 TO K7 WORKSHOP MANUAL
HONDA 750cc SHOC 4 CYL 1969-1978 K0~K8 WORKSHOP MANUAL
HONDA C100 SUPER CUB FACTORY WORKSHOP MANUAL
HONDA C110 SPORT CUB 1962-1969 FACTORY WORKSHOP MANUAL
HONDA TWINS & SINGLES 50cc THRU 305cc 1960-1966 (BOOK OF)
HONDA TWINS ALL MODELS 125cc THRU 450cc UP TO 1968 (BOOK OF)
INDIAN PONYBIKE, BOY RACER & PAPOOSE ILL PARTS LIST & SALES LIT
J.A.P. ENGINES 1927-1952 & MOTORCYCLES 1934-1952 (BOOK OF)
MATCHLESS 1931-1939 ALL MODELS 250cc THRU 990cc (BOOK OF)
MATCHLESS 1945-1956 350 & 500cc SINGLES (BOOK OF)
MATCHLESS 1955-1966 350 & 500cc SINGLES (BOOK OF)
MATCHLESS 1957-1966 FACTORY WSM - ALL SINGLES & TWINS
NEW IMPERIAL ALL SV & OHV FROM 1935 ONWARDS (BOOK OF)
NORTON 1932-1939 PREWAR MODELS (BOOK OF)
NORTON 1932-1947 (BOOK OF)
NORTON 1938-1956 (BOOK OF)
NORTON 1955-1963 MODELS 19, 50 & ES2 (BOOK OF)
NORTON 1955-1965 DOMINATOR TWINS (BOOK OF)
NORTON 1960-1970 TWIN CYLINDER FACTORY WORKSHOP MANUAL
NORTON 1970-1975 COMMANDO 850 & 750cc FACTORY WSM
NORTON 1975-1978 MK 3 COMMANDO 850 cc FACTORY WSM
PANTHER 1932-1958 LIGHTWEIGHT MODELS 250 & 350cc (BOOK OF)
PANTHER 1938-1966 HEAVYWEIGHT MODELS 600 & 650cc (BOOK OF)
RALEIGH MOTORCYCLES 1919-1933 (BOOK OF)
ROYAL ENFIELD 1934-1946 SINGLES & V TWINS (BOOK OF)
ROYAL ENFIELD 1937-1953 SINGLES & V TWINS (BOOK OF)
ROYAL ENFIELD 1946-1962 SINGLES (BOOK OF)
ROYAL ENFIELD 1958-1966 250cc & 350cc SINGLES (SECOND BOOK OF)
ROYAL ENFIELD 1962-1970 INTERCEPTOR WSM'S & PARTS (Compilation)
RUDGE 1933-1939 (BOOK OF)
SUNBEAM 1928-1939 (BOOK OF)
SUNBEAM 1946-1957 S7 & S8 (BOOK OF)
SUZUKI 50cc & 80cc UP TO 1966 (BOOK OF)
SUZUKI T10 1963-1967 FACTORY WORKSHOP MANUAL
SUZUKI T20 & T200 1965-1969 FACTORY WORKSHOP MANUAL
SUZUKI TWINS 1962 ONWARDS 125-500cc WORKSHOP MANUAL
TRIUMPH 1935-1949 SINGLES & TWINS (BOOK OF)
TRIUMPH 1937-1951 (WORKSHOP MANUAL)
TRIUMPH 1945-1955 FACTORY WORKSHOP MANUAL
TRIUMPH 1945-1959 TWINS (BOOK OF)
TRIUMPH 1956-1969 TWINS (BOOK OF)
TRIUMPH 1963-1970 UNIT CONSTRUCTION 650cc FACTORY WSM
TRIUMPH 1963-1974 UNIT CONSTRUCTION 350-500cc FACTORY WSM
TRIUMPH 1968-1974 TRIDENT T150 & T150V FACTORY WSM
VELOCETTE 1925-1970 ALL SINGLES & TWINS (BOOK OF)
VILLIERS ENGINE UP TO 1959 INC. 3 WHEELERS (BOOK OF)
VILLIERS ENGINE UP TO 1969 (BOOK OF)
VINCENT 1935-1955 (WORKSHOP MANUAL)
YAMAHA 1961-1967 YA5 & YA6 (WORKSHOP MANUAL & ILL PARTS LIST)
YAMAHA 1971-1972 JT1& JT2 (WORKSHOP MANUAL & ILL PARTS LIST)

www.VelocePress.com

VELOCEPRESS TECHNICAL BOOKS – MOTORCYCLE

1930'S BRITISH MOTORCYCLE CARBS & ELEC COMPONENTS (BOOK OF)
1930'S BRITISH MOTORCYCLE ENGINES (OVERHAUL & MAINTENANCE)
1930'S BRITISH MOTORCYCLE GEARBOXES & CLUTCHES (BOOK OF)
CATALOG OF BRITISH MOTORCYCLES (1951 MODELS)
LUCAS ELECTRONICS BRITISH M/CYCLES REPAIR & PARTS (1950-1977)
MOTORCYCLE ENGINEERING (P.E. Irving)
MOTORCYCLE ROAD TESTS 1949-1953 (Motor Cycle Magazine UK)
SPEED AND HOW TO OBTAIN IT (Motor Cycle Magazine UK)
TUNING FOR SPEED (P.E. Irving)
WIPAC (COMBO) MANUAL NUMBER 3 + M/CYCLE & SCOOTER MANUAL

VELOCEPRESS MANUALS – SCOOTERS BY MAKE

BSA SUNBEAM SCOOTER WORKSHOP MANUAL 1959-1965
BSA SUNBEAM SCOOTER 1959-1965 (BOOK OF)
LAMBRETTA 1947-1957 ALL 125 & 150cc MODELS (BOOK OF)
LAMBRETTA 1957-1970 LI & TV MODELS (SECOND BOOK OF)
NSU PRIMA 1956-1964 ALL MODELS (BOOK OF)
TRIUMPH TIGRESS SCOOTER WORKSHOP MANUAL 1959-1965
TRIUMPH TIGRESS SCOOTER (BOOK OF)
VESPA 1951-1961 (BOOK OF)
VESPA 1955-1963 125 & 150cc & GS MODELS (SECOND BOOK OF)
VESPA 1955-1968 GS & SS (BOOK OF)
VESPA 1963-1972 90, 125 & 150cc (THIRD BOOK OF)

VELOCEPRESS MANUALS – MOPEDS & MOTORIZED BICYCLES

CYCLEMOTOR (BOOK OF)
NSU QUICKLY 1953-1963 ALL MODELS (BOOK OF)
PUCH MAXI N & S MAINTENANCE & REPAIR (3 MANUAL COMPILATION)
RALEIGH MOPEDS 1960-1969 (BOOK OF)

VELOCEPRESS MANUALS - THREE WHEELER'S

BOND MINICAR THREE WHEELER 1948-1967 (BOOK OF)
BMW ISETTA FACTORY WORKSHOP MANUAL
BSA THREE WHEELER (BOOK OF)
RELIANT REGAL THREE WHEELER 1952-1973 (BOOK OF)
VINTAGE MORGAN THREE WHEELER (BOOK OF)

VELOCEPRESS MANUALS – AUTOMOBILE BY MAKE

ALFA ROMEO GIULIA WORKSHOP MANUAL 1300 TO 2000cc 1962-1975
ALFA ROMEO GIULIA TECH MANUAL CARBURETED CARS FROM 1962
ALFA ROMEO GIULIA TECH MANUAL FUEL INJECTED CARS FROM 1969
ALFA ROMEO GIULIETTA & GIULIA 750 & 101 SERIES 1955-1965 WSM
AUSTIN-HEALEY SPRITE & MG MIDGET WORKSHOP MANUAL 1958-1971
BMW 600 LIMOUSINE FACTORY WORKSHOP MANUAL
BMW 600 LIMOUSINE OWNERS HAND BOOK & SERVICE MANUAL
BMW 2000 & 2002 1966-1976 WORKSHOP MANUAL
CORVAIR 1960-1969 WORKSHOP MANUAL
CORVETTE V8 1955-1962 WORKSHOP MANUAL
FERRARI 250/GT SERVICE & MAINTENANCE MANUAL
FIAT 500 FACTORY WORKSHOP MANUAL 1957-1973
FIAT 600, 600D & MULTIPLA FACTORY WORKSHOP MANUAL 1955-1969
JAGUAR E-TYPE 3.8 & 4.2 SERIES 1 & 2 WORKSHOP MANUAL
JAGUAR MK 7, 8, 9 & XK120, 140, 150 WORKSHOP MANUAL 1948-1961
METROPOLITAN FACTORY WORKSHOP MANUAL
MGA & MGB OWNERS HANDBOOK & WORKSHOP MANUAL
MG MIDGET TC, TD, TF & TF1500 WORKSHOP MANUAL
PORSCHE 356 1948-1965 WORKSHOP MANUAL
PORSCHE 911 2.0, 2.2, 2.4 LITRE 1964-1973 WORKSHOP MANUAL
PORSCHE 911 2.7, 3.0, 3.2 LITRE 1973-1989 WORKSHOP MANUAL
PORSCHE 912 WORKSHOP MANUAL
TRIUMPH TR2, TR3, TR4 1953-1965 WORKSHOP MANUAL
VOLKSWAGEN TRANSPORTER, TRUCKS & WAGONS 1950-1979 WSM
VOLVO 1944-1968 ALL MODELS WORKSHOP MANUAL

VELOCEPRESS TECHNICAL BOOKS - AUTOMOBILE

FERRARI OWNER'S HANDBOOK
HOW TO BUILD A FIBERGLASS CAR
HOW TO BUILD A RACING CAR
HOW TO RESTORE THE MODEL 'A' FORD
MASERATI OWNER'S HANDBOOK
PERFORMANCE TUNING THE SUNBEAM TIGER
SOUPING THE VOLKSWAGEN
SOLEX CARBURETORS (EMPHASIS ON UK & EU AUTOMOBILES)
SU CARBURETORS (EMPHASIS ON UK AUTOMOBILES)
WEBER CARBURETORS (EMPHASIS ON ALFA & FIAT)

VELOCEPRESS BOOKS & GUIDES - AUTOMOBILE

COMPLETE CATALOG OF JAPANESE MOTOR VEHICLES
FERRARI 308 SERIES BUYER'S AND OWNER'S GUIDE
FERRARI BROCHURES AND SALES LITERATURE 1968-1989
FERRARI SERIAL NUMBERS PART I - ODD NUMBERS TO 21399
FERRARI SERIAL NUMBERS PART II - EVEN NUMBERS TO 1050
HENRY'S FABULOUS MODEL "A" FORD
MASERATI BROCHURES AND SALES LITERATURE

VELOCEPRESS BOOKS – RACING

CARRERA PANAMERICANA - MEXICAN ROAD RACE (BOOK OF)
DIALED IN - THE JAN OPPERMAN STORY
VEDA ORR'S NEW REVISED HOT ROD PICTORIAL